Critical Phishing Defense Strategies and Digital Asset Protection

Brij B. Gupta
Asia University, Taiwan

IGI Global
Scientific Publishing
Publishing Tomorrow's Research Today

Vice President of Editorial Melissa Wagner
Managing Editor of Acquisitions Mikaela Felty
Managing Editor of Book Development Jocelynn Hessler
Production Manager Mike Brehm
Cover Design Phillip Shickler

Published in the United States of America by
IGI Global Scientific Publishing
701 East Chocolate Avenue
Hershey, PA, 17033, USA
Tel: 717-533-8845
Fax: 717-533-8661
Website: https://www.igi-global.com E-mail: cust@igi-global.com

Library of Congress Cataloging-in-Publication Data

Names: Gupta, Brij B., 1982- editor.
Title: Critical phishing defense strategies and digital asset protection / edited by: Brij Gupta.
Description: Hershey PA : IGI Global Scientific Publishing, [2025] | Includes bibliographical references. | Summary: "This book covers the fundamentals of phishing, including common tactics and techniques used by attackers. It then progresses to explore advanced detection and prevention methods, offering practical solutions and best practices for defending against these malicious activities"-- Provided by publisher.
Identifiers: LCCN 2024054412 (print) | LCCN 2024054413 (ebook) | ISBN 9798369387849 (hardcover) | ISBN 9798369387856 (paperback) | ISBN 9798369387863 (ebook)
Subjects: LCSH: Phishing--Prevention. | Computer security.
Classification: LCC HV6773.15.P45 C75 2025 (print) | LCC HV6773.15.P45 (ebook) | DDC 364.16/32--dc23/eng/20250129
LC record available at https://lccn.loc.gov/2024054412
LC ebook record available at https://lccn.loc.gov/2024054413

British Cataloguing in Publication Data
A Cataloguing in Publication record for this book is available from the British Library.

To my beloved family, whose steadfast support and encouragement have been my guiding light throughout this journey.

Brij B. Gupta

Table of Contents

Detailed Table of Contents

Phishing remains a significant cybersecurity threat, targeting individuals and organizations to access confidential data. As techniques evolve, innovative protective measures are essential. This paper offers a detailed overview of phishing defense strategies, focusing on both technological solutions and human-centered approaches. Multi-layered defenses, blending traditional security with user education, are vital for mitigating risks. Simulated phishing exercises and ongoing training empower employees to recognize and respond to threats, strengthening the human aspect of cybersecurity. Leadership commitment and open communication are crucial for cultivating a strong security culture, encouraging staff to report suspicious activities. Continuous evaluation and updates to defenses are necessary to adapt to evolving threats. Real-world case studies, such as the 2020 Twitter breach and the SolarWinds attack, highlight the severe impacts of phishing, reinforcing the need for a proactive that combines technology, education, and risk management to protect digital assets effectively.

This chapter explores the evolution of phishing detection methods, present traditional, advanced, and hybrid approaches. Traditional methods provide a base layer of defense, but their effectiveness is limited against adaptive attacks. Advanced techniques employ machine learning (ML) and deep learning (DL) to enhance detection accuracy and leveraging data-driven models that analyze URL structures, email content, and website behavior. Hybrid models combine multiple techniques to optimize performance.

Case studies illustrate the practical application of these methodologies in various domains which include the use of convolutional neural networks (CNNs), long short-term memory networks (LSTMs), and ensemble algorithms such as Random Forests and Gradient Boosting, achieving detection accuracies exceeding 97% in many cases. Research also highlights on large language models (LLMs) and Universal Adversarial Perturbation (UAP) techniques, for detecting advanced phishing strategies. Challenges in phishing detection include imbalanced datasets and real-time detection requirements.

Phishing is a dangerous online fraud tactic that tricks individuals into disclosing personal information, like usernames, passwords, and credit card numbers. It often appears through fake emails, messages, or websites designed to lure victims into sharing sensitive data. This illegal activity can cause significant financial losses for businesses and consumers, while also damaging trust in online transactions. Anti-phishing tools, such as SpamTitan and Barracuda Sentinel, use advanced algorithms and machine learning to detect and block phishing attempts in real time, protecting users from data breaches and financial harm. These solutions also offer user training to increase awareness of phishing tactics, enhancing defenses. Emphasizing the need for comprehensive anti-phishing strategies, it shows how organizations can safeguard sensitive information and maintain customer trust in a digital world. It explores technologies and methods for building a robust framework against phishing, detailing innovative ways to secure communication systems and ensure data integrity.

The use of IoT and smart devices has increased day by day. The connections and automations are easily made in the digital world by the use of IoT and smart devices. But, the frequency of phishing attacks on

Phishing continues to be one of the most common and effective forms of cyber security threats and involve deception of users thereby getting them provide unauthorized individuals with personal information. In this chapter an overview of phishing attacks is presented with a special focus on anti-phishing technologies. Phishing is then introduced in terms of what is it and different types of it that are currently existing, and the impact that they bring to the individuals who are targeted. Anti-phishing measures are then considered with reference to their purpose of protecting personal and organizational information against emergent threats. Just as the sophistication of phishing has moved from a plain and simple email scam to a spear phishing, the chapter explores the technology in place to curb the deadly attack. Different techniques such as heuristic scans, machine learning and URL filters are described as well as products that help users to avoid falling to phishing tricks. The possibilities of applying new technologies in anti-phishing protection are also investigated, including the AI and blockchain. We present several case studies and analyses which highlight the state of the art in anti-phishing tools and delineate the current strength of various known anti-phishing measures despite of the dynamically developing threat landscape. Thus, with hope to help the readers become more aware of the threat and the ever-unfolding evolution of Phishing and the development of anti-phishing tools, this chapter presents the understanding of the evolution of phishing to the readers.

Phishing attacks are among the most prevalent and dangerous cyber threats, exploiting both technological and human vulnerabilities to access sensitive information. As phishing techniques evolve, organizations must implement various detection strategies to stay ahead of cybercriminals. This chapter delves into phishing detection methods, covering traditional approaches like signature-based detection and content filtering, alongside advanced strategies such as heuristic analysis, machine learning, and artificial intelligence (AI). It evaluates the strengths, limitations, and practical applications of these methods in real-world scenarios. Additionally, the chapter explores emerging technologies like Natural Language

Processing (NLP), blockchain, and behavioral analysis that are redefining phishing detection. By combining traditional and modern techniques, organizations can enhance their ability to identify and prevent phishing attacks, strengthening their overall cybersecurity.

Phishing attacks are a major cybersecurity threat, exploiting human vulnerabilities by manipulating trust to access sensitive information. As phishing tactics evolve, the demand for advanced anti-phishing technologies has surged. This paper examines key measures such as email filters, SSL/TLS certificates, DNS-based authentication, multi-factor authentication, and URL filtering to protect against phishing. Advanced methods like machine learning, AI-driven analysis, and real-time threat detection have improved phishing prevention. It also discusses browser-based, cloud-based, and email security tools for mitigating risks. The paper highlights challenges such as evolving tactics, email filtering limitations, and user negligence, emphasizing the need for ongoing innovation in strategies. Future trends like AI, biometrics, and deep learning for threat intelligence are explored, showing potential to enhance phishing defense. A holistic approach integrating technology, protocols, and user awareness is advocated to combat phishing effectively at both individual and organizational levels.

Cryptography has a crucial role in maintaining the security of sensitive information on digital assets. By applying strong encryption techniques, cryptography converts data into a format that is not easily read by unauthorized parties. This not only minimizes the risk of illegal access or hacking, but also ensures that information can only be accessed by parties who have the appropriate keys. Decryption techniques then allow legitimate recipients to restore the data to its original form. cryptography uses complex mathematical algorithms to convert original data into a secure, encrypted form. This applies not only to data storage in secure repositories, but also to data transmission over communications networks. Thus, the application of cryptography is not only a prerequisite for protecting sensitive information, but also for ensuring trust in data exchange in the digital era. Cryptography is the main foundation in maintaining the security of sensitive information on digital assets.

Phishing is still one of the most common and dangerous types of cyber threats, and it keeps getting more sophisticated. The increasing prevalence of phishing attempts has made it necessary for enterprises across the globe to prioritize the development of offensive and defensive cybersecurity solutions. This case study explores the current state of phishing and the developments in cyber protection tactics that have accompanied them, showcasing actual situations in which businesses have successfully reduced these risks. Phishing uses human psychology to trick people into disclosing private data, such as login passwords, bank account details, or other personal information. It frequently takes the form of official correspondence. A more advanced variation called spear-phishing is more difficult to identify and counter since it uses carefully constructed communications that are targeted at certain people or companies. More proactive threat identification and response are now possible thanks to the integration of AI and ML with conventional SIEM systems.

In an era, health monitoring technologies are increasingly powered by smart devices and applications, ensuring the privacy and security of sensitive health data is a critical challenge. The chapter begins with an introduction to precise health monitoring, highlighting the importance of smart devices and mobile applications in tracking patient health. The chapter delves into the key challenges posed by the volume, sensitivity, and complexity of health data, examining privacy during data collection and sharing. The challenges is addressed by optimizing data security in health monitoring, such as data encryption techniques to protect patient identities. Blockchain technology is used for secure health data sharing. Authentication and access control mechanisms are explored to protect health data. As healthcare systems handle increasing volumes of data, the chapter discusses the role of cloud computing to achieve scalability. The chapter concludes by emphasizing the importance of balancing cloud computing to optimize both scalability and efficiency in health monitoring applications

Cloud computing has provided enormous opportunities for small and medium-sized enterprises (SMEs) to digitalize their business processes. However, with increasing cloud computing adoption, security and privacy threats are on the rise. The aim of this book chapter is to examine the nature and the impact of cyber security threats to SMEs. In particular, by employing a quantitative approach, conducting a survey of 289 SMEs in Australia, this paper examines the cyber security practices, measures, and suggest solutions for effective cyber security practices in cloud environments. The findings highlight the most frequent cyber security threats faced by. SMEs and demonstrate the significant differences in cloud security practice measures among micro enterprises, small, and medium-sized enterprises.

The rapid adoption of IoT-based healthcare devices has revolutionized the medical industry by enabling real-time monitoring and data collection, yet it raises significant privacy and security concerns. These devices are vulnerable to various cyber-attacks, including man-in-the-middle attacks, spoofing, and data injection, which can compromise sensitive patient information and disrupt critical healthcare operations. To address these challenges, this study explores the application of deep learning techniques, particularly ResNet-50, to classify unforeseen cyber-attacks in IoT-based healthcare systems. The WUSTL-EHMS-2020 dataset, containing biometric data and network flow metrics, is utilized for experimentation. Preprocessing steps like normalization and feature engineering ensure compatibility with the model. ResNet-50, with its residual learning mechanism, effectively extracts complex patterns and generalizes to previously unseen attacks. The model's performance is evaluated using accuracy, precision, recall, and F1-score, demonstrating its ability to identify cyber-attacks while minimizing false positives and negatives. This research underscores the importance of advanced deep learning frameworks in enhancing the security and reliability of IOT-based healthcare systems.

Chapter examines urgent need to address cyber threats by reassessing conventional security techniques & arguing in favor of a large degree of automation & incorporation of AI & ML. Though it acknowledges associated issues, AI highlights cybersecurity defences by strengthening them, despite worries about potential misuse by criminals. While technologies have made jobs more automated, they have exposed systems to flaws. AI's widespread use has made attacks worse, which has led to revaluation of traditional & modern defences. It emphasizes AI's role in cybersecurity by showcasing its capacity to manage enormous datasets, adapt in real-time, & quickly detect risks. It highlights the significance of AI globally

Foreword

In an era where digital transactions, communication, and business operations are deeply integrated into our daily lives, cybersecurity threats have evolved at an alarming rate. Among these threats, phishing remains one of the most deceptive and damaging cyberattacks, targeting individuals, businesses, and institutions worldwide. The ability to detect, prevent, and mitigate phishing attacks is no longer optional—it is a necessity. This book, Critical Phishing Defense Strategies and Digital Asset Protection, serves as a timely and essential resource in addressing these growing cybersecurity challenges.

This book brings together an exceptional collection of research, insights, and practical strategies aimed at fortifying digital ecosystems against phishing threats. The comprehensive scope of its 16 chapters covers foundational aspects of phishing defense, advanced detection techniques, and the role of emerging technologies such as artificial intelligence, blockchain, and cryptography in safeguarding digital assets. It also explores phishing defense in various domains, including IoT networks, social media, and cloud computing, making it a versatile and invaluable reference for researchers, cybersecurity professionals, policymakers, and organizations striving to enhance their security posture.

One of the book's significant strengths is its multidisciplinary approach, blending theoretical foundations with real-world applications. The chapters on deep learning, machine learning, and AI-driven phishing detection methods highlight the cutting-edge advancements in cybersecurity, while discussions on psychological triggers and case studies provide crucial insights into the human factors influencing cyber threats. The inclusion of empirical studies and best practices ensures that readers gain both academic knowledge and actionable strategies to combat phishing attacks effectively.

As we navigate an increasingly interconnected and digital world, cybersecurity resilience must be at the forefront of technological advancement and policy formulation. This book is a testament to the collaborative effort of esteemed researchers and practitioners who have dedicated their expertise to addressing one of the most persistent threats in cyberspace. It is not just a scholarly contribution but a roadmap for the future of phishing defense and digital asset protection.

I am confident that this book will serve as a guiding resource for students, professionals, and researchers in the cybersecurity field. By equipping readers with the necessary knowledge and tools, it plays a crucial role in strengthening global cyber defense strategies against phishing attacks.

I congratulate the editors, authors, and contributors for compiling this remarkable volume and for their dedication to advancing cybersecurity research. I hope that readers will find this book enlightening, insightful, and instrumental in enhancing their understanding and implementation of phishing defense strategies.

Jinsong Wu

School of Artificial Intelligence, Guilin University of Electronic Technology (GUET), Guilin, China, & Department of Electrical Engineering, University of Chile, Santiago, Chile

Preface

Phishing attacks have emerged as one of the most persistent and evolving cybersecurity threats, posing significant risks to individuals, businesses, and critical infrastructures worldwide. As cybercriminals refine their tactics, leveraging advanced techniques such as artificial intelligence, deep learning, and social engineering, the need for robust phishing defense strategies has never been more critical. This book, "Critical Phishing Defense Strategies and Digital Asset Protection," is a comprehensive guide that brings together cutting-edge research, innovative methodologies, and practical insights to strengthen cybersecurity frameworks against phishing attacks.

The book comprises 16 chapters, each addressing different dimensions of phishing threats and digital asset protection. It begins with a foundational exploration of phishing defense strategies, providing readers with a strong theoretical background before progressing into detection and prevention mechanisms that incorporate smart devices, IoT networks, and social media platforms. Advanced methodologies, including deep learning, machine learning, cryptographic security, and blockchain-based solutions, are discussed to showcase how modern technologies are shaping anti-phishing defenses. Additionally, the book highlights real-world case studies, psychological triggers behind phishing attacks, and strategies for mitigating risks in cloud computing and healthcare environments.

This book serves as a valuable resource for cybersecurity professionals, researchers, policymakers, and students who seek to understand and implement state-of-the-art phishing defense mechanisms. By bridging the gap between theoretical knowledge and practical applications, it equips readers with the necessary tools to combat phishing threats effectively and secure digital assets in an increasingly interconnected world.

We extend our sincere gratitude to the contributors, reviewers, and professionals whose expertise has shaped this book. Their dedication and research efforts have enabled us to present a rich compilation of knowledge that will aid in the ongoing battle against phishing threats. We hope this book serves as an essential guide and inspires further advancements in cybersecurity.

Brij B. Gupta
Editor

Acknowledgement

I would like to express my sincere gratitude to everyone who has contributed to the completion of this book, Critical Phishing Defense Strategies and Digital Asset Protection. This endeavor would not have been possible without the invaluable support, guidance, and dedication of many individuals.

First and foremost, I extend my heartfelt appreciation to the authors and reviewers of each chapter. Their expertise, insightful feedback, and unwavering commitment have played a crucial role in shaping the depth and quality of this book. Their contributions have been instrumental in ensuring that this volume serves as a comprehensive resource in the field.

I am also profoundly grateful to the team at IGI Global Publishing for their continuous support, technical expertise, and encouragement throughout this journey. Their professional guidance and commitment have been invaluable in bringing this project to fruition.

A special note of thanks goes to my family, whose unwavering love, patience, and encouragement have been a constant source of strength. Their support has sustained me through the challenges of this endeavor and has been instrumental in its successful completion.

Lastly, I am deeply thankful to the Almighty for granting me the strength, resilience, and determination to navigate this journey and see this work through to completion.

To all those who have contributed in various ways, I extend my deepest gratitude. Your support and efforts are truly appreciated.

Brij B. Gupta

January 24, 2025

Chapter 1
Foundations of Phishing Defense:
Comprehensive Strategies for Digital Asset Protection

Raj Kanwar
Chandigarh College of Engineering and Technology, Panjab University, Chandigarh, India

Sumit Bawa
https://orcid.org/0009-0008-5152-2067
Zscaler, Inc., India

Sunil K. Singh
https://orcid.org/0000-0003-4876-7190
Chandigarh College of Engineering and Technology, Panjab University, Chandigarh, India

Sudhakar Kumar
https://orcid.org/0000-0001-7928-4234
Chandigarh College of Engineering and Technology, Panjab University, Chandigarh, India

Chandra Kumari Subba
Sikkim University, India

Varsha Arya
Hong Kong Metropolitan University, Hong Kong

Abhay Ratnaparkhi
IBM, Austin, USA

ABSTRACT

Phishing remains a significant cybersecurity threat, targeting individuals and organizations to access confidential data. As techniques evolve, innovative protective measures are essential. This paper offers a detailed overview of phishing defense strategies, focusing on both technological solutions and human-centered approaches. Multi-layered defenses, blending traditional security with user education, are vital for mitigating risks. Simulated phishing exercises and ongoing training empower employees to recognize and respond to threats, strengthening the human aspect of cybersecurity. Leadership commitment and open communication are crucial for cultivating a strong security culture, encouraging staff to report suspicious activities. Continuous evaluation and updates to defenses are necessary to adapt to evolving threats. Real-world case studies, such as the 2020 Twitter breach and the SolarWinds attack, highlight the severe impacts of phishing, reinforcing the need for a proactive that combines technology, education, and risk management to protect digital assets effectively.

DOI: 10.4018/979-8-3693-8784-9.ch001

INTRODUCTION

Phishing (Thakur, K. et al., 2024) has become one of the most widespread and dangerous methods used by cybercriminals to exploit weaknesses in digital communication. By impersonating legitimate entities, attackers trick individuals into revealing sensitive information, such as login details, financial records, or personal identification. As phishing techniques continue to advance, growing more sophisticated and harder to detect, they represent an increasing threat to both organizations and individuals. In response, the need for robust and adaptive defense mechanisms has become paramount to protect sensitive data and preserve the integrity of digital systems. Traditional security measures, such as spam filters and firewalls, are proving less effective against modern phishing attacks, which employ advanced psychological manipulation and social engineering tactics. Cybercriminals often craft highly convincing messages and counterfeit websites designed to prompt victims into making rushed, uninformed decisions. To address these evolving threats, organizations must adopt innovative strategies that combine cutting-edge technologies, like artificial intelligence (AI) and machine learning (ML), with proactive, human-focused defense approaches.

This research explores the components of a comprehensive phishing defense strategy, combining AI-driven detection systems, behavioral analysis, and ongoing employee education. It highlights the importance of a multi-layered approach, emphasizing the critical role that technology and user awareness play in defending against the ever-changing landscape of phishing attacks. Our analysis begins by examining the prevalence and design of phishing kits, as observed in the dataset retrieved from Cofense, Inc. during the first half of 2016. Phishing kits (Abbas, A. (2024)), which are deployable software packages used by attackers to host fraudulent websites, provide a unique vantage point into how attackers circumvent detection by using server-side evasion techniques. These kits often contain directives in .htaccess files or other configuration scripts that allow attackers to control who can access the phishing site. This not only facilitates the evasion of automated phishing detection systems but also offers insight into which organizations are being targeted based on the filters embedded within the configuration. For instance, many kits deploy filtering rules that block visits from known security researchers, government bodies, or specific geographic regions, thus delaying the blacklisting of their malicious sites.

In addition to understanding the configuration of phishing kits, we analyze over 170,000 phishing URLs submitted to the Anti-Phishing Working Group (APWG) (Afridi, S. (2024)) during the first half of 2017. This data reveals that attackers often rely on compromised domains, rather than registering new ones, to host phishing content. By exploiting vulnerabilities in legitimate websites, phishers can bypass the need to invest in new domain registrations, which often triggers scrutiny by domain registrars and security vendors. Our study highlights that a significant portion of phishing attacks are deployed on previously compromised infrastructure, making detection more difficult for conventional security systems. To further our understanding of these attacks, we developed an innovative URL classification scheme that takes into account both the structure of the URL and the age of the associated domain. This novel approach allows us to fingerprint phishing attacks by combining URL patterns with domain metadata, thus improving detection rates. Our classification model shows that phishers often craft URLs to appear legitimate, either by including brand names or using URL shortening services. Additionally, older domains—whether compromised or newly registered—are often used to build trust with potential victims, as these domains are less likely to raise suspicion compared to freshly created ones.

Analyzing these datasets helps us draw important conclusions regarding the motivations and methods of phishers. By observing trends in phishing kit distribution and URL usage, we gain a deeper understanding of how phishing operations are structured and maintained over time. Our findings also emphasize the importance of examining both the client-side and server-side components of phishing attacks. While much of the existing anti-phishing research focuses on detecting phishing content presented to users, this study reveals that attackers are equally focused on avoiding detection by the defenders. As discussed in Section IV, phishers utilize sophisticated techniques such as obfuscating server configurations, randomizing URLs (Hera, J. (2024)), and employing URL redirection to avoid blacklist inclusion for as long as possible. Our research holds significant value for organizations dedicated to anti-phishing efforts. By shedding light on the various evasion techniques used by phishers, we provide actionable insights that can enhance incident response protocols. Our proposed URL classification model, when integrated into existing anti-phishing systems, can improve the speed and accuracy of identifying phishing attacks, ultimately reducing the window of vulnerability for potential victims. Moving forward, this research lays the groundwork for future studies that will evaluate the long-term effectiveness of phishing evasion techniques and propose even more robust countermeasures.

In understanding the anatomy of phishing attacks, we reiterate the importance of recognizing the full spectrum of tools at a phisher's disposal. Phishing kits lower the barrier to entry, enabling even unskilled attackers to launch effective scams. The widespread availability of such kits contributes to the growing prevalence of phishing and the increasing sophistication of these attacks. Furthermore, the compromised infrastructure commonly used by phishers highlights a critical area for improvement in the cybersecurity landscape. By focusing on strengthening the security of legitimate web servers and improving domain registration vetting processes, anti-phishing (Wang, M., & Song, L. (2021)) entities can reduce the avenues available for phishers to exploit.

2. UNDERSTANDING THE PHISHING THREAT LANDSCAPE

The phishing threat landscape presents substantial risks to both individuals and multinational corporations (MNCs), making it a widespread and dangerous form of cybercrime. For everyday individuals, phishing attacks often result in the theft of personal data, including credit card information, passwords, or social security numbers, leading to financial losses, identity theft, and emotional distress. These attacks are typically disguised as legitimate communications from trusted entities, making them difficult for unsuspecting users to identify. On a larger scale, MNCs face even greater challenges, as successful phishing attempts can compromise vast amounts of sensitive corporate information, lead to financial fraud, and cause severe operational disruptions. The financial and reputational damage to such organizations can be immense, with losses potentially reaching millions of dollars. Whether aimed at individuals or large corporations, phishing attacks exploit human vulnerabilities, highlighting the necessity for both everyday users and large enterprises to implement robust defense strategies to reduce risks.

2.1. Email Snaps

Email phishing is the most common and widely recognized form of phishing attack, in which attackers send deceptive emails that are disguised as legitimate communications from trusted entities, such as banks, online retailers, or social media platforms. These emails often convey a sense of urgency or importance, prompting recipients to take immediate action, such as resetting passwords or confirming account information. The emails may contain malicious (Nair, S. S. (2024)) links that direct users to counterfeit websites designed to imitate the appearance of legitimate sites. Once users enter sensitive details, like passwords or credit card information, attackers harvest the data. To make the emails appear legitimate, attackers use tactics like email spoofing, where they alter the "from" field to make it seem as if the email is from a reliable source. They also incorporate realistic logos and official-sounding language to mimic the communication style of the genuine organization, making it harder for recipients to identify the email as fraudulent. Fig.1. depicts schematic representation of the categorization of cyber threats.

Figure 1. Schematic representation of the Categorization of cyber threats.

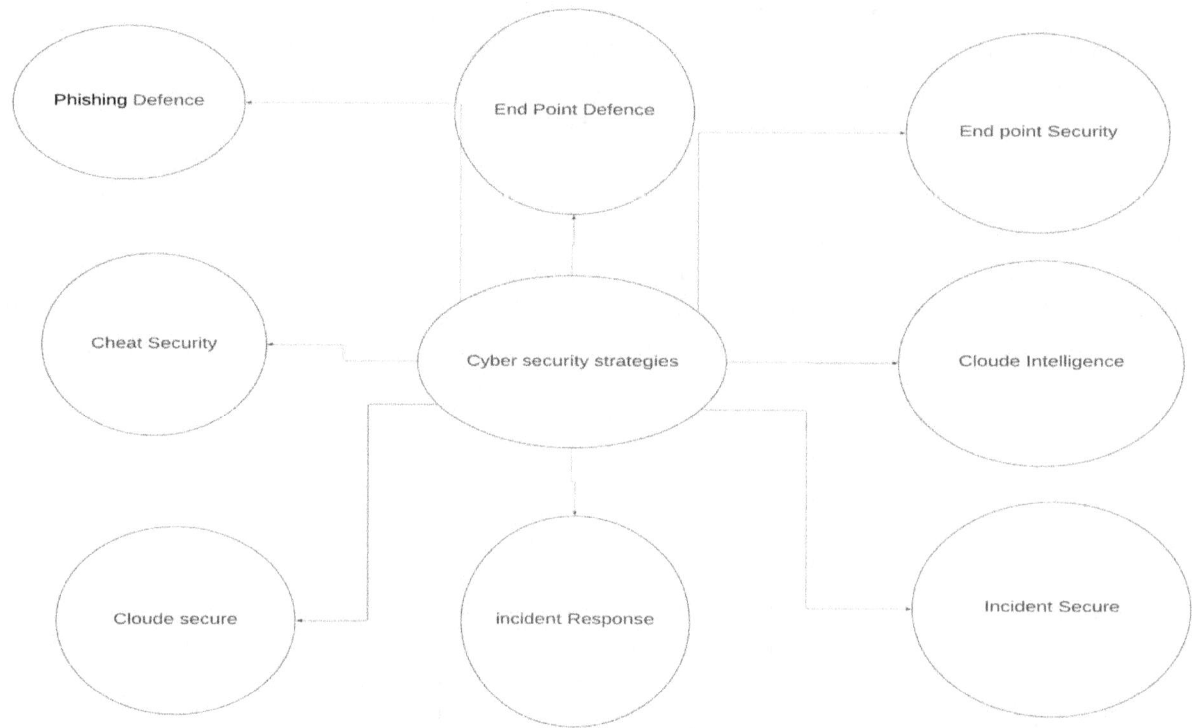

2.2. Spear Phishing

The phishing attack life cycle begins with the attack launch phase, where the phishing attempt is initiated, typically through malicious emails, links, or websites. Once the attack is in motion, it progresses to the User interaction stage, in which the victim is deceived into engaging with the fraudulent content, often leading to credential theft. At this stage, attackers acquire unauthorized access to sensitive information, such as usernames, passwords, or financial data. Fig.2. depicts costs related to phishing email defenses.

Figure 2. Costs Related to Phishing Email Defenses

Technique	Prevention Measures	Tools/Technologies
Email Filtering	- Implement robust email filtering systems to detect and block phishing emails. - Train employees on recognizing phishing emails and reporting them.	- Advanced Threat Protection (ATP) - Security Awareness Training
Web Page Inspection	- Regularly inspect and validate the legitimacy of web pages. - Use secure connections (HTTPS) and multi-factor authentication (MFA).	- Web Browsers - SSL/TLS Certificates
Domain Verification	- Verify email sender domains and use DMARC to prevent domain spoofing.	- DMARC (Domain-based Message Authentication, Reporting, and Conformance)
URL Inspection	- Implement URL filtering to block access to known phishing websites. - Educate users about the risks of clicking on suspicious links.	- URL Filtering Software
User Training	- Conduct regular security awareness training to educate users about phishing threats and best practices. - Use simulations and real-world scenarios to train users to identify and respond to phishing attempts.	- Security Awareness Training Platforms
Incident Response	- Establish clear incident response procedures to quickly investigate and contain phishing attacks. - Implement a system for tracking and reporting phishing incidents.	- Security Information and Event Management (SIEM)
Behavioral Analytics	- Monitor user behavior for anomalies that may indicate a phishing attack. - Use machine learning algorithms to detect unusual patterns.	- User and Entity Behavior Analytics (UEBA)
Multi-Factor Authentication (MFA)	- Require multiple forms of authentication to access sensitive accounts. - Use strong passwords and unique passwords for each account.	- Authentication Apps (e.g., Google Authenticator)
Patch Management	- Regularly update software and systems to patch vulnerabilities that could be exploited by phishers.	- Patch Management Software

After credentials are compromised, Defensive Measures come into play to mitigate potential damage. These include User Education, where individuals are trained to recognize phishing attempts, Email Filtering systems that detect and block phishing emails before they reach users, and Multi-Factor Authentication (MFA), which adds a layer of security by requiring multiple forms of verification(Badwa, E. et al., 2024), even if credentials are stolen. The attack lifecycle underscores the importance of employing multi-layered defensive strategies to counter phishing at various stages of the attack. Spear phishing, a more targeted form of phishing, focuses on specific individuals or groups within an organization. Unlike broad phishing campaigns, which target a large pool of random people, spear phishing is personalized, often using information like the target's name, job title, work contacts, and recent activities. Attackers conduct thorough research on the target, using social media profiles, professional networks, and previous public statements to craft convincing emails that appear to come from trusted sources, such as a supervisor, coworker, or business associate. Due to its personalized nature, victims are more likely to fall for spear phishing attempts. For instance, a CEO might receive an email that looks like it's from the company's legal team, requesting confidential financial information(Basit, A. et al., 2021) or login credentials. This precise targeting makes spear phishing one of the most successful and damaging phishing techniques, particularly in corporate environments.

2.3. CEO fraud

Whaling is a specialized form of phishing aimed at high-ranking executives or senior leaders within an organization, often called "whales" due to their significance in the company. Cybercriminals create highly sophisticated and well-researched emails that imitate official business correspondence. These emails frequently involve requests for substantial financial transactions, confidential information, or access to critical systems. Since whaling attacks target top-level management(Jain, A. K., & Gupta, B. B. (2022), Kumar, R. et al., 2025), they can cause considerable financial loss and reputational harm. Unlike standard phishing, which uses a broad approach, whaling demands in-depth knowledge of the corporate hierarchy and the personal routines of the executive. Attackers might pose as legal counsel seeking sensitive documents or a trusted vendor requesting an urgent wire transfer. Because these attacks target busy executives who may have limited time to carefully review each email, they are often particularly successful.

2.4. Clone Phishing

Clone phishing is a sophisticated technique where attackers generate an almost identical replica of a legitimate email that a victim has previously received. The cloned email may resemble the original message from a trusted sender but features modified attachments or links that direct users to harmful sites. Since the email seems to be part of an ongoing conversation, the recipient is more inclined to trust it and interact with its content without hesitation. For instance, an individual might receive a subsequent email that appears to be from a legitimate service provider, requesting them to download an updated invoice or click a link for further information. Because the initial email was genuine, users often presume the follow-up is legitimate as well, enabling attackers to circumvent initial skepticism and deceive them into downloading malware or revealing sensitive information.

2.5. Vishing (Voice Phishing)

Vishing is a form of phishing that takes place over the phone, where attackers attempt to deceive victims into disclosing personal information or transferring funds. Cybercriminals frequently impersonate representatives from banks, government agencies, or technical support teams. They employ tactics like caller ID spoofing to make it seem as though the call is originating from a legitimate number. For instance, a victim might receive a call from someone claiming to be a bank official (Oest, A. et al., 2018), stating that there has been suspicious activity on their account. The caller then asks for verification of account numbers, PINs, or even Social Security numbers. Vishing attacks can be particularly effective because they often instill a sense of urgency or fear, prompting the victim to act without careful consideration. Unlike email phishing, vishing involves real-time interaction, making it harder for the victim to recognize the fraud.

2.6 Smishing (SMS Phishing)

Smishing involves sending deceptive messages via SMS (text messaging) to trick individuals into revealing sensitive information or clicking on harmful links. Much like email phishing, these messages seem to originate from trusted sources such as banks, delivery services, or retailers. The text often contains a call to action, such as “click here to claim your prize” or “verify your account by clicking the link.” Smishing is particularly hazardous because mobile users are more inclined to trust text messages, and the smaller screen size may make it more difficult to recognize phishing attempts. The simplicity and widespread use of SMS make it an appealing channel for cybercriminals (Berghel, H. et al., 2007). For instance, a smishing message might state that a delivery is pending confirmation and direct the recipient to a fraudulent website that gathers personal information. Attackers may also take advantage of mobile payment systems, deceiving users into sending money directly from their accounts.

Figure 3. depicts phishing attack lifecycle.

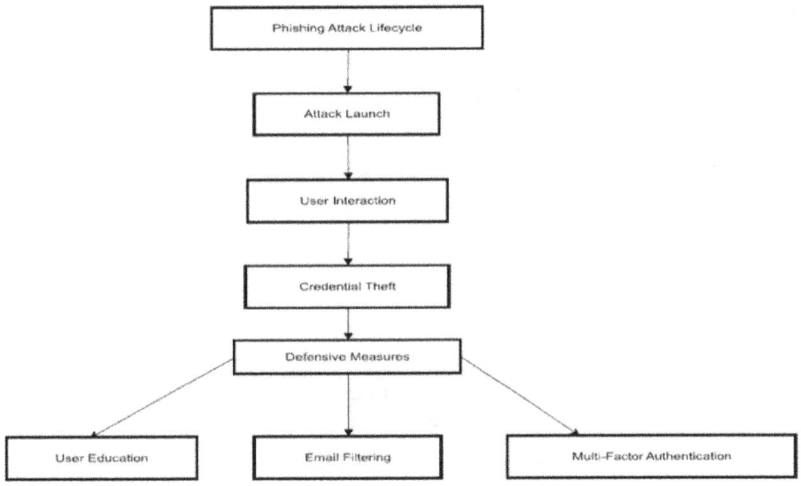

2.7. Pharming

Pharming is a sophisticated form of phishing where attackers redirect web traffic from legitimate websites to fraudulent ones, even when users enter the correct URL. This is usually done by exploiting vulnerabilities in DNS (Domain Name System) (Kamachi, C. (2014)) settings. Pharming differs from other types of phishing because it targets the infrastructure rather than directly tricking individuals. Once a user enters their login credentials on the fake website, the attackers capture the data. Since users have no way of knowing they've been redirected to a malicious site, pharming can be highly effective in harvesting sensitive information like passwords, credit card details, or other personal data. For instance, a user might type in the URL of their bank, but due to compromised DNS settings, they are directed to a fraudulent site that looks identical to the real one.

2.8. Angler Phishing

Angler phishing is a social media-based phishing attack where cybercriminals (Williams, J. et al., 2021) pose as customer service representatives or trusted organizations to deceive users into providing sensitive information. This form of phishing often occurs on platforms like Twitter or Facebook. Attackers monitor public posts where users express dissatisfaction or complaints about a service. They then impersonate the official customer support account and respond to the victim, providing fake support links that lead to phishing websites. Angler phishing exploits the trust users place in online support teams and the immediacy of social media interactions. For example, a user might tweet about an issue with their bank account, and a fake support account will reply with a link, claiming it will resolve the issue. Victims who fall for these scams may end up providing login credentials, which the attacker can then use for identity theft or financial fraud.

2.9 Consequences of Phishing Breaches

Phishing breaches have far-reaching (Sharif, F. (2024)) consequences that affect individuals, organizations, and even national security. These consequences can be categorized into financial, operational, reputational, legal, and psychological impacts.

2.9.1. Financial Consequences

Direct Financial Loss: Phishing attacks that target financial data, such as credit card numbers or bank account information, can result in immediate theft of funds. For example, in Business Email Compromise (BEC) scams (Moore, T. W., & Clayton, R. (2011)), attackers trick organizations into transferring large sums of money to fraudulent accounts. Cost of Remediation: After a breach, companies incur significant costs in recovering from the incident. This includes forensic investigations, restoring data, rebuilding systems, and enhancing security to prevent future attacks. Ransomware and Data Theft: Phishing is a common entry point for ransomware attacks. Once inside, attackers can encrypt sensitive data and demand a ransom to unlock it. Even after paying the ransom, businesses might face prolonged downtime and potential data loss. Business Disruption: Phishing attacks can cause operational downtime, leading to loss of revenue, decreased productivity, and missed business opportunities. For instance, if critical systems are compromised or employees cannot access essential tools due to an attack, it disrupts normal operations. Insurance Premiums and Coverage: Cybersecurity insurance may cover some costs related to a breach, but frequent or severe breaches can increase premiums. Moreover, some phishing-related incidents may fall outside the scope of coverage, adding to the overall cost for the business.

Example: In 2020, Twitter suffered a phishing attack that led to hackers gaining control of high-profile accounts, resulting in financial losses and reputational damage. While the direct financial loss was limited, the overall cost of managing the breach, improving security, and dealing with lawsuits(Naqvi, B. et al., 2023) escalated the expenses significantly.

2.9.2. Reputational Damage

The erosion of trust and harm to an organization's reputation can be both severe and enduring:

Loss of Customer Trust: Customers depend on companies to safeguard their personal information. A phishing incident that compromises sensitive customer data can significantly diminish this trust. Many customers may choose to sever ties with the organization, concerned that their information could be mishandled once more.

Brand Damage: A phishing attack, especially a high-profile one, can tarnish a company's image. News of the breach can spread quickly, leading to negative press coverage, social media backlash, and damage to the brand's reputation. Rebuilding trust after such incidents can take years and may never fully recover. Loss of Competitive Advantage: If intellectual property or sensitive business data is stolen through phishing, competitors could gain an unfair advantage. The loss of trade secrets or proprietary information can weaken a company's position in the market. Decline in Stock Prices: Publicly traded companies often experience a decline in stock value following a significant data breach. Investors may lose confidence in the company's security measures and its ability to safeguard critical assets.

Example: In 2014, the Sony Pictures phishing breach resulted in massive reputational damage(Alabdan, R. (2020)), with leaked private emails, unreleased films, and sensitive employee information, all contributing to a negative public perception of the company.

3. TECHNICAL DEFENSES AGAINST PHISHING

3.1. Email Filtering and Security

Email serves as the most prevalent vector for phishing attacks, making email filtering and security critical components of technical defense. Advanced email filtering solutions utilize a combination of spam filters, heuristic analysis, and machine learning algorithms to detect and block phishing emails before they enter users' inboxes. These filters scrutinize email metadata, verify known malicious URLs, and evaluate the content for suspicious characteristics, such as domain spoofing, unusual attachments, or phishing keywords. Key protocols like Domain-based Message Authentication, Reporting, and Conformance (DMARC), Sender Policy Framework (SPF), and DomainKeys Identified Mail (DKIM) help validate the authenticity of an email sender, preventing attackers from masquerading(da Silva et al., 2020) as trusted domains. Furthermore, some security tools employ sandboxing to open and analyze potentially harmful attachments within a secure, isolated environment. By implementing these layers of protection, organizations can significantly decrease the number of phishing emails that reach users, thereby lowering the chances of a successful attack.

3.2. Web Filtering

Web filtering is a crucial defense mechanism that prevents users from accessing malicious websites often linked in phishing emails or other forms of communication. Web filters analyze URLs and block access to known phishing sites, malware distribution domains, and other harmful content. These systems frequently utilize DNS (Amiri, I. S. et al., 2014) filtering, which prevents connections to websites identified as malicious by cross-referencing them with databases of known harmful domains. Moreover, contemporary web filtering tools integrate real-time threat intelligence feeds to identify and block newly emerging phishing websites, which often have a brief lifespan to evade detection. Some web filters also examine the content of web pages in real time, scanning for deceptive login forms, script injections, or malware. By restricting access to these hazardous websites, web filtering helps protect users who may inadvertently click on malicious links in phishing attempts, thereby lowering the risk of credential theft or malware infections (Huang, H. et al., 2009).

3.3. Endpoint Protection and Threat Intelligence

Endpoint protection solutions play a vital role in safeguarding against phishing attacks by monitoring devices (endpoints) for malicious activities and preventing the installation of malware. Modern endpoint protection platforms (EPP) utilize behavioral analysis, machine learning, and signature-based detection to identify and block phishing-related threats, such as malware that could be delivered through phishing emails. Additionally, these solutions can recognize and respond to indicators of compromise (IoCs), such as unusual processes, unexpected network connections, or alterations in system files, which may suggest that an endpoint has been compromised through phishing. Endpoint Detection and Response (EDR) tools take this a step further by providing real-time monitoring and rapid incident response capabilities to contain and remediate threats before they can spread. Integrating threat intelligence enhances endpoint protection by offering real-time insights into emerging phishing tactics, malicious URLs, and phishing kits used by attackers. This proactive strategy enables organizations to stay ahead of evolving phishing campaigns and continually strengthen their defenses.

4. USER TRAINING AND AWARENESS

4.1. Phishing Simulations

Phishing simulations are an effective method for increasing employee awareness and enhancing their ability to recognize phishing attempts. In these simulations, IT or security teams distribute fake phishing emails (Oest, A. et al., 2020) that replicate real-world attacks to evaluate whether employees can identify and avoid them. These controlled assessments help gauge employees' vulnerability to phishing and provide immediate feedback and education. Employees who fall for the simulated phishing emails are typically directed to training resources that highlight the warning signs they overlooked and how to better identify phishing attempts in the future. By regularly implementing phishing simulations, organizations can monitor progress, decrease the likelihood of human error, and bolster their overall cybersecurity posture. These exercises also foster a culture of vigilance, engaging employees as active participants in the organization's defense strategy. Table1 explains various past Cybercrime happenings. Table 1 lists few past cybercrime happenings.

Table 1. Past Cybercrime Happenings

Company/Organization	Year	Type of Attack	Detection Methods	Preventive Measures
Acorn Financial Services	2022	Phishing	Email analysis	Anti-phishing tools
Ubiquiti Networks	2021	Phishing	IT monitoring	Enhanced IT security measures and protocols
Twitter	2020	Spear-phishing	System audit	Improved security protocols and employee training
Wipro	2019	Phishing	Email analysis	Security measures and employee awareness training
Atlanta	2018	Phishing	Intrusion detection	Enhanced security measures and improved user training
Enigma ICO	2017	Phishing	Transfer tracking	Improved security measures and user education
DNC	2016	Spear-phishing	Email scanning	Strengthened security measures and employee education
Crelan Bank	2016	Phishing	Transaction monitoring	Security training and improved transaction security
Anthem Inc.	2015	Data Breach	System monitoring	Improved security systems and protocols
Gmail and AOL	2014	Phishing	User monitoring	Increased user awareness and stronger security measures
Target	2013	Phishing	Vendor monitoring	Strengthened vendor security checks and enhanced network security
LinkedIn	2012	Phishing	User behavior analysis	Two-factor authentication and password strengthening
RSA	2011	Spear-phishing	Malware scanning	Improved security protocols and employee training
Equifax	2017	Data Breach	System monitoring	Improved security systems and protocols
Colonial Pipeline	2021	Ransomware	Network monitoring	Improved network security and backups
Microsoft Exchange Server	2021	Exploit	Vulnerability scanning	Software patching and updates
SolarWinds	2020	Supply Chain Attack	Intrusion detection	Improved supply chain security and monitoring
Uber	2016	Data Breach	Data loss prevention	Improved data security and encryption

4.2. Security Awareness Programs

Security awareness programs (Singh, T. et al., 2025) provide a systematic approach to educating employees about cybersecurity threats, including phishing. These programs deliver ongoing training that addresses various topics such as identifying phishing emails, practicing safe browsing habits, and employing secure password practices. By incorporating a range of learning methods including interactive workshops, e-learning modules, videos, and quizzes, organizations can engage employees at all levels and ensure that the training is both comprehensive and accessible. Regular updates to these programs are crucial to address emerging phishing tactics, such as spear phishing and social engineering (Sharma, A. et al., 2024), that change over time. Security awareness programs also help cultivate a security-first mindset among employees, encouraging them to be vigilant with suspicious emails and proactive in reporting potential threats. This continuous education not only mitigates the risk of phishing attacks but also strengthens the overall cybersecurity culture within the organization.

4.3. Incident Reporting Channels

An effective phishing defense strategy requires clear and accessible incident reporting channels for employees. These channels allow employees to report suspicious emails, links, or activities without fear of retribution. Having a well-established and easy-to-use reporting process ensures that potential phishing threats are quickly identified and handled before they can escalate into a security breach. Incident reporting channels can be as simple as a designated email address or integrated within existing IT helpdesk platforms. This work emphasizes the importance of robust cybersecurity frameworks (Kumar, S. et al., 2024), essential for developing comprehensive phishing defense strategies. The integration of advanced security measures and awareness can significantly mitigate phishing threats. Some organizations also use automated reporting tools embedded within email clients, enabling employees to flag suspicious messages with a single click. Timely reporting not only helps contain phishing threats but also enables the security team to investigate and, if necessary, alert the rest of the organization about a potential phishing campaign. Establishing these channels reinforces the importance of vigilance and ensures that employees play an active role in the organization's defense against phishing.

5. INCIDENT RESPONSE AND RECOVERY

5.1 The Phishing Incident Response Playbook

It is a predefined collection of procedures designed to assist organizations in effectively managing and responding to phishing incidents. When a phishing attack is identified, prompt and coordinated action is essential to minimize damage. The playbook outlines the steps to determine the scope of the attack, contain the threat, and prevent further spread. This typically involves isolating compromised accounts, blocking malicious domains, and removing harmful emails from employee inboxes. The playbook should also provide guidelines for gathering evidence, conducting forensic analysis, and evaluating the potential impact of the attack on systems and data. By having a clear and well-rehearsed incident response plan, organizations can reduce the time required to respond to phishing threats, ensuring swift mitigation while minimizing operational disruption. Regular updates and drills utilizing the playbook ensure that the team is prepared for various phishing scenarios (Setia, H. et al., 2024), including more sophisticated spear phishing or business email compromise (BEC) attempts.

5.2 Recovery Solutions

Backup and recovery solutions are essential for mitigating the long-term effects of a successful phishing attack, especially when the attack involves ransomware or data theft. Regularly backing up critical systems and data ensures that, in the event of a breach, organizations can swiftly restore operations without substantial data loss. Backups should be stored in a secure, isolated environment, separate from the organization’s main network, to prevent attackers from compromising them. Automated, frequent backups are vital for minimizing data loss, and organizations should routinely test their recovery processes to confirm that they function as intended during a crisis. In the event of ransomware deployed through phishing, having a dependable backup can be the key to avoiding payment of a ransom to regain access to encrypted data(Kumar, S. et al., 2024; Aggarwal, T. et al., 2024) or restoring systems without engaging with attackers. Making backup and recovery plans a fundamental part of an organization's overall incident response strategy facilitates quicker recovery from phishing incidents and ensures business continuity.

5.3 Communication and PR Management

Effective communication and public relations (PR) management (Chhabra, A. et al., 2024) are essential components of a phishing incident response, particularly when sensitive customer or company information has been compromised. Clear and transparent communication helps to maintain trust with clients, partners, and stakeholders while managing the organization's reputation. As soon as a phishing attack is confirmed, organizations must coordinate internal communication to inform employees about the threat, provide instructions to prevent further spread, and clarify any immediate actions required. Externally, the organization must be ready to disclose the breach to affected parties, regulatory bodies, and the media in a timely and responsible manner, in accordance with legal obligations. Crafting well-prepared, empathetic messages helps to reassure customers and stakeholders that the incident is being handled with urgency and professionalism. Proactively managing communication and PR in the wake of a phishing attack helps control the narrative, reduce panic, and mitigate reputational damage.

The Phishing Defense Strategy Framework (illustrated in Fig.4) highlights two key pillars in combating phishing attacks: User Education and Organizational Culture. User Education focuses on empowering employees (Kumar, R. et al., 2024) with the knowledge and skills to detect phishing attempts through structured Training Programs and hands-on Phishing Simulations (Vats, T. et al., 2024) that mimic real-world scenarios, reinforcing their ability to respond effectively. On the other hand, Organizational Culture plays a crucial role in sustaining these efforts, driven by Leadership Commitment to prioritize cybersecurity initiatives and fostering Open Communication within the organization. This culture encourages employees to report suspicious activities, creating a proactive environment. Together, these elements create a comprehensive and resilient phishing defense strategy that integrates both human and organizational efforts.

Figure 4. Phishing Defense Strategy Framework

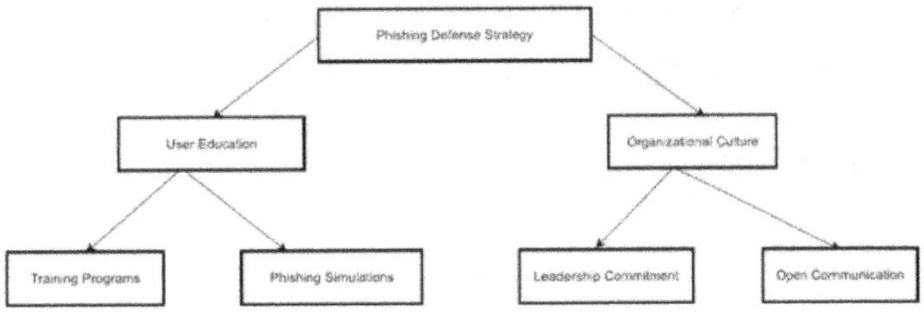

6. GOVERNANCE, RISK, AND COMPLIANCE

6.1. Data Protection Regulations

Compliance with data protection regulations (**Setia, H. et al., 2024**) is a crucial aspect of governance in phishing defense. These regulations, such as the General Data Protection Regulation (GDPR) in Europe and the California Consumer Privacy Act (CCPA) in the U.S., establish stringent guidelines regarding how organizations must safeguard personal data, manage breaches, and notify affected parties in the event of an incident. Phishing attacks often result in unauthorized access to sensitive information, making compliance with these regulations essential to avoid substantial fines and legal repercussions(Sharma, A. et al., 2023). To meet these requirements, organizations must implement robust security measures, such as encryption and access controls, to protect data from phishing-related breaches. The development of a cybersecurity model(Vats, T. et al., 2024) utilizing cloud cryptography(Rajput, D. et al., 2024) underscores the importance of securing data transmission against phishing attacks, reinforcing the necessity for layered defenses in cybersecurity. Additionally, many regulations mandate timely breach notification protocols, requiring clear communication with regulators and impacted individuals. By integrating data protection obligations into their overall cybersecurity strategy, organizations can mitigate legal risks and ensure they are well-prepared to meet regulatory requirements in the event of a phishing attack.

6.2. Risk Management Frameworks

A robust risk management framework enables organizations to identify, assess, and mitigate the risks associated with phishing attacks. This framework offers a structured approach to understanding the potential impact of phishing threats and prioritizing defenses based on the likelihood and severity of an attack. Frameworks such as the NIST (National Institute of Standards and Technology) Cybersecurity Framework or ISO 27001 guide organizations in implementing security controls(Sharma, A. et al., 2021, Singh, M. et al., 2021), identifying vulnerabilities(Singh, S. K. et al., 2025), and preparing response plans specifically tailored to phishing risks. Organizations utilize these frameworks to evaluate their exposure to phishing threats, develop suitable mitigation strategies (including technical defenses and employee training), and ensure continuous monitoring and adaptation as the threat landscape changes. By consistently evaluating phishing risks and applying controls that are proportionate to those risks, a comprehensive framework ensures that organizations remain resilient against evolving phishing tactics.

6.3. Regular Audits and Policy Updates

Regular audits and policy updates are crucial for sustaining an effective phishing defense strategy over time. Cybersecurity audits evaluate an organization's current defenses, identify gaps in its phishing prevention and response capabilities, and ensure compliance with applicable standards and regulations. These audits can be conducted internally or by third-party experts who assess technical safeguards, employee awareness programs, and incident response procedures. Alongside audits, security policies (Singh, N. et al., 2024; Singh, A. et al., 2025) must be frequently updated to reflect the latest phishing trends and tactics, as attackers continuously adapt their methods. For instance, policies regarding acceptable email use, incident reporting, and authentication procedures should be reviewed and refined in light of emerging phishing threats or technological advancements. Regular audits and policy updates guarantee that organizations remain agile and proactive in their defense efforts, continually enhancing their resilience against phishing.

7. CASE STUDIES AND RECENT PHISHING ATTACKS

Phishing attacks continue to evolve, posing significant threats to organizations across the globe. As evidenced by recent high-profile breaches, attackers employ a range of techniques, including exploiting global events, targeting supply chains, and manipulating cloud and SaaS environments. This section examines several notable case studies, analyzes their impacts, and highlights the solutions and precautions adopted by affected organizations to mitigate such threats in the future. The classification of web pages based on attractiveness through supervised learning can be linked to the identification of phishing attempts, underscoring the necessity for advanced techniques in phishing detection and prevention.

Widespread Phishing during Global Events

Phishing attacks have escalated during global events, with attackers exploiting public fear, uncertainty, and misinformation. A prominent example occurred during the COVID-19 pandemic when cybercriminals initiated phishing campaigns related to health information (Thakur, R. et al., 2025), economic relief efforts, and vaccine updates. According to the Cybersecurity and Infrastructure Security Agency (CISA), there was a significant rise in phishing emails impersonating health organizations, such as the World Health Organization (WHO) and the Centers for Disease Control and Prevention (CDC). These emails frequently contained malicious links or attachments, aiming to deceive users into disclosing sensitive information or downloading malware.

Solutions and Precautions:

In response to the rise in COVID-19-related phishing attacks, organizations adopted improved email filtering solutions to block malicious emails and educated employees about the risks associated with such phishing attempts. Security awareness programs became crucial, teaching staff how to recognize phishing emails and verify information from trusted sources. Additionally, organizations stressed the significance of using multi-factor authentication (MFA) to secure accounts, thereby decreasing the likelihood of unauthorized access, even if credentials were compromised. By fostering a culture of cybersecurity vigilance and implementing technical defenses, organizations successfully mitigated the impact of these opportunistic attacks. Fig.5. explains organizational cybersecurity culture model.

Figure 5. Organizational Cybersecurity Culture Model

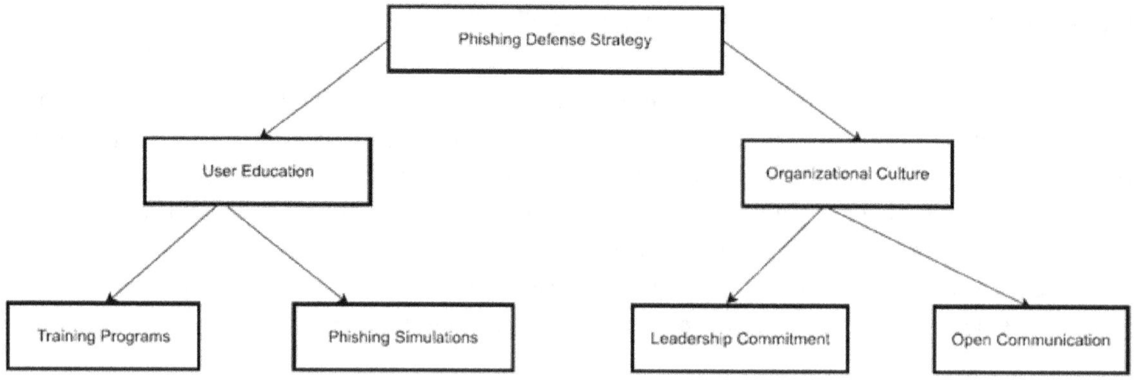

The Organizational Cybersecurity Culture Model delineates the essential components necessary for building and sustaining a robust cybersecurity culture within an organization. At the heart of this model is Cybersecurity Culture, which is reinforced by three vital pillars: Leadership, Employee Engagement, and Communication. Leadership is crucial in establishing and nurturing this culture by providing the necessary Support and Commitment to prioritize cybersecurity initiatives. Employee Engagement is promoted through comprehensive Training Programs, ensuring that staff are adequately prepared to identify and address cybersecurity threats. Equally significant is Communication, which encompasses the establishment of Reporting Channels that allow employees to efficiently report suspicious activities and incidents. Together, these elements foster a proactive and resilient cybersecurity culture, motivating all levels of the organization to actively contribute to the protection of sensitive information.

Twitter's 2020 Attack

In July 2020, Twitter fall victim to a major phishing attack that compromised high-profile accounts, including those of former President Barack Obama, billionaire Elon Musk, and tech entrepreneur Bill Gates. The attackers utilized social engineering techniques to deceive Twitter employees into divulging their login credentials, allowing them to access internal systems. Once inside, they reset passwords and took control of the targeted accounts. The attackers exploited the compromised accounts to solicit Bitcoin payments from followers, leading to financial losses and significant reputational damage for Twitter.

Solutions and Precautions:

After the breach, Twitter instituted a series of security measures to prevent similar incidents from occurring in the future. The company strengthened its internal security protocols by restricting employee access to sensitive systems and mandating multi-factor authentication (MFA) for all staff members. Twitter also undertook a thorough review of its security policies, highlighting the significance of training employees to recognize social engineering tactics. Furthermore, the company enhanced transparency regarding its incident response processes, providing updates to users and stakeholders about the actions taken to address the breach. By reinforcing its security posture and raising awareness among employees, Twitter sought to restore trust and safeguard its platform from future threats.

2019 Toyota Boshoku Corporation Breach

In 2019, Toyota Boshoku Corporation, a global automotive components supplier, fell victim to a phishing attack that exposed sensitive employee data. Cybercriminals targeted the company's payroll department, sending phishing emails designed to mimic official communications. When employees clicked on malicious links, their credentials were compromised, leading to unauthorized access to sensitive payroll information(Kaur, H. et al., 2025). The breach highlighted the vulnerabilities that exist within supply chains, particularly in industries reliant on extensive collaboration between multiple partners.

Solutions and Precautions:

In reaction to the breach, Toyota Boshoku improved its cybersecurity training programs to educate employees about the threats posed by phishing and social engineering(Sarin, S. et al., 2024). The company instituted more robust access controls and multi-factor authentication for sensitive systems, ensuring that unauthorized access would be prevented even if credentials were compromised. Furthermore, the organization invested in advanced email filtering solutions to identify and block phishing attempts effectively. By cultivating a culture of awareness and implementing technical safeguards, Toyota Boshoku aimed to reduce future risks and safeguard sensitive employee information.

2016 Snapchat Payroll Attack

In 2016, Snapchat (Snap Inc.) became a victim of a phishing attack aimed at the company's payroll department. An attacker impersonated the CEO and sent an email to a payroll employee, requesting confidential information regarding employee salaries and personal details. The employee, convinced they were adhering to legitimate instructions, provided the requested information, leading to a data breach(Li, S. et al., 20222) that compromised sensitive employee records.

Solutions and Precautions:

In reaction to the incident, Snapchat bolstered its employee training programs to highlight the necessity of verifying requests for sensitive information. The company adopted stricter email authentication measures, including DMARC and SPF, to deter unauthorized emails from being dispatched from compromised accounts. Additionally, Snapchat assessed and fortified its internal communication protocols to guarantee that sensitive requests were managed securely and verified through alternative channels. By raising awareness and securing communication pathways(Hu, B. et al., 2022), Snapchat sought to mitigate the risk of similar phishing incidents occurring in the future.

SolarWinds Chain Attack

The SolarWinds supply chain breach, identified in late 2020, marked one of the most substantial cybersecurity incidents in history. Attackers infiltrated SolarWinds' Orion software, embedding malicious code into software updates that were subsequently disseminated to thousands of clients, including government entities and major corporations. This access allowed the attackers to engage in espionage and exfiltrate sensitive information(Kumbhojkar, N. R., & Menon, A. B. (2022)). Phishing played a crucial role in the attack, as the perpetrators employed social engineering techniques to secure initial access to SolarWinds' systems and, ultimately, to the networks of its customers.

Solutions and Precautions:

In reaction to the breach, SolarWinds initiated a thorough security revamp, prioritizing improvements in its software development practices(Bhardwaj, A., & Kaushik, K. (2022)) to avert similar incidents in the future. The company established more rigorous code review procedures and introduced tighter security controls within its development environments. Moreover, SolarWinds collaborated with law enforcement and cybersecurity firms to investigate the breach and offer support to impacted customers. This incident also encouraged organizations to reevaluate their supply chain security, prompting many to adopt risk management frameworks that stress comprehensive vetting of third-party vendors and the implementation of strict security measures throughout the supply chain.

Microsoft Office 365 Phishing Campaign (2020)

In 2020, Microsoft reported a significant phishing campaign targeting Office 365 users, wherein attackers used email spoofing to impersonate legitimate accounts. The campaign involved sending emails containing links to fake login pages (Girdhar, M. et al., 2023) designed to harvest users' credentials. These phishing emails often contained messages that created a sense of immediate urgency, prompting users to act rapidly without verifying the sender's identity. The campaign successfully compromised numerous accounts, allowing attackers to access sensitive information and conduct further phishing attempts within organizations.

Solutions and Precautions:

In response to the campaign, Microsoft intensified its efforts to educate users about recognizing phishing attempts, providing guidance on identifying suspicious emails and URLs. The company also implemented advanced threat protection features (Chokkappagari R. (2024)) within Office 365 to detect and block malicious emails. Multi-factor authentication was strongly recommended for all users to enhance account security. Furthermore, organizations were encouraged to adopt security awareness training programs to cultivate a culture of vigilance among employees. By emphasizing user education and implementing technical safeguards, Microsoft and its users aimed to significantly reduce the effectiveness of phishing campaigns targeting Office 365. The proposed SMART Protocol (Spoorthi K.S. (2024)) for vehicular IoT(Gupta, H. et al. 2024, Kumar, R. et al., 2024) networks illustrates the necessity of incorporating security metrics and authentication mechanisms to counter phishing attacks in emerging technology domains.

8. CONCLUSION

As the digital landscape becomes increasingly interconnected, the risk of phishing attacks continues to present significant challenges to both organizations and individuals. Cybercriminals are constantly adapting their tactics, making it essential for organizations to implement comprehensive and flexible defense strategies against these persistent threats. A multi-pronged approach is vital, integrating advanced technologies, strong user education, and a culture of cybersecurity awareness within the organization. Investing in state-of-the-art technologies such as artificial intelligence and machine learning can significantly enhance phishing detection capabilities. The examination of cyber-physical systems underscores the necessity of a holistic security approach, including phishing defense strategies, to safeguard integrated systems from various cyber threats(Jain, A. K., & Gupta, B. B. (2022)). These technologies process vast amounts of data to identify anomalies and provide insights that guide proactive security measures, enabling organizations to detect and respond to phishing attempts with greater accuracy and speed. However, relying solely on technology is insufficient; it must be complemented by comprehensive user education programs that empower employees to recognize, report, and respond effectively to phishing threats. Cultivating a culture of cybersecurity vigilance through continuous training, simulations, and awareness campaigns ensures that employees are well-equipped to identify suspicious activities and take appropriate actions. Furthermore, implementing robust practices such as Multi-Factor Authentication (MFA) strengthens defenses against credential theft(Gupta, B. B. et al., 2021), which is a common objective of phishing attacks. By necessitating multiple forms of verification, organizations can protect sensitive information even if attackers manage to compromise user passwords. The effectiveness of MFA is amplified when paired with educational initiatives that foster a deeper understanding of cybersecurity among employees, reinforcing their commitment to safeguarding organizational assets . Continuous improvement becomes a vital principle in sustaining effective phishing defenses. Organizations must routinely evaluate their security protocols, adapt to emerging threats, and implement feedback loops (Gupta & Jain, 2020) to refine their strategies. Iterative training programs that reflect the latest phishing trends and tactics help to reinforce the human element of cybersecurity, ensuring employees remain vigilant and informed.

Ultimately, a comprehensive phishing defense strategy necessitates collaboration and commitment across all levels of an organization. By creating an environment that encourages open communication regarding cybersecurity risks and recognizing proactive behaviors, organizations foster a sense of shared responsibility among all employees. Leadership commitment to cybersecurity and a culture of awareness are vital in empowering employees to actively participate in protecting sensitive information. As organizations navigate the complexities of the digital world, embracing innovation(Sahoo et al., 2020) and maintaining a proactive stance will be essential in mitigating the risks associated with phishing attacks. By integrating advanced technologies, robust training programs, and a commitment to continuous improvement, organizations can significantly enhance their security posture, effectively safeguarding their assets against the ever-present threat of phishing. In doing so, they can cultivate a resilient cybersecurity environment where both organizations and individuals can thrive securely.

REFERENCES

Abbas, A. (2024). Evolving Phishing Defense: Innovative Defense Mechanisms and Effective Measurement Strategies.

Afridi, S. (2024). Revolutionizing Phishing Defense: A Comprehensive Overview of Defense Mechanisms and Measurement Strategies.

Aggarwal, T., Kumar, S., Singh, S. K., Gupta, B. B., Nedjah, N., & Castiglione, A. (2024). Zero Knowledge Proofs and Their Applications in Cryptography: Advancements, Challenges, and Future Aspects. In *Innovations in Modern Cryptography* (pp. 55-74). IGI Global.

Alabdan, R. (2020). Phishing attacks survey: Types, vectors, and technical approaches. *Future Internet*, 12(10), 168. DOI: 10.3390/fi12100168

Amiri, I. S., Akanbi, O. A., & Fazeldehkordi, E. (2014). *A machine-learning approach to phishing detection and defense*. Syngress.

Badwa, E., Singh, S. K., Kumar, S., Chilkoti, V., Arya, V., & Chui, K. T. (2024). Deep Learning Model for Digital Forensics Face Sketch Synthesis. In *Digital Forensics and Cyber Crime Investigation* (pp. 168–195). CRC Press.

Basit, A., Zafar, M., Liu, X., Javed, A. R., Jalil, Z., & Kifayat, K. (2021). A comprehensive survey of AI-enabled phishing attacks detection techniques. *Telecommunication Systems*, 76(1), 139–154. DOI: 10.1007/s11235-020-00733-2 PMID: 33110340

Berghel, H., Carpinter, J., & Jo, J. Y. (2007). Phish phactors: Offensive and defensive strategies. *Advances in Computers*, 70, 223–268. DOI: 10.1016/S0065-2458(06)70005-5

Bhardwaj, A., & Kaushik, K. (2022). Predictive analytics-based cybersecurity framework for cloud infrastructure. [IJCAC]. *International Journal of Cloud Applications and Computing*, 12(1), 1–20. DOI: 10.4018/IJCAC.297106

Chhabra, A., Singh, S. K., Sharma, A., Kumar, S., Gupta, B. B., Arya, V., & Chui, K. T. (2024). Sustainable and intelligent time-series models for epidemic disease forecasting and analysis. *Sustainable Technology and Entrepreneurship*, 3(2), 100064. DOI: 10.1016/j.stae.2023.100064

Chokkappagari, R. (2024). How AI Detects Phishing Scams, Insights2Techinfo, pp.1, https://insights2techinfo.com/how-ai-detects-phishing-scams/

da Silva, C. M. R., Feitosa, E. L., & Garcia, V. C. (2020). Heuristic-based strategy for Phishing prediction: A survey of URL-based approach. *Computers & Security*, 88, 101613. DOI: 10.1016/j.cose.2019.101613

Girdhar, M., Singh, S. K., Kumar, S., Mahto, D., Sharma, S. K., Gupta, B. B., & Chui, K. T. (2023, November). Exploring Advanced Neural Networks For Cross-Corpus Fake News Detection. In *Proceedings of the 5th International Conference on Information Management & Machine Intelligence* (pp. 1-6). DOI: 10.1145/3647444.3652457

Gupta, B. B., & Jain, A. K. (2020). Phishing attack detection using a search engine and heuristics-based technique. [JITR]. *Journal of Information Technology Research*, 13(2), 94–109. DOI: 10.4018/JITR.2020040106

Gupta, B. B., Yadav, K., Razzak, I., Psannis, K., Castiglione, A., & Chang, X. (2021). A novel approach for phishing URLs detection using lexical based machine learning in a real-time environment. *Computer Communications*, 175, 47–57. DOI: 10.1016/j.comcom.2021.04.023

Gupta, H., Singh, S. K., Kumar, S., Sharma, K., Saini, H., Gupta, B. B., Arya, V., & Chui, K. T. (2024). Variance-driven security optimisation in industrial IoT sensors. *IET Networks*, ntw2.12139. DOI: 10.1049/ntw2.12139

Hera, J. (2024). Phishing Defense Mechanisms: Strategies for Effective Measurement and Cyber Threat Mitigation.

Hu, B., Gaurav, A., Choi, C., & Almomani, A. (2022). Evaluation and comparative analysis of semantic web-based strategies for enhancing educational system development. [IJSWIS]. *International Journal on Semantic Web and Information Systems*, 18(1), 1–14. DOI: 10.4018/IJSWIS.302895

Huang, H., Tan, J., & Liu, L. (2009, June). Countermeasure techniques for deceptive phishing attack. In *2009 International Conference on New Trends in Information and Service Science* (pp. 636-641). IEEE.

Jain, A. K., & Gupta, B. B. (2022). A survey of phishing attack techniques, defence mechanisms and open research challenges. *Enterprise Information Systems*, 16(4), 527–565. DOI: 10.1080/17517575.2021.1896786

Jain, A. K., & Gupta, B. B. (2022). A survey of phishing attack techniques, defence mechanisms and open research challenges. *Enterprise Information Systems*, 16(4), 527–565. DOI: 10.1080/17517575.2021.1896786

Kamachi, C. (2014). *A Phishing Layered Defense Framework: A Holistic Approach to the Phishing Problem*. Idaho State University.

Kaur, H., Singh, S. K., Chhabra, A., Bhardwaj, V., Saini, R., Kumar, S., & Arya, V. (2025). Chaotic Watermarking for Tamper Detection: Enhancing Robustness and Security in Digital Multimedia. In Digital Forensics and Cyber Crime Investigation (pp. 101-128). CRC Press.

Kumar, R., Singh, S. K., Lobiyal, D. K., & Kumar, S. (2025). Secure and cost-effective key management scheme for the Internet of Things-supported WSN. In *Uncertainty in Computational Intelligence-Based Decision Making* (pp. 277–292). Academic Press. DOI: 10.1016/B978-0-443-21475-2.00012-6

Kumar, R., Singh, S. K., Lobiyal, D. K., Kumar, S., & Jawla, S. (2024). Security Metrics and Authentication-based RouTing (SMART) Protocol for Vehicular IoT Networks. *SN Computer Science*, 5(2), 236. DOI: 10.1007/s42979-023-02566-7

Kumar, S., Singh, S. K., Chilkoti, V., Arya, V., Chui, K. T., & Gupta, B. B. (2024). Metaversal 6G: Deciphering Complex Requirements and Multivariate KPIs in High-Performance Computing. *Procedia Computer Science*, 238, 914–919. DOI: 10.1016/j.procs.2024.06.112

Kumar, S., Singh, S. K., Gupta, B. B., Psannis, K., & Wu, J. (2024). Homomorphic Encryption in Smart City Applications for Balancing Privacy and Utility. In *Innovations in Modern Cryptography* (pp. 241–269). IGI Global. DOI: 10.4018/979-8-3693-5330-1.ch010

Kumbhojkar, N. R., & Menon, A. B. (2022). Integrated predictive experience management framework (IPEMF) for improving customer experience: In the era of digital transformation. [IJCAC]. *International Journal of Cloud Applications and Computing*, 12(1), 1–13. DOI: 10.4018/IJCAC.2022010107

Li, S., Qin, D., Wu, X., Li, J., Li, B., & Han, W. (2022). False alert detection based on deep learning and machine learning. [IJSWIS]. *International Journal on Semantic Web and Information Systems*, 18(1), 1–21. DOI: 10.4018/IJSWIS.313190

Moore, T. W., & Clayton, R. (2011). The impact of public information on phishing attack and defense. *Communications & Stratégies*, (81), 45–68.

Nair, S. S. (2024). Securing Against Advanced Cyber Threats: A Comprehensive Guide to Phishing, XSS, and SQL Injection Defense. *Journal of Computer Science and Technology Studies*, 6(1), 76–93. DOI: 10.32996/jcsts.2024.6.1.9

Naqvi, B., Perova, K., Farooq, A., Makhdoom, I., Oyedeji, S., & Porras, J. (2023). Mitigation strategies against the phishing attacks: A systematic literature review. *Computers & Security*, 132, 103387. DOI: 10.1016/j.cose.2023.103387

Oest, A., Safei, Y., Doupé, A., Ahn, G. J., Wardman, B., & Warner, G. (2018, May). Inside a phisher's mind: Understanding the anti-phishing ecosystem through phishing kit analysis. In *2018 APWG Symposium on Electronic Crime Research (eCrime)* (pp. 1-12). IEEE. DOI: 10.1109/ECRIME.2018.8376206

Oest, A., Zhang, P., Wardman, B., Nunes, E., Burgis, J., Zand, A., . . . Ahn, G. J. (2020). Sunrise to sunset: Analyzing the end-to-end life cycle and effectiveness of phishing attacks at scale. In *29th {USENIX} Security Symposium ({USENIX} Security 20)*.

Rajput, D., Singh, S. K., Kumar, S., Manro, D., Bansal, S., Arya, V., & Chui, K. T. (2024). Applying Visual Cryptography to Decrypt Data Using Human Senses. In *Innovations in Modern Cryptography* (pp. 376–404). IGI Global. DOI: 10.4018/979-8-3693-5330-1.ch016

Sahoo, S. R., Gupta, B. B., Choi, C., Hsu, C. H., & Chui, K. T. (2020). Behavioral analysis to detect social spammer in online social networks (OSNs). In Computational Data and Social Networks: 9th International Conference, CSoNet 2020, Dallas, TX, USA, December 11–13, 2020 [Springer International Publishing.]. *Proceedings*, 9, 321–332.

Sarin, S., Singh, S. K., Kumar, S., Goyal, S., Gupta, B. B., Arya, V., & Chui, K. T. (2024). SEIR-driven semantic integration framework: Internet of Things-enhanced epidemiological surveillance in COVID-19 outbreaks using recurrent neural networks. IET Cyber-Physical Systems: Theory & Applications.

Setia, H., Chhabra, A., Singh, S. K., Kumar, S., Sharma, S., Arya, V., Gupta, B. B., & Wu, J. (2024). Securing the road ahead: Machine learning-driven DDoS attack detection in VANET cloud environments. *Cyber Security and Applications*, 2, 100037. DOI: 10.1016/j.csa.2024.100037

Sharif, F. (2024). Enhancing Cybersecurity Resilience: Phishing Defense and the Importance of Measurement Strategies.

Sharma, A., Singh, S. K., Chhabra, A., Kumar, S., Arya, V., & Moslehpour, M. (2023). A novel deep federated learning-based model to enhance privacy in critical infrastructure systems. [IJSSCI]. *International Journal of Software Science and Computational Intelligence*, 15(1), 1–23. DOI: 10.4018/IJSSCI.334711

Sharma, A., Singh, S. K., Kumar, S., Chhabra, A., & Gupta, S. (2021, September). Security of android banking mobile apps: Challenges and opportunities. In *International conference on cyber security, privacy and networking* (pp. 406-416). Cham: Springer International Publishing.

Sharma, A., Singh, S. K., Kumar, S., Thakur, R., Gupta, B. B., & Arya, V. (2024). IoT-enabled smart farming with Industry 5.0. *Journal of High Speed Networks*, (Preprint), 1-20.

Singh, A., Singh, S. K., Chhabra, A., Singh, G., Kumar, S., & Arya, V. (2025). Detailed Evolution Process of CNN-Based Intrusion Detection in the Context of Network Security. In Digital Forensics and Cyber Crime Investigation (pp. 70-87). CRC Press.

Singh, M., Singh, S. K., Kumar, S., Madan, U., & Maan, T. (2021, September). Sustainable framework for metaverse security and privacy: Opportunities and challenges. In *International Conference on Cyber Security, Privacy and Networking* (pp. 329-340). Cham: Springer International Publishing.

Singh, N., Singh, S. K., Kumar, S., Rawat, Y., Arya, V., Bansal, R., & Chui, K. T. (2024). Next Gen Security With Quantum-Safe Cryptography. In *Innovations in Modern Cryptography* (pp. 131–164). IGI Global. DOI: 10.4018/979-8-3693-5330-1.ch006

Singh, S. K., Kumar, S., Garg, S., Arora, S., Sharma, S. K., Arya, V., & Chui, K. T. (2025). Blockchain-Based Data Security in Smart Cities: Ensuring Data Integrity and Trustworthiness. In Digital Forensics and Cyber Crime Investigation (pp. 17-41). CRC Press.

Singh, T., Kumar, S., Singh, S. K., Gupta, B. B., Wu, J., & Castiglione, A. (2025). Enhancing Autonomous System Security With AI and Secure Computation Technologies. In *AI Developments for Industrial Robotics and Intelligent Drones* (pp. 159–186). IGI Global Scientific Publishing. DOI: 10.4018/979-8-3693-2707-4.ch008

Spoorthi, K. S. (2024) Generative AI in Personalized Medicine, Insights2Techinfo, pp.1, https://insights2techinfo.com/ai-solutions-for-phishing-protection/

Thakur, K., Shan, J., & Pathan, A. S. K. (2018). Innovations of phishing defense: The mechanism, measurement and defense strategies. *International Journal of Communication Networks and Information Security*, 10(1), 19–27.

Thakur, R., Kumar, S., Singh, S. K., Singla, K., Sharma, S. K., & Arya, V. (2025). Cyber Synergy: Unlocking the Potential Use of Biometric Systems and Multimedia Forensics in Cybercrime Investigations. In Digital Forensics and Cyber Crime Investigation (pp. 241-267). CRC Press.

Vats, T., Kumar, S., Singh, S. K., Madan, U., Preet, M., Arya, V., Bansal, R., & Almomani, A. (2024). Navigating the landscape: Safeguarding privacy and security in the era of ambient intelligence within healthcare settings. *Cyber Security and Applications*, 2, 100046. DOI: 10.1016/j.csa.2024.100046

Wang, M., & Song, L. (2021). Efficient defense strategy against spam and phishing email: An evolutionary game model. *Journal of Information Security and Applications*, 61, 102947. DOI: 10.1016/j.jisa.2021.102947

Williams, J., King, J., Smith, B., Pouriyeh, S., Shahriar, H., & Li, L. (2021). Phishing prevention using defense in depth. In *Advances in Security, Networks, and Internet of Things: Proceedings from SAM'20, ICWN'20, ICOMP'20, and ESCS'20* (pp. 101-116). Springer International Publishing. DOI: 10.1007/978-3-030-71017-0_8

Chapter 2
Phishing Detection Methods

Sally D. Abualgasim
https://orcid.org/0000-0003-4154-8112
University of Gezira, Sudan

Zeinab E. Ahmed
https://orcid.org/0000-0002-6144-8533
University of Gezira, Sudan

ABSTRACT

This chapter explores the evolution of phishing detection methods, present traditional, advanced, and hybrid approaches. Traditional methods provide a base layer of defense, but their effectiveness is limited against adaptive attacks. Advanced techniques employ machine learning (ML) and deep learning (DL) to enhance detection accuracy and leveraging data-driven models that analyze URL structures, email content, and website behavior. Hybrid models combine multiple techniques to optimize performance. Case studies illustrate the practical application of these methodologies in various domains which include the use of convolutional neural networks (CNNs), long short-term memory networks (LSTMs), and ensemble algorithms such as Random Forests and Gradient Boosting, achieving detection accuracies exceeding 97% in many cases. Research also highlights on large language models (LLMs) and Universal Adversarial Perturbation (UAP) techniques, for detecting advanced phishing strategies. Challenges in phishing detection include imbalanced datasets and real-time detection requirements.

1. INTRODUCTION

In recent years, phishing attacks have emerged as a critical concern, given that millions of users manage sensitive information online while numerous phishing schemes attempt to compromise this data. Phishing constitutes a form of social engineering aimed at unlawfully obtaining user credentials, such as login details and credit card numbers, by impersonating trusted entities(Zieni et al., 2023). To address increasingly sophisticated phishing schemes, detection methodologies have advanced significantly (Hussain et al., 2023). Traditional, reactive systems, such as Microsoft SmartScreen and Google Safe Browsing, utilize blacklists of known malicious URLs and are generally effective with low false-positive rates. However, their reliance on regular updates introduces potential vulnerability windows. Phishing attacks also manifest in varied forms, including spear phishing, whaling, vishing, smishing, and

DOI: 10.4018/979-8-3693-8784-9.ch002

pharming. Detection techniques encompass a range of approaches, from whitelisting and blacklisting to content-based, URL-based, visual similarity, and machine-learning-based methods (Kalaharsha & Mehtre, 2021).

In the context of widespread digital information storage, phishing schemes primarily seek to manipulate users into divulging their sensitive data. Phishing remains one of the most prevalent and impactful tactics deployed by cybercriminals against businesses, frequently targeting corporate email systems due to their high-value information. To aid organizations in strengthening their defenses, Kaspersky offers in-depth analyses of phishing attack methods. An effective strategy for identifying phishing attempts involves scrutinizing domain names for misspellings or subtle anomalies, as phishing websites often imitate legitimate domains closely, with minor alterations to characters or language. Detection systems thus focus on identifying these subtle deviations to flag potentially harmful URLs (Remya et al., 2024). Phishing attacks come in various forms, including email phishing, spear phishing, whaling, smishing (SMS phishing), vishing (voice phishing), clone phishing, pharming, angler phishing (social media scams), and CEO fraud. Each type exploits different platforms or personal details to deceive victims, aiming to steal sensitive information or prompt unauthorized transactions. Figure 1 categorizes various Phishing Detection Methods into three main approaches: Traditional Phishing Detection Methods, Advanced Phishing Detection Techniques, and Hybrid and Data Mining Methods (Yang et al., 2021).

1. Traditional Phishing Detection Methods: This category includes conventional approaches to phishing detection, focusing on simpler, less computationally intensive techniques(Baadel et al., 2021a) .
    - Legal, Educational, and Awareness methods aim to educate users about phishing risks and enforce laws to deter phishing attempts.
    - Blacklist and Whitelist Methods involve maintaining lists of known phishing or trusted sites to block or allow access, respectively.
    - Visual Similarities Methods detect phishing by comparing visual elements of websites to known legitimate sites to spot imitations.
    - Search Engine Methods use search engines to identify potentially fraudulent websites by examining their presence and ranking.
2. Advanced Phishing Detection Techniques: These methods are more sophisticated and often utilize content analysis or heuristic approaches. Content-Based and Heuristic Methods analyze the content, structure, or metadata of emails and websites to identify signs of phishing. Heuristic methods look for suspicious patterns or elements based on pre-defined rules(Elgharbi et al., 2024).
3. Hybrid and Data Mining Methods: This approach combines different techniques to improve detection accuracy and adaptability, often employing machine learning and artificial intelligence. Machine Learning, Deep Learning Methods apply algorithms that can learn from data, adapt to new phishing techniques, and detect subtle, complex patterns that traditional methods might miss. Hybrid and Data Mining Methods further leverage multiple techniques, blending data-driven and rule-based approaches to optimize detection performance. These methods are particularly effective in detecting novel or adaptive phishing tactics(Priya et al., 2024).

This classification highlights a spectrum of phishing detection methods, from traditional and rule-based to adaptive, data-driven approaches, showing the evolution of strategies to combat increasingly sophisticated phishing threats.

Figure 1. Phishing Detection Methods

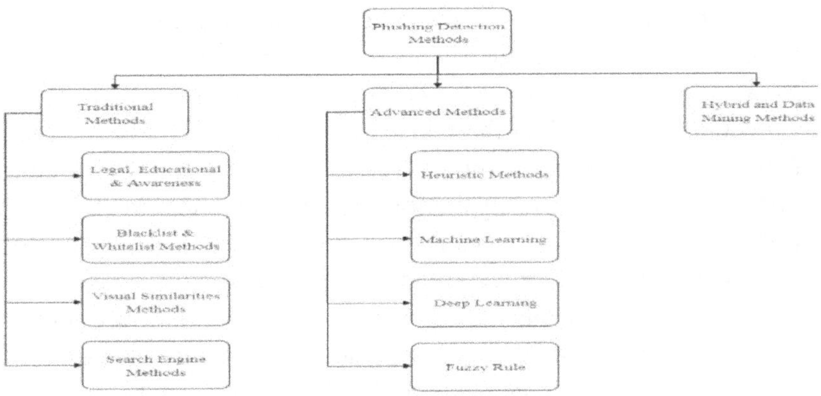

1.1. Impact on Digital Assets and Cybersecurity

Phishing attacks exert a substantial impact on digital assets and cybersecurity by posing persistent threats to network integrity. Such attacks compromise sensitive information, degrade the effectiveness of detection models, and reduce their longevity as attackers develop adaptive strategies to circumvent existing security measures (Zhu et al., 2024). Phishing incidents frequently lead to data breaches, unauthorized transactions, and malware infections, directly undermining the integrity of digital assets. Consequently, cybersecurity defenses require advanced, adaptive models capable of accurately identifying and mitigating phishing threats to secure digital environments.

Digital asset protection necessitates strategic defenses against an array of cyber threats, including malware, phishing, ransomware, distributed denial of service (DDoS) attacks, and password breaches (Zhang et al., 2024). Effective protection mechanisms encompass a range of security measures such as access control, antivirus and antimalware software, encryption protocols, backup systems, data loss prevention (DLP) tools, digital rights management (DRM), firewalls, password security protocols, multi-factor authentication (MFA), and website security enhancements. These measures are essential for organizations aiming to maintain a robust defense against cyber threats and protect valuable digital resources.

1.2. Motivation and Contributions.

Phishing has emerged as one of the most concerning cyber-attacks, especially when sensitive and critical data are handled within digital environments. A primary area of focus in combating these threats lies in the development and advancement of phishing detection methods. Despite companies relying heavily on technology to secure their valuable assets, they often overlook the role of human awareness and involvement in organizational security. Particularly, in 2012, the top vulnerabilities facing organizations included third-party access, the widespread use of mobile devices, and inadequate human awareness, all underscoring a critical human factor in cybersecurity.

The urgency of addressing phishing is underscored by alarming statistics. The FBI's Internet Crime Complaint Center (IC3) reported over 20,000 phishing-related complaints in a recent year, with compromised email accounts leading to financial losses exceeding $1.2 billion (Saravanan & Subramanian, 2020). Phishing attacks have increased by an average of 33% annually since 2015, with the expansion of internet use and remote work doubling the rate of incidents by 2022. December 2021 recorded an unprecedented 316,747 attacks, marking the highest monthly total in the Anti-Phishing Working Group's (APWG) history (APWG, 2021). Financial institutions remain a primary target, with bank-related phishing accounting for 23.2% of all phishing attacks reported in the fourth quarter of 2021 (Remya, Pillai, Arjun, et al., 2024). Figure 2 illustrates the distribution of phishing attacks across various industries in Q1 2024. Social media platforms were the most targeted, accounting for 38% of phishing attempts. This distribution emphasizes that cybercriminals prioritize industries with high user engagement and financial transactions. This study aims to contribute to the field of cybersecurity by examining and enhancing phishing detection methodologies to address the rising frequency and sophistication of phishing threats. The insights gained are intended to support organizations in strengthening their defenses against this pervasive form of cyber-attack.

Figure 2. Most targeted industries for phishing in Q1 2024

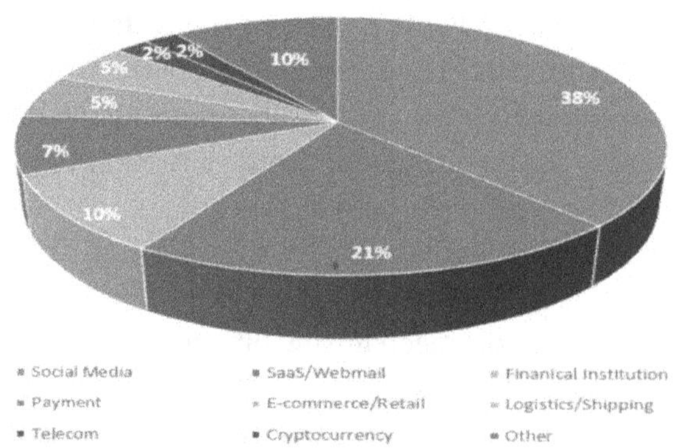

2. TRADITIONAL PHISHING DETECTION METHODS

In this section will be discuss foundational approaches for identifying and mitigating phishing attacks. These methods are typically rule-based, relying on predefined lists, patterns, and characteristics to identify potential threats. While they may lack the adaptability of advanced, data-driven techniques, traditional methods remain widely utilized due to their simplicity, efficiency, and effectiveness in detecting known phishing threats. Such approaches include legal, educational, and awareness initiatives aimed at informing users about phishing risks, along with technical measures such as blacklists, whitelists, visual similarity assessments, and search engine-based detection. Serving as a reliable first line of defense, traditional phishing detection methods play a critical role in protecting users and organizations against the dynamic threat landscape(Abdillah et al., 2022).

2.1. Legal, Educational, and Awareness.

These traditional methods collectively aim to reduce phishing attacks by combining legal deterrence, practical user education, and ongoing awareness efforts.

- Legal measures play a crucial role in combating phishing, as they delineate stringent regulations and sanctions designed to discourage cybercriminal behavior (Qabajeh et al., 2018). Numerous nations, including the United States, United Kingdom, Canada, and Australia, have instituted anti-phishing legislation that imposes severe penalties, encompassing fines and incarceration, on individuals convicted of engaging in phishing activities. Such statutes not only engender a deterrent effect by rendering phishing a prosecutable offense but also empower organizations to pursue legal recourse against perpetrators (Alkhalil et al., 2021a). Furthermore, international partnerships, such as Microsoft's accord with the Australian government, seek to bolster cross-border enforcement and fortify global defenses against cybercrime. Nevertheless, the implementation of these laws on an international scale presents significant challenges due to jurisdictional intricacies and the anonymity frequently exploited by offenders.
- Educational initiatives play a pivotal role in mitigating the efficacy of phishing attacks by augmenting users' awareness and detection competencies. Numerous organizations enact extensive training programs that incorporate simulated phishing exercises, wherein employees encounter realistic phishing scenarios within a controlled setting (Alharbi et al., 2022a). These exercises significantly enhance users' capacity to discern warning signs and identify deceptive communications. Academic institutions and organizations similarly implement such methodologies, executing integrated training that evaluates vulnerability to phishing endeavors. Furthermore, innovative strategies such as interactive anti-phishing games actively engage users through authentic scenarios, effectively instructing them on how to detect phishing threats. These scenario-based techniques permit users to hone their skills in recognizing phishing attempts, thereby markedly diminishing their susceptibility(Alanezi, 2021). Collectively, these educational initiatives cultivate a security-aware culture, equipping individuals with the requisite skills to thwart phishing assaults.
- Awareness initiatives are pivotal in promoting sustained vigilance towards phishing attacks(Baadel et al., 2021b). Through systematic campaigns and community-oriented resources, individuals remain apprised of the most recent phishing methodologies and prevention tactics. Platforms such as PhishTank and the Anti-Phishing Working Group (APWG) provide contemporaneous data regarding reported phishing websites and emerging threats, thereby establishing a communal knowledge repository. Numerous organizations also implement alert systems that inform users of potentially harmful URLs, thereby augmenting the collective capacity to identify and evade phishing scams. These endeavors foster a culture of security awareness, enabling individuals to discern, report, and thwart phishing attempts, thus contributing to a more secure online ecosystem(Alkhalil et al., 2021a).

2.2. Blacklist and Whitelist Methods

A blacklist is a list of entities, such as websites or IP addresses, that are identified as malicious, harmful, or unauthorized, and are therefore blocked or restricted from access. A whitelist is a list of trusted entities or items that are considered safe, authorized, or allowed access, while all others are restricted or blocked(He et al., 2024). Blacklist-based phishing detection maintains a list of known phishing sites and blocks access to them. Regular updates ensure new phishing URLs are added, and incoming site requests are checked against the blacklist. While effective and easy to implement, this method can be bypassed by frequently changing URLs(Azeez et al., 2021). Web browsers like Microsoft Edge, Firefox, and Chrome use both whitelists (valid sites) and blacklists (fraudulent sites) to prevent phishing but require frequent updates to stay effective. A key limitation is that even slight URL modifications may evade detection(Safi & Singh, 2023).

Blacklists exhibit two fundamental limitations: they are incapable of identifying newly established domains and necessitate an alternative classification methodology for their updates. The effectiveness of blacklists is constrained, particularly since a significant number of phishing domains do not recur, rendering detection solely based on blacklists less precise. In 2023, Two primary methodologies (human and machine-driven) are employed to evaluate domains; however, both encounter inherent limitations. The obtained results, during the 10-year time from 2013 to 2022, show that domain blacklist is a relevant detection technique with a capacity to detect between 15% and 20%, except the last year which the efficacy let fall to less than 7%. Consequently, blacklists encounter challenges in adapting effectively, thereby necessitating a composite approach that is progressively essential for dependable phishing detection (Skula & Kvet, 2023).

In 2017 the Simhash algorithm was used to generate fingerprint for each website. Two Experiments were conducted, one for fingeprint generation of Blacklist URL and the other for detection of replicated phishing websites. The experimentation was detected 84.36% from Experiment 1 and 62.10% from Experiment 2 of phishing sites as replicas of other phishing websites with manipulated content while maintaining zero false positive rate. The method is similar to that of traditional blacklist with and also it can detect replicated and manipulated phishing sites efficiently. (Rao & Pais, 2017).

The primary operational and functional prerequisite for whitelisting entails the comparison of an input received through the defense solution interface with the signatures contained within the extant whitelist database, thereby assisting the control module in determining the appropriateness of granting or rejecting the input, as illustrated in Figure 3, and subsequently transmitting the decision back to the defense application to either authorize or disallow the input (Bayer et al., 2023). Whitelisting methodologies establish reliable databases to delineate sanctioned files, applications, or behaviors, predicated on criteria such as file pathways, digital certifications, or behavioral patterns (NIST SP 800-167). Instruments such as VirusTotal employ the National Software Reference Library (NSRL) whitelist to mitigate false positive occurrences (Medhat et al., 2023). Despite their efficacy in bolstering security, the processes of maintaining and updating whitelists present significant challenges. Whitelisting is indispensable in cybersecurity frameworks to obstruct unauthorized access and guarantee that only verified applications function, thereby enhancing defenses against cyber threats (Ishtaiwi et al., 2024).

Figure 3. Process for Whitelist

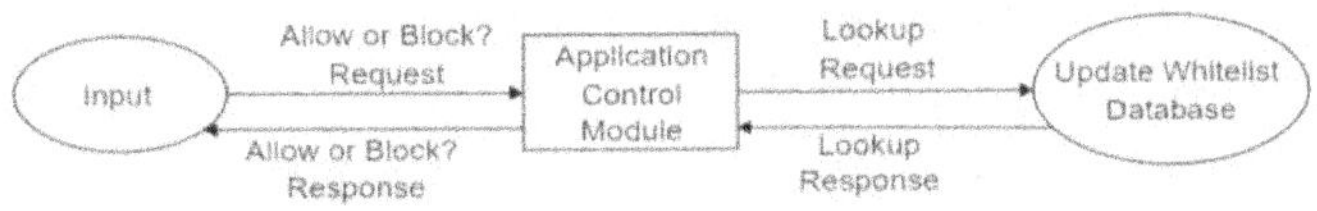

2.3. Visual Similarities Methods.

The visual similarity methodology assesses both dubious and bona fide websites through an analysis of diverse visual components, given that phishing websites are meticulously crafted to closely imitate legitimate ones (Safi & Singh, 2023). This methodology evaluates attributes such as Cascading Style Sheets (CSS), textual arrangement, underlying source code, logos, and visual representations to identify resemblances. Nevertheless, due to its dependence on juxtaposing a questionable site with previously archived pages, this approach is inadequate against zero-hour phishing assaults (Niu & Wu, 2024).

S. Remya et al. presented a novel residual pipelining technique that augments conventional detection methodologies. This technique encompasses the extraction of URL characteristics alongside selected sentiment-oriented features, subsequently transforming them into a matrix and generating a hybrid feature set to enhance detection efficacy. Comprehensive testing disclosed that this methodology attained a remarkable accuracy of 98.295%, exceeding that of traditional approaches (Remya, Pillai, Nair, et al., 2024).

These methodologies based on visual similarity are contingent upon comparisons with a repository of resources, such as visual representations, logos, and design styles, yet encounter difficulties in identifying phishing endeavors on non-whitelisted domains or phishing sites featuring modified whitelisted content. Owing to their considerable computational requirements, these techniques pose implementation challenges on the client side. To bolster detection rates, heuristic features, including indicators derived from URLs and source code, are integrated to identify non-blacklisted phishing sites. Empirical findings reveal that blacklist filters in isolation detect only 55.58% of phishing sites that mimic existing ones. An ensemble model incorporating Random Forest, Extra Trees, and XGBoost was proposed, amalgamating blacklist and heuristic filters, achieving an accuracy of 98.72% and a Matthews Correlation Coefficient (MCC) of 97.39%. This model was operationalized as a Chrome extension, "BlackPhish," offering real-time protection against phishing threats and surpassing the performance of existing anti-phishing solutions in terms of accuracy and MCC (Rao & Pais, 2017) .

2.4. Search Engine Methods

The search engine-oriented phishing detection methodology employs search engines to discern phishing websites by scrutinizing site content and juxtaposing it with established legitimate entities (Azeez et al., 2021). This technique encompasses the validation of webpage authenticity through search engine results, evaluating salient phrases, lexical signatures, and content patterns. Upon the submission of a potentially nefarious URL, search engines ascertain whether the webpage's content corresponds with recognized legitimate sources, thereby facilitating real-time phishing identification.

A salient strategy within this framework is the employment of black hat SEO techniques by cyber-criminals, whereby they enhance malicious websites to achieve elevated rankings in search results. This phenomenon can inadvertently expose users to phishing webpages during their routine searches for goods or services (Alkhalil et al., 2021b). The efficacy of search engine-based detection is attributed to its remarkable precision in recognizing established phishing indicators such as logos, URLs, and textual elements (Alanezi, 2021) . Nevertheless, it encounters challenges when phishing websites are hosted on compromised servers or obscure domains, as this may adversely affect the true negative rate.

Innovative methodologies, like those proposed by Ramesh et al., enhance search engine-based detection by identifying target domains through analytical processes (Ramesh et al., 2017). By summing rows and columns, they create a "parasitic matrix" to illustrate connections between a phishing site and its target. Although promising, this approach encounters scalability issues with large datasets and may yield inaccurate results if the initial data correlations are flawed. Additionally, it may struggle to adapt to the constantly evolving nature of phishing tactics and web designs.

3. ADVANCED PHISHING DETECTION TECHNIQUES

In this section dedicated to advanced phishing detection methodologies, we investigate sophisticated phishing detection techniques that transcend conventional methods to effectively counter the increasingly intricate nature of phishing assaults. In contrast to traditional strategies that depend on blacklists or rudimentary rule-based frameworks, advanced techniques integrate more elaborate methodologies, encompassing machine learning, artificial intelligence, and heuristic analysis. These approaches evaluate a diverse array of indicators, including behavioral patterns, sentiment attributes, URL characteristics, and website content, to discern phishing threats with heightened precision and immediacy. By utilizing data-driven models and adaptive algorithms, advanced phishing detection methodologies are more adept at identifying previously unknown, zero-hour phishing attacks that circumvent traditional filters. As phishing strategies continue to evolve in complexity, these advanced methodologies offer an essential layer of defense, thereby improving both detection accuracy and adaptability within the contemporary cyber threat environment.

3.1. Content-Based and Heuristic Methods

Content-based and heuristic methodologies are predicated on the examination of inherent characteristics of phishing websites, thereby facilitating the differentiation of these malicious entities from legitimate counterparts through the analysis of specific attributes. Such methodologies aggregate data from a multitude of sources, including but not limited to URLs, textual content, DNS records, digital certificates, and patterns of web traffic (Ishtaiwi et al., 2024). The ability of these methodologies is conditional upon the selection of features, the quality of training data, and the classification algorithms employed. A significant merit of heuristic approaches lies in their capacity to detect zero-hour phishing attacks, rendering them exceptionally responsive to the continually advancing tactics employed by phishers (Dafni Rose et al., 2024).

E. Anupriya et al. exposed a methodology for the identification of authentic profiles through the analysis of patterns within extensive datasets, thereby enhancing the detection of fraudulent accounts with efficacy. The graph adjacency matrix was utilized, followed by the PCA algorithm. The obtained result was 74% normal users and 28% frauds (Anupriya et al., 2022). Furthermore, as DDoS attacks exhibit increasing sophistication, scholars such as (Chinnasamy et al., 2023) have devised heuristic-based strategies to confront these challenges, utilizing web traffic metrics and URL parameters. Parekh et al. employed a Random Forest algorithm on the PhishTank dataset, concentrating on 31 URL features, thereby attaining an accuracy rate of approximately 95%. Despite this efficacy, the investigation underscored certain limitations attributable to the finite number of URL features employed during the evaluation process (Parekh et al., 2018). Ding et al. introduced a hybrid Search & Heuristic Rule & Logistic Regression (SHLR) methodology aimed at enhancing filtering efficiency (Ding et al., 2019). The SHLR framework comprises a tripartite process: it first conducts a search for title tags to ascertain legitimacy via the Baidu search engine, subsequently applying heuristic rules to evaluate character features should additional verification prove necessary. Ultimately, a logistic regression classifier evaluates the remaining pages to bolster detection accuracy. This methodology successfully filters 61.9% of legitimate pages while identifying 22.9% of phishing pages, culminating in an overall detection accuracy of 98.9% (Ding et al., 2019). These content-based and heuristic methodologies persist in their pivotal role in phishing detection by harnessing machine learning, heuristic principles, and hybrid techniques to maintain a proactive stance against the perpetually evolving landscape of phishing strategies.

3.2. Machine Learning, Deep Learning Methods

Machine learning has become a widely used method for detecting phishing websites. This approach involves collecting attributes such as URL details, website structure, and JavaScript features, which help represent phishing URLs and associated sites (Singh et al., 2020). Phishing datasets are subsequently developed based on these selected features, and classifiers are trained to detect phishing sites. Pathmanaban et al. commonly used classifiers include the Bayes model, Support Vector Machine (SVM), Association Rules, Logistic Regression (LR), and neural networks, a hybrid approach was adopted to enhance the results and efficiency of the machine learning models. The highest and most efficient results were achieved with the proposed approach, with an accuracy of 98.12%, precision of 97.31%, recall of 96.33%, specificity of 96.55%, and F1-score of 95.89% (Pathmanaban et al., 2024). Although machine learning methods effectively learn data classification, public phishing datasets often contain duplicate entries and irrelevant features, which can cause overfitting. Moreover, excessive or uninformative features may increase classifier size and lower detection accuracy, ultimately impacting classifier performance (Zhu et al., 2020). This method is particularly effective with Big Data due to its high velocity, variety, volume, value, and veracity. Figure 4 illustrates the operation of the machine learning model. In 2024 six classical machine-learning models (RFs, decision trees, SVMs, naive Bayes, logistic regression, and KNN) were benchmarked for discrimination capability. The RF classifier achieves over 97% accuracy, other algorithms also exhibit strong accuracies around 91-95%, indicating machine learning's versatility for phishing challenges (Ishtaiwi et al., 2024). Chinnasamy et al. has been applied Machine learning architectures, the best outcome was generated by the Decision Tree algorithm, which had a 99.77% accuracy rate (Chinnasamy et al., 2024).

Deep learning (DL) centers on layered models like deep neural networks and reinforcement learning (Thakur et al., 2023). Methods such as convolutional neural networks (CNNs), recurrent neural networks (RNNs), long short-term memory (LSTM), and auto-encoders are selected based on specific data types and applications. Unlike ML, which can perform well with smaller datasets, DL relies on substantial data volumes to achieve high accuracy. This need, coupled with DL's complex architecture, requires significant computational resources. Technologies like Graphics Processing Unit (GPUs) support parallel processing, boosting efficiency, yet DL training times can still extend from hours to months, whereas ML models often train more quickly. Experimental results showed that CNN had the highest performance, with 98.74% accuracy for phishing attacks and RNN with 95.1% accuracy (Sahingoz et al., 2024). Deep Neural Networks are expected to outperform traditional Machine Learning methods in phishing website detection. Common Deep Learning algorithms applied in this field include the Deep Neural Network, Recurrent Neural Network, Feed-Forward Deep Neural Network, Limited Boltzmann Machine, Convolutional Neural Network, Deep Belief Network, and Deep Auto-Encoder. Each of these algorithms offers advanced capabilities for identifying complex patterns in phishing data (Alsubaei et al., 2024).

Figure 4. Phishing Attack Detection Using Machine Learning

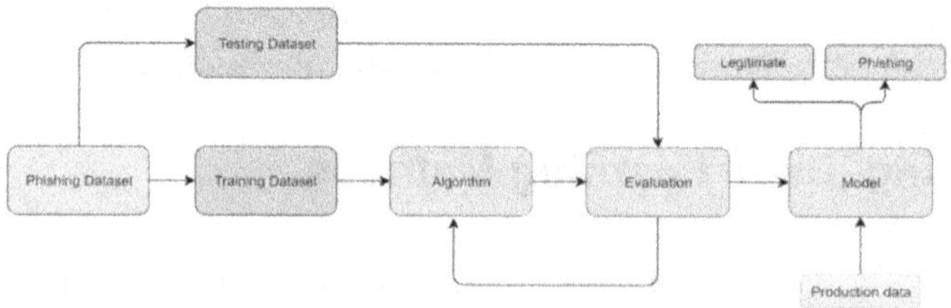

3.3. Hybrid Methods

A hybrid approach to phishing detection combines multiple classification techniques, aiming to improve the accuracy of identifying malicious websites across the internet. For instance, a hybrid model may apply an initial algorithm to train the dataset, then pass the results to a secondary algorithm for further refinement (Do et al., 2022). This layered process often yields greater accuracy than using individual algorithms in isolation, highlighting the strength of this integrative method. In the evolving cybersecurity landscape, hybrid models are essential, as singular approaches can expose vulnerabilities that cybercriminals may exploit, with an accuracy of 98.8% (Dubey & Makwana, 2024). By combining different techniques, hybrid models capitalize on the strengths of each, addressing limitations and providing a more reliable classification of phishing threats. The accuracy results obtained around 97.4% -100% (Siva et al., 2024). This comprehensive approach not only enhances detection accuracy but also offers a more resilient framework for combating increasingly complex cyber threats, representing a significant advancement in cybersecurity. Therefore, exploring and adopting hybrid models is critical to improving the efficacy of malicious website detection (Bountakas & Xenakis, 2023).

4. CASE STUDIES AND APPLICATIONS

Applications and case studies in phishing detection explore diverse strategies and techniques for identifying and mitigating phishing attacks. These studies often focus on the effectiveness of heuristic-based and machine learning methods in detecting phishing emails, websites, and URLs. They address the challenges and successes of implementing these methods in practical scenarios, evaluating their performance with real-world data. The primary goal is to enhance the accuracy and efficiency of phishing detection systems, offering better protection against cyber threats. By examining various artificial intelligence approaches, including scenario-based methods, machine learning, deep learning, and hybrid learning, these investigations provide valuable insights into combating phishing attacks effectively.

4.1. Case Studies

Phishing attacks remain a significant cybersecurity challenge, exploiting user trust to compromise sensitive information. The rapid advancement of artificial intelligence (AI) has opened new frontiers in developing robust solutions to detect and mitigate these threats. This section explores various AI-driven methods for phishing detection, including machine learning, deep learning, hybrid approaches, and scenario-based techniques. By examining these methodologies through detailed case studies, we aim to provide a comprehensive understanding of their effectiveness and practical applications in combating phishing attacks. The survey presented in this section highlights the strengths and limitations of each approach, offering valuable insights into their potential for improving cybersecurity frameworks.

Advanced Phishing Detection Techniques

Siva et al. emphasizes machine learning (ML) as a critical tool for detection, employing mixed algorithms and URL analysis to adapt to evolving challenges. The study explores advanced ML techniques, including Random Forest, Gradient Boosting, and ensemble methods like Stacking Classifiers, with hybrid LSD models showing promise. The best accuracy results obtained was 100% for with hybrid LSD and Stacking Classifiers and 97.4% for, Gradient Boosting (Siva et al., 2024). Chinnasamy et al. explored various techniques, including supervised machine learning, deep learning models like RNNs and CNNs, and anomaly detection, to enhance phishing detection (Chinnasamy et al., 2024). Hybrid approaches, such as combining logistic regression, SVM, and decision trees, have shown improved accuracy. Studies also highlight the effectiveness of LSTM, CNN, and C-LSTM in analyzing phishing websites and emails. Proposed systems integrate deep learning, continuous updates, and compliance with data security laws. Features include real-time data collection, multi-channel notifications, and user-friendly designs, ensuring adaptability and robust protection. Ethical AI practices and interdisciplinary collaboration are emphasized for addressing privacy concerns and strengthening cybersecurity frameworks.

E-banking's convenience is overshadowed by sophisticated phishing attacks targeting sensitive financial information. To combat this, authors proposed advanced detection system leverages data mining, machine learning, and ensemble methods like Random Forests and LSTM for robust and efficient phishing detection (Siva Reddy et al., 2024). By integrating hand-crafted and deep features, the model adapts to evolving threats with high accuracy. Using a comprehensive dataset enriched by sources like Common Crawl, preprocessing ensures data quality, while techniques like Word2Vec enable semantic URL analysis, and LSTM captures temporal patterns. Ensemble methods enhance stability and mitigate overfitting through mechanisms like bagging and voting. Haq et al. proposed a deep learning-based method for detecting phishing URLs using a 1D convolutional neural network (CNN) (Haq et al., 2024). The model is trained on features extracted from URLs and evaluates the system using data from PhishTank, UNB, and Alexa. The study generated 200,000 phishing URLs and 200,000 legitimate URLs for testing. Experimental results showed that the CNN-based approach significantly outperformed traditional models for URL-based phishing detection, achieving an impressive accuracy rate of 99.7%. Authors introduced a novel approach combining convolutional neural networks (CNNs) with deep Q-networks (DQNs) and attention mechanisms, leveraging word2vec, PCA, and natural language processing (NLP) for enhanced feature extraction and classification (Birthriya et al., 2024). The proposed methodology demonstrated superior accuracy (99.75%) and robustness, with a low false positive rate (0.25%) and high AUC (0.9975), effectively distinguishing phishing from legitimate URLs. By addressing challenges like parameter tuning and computational intensity, this study highlights the potential of hybrid models to improve phishing detection. In 2024 Trad & Chehab compares the efficacy of large language models (LLMs) like Claude 2 and GPT-3.5-turbo in identifying phishing URLs, aiming to determine whether generalized LLMs can replace task-specific models for phishing detection. Two methods were tested: fine-tuning and prompt engineering. The authors explored various prompt-engineering techniques, such as zero-shot, role-playing, and chain-of-thought prompting, using chat models like GPT-3.5-turbo and Claude 2. With a test set of 1000 samples, rapid engineering yielded the best results, achieving an F1-score of 92.74%. The study found that fine-tuning base LLMs like GPT-2, Bloom, LLaMA, and DistilGPT-2 improved their performance, with GPT-2 (medium) outperforming prompt-engineered versions. The findings highlight that while LLMs with prompt engineering can perform well, task-specific models provide superior accuracy, emphasizing the importance of tailored models for phishing detection (Trad & Chehab, 2024). Talukder et al. evaluated Naive Bayes classifiers using the Kaggle dataset, distinguishing "Good" and "Bad" URLs through vectorization and tokenization (Talukder et al., 2024). Complement Naive Bayes outperformed others, achieving 96% precision and 90% recall for phishing detection. While results are promising, limitations include language dependency and the need for metaheuristic optimization in future work. Integrating enhanced databases and alert systems may bolster phishing prevention efforts.

By this article advanced phishing detection techniques were focusing on similarity-based methods and prototype learning to address evolving attack strategies (Purwanto et al., 2022). The research highlights normalized compression distance (NCD) for identifying shared patterns in phishing websites, which often reuse HTML templates. Prototype-based learning, a feature-free method using real data samples as cluster representatives, improves efficiency with a greedy clustering algorithm and enables incremental learning to adapt to new data over time. The PhishSim system classifies websites by comparing their NCD similarity to known phishing prototypes, achieving a high AUC score, a true positive rate of nearly 90%, and a low false positive rate of 0.58%. (Purwanto et al., 2022).This paper addressed phishing attack detection through machine learning approaches, highlighting their superiority over traditional methods (Olukoya et al., 2024). Emphasis is placed on the importance of feature selection in enhancing model efficiency. To this end, an ensemble feature selection framework was introduced, which effectively reduced the number of features while achieving an accuracy of 98.4%.

Hybrid Phishing Detection Methods

This study leverages machine learning and the Horse Herd Optimization (HHO) algorithm for phishing detection, emphasizing feature selection (Hemannth et al., 2024). HHO, inspired by horse herding behavior, optimizes feature subsets, guiding model performance. Random Forest, known for handling high-dimensional data, complements HHO, providing robust predictions and feature importance insights. Data collection involves URLs, categorized by external services and structure, with pre-processing steps to remove duplicates, convert categorical data, and filter short URLs. The dataset, equally split between phishing and legitimate URLs, is divided into training (80%) and testing (20%) sets. Evaluation metrics reveal the model's accuracy (97%), precision (0.97), recall (0.97), and F1 score (0.97), with the area under the curve of the receiver operating characteristic (AUC-ROC) curve confirming robustness. Future enhancements include parameter optimization, ensemble methods, and integrating email content and webpage analysis to improve phishing detection (Hemannth et al., 2024). Catal et al. conducted a systematic literature review (SLR) on deep learning techniques for phishing detection by addressing nine research questions (Catal et al., 2022). They found that email content, URLs, website data, and third-party information were commonly used data sources, with supervised deep learning methods being predominant. The most popular algorithms were deep neural networks (DNN), convolutional neural networks (CNN), and recurrent/long short-term memory networks (RNN/LSTM), with DNN and hybrid models performing the best. Notably, 72% of studies did not use feature selection, and while PhishTank was a common dataset, nearly half of the studies lacked a specified framework, though Keras and TensorFlow were widely used (Catal et al., 2022).

Cybercriminals exploit urgency and trust, making detection challenging for conventional methods (Sawant et al., 2024). The rise in phishing is linked to free hosting services and social media. A proposed solution leverages machine learning (ML) and deep learning to analyze URLs, combining a browser extension and web application for real-time alerts and detailed URL analysis. Using datasets with over 650,000 URLs, the approach extracts URL components for training CNN and hybrid models like CNN-LSTM, achieving high accuracy (97%). Integrated with Flask, the system offers scalable, user-friendly protection. Bezerra et al. investigated the development of a machine learning-based model for detecting phishing emails within the e-governance platform, E-goi (Bezerra et al., 2024) . Phishing emails constituted less than 1% of the dataset, which was collected from E-goi servers. After rigorous data selection and feature extraction based on email content, the study evaluated multiple models to handle the dataset's imbalance. Various under-sampling techniques were explored to enhance the model's ability to identify phishing emails effectively. The final neural network model demonstrated the capability to detect over 80% of phishing emails while maintaining the integrity of legitimate emails sent to E-goi clients, ensuring reliable performance in the email system (Bezerra et al., 2024).

Alsarhan et al. employed Random Forest (RF) and machine learning (ML) to develop a phishing detection model with 97% accuracy (Alsarhan et al., 2024). Key metrics, including precision, recall, and F1-score, confirm its effectiveness. Automated feature selection and importance scoring improve classification. Evaluation via ROC curve and AUC highlights robust performance. Authors introduced a phishing URL detection method leveraging ResMLP, incorporating residual pipelining to enhance detection accuracy (Remya, Pillai, Nair, et al., 2024). The approach analyzes URL features and sentiments for classification, achieving an impressive 98.29% accuracy. Additionally, domain age analysis contributes to the model's robustness and efficiency. Future research aims to address resilience against adversarial attacks. This paper proposed a Universal Adversarial Perturbation (UAP)-based method to detect such triggers in phishing detection models (Nishiura et al., 2024). By analyzing perturbation-induced distortions in decision boundaries, the method identifies and locates triggers, enhancing backdoor attack detection. Tested on 32,272 URLs with various trigger scenarios, the method demonstrated success in identifying malicious data without false positives, even under clean conditions.

Traditional Phishing Detection Methods

Tan et al. examined advancements in identity-based phishing detection methods, which verify websites by querying search engines with brand logos or keywords (Tan et al., 2023). While these techniques achieve high true positive rates, they often face false positives due to limited textual content on websites, making keyword extraction difficult. The study introduced "colorfulness" as a key factor in logo identification and proposes a hybrid method combining visual and textual identity checks to enhance accuracy and reduce false positives. Approach involves logo detection, feature extraction, and textual identity verification, with a fallback to textual discovery if logo detection fails. A 3-tier identity matching module improves accuracy, especially for country-specific websites. Experimental results showed a true positive rate of 99.4% and a true negative rate of 97.8%, outperforming visual or textual-only methods (Tan et al., 2023). Authors investigated factors influencing phishing susceptibility and the role of cue use in identifying phishing emails (Sturman et al., 2023). The study found that higher cue utilization, such as recognizing phishing characteristics (e.g., spelling errors, unusual sender addresses), improves the ability to distinguish between phishing and legitimate emails, especially when participants are aware of phishing base rates. Time constraints reduced detection accuracy, with more time leading to better cue use. The research suggests that cue-based training, combined with knowledge-based training, can enhance phishing detection skills. Two experiments were conducted: in the second, participants were aware of phishing emails, while in the first, they were unaware. Both studies showed that while increased cue use improved detection, it also led to a higher bias for labeling emails as phishing. The findings highlight the importance of cue use in phishing detection and recommend that training programs focus on improving this skill to strengthen cybersecurity (Sturman et al., 2023).

4.2. Main Application of Phishing Detection Method

Phishing detection techniques are widely used in many different fields to shield users from online dangers. Here are some of the primary applications:

- Email Security: there are two main ways to secure emails. Firstly, spam filters where phishing emails are detected and blocked before they reach the user's mailbox by integrating phishing detection algorithms with spam filters. Secondly, Email Gateways, these systems analyze incoming and outgoing emails for phishing content, preventing malicious emails from being delivered.
- Web Browsers: URL Filtering, which browsers use phishing detection technologies to examine URLs and notify users if they are about to visit a known or suspected phishing site. Also, Safe Browsing Services by keeping track of phishing websites and warning users when they try to access them, services like Google Safe Browsing offer real-time security.
- Financial Institutions: Phishing detection is used by banks and other financial institutions to keep an eye on transactions for indications of fraud linked to phishing. And to inform consumers about

phishing hazards and how to prevent them, financial institutions frequently employ phishing detection systems by consumer education (Wei & Sekiya, 2022).

- Enterprise Security: Initially, Network Security to keep an eye on network activity and identify phishing attempts directed at staff members, organizations implement phishing detection systems. And security awareness training to teach staff members how to spot and handle phishing attempts by simulating phishing attacks in Businesses (Wu et al., 2022).
- Mobile Security: Phishing detection techniques are included into mobile security applications to shield users' smartphones and tablets against phishing scams. Phishing detection is used by mobile carriers and apps to filter out phishing SMS messages (Zheng et al., 2024).
- Social Media: Phishing detection is a tool used by social media platforms to detect and stop phishing attacks that aim to compromise user accounts. And content monitoring to stop harmful links from spreading, platforms keep an eye out for phishing content in posts and messages (Alharbi et al., 2022b).

By identifying and stopping phishing attempts in a variety of settings, these applications contribute to the protection of users' financial information, personal information, and general online security (Shahrivari et al., 2020).

5. CHALLENGES AND FUTURE DIRECTIONS

Phishing detection methods face numerous challenges, particularly due to the rapid evolution of phishing techniques. Here are some major challenges:

- **Data Labeling**: One of the key hurdles in phishing detection research is acquiring high-quality, labelled datasets for training and evaluation. Phishing datasets are often scarce, outdated, or incomplete, and manually labelling phishing emails or websites is time-consuming and prone to errors (Subasi & Kremic, 2020).
- **Imbalanced Datasets**: Phishing emails and websites are relatively rare compared to legitimate ones, leading to highly imbalanced datasets. This imbalance can negatively impact the performance of detection models, making it difficult to develop accurate classifiers without overfitting to the majority class (Tusher et al., 2024).
- **Multimodal Phishing**: Phishing attacks are not restricted to emails and websites; they can also occur through SMS, voice calls, social media, and other platforms. Creating unified detection systems that can handle multiple types of phishing attacks is a significant challenge.
- **Real-Time Detection**: Detecting phishing attempts in real time is a critical challenge, especially with the growing volume of data. Phishing detection systems must be both accurate and fast, able to process large datasets without significant delays (Patil et al., 2024).
- **Collaboration Across Domains**: Phishing detection is an interdisciplinary problem involving cybersecurity, machine learning, and human-computer interaction. Effective solutions require collaboration across these fields, but research is often siloed, which slows down innovation and progress (Sarker et al., 2024).

Phishing remains one of the most persistent cybersecurity threats, and while significant progress has been made in phishing detection techniques, there is still ample room for innovation and improvement. Below are several promising directions for future research in the field of phishing detection:

- **Advancement of Machine Learning and Deep Learning Models**: Hybrid models that combine multiple machine learning techniques, such as ensemble methods and deep learning with traditional rule-based approaches, can enhance phishing detection accuracy by leveraging the strengths of each method (Patil et al., 2024). For example, deep neural networks can extract features from raw data like HTML code or URLs, which are then classified using classical machine learning techniques. Additionally, reinforcement learning can create adaptive models that continuously improve by learning from new phishing tactics over time, while transfer learning offers the potential to transfer knowledge across different phishing campaigns, enabling effective detection even with limited labeled data from new attack vectors.
- **Behavioral and Context-Aware Detection Systems**: Future research in phishing detection could focus on analyzing user behavior patterns through User Behavior Analytics (UBA) to identify deviations from normal activity that may signal phishing attempts. Additionally, enhancing phishing detection systems with contextual awareness, such as considering factors like time of day, email frequency, or recent activities, could help distinguish legitimate communications from phishing. For example, sudden spikes in unsolicited emails or unusual domain usage could serve as indicators of phishing attacks (Gupta et al., 2018).
- **Integration of Threat Intelligence**: Collaborative detection in phishing detection systems involves integrating threat intelligence feeds from diverse sources, such as cybersecurity organizations, private sector entities, and government agencies, to improve detection accuracy by leveraging shared insights on phishing trends, malicious domains, and email signatures. Additionally, crowdsourcing phishing reports from users and organizations can enhance detection models, enabling real-time identification of emerging phishing campaigns and helping to stay ahead of evolving threats (Basit et al., 2021).
- **Phishing via Voice and Video Communications**: As voice and video communication platforms (e.g., Voice over IP, video conferencing) become more widely used, phishing attacks are increasingly targeting these mediums. Future research could focus on detecting phishing attempts through the analysis of audio and video content, as well as communication patterns. A promising area for development is voice phishing detection, where techniques like voice biometrics, speech recognition, and NLP could be employed to identify suspicious or malicious voice phishing attempts (Catal et al., 2022) .
- **Privacy Preserving Phishing Detection**: Federated learning and differential privacy are promising techniques for improving phishing detection while addressing privacy concerns. Federated learning enables the training of machine learning models without directly sharing sensitive user data, allowing for enhanced phishing detection without compromising privacy. Similarly, differential privacy can be integrated into phishing detection systems to protect users' personal information by adding noise to datasets, thereby reducing the risks associated with collecting large amounts of user data for training purposes. Both approaches aim to balance privacy with effective phishing detection.
- **Phishing Detection for Emerging Technologies**: As blockchain technology and cryptocurrencies gains popularity, phishing attacks targeting these areas are becoming more prevalent. Research

could focus on developing specialized detection methods for blockchain-related phishing threats. Additionally, the rise of AI tools capable of generating realistic content, such as GPT models and deepfakes, presents new challenges in detecting AI-generated phishing attempts. As a result, there is an emerging need for research to create effective detection techniques for identifying AI-driven phishing content (Kulkarni et al., 2024).

In summary, phishing detection is an evolving field that requires continual adaptation to counter the increasingly sophisticated tactics of cybercriminals. The future of phishing detection lies in developing more intelligent, and adaptive detection systems, integrating emerging technologies, and maintaining a focus on user privacy and system explainability. With a collaborative and multidisciplinary approach, it is possible to make significant strides toward reducing the impact of phishing attacks in the coming years.

6. CONCLUSION

Phishing attacks continue to pose a persistent threat to cybersecurity, leveraging both technical subterfuge and social engineering to exploit human trust and vulnerabilities. This chapter has comprehensively examined the landscape of phishing detection methodologies, focusing on their evolution, effectiveness, and adaptability in combating increasingly sophisticated attack strategies. Traditional phishing detection methods, including blacklisting, whitelisting, and visual similarity analysis, remain widely used due to their simplicity and efficiency. However, their reliance on static data limits their efficacy against zero-hour attacks and dynamically evolving phishing tactics. For instance, blacklists often fail to detect newly created phishing domains, while whitelists, though effective in providing controlled access, suffer from scalability challenges. The integration of visual similarity methods addresses some gaps, but their dependency on archived legitimate sites reduces their applicability to novel phishing strategies. Advanced detection techniques, incorporating machine learning (ML) and deep learning (DL), have demonstrated remarkable progress in overcoming the limitations of traditional approaches. These methods analyze complex patterns in URLs, email content, and website metadata, offering adaptive capabilities for zero-hour attack detection. Innovations such as CNNs, LSTMs, and hybrid deep learning models achieve exceptional accuracy by extracting and analyzing intricate features, addressing the dynamic nature of phishing threats. The use of heuristic rules and feature selection techniques further enhances the robustness of ML models, reducing false positives and improving overall efficiency. Hybrid models represent a significant advancement, combining the strengths of traditional and advanced methodologies. These approaches integrate ML with heuristic techniques, ensemble learning, and feature optimization to address the inherent limitations of individual models. For example, the use of Random Forests and ensemble methods like Stacking Classifiers provides enhanced accuracy and stability, while models employing the Horse Herd Optimization (HHO) algorithm showcase the potential of nature-inspired techniques in optimizing phishing detection. Case studies across diverse domains, including e-banking, email systems, and social media platforms, highlight the practical application of these methodologies. The use of hybrid models to address financial phishing, as well as deep learning approaches for email and URL-based phishing detection, illustrates their effectiveness in real-world scenarios. Additionally, emerging research emphasizes the role of large language models (LLMs) such as GPT-3.5-turbo and Claude 2 in phishing detection, leveraging advanced prompt engineering and fine-tuning techniques to achieve high F1 scores. These studies underscore the potential of task-specific and generalized AI models in enhancing phishing detection frameworks. Despite these advancements, phishing detection faces significant challenges. Imbalanced datasets, limited access to high-quality labeled data, and the need for real-time detection continue to hinder model performance. Privacy concerns further complicate the development of collaborative detection systems, emphasizing the importance of federated learning and differential privacy in maintaining user confidentiality. Future research must focus on adaptive and privacy-conscious models, integrating interdisciplinary approaches to tackle the multifaceted nature of phishing. Advancements in behavioral analytics, threat intelligence integration, and the detection of phishing in emerging technologies, such as blockchain and AI-generated content, represent promising directions. Moreover, the development of scalable, real-time detection systems that can address multimodal phishing threats, including voice and video communications, is critical for maintaining cybersecurity resilience.

REFERENCES

Abdillah, R., Shukur, Z., Mohd, M., & Murah, T. M. Z. (2022). Phishing Classification Techniques: A Systematic Literature Review. In *IEEE Access* (Vol. 10, pp. 41574–41591). Institute of Electrical and Electronics Engineers Inc. DOI: 10.1109/ACCESS.2022.3166474

Alanezi, M. (2021). Phishing Detection Methods: A Review. *Technium Science*. www.techniumscience.com

Alharbi, A., Alotaibi, A., Alghofaili, L., Alsalamah, M., Alwasil, N., & Elkhediri, S. (2022a). Security in Social-Media: Awareness of Phishing Attacks Techniques and Countermeasures. *Proceedings of 2022 2nd International Conference on Computing and Information Technology, ICCIT 2022*, 10–16. DOI: 10.1109/ICCIT52419.2022.9711640

Alharbi, A., Alotaibi, A., Alghofaili, L., Alsalamah, M., Alwasil, N., & Elkhediri, S. (2022b). Security in Social-Media: Awareness of Phishing Attacks Techniques and Countermeasures. *Proceedings of 2022 2nd International Conference on Computing and Information Technology, ICCIT 2022*, 10–16. DOI: 10.1109/ICCIT52419.2022.9711640

Alkhalil, Z., Hewage, C., Nawaf, L., & Khan, I. (2021a). Phishing Attacks: A Recent Comprehensive Study and a New Anatomy. In *Frontiers in Computer Science* (Vol. 3). Frontiers Media S.A. DOI: 10.3389/fcomp.2021.563060

Alkhalil, Z., Hewage, C., Nawaf, L., & Khan, I. (2021b). Phishing Attacks: A Recent Comprehensive Study and a New Anatomy. In *Frontiers in Computer Science* (Vol. 3). Frontiers Media S.A. DOI: 10.3389/fcomp.2021.563060

Alsarhan, A., Al-Aiash, I., Al-Fraihat, D., Aljaidi, M., & Abu Laila, D. A. A. H. (2024). Expert Phishing Detection System. *Proceedings of the 2024 IEEE International Conference on Industry 4.0, Artificial Intelligence, and Communications Technology, IAICT 2024*, 54–59. DOI: 10.1109/IAICT62357.2024.10617460

Alsubaei, F. S., Almazroi, A. A., & Ayub, N. (2024). Enhancing Phishing Detection: A Novel Hybrid Deep Learning Framework for Cybercrime Forensics. *IEEE Access : Practical Innovations, Open Solutions*, 12, 8373–8389. DOI: 10.1109/ACCESS.2024.3351946

Anupriya, E., Kumaresan, N., Suresh, V., Dhanasekaran, S., Ramprathap, K., & Chinnasamy, P. (2022). Fraud Account Detection on Social Network using Machine Learning Techniques. *2022 International Conference on Advancements in Smart, Secure and Intelligent Computing (ASSIC)*, 1–4. DOI: 10.1109/ASSIC55218.2022.10088336

Azeez, N. A., Misra, S., Margaret, I. A., Fernandez-Sanz, L., & Abdulhamid, S. M. (2021). Adopting automated whitelist approach for detecting phishing attacks. *Computers & Security*, 108, 102328. Advance online publication. DOI: 10.1016/j.cose.2021.102328

Baadel, S., Thabtah, F., & Lu, J. (2021a). Cybersecurity awareness: A critical analysis of education and law enforcement methods. *Informatica (Slovenia)*, 45(3), 335–345. DOI: 10.31449/inf.v45i3.3328

Baadel, S., Thabtah, F., & Lu, J. (2021b). Cybersecurity awareness: A critical analysis of education and law enforcement methods. *Informatica (Slovenia)*, 45(3), 335–345. DOI: 10.31449/inf.v45i3.3328

Basit, A., Zafar, M., Liu, X., Javed, A. R., Jalil, Z., & Kifayat, K. (2021). A comprehensive survey of AI-enabled phishing attacks detection techniques. In *Telecommunication Systems* (Vol. 76, Issue 1, pp. 139–154). Springer. DOI: 10.1007/s11235-020-00733-2

Bayer, J., Maroofi, S., Hureau, O., Duda, A., & Korczynski, M. (2023). Building a Resilient Domain Whitelist to Enhance Phishing Blacklist Accuracy. *ECrime Researchers Summit, ECrime*. DOI: 10.1109/eCrime61234.2023.10485549

Bezerra, A., Pereira, I., Rebelo, M. Â., Coelho, D., de Oliveira, D. A., Costa, J. F. P., & Cruz, R. P. M. (2024). A case study on phishing detection with a machine learning net. *International Journal of Data Science and Analytics*. Advance online publication. DOI: 10.1007/s41060-024-00579-w

Birthriya, S. K., Ahlawat, P., & Jain, A. K. (2024). Phishing URL Detection using Deep Q-Networks with Convolutional Neural Networks. *2024 International Conference on Intelligent Systems for Cybersecurity, ISCS 2024*. DOI: 10.1109/ISCS61804.2024.10581203

Bountakas, P., & Xenakis, C. (2023). HELPHED: Hybrid Ensemble Learning PHishing Email Detection. *Journal of Network and Computer Applications*, 210, 103545. Advance online publication. DOI: 10.1016/j.jnca.2022.103545

Catal, C., Giray, G., Tekinerdogan, B., Kumar, S., & Shukla, S. (2022). Applications of deep learning for phishing detection: A systematic literature review. *Knowledge and Information Systems*, 64(6), 1457–1500. DOI: 10.1007/s10115-022-01672-x PMID: 35645443

Chinnasamy, P., Devika, S., Balaji, V., Dhanasekaran, S., Jebamani, B. J. A., & Kiran, A. (2023). BD-DoS: Blocking Distributed Denial of Service Flooding Attacks With Dynamic Path Detectors. *2023 International Conference on Computer Communication and Informatics (ICCCI)*, 1–5. DOI: 10.1109/ICCCI56745.2023.10128499

Chinnasamy, P., Krishnamoorthy, P., Alankruthi, K., Mohanraj, T., Kumar, B. S., & Chandran, L. (2024). AI Enhanced Phishing Detection System. *2024 IEEE International Conference on Intelligent Techniques in Control, Optimization and Signal Processing, INCOS 2024 - Proceedings*. DOI: 10.1109/INCOS59338.2024.10527485

Dafni Rose, J., Jennifer Nissitta, M., & Jaya Prabha, S. (2024). Next-Gen Phishing Detection System Based on Federated Learning Integrated CNN-LSTM for SMS Communication. *Proceedings - 2024 5th International Conference on Intelligent Communication Technologies and Virtual Mobile Networks, ICICV 2024*, 367–372. DOI: 10.1109/ICICV62344.2024.00064

Ding, Y., Luktarhan, N., Li, K., & Slamu, W. (2019). A keyword-based combination approach for detecting phishing webpages. *Computers & Security*, 84, 256–275. DOI: 10.1016/j.cose.2019.03.018

Do, N. Q., Selamat, A., Krejcar, O., Herrera-Viedma, E., & Fujita, H. (2022). Deep Learning for Phishing Detection: Taxonomy, Current Challenges and Future Directions. *IEEE Access : Practical Innovations, Open Solutions*, 10, 36429–36463. DOI: 10.1109/ACCESS.2022.3151903

Dubey, M., & Makwana, R. R. S. (2024). Enhancing Web Security: Hybrid Deep Learning Model for Robust URL Phishing Detection. *2024 IEEE International Conference on Interdisciplinary Approaches in Technology and Management for Social Innovation, IATMSI 2024*. DOI: 10.1109/IATMSI60426.2024.10502735

Elgharbi, S. E., Ait Yahia, M., & Ouchani, S. (2024). Online Phishing Detection: A Heuristic-Based Machine Learning Framework. *2024 13th Mediterranean Conference on Embedded Computing, MECO 2024*. DOI: 10.1109/MECO62516.2024.10577848

Gupta, B. B., Arachchilage, N. A. G., & Psannis, K. E. (2018). Defending against phishing attacks: Taxonomy of methods, current issues and future directions. *Telecommunication Systems*, 67(2), 247–267. DOI: 10.1007/s11235-017-0334-z

Haq, Q. E., Faheem, M. H., & Ahmad, I. (2024). Detecting Phishing URLs Based on a Deep Learning Approach to Prevent Cyber-Attacks. *Applied Sciences (Basel, Switzerland)*, 14(22), 10086. DOI: 10.3390/app142210086

He, D., Lv, X., Zhu, S., Chan, S., & Choo, K. K. R. (2024). A Method for Detecting Phishing Websites Based on Tiny-Bert Stacking. *IEEE Internet of Things Journal*, 11(2), 2236–2243. DOI: 10.1109/JIOT.2023.3292171

Hemannth, P., Chinta, M., Satya, S. S., & Sri Aneelaja Devasena, P. (2024). A Phishing URL Detection Model based on Horse Herd Optimization and Random Forest Algorithms. *Proceedings - 2024 4th International Conference on Pervasive Computing and Social Networking, ICPCSN 2024*, 926–931. DOI: 10.1109/ICPCSN62568.2024.00156

Hussain, M., Cheng, C., Xu, R., & Afzal, M. (2023). CNN-Fusion: An effective and lightweight phishing detection method based on multi-variant ConvNet. *Information Sciences*, 631, 328–345. DOI: 10.1016/j.ins.2023.02.039

Ishtaiwi, A., Ali, A. M., Al-Qerem, A., Sabahean, M., Alzubi, B., Almomani, A., Alauthman, M., Aldweesh, A., & Al Khaldy, M. A. (2024). Next-Gen Phishing Defense Enhancing Detection With Machine Learning and Expert Whitelisting/Blacklisting. *International Journal of Cloud Applications and Computing*, 14(1), 1–17. Advance online publication. DOI: 10.4018/IJCAC.353301

Kalaharsha, P., & Mehtre, B. M. (2021). Detecting Phishing Sites-An Overview. *ArXiv Preprint ArXiv:2103.12739*. https://doi.org//arXiv.2103.12739DOI: 10.48550

Kulkarni, A., Balachandran, V., & Das, T. (2024). Phishing Webpage Detection: Unveiling the Threat Landscape and Investigating Detection Techniques. *IEEE Communications Surveys and Tutorials*, 1. Advance online publication. DOI: 10.1109/COMST.2024.3441752

Medhat, M., Sayed, S. G., Abd-Alhalem, S. M., & Takieldeen, A. E. (2023). Whitelisting Requirements for Effective Cyber Defense Solutions. *2023 International Telecommunications Conference, ITC-Egypt 2023*, 484–489. DOI: 10.1109/ITC-Egypt58155.2023.10206403

Nishiura, K., Kimura, T., & Cheng, J. (2024). Backdoor Trigger Detection Using Adversarial Perturbation for Deep-learning Phishing Detector. *International Conference on Information Networking*, 506–508. DOI: 10.1109/ICOIN59985.2024.10572156

Niu, T., & Wu, B. (2024). Visual-based Phishing Website Recognition. *IMCEC 2024 - IEEE 6th Advanced Information Management, Communicates,Electronic and Automation Control Conference*, 992–997. DOI: 10.1109/IMCEC59810.2024.10575293

Olukoya, B. M., Aderemi, E. T., Olabisi, P. O., Osobukola, A. A., Oluwaseyi, A. A. V., Ogundokun, R. O., Olaniyi, O. A., & Olowe, O. T. (2024). An Improved Webpage Phishing Detection Based on an Ensemble Feature Selection and Multilevel Techniques. *International Conference on Science, Engineering and Business for Driving Sustainable Development Goals, SEB4SDG 2024*. DOI: 10.1109/SEB4SDG60871.2024.10629961

Parekh, S., Parikh, D., Kotak, S., & Sankhe, S. (2018). A New Method for Detection of Phishing Websites: URL Detection. *2018 Second International Conference on Inventive Communication and Computational Technologies (ICICCT)*, 949–952. DOI: 10.1109/ICICCT.2018.8473085

Pathmanaban, J., James, P. G., Ashok, P., Ragesh, B., Aakash, S., & Kaushik, N. (2024). Phishing Website Detection Using Machine Learning. *Proceedings of the 2nd IEEE International Conference on Networking and Communications 2024, ICNWC 2024*. DOI: 10.1109/ICNWC60771.2024.10537279

Patil, D., Rane, N. L., Desai, P., & Rane, J. (2024). Machine learning and deep learning: Methods, techniques, applications, challenges, and future research opportunities. In *Trustworthy Artificial Intelligence in Industry and Society*. Deep Science Publishing., DOI: 10.70593/978-81-981367-4-9_2

Priya, S., Gutema, D., & Singh, S. (2024). A Comprehensive Survey of Recent Phishing Attacks Detection Techniques. *2024 5th International Conference on Innovative Trends in Information Technology, ICITIIT 2024*. DOI: 10.1109/ICITIIT61487.2024.10580446

Purwanto, R. W., Pal, A., Blair, A., & Jha, S. (2022). PhishSim: Aiding Phishing Website Detection With a Feature-Free Tool. *IEEE Transactions on Information Forensics and Security*, 17, 1497–1512. DOI: 10.1109/TIFS.2022.3164212

Qabajeh, I., Thabtah, F., & Chiclana, F. (2018). A recent review of conventional vs. automated cybersecurity anti-phishing techniques *. *Computer Science Review*, 29, 44–55. DOI: 10.1016/j.cosrev.2018.05.003

Ramesh, G., Gupta, J., & Gamya, P. G. (2017). Identification of phishing webpages and its target domains by analyzing the feign relationship. *Journal of Information Security and Applications*, 35, 75–84. DOI: 10.1016/j.jisa.2017.06.001

Rao, R. S., & Pais, A. R. (2017). An enhanced blacklist method to detect phishing websites. *Lecture Notes in Computer Science (Including Subseries Lecture Notes in Artificial Intelligence and Lecture Notes in Bioinformatics), 10717 LNCS*, 323–333. DOI: 10.1007/978-3-319-72598-7_20

Remya, S., Pillai, M. J., Arjun, C., Ramasubbareddy, S., & Cho, Y. (2024). Enhancing Security in LLNs Using a Hybrid Trust-Based Intrusion Detection System for RPL. *IEEE Access: Practical Innovations, Open Solutions*, 12, 58836–58850. DOI: 10.1109/ACCESS.2024.3391918

Remya, S., Pillai, M. J., Nair, K. K., Rama Subbareddy, S., & Cho, Y. Y. (2024). An Effective Detection Approach for Phishing URL Using ResMLP. *IEEE Access: Practical Innovations, Open Solutions*, 12, 79367–79382. DOI: 10.1109/ACCESS.2024.3409049

Safi, A., & Singh, S. (2023). A systematic literature review on phishing website detection techniques. *Journal of King Saud University. Computer and Information Sciences*, 35(2), 590–611. DOI: 10.1016/j.jksuci.2023.01.004

Sahingoz, O. K., Buber, E., & Kugu, E. (2024). DEPHIDES: Deep Learning Based Phishing Detection System. *IEEE Access : Practical Innovations, Open Solutions*, 12, 8052–8070. DOI: 10.1109/ACCESS.2024.3352629

Saravanan, P., & Subramanian, S. (2020). A Framework for Detecting Phishing Websites using GA based Feature Selection and ARTMAP based Website Classification. *Procedia Computer Science*, 171, 1083–1092. DOI: 10.1016/j.procs.2020.04.116

Sarker, O., Jayatilaka, A., Haggag, S., Liu, C., & Babar, M. A. (2024). A Multi-vocal Literature Review on challenges and critical success factors of phishing education, training and awareness. *Journal of Systems and Software*, 208, 111899. Advance online publication. DOI: 10.1016/j.jss.2023.111899

Sawant, S., Savakhande, R., Sankhe, O., & Tamboli, S. (2024). Phishing Detection by integrating Machine Learning and Deep Learning. *In 2024 11th International Conference on Computing for Sustainable Global Development (INDIACom) (Pp. 1078-1083).*

Singh, S., Singh, M. P., & Pandey, R. (2020). Phishing Detection from URLs Using Deep Learning Approach. *2020 5th International Conference on Computing, Communication and Security (ICCCS)*, 1–4. DOI: 10.1109/ICCCS49678.2020.9277459

Siva, N., Sivaiah, B. V., Reddy, S. S. K., Irfan, S., Kumar, U. P., & Nayagara, S. N. (2024). Phishing Detection System through Hybrid Machine Learning Based on URL. *2024 5th International Conference for Emerging Technology, INCET 2024*. DOI: 10.1109/INCET61516.2024.10593373

Siva Reddy, N. V., Rohith Saai, A. R., Ramanujan, T. V., Reddy, N. R. K., & Pramila, R. P. (2024). A Robust Approach to E-Banking Phishing Detection using Ensemble Methods and LSTM. *2024 International Conference on Cognitive Robotics and Intelligent Systems, ICC - ROBINS 2024*, 856–863. DOI: 10.1109/ICC-ROBINS60238.2024.10533883

Skula, I., & Kvet, M. "Domain Blacklist Efficacy for Phishing Web-page Detection Over an Extended Time Period," 2023 33rd Conference of Open Innovations Association (FRUCT), Zilina, Slovakia, 2023, pp. 257-263, doi: DOI: 10.23919/FRUCT58615.2023.10142999

Sturman, D., Valenzuela, C., Plate, O., Tanvir, T., Auton, J. C., Bayl-Smith, P., & Wiggins, M. W. (2023). The role of cue utilization in the detection of phishing emails. *Applied Ergonomics*, 106, 103887. Advance online publication. DOI: 10.1016/j.apergo.2022.103887 PMID: 36037654

Subasi, A., & Kremic, E. (2020). Leveraging AI and machine learning for societal challenges, cas 2019 comparison of adaboost with multiboosting for phishing website detection. *Procedia Computer Science*, 168, 272–278. DOI: 10.1016/j.procs.2020.02.251

Talukder, A. R., Alam, F., Mim, S. T., & Al Emon, M. A. (2024). Detecting Phishing Websites using Naive Bayes Classification. *2024 3rd International Conference on Advancement in Electrical and Electronic Engineering, ICAEEE 2024*. DOI: 10.1109/ICAEEE62219.2024.10561829

Tan, C. C. L., Chiew, K. L., Yong, K. S. C., Sebastian, Y., Than, J. C. M., & Tiong, W. K. (2023). Hybrid phishing detection using joint visual and textual identity. *Expert Systems with Applications*, 220, 119723. Advance online publication. DOI: 10.1016/j.eswa.2023.119723

Thakur, K., Ali, M. L., Obaidat, M. A., & Kamruzzaman, A. (2023). A Systematic Review on Deep-Learning-Based Phishing Email Detection. In *Electronics (Switzerland)* (Vol. 12, Issue 21). Multidisciplinary Digital Publishing Institute (MDPI). DOI: 10.3390/electronics12214545

Trad, F., & Chehab, A. (2024). Prompt Engineering or Fine-Tuning? A Case Study on Phishing Detection with Large Language Models. *Machine Learning and Knowledge Extraction*, 6(1), 367–384. DOI: 10.3390/make6010018

Tusher, E. H., Ismail, M. A., Rahman, M. A., Alenezi, A. H., & Uddin, M. (2024). Email Spam: A Comprehensive Review of Optimize Detection Methods, Challenges, and Open Research Problems. In *IEEE Access*. Institute of Electrical and Electronics Engineers Inc., DOI: 10.1109/ACCESS.2024.3467996

Wei, Y., & Sekiya, Y. (2022). Sufficiency of Ensemble Machine Learning Methods for Phishing Websites Detection. *IEEE Access : Practical Innovations, Open Solutions*, 10, 124103–124113. DOI: 10.1109/ACCESS.2022.3224781

Wu, J., Yuan, Q., Lin, D., You, W., Chen, W., Chen, C., & Zheng, Z. (2022). Who Are the Phishers? Phishing Scam Detection on Ethereum via Network Embedding. *IEEE Transactions on Systems, Man, and Cybernetics. Systems*, 52(2), 1156–1166. DOI: 10.1109/TSMC.2020.3016821

Yang, R., Zheng, K., Wu, B., Wu, C., & Wang, X. (2021). Phishing Website Detection Based on Deep Convolutional Neural Network and Random Forest Ensemble Learning. *Sensors (Basel)*, 21(24), 8281. DOI: 10.3390/s21248281 PMID: 34960375

Zhang, Z., Devaraj, M., Bai, X., & Lu, H. (2024). Ethereum Phishing Scams Detection: A Survey. *Proceedings - 2024 International Conference on Artificial Intelligence and Digital Technology, ICAIDT 2024*, 70–75. DOI: 10.1109/ICAIDT62617.2024.00023

Zheng, H., Ma, M., Ma, H., Chen, J., Xiong, H., & Yang, Z. (2024). TEGDetector: A Phishing Detector That Knows Evolving Transaction Behaviors. *IEEE Transactions on Computational Social Systems*, 11(3), 3988–4000. DOI: 10.1109/TCSS.2023.3323512

Zhu, E., Cheng, K., Zhang, Z., & Wang, H. (2024). PDHF: Effective phishing detection model combining optimal artificial and automatic deep features. *Computers & Security*, 136, 103561. Advance online publication. DOI: 10.1016/j.cose.2023.103561

Zhu, E., Ju, Y., Chen, Z., Liu, F., & Fang, X. (2020). DTOF-ANN: An Artificial Neural Network phishing detection model based on Decision Tree and Optimal Features. *Applied Soft Computing*, 95, 106505. DOI: 10.1016/j.asoc.2020.106505

Zieni, R., Massari, L., & Calzarossa, M. C. (2023). Phishing or Not Phishing? A Survey on the Detection of Phishing Websites. *IEEE Access : Practical Innovations, Open Solutions*, 11, 18499–18519. DOI: 10.1109/ACCESS.2023.3247135

Chapter 3
Phishing Prevention Solutions and Mechanisms

Abhavya Muku
Chandigarh College of Engineering and Technology, Panjab University, Chandigarh, India

Sunil K. Singh
https://orcid.org/0000-0003-4876-7190
Chandigarh College of Engineering and Technology, Panjab University, Chandigarh, India

Sudhakar Kumar
https://orcid.org/0000-0001-7928-4234
Chandigarh College of Engineering and Technology, Panjab University, Chandigarh, India

Ankita Sharma
https://orcid.org/0009-0003-9477-3126
Chandigarh College of Engineering and Technology, Panjab University, Chandigarh, India

Pooja Rai
Department of Computer Science, New Alipore College, Kolkata, India

Biraj Upadhyaya
Sikkim Manipal Institute of Technology, India

Sunil Kumar Sharma
S.E. Railway, India

Vandana Sharma
Chandigarh College of Engineering and Technology, Panjab University, Chandigarh, India

ABSTRACT

Phishing is a dangerous online fraud tactic that tricks individuals into disclosing personal information, like usernames, passwords, and credit card numbers. It often appears through fake emails, messages, or websites designed to lure victims into sharing sensitive data. This illegal activity can cause significant financial losses for businesses and consumers, while also damaging trust in online transactions. Anti-phishing tools, such as SpamTitan and Barracuda Sentinel, use advanced algorithms and machine learning to detect and block phishing attempts in real time, protecting users from data breaches and financial harm. These solutions also offer user training to increase awareness of phishing tactics, enhancing defenses. Emphasizing the need for comprehensive anti-phishing strategies, it shows how organizations can safeguard sensitive information and maintain customer trust in a digital world. It explores technologies and methods for building a robust framework against phishing, detailing innovative ways to secure communication systems and ensure data integrity.

DOI: 10.4018/979-8-3693-8784-9.ch003

1. INTRODUCTION

Phishing is a form of cybercrime that involves fraudulent attempts to obtain sensitive information by impersonating trustworthy entities in electronic communications. These deceptive tactics often occur through emails, text messages, or fake websites designed to appear legitimate(L. J. Singh & Imphal, 2018). Attackers craft convincing messages that appear to originate from reputable organizations—such as banks, social media platforms, or online service providers—luring victims to click on malicious links or download harmful attachments. Once individuals share their information, cybercriminals can exploit it for identity theft, financial fraud, or unauthorized access to accounts(Mohammed et al., 2023).

To counter these threats, phishing prevention measures and solutions are essential for safeguarding individuals and organizations. These solutions employ advanced techniques such as machine learning, AI-based detection, and real-time email filtering to block phishing attempts before they can cause harm. Email filtering systems identify suspicious content or URLs, while multi-factor authentication (MFA) provides an additional security layer to prevent unauthorized access(Mohammed et al., 2023; M. Singh et al., 2023), even if login credentials are compromised. Advanced neural networks can be explored for cross-corpus fake news detection by leveraging their ability to generalize across diverse datasets, enabling accurate identification of misinformation across different sources.(Girdhar et al., 2023)

The growing sophistication of phishing attacks necessitates the integration of advanced security measures, including behavioral analytics, URL monitoring, and real-time threat intelligence. Additionally, incorporating biometric authentication and multimedia forensics strengthens phishing prevention by ensuring reliable user verification and comprehensive analysis of phishing incidents.

As technology and digital communication expand, the attack surface for cybercriminals grows, making it imperative to adopt multi-layered solutions. Next-generation advancements in cyber-physical systems and digital twins focus on integrating real-time data processing, enhanced interoperability, and intelligent automation to improve system resilience and adaptability(Vats & Kumar, 2021). Phishing attacks not only lead to direct financial losses but also cause reputational damage and erode consumer trust. Organizations must deploy robust anti-phishing measures to protect sensitive data, mitigate risks, and maintain cybersecurity(Goyal et al., 2023).

This chapter explores the landscape of phishing threats, focusing on innovative solutions and strategies to combat phishing attacks. It highlights the importance of leveraging advanced technologies, educating users, and implementing comprehensive frameworks to ensure secure and trustworthy digital environments(Goyal et al., 2023).

Figure 1. Working of phishing attack

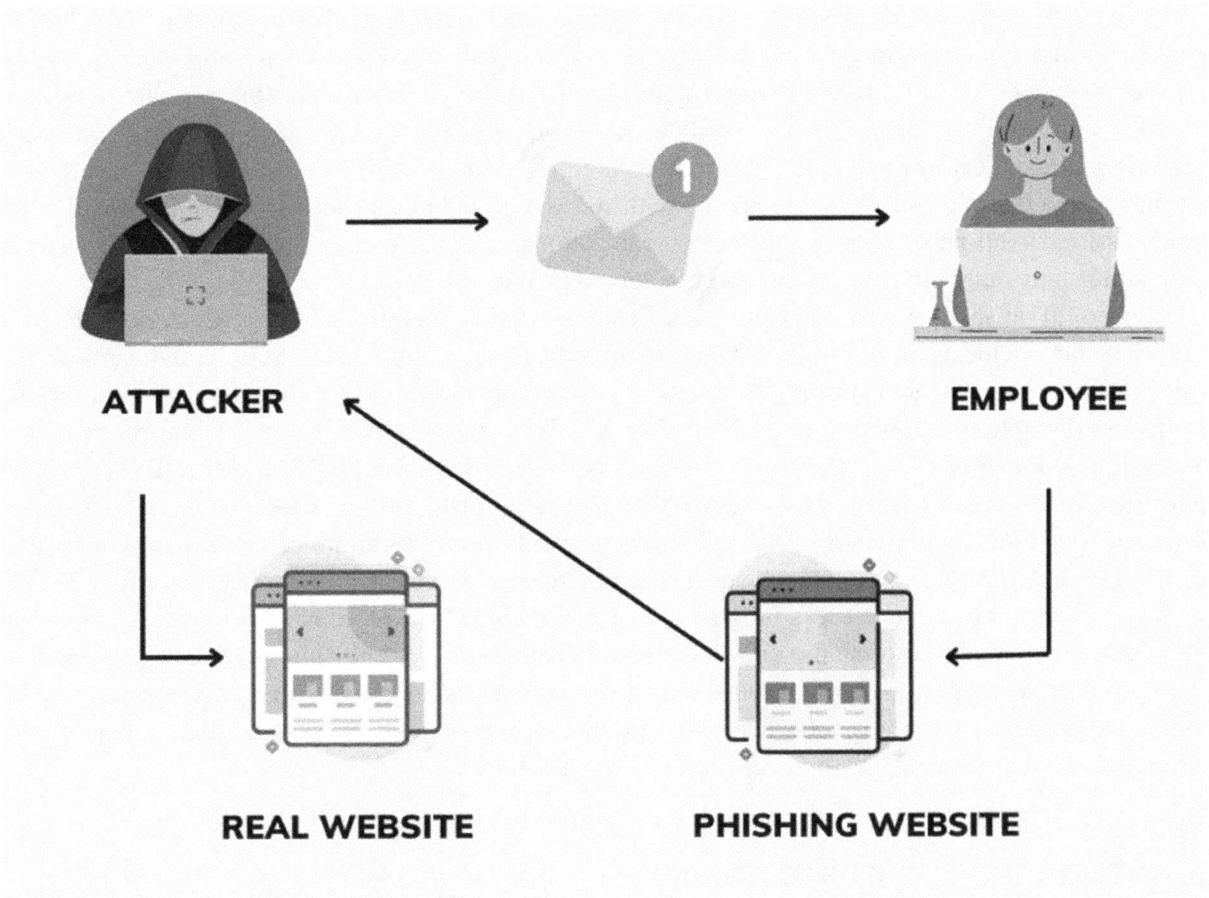

The diagram (figure 1) illustrates how a phishing attack works. It starts with an attacker sending a fake email to an employee. When the employee gets the email, they might click on a link inside it. If they do, they could be sent to a phishing website that looks like a real one, where their personal information could be stolen. However, if the employee realizes the email is a scam and ignores it, they can avoid getting tricked. Now we will explain the importance of anti phishing.

2. IMPORTANCE OF ANTI PHISHING

Phishing attacks primarily aim to steal sensitive personal information, such as usernames, passwords, credit card numbers, and other financial data. By implementing anti-phishing technologies, organizations and individuals can safeguard their confidential information from falling into the hands of cybercriminals(Alkhalil et al., 2021a). This protection helps prevent identity theft and financial fraud. Phishing can lead to substantial financial losses for both individuals and organizations. Businesses may face direct monetary losses from unauthorized transactions or costly remediation efforts following a successful attack.

For individuals, falling victim to phishing scams can result in drained bank accounts or credit card fraud. Anti-phishing strategies reduce the likelihood of such incidents, ultimately preserving financial resources.

Organizations that suffer phishing attacks may experience damage to their reputation and a loss of consumer trust. Customers are less likely to engage with companies that have been compromised, fearing for their own security. By effectively implementing anti-phishing measures, businesses can maintain a positive reputation and foster trust among their customers, which is vital for long-term success. Many industries are subject to regulations that require the protection of sensitive data, such as healthcare, finance(Vats et al., 2024). Non-compliance with these regulations can lead to hefty fines and legal repercussions. Anti-phishing measures help organizations meet these compliance standards, ensuring they protect customer information and avoid potential penalties.

Successful phishing attacks can cause significant operational disruptions for organizations. Recovery from such incidents often involves extensive investigations, system restorations, and downtime. By implementing effective anti-phishing solutions, organizations can minimize the risk of attacks and the associated disruptions, allowing them to maintain productivity and efficiency. Anti-phishing measures are a critical component of a comprehensive cybersecurity strategy(Jaswal & Malhotra, 2022). By addressing phishing threats, organizations can strengthen their overall security posture, making it more difficult for attackers to exploit vulnerabilities. This proactive approach fosters a culture of security awareness and encourages individuals to be vigilant against potential threats(A. Sharma, Singh, Kumar, et al., 2023).

Lastly, education and awareness programs are often included in anti-phishing strategies, providing individuals and employees with the knowledge to recognize and avoid phishing attempts. These initiatives promote safe online practices, reduce the chances of successful attacks, and empower users to be vigilant against potential threats. By fostering a culture of security awareness, organizations can create a more resilient defense against phishing and other cyberattacks.

3. ANTI PHISHING TECHNOLOGIES

Anti-phishing prevention and solutions are specialized strategies, tools, and methodologies aimed at combating phishing attacks that attempt to deceive individuals into sharing sensitive information by impersonating legitimate organizations or individuals. These solutions enhance cybersecurity by leveraging advanced technologies and promoting awareness to detect, prevent, and respond to phishing threats effectively. Phishing prevention employs sophisticated algorithms, machine learning models, and authentication protocols to safeguard users and organizations. These solutions focus on blocking malicious emails, verifying the legitimacy of URLs, and ensuring secure communication between users and websites. By adopting a multi-layered defense strategy, organizations can mitigate the risks associated with phishing attacks.

Phishing prevention solutions begin by analyzing incoming emails for indicators of phishing, such as suspicious sender addresses or content requesting personal information. URL analysis tools cross-check embedded links against databases of known phishing sites, while email scanning tools inspect attachments for harmful files. Behavioral monitoring solutions detect unusual activities, such as logging in from unfamiliar locations or clicking suspicious links, providing early warnings for potential phishing attempts. To enhance protection, solutions such as **two-factor authentication (2FA)** are widely adopted. This mechanism requires users to verify their identity through an additional step, such as entering a code sent to their phone. Additionally, email authentication technologies like **DMARC**, **SPF**, and **DKIM** ensure that emails originate from legitimate sources and prevent tampering(B. B. Gupta et al., 2018). Organizations also use technologies such as **machine learning-based email filtering systems**, **real-time URL monitoring**, and **encryption protocols like SSL/TLS** to create a robust defense(B. B. Gupta et al., 2018). These are complemented by human-centric solutions, including **user training programs**, **phishing simulations**, and **incident response plans** to foster a culture of awareness and preparedness. By integrating technological and educational measures, phishing prevention and solutions provide a comprehensive shield, ensuring a secure and trustworthy digital environment.

The diagram(figure 2) below illustrates two primary methods of phishing detection: User Awareness and Software Detection. The User Awareness approach emphasizes educating and training users to identify phishing attempts through simulated attacks, awareness programs, and learning to recognize suspicious elements like unusual URLs, attachments, or urgent requests. On the other hand, Software Detection(A. Sharma, Singh, Badwal, et al., 2023) is an automated approach that consists of several techniques. Blacklist/Whitelist systems flag emails based on predefined trusted or blocked sources, while Heuristics rely on rule-based systems to detect common phishing characteristics such as certain keywords or patterns in emails(Das et al., 2019; Jain & Gupta, 2018a) . Visual Similarity techniques compare the visual appearance of phishing attempts with legitimate emails or websites, spotting subtle differences like altered logos or domain names. Machine Learning employs AI algorithms trained on large datasets to identify phishing by recognizing patterns of attacks, continuously improving over time(Peñalvo, Maan, et al., 2022). Advancements in CNN-based models have significantly improved the detection of phishing attempts by accurately identifying patterns in malicious activities, providing more robust defenses against evolving phishing tactics.(Kaur et al., 2021)

Figure 2. Different Phishing Detection Methods

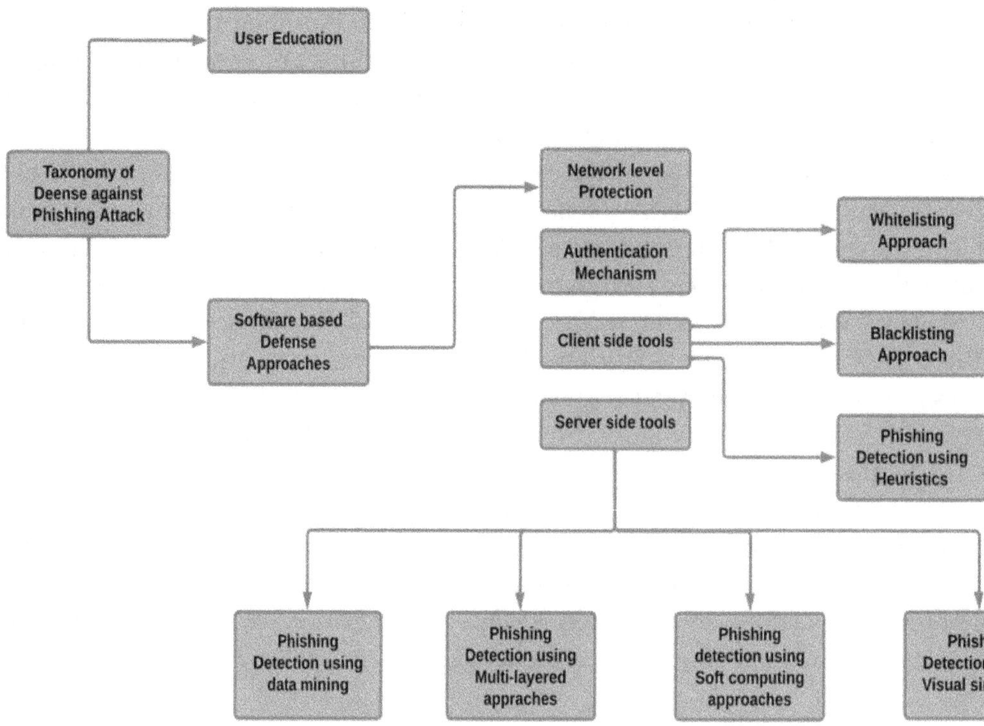

Finally, Hybrid Approaches combine multiple methods like heuristics, machine learning, and visual similarity to enhance detection accuracy. This categorization demonstrates both human-centered and technology-driven strategies to combat phishing. Here are the different anti phishing technologies:

3.1 Technological Solutions for Phishing Prevention

Phishing prevention involves implementing strategies and technologies to safeguard users and organizations from phishing attacks. These attacks aim to deceive individuals into sharing sensitive information like login credentials, financial details, or personal data. Below are some key solutions for phishing prevention:

3.1.1 Email filtering:

Email filtering systems scan incoming emails using a sophisticated combination of rules, algorithms, heuristics, and machine learning models to detect phishing attempts and other forms of email-based threats.

The system compares the sender's email address with a blacklist of known malicious addresses. It also employs domain spoofing detection techniques, analyzing whether the sender is attempting to impersonate a trusted domain. For example, an email claiming to be from "support@paypall.com" (note the extra 'l') would be flagged as suspicious.

The email's content is examined for common phishing indicators, such as requests for sensitive information (passwords, financial data) or language that creates a false sense of urgency (e.g., "Your account has been compromised, act now!"). Advanced filters can identify sophisticated language patterns used in phishing attacks and detect suspicious phrases.

Attachments are a common vector for malware delivery. Email filters scan these attachments for known malicious file types, such as executable files (.exe), or malicious scripts embedded within seemingly harmless files like PDFs or Word documents. Some filters even have the capability to open and analyze attachments in a sandbox environment before delivery. Any links embedded in the email are scrutinized to ensure they lead to legitimate websites. Filters analyze URL structures, looking for signs of phishing attempts, such as slight misspellings of domain names (e.g., "google.com" vs. "g00gle.com"). They also compare the URLs to databases of known phishing domains and detect whether the link redirects the user to another site, which is a common tactic used in phishing schemes.

Machine learning algorithms play a key role in improving the accuracy of email filtering over time. These systems are trained with enormous datasets of both legitimate and fraudulent emails, allowing them to detect new, evolving phishing techniques(Chhabra et al., 2024; Setia et al., 2024). As users report phishing emails or false positives, the machine learning model updates itself to reduce future mistakes.

3.1.2 AI phishing detection:

AI-based phishing detection systems are highly effective at spotting phishing attempts by leveraging machine learning algorithms. These systems are trained on vast datasets containing both phishing and legitimate emails. Over time, they learn to recognize subtle patterns, behaviors, and anomalies that differentiate phishing emails from genuine communication. Here's a breakdown of how they operate:

Figure 3. AI based phishing detection

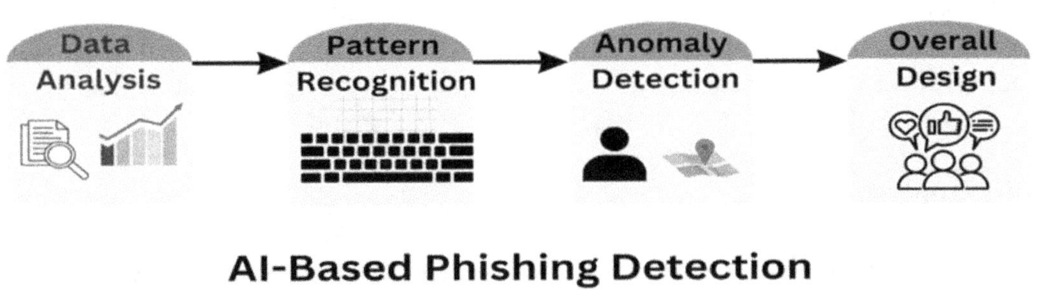

- **Data Analysis:** AI phishing detection systems begin by gathering and analyzing vast amounts of data from multiple sources(Jain & Gupta, 2019). This includes email metadata, such as the sender's address, IP information, and headers, which help in identifying whether the email originates from a trusted or suspicious source(T. Aggarwal et al., 2024). The content of the email, including the text, attachments, and embedded links, is thoroughly analyzed to spot keywords, phrases, and patterns commonly associated with phishing attempts. Additionally, AI systems track user behavior, such as login attempts and click patterns, to understand if the behavior deviates from the norm. By processing this extensive data, AI can detect phishing even in emails that may appear genuine to a human reader.

- **Pattern Recognition:** Once the data is collected, AI phishing systems rely on sophisticated pattern recognition to identify phishing attempts. These systems are trained to recognize specific language patterns, such as the use of urgent calls to action or requests for sensitive information, which are hallmarks of phishing attacks. AI also analyzes deceptive URLs that may closely mimic legitimate domains, spotting subtle differences like character substitutions. In addition, AI detects recurring issues like poor grammar or awkward syntax that often appear in phishing emails. By identifying these common patterns, AI systems can flag suspicious emails that may otherwise bypass traditional filters.
- **Pattern Recognition:** Pattern recognition is a critical capability of AI in combating phishing emails, as it can identify recurring patterns that traditional filters might miss. One of the key aspects is the detection of specific language; phishing emails often use common vocabulary, such as requests for confidential information or references to financial transactions. AI systems are trained to recognize these triggers, even spotting subtle variations in commonly used phrases. Additionally, AI can analyze deceptive URLs that may appear legitimate but contain slight misspellings, like changing "paypal.com" to "paypa1.com." By comparing these URLs against known phishing links and analyzing their structure, AI enhances detection accuracy. Furthermore, AI systems can flag phishing attempts based on grammar and syntax errors, which are prevalent in these fraudulent emails, as they often exhibit poor grammar or unnatural sentence structures.
- **Anomaly Detection:** In addition to identifying patterns, AI phishing detection heavily relies on anomaly detection, which focuses on spotting behaviors that deviate from a user's normal activity. For example, if a user typically logs in from a specific location (like the U.S.) and suddenly tries to log in from a different country, this unusual activity would raise a red flag. Similarly, unfamiliar login patterns are another common indicator of phishing. If an employee attempts to access their email at an odd time of day or from an unrecognized device, the AI system will consider this behavior abnormal and potentially suspicious. By monitoring these anomalies, AI systems can effectively detect phishing attempts that rely on exploiting user behavior rather than the content of the email itself.

3.1.3 URL analysis

URL analysis tools are designed to evaluate the web addresses (URLs) found in emails or visited by users to detect phishing sites. Many URL analysis tools rely on maintaining extensive lists of known phishing sites. If a URL found in an email or accessed by a user matches one on the blacklist, it is automatically flagged or blocked to prevent access. This provides immediate protection against previously identified phishing sites.

Heuristic methods allow the tool to detect phishing attempts by verifying the structure of the URL. Phishers often create URLs that closely mimic trusted websites, changing small details like replacing letters or adding extra characters (e.g., "amazon.com" might be altered to "amaz0n.com"). The heuristic analysis spots these irregularities in domain names, subdomains, or URL paths, flagging potentially harmful links before a user can click on them.

URL analysis tools also use Domain Name System (DNS) lookups to verify the legitimacy of a website's domain. By checking the DNS records, the tool can ensure that the domain name corresponds to its claimed identity. If there's a discrepancy between the domain name and its DNS information, the URL may be marked as suspicious. Some systems go beyond simply evaluating the URL itself by checking the content of the linked website in real-time. If the site contains suspicious elements, such as forms requesting sensitive information like usernames, passwords, or credit card details, the tool flags the site as a phishing attempt. This real-time check ensures that users are not tricked into entering personal information on malicious sites.

3.1.4 Two-Factor Authentication:

Two-factor authentication (2FA) enhances security by requiring two different forms of verification during the login process. This additional layer protects user accounts even if an attacker manages to obtain the user's password (Jain & Gupta, 2018b). 2FA improves security by demanding two types of verification on login(Petsas et al., 2015). This additional layer protects user accounts even if an attacker obtains the password. The two factors involved in 2FA are:

- **Something You Know:** The first step in the login process is the user entering their password. This serves as the primary form of authentication that verifies the user's identity.
- **Something You Have:** After successfully entering the password, the system prompts for a second form of authentication. This could be a temporary code sent to the user's mobile phone via SMS, an email containing a verification link, or a one-time code generated by an authentication app (such as Google Authenticator or Authy). This second factor ensures that even if someone has the password, they cannot access the account without the code.
- **Physical Tokens:** In some systems, users can opt for physical tokens to verify their identity. This includes smart cards, USB keys, or other hardware devices that generate authentication codes. These tokens are typically required to be physically present for successful login, adding another layer of security.

Figure 4. Work flow of two factor authentication

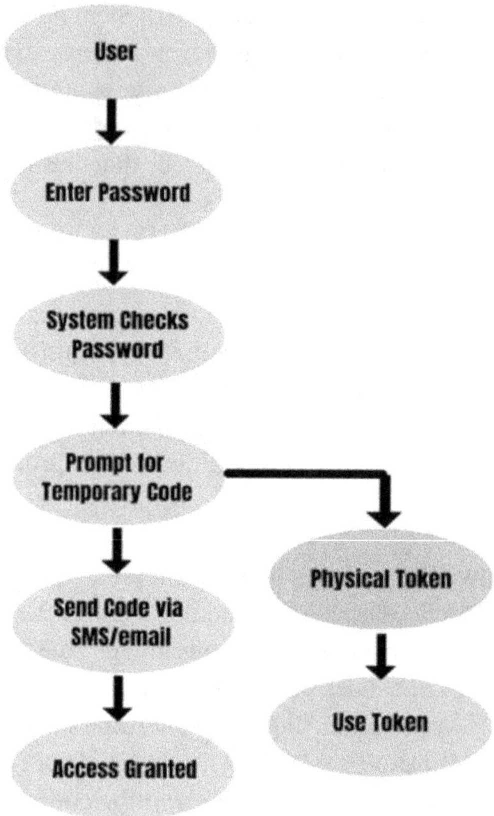

3.1.5 Domain-Based Message Authentication, Reporting & Conformance:

DMARC is an email authentication mechanism that combat domain spoofing, which occurs when malicious actors send emails that look to be from a trustworthy domain. DMARC works in conjunction with two other email authentication methods: Sender Policy Framework (SPF) and Domain Keys Identified Mail (DKIM)(Hu et al., 2018).

SPF and DKIM play crucial roles in the functioning of Domain-based Message Authentication, Reporting & Conformance (DMARC)(Ashiq et al., 2023). DMARC first verifies that emails claiming to be from a specific domain are sent from authorized servers by checking the domain's SPF records, which list the IP addresses of servers permitted to send emails on behalf of that domain. If an email originates from an unauthorized server, DMARC flags it as suspicious, enhancing the protection against spoofing. Additionally, DMARC checks the DKIM signature found in the email header. DKIM employs cryptographic signatures to ensure that the email content remains intact and unaltered during transmission. By validating this signature, DMARC can confirm the email's integrity, thereby ensuring that it has not been tampered with by a third party. Together, these mechanisms fortify email authentication and enhance the security of digital communications

One of the key features of DMARC is its policy enforcement capability. Domain owners can specify how their email should be handled if it fails DMARC checks. They can choose from several actions:

- **Reject:** Emails that do not pass DMARC authentication are rejected outright and not delivered to the recipient.
- **Quarantine:** Suspicious emails are placed in a quarantine or spam folder for further review.
- **Allow:** Emails that fail the checks can still be delivered but may be tagged for review.

By implementing DMARC, organizations can significantly reduce the likelihood of phishing emails that attempt to spoof their domain, as unauthorized emails are automatically blocked or marked as spam.

3.1.6 Secure Sockets Layer & Transport Layer Security:

SSL and TLS are cryptographic technologies intended to safeguard communications over a computer network, such as the internet. They play a critical role in protecting sensitive data transmitted between a web browser and a server(THOMAS & Essentials, 2000). Here's how these protocols function:

SSL/TLS encrypts the data exchanged during transmission. This means that even if a hostile actor intercepts the conversation, they cannot read the data being sent. The encryption process uses complex algorithms to scramble the data into a format that is unreadable without the correct decryption key, thus ensuring confidentiality. These protocols also provide authentication, ensuring that users are communicating with the legitimate website rather than an imposter. When a user connects to a website secured by SSL/TLS, the server presents a digital certificate known as an SSL/TLS certificate(Oppliger, 2023). This certificate contains information about the website's identity and is issued by a trusted Certificate Authority (CA). The user's browser checks this certificate for authenticity, ensuring that it is valid and that the website is genuine. SSL/TLS protocols ensure data integrity during transmission, meaning that the information cannot be altered or tampered with without detection. Each message delivered over an SSL/TLS connection includes a checksum, which allows the recipient to ensure that the data received matches what was sent. This is especially significant in activities like online banking, where data accuracy is crucial.

Table 1. Anti-phishing techniques

Technology	Core Functionality	Benefits	Limitation	Example Implementation
Email Filtering	Scans emails for suspicious content, URLs, and attachments. Uses machine learning and heuristics for detection.	Prevents phishing emails from reaching inboxes.	May produce false positives or miss highly sophisticated attacks.	SpamTitan, Microsoft Defender for Office 365
AI-Based Phishing Detection	Uses machine learning algorithms to detect phishing patterns in real-time.	Adapts to new phishing tactics, highly accurate.	Requires large datasets and significant computational power for training and detection.	Google Safe Browsing, Barracuda Sentinel
URL Analysis	Evaluates URL structures and DNS records to detect spoofed or malicious links.	Blocks access to known phishing sites.	Relies on updated databases; can miss newly created phishing URLs.	PhishTank, Google Safe Browsing
Two-Factor Authentication	Adds an extra layer of verification during user login (e.g., SMS codes, authentication apps).	Protects even if credentials are compromised.	Can be inconvenient for users; SMS codes are vulnerable to interception.	Google Authenticator, Authy
DMARC	Authenticates email senders using SPF and DKIM protocols. Prevents domain spoofing.	Prevents impersonation attacks, ensures email integrity.	Requires proper configuration; limited adoption by organizations.	Agari, Microsoft Defender for Office 365
SSL/TLS	Encrypts data transmission between browsers and servers.	Ensures data confidentiality and integrity.	Cannot protect if phishing occurs over unsecured websites or social engineering techniques.	HTTPS protocols in web browsers
Phishing Simulations	Educates users by simulating phishing attacks. Trains them to recognize phishing attempts.	Improves employee awareness, reduces human error.	Depends on regular training to remain effective; does not directly block phishing attacks.	Barracuda Sentinel, KnowBe4

3.1.7 Anti Phishing Tools:

Anti-phishing tools are specialized security solutions designed to protect individuals and organizations from phishing attacks, which are fraudulent attempts to steal sensitive information by impersonating legitimate sources(Alkhalil et al., 2021b). These tools employ various techniques to detect and block phishing emails, malicious websites, and harmful attachments before they can cause harm. From email security platforms to browser-based protections, anti-phishing tools help identify suspicious activity, analyze email content, and prevent users from clicking on dangerous links. By integrating these technologies, businesses and individuals can strengthen their defenses against increasingly sophisticated phishing threats, ensuring safer online interactions.

WORKING OF ANTI PHISHING TOOLS:

Anti-phishing tools work by scanning emails, websites, and online interactions to spot and block phishing attempts. They check email content, attachments, and links for signs of phishing, such as unusual sender addresses or requests for personal information. These tools use advanced algorithms and databases of known phishing sites to identify and block suspicious activities.They also maintain updated databases of known phishing sources to stay ahead of emerging threats. They often use machine learning to improve detection, learning from past attacks to recognize new threats. Some tools offer real-time monitoring and alert users immediately when they detect potential risks(P. Sharma et al., 2022a). Additionally, anti-phishing tools can include two-factor authentication and encryption to ensure that even if a phishing attempt occurs, attackers cannot easily access sensitive data. By combining multiple layers of protection, these tools provide comprehensive security, keeping users safe from phishing attacks.

Figure 5. Important features of anti-phishing software

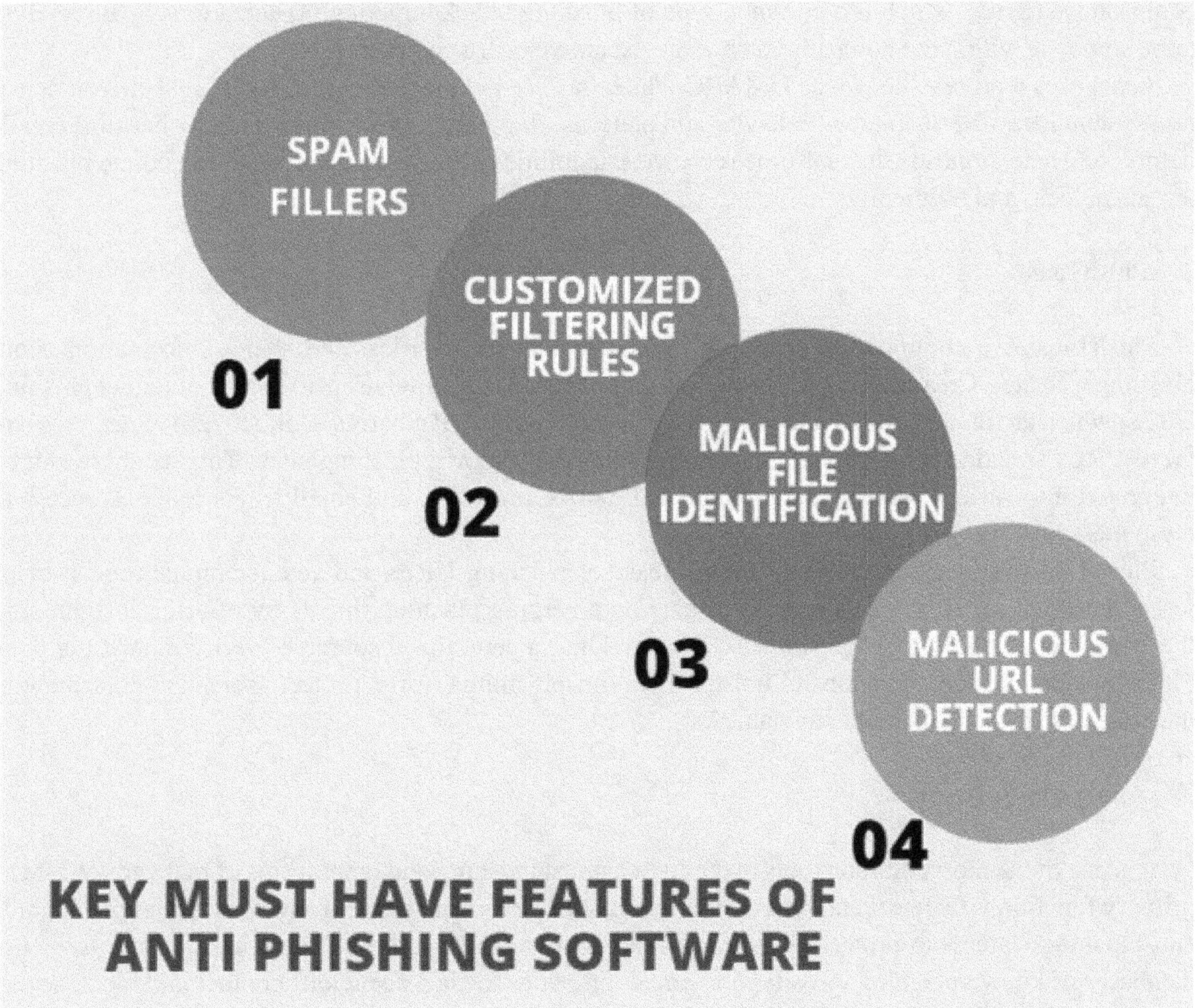

The diagram (figure 5) above explains how Anti-phishing software is essential for protecting users from deceptive online threats. Key features include **spam filters**, which block unsolicited emails that often carry phishing attacks, and **customized filtering rules**, allowing users to tailor their security settings to specific needs. The software also provides **malicious file identification**, detecting harmful attachments before they can be opened, and **malicious URL detection**, which identifies dangerous links leading to fraudulent websites. Together, these features create a comprehensive shield against phishing attempts, safeguarding sensitive information and preventing cyberattacks. Different anti phishing tools are explained below in detail:

1. Agari

Agari is a cutting-edge email security platform designed to protect organizations from advanced phishing threats. It leverages artificial intelligence and machine learning to analyze email communications, authenticate senders, and prevent impersonation attacks. Agari primarily focuses on business email compromise (BEC), which is a common type of phishing attack targeting organizations by pretending to be someone within the company, such as an executive or trusted partner.

Agari uses a process known as DMARC which has been explained earlier.Agari's AI-driven detection system identifies suspicious behavior and patterns, flagging or blocking potentially harmful emails before they reach inboxes. Its real-time response capabilities allow organizations to remediate phishing threats quickly and efficiently.

2. PhishTank

PhishTank is a community-driven platform that collects, verifies, and shares information about phishing websites. Created by OpenDNS (now part of Cisco), it allows users to submit potential phishing URLs, which are then reviewed and verified by the community (P. Sharma et al., 2022b). Once verified, these URLs are added to a publicly available database of known phishing sites. This database can be integrated into various security solutions like firewalls, browsers, and email filters to block access to these malicious websites.

PhishTank serves as both a real-time database of phishing URLs and an educational tool. It helps researchers and security teams stay up-to-date on emerging phishing threats by offering insights into the latest tactics used by cybercriminals. By providing a centralized source of verified phishing data, PhishTank enables organizations to bolster their anti-phishing efforts, protect users, and contribute to the collective fight against phishing attacks.

3. Anti-Virus Software

It is one of the most common tools in the fight against phishing and other forms of malware. While its primary function is to detect and remove malicious software, many modern anti-virus programs include anti-phishing features to protect users from fraudulent websites and phishing emails. These tools use databases of known phishing websites and email templates to flag suspicious content and block access to malicious websites (Rao & Nayak, 2014).

In addition to scanning for phishing threats, anti-virus software often includes real-time protection features that monitor network traffic, web activity, and email communication for signs of phishing. Some of the most popular anti-virus programs, such as Norton, McAfee, and Kaspersky, provide browser extensions that help users avoid phishing sites by checking the safety of URLs before they click. Advanced anti-virus software may also use machine learning algorithms to detect new phishing attempts by identifying unusual or suspicious behavior that deviates from typical patterns.

4. Microsoft Defender for Office 365

Microsoft Defender is a cloud-based security solution designed to protect organizations using Microsoft's Office 365 suite from phishing attacks, malware, and other threats. It provides advanced email protection by filtering out malicious content, scanning attachments, and checking URLs in real-time to prevent users from interacting with phishing websites.

One of the main characteristics of Microsoft Defender for Office 365 is its ability to safeguard against zero-day threats—new, previously unknown types of attacks that exploit vulnerabilities before a fix is available (Lakshmi, 2019). Using AI and machine learning, Microsoft Defender detects abnormal behavior patterns in emails and automatically quarantines suspicious messages. The tool also offers phishing simulations that organizations can use to educate employees about phishing threats, helping to build a stronger security culture (Rasmusen et al., 2022). Microsoft Defender integrates seamlessly with other Microsoft security products, providing comprehensive protection and enabling centralized management for IT teams. This makes it a powerful solution for organizations of all sizes looking to defend against email-based phishing attacks.

5. Google Safe Browsing

It is a security tool designed to safeguard consumers from online risks such as phishing and malware. It works by maintaining an up-to-date list of dangerous websites, including phishing sites, which are flagged when users attempt to visit them through browsers like Google Chrome or Firefox (Bell & Komisarczuk, 2020). When a user encounters a known phishing website, Safe Browsing triggers a warning page that alerts the user to the danger and offers an option to return to safety.

The system constantly scans the web for new threats, adding malicious URLs to its database and sharing that data with other services and products that utilize Safe Browsing. In addition to protecting individuals, Google Safe Browsing also provides APIs that developers can integrate into their own applications to protect users from phishing and malware. By delivering real-time protection to millions of users worldwide, Google Safe Browsing is one of the most widely used anti-phishing tools. Its seamless integration into web browsers ensures that users are alerted before they can fall victim to phishing scams.

6. SpamTitan

SpamTitan is a powerful email filtering solution designed to protect organizations from phishing, malware, and other email-borne threats. It uses advanced spam filtering algorithms to block unwanted and harmful emails before they reach users' inboxes. SpamTitan offers multi-layered security by scanning email content, attachments, and URLs for signs of phishing attempts. Its real-time threat intelligence database helps identify and block new phishing campaigns as soon as they are discovered. Efficient hardware-supported and parallelized architectures can enhance phishing prevention by accelerating real-time threat detection, enabling intelligent systems to process large volumes of data simultaneously while minimizing speculative execution overheads.(I. Singh et al., 2022)

SpamTitan's ability to detect phishing emails is enhanced by its machine learning capabilities, which analyze email patterns and behaviors to spot anomalies that indicate phishing. It also provides detailed reporting features, allowing administrators to monitor phishing attempts and other threats within the organization. The tool is easy to deploy and integrates well with most email platforms, making it a popular choice for businesses seeking comprehensive email security. In addition to its anti-phishing features, SpamTitan offers protection against other email-based threats, including ransomware and spam.

7. Barracuda Sentinel

Barracuda Sentinel is an AI-powered email security solution designed to protect organizations from phishing, spear-phishing, and business email compromise (BEC) attacks. It works in real-time by scanning incoming emails for signs of fraud and impersonation. Barracuda Sentinel uses machine learning models to detect anomalous email behaviors, such as spoofed domains or unusual sender patterns, helping to block phishing emails before they reach the recipient's inbox (Mengi et al., 2023).One of Barracuda Sentinel's standout features is its ability to prevent account takeover (ATO) attacks. ATO occurs when cybercriminals gain access to legitimate user accounts and use them to launch phishing campaigns from within an organization (Yi & Kamsin, 2022). Barracuda Sentinel continuously monitors email activity for signs of compromise and alerts administrators if an account shows suspicious activity.In addition to protecting against phishing, Barracuda Sentinel offers user training tools. It can simulate phishing attacks to educate employees, making them more adept at spotting phishing emails and improving overall security awareness in the workplace.

Benefits of using phishing prevention technologies tools:

Anti-phishing technologies provide numerous significant benefits that greatly enhance online security and user safety. These benefits include **Increased Security**, offering a robust layer of protection against phishing attacks This protects unwanted access to critical information, including passwords, credit card numbers, and personal data. They enable **Early Detection and Prevention** by analyzing emails and links in real time, swiftly identifying and blocking phishing attempts before users interact with them, significantly reducing the likelihood of falling victim to scams. Many anti-phishing solutions also focus on **User Education**, training users to recognize phishing attempts and empowering them to make safer online choices. Organisations that implement effective anti-phishing measures experience **Improved Trust**, as users are more likely to trust communications from companies that actively protect against phishing threats.

Additionally, these technologies lead to **Reduced Financial Losses** by preventing successful phishing attacks, helping organisations avoid costs associated with fraud, data breaches, and recovery efforts. They also ensure **Compliance with Regulations**, as many industries have requirements for robust data protection measures, reducing legal risks. The **Enhanced Incident Response** capabilities allow users to flag suspicious emails, providing valuable feedback to improve detection algorithms.

Figure 6. Benefits of anti-phishing technologies

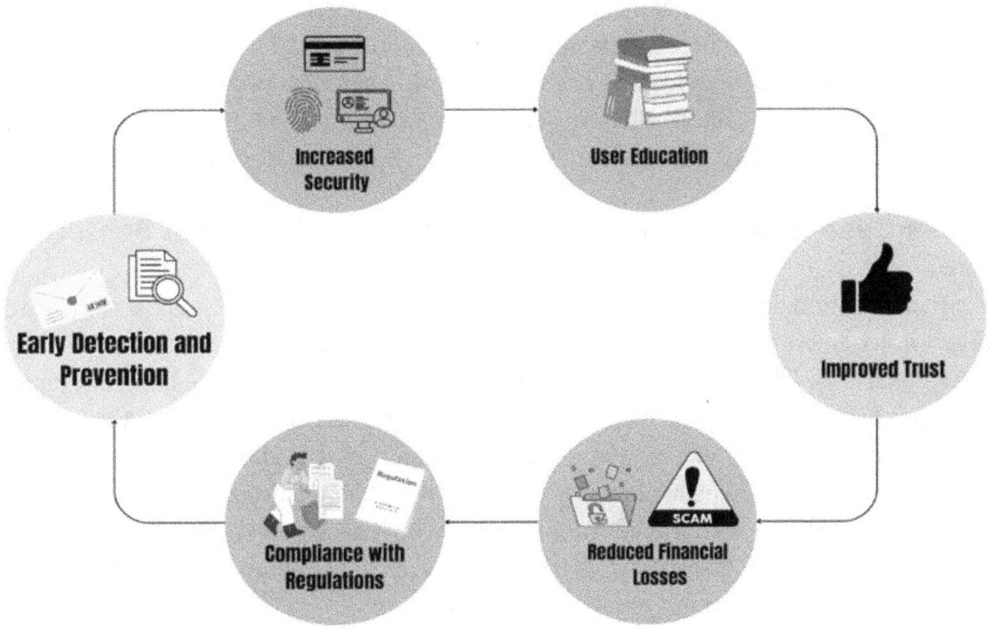

Here are some key advantages of using anti-phishing tools and services, which can help safeguard against phishing attacks:

Table 2. Features of phishing prevention tools

BENEFITS	DESCRIPTION
Threat Prevention	Protects against phishing attacks, reducing risks of financial loss, data breaches, and identity theft.
Real-time Identification	Quickly detects phishing attempts, preventing users from falling victim to scams (A. Aggarwal et al., 2012).
Enhanced Security	Strengthens overall cybersecurity by improving defences against a prevalent online threat.
Minimised Business Disruption	Prevents successful phishing attempts, so ensuring business continuity and productivity.
Data Security	Protects sensitive information, maintains customer trust, and complies with privacy regulations.
Cost Efficiency	Reduces the costs associated with data breaches and fraud-related occurrences, resulting in substantial savings.
User Training	Offers educational initiatives to help people spot and report phishing attacks.

4. CASE STUDY

Two case studies are discussed that illustrate the contrasting outcomes of anti-phishing mechanisms—one highlighting a successful implementation of advanced tools and strategies, and the other showcasing the consequences of inadequate defenses. These real-world examples provide valuable insights into the effectiveness of technologies like AI-based detection and Multi-Factor Authentication (MFA) while underscoring the critical role of user training and timely response in combating phishing threats.

4.1 Success Case Study: Barracuda Sentinel in the Financial Sector

A leading multinational bank operating in over 30 countries faced a surge in sophisticated phishing attacks targeting its employees and customers. Spear-phishing emails were used to impersonate senior executives (e.g., CEO or CFO) and requested unauthorized fund transfers. Phishing attempts also aimed to steal customer data by redirecting them to fake login pages resembling the bank's website. The bank faced significant cybersecurity challenges related to phishing, as traditional spam filters were unable to detect highly personalized spear-phishing emails . This left customers and employees vulnerable to attacks. Domain spoofing was another major issue, with attackers using deceptive domains such as "bank-secure.com" instead of "bank.com" to trick victims. Existing email security tools generated a high number of false positives, disrupting regular operations.

Additionally, the absence of real-time incident response mechanisms caused delays in neutralizing phishing attempts effectively. To address these issues, the bank implemented **Barracuda Sentinel**, an AI-powered anti-phishing tool, as part of its enhanced cybersecurity strategy. The tool provided real-time email analysis to detect anomalies in sender behavior, content patterns, and domain authenticity. To combat domain spoofing, the bank adopted **DMARC** (Domain-based Message Authentication, Reporting, and Conformance) policies, which effectively prevented impersonation. Automated incident response was introduced to quarantine suspicious emails, reducing the need for manual intervention. Furthermore, simulated phishing attacks and training sessions improved employee awareness and their ability to recognize phishing attempts(Rasmusen et al., 2022).

4.2 Failure Case Study: Lack of Multi-Factor Authentication (MFA) in a Government Agency

A regional government agency responsible for managing citizen data was targeted in a large-scale phishing campaign. Attackers sent fraudulent emails impersonating IT administrators, asking employees to reset their passwords through fake login pages. The phishing campaign aimed to gain access to the agency's database containing sensitive personal information. The agency faced several vulnerabilities that made it susceptible to phishing attacks. It relied on outdated email filtering software incapable of detecting personalized phishing attempts. Employees were largely unaware of phishing risks and frequently clicked on suspicious links. Additionally, the agency had not implemented Multi-Factor Authentication (MFA), leaving accounts open to credential theft. Compounding these issues, there was no incident response plan in place to address breaches swiftly(P. Sharma et al., 2022c). Attackers successfully exploited these weaknesses by tricking multiple employees into revealing their credentials through phishing emails.

Using these compromised accounts, the attackers gained access to the agency's database and exfiltrated over 1.2 million citizen records, including names, addresses, and Social Security Numbers.

The attack had devastating consequences:

- Data Breach: Over 1.2 million sensitive citizen records were leaked, causing significant reputational damage to the agency.
- Financial Loss: The agency faced lawsuits and regulatory fines, with total costs exceeding $10 million.
- Delayed Detection: The breach went undetected for weeks, giving attackers time to exploit the stolen data further.
- Public Backlash: Citizens lost trust in the agency's ability to protect their information, leading to widespread criticism.

5. FUTURE TRENDS IN ANTI PHISHING TECHNOLOGIES AND TOOLS

As phishing attacks become more advanced, new technologies are being developed to improve protection against them. Here are some important trends shaping the future of anti-phishing tools:

Table 3. Future Trends in Anti-Phishing Technologies and Tools

Sr. No	Future Trend	Description
1.	AI and Machine Learning	AI systems learn from data and recognize phishing patterns, while machine learning improves detection over time(K. Aggarwal, Singh, Chopra, Kumar, et al., 2022; I. Singh et al., 2022). AI helps automate detection and requires minimal human intervention. AI helps automate detection and requires minimal human intervention. AI helps automate detection and requires minimal human intervention. Linux include the integration of AI-driven threat detection, automated real-time email analysis, advanced machine learning algorithms for anomaly detection, and enhanced open-source tools for proactive security monitoring and response.(S. K. Singh, 2021)
2.	Predictive Analytics	Uses past data to predict future phishing attacks, allowing preventive measures before attacks happen. Predictive models also help prioritize high-risk individuals or departments.
3.	Continuous Updates and Adaptations	Anti-phishing tools are regularly updated to stay effective against new phishing techniques. Dynamic updates allow systems to respond instantly to emerging phishing threats.
4.	Behavioural Analysis	Tracks user behavior (e.g., login times, device usage) to detect unusual activity that may indicate phishing. It also monitors changes in communication patterns to identify compromised accounts.
5.	Real-Time Threat Intelligence	Combines live data from global security networks to detect and block phishing attacks in real time. Helps organizations receive immediate updates on phishing campaigns worldwide.
6.	Natural Language Processing (NLP)	NLP helps analyze email language to detect phishing by spotting suspicious or unusual language patterns. It can identify social engineering tactics, like impersonation, used in phishing emails (K. Aggarwal, Singh, Chopra, & Kumar, 2022).
7.	Phishing Simulation and User Training	Companies simulate phishing attacks to train employees to recognize and report phishing attempts. Regular simulations improve employee awareness and help prevent future attacks.

continued on following page

Table 3. Continued

Sr. No	Future Trend	Description
8.	Advanced Email Authentication Protocols	Stronger authentication methods like DMARC, SPF, and DKIM are used to verify legitimate senders and block phishing emails. These protocols help prevent email spoofing and reduce false positives(Kolagotla, 2021).
9.	Cloud-Based Anti-Phishing Solutions	Cloud-based tools offer scalable and flexible protection, allowing organizations to detect phishing across multiple devices and locations. These solutions provide seamless integration with existing IT infrastructure(A. Gupta et al., 2017; Iqbal et al., 2016).
10.	Mobile Device Protection	As phishing spreads to mobile platforms, anti-phishing tools are expanding to cover mobile devices and apps. Protection includes detecting phishing links sent via SMS, social media, or mobile apps.(Peñalvo, Sharma, et al., 2022)

6. CONCLUSION

Phishing Prevention tools and technologies are indispensable in the fight against increasingly sophisticated phishing attacks. Solutions like email filtering, AI-driven phishing detection, URL analysis, and two-factor authentication provide organizations with multi-layered defenses to safeguard sensitive data and prevent malicious activities. Tools such as DMARC, Agari, PhishTank, Microsoft Defender for Office 365, SpamTitan, and Barracuda Sentinel offer comprehensive protection by continuously monitoring and blocking phishing attempts in real time. An explainable context-aware IoT framework, leveraging a human digital twin, can enhance phishing prevention in healthcare by providing real-time, personalized threat detection and response based on user behavior and context.(Kumar et al., 2024; Vats et al., 2023). The benefits of using these technologies extend beyond immediate threat mitigation, as they enhance overall cybersecurity, maintain business continuity, protect sensitive information, and generate significant cost savings by preventing data breaches and fraud. As phishing techniques evolve, future advancements in AI and machine learning will be critical for staying ahead of emerging threats. These tools will continue to refine their ability to detect patterns, learn from new threats, and adapt more quickly to changing cybercriminal strategies. By investing in and adopting these advanced technologies, organizations can not only secure their operations but also empower users through awareness programs, making the digital ecosystem safer and more resilient for everyone(Valdez-De-Leon, 2019). Ultimately, the continued evolution of anti-phishing solutions will be key to protecting businesses and individuals in an increasingly interconnected world.

REFERENCES

Aggarwal, A., Rajadesingan, A., & Kumaraguru, P. (2012). PhishAri: Automatic realtime phishing detection on twitter. *2012 eCrime Researchers Summit*, 1–12. https://ieeexplore.ieee.org/abstract/document/6489521/

Aggarwal, K., Singh, S. K., Chopra, M., & Kumar, S. (2022). Role of social media in the COVID-19 pandemic: A literature review. *Data Mining Approaches for Big Data and Sentiment Analysis in Social Media*, 91–115.

Aggarwal, K., Singh, S. K., Chopra, M., Kumar, S., & Colace, F. (2022). Deep Learning in Robotics for Strengthening Industry 4.0.: Opportunities, Challenges and Future Directions. In Nedjah, N., Abd El-Latif, A. A., Gupta, B. B., & Mourelle, L. M. (Eds.), *Robotics and AI for Cybersecurity and Critical Infrastructure in Smart Cities* (Vol. 1030, pp. 1–19). Springer International Publishing., DOI: 10.1007/978-3-030-96737-6_1

Aggarwal, T., Kumar, S., Singh, S. K., Gupta, B. B., Nedjah, N., & Castiglione, A. (2024). Zero Knowledge Proofs and Their Applications in Cryptography: Advancements, Challenges, and Future Aspects. In *Innovations in Modern Cryptography* (pp. 55–74). IGI Global. https://www.igi-global.com/chapter/zero-knowledge-proofs-and-their-applications-in-cryptography/354035

Alkhalil, Z., Hewage, C., Nawaf, L., & Khan, I. (2021b). Phishing attacks: A recent comprehensive study and a new anatomy. *Frontiers of Computer Science*, 3, 563060. DOI: 10.3389/fcomp.2021.563060

Ashiq, M. I., Li, W., Fiebig, T., & Chung, T. (2023). You've Got Report: Measurement and Security Implications of {DMARC} Reporting. *32nd USENIX Security Symposium (USENIX Security 23)*, 4123–4137. https://www.usenix.org/conference/usenixsecurity23/presentation/ashiq

Bell, S., & Komisarczuk, P. (2020). An Analysis of Phishing Blacklists: Google Safe Browsing, OpenPhish, and PhishTank. *Proceedings of the Australasian Computer Science Week Multiconference*, 1–11. DOI: 10.1145/3373017.3373020

Chhabra, A., Singh, S. K., Sharma, A., Kumar, S., Gupta, B. B., Arya, V., & Chui, K. T. (2024). Towards Sustainable Consumer Electronics: DL-based SoH and RUL Prediction for E-Waste Reduction. *2024 IEEE International Conference on Consumer Electronics (ICCE)*, 1–4. https://ieeexplore.ieee.org/abstract/document/10444466/

Das, A., Baki, S., El Aassal, A., Verma, R., & Dunbar, A. (2019). SoK: A comprehensive reexamination of phishing research from the security perspective. *IEEE Communications Surveys and Tutorials*, 22(1), 671–708. DOI: 10.1109/COMST.2019.2957750

Girdhar, M., Singh, S. K., Kumar, S., Mahto, D., Sharma, S. K., Gupta, B. B., Arya, V., & Chui, K. T. (2023). Exploring Advanced Neural Networks For Cross-Corpus Fake News Detection. *Proceedings of the 5th International Conference on Information Management & Machine Intelligence*, 1–6. DOI: 10.1145/3647444.3652457

Goyal, S., Singh, S. K., Kumar, S., Sarin, S., Gupta, B. B., Arya, V., & Chui, K. T. (2023). Hyperdimensional Consumer Pattern Analysis with Quantum Neural Architectures using Non-Hermitian Operators. *Proceedings of the 5th International Conference on Information Management & Machine Intelligence*, 1–5. DOI: 10.1145/3647444.3652458

Gupta, B. B., Arachchilage, N. A. G., & Psannis, K. E. (2018). Defending against phishing attacks: Taxonomy of methods, current issues and future directions. *Telecommunication Systems*, 67(2), 247–267. DOI: 10.1007/s11235-017-0334-z

Hu, H., Peng, P., & Wang, G. (2018). Towards understanding the adoption of anti-spoofing protocols in email systems. *2018 IEEE Cybersecurity Development (SecDev)*, 94–101. https://ieeexplore.ieee.org/abstract/document/8543392/

Iqbal, S., Kiah, M. L. M., Dhaghighi, B., Hussain, M., Khan, S., Khan, M. K., & Choo, K.-K. R. (2016). On cloud security attacks: A taxonomy and intrusion detection and prevention as a service. *Journal of Network and Computer Applications*, 74, 98–120. DOI: 10.1016/j.jnca.2016.08.016

Jain, A. K., & Gupta, B. B. (2018a). Towards detection of phishing websites on client-side using machine learning based approach. *Telecommunication Systems*, 68(4), 687–700. DOI: 10.1007/s11235-017-0414-0

Jain, A. K., & Gupta, B. B. (2018b). Two-level authentication approach to protect from phishing attacks in real time. *Journal of Ambient Intelligence and Humanized Computing*, 9(6), 1783–1796. DOI: 10.1007/s12652-017-0616-z

Jain, A. K., & Gupta, B. B. (2019). A machine learning based approach for phishing detection using hyperlinks information. *Journal of Ambient Intelligence and Humanized Computing*, 10(5), 2015–2028. DOI: 10.1007/s12652-018-0798-z

Jaswal, S., & Malhotra, M. (2022). Afttm: Agent-based fault tolerance trust mechanism in cloud environment. [IJCAC]. *International Journal of Cloud Applications and Computing*, 12(1), 1–12. DOI: 10.4018/IJCAC.297105

Kaur, P., Singh, S. K., Singh, I., & Kumar, S. (2021). Exploring convolutional neural network in computer vision-based image classification. *International Conference on Smart Systems and Advanced Computing (Syscom-2021)*. https://ceur-ws.org/Vol-3080/21.pdf

Kolagotla, R. R. (2021). *Enhancing the security of an E-mail by DMARC and DNS data* [PhD Thesis, Dublin, National College of Ireland]. https://norma.ncirl.ie/5176/

Kumar, R., Singh, S. K., Lobiyal, D. K., Kumar, S., & Jawla, S. (2024). Security Metrics and Authentication-based RouTing (SMART) Protocol for Vehicular IoT Networks. *SN Computer Science*, 5(2), 236. DOI: 10.1007/s42979-023-02566-7

Lakshmi, V. (2019). *Beginning Security with Microsoft Technologies: Protecting Office 365, Devices, and Data*. Apress., DOI: 10.1007/978-1-4842-4853-9

Mengi, G., Singh, S. K., Kumar, S., Mahto, D., & Sharma, A. (2023). Automated Machine Learning (AutoML): The Future of Computational Intelligence. In Nedjah, N., Martínez Pérez, G., & Gupta, B. B. (Eds.), *International Conference on Cyber Security, Privacy and Networking (ICSPN 2022)* (Vol. 599, pp. 309–317). Springer International Publishing. DOI: 10.1007/978-3-031-22018-0_28

Mohammed, A. H. Y., Dziyauddin, R. A., & Latiff, L. A. (2023). Current multi-factor of authentication: Approaches, requirements, attacks and challenges. *International Journal of Advanced Computer Science and Applications*, 14(1). Advance online publication. http://eprints.utm.my/105361/1/AliHameedYassirMohammed2023_CurrentMultiFactorofAuthenticationApproaches.pdf. DOI: 10.14569/IJACSA.2023.0140119

Oppliger, R. (2023). *SSL and TLS: Theory and Practice.* Artech House. https://books.google.com/books?hl=en&lr=&id=TOnNEAAAQBAJ&oi=fnd&pg=PP1&dq=31.%09Oppliger,+R.+(2023).+SSL+and+TLS:+Theory+and+Practice.+Artech+House.&ots=8auA5Xm50B&sig=FdKkuhxigQlNaznl5w4IdTTskhA

Peñalvo, F. J. G., Maan, T., Singh, S. K., Kumar, S., Arya, V., Chui, K. T., & Singh, G. P. (2022). Sustainable stock market prediction framework using machine learning models. [IJSSCI]. *International Journal of Software Science and Computational Intelligence*, 14(1), 1–15. DOI: 10.4018/IJSSCI.313593

Peñalvo, F. J. G., Sharma, A., Chhabra, A., Singh, S. K., Kumar, S., Arya, V., & Gaurav, A. (2022). Mobile cloud computing and sustainable development: Opportunities, challenges, and future directions. [IJCAC]. *International Journal of Cloud Applications and Computing*, 12(1), 1–20. DOI: 10.4018/IJCAC.312583

Petsas, T., Tsirantonakis, G., Athanasopoulos, E., & Ioannidis, S. (2015). Two-factor authentication: Is the world ready?: quantifying 2FA adoption. *Proceedings of the Eighth European Workshop on System Security*, 1–7. DOI: 10.1145/2751323.2751327

Rao, U. H., & Nayak, U. (2014). *The InfoSec handbook: An introduction to information security*. Springer Nature. https://library.oapen.org/bitstream/handle/20.500.12657/28165/1/1001829.pdf

Rasmusen, S. C., Penz, M., Widauer, S., Nako, P., Kurteva, A., Roa-Valverde, A., & Fensel, A. (2022). Raising consent awareness with gamification and knowledge graphs: An automotive use case. [IJSWIS]. *International Journal on Semantic Web and Information Systems*, 18(1), 1–21. DOI: 10.4018/IJSWIS.300820

Setia, H., Chhabra, A., Singh, S. K., Kumar, S., Sharma, S., Arya, V., Gupta, B. B., & Wu, J. (2024). Securing the road ahead: Machine learning-driven DDoS attack detection in VANET cloud environments. *Cyber Security and Applications*, 2, 100037. DOI: 10.1016/j.csa.2024.100037

Sharma, A., Singh, S. K., Badwal, E., Kumar, S., Gupta, B. B., Arya, V., Chui, K. T., & Santaniello, D. (2023). Fuzzy based clustering of consumers' big data in industrial applications. *2023 IEEE International Conference on Consumer Electronics (ICCE)*, 01–03. https://ieeexplore.ieee.org/abstract/document/10043451/

Sharma, A., Singh, S. K., Kumar, S., Chhabra, A., & Gupta, S. (2023). Security of Android Banking Mobile Apps: Challenges and Opportunities. In Nedjah, N., Martínez Pérez, G., & Gupta, B. B. (Eds.), *International Conference on Cyber Security, Privacy and Networking (ICSPN 2022)* (Vol. 599, pp. 406–416). Springer International Publishing. DOI: 10.1007/978-3-031-22018-0_39

Sharma, P., Dash, B., & Ansari, M. F. (2022a). Anti-phishing techniques–a review of Cyber Defense Mechanisms. *International Journal of Advanced Research in Computer and Communication Engineering*, 3297(7), 2007. DOI: 10.17148/IJARCCE.2022.11728

Singh, I., Singh, S. K., Singh, R., & Kumar, S. (2022). Efficient loop unrolling factor prediction algorithm using machine learning models. *2022 3rd International Conference for Emerging Technology (INCET)*, 1–8. https://ieeexplore.ieee.org/abstract/document/9825092/

Singh, L. J., & Imphal, N. (2018). A survey on phishing and anti-phishing techniques. [IJCST]. *International Journal of Computer Science Trends and Technology*, 6(2), 62–68.

Singh, M., Singh, S. K., Kumar, S., Madan, U., & Maan, T. (2023). Sustainable Framework for Metaverse Security and Privacy: Opportunities and Challenges. In Nedjah, N., Martínez Pérez, G., & Gupta, B. B. (Eds.), *International Conference on Cyber Security, Privacy and Networking (ICSPN 2022)* (Vol. 599, pp. 329–340). Springer International Publishing. DOI: 10.1007/978-3-031-22018-0_30

Singh, S. K. (2021). *Linux yourself: Concept and programming*. Chapman and Hall/CRC. https://www.taylorfrancis.com/books/mono/10.1201/9780429446047/linux-sunil-singh

Thomas, S., & Essentials, T. L. S. (2000). *Securing the Web*. John Wiley. https://pages.cs.wisc.edu/~jha/course-archive/642-spring-2007/SLIDES/ssl.ps

Valdez-De-Leon, O. (2019). How to develop a digital ecosystem: A practical framework. *Technology Innovation Management Review*, 9(8), 43–54. DOI: 10.22215/timreview/1260

Vats, T., & Kumar, S. (2021). *Next-generation towards construction of cyber-physical systems and digital twins*. Insights2Techinfo. https://insights2techinfo.com/next-generation-towards-construction-of-cyber-physical-systems-and-digital-twins/

Vats, T., Kumar, S., Singh, S. K., Madan, U., Preet, M., Arya, V., Bansal, R., & Almomani, A. (2024). Navigating the landscape: Safeguarding privacy and security in the era of ambient intelligence within healthcare settings. *Cyber Security and Applications*, 2, 100046. DOI: 10.1016/j.csa.2024.100046

Vats, T., Singh, S. K., Kumar, S., Gupta, B. B., Gill, S. S., Arya, V., & Alhalabi, W. (2023). RETRACTED ARTICLE: Explainable context-aware IoT framework using human digital twin for healthcare. *Multimedia Tools and Applications*, 83(22), 62489–62490. DOI: 10.1007/s11042-023-16922-5

Yi, C. X., & Kamsin, D. (2022). Research of Detection and Prevention of Phishing and Proposal of Phishing Detector Solution. *Journal of Applied Technology and Innovation*, 6(3), 1–5.

Chapter 4
Phishing Detection and Prevention in Smart Devices and IoT Networks

Achit Katiyar
International Center for AI and Cyber Security Research and Innovations (CCRI), Asia University, Taichung, Taiwan

Akshat Gaurav
https://orcid.org/0000-0002-5796-9424
International Center for AI and Cyber Security Research and Innovations (CCRI), Asia University, Taichung, Taiwan

Brij B. Gupta
https://orcid.org/0000-0003-4929-4698
Asia University, Taiwan

Moon Jusung
https://orcid.org/0009-0004-2513-9364
International Center for AI and Cyber Security Research and Innovations (CCRI), Asia University, Taichung, Taiwan

ABSTRACT

The use of IoT and smart devices has increased day by day. The connections and automations are easily made in the digital world by the use of IoT and smart devices. But, the frequency of phishing attacks on these devices has grown day by day. This chapter focuses on the increasing situation of phishing in the environments of the IoT and smart devices. Also, paper provides the explanation of the challenges given by the IoT and smart devices. The paper explore that how the phishing attacks have been changed in order to aim the existing weaknesses within the IoT environments. Advantages of these devices in terms of connectivity and user-friendly interfaces are also discussed. Moving a step further than the risk valuation, this paper aims at explaining the details about current state of art in the detection and prevention strategies. There are some problems in which fundamental security protocols may be problematic to enforce.

DOI: 10.4018/979-8-3693-8784-9.ch004

1. INTRODUCTION

Phishing is one of the oldest and most common forms of the cyber-attacks (Ishtaiwi et al., 2024). It aimed the individuals via email to manipulate them. Target of the phishing is to get the sensitive information like passwords or financial details of the individuals. IoT means to the growing network of physical devise, vehicles, appliances and other smart systems. Figure 1 presents the global phishing statistics breakdown.

1.1 Definition of Phishing

Phishing is a cybercrime strategy. In this cybercrime method, attackers steal the personal information online without any direct contact. This cybercrime involves the deceptive communications to trick individuals into revealing the sensitive information like login details, financial details etc (Zhou et al., 2024).

Cyber criminals commonly use phisher as a tool of attacking the users and get their personal data by misleading them through social engineering and technical means (Gaurav et al., 2024). These attacks have developed since their inception in the mid-1990s where the attackers get more innovative in their techniques such as fake websites and fake communications (Priya et al., 2024) (Al-Sinayyid et al., 2023; Surianarayanan & Chelliah, 2023).

Figure 1. Global Phishing Statistics Breakdown - 2023

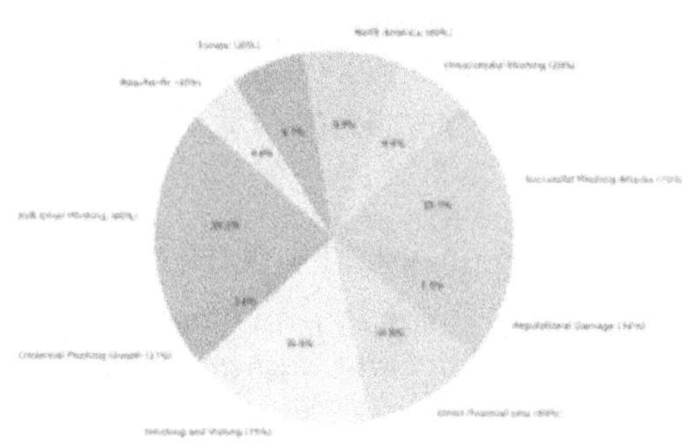

The type of phishing has evolved to many forms, especially spear phishing, whale phishing, and email spoofing that tend to reach out to different categories of users (Al-Sinayyid et al., 2023; Li et al., 2024). With advances in the use of internet, the cases of phishing have surged since the attackers use different techniques to exploit the identified weaknesses (Priya et al., 2024).

It has been possible to apply different detection techniques like machine learning techniques to enhance the effect detection of phishing attempts in which different accuracy rates have been realized.

Evolution of Phishing Techniques:

The evaluation of phasing attacks is represented in Figure 2.

- **Initial Methods:** Initial phishing schemes only included a large number of emails sent to people in order to prompt them into revealing data about themselves (Journals, n.d.).
- **Targeted Attacks:** In addition to this, the authors state that spear phishing has emerged as a newer and improved method with the concentration on high target individuals or entities (Ghazi-Tehrani & Pontell, 2022; Gupta et al., 2024).
- **Technological Advancements:** The advancement in technology has also helped in the carrying out of the phisher and the discovering of new tactics such as the deepfakes as seen in the article (Ghazi-Tehrani & Pontell, 2022) and (Cui et al., 2018).

Figure 2. Rise of Phishing attacks

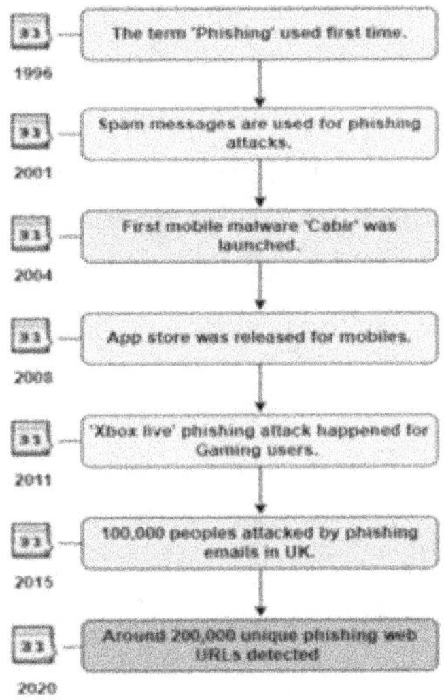

1.2 IoT and Smart Devices

Internet of Things commonly (IoT) can be described as the linkages or interfaces between physical things or computing machines that can exchange information over the Internet (AlShaikh et al., 2023). IoT environment contains smart devices which are fitted with sensors and software programs for operation on their own.

IoT includes almost any type of connected devices: household devices, factory and industry tools, and many more that possess communication abilities and can equally be operated without physical presence (R et al., 2023; Stergiou et al., 2022). Smart devices therefore refers to these devices which are capable of perceiving, capturing, analysing and acting on data in a way that it can be more useful to mankind and organisationally more functional (Jain et al., 2022; M, n.d.; Nirmal et al., 2024).

Examples of Smart Devices:

- **Home Automation:** Smart devices like smart thermostats and door cameras and the devices that are now controllable through the internet (R et al., 2023) (Abinayasree, 2024).
- **Wearable technology:** Activity trackers that are used to monitor the general health status and performance, body fat, pulse rates and so on (Abinayasree, 2024).
- **Connected Vehicles:** Self-driving cars to have sensors for navigation and other safety functions (Nirmal et al., 2024).

Huge advantages are connected with IoT and smart devices use, but enhanced data security danger and privacy issues are still topical, so proper protective actions are needed (Usha et al., 2022).

IoT is becoming more influential in shaping contemporary society's communication and can lead to improvement of performance in a number of industries. Smart homes, health care, industries, and smart city are some of the applications where devices pull and push data for better customer interaction and function.

Key Areas of Growth:

- **Healthcare:** With the usage of IoT patient can be monitored remotely and smart medical devices improve patient's condition ("The Internet of Things (IoT)," 2024). As represented in Figure 3.

Figure 3. Applications of IoT in Healthcare

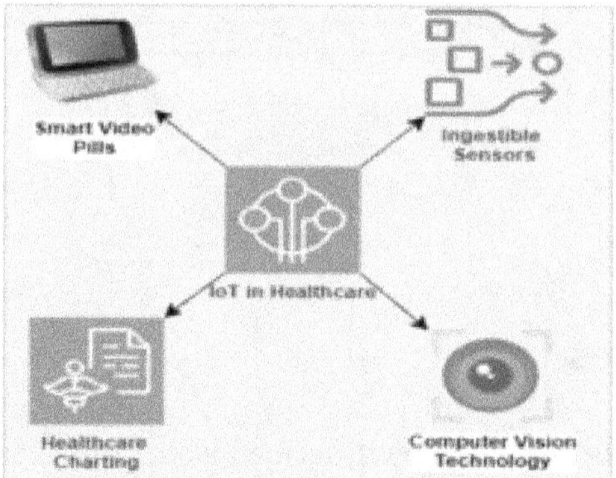

- **Manufacturing:** The incorporation of IoT in the industrial application has resulted in what is known as smart factories improving the sort of predictive maintenance routines and supply chain (Bhaskar et al., 2024) (Figure 4).

Figure 4. Applications of IoT in Manufacturing

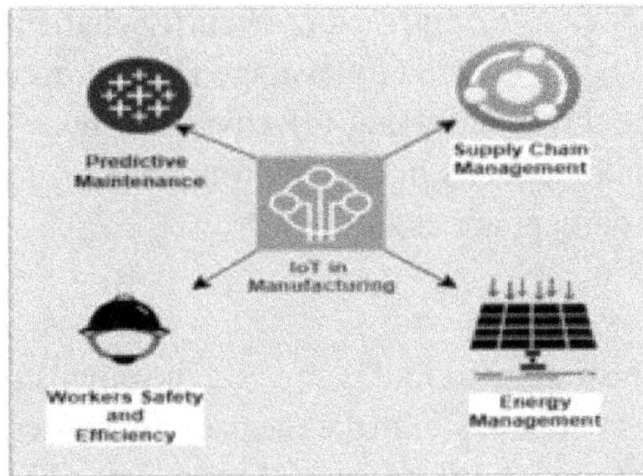

- **Smart Cities:** Smart city IoT applications enhance traffic control and efficient use of energy in city infrastructure to be sustainable ("The Internet of Things (IoT)," 2024). As represented in Figure 5.

Figure 5. Applications of IoT in Smart Cities

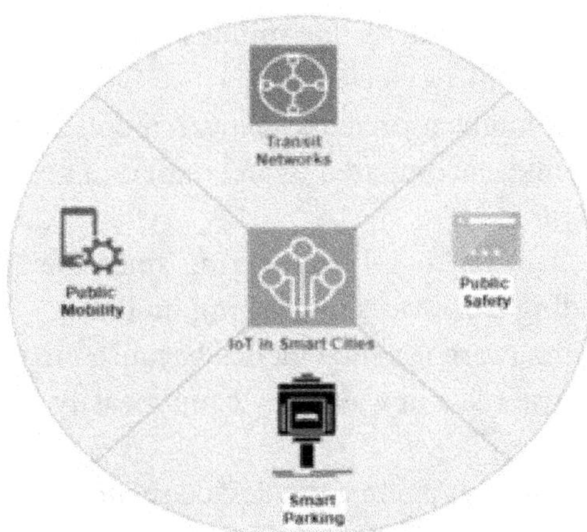

2. THE INTERSECTION OF PHISHING AND IOT

The phishing attacks in IoT devices brings serious security challenges. Fraudulent email and website strategies aimed at users are being evolved to leverage flaws present in IoT systems. This blending requires a better awareness of the threats targeting IoT environments.

There are many type of Phishing attacks in IoT environments, as represented in Figure 5. Some of the phishing attacks in IoT environment are as follows:

- *Email phishing:*
  - Phishing is a common strategy to fool people on the emails pretended they are actually from other genuine services with aims to make the user give away some information or user name and password regarding to the IoT devices (Abbas et al., 2021).
  - There are even more IoT devices than ever before, meaning there are plenty of possible targets, and people are likely to be less protective of their data when dealing with smart objects (Abomhara et al., 2021).
- *SMS Phishing (Smishing):*
  - Smishing is a form of phishing that utilizes Short Messaging Systems hence the name SMS to send messages that look as if they were sent by known senders hence encouraging subscribers to click on links that are harmful or offer personal information.
  - This method is useful as most IoT devices have their setting accessed through a mobile interface where they can be attacked (Foozy et al., 2013).
- *Voice Phishing (Vishing):*
  - Vishing is a type of phone call attack that mimics some kind of official body to trap users into providing information on IoT devices.
  - The nature of voice communication makes it even more effective because the user is likely to believe the call is genuine as compared to an email or a text message (Alkhalil et al., 2021).
- *Social Engineering Techniques:*
  - Phishing is heavily reliant on social engineering since the attacker relies on the user's mistakes including providing passwords or clicking on links.
  - Users of IoT devices are aware for such tactics because the use of such devices in their daily life exposes them to those risks in ways they cannot easily observe (Xenofontos et al., 2022).

The IoT has its own threats, which act against the device security mainly because of the lack of protection mechanisms. Some of the identified risks are insecurity with little or no provisions for security, credentialed systems with default logins, outdated software, and insecure connection.

- *Lack of Robust Security Measures:*
  - Most developed IoT devices have no security facilities built into their systems, which makes them vulnerable to hackers (Samaila et al., 2017).
  - Due to the dual nature of IoT, issues with security cannot be solved through traditional solutions and need innovative solutions (Samaila et al., 2017).
- *Default Credentials and Weak Passwords:*
  - Most of the gadgets come with factory-set user names and passwords, which are not changed and therefore present easy grounds for exploitation (Costa et al., 2024).

This problem has been attributed to serious security threats such as large-scale DDoS attacks (Costa et al., 2024).

- *Unpatched Software and Firmware:*
  Most IoT devices are constantly running on now condemned firmware which exposes them to hackers (Girma, 2018).
  Because of the limited resources of these devices, usual alterations are rarely made although they can significantly enhance mode performance (Ahmed et al., 2017).
- *Insecure communication Channels:*
  Most IoT devices are on networks that make their data equally easy for any party to intercept (Jurcut et al., 2020).
  This vulnerability is however combined by the fact that most communication protocols do not use encryption (Jurcut et al., 2020).

Apart from these vulnerabilities, critics note that the clients and markets of IoT are still growing, with development in the IoT sector constant, and when demand arises for safer devices, the measures will be developed.

3. CASE STUDIES

In this section of the paper, we analysis relevant case studies.

The Mirai Botnet Incident (2016): While, one of the recent IoT cyber-attack that occurred in the year 2016 was the Mirai Botnet attack. It was discovered in August of 2016 and has been behind some of the largest DDoS attacks ever to take place. Mirai operates by targeting IoT devices with improperly set up security parameters with a brute force method for gaining administrative access.

Mirai was designed to primarily attack IoT devices to include routers, cameras and digital video recorders (DVRs) through weak credentials used to control them from remote locations. Threat attackers launched phishing emails that forced the targets to disclose facts that include default IoT credentials. After compromise the devices became botnet and were used for large scale Distributed Denial of Service (DDoS) cyber-attacks on a number of websites and servers around the world (Kolias et al., 2017).

The Ring Camera Hack (2019): One other major type of phishing attack was targeting Ring smart cameras. Phishing emails were sent right to the users and once logged in, hackers gained control over home surveillance systems of the families (Pétursson, 2023).

This led to privacy violation cases in which the attackers were able to interface with people through the device's own cameras. It exposed personal information and members of approximately thousand households to danger. Apart from the distress of the event, weaknesses such as poor password practices and phishing vulnerability of IoT environment were demonstrated (Budimir et al., 2021).

Targeted Phishing on Industrial IoT (IIoT) (2020): In 2020, the IIoT systems have been on the receiving end of phishing attacks than other categories of cyber-attacks. That is how the attackers simulated phishing on email accounts of employees of industrial firms to penetrate the systems and leave malware on the networks connected to the critical infrastructure. These attacks resulted in unauthorized access to IIoT networks, which have threats to manufacturing systems and utilities (Sisinni et al., 2018).

These attacks were not just limited to controlling confidential data; they threatened real assets of a nation, the security of infrastructures like energy stations and manufacturing facilities. The response included steps of securing IIoT and increased investments to cybersecurity for IIoT spaces (Tsiknas et al., 2021).

Table 1 presents some phishing attack detection models

Table 1. Phishing Attack Detection Models

Authors and Year	Methods	Solutions
(Shueb et al., 2024)	Blockchain-based token system structured for IoT devices with the access control and verification for phishing defence.	Token-tagged blockchain for IoT security, reducing phishing in airport and transit IoT devices.
(Liu et al., 2024)	Anti-phishing mechanisms in healthcare IoT using encryption for sensitive Electronic Medical Records (EMRs).	Encryption and access control mechanisms to prevent phishing attacks on medical IoT data.
(Gnana Jeslin et al., 2024)	Blockchain and ML-based Privacy Intrusion Detection System for smart networks with an emphasis on phishing threat prevention.	Combined blockchain and ML solution to secure IoT smart networks against phishing and privacy intrusions.
(N. Fatima et al., 2024)	AI-based phishing detection model tailored for IoT devices in smart homes, focusing on detecting malicious network behaviour.	AI-driven monitoring for real-time phishing detection in smart home IoT systems.

4. TECHNOLOGICAL AND HUMAN FACTORS

IoT device security depends on by both technical and human variables. The flexibility of IoT systems to cyber threats is determined by both technological aspects, namely, the architecture of these systems and their characteristic network vulnerabilities. In this time, human factors such as user's behaviour, awareness and susceptibility to social engineering (SE) strategies have very high influence in IoT environments security because IoT devices are no longer passive components. In developing effective strategies for safeguarding the IoT against evolving cyber risks, we need to understand from both dimensions.

4.1 Technological Factors

IoT systems are comprised by a large number of interconnected physical devices that communicate via Interconnecting networks. They are simple sensors up to complex smart devices, which are involved in the IoT ecosystem. Because of limited security resource, IoT devices can be easily compromised, and attackers can exploit these vulnerabilities to fuel phishing scheme targeting unsuspecting users. Safeguarding IoT systems from cyber threats requires an understanding, and an ability to address, these architectural weaknesses. The combined limitations in IoT architecture and the big networks in which they are deployed are presenting users with an entirely new set of security risks that can be addressed through both technical and procedural measures.

4.1.1 IoT architecture and security flaws

IoT networks have their own architecture and as such bring out distinct security challenges, particularly given the diversity (and sometimes resource limitation) of connected devices. However, these limitations prevent early adoption of advanced security protocol for many of the IoT systems, making them prone to phishing attacks. Using these vulnerabilities in sectors that transmit data on sensitive patient information, they could put our data at risk through data breaches and system disruptions. There is one solution that is integration with Blockchain technology. This combination can enhance data transparency, integrity and also mitigating phishing risks within industrial IoT systems (Bouijij & Berqia, 2024). In addition, IoT devices in smart home spaces are specifically vulnerable. It is because of the limited security protocols on consumer-grade devices. This allows phishing attack to invade home networks and exploit connected devices (Asadi et al., 2024).

4.1.2 Network Vulnerabilities

Network vulnerabilities within IoT environments shows another significant risk factor for phishing. IoT devices usually use Wi-Fi or similar connectivity. So, if these networks are not properly secured then these networks would be exposed to unauthorized access. For example, Wi-Fi enabled IoT devices are exactly prone to phishing attacks because attackers can exploit insecure network connections to obtain sensitive information or invade the other connected devices (Nurdin et al., 2024). There is an emerging security strategy which involves the use of deception methods within IoT networks. For example, creating false checkpoints that can mislead attackers. Deception-based security represents an additional defences layer, that makes tough to execute phishing tricks by attackers (Chaturvedi et al., 2024).

4.2 Human Factors

Technical vulnerabilities are important factors in IoT phishing susceptibility as well, but so too are human factors. All of user behaviour, awareness and the effectiveness of social engineering play a big part when it comes to the effectiveness of an IoT networks defence against phishing. Phishing tactics are often not known to many users and they don't have any cybersecurity training, so they are more prone to phishing attempts. Mitigating these human centred risks is an essential component to a complete defense strategy to phishing attacks.

4.2.1 User Behaviour and Awareness

User awareness and behaviour particularly affect the possibility of falling victim to phishing attacks. IoT users are not completely aware in identification of phishing strategies. This makes them vulnerable to scams. Research has shown that ongoing proper education and awareness campaigns can enhance the user's ability to recognize and respond to phishing strategies. For example, studies represent that cybersecurity education can help users to identify the suspicious behaviour. Because of this, the risk of phishing attacks within IoT networks would be reduced (Candra et al., 2024). Further, Behavioural monitoring tools can detect deviations in the user interaction patterns. This provides the alerts to users on-time and helping them to avoid the phishing scams (Alessa et al., 2024).

4.2.2 Role of Social Engineering

Social engineering is a key strategy that used in phishing attacks on IoT devices. This strategy leverages the trust of users in known interfaces and established brands. Attackers usually manipulates the users by developing deceptive message or fake login prompts. These messages or fake prompts appear authentic and trick the users into providing sensitive information. Phishing attacks within IoT environments frequently include copying trusted entities, exploiting the user's sense of knowing urgency to make the attack easier (Rahman et al., 2024). By applying the educational programs and anti-phishing workshops, users can become more attentive to recognize and resist social engineering strategies in IoT context (*Vol. 5 No. 11 (2024)*, n.d.).

5. DETECTION AND PREVENTION STRATEGIES

In today's world, IoT and smart devices are powering homes, workplaces and banks. Their uses are growing very rapidly. These devices are very convenience for the human life but also open ways for cyber threats like phishing attacks. Phishing in IoT is not only technical risk but also a threat that targets both technology and people using it. Attackers create deceptive tactics to trick users into letting them access the user's own device or networks. As a result, the protection of IoT devices against phishing requires an intersection of comprehensive technology and human caution. In this section, some detection and prevention approach are explored. By combining these strategies, a multi-layered shield will be created. This layer makes IoT devices safer and smarter.

5.1 Technological Solutions:

5.1.1 Intrusion detection systems (IDS):

Intrusion detection systems (IDS) play a crucial role in the IoT security. It provides the continuous monitoring and identifying unauthorized access or abnormal behaviour within a network. IDS solutions are specifically suited to IoT ecosystems where the diversity of devices and protocols that comprise them can make security enforcement challenging. Two primary approaches of Intrusion Detection system in IoT are Signature-Based systems and Anomaly-Based systems. Signature-Based systems detect the known attack patterns. Anomaly-Based systems monitor deviations from normal traffic patterns and helping to identify new phishing attacks (Heidari & Jabraeil Jamali, 2023). IDS has become an integral part of industrial IoT environments especially with the use of AI for better accuracy harnessing the use of machine learning models that analyses large volumes of data in real time to detect sophisticated phishing attempts (Shahin et al., 2024).

5.1.2 Network segmentation and firewalls:

Network segmentation is another defensive layer by isolating IoT devices into smaller sub-networks. This strategy helps to reduce the potential spread of spam attacks. If a user chooses to embed an IoT device into a segmented network, the phishing breach is restricted to a single critical area and attackers are only visible to that device. Network segmentation is specifically important in industrial IoT (IIoT). In industrial IoT, high-value data and critical infrastructure are at high risk. IDS is integrated with firewalls to manage data flow over this segmented piece of network to block off phishing vectors using open network ports or unauthorized access attempts. These strategies develop a robust IoT security framework and help to balance the open communication for device functionality with restrictive policies to phishing attacks (Yatagha et al., n.d.). Some more prevention strategies are presented in Table 2.

Table 2. Ongoing Detection of Phishing attacks in IoT Devices

Phishing Attacks	Preventive Techniques	Evaluation
Credential Harvesting	Multi-factor authentication (MFA) integrated with AI for risk assessment.	Reduction in unauthorized access incidents.
Fake Login Pages	Real-time page verification using blockchain and secure public key infrastructure.	Detection speed and reliability of source verification.
Malicious Attachments	Deep learning-based malware detection in IoT attachments.	Performance in real-time file scanning.
URL Spoofing	Machine Learning for URL classification and anomaly detection.	Accuracy in identifying legitimate vs. malicious URLs.
Voice Phishing (Vishing)	Voice recognition AI for anomaly detection in caller behaviour.	Accuracy in identifying suspicious caller patterns.

5.2 Human-Centric Approaches

5.2.1 User education and awareness programs:

Prevention of the phishing in the IoT environment relies not only on high technological defenses but also on informed users, who are given knowledge about the suspicious activities and trained to react to them. This includes a core element of user education with the goal of understanding common phishing tactics and relevant IoT related threat. Organizations can reduce phishing breach likelihood by regularly training users to identify phishing attempts through regular training (Chaudhary, 2016). Recent studies have shown that training should include practical exercises and simulations which are similar to real world phishing scenarios with which to increase user recognition of phishing attempts (Dine, 2024).

5.2.2 Training on recognizing phishing attempts

To be effective, phishing awareness must target types of attacks users might see in IoT contexts. It trains users to determine phishing emails and social engineering ways to attempt to exploit the vulnerabilities of smart devices. Also, hands on training sessions using phishing simulation will help users learn what is normal for them and what tells them something is not right such as link that is not obvious and maybe the request to provide your device access. It's also important to keep the training content up to date, so that phishing tactics always have an active target: new security measures or exploiting new device capabilities can't be learned quickly enough by the attackers (Abbas et al., 2021).

5.2.3 Best practices for IoT security:

For users in IoT environments, best practice is to secure device configurations (such as two-factor authentication) and be careful of network connections. The biggest phishing threats to an IoT system can be mitigated by educating users to use a unique password for every device, not update firmware in IoT systems regularly, and avoid installing unauthorized IoT apps.

6. FUTURE TRENDS AND CHALLENGES

Phishing is an active threat that has become sophisticated with spread of IoT devices across industries, and the cybersecurity landscape of IoT is always changing. IoT platforms are a new direction for phishing, running on sophisticated attacks designed to make device communications appear as if they came from a specific remote host, steal data, or allow remote access to a device. With the quick rise of IoT, both vulnerabilities and new solutions come and hence we need awareness and their proactive defense. In this section, we discuss advancements in the field of security of IoT.

6.1 Emerging Threats:

6.1.1 Evolution of phishing techniques

Phishing strategies have grown more tough and now targeting IoT devices with unique sophistication. Because IoT keeps growing, attackers increasingly misuse networked devices that often lack strong security control and carry out even more sophisticated phishing attempts. In this context, Table 4 presented challenges in IoT devices against Phishing attacks. In healthcare IoT, phishing attacks can result in unauthorized access to the sensitive data related with health data. This happens because of vulnerabilities of centralized device management systems, highlighting the need of decentralized, secure protocols (S. Fatima et al., 2023). The finance industry is seeing a rise in phishing tactics aimed at IoT enabled payment and transaction device. Phishing usually exploit the device connectivity features to launch fraud attacks (Thirumagal et al., 2024). Cyber Physical Systems (CPS) become increasingly embedded with IoT and phishing threats keep growing; we thus need consistent phishing detection development (Bhushan et al., 2024).

Table 3. Challenges in IoT devices against Phishing Attacks

Phishing Attacks	Challenges	Remarks
Credential Harvesting	Limited IoT security interfaces make phishing more likely as users often overlook device alerts.	Training on IoT Risk is still weak.
Social Engineering	Robust authentication mechanisms are missing in IoT devices that allow attackers to impersonate a legitimate user easier.	To mitigate this risk devices, need more enhanced identity verification.
Spear Phishing on IoT Systems	Device specific vulnerabilities can be exploited in targeted attacks, and detection thence becomes complex.	Basic security frameworks for IoT do not yet explicitly deal with highly specialized attack patterns.

continued on following page

Table 3. Continued

Phishing Attacks	Challenges	Remarks
Man-in-the-Middle Attacks	MITM phishing exists through weak encryption and session hijacking vulnerabilities.	The most important facts in securing the IoT devices are the stronger encryption protocols and session security.
Firmware Phishing	IoT firmware are targeted by attackers in order to inject malicious software into IoT devices.	All IoT systems should use safe update practice and firmware verification protocols.

6.1.2 New vulnerabilities in upcoming IoT technologies

New IoT technologies keep coming out and vulnerabilities are found that attackers are quick to exploit. The reason why IoT advancements, such as connected cars or smart home systems, often take a backseat in the race, sacrificing functionality for security, is because phishers discovered how to enter these gaps. For example, in connected vehicles, phishing attacks involve in-vehicle communication systems which are necessary, but under protected (Kolasani, 2024). Similar to this, in smart home platform such as IoT devices like smart thermostats and security cameras are common phishing targets since they are easy to breach as they have limited traditional (example: strong password) authentication methods (S. Fatima et al., 2023). New IoT devices continue to be vulnerable without a secure communication framework, so the priority is security enhanced designs (*Communication Technologies and Security Challenges in IoT*, n.d.).

6.2 Advancements in Security Technologies

6.2.1 AI and machine learning for phishing detection:

By automating and improving the threat identification in IoT devices, an impact is created with respect to phishing detection through AI and ML. Through these technologies, IoT devices are capable of detecting and blocking phishing attacks in real time. This increases the efficiency of a security results. ML based algorithms have good accuracy in prediction of phishing risks. This results the extremely low false positives and quick response to the real threats (Thirumagal et al., 2024). There is another aspect of the benefit of using AI driven platforms that is adaptive threat detection. Adaptive threat detection shows how systems can learn from the past phishing patterns to better protect the future defenses (Gunjan et al., 2024). There are some other technologies that are crucial to prevent the phishing. AI and ML play an important role in the integration of ani-phishing protocols in cyber physical systems (CPS) (Bhushan et al., 2024).

6.2.2 Blockchain for secure IoT communication

Blockchain technology results robust solutions for securing IoT communications against phishing by giving a decentralized and tamper-resistant framework. IoT networks require secure data exchange among many devices. Blockchain-based authentication can eliminate the single points failure and makes the phishing attempts less active. Blockchain application in IoT healthcare devices protects the patient data. This makes it resistant to unauthorized access through secure and immutable records (S. Fatima et al., 2023). Blockchain can create trust zones among connected devices in smart transportation systems. In these trust zones, each transaction and communication between IoT devices is verified (*Communication Technologies and Security Challenges in IoT*, n.d.). Blockchain integration in connected cars ensures data authenticity and secure vehicle-to-vehicle communication. This helps to shield the systems from phishing induced breaches (Kolasani, 2024).

7. CONCLUSION

IoT environment is vulnerable to phishing attacks as IoT devices usually have weak security. New entry points for the attackers are presented by IoT devices used in homes, healthcare, and industry. It is Blockchain technology which can be used against phishing, as it provides the decentralized, secure verification for IoT devices. Building trust without a central authority in blockchain has been a way to minimize vulnerability of any IoT network. Phishing detection in IoT is made stronger with the help of machine learning which identifies suspicious behaviour patterns in devices. These models detects the attack in real time, and adapt to new phishing tactics for continuous protection for users. In healthcare, there are smart devices and their security needs have some speciality, its security needs are in the form of phishing protections to secure sensitive data. A stronger and resilient IoT security framework is built by integrating blockchain, machine learning and multi-layer authentication. The combination of these methods will serve to create a secure and trustworthy IoT ecosystem of the future.

REFERENCES

Abbas, S. G., Vaccari, I., Hussain, F., Zahid, S., Fayyaz, U. U., Shah, G. A., Bakhshi, T., & Cambiaso, E. (2021). Identifying and Mitigating Phishing Attack Threats in IoT Use Cases Using a Threat Modelling Approach. *Sensors (Basel)*, 21(14), 14. Advance online publication. DOI: 10.3390/s21144816 PMID: 34300556

Abinayasree, C. (2024, May)"INTERNET OF THINGS", Futuristic Trends in Artificial Intelligence Volume 3 Book 5,IIP Series, Volume 3, Page no.185-192, e-ISBN: 978-93-6252-373-0, DOI/Link: https://www.doi.org/10.58532/V3BBAI5P3CH5

Abomhara, M., Køien, G., & Alghamdi, M. (2021). *Cyber Security and the Internet of Things: Vulnerabilities*. Threats, Intruders and Attacks.

Ahmed, I., Saleel, A. P., Beheshti, B., Khan, Z. A., & Ahmad, I. (2017). Security in the Internet of Things (IoT). *2017 Fourth HCT Information Technology Trends (ITT)*, 84–90. DOI: 10.1109/CTIT.2017.8259572

Al-Sinayyid, A., Ali Jewel, M. J., Mannuru, V., & Sasidhar, K. (2023). Defending Characteristics and Attribution Analysis for Phishing Attacks. *2023 International Conference on Computational Science and Computational Intelligence (CSCI)*, 868–874. DOI: 10.1109/CSCI62032.2023.00145

Alessa, K., Alhetelah, B., Alazman, G., Bader, A., Alhomeed, N., Almubarak, L., & Almulla, F. (2024). Browser-in-the-Browser (BitB) Attack: Case Study. *Journal of Engineering Research and Sciences*, 3(5), 14–22. DOI: 10.55708/js0305002

Alkhalil, Z., Hewage, C., Nawaf, L., & Khan, I. (2021). Phishing Attacks: A Recent Comprehensive Study and a New Anatomy. *Frontiers of Computer Science*, 3, 563060. Advance online publication. DOI: 10.3389/fcomp.2021.563060

AlShaikh, M., Alsemaih, W., Alamri, S., & Ramadan, Q. (2023). Using supervised learning to detect command and control attacks in IoT. *International Journal of Cloud Applications and Computing*, 14(1), 1–19. Advance online publication. DOI: 10.4018/IJCAC.334214

Asadi, M., Jamali, M. A. J., Heidari, A., & Navimipour, N. J. (2024). Botnets Unveiled: A Comprehensive Survey on Evolving Threats and Defense Strategies. *Transactions on Emerging Telecommunications Technologies*, 35(11), e5056. DOI: 10.1002/ett.5056

Bhushan, B., Sharma, S. K., Nand, P., Shankar, A., & Obaid, A. J. (Eds.). (2024). *Emerging Trends for Securing Cyber Physical Systems and the Internet of Things*. CRC Press., DOI: 10.1201/9781003474111

Bouijij, H., & Berqia, A. (2024). Enhancing IOT security: Proactive phishing website detection using Deep Neural Networks case study: smart home. *Journal of Telecommunications and the Digital Economy*, 12(1), 446–462. DOI: 10.18080/jtde.v12n1.822

Budimir, S., Fontaine, J. R. J., Huijts, N. M. A., Haans, A., Loukas, G., & Roesch, E. B. (2021). Emotional Reactions to Cybersecurity Breach Situations: Scenario-Based Survey Study. *Journal of Medical Internet Research*, 23(5), e24879. DOI: 10.2196/24879 PMID: 33978591

Chaturvedi, R., Tyagi, N., Pateria, J., & Tyagi, L. K. (2024). Exploring Deception Techniques in Safeguarding IoT Networks from Intruders. *2024 International Conference on Communication, Computer Sciences and Engineering (IC3SE)*, 348–353. DOI: 10.1109/IC3SE62002.2024.10593377

Chaudhary, S. (2016). *The Use of Usable Security and Security Education to Fight Phishing Attacks*. Tampere University Press. https://trepo.tuni.fi/handle/10024/100073

Communication Technologies and Security Challenges in IoT. (n.d.). Springerprofessional.De. Retrieved November 7, 2024, from https://www.springerprofessional.de/en/communication-technologies-and-security-challenges-in-iot/26911724

Costa, L., Barros, J. P., & Tavares, M. (2024). *Vulnerabilities in IoT Devices for Smart Home Environment*. 615–622. https://www.scitepress.org/Link.aspx?doi=10.5220/0007583306150622

Cui, Q., Jourdan, G.-V., Bochmann, G. V., Onut, I.-V., & Flood, J. (2018). Phishing Attacks Modifications and Evolutions. In Lopez, J., Zhou, J., & Soriano, M. (Eds.), *Computer Security* (pp. 243–262). Springer International Publishing., DOI: 10.1007/978-3-319-99073-6_12

Dine, F. (2024). *Enhancing Phishing Threat Detection and Resilience: Leveraging Machine Learning, AI, and User Education in Cybersecurity*. DOI: 10.13140/RG.2.2.20865.26728

Fatima, N., Ashraf, M., Tehseen, R., Omer, U., Sabahat, N., Javaid, R., Yousaf, M., Mehr, M., & Zaheer, A. (2024). AI-Powered Phishing Detection and Mitigation for IoT-Based Smart Home Security. *Journal of Computing & Biomedical Informatics*. https://www.jcbi.org/index.php/Main/article/view/724

Fatima, S., Hussain, S., Shahzadi, N., Din, B. U., Sajjad, W., & Ali, R. (2023). A Secure BlockChain Based Application For Health Records. *2023 2nd International Conference on Emerging Trends in Electrical, Control, and Telecommunication Engineering (ETECTE)*, 1–6. DOI: 10.1109/ETECTE59617.2023.10396794

Fawaz, M. M. (2022). Applications and Security Aspects of Internet of Things for Way of Smart World. i-Manager's Journal on Embedded Systems, 11(1), 33.

Foozy, C. F. M., Ahmad, R., & Abdollah, M. F. (2013). *Phishing detection taxonomy for mobile device*. https://www.semanticscholar.org/paper/Phishing-detection-taxonomy-for-mobile-device-Foozy-Ahmad/673ce7697a8e419807241bbeb99268afebe7bbfe

Gaurav, A., Bansal, S., Chui, K. T., Alhomoud, A., Arya, V., Psannis, K., & Attar, R. W. (2024). Optimized AI-driven semantic web approach for enhancing phishing detection in e-commerce platforms. *International Journal on Semantic Web and Information Systems*, 20(1), 1–13. Advance online publication. DOI: 10.4018/IJSWIS.359767

Ghazi-Tehrani, A. K., & Pontell, H. N. (2022). Phishing Evolves: Analyzing the Enduring Cybercrime. In *The New Technology of Financial Crime*. Routledge. DOI: 10.4324/9781003258100-3

Girma, A. (2018). Analysis of Security Vulnerability and Analytics of Internet of Things (IOT) Platform. In Latifi, S. (Ed.), *Information Technology—New Generations* (pp. 101–104). Springer International Publishing., DOI: 10.1007/978-3-319-77028-4_16

Gunjan, V. K., Ansari, M. D., Usman, M., & Nguyen, T. (Eds.). (2024). *Modern Approaches in IoT and Machine Learning for Cyber Security: Latest Trends in AI.* Springer International Publishing., DOI: 10.1007/978-3-031-09955-7

Gupta, B. B., Gaurav, A., Arya, V., Attar, R. W., Bansal, S., Alhomoud, A., & Chui, K. T. (2024). Advanced BERT and CNN-Based Computational Model for Phishing Detection in Enterprise Systems. *CMES-Computer Modeling in Engineering & Sciences, 141*(3). https://search.ebscohost.com/login.aspx?direct=true&profile=ehost&scope=site&authtype=crawler&jrnl=15261492&AN=180704148&h=nmVHJrTMipdhrLOTFnmG4b%2BhsSD91AL1%2BVZyNbZh3byamFOz5Nj%2BzSBmoRbjzP2gcplLyMC210CKfroA6Ysa6A%3D%3D&crl=c

Heidari, A., & Jabraeil Jamali, M. A. (2023). Internet of Things intrusion detection systems: A comprehensive review and future directions. *Cluster Computing*, 26(6), 3753–3780. DOI: 10.1007/s10586-022-03776-z

Ishtaiwi, A., Ali, A. M., Al-Qerem, A., Sabahean, M., Alzubi, B., Almomani, A., Alauthman, M., Aldweesh, A., & Al Khaldy, M. A. (2024). Next-Gen Phishing Defense Enhancing Detection With Machine Learning and Expert Whitelisting/Blacklisting. [IJCAC]. *International Journal of Cloud Applications and Computing*, 14(1), 1–17. DOI: 10.4018/IJCAC.353301

Jain, A. K., Gupta, B. B., Kaur, K., Bhutani, P., Alhalabi, W., & Almomani, A. (2022). A content and URL analysis-based efficient approach to detect smishing SMS in intelligent systems. *International Journal of Intelligent Systems*, 37(12), 11117–11141. DOI: 10.1002/int.23035

Jeslin, J. G., Maheswari, G. U., Amutha, S., Vargheese, M., Rajeshkumar, C., & Valarmathi, S. (2024, April). Securing Smart Networks and Privacy Intrusion Detection System Utilizing Blockchain and Machine Learning. In 2024 2nd International Conference on Networking and Communications (ICNWC) (pp. 1-9). IEEE.

Journals, M. (n.d.). *PHISHING: AN EVOLVING THREAT*. Retrieved September 19, 2024, from https://www.academia.edu/10723684/PHISHING_AN_EVOLVING_THREAT

Jurcut, A., Niculcea, T., Ranaweera, P., & Le-Khac, N.-A. (2020). Security Considerations for Internet of Things: A Survey. *SN Computer Science*, 1(4), 193. DOI: 10.1007/s42979-020-00201-3

Kolasani, S. (2024). Connected Cars and Autonomous Vehicles: Personalizing Owner/Customer Experiences and Innovation using AI, IoT, Blockchain, and Big Data. *International Numeric Journal of Machine Learning and Robots, 8*(8), Article 8.

Kolias, C., Kambourakis, G., Stavrou, A., & Voas, J. (2017). DDoS in the IoT: Mirai and Other Botnets. *Computer, 50*(7), 80–84. *Computer*. Advance online publication. DOI: 10.1109/MC.2017.201

Li, Z., Yu, X., & Zhao, Y. (2024). A web semantic mining method for fake cybersecurity threat intelligence in open source communities. *International Journal on Semantic Web and Information Systems*, 20(1), 1–22. Advance online publication. DOI: 10.4018/IJSWIS.350095

Liu, S., Wang, Z., Kumari, S., Lv, J., & Chen, C.-M. (2024). Provably Secure Anti-Phishing Scheme for Medical Information in Smart Healthcare. *IEEE Internet of Things Journal*, 1–1. *IEEE Internet of Things Journal*, 11(23), 38086–38097. Advance online publication. DOI: 10.1109/JIOT.2024.3445375

Nirmal, B., Shah, M., Azrour, M., Mabrouki, J., & Guezzaz, A. (2024). A Systematic Study on Implementation of Smart Devices for Sustainable Environment. In Azrour, M., Mabrouki, J., & Guezzaz, A. (Eds.), *Sustainable and Green Technologies for Water and Environmental Management* (pp. 189–213). Springer Nature Switzerland., DOI: 10.1007/978-3-031-52419-6_15

Nurdin, M., Pranandi, A., F, U. D., Hermawan, Y., & Fadlapi, R. (2024). SERANGAN PHISING WIFI MENGGUNAKAN ESP8266: REPLIKASI JARINGAN UNTUK PENANGKAPAN INFORMASI OTENTIKASI. *HUMANITIS: Jurnal Homaniora, Sosial Dan Bisnis, 2*(7), Article 7.

Pétursson, A. (2023). *Ethical Hacking of a Ring Doorbell.* KTH Royal Institute of Technology. https://urn.kb.se/resolve?urn=urn:nbn:se:kth:diva-325834

Priya, S., Gutema, D., & Singh, S. (2024). A Comprehensive Survey of Recent Phishing Attacks Detection Techniques. *2024 5th International Conference on Innovative Trends in Information Technology (ICITIIT)*, 1–6. DOI: 10.1109/ICITIIT61487.2024.10580446

Rahman, R., Zulfattah, A. K., & Haslinda, H. (2024). MENINGKATKAN KEAMANAN EDGE COMPUTING DAN IOT DENGAN UBUNTU DARI ANCAMAN REAL-TIME. *Jurnal Riset Sistem Informasi*, 1(4), 4. Advance online publication. DOI: 10.69714/kw984551

Rajarajeswari, R., Suchitra, D., Praveena, V., & Karthik, S. (2023). IoT Integrated Advanced Mor-Sockets for Smart Devices (No. 2023-28-0150). SAE Technical Paper.

Samaila, M. G., Neto, M., Fernandes, D. A. B., Freire, M. M., & Inácio, P. R. M. (2017). Security Challenges of the Internet of Things. In Batalla, J. M., Mastorakis, G., Mavromoustakis, C. X., & Pallis, E. (Eds.), *Beyond the Internet of Things: Everything Interconnected* (pp. 53–82). Springer International Publishing., DOI: 10.1007/978-3-319-50758-3_3

Shahin, M., Maghanaki, M., Hosseinzadeh, A., & Chen, F. F. (2024). Advancing Network Security in Industrial IoT: A Deep Dive into AI-Enabled Intrusion Detection Systems. *Advanced Engineering Informatics*, 62, 102685. DOI: 10.1016/j.aei.2024.102685

Shueb, M. M., Yang, C., & Che, X. (2024). An Innovative Design for Improving U.S. Airports' Cybersecurity Based on Blockchain Technology. *2024 Systems and Information Engineering Design Symposium (SIEDS)*, 232–237. DOI: 10.1109/SIEDS61124.2024.10534684

Sisinni, E., Saifullah, A., Han, S., Jennehag, U., & Gidlund, M. (2018). Industrial Internet of Things: Challenges, Opportunities, and Directions. *IEEE Transactions on Industrial Informatics*, 14(11), 4724–4734. DOI: 10.1109/TII.2018.2852491

Stergiou, C. L., Psannis, K. E., & Gupta, B. B. (2022). InFeMo: Flexible Big Data Management Through a Federated Cloud System. *ACM Transactions on Internet Technology*, 22(2), 1–22. DOI: 10.1145/3426972

Surianarayanan, C., & Chelliah, P. R. (2023). Integration of the internet of things and cloud: Security challenges and solutions—A review. *International Journal of Cloud Applications and Computing*, 13(1), 1–30. Advance online publication. DOI: 10.4018/IJCAC.325624

The Internet of Things (IoT). (2024). The Internet of Things (IoT): Transformations and Challenges in the Modern World. *African Journal of Biological Sciences*, 6(3). Advance online publication. DOI: 10.48047/AFJBS.6.3.2024.764-769

Thirumagal, P. G., Das, T., Das, S., Khatri, E. S. K., & Rani, S. (2024). The Role of IoT in Revolutionizing Payment Systems and Digital Transactions in Finance. *2024 5th International Conference on Recent Trends in Computer Science and Technology (ICRTCST)*, 171–176. DOI: 10.1109/ICRTCST61793.2024.10578351

Tsiknas, K., Taketzis, D., Demertzis, K., & Skianis, C. (2021). Cyber Threats to Industrial IoT: A Survey on Attacks and Countermeasures. *IoT*, 2(1), 1. Advance online publication. DOI: 10.3390/iot2010009

Usha, G., Jeyasudha, J., Karthikeyan, H., & Vimal Cruz, M. (2022). A Smart and Secure IoT devices Using Machine Learning Algorithm. *2022 IEEE 2nd Mysore Sub Section International Conference (MysuruCon)*, 1–8. DOI: 10.1109/MysuruCon55714.2022.9972586

Vol. 5 No. 11 (2024): South Florida Journal of Development, Miami, v. 5, n. 11, 2024 | South Florida Journal of Development. (n.d.). Retrieved November 4, 2024, from https://ojs.southfloridapublishing.com/ojs/index.php/jdev/issue/view/117

Xenofontos, C., Zografopoulos, I., Konstantinou, C., Jolfaei, A., Khan, M. K., & Choo, K.-K. R. (2022). Consumer, Commercial, and Industrial IoT (In)Security: Attack Taxonomy and Case Studies. *IEEE Internet of Things Journal, 9*(1), 199–221. *IEEE Internet of Things Journal.* Advance online publication. DOI: 10.1109/JIOT.2021.3079916

Yatagha, R., Waedt, K., Schindler, J., & Kirdan, E. (n.d.). *Security challenges and best practices for resilient IIoT Networks: Network Segmentation.*

Zhou, L., Gaurav, A., Arya, V., Attar, R. W., Bansal, S., & Alhomoud, A. (2024). Enhancing phishing detection in semantic web systems using optimized deep learning models. *International Journal on Semantic Web and Information Systems*, 20(1), 1–13. Advance online publication. DOI: 10.4018/IJSWIS.361772

Chapter 5
Defending Against Phishing Attacks on Social Media: A Multi-Layered, User-Driven Security Solution

Usharani Bhimavarapu
https://orcid.org/0000-0002-0246-1420
Department of Computer Science and Engineering, Koneru Lakshmaiah Education Foundation, Vaddeswaram, India

ABSTRACT

Phishing in the Age of Mobile Devices and Social Media presents a growing threat to online security, as attackers increasingly target users through social platforms and mobile applications. The widespread use of these technologies has created new vulnerabilities, as phishing schemes exploit both personal data and trust-based interactions. This paper proposes a novel security system designed to protect social network users from unauthorized access by leveraging advanced authentication mechanisms, real-time monitoring, and proactive countermeasures. The system integrates features such as password-based login with camera-based identity verification upon failed login attempts, secure email notifications, and user-controlled security actions, such as remote logout and account locking. By providing users with enhanced control over their account security, the proposed system offers a robust defense against phishing attacks and other unauthorized access threats.

INTRODUCTION

Phishing in the Age of Mobile Devices and Social Media has become an increasingly prevalent threat, exploiting the vast reach and connectivity offered by modern communication platforms. With the rise of mobile devices and the widespread use of social media, attackers have found new opportunities to deceive users into disclosing sensitive information, often by masquerading as legitimate sources. Phishing attacks target both personal data and trust, using sophisticated tactics such as fake login pages, deceptive messages, and social engineering. As users become more reliant on their mobile devices and social media accounts for communication, shopping, and banking, the risk of falling victim to such attacks has grown significantly. This paper explores how these evolving threats challenge traditional security measures and

DOI: 10.4018/979-8-3693-8784-9.ch005

proposes a novel security system that integrates user authentication, real-time monitoring, and proactive countermeasures to combat phishing in the mobile and social media era.

Protecting Social Networking Platforms from Security Attacks is a critical concern in today's digital landscape, where millions of users rely on these platforms for communication, information sharing, and entertainment. These platforms are prime targets for various security threats, including phishing, account hijacking, data breaches, and social engineering attacks. The complexity of these threats has grown with the increasing sophistication of cybercriminals, who exploit vulnerabilities in platform security systems, user behaviors, and application flaws. To safeguard users and maintain trust, it is essential to implement a multi-layered security approach that includes strong authentication mechanisms, real-time monitoring, and proactive countermeasures. This paper proposes a comprehensive security solution that combines password protection with advanced features like camera-based identity verification, real-time alerts, and user-driven security actions, such as remote logouts and account locking, to protect social networking platforms from evolving security threats.

There are several models designed to protect social networking platforms from security attacks, each with its strengths and limitations. Multi-Factor Authentication (MFA) enhances security but is vulnerable to SIM-swapping attacks (Aleisa et al., 2020). Intrusion Detection Systems (IDS) help detect unauthorized access, though they can generate false positives (Ali et al., 2022). Behavioral Analysis, while effective in anomaly detection, raises privacy concerns and relies on large datasets (Almolhis et al., 2020). Biometric Authentication provides strong security but is vulnerable to spoofing and is resource-intensive (Babun et al., 2018). Data Encryption secures communications but can be bypassed if mismanaged (Bhandari & Jusas, 2020). AI-Based Threat Detection offers advanced protection but faces ethical and transparency issues (Curtis, 2021). Social Engineering Awareness educates users but is limited by varying user awareness (Elhoseny et al., 2021). Network Segmentation reduces exposure during breaches but complicates system architecture (Ferrag et al., 2022). Cloud-Based Security Systems scale well but are susceptible to shared resource attacks (Hassija et al., 2019). Security Information and Event Management (SIEM) tools monitor threats but require expertise to manage effectively (Intersog, 2021). Threat Intelligence Sharing improves detection but can overwhelm users with data (Koroniotis et al., 2017). User Access Control ensures that only authorized users can access sensitive data but may lead to usability issues (Li et al., 2019). Endpoint Protection secures devices but is less effective against phishing (Marturana et al., 2012). Password Management Systems encourage strong passwords but depend on user adoption (McGraw et al., 2020). Real-Time Monitoring tracks suspicious activity but can overwhelm users with alerts (Mohammad, 2018). Phishing Detection Tools identify fake content but struggle with sophisticated phishing techniques (Mohiuddin & Almogren, 2020). Incident Response Plans ensure a swift reaction to threats but can be ineffective without proper training (Muñoz et al., 2018). Vulnerability Scanning detects system weaknesses but overlooks human error (Naveen & Kounte, 2019). Blockchain for Identity Management enhances security but faces scalability challenges (Nolle, 2021). Data Loss Prevention Systems reduce data leaks but can generate false positives (Qadir & Varol, 2020). Zero Trust Architecture validates all users but complicates network management (Rahman et al., 2020). Firewalls and Web Application Firewalls (WAF) protect against network intrusions but may not prevent sophisticated attacks (Red Hat, 2022). Mobile Device Management (MDM) secures devices but limits user autonomy (Sachdeva & Ali, 2022). Content Filtering blocks harmful content but may restrict legitimate communications (Shah, 2022). Finally, AI-Based Phishing Simulation helps train users but depends on accurate simulations (Shakeel et al., 2021). Each model requires constant updates and integration to address the evolving landscape of cyber threats.

The proposed system addresses several limitations found in existing models for protecting social networking platforms from security attacks. For example, Multi-Factor Authentication (MFA) is effective but can be bypassed by SIM-swapping attacks (Soltani & Seno, 2019). To counter this, the proposed system enhances MFA by incorporating real-time facial recognition and behavior-based anomaly detection, making it more resilient to fraudsters. Intrusion Detection Systems (IDS) can generate false positives, leading to user inconvenience (Tallón-Ballesteros & Riquelme, 2014), but the proposed system uses adaptive algorithms that continuously learn and improve, minimizing false alarms.

Behavioral analysis, while useful for anomaly detection, faces challenges related to privacy concerns and reliance on extensive user data (Vennam, 2020). The system addresses this by processing data locally on the user's device, ensuring that sensitive information is not exposed while maintaining privacy. Additionally, while biometric authentication is typically resource-intensive and susceptible to spoofing (Yen et al., 2018), the proposed system integrates multi-modal biometrics, combining fingerprint, voice, and facial recognition, to enhance accuracy and reduce spoofing risks.

Existing data encryption techniques can be bypassed with poor implementation. In response, the proposed system integrates end-to-end encryption with decentralized key management, offering stronger protection against interception. While AI-Based Threat Detection has proven to be effective, it faces challenges in transparency and ethical concerns. To mitigate this, the proposed system uses explainable AI (XAI), which provides clear explanations for security actions, enhancing user trust.

In addition, the system includes real-time monitoring and alerts for suspicious activities, which are often overwhelming for users. To address this, the system uses a smart alerting mechanism that prioritizes notifications based on severity, ensuring that users only receive alerts for critical incidents. Lastly, phishing detection tools struggle with sophisticated attacks, but the proposed system utilizes a hybrid approach, combining machine learning with human-in-the-loop verification, to improve detection rates and reduce false negatives.

Through these innovations, the proposed system provides a more robust and user-friendly solution to the limitations of existing models, enhancing security and user experience on social networking platforms.

MATERIALS AND METHODOLOGY

The methodology of the proposed system focuses on integrating advanced security measures to protect social media users from phishing and unauthorized access. It begins with secure user authentication through hashed passwords and optional multi-factor authentication. In case of incorrect password entries, a camera-based identity verification system is triggered, capturing the image of the user. Real-time email alerts are sent to legitimate users to notify them of suspicious activity. Users are empowered to take immediate countermeasures, such as remote logouts and account locking, through an intuitive interface. The system is designed to be scalable and adaptable to various social media platforms for enhanced security.

Material

A survey was conducted with 25 participants from diverse age groups and educational backgrounds to explore their experiences while using social networking platforms. The participants were asked a series of questions aimed at understanding the challenges they faced and their familiarity with these platforms. The survey focused on identifying the types of violations users encountered, such as harassment, hate speech, privacy breaches, or exposure to misinformation. Participants were also asked to specify where these violations occurred, allowing the identification of platform-specific issues across popular networks like Facebook, Twitter, and Instagram. Additionally, the survey sought to assess the participants' level of expertise with social media, examining whether they had sufficient knowledge and experience to navigate these platforms effectively and respond to violations. This comprehensive approach provided valuable insights into the challenges users face in the social media landscape.

Proposed Frame Work

The proposed system enhances security measures for social networking platforms by incorporating advanced, multi-layered authentication protocols and real-time threat mitigation mechanisms. These security features are designed to identify and prevent unauthorized access while giving users control over their personal data and privacy settings.

A central aspect of the system is advanced biometric authentication, which goes beyond traditional password-based systems. It employs multi-modal biometrics, including facial recognition, fingerprint scanning, and voice verification (Curtis, 2021). This multi-layered approach ensures that even if one biometric factor is compromised, others can still provide an additional layer of security. Additionally, behavioral analytics is used to continuously monitor user actions and detect anomalies that may indicate malicious activity. This system can adapt and learn from user behavior patterns, making it more resilient to evolving threats (Almolhis et al., 2020).

The system also integrates real-time intrusion detection and alerting. If a user enters an incorrect password, the system's proactive intrusion detection mechanism activates automatically. An integrated high-resolution camera captures an image of the individual attempting access. This captured image is securely stored for future verification or investigation (Ferrag et al., 2022). In addition, the system sends an alert email to the legitimate user, notifying them of the potential breach in real-time. This feature is especially valuable for users who may not immediately notice suspicious activity.

To further empower the user, the system offers a set of countermeasures that can be taken immediately. If unauthorized access is detected, the user can perform actions such as disconnecting their device from the internet, remotely logging out of all active sessions, or even triggering an account lockdown. These features ensure that, even if an attack occurs, the user has control and can act swiftly to mitigate the threat.

The system also introduces a location control feature, which allows users to enable or disable location tracking based on their preferences. This ensures that users can maintain control over their geographical data, providing a greater sense of privacy and reducing the risk of location-based attacks.

Moreover, the system implements end-to-end encryption for data storage and communication, making it virtually impossible for attackers to intercept sensitive information. By ensuring that all user data, including passwords, personal information, and biometric data, is encrypted both at rest and in transit, the system strengthens its defense against potential breaches.

Lastly, the use of multi-factor authentication (MFA) adds an extra layer of protection. Even if a hacker gains access to a user's password, they would still need additional authentication factors, such as a biometric scan or a one-time passcode sent to the user's phone. This significantly reduces the risk of successful attacks like SIM swapping or credential stuffing.

By combining these diverse techniques—advanced biometrics, behavioral analysis, real-time alerts, location control, encryption, and MFA—the proposed system provides a robust and adaptive security framework. This ensures that social networking platforms remain resilient to various cyberattacks while empowering users with control over their privacy and security.

Working Mechanism Of The Proposed Frame Work

The proposed system operates through a multi-layered mechanism designed to detect unauthorized access attempts and provide users with real-time control over their account security. Below is an overview of its working mechanism:

1. User Authentication:

The system begins with standard user authentication, where the user inputs their credentials (username and password) to access their account. These credentials are securely validated against encrypted data stored in the database.

2. Incorrect Password Handling:

If the user enters an incorrect password on the first attempt, the system activates its security measures. An integrated camera captures an image of the individual attempting to gain access. This image is stored in the system database for further analysis and verification.

3. Real-Time Alerts:

Upon detecting an incorrect password entry, the system immediately sends a notification email to the legitimate user, informing them of the failed attempt. This email contains details such as the timestamp, location (if enabled by the user), and the captured image of the individual attempting access.

4. User-Controlled Countermeasures

In case of an unauthorized access attempt, the system allows the legitimate user to take immediate action. Through the notification email or a dedicated security interface, users can:

- Disconnect their device from the internet to prevent further access.
- Log out from all active sessions across social networking platforms.
- Lock down their account temporarily to restrict access until the issue is resolved.

5. Location Privacy:

Users have the option to enable or disable location tracking based on their privacy preferences. If enabled, the system records the location of access attempts, aiding in the identification of unauthorized activities.

6. Technical Support Access:

User data is stored in a secure, encrypted database, and only authorized technical support personnel can access it, ensuring the confidentiality of sensitive information.

7. Continuous Monitoring and Analysis:

The system continuously monitors login attempts and activities for unusual patterns. Repeated incorrect attempts or access from unfamiliar devices trigger additional security checks and alerts.

By integrating real-time intrusion detection, user notifications, and responsive countermeasures, the proposed system provides a robust framework for safeguarding user accounts against unauthorized access and potential cyber threats.

The software development process for the proposed system involves designing and integrating multiple modules to establish a comprehensive security framework. At the core is the Authentication Module, which secures user login by implementing hashed password storage using cryptographic algorithms like bcrypt or SHA-256. It also handles incorrect login attempts by triggering additional security measures. Multi-factor authentication (MFA) is incorporated as an optional feature for enhanced protection. The Camera Integration Module activates upon the first incorrect password entry, capturing an image of the individual using libraries like OpenCV. The captured images are optimized for resolution and securely stored to ensure efficient usage.

The Notification System plays a pivotal role by sending real-time alerts to legitimate users through email, using SMTP servers or cloud-based services like SendGrid or AWS SES. The alerts include details such as the timestamp, location (if enabled), and the captured image. An optional mobile push notification system can be integrated for faster delivery. The Countermeasure Module empowers users to secure their accounts proactively. Through a user-friendly interface, they can remotely log out of active sessions, temporarily lock their accounts, or initiate an emergency freeze to halt all account activity until re-authentication.

To securely store user credentials, logs, and captured images, the Database Management Module uses a robust storage system, such as PostgreSQL or MongoDB. Sensitive data is encrypted using AES-256 encryption, ensuring data integrity and security. Collectively, these modules work seamlessly to create a user-focused and highly secure system capable of detecting and countering unauthorized access attempts effectively.

EXPERIMENTAL RESULTS

The system configuration for conducting the experiments in this study was built on a Windows 11 environment to ensure compatibility with modern software requirements and hardware components. The system was equipped with an Intel Core i7 processor (11th Gen), 16GB of RAM, and a 512GB SSD, offering sufficient processing power and memory for running the proposed security models without performance degradation. The Windows 11 operating system provides a robust platform with integrated security features, such as enhanced encryption, secure boot, and support for the latest multi-factor authentication protocols, which align with the security requirements of the proposed system.

The security testing was executed using a variety of social media platforms to assess their vulnerability to potential attacks, with emphasis on both user authentication mechanisms and intrusion detection methods. The experiments were conducted under controlled conditions, simulating different attack scenarios such as brute-force password guessing, phishing, and unauthorized login attempts. System responses, including the time to detect attacks, the recovery time, and the effectiveness of countermeasures (like session termination and account lockdown), were recorded and analyzed to compare the robustness of each platform's security architecture.

By leveraging the advanced features of Windows 11, such as Windows Defender and its integration with Microsoft security protocols, we ensured that the test environment was both secure and representative of real-world conditions, providing reliable data for evaluating the security measures implemented on the social media platforms.

Table 1 presents the demographic characteristics of the survey participants. In terms of age, the largest group of participants is within the 25-34 age range, representing 40% of the sample, followed by the 18-24 age group at 32%. The 35-44 age group accounts for 16%, while the 45+ group has the smallest representation at 12%. Regarding gender, there is a fairly balanced distribution, with 52% of participants identifying as female and 48% as male. The survey also collected data on education levels. The majority of participants hold a Bachelor's Degree (52%), followed by those with a Master's Degree (28%). A smaller portion of the sample has a High School education (12%), and only 8% hold a Doctorate. As for usage frequency, a significant portion of the participants (72%) reported using social media daily, while 24% use it weekly, and 4% use it monthly. Lastly, the table also shows location tracking preferences, with 64% of users enabling location tracking and 36% opting to keep it disabled. This demographic distribution provides valuable insights into the sample's characteristics, offering a clearer understanding of the target audience's behaviors and preferences.

Table 1. Characteristics of Demographics data

Demographic Attribute	Category	Frequency	Percentage (%)
Age	18-24	8	32%
	25-34	10	40%
	35-44	4	16%
	45+	3	12%
Gender	Male	12	48%
	Female	13	52%
Education Level	High School	3	12%
	Bachelor's Degree	13	52%
	Master's Degree	7	28%
	Doctorate	2	8%
Usage Frequency	Daily	18	72%
	Weekly	6	24%
	Monthly	1	4%
Location Tracking	Enabled	16	64%
	Disabled	9	36%

Table 2 outlines the complexity of passwords, comparing different types of passwords based on their average length, security strength, hacking resistance, ease of recall, and provides examples of each password type.Starting with simple passwords, which typically range from 6 to 8 characters, these passwords are considered weak due to their vulnerability to common attacks, such as brute-force or dictionary attacks. They are easy to recall but have low hacking resistance, making them highly susceptible to being guessed or cracked. Examples of simple passwords include “123456” and “password”. Moderately complex passwords are between 8 to 12 characters long and are classified as having medium security strength. They provide a moderate level of hacking resistance, but they can still be vulnerable to guessing over time. These passwords are relatively easy to recall. Examples include “MyDog@123” and “Apple$2023”.Complex passwords, ranging from 12 to 16 characters, are deemed strong due to their resistance against brute-force attacks. However, these passwords are harder to recall without the assistance of a password manager. Examples include "h#8d@59V&%zJg7". The very complex passwords, which are over 16 characters and often paired with multi-factor authentication (MFA), offer the highest security, providing very high hacking resistance. These passwords are nearly impossible to crack without MFA, although they are extremely difficult for users to remember without a password manager. An example is "P@ssw0rD!75#Q#" with MFA .Lastly, passphrases, typically over 20 characters and often incorporating a mix of symbols and upper/lowercase letters, provide very strong security and very high hacking resistance, especially when used with mixed case and special characters. However, they are also hard to recall without a password manager. An example of a passphrase is "Purple$Rabbit3!Jumps". Each password type is categorized according to its level of complexity and associated security features, demonstrating the trade-offs between security strength, ease of recall, and hacking resistance.

Table 2. Complexity of passwords

Password Type	Average Length	Security Strength	Hacking Resistance	Ease of Recall	Example
Simple Password	6-8 characters	Weak	Low (easy to guess or crack)	Easy to recall	"123456", "password"
Moderately Complex Password	8-12 characters	Medium	Moderate (possible to guess with time)	Fairly easy to recall	"MyDog@123", "Apple$2023"
Complex Password	12-16 characters	Strong	High (resistant to brute force attacks)	Difficult to recall without a password manager	"h#8d@59V&%zJg7"
Very Complex Password (with MFA)	16+ characters	Very Strong	Very High (near impossible to crack without MFA)	Extremely difficult to recall without a manager	"P@ssw0rD!75#Q#" with MFA
Passphrase	20+ characters	Very Strong	Very High (especially with symbols and mixed case)	Hard to recall without a password manager	"Purple$Rabbit3!Jumps"

Table 3 presents an analysis of hacked social networks, detailing the average time to detect hacks, account recovery time, potential financial loss, security measures in place, and user control for various platforms. For Facebook, the average time to detect a hack is between 15-30 minutes, with account recovery taking approximately 1-3 days. The potential financial loss can be high, especially for business accounts. Facebook offers 2FA, account lockout, and email alerts as its primary security measures. However, users have minimal control over detection, and recovery is user-initiated. Instagram detects hacks in 10-25 minutes, and account recovery takes 1-2 days. The potential financial loss is medium, mostly relating to personal data theft. Instagram also uses 2FA, account lockout, and email alerts for security. User control is limited to user-initiated recovery, with minimal control over hack detection. For Twitter, the average detection time is 10-20 minutes, with recovery taking 1-3 days. The potential financial loss is medium, primarily affecting tweets and reputation. Twitter implements 2FA and suspicious activity alerts but offers limited control for users, who must often rely on external reporting for resolution. On TikTok, hacks are typically detected in 15-30 minutes, and recovery takes 1-2 days. The potential loss is medium, mostly from account takeover. TikTok provides 2FA, account recovery options, and user-driven recovery. Alerts are triggered for user awareness.For YouTube, it takes 20-35 minutes to detect a hack, and recovery usually spans 1-2 days. The financial loss can be high, particularly affecting content monetization. YouTube also uses 2FA, email alerts, and account lockout. Similar to others, recovery is user-initiated, with limited control over hack detection. In Snapchat, hacks are detected quickly, usually within 5-15 minutes, and recovery takes 1-2 days. The potential financial loss is low, limited mostly to personal data. 2FA, email alerts, and account lockout are implemented, with user-driven recovery and alerts.For LinkedIn, detection takes 10-25 minutes, and recovery occurs in 1-3 days. The potential financial loss is medium, particularly affecting professional reputation. LinkedIn employs 2FA and suspicious activity alerts, but user control over detection is limited.Lastly, WhatsApp detects hacks in 10-15 minutes, with recovery within 1-2 days. The potential financial loss is low, with risks related to account takeover and messaging. WhatsApp offers 2FA and session management, providing users high control over recovery through session termination.

Table 3. Hacked social networks

Social Media Platform	Average Time to Detect Hack	Time to Recover Account	Potential Financial Loss	Security Measures in Place	User Control
Facebook	15-30 minutes	1-3 days	High (especially for business accounts)	2FA, Account Lockout, Email Alerts	User-initiated recovery, minimal control over detection
Instagram	10-25 minutes	1-2 days	Medium (mainly personal data theft)	2FA, Account Lockout, Email Alerts	User-initiated recovery, minimal control over detection
Twitter	10-20 minutes	1-3 days	Medium (impacts tweets, reputation)	2FA, Suspicious Activity Alerts	Limited, requires external reporting
TikTok	15-30 minutes	1-2 days	Medium (mainly account takeover)	2FA, Account Recovery Options	User-driven recovery, alerting
YouTube	20-35 minutes	1-2 days	High (loss of content monetization)	2FA, Email Alerts, Account Lockout	User-initiated recovery, minimal control over detection
Snapchat	5-15 minutes	1-2 days	Low (limited to personal data)	2FA, Email Alerts, Account Lockout	User-driven recovery, alerting
LinkedIn	10-25 minutes	1-3 days	Medium (impacts professional reputation)	2FA, Suspicious Activity Alerts	Limited user control over detection
WhatsApp	10-15 minutes	1-2 days	Low (account takeover, messaging)	2FA, Session Management	High control (via session termination)

Table 4 presents the average daily time social media users spend on popular platforms and outlines the primary usage behavior, platform focus, and device usage preference for each platform. On Facebook, users typically spend 35-45 minutes per day, engaging in activities such as content browsing, messaging, and sharing. This platform is focused on general social networking, with a preference for mobile usage (70%) over desktop (30%). Instagram users spend 30-40 minutes daily, primarily for sharing photos, videos, and stories. Instagram's focus is on visual content sharing, and users favor mobile devices (85%) for their engagement. On Twitter, users allocate 15-25 minutes each day, mostly reading tweets, retweeting, and interacting. The platform focuses on news and microblogging, with mobile usage (75%) dominating over desktop (25%). For TikTok, users spend 50-60 minutes per day, mainly watching videos and creating content. TikTok focuses on short-form video sharing, with an overwhelming preference for mobile use (90%). YouTube users dedicate 60-80 minutes each day to watching videos, liking, and commenting. As a video streaming platform, it also has a significant mobile usage preference (70%) over desktop (30%).On Snapchat, users spend 25-35 minutes daily, engaging in messaging and photo sharing via snaps and stories. The platform focuses on messaging and photo sharing, with mobile usage (95%) being predominant. LinkedIn users engage for 15-20 minutes daily, primarily for professional networking and job searching. The platform focuses on business networking, with a preference for desktop usage (60%), although mobile usage (40%) is also notable. Lastly, WhatsApp users spend 25-40 minutes per day, primarily for messaging and voice/video calling. It focuses on communication and messaging, with mobile usage (95%) being the overwhelming preference.

Table 4. Average daily time social media users spend on popular platforms.

Social Media Platform	Average Daily Usage (Minutes)	Primary Usage Behavior	Platform Focus	Device Usage Preference
Facebook	35-45 minutes	Content browsing, messaging, and sharing	General social networking	Mobile (70%), Desktop (30%)
Instagram	30-40 minutes	Sharing photos/videos, stories	Visual content sharing	Mobile (85%)
Twitter	15-25 minutes	Reading tweets, retweeting, interactions	News and microblogging	Mobile (75%), Desktop (25%)
TikTok	50-60 minutes	Watching videos, creating content	Short-form video sharing	Mobile (90%)
YouTube	60-80 minutes	Watching videos, liking, commenting	Video streaming	Mobile (70%), Desktop (30%)
Snapchat	25-35 minutes	Sending snaps, creating stories	Messaging & photo sharing	Mobile (95%)
LinkedIn	15-20 minutes	Professional networking, job searching	Business networking	Desktop (60%), Mobile (40%)
WhatsApp	25-40 minutes	Messaging, voice/video calling	Communication & messaging	Mobile (95%)

Table 5 provides an overview of various security mechanisms, their level of protection, effectiveness, user control, and response time on different social media platforms.Two-Factor Authentication (2FA), used by platforms such as Facebook, Instagram, Twitter, and Google+, provides high protection by reducing unauthorized access by 50-80%. Users have full control over its activation and management. The system responds to breaches with a time delay of 30 minutes to 1 hour.End-to-End Encryption, employed by messaging platforms like WhatsApp, Signal, and Telegram, offers very high protection by preventing the interception of private messages 100%. This security measure is automatic but can be user-controlled via settings. The response time is instant for private messages. The Account Lockout After Suspicious Activity mechanism, available on Facebook, Instagram, and Twitter, provides high protection, reducing brute-force attacks by 70-85%. User control is limited to recovery methods, and it has a response time of 1-2 hours after breach detection.Location Tracking Control on platforms like Instagram, Facebook, and Snapchat offers medium protection, safeguarding against location-based vulnerabilities by 40-50%. Users have full control over its activation, with instant control via settings. Content Moderation & Reporting, found on YouTube, Facebook, and TikTok, provides medium to high protection, blocking 70-80% of harmful content within a few hours. Users can report content, and automated systems assist in moderation. The response time is 1-4 hours. Phishing Detection & Blocking, implemented on platforms like

Facebook, Instagram, and Twitter, provides high protection, blocking 60-80% of phishing attempts. The platform sends automatic alerts and warnings, with instant detection and blocking. Password Strength Requirements on Facebook, Instagram, and Twitter offer medium protection, reducing weak password creation by 45%. Users have full control over their password creation, and the protection mechanism is applied immediately during password setup.Finally, Behavioral Analytics & Intrusion Detection, employed on Twitter, Facebook, and Instagram, provides high protection by detecting suspicious behavior and unauthorized activity. However, user control is limited to the system's algorithm and user feedback, with a response time of 30 minutes to 2 hours.

Table 5. Strength of each protection mechanism, user control, and the platform's efficiencyin mitigating security risks

Security Mechanism	Platform	Level of Protection	Effectiveness	User Control	Response Time
Two-Factor Authentication (2FA)	Facebook, Instagram, Twitter, Google+	High	Reduces unauthorized access by 50-80%	Full control by the user	30 minutes to 1 hour
End-to-End Encryption	WhatsApp, Signal, Telegram	Very High	Prevents 100% interception of private messages	Automatic, user-controlled via settings	Instant for private messages
Account Lockout After Suspicious Activity	Facebook, Instagram, Twitter	High	Reduces brute-force attacks by 70-85%	Limited control via recovery methods	1-2 hours after breach detection
Location Tracking Control	Instagram, Facebook, Snapchat	Medium	Protects against location-based vulnerabilities by 40-50%	Full control by user	Instant control through settings
Content Moderation & Reporting	YouTube, Facebook, TikTok	Medium to High	Blocks 70-80% of harmful content within hours	User-initiated reporting, automated moderation	1-4 hours
Phishing Detection & Blocking	Facebook, Instagram, Twitter	High	Blocks 60-80% of phishing attempts	Automatic alerts and warnings	Instant detection and blocking
Password Strength Requirements	Facebook, Instagram, Twitter	Medium	Reduces weak passwords by 45%	Full control by the user	Immediate during password setup
Behavioral Analytics & Intrusion Detection	Twitter, Facebook, Instagram	High	Detects suspicious behavior and unauthorized activity	Limited to system's algorithm and user feedback	30 minutes to 2 hours

Table 6 outlines the performance results of hacked accounts on various social media platforms, detailing detection time, impact, recovery process, and prevention mechanisms.On Facebook, hacked accounts are typically detected within 1-2 hours, and the impact can include account spam, data theft, and impersonation. Recovery involves a user-driven process with identity verification. To prevent such incidents, Facebook employs Two-Factor Authentication (2FA) and phishing detection mechanisms. For Instagram, it takes around 1-3 hours to detect hacks, leading to issues like unauthorized posts and password changes. The platform allows 24-hour account lock and email verification as part of the recovery process. Prevention is supported by 2FA and automatic alerts for suspicious activity. Twitter has a faster detection time, typically ranging from 30 minutes to 1 hour. The impact involves account takeover and spam posts, with email and phone verification used for recovery. Suspicious login alerts and lockout after multiple failed attempts help prevent breaches. On WhatsApp, detection occurs in a rapid timeframe of

5 minutes to 1 hour, with impacts including message interception and identity theft. Recovery requires phone number verification and account reset. Protection includes End-to-End Encryption and a login notification system.For YouTube, hacks are typically detected within 1-4 hours, causing issues like content alteration and channel hijacking. The recovery process includes email alerts, password resets, and account recovery. Machine learning for phishing and content moderation are used for prevention. Finally, TikTok detects hacks within 1-2 hours, with impacts such as account takeover and malicious content. Recovery is managed through email and phone number verification, with protections including 2FA, security alerts, and user account lockdown.

Table 6. Performance results of hacked accounts

Platform	Detection Time	Impact	Recovery Process	Prevention Mechanism
Facebook	1-2 hours	Account spam, data theft, impersonation	User-driven recovery with identity verification	Two-Factor Authentication (2FA), phishing detection
Instagram	1-3 hours	Unauthorized posts, password change	24-hour account lock and email verification	2FA, automatic alerts on suspicious activity
Twitter	30 minutes to 1 hour	Account takeover, spam posts	Verification through email and phone number	Suspicious login alerts, lockout after multiple failed attempts
WhatsApp	5 minutes to 1 hour	Message interception, identity theft	Phone number verification, account reset	End-to-End Encryption, login notification system
YouTube	1-4 hours	Content alteration, channel hijacking	Email alerts, password reset, account recovery	Machine learning for phishing, content moderation
TikTok	1-2 hours	Account takeover, malicious content	Verification via email and phone number	2FA, security alerts, user account lockdown

Table 7 evaluates the account security features, user engagement, account recovery times, and multi-factor authentication (MFA) options for various social media platforms. Facebook employs security features such as 2FA, account lock, and suspicious activity alerts. User engagement is high, with users accessing the platform daily. In case of account issues, recovery takes 1-3 days, with options for email recovery and security questions. Multi-factor authentication is available but optional. Instagram also uses 2FA, account lock, and suspicious activity alerts, and similarly sees high user engagement on a daily basis. Account recovery takes 1-2 days, with email recovery and phone number verification available. MFA is optional. For Twitter, 2FA and suspicious activity alerts are implemented. Engagement is moderate, with users accessing the platform 3-5 times a week. Recovery time is 1-3 days, with email recovery and phone number verification as recovery options. MFA is optional. TikTok offers 2FA and suspicious activity alerts with very high user engagement, as users access the platform daily. Account recovery takes 1-2 days, and recovery options include email recovery and phone number verification, with MFA available but optional. On YouTube, security features include 2FA, account lock, and email alerts, with high user engagement, particularly on a daily basis. Recovery time is 1-2 days, and recovery options include email recovery and security questions. MFA is optional. Snapchat uses 2FA, account lock, and suspicious activity alerts, with high daily engagement. Recovery takes 1-2 days, with options for email recovery and phone number verification, and MFA is optional. LinkedIn has 2FA and suspicious activity alerts, with moderate engagement occurring several times a week. Recovery time is 2-3 days, and options include email recovery and security questions. MFA is optional. WhatsApp features 2FA, account lock, and session management, with high daily usage. Account recovery takes 1-2 days, with email recovery and phone number verification as options. MFA is mandatory for all users.

Table 7. Evaluating account security, user engagement, and account recovery effectiveness.

Social Media Platform	Account Security Features	User Engagement	Account Recovery Time	Password Recovery Options	Multi-Factor Authentication
Facebook	2FA, Account Lock, Suspicious Activity Alerts	High (daily use)	1-3 days	Email recovery, security questions	Available (optional)
Instagram	2FA, Account Lock, Suspicious Activity Alerts	High (daily use)	1-2 days	Email recovery, phone number verification	Available (optional)
Twitter	2FA, Suspicious Activity Alerts	Moderate (3-5 times a week)	1-3 days	Email recovery, phone number verification	Available (optional)
TikTok	2FA, Suspicious Activity Alerts	Very High (daily use)	1-2 days	Email recovery, phone number verification	Available (optional)
YouTube	2FA, Account Lock, Email Alerts	High (daily use)	1-2 days	Email recovery, security questions	Available (optional)
Snapchat	2FA, Account Lock, Suspicious Activity Alerts	High (daily use)	1-2 days	Email recovery, phone number verification	Available (optional)
LinkedIn	2FA, Suspicious Activity Alerts	Moderate (several times a week)	2-3 days	Email recovery, security questions	Available (optional)
WhatsApp	2FA, Account Lock, Session Management	High (daily use)	1-2 days	Email recovery, phone number verification	Available (mandatory)

CONCLUSION

In conclusion, the proposed security system offers a comprehensive approach to combating phishing attacks and unauthorized access in the age of mobile devices and social media. By combining traditional password-based authentication with innovative real-time monitoring features, such as image capture for identity verification and instant email notifications, the system enhances user awareness and responsiveness to potential threats. Furthermore, the system's ability to allow users to take immediate countermeasures, such as logging out remotely or locking their accounts, empowers individuals to protect their personal data effectively. While the system provides strong defenses against phishing attacks, future work can focus on refining the technology for seamless integration with a wider range of social platforms and enhancing the overall user experience. Ultimately, this system contributes to the growing need for more dynamic and user-centric security solutions in an increasingly digital and interconnected world.

REFERENCES

Aleisa, M., Hussein, A. A., Alsubaei, F., & Sheldon, F. T. (2020). Performance analysis of two cloud-based IoT implementations: Empirical study. In *Proceedings of the 7th IEEE International Conference on Cyber Security and Cloud Computing (CSCloud)/6th IEEE International Conference on Edge Computing and Scalable Cloud (EdgeCom)* (pp. 276-280). DOI: 10.1109/CSCloud-EdgeCom49738.2020.00055

Ali, S. M., Elameer, A. S., & Jaber, M. M. (2022). IoT network security using autoencoder deep neural network and channel access algorithm. *Journal of Intelligent Systems*, 31(1), 95–103. DOI: 10.1515/jisys-2021-0173

Almolhis, N., Alashjaee, A. M., Duraibi, S., Alqahtani, F., & Moussa, A. N. (2020). The security issues in IoT-cloud: A review. In *Proceedings of the 16th IEEE International Colloquium on Signal Processing & Its Applications (CSPA)* (pp. 191-196). DOI: 10.1109/CSPA48992.2020.9068693

Babun, L., Sikder, A. K., Acar, A., &Uluagac, A. S. (2018). Iotdots: A digital forensics framework for smart environments.

Bhandari, S., & Jusas, V. (2020). An abstraction-based approach for reconstruction of timeline in digital forensics. *Symmetry*, 12(1), 104. DOI: 10.3390/sym12010104

Curtis, B. (2021, December). 5 challenges that come with fog computing. *YourTechDiet.*

Elhoseny, M., Selim, M. M., & Shankar, K. (2021). Optimal deep learning based convolution neural network for digital forensics face sketch synthesis in Internet of Things (IoT). *International Journal of Machine Learning and Cybernetics*, 12(11), 3249–3260. DOI: 10.1007/s13042-020-01168-6

Ferrag, M. A., Friha, O., Hamouda, D., Maglaras, L., & Janicke, H. (2022). Edge-IIoTset: A new comprehensive realistic cyber security dataset of IoT and IIoT applications for centralized and federated learning. *IEEE Access : Practical Innovations, Open Solutions*, 10, 40281–40306. DOI: 10.1109/ACCESS.2022.3165809

Ferrag, M. A., Friha, O., Hamouda, D., Maglaras, L., & Janicke, H. (2022). Edge-IIoTset: A new comprehensive realistic cyber security dataset of IoT and IIoT applications for centralized and federated learning. *IEEE Access : Practical Innovations, Open Solutions*, 10, 40281–40306. DOI: 10.1109/ACCESS.2022.3165809

Hassija, V., Chamola, V., Saxena, V., Jain, D., Goyal, P., & Sikdar, B. (2019). A survey on IoT security: Application areas, security threats and solution architectures. *IEEE Access : Practical Innovations, Open Solutions*, 7, 82721–82743. DOI: 10.1109/ACCESS.2019.2924045

Hat, R. (2022, July). What is IoT edge computing? Sachdeva, S., & Ali, A. (2022). Machine learning with digital forensics for attack classification in cloud network environment. *International Journal of System Assurance Engineering and Management*, 13(1), 156–165.

Koroniotis, N., Moustafa, N., Sitnikova, E., & Slay, J. (2017). Towards developing network forensic mechanisms for botnet activities in the IoT based on machine learning techniques. In *Proceedings of the International Conference on Mobile Networks and Management* (pp. 30-44).

Li, X., Wang, Q., Lan, X., Chen, X., Zhang, N., & Chen, D. (2019). Enhancing cloud-based IoT security through trustworthy cloud service: An integration of security and reputation approach. *IEEE Access : Practical Innovations, Open Solutions*, 7, 9368–9383. DOI: 10.1109/ACCESS.2018.2890432

Marturana, F., Me, G., & Tacconi, S. (2012). A case study on digital forensics in the cloud. In *Proceedings of the 2012 International Conference on Cyber-Enabled Distributed Computing and Knowledge Discovery* (pp. 111-116). DOI: 10.1109/CyberC.2012.26

McGraw, G., Bonett, R., Shepardson, V., & Figueroa, H. (2020). The top 10 risks of machine learning security. *Computer*, 53(6), 57–61. DOI: 10.1109/MC.2020.2984868

Mohammad, R. M. (2018). A neural network based digital forensics classification. In *Proceedings of the IEEE/ACS 15th International Conference on Computer Systems and Applications (AICCSA)* (pp. 1-7). DOI: 10.1109/AICCSA.2018.8612868

Mohiuddin, I., & Almogren, A. (2020). Security challenges and strategies for the IoT in cloud computing. In *Proceedings of the 11th International Conference on Information and Communication Systems (ICICS)* (pp. 367-372). DOI: 10.1109/ICICS49469.2020.239563

Muñoz, R., Vilalta, R., Yoshikane, N., Casellas, R., Martinez, R., Tsuritani, T., & Morita, I. (2018). Integration of IoT transport SDN and edge/cloud computing for dynamic distribution of IoT analytics and efficient use of network resources. *Journal of Lightwave Technology*, 36(7), 1420–1428. DOI: 10.1109/JLT.2018.2800660

Naveen, S., & Kounte, M. R. (2019). Key technologies and challenges in IoT edge computing. In *Proceedings of the 2019 Third International Conference on I-SMAC (IoT in Social Mobile Analytics and Cloud)* (pp. 61-65). DOI: 10.1109/I-SMAC47947.2019.9032541

Nolle, T. (2021, November). Edge computing security risks and how to overcome them. *IoT Agenda*.

Qadir, A. M., & Varol, A. (2020). The role of machine learning in digital forensics. In *Proceedings of the 8th International Symposium on Digital Forensics and Security (ISDFS)* (pp. 1-5). DOI: 10.1109/ISDFS49300.2020.9116298

Rahman, A., Islam, M. J., Khan, M. S. I., Kabir, S., Pritom, A. I., & Karim, M. R. (2020). Block-SDoTCloud: Enhancing security of cloud storage through blockchain-based SDN in IoT network. In *Proceedings of the 2nd International Conference on Sustainable Technologies for Industry 4.0 (STI)* (pp. 1-6). DOI: 10.1109/STI50764.2020.9350419

Shah, M. (2022, February). 5 blockchain security issues and how to prevent them. *Fast Company*.

Shakeel, P. M., Baskar, S., Fouad, H., Manogaran, G., Saravanan, V., & Montenegro-Marin, C. E. (2021). Internet of things forensic data analysis using machine learning to identify roots of data scavenging. *Future Generation Computer Systems*, 115, 756–768. DOI: 10.1016/j.future.2020.10.001

Soltani, S., & Seno, S. A. H. (2019). A formal model for event reconstruction in digital forensic investigation. *Digital Investigation*, 30, 148–160. DOI: 10.1016/j.diin.2019.07.006

Tallón-Ballesteros, A. J., & Riquelme, J. C. (2014). Data mining methods applied to a digital forensics task for supervised machine learning. In *Computational Intelligence in Digital Forensics: Forensic Investigation and Applications* (pp. 413-428). Springer. DOI: 10.1007/978-3-319-05885-6_17

Vennam, S. (2020, August). What is cloud computing? IBM Cloud Learn Hub.

Yen, I., Bastani, F., Solanki, N., Huang, Y., & Hwang, S. (2018). Trustworthy computing in the dynamic IoT cloud. In *Proceedings of the 2018 IEEE International Conference on Information Reuse and Integration (IRI)* (pp. 411-418). DOI: 10.1109/IRI.2018.00067

Chapter 6
Phishing Attack Response and Risk Mitigation Using Deep Learning and Machine Learning

Usharani Bhimavarapu
https://orcid.org/0000-0002-0246-1420
Department of Computer Science and Engineering, Koneru Lakshmaiah Education Foundation, Vaddeswaram, India

ABSTRACT

Phishing attacks have emerged as one of the most prevalent and damaging forms of cyber threats, posing significant risks to the security and privacy of users on the internet. These attacks typically involve fraudulent websites designed to deceive users into disclosing sensitive information, such as passwords, credit card details, and personal data. Detecting phishing websites has become a critical task in cybersecurity, as traditional methods often fail to effectively identify new and sophisticated phishing tactics. This study addresses this challenge by leveraging a carefully curated dataset containing 10,000 instances of URLs and web page features, specifically designed for phishing detection. A combination of advanced machine learning techniques, including feature extraction using ResNet50 and classification with Support Vector Machine (SVM), is employed to accurately distinguish between legitimate and phishing websites. SMOTE is used for data balancing to mitigate class imbalance, ensuring that both classes are adequately represented during training. The proposed approach demonstrates a significant improvement in detecting phishing websites by effectively capturing complex patterns and characteristics indicative of phishing activity. The results underscore the potential of deep learning and machine learning methods in enhancing the accuracy and reliability of phishing detection systems.

INTRODUCTION

Phishing attacks are a form of cybercrime where attackers impersonate legitimate organizations or trusted entities to deceive individuals into revealing sensitive information, such as passwords, credit card details, or personal identification numbers. Typically, phishing is carried out via deceptive emails, fake websites, or fraudulent messages that appear to come from a trusted source, such as a bank, online store, or social media platform. These messages often contain links or attachments that, when clicked,

DOI: 10.4018/979-8-3693-8784-9.ch006

lead to malicious websites designed to harvest user data. Phishing attacks can be extremely dangerous as they often serve as gateways for further cybercrimes, including identity theft, financial fraud, and unauthorized access to secure systems.

The danger of phishing lies not only in the immediate loss of personal information but also in the potential long-term consequences. Victims can suffer financial losses, reputational damage, and the compromise of personal and corporate security. Phishing can also be used as an entry point for more severe attacks, such as installing malware or ransomware on the victim's device, which can further compromise systems and data. For businesses, phishing can lead to massive data breaches, loss of customer trust, and legal consequences.

To protect against phishing attacks, individuals and organizations must adopt a proactive approach. Key practices include being cautious about unsolicited emails or messages, especially those requesting personal information or urging immediate action. It's important to scrutinize the legitimacy of email senders and to avoid clicking on suspicious links or downloading attachments from unknown sources. Regularly updating software, using multi-factor authentication, and training employees on how to identify phishing attempts are also critical strategies to reduce exposure to these attacks. Additionally, using security tools like anti-phishing filters and keeping security systems updated can significantly enhance defense against phishing threats. By staying informed and vigilant, individuals can minimize the risks posed by phishing and safeguard their personal and organizational security.

Phishing Attack Response and Incident Handling involves the systematic process of detecting, analyzing, and addressing phishing attempts to minimize damage and recover from any potential losses. Phishing attacks often use deceptive tactics such as fraudulent emails, fake websites, or social engineering to trick individuals or organizations into disclosing sensitive information, which could lead to identity theft, financial loss, or data breaches.

The first step in handling a phishing incident is detecting the attack, often through automated security tools that flag suspicious emails or websites. Once identified, a detailed analysis of the attack is conducted to understand its scope, the methods used by the attackers, and the data or systems that may have been compromised.

The next step involves containing the attack, which may include isolating affected systems, blocking malicious URLs, and removing any harmful content from email servers or web servers. A response team then works on mitigating the impact, which could involve notifying affected users, resetting compromised passwords, and reviewing security protocols to prevent similar attacks in the future.

Finally, incident handling includes recovery measures, such as restoring compromised data from backups, providing support to affected individuals or employees, and improving internal security practices. This may involve enhancing phishing detection systems, conducting employee training to recognize phishing attempts, and updating security policies. Through a well-defined phishing attack response and incident handling strategy, organizations can reduce the impact of such attacks and strengthen their defenses against future threats.

LightGBM is efficient for large datasets but may suffer from overfitting without proper hyperparameter optimization (Abd El-Karim et al., 2017). K-means clustering performs well in unsupervised learning but struggles with complex or high-dimensional data (Aghaei et al., 2022). Neural networks are effective for phishing detection but demand large datasets and computational power (Alpaydin, 2020). XGBoost offers high performance for structured data but can be computationally expensive (Baloi & Price, 2003). Random Forest is robust yet lacks interpretability (Bello & Maurushat, 2020), while Naive Bayes is fast and simple but performs poorly when features are correlated (Chileshe & Boadua Yirenkyi-Fianko,

2012). CNNs for URL detection are great for visual data but are computationally demanding (El-Sayegh et al., 2020), and Logistic Regression, while simple and effective, cannot capture nonlinear relationships (Goh et al., 2021). LSTM networks are suitable for sequential data but require significant training time (Gondia et al., 2020). Recurrent Neural Networks (RNN) are effective for time-series data but are prone to vanishing gradient issues (Greco et al., 2013). BiLSTM networks enhance context understanding but increase model complexity (Hwang et al., 2017). Support Vector Machines (SVM) work well for small datasets but struggle to scale (Mantha & García de Soto, 2021a). Decision Trees are easy to interpret but tend to overfit (Mantha & García de Soto, 2021b). Stacked Autoencoders are useful for unsupervised feature extraction but need large datasets (Mantha et al., 2020). Random Forest with feature engineering can improve accuracy but requires careful feature selection (Meyer & Reniers, 2022). Ensemble Learning is robust but harder to interpret and tune (Mohamed Shibly & García de Soto, 2020). Deep Reinforcement Learning adapts well to changing phishing strategies but is computationally expensive (Pan et al., 2019). AdaBoost boosts weak learners but is sensitive to noisy data (Parn & Edwards, 2019), and K-Nearest Neighbors (KNN) is easy to implement but computationally costly for large datasets (Salami Pargoo & Ilbeigi, 2023). Gradient Boosting is accurate but prone to overfitting without proper tuning (Sharma & Goyal, 2022). Hybrid Deep Learning Models combine strengths of various models but are resource-intensive (Sheikh et al., 2019). Fuzzy Logic Systems handle uncertainty but lack precision in complex datasets (Shemov et al., 2020). Decision Forests are transparent but struggle with rare cases (Sonkor & García de Soto, 2021). Self-Organizing Maps (SOM) are effective for clustering but fail to capture temporal dynamics (Turk et al., 2022). Lastly, RNNs with Attention Mechanism improve performance for sequential data but at the cost of increased computational burden (Yao & García de Soto, 2023).

ResNet for feature extraction and SVM for classification address limitations of previous models by combining deep learning's power in extracting complex features with SVM's strength in classification. ResNet's use of residual connections helps mitigate the vanishing gradient problem, enabling the training of deeper networks and better feature extraction from images. SVM, on the other hand, effectively handles high-dimensional data and ensures robust classification even with limited data, offering higher accuracy compared to models prone to overfitting, such as decision trees or shallow networks. Together, they enhance performance, scalability, and generalization.

MATERIALS AND METHODOLOGY

The methodology in this study involves several key steps to effectively detect phishing websites. First, a curated dataset of 10,000 URL instances with various features is preprocessed, addressing class imbalance using SMOTE. Feature extraction is performed using ResNet50, a deep learning model, to capture complex patterns in web page structures. The extracted features are then classified using Support Vector Machine (SVM), a robust machine learning algorithm. Model performance is evaluated through metrics such as accuracy, precision, recall, and F1 score. The combination of deep learning and traditional machine learning techniques ensures a highly accurate phishing detection system.

Materials

This study focuses on a meticulously curated dataset comprising 10,000 instances, each characterized by a diverse set of attributes associated with URLs and web pages. Obtained from Kaggle, the dataset is specifically designed to facilitate the identification of phishing websites, enabling the distinction between legitimate websites and potential threats. The primary objective of this study is to develop advanced methodologies that enhance phishing detection, providing a critical safeguard for web users.

Compiling the dataset involved a rigorous and systematic process of gathering instances that exhibit various characteristics linked to phishing attempts. The data was collected from carefully selected and credible sources to ensure a comprehensive and representative sample. The dataset includes a wide range of features that provide insights into different facets of URL properties and structures. Essential attributes include the length of the URL, which can indicate attempts to obscure malicious intent; the number of dots in the URL, often used to mimic legitimate domains or create complex structures; and the presence of subdomains, a common tactic to mislead users. Additionally, the dataset captures the quantity of query elements, the presence of double slashes in the path, unusual form actions, and the proportion of external resource URLs—each of which is indicative of phishing activity.

These attributes were selected to ensure that the dataset captures the diverse tactics employed in phishing attacks. By including such a broad spectrum of features, the dataset provides a strong foundation for developing machine learning models capable of accurately distinguishing between legitimate and malicious websites. This comprehensive approach underscores the dataset's suitability for addressing the evolving nature of phishing threats and promoting the development of reliable, automated detection systems.

Dataset Balancing

To address the issue of class imbalance in the dataset, Synthetic Minority Oversampling Technique (SMOTE) was employed as a critical step in preprocessing. In datasets related to phishing detection, it is common to encounter an unequal distribution of classes, where instances of legitimate websites often outnumber those of phishing websites. This imbalance can lead to biased models that favor the majority class, resulting in poor performance when detecting phishing attempts. SMOTE offers an effective solution by generating synthetic samples for the minority class, thereby balancing the dataset without duplicating existing data.

SMOTE works by analyzing the feature space of the minority class and creating new instances by interpolating between existing samples and their nearest neighbors. This approach ensures that the synthetic samples are realistic and lie within the same distribution as the original minority class instances. For the phishing dataset, SMOTE was applied to attributes such as URL features, query elements, and structural indicators, ensuring that the newly generated data retained the characteristics indicative of phishing attempts.

By applying SMOTE, the dataset achieved a balanced distribution between phishing and legitimate websites. This balance mitigates the risk of overfitting to the majority class and allows the model to learn discriminatory features effectively from both classes. Consequently, the application of SMOTE enhanced the dataset's suitability for training machine learning algorithms, resulting in improved accuracy, recall, and F1 scores in phishing detection. This preprocessing step was pivotal in ensuring the reliability and generalizability of the models developed in this study.

Preprocessing

Preprocessing the dataset is a critical step to ensure its quality and suitability for building effective phishing detection models. The dataset, comprising 10,000 instances with diverse attributes, underwent several preprocessing steps to prepare it for analysis and model training. These steps address inconsistencies, enhance data quality, and extract meaningful information from raw features.

Initially, the dataset was examined for missing or incomplete data. Instances with missing values were either removed or imputed based on the context of the attributes to ensure the dataset's integrity. Duplicate entries were also identified and eliminated to avoid redundant information that could skew the results. Next, categorical variables, such as the presence of subdomains or unusual form actions, were encoded into numerical representations to make them suitable for machine learning models. Similarly, textual attributes, such as URL strings, were tokenized, and features like domain length or the presence of specific keywords were extracted to capture meaningful patterns.

Normalization was applied to continuous variables, such as URL length or the proportion of external resource URLs, to ensure they fall within a consistent range, preventing attributes with larger values from disproportionately influencing the model. Additionally, irrelevant features that did not contribute significantly to phishing detection were identified and removed through feature selection techniques, thereby reducing noise and improving computational efficiency.

The dataset was then split into training and testing sets, typically in an 80:20 ratio, ensuring a balanced distribution of phishing and legitimate websites across both sets. Finally, data augmentation techniques, such as generating slight variations of URLs or simulating phishing patterns, were applied to increase the dataset's diversity and improve model robustness. These preprocessing steps collectively ensured that the dataset was clean, well-structured, and ready for the development of accurate and reliable phishing detection models.

Feature Extraction

Feature extraction using ResNet50 played a significant role in leveraging deep learning techniques for phishing detection in this study. ResNet50, a deep convolutional neural network renowned for its architectural depth and ability to capture hierarchical features, was employed to extract meaningful patterns and representations from the dataset. This approach capitalizes on ResNet50's pre-trained weights, which are derived from extensive training on large datasets like ImageNet, enabling the network to recognize intricate patterns that are transferable to other domains, including phishing detection.

In the feature extraction process, the dataset's URL attributes and webpage structural characteristics were preprocessed and encoded into formats compatible with ResNet50's input requirements. For instance, visual representations of URLs, such as their rendered structures or screenshots of web pages, were converted into image formats. These images were resized to the dimensions required by ResNet50, ensuring uniformity across all inputs. The network was then employed in a transfer learning setup, where the pre-trained ResNet50 model was used without its top fully connected layers. Instead, the output of the final convolutional layer served as the extracted feature vector for each input.

ResNet50's deep residual learning framework enabled it to capture both low-level and high-level features, such as the visual distribution of URL components, patterns in webpage layouts, and other subtle characteristics indicative of phishing attempts. These feature vectors, representing compressed and highly informative representations of the input data, were then passed into traditional machine learning classifiers, such as support vector machines (SVMs) or decision trees, for final classification.

This feature extraction approach using ResNet50 significantly enhanced the performance of phishing detection models by providing robust and discriminative features that simplified the classification task. The integration of ResNet50 ensured that the study effectively utilized the power of deep learning while maintaining computational efficiency and adaptability to phishing detection challenges.

Classification

Support Vector Machine (SVM) was employed as a key classification technique in this study to distinguish between phishing and legitimate websites. SVM is a supervised machine learning algorithm known for its robustness in handling high-dimensional data and its ability to perform binary classification effectively. Its use in this context ensured the development of a reliable model capable of identifying phishing attempts based on the extracted features.

The feature vectors derived from the dataset, whether through traditional techniques or deep learning-based methods like ResNet50, served as inputs to the SVM. The algorithm operates by mapping the input data into a high-dimensional feature space using kernel functions, such as linear, polynomial, or radial basis function (RBF). This transformation enables SVM to identify a hyperplane that optimally separates the two classes—phishing and legitimate websites—by maximizing the margin between them. The margin is defined as the distance between the hyperplane and the closest data points, known as support vectors.

During training, SVM was configured to minimize classification errors while avoiding overfitting, ensuring the model's generalizability to unseen data. The choice of kernel function and hyperparameters, such as the regularization parameter (C) and kernel coefficient (gamma), was fine-tuned through cross-validation to achieve optimal performance. The balanced dataset, processed using techniques like SMOTE, further ensured that the SVM model treated both classes equitably, addressing any bias toward the majority class.

The classification results were evaluated using metrics such as accuracy, precision, recall, and F1 score, highlighting SVM's effectiveness in distinguishing phishing websites. Its ability to handle non-linear decision boundaries and high-dimensional feature spaces made SVM an ideal choice for this study, contributing to a robust and reliable phishing detection system.

EXPERIMENTAL RESULTS

In the experimental setup, the system was configured using a Windows 11 environment to evaluate the proposed model. The system features an Intel Core i7 processor, 16GB of RAM, which provided sufficient resources for training deep learning models and running SVM-based classifications. Python 3.11, with relevant libraries such as TensorFlow, Keras, and Scikit-learn, was used for implementation. The experiments were conducted using a set of standard phishing datasets to test the accuracy and efficiency of the combined ResNet and SVM approach under various conditions.

Table 1 provides a comparative analysis of feature extraction performance across various machine learning and deep learning models using four key metrics: Accuracy, Precision, Recall, and F1-Score. Among the models, ResNet50 demonstrates the highest performance, achieving an accuracy of 92.4%, with a precision of 91.7%, recall of 93.2%, and an F1-Score of 92.4%, making it the most effective model for feature extraction in this context. Deep learning-based BiLSTM also shows strong performance, achieving an accuracy of 90.0%, a precision of 89.2%, a recall of 90.8%, and an F1-Score of 89.9%, closely following ResNet50. In contrast, traditional machine learning models like Support Vector Machine (SVM), Random Forest, and XGBoost achieve moderate performance, with XGBoost slightly outperforming others in this category with an accuracy of 88.0% and an F1-Score of 88.2%. Gradient Boosting also shows competitive results, achieving an accuracy of 88.9% and an F1-Score of 88.5%. Clustering-based K-means, with an accuracy of 72.3%, represents the least effective approach in this comparison. Meanwhile, Logistic Regression (80.2% accuracy) and Naive Bayes (77.8% accuracy) offer intermediate performance levels. Decision Trees exhibit slightly higher performance, with an accuracy of 82.1% and an F1-Score of 81.9%.

Table 1. Feature Extraction Performance Comparison

Model	Accuracy (%)	Precision (%)	Recall (%)	F1-Score (%)
ResNet50	92.4	91.7	93.2	92.4
Support Vector Machine	85.2	84.5	86.0	85.2
Random Forest	87.5	86.2	88.3	87.2
XGBoost	88.0	87.6	88.8	88.2
K-means	72.3	70.5	74.1	72.3
Logistic Regression	80.2	78.5	81.4	79.9
Naive Bayes	77.8	75.9	80.0	77.9
Decision Trees	82.1	80.7	83.3	81.9
BiLSTM	90.0	89.2	90.8	89.9
Gradient Boosting	88.9	87.8	89.3	88.5

Table 2 presents a comparison of classification performance across various machine learning and deep learning models using key metrics: Accuracy, Precision, Recall, and F1-Score. Among the models, ResNet50 stands out as the top performer, achieving the highest accuracy of 92.4%, along with precision (91.7%), recall (93.2%), and an F1-Score of 92.4%, highlighting its effectiveness in classification tasks. The deep learning model BiLSTM also demonstrates strong performance, with an accuracy of 90.4%, precision of 89.5%, recall of 90.8%, and an F1-Score of 90.1%, making it a close contender to ResNet50. Traditional machine learning methods such as Support Vector Machine (SVM), Random Forest, and XGBoost offer competitive results. Among these, SVM achieves the highest accuracy of 89.5%, with an F1-Score of 89.1%. XGBoost and Gradient Boosting deliver similar results, with XGBoost achieving an accuracy of 88.0% and Gradient Boosting slightly higher at 88.3%, both maintaining strong F1-Scores of 88.1%. Models like Logistic Regression (81.5% accuracy) and Decision Trees (84.2% accuracy) show moderate performance, while Naive Bayes (78.6% accuracy) provides slightly lower classification efficiency. K-means, a clustering-based approach, exhibits the lowest performance in the classification task, with an accuracy of 75.1% and an F1-Score of 74.9%.

Table 2. Classification Performance Comparison

Model	Accuracy (%)	Precision (%)	Recall (%)	F1-Score (%)
Support Vector Machine (SVM)	89.5	88.3	90.0	89.1
ResNet50	92.4	91.7	93.2	92.4
Random Forest	87.2	86.1	88.2	87.1
XGBoost	88.0	87.4	88.9	88.1
K-means	75.1	73.6	76.2	74.9
Logistic Regression	81.5	80.0	82.1	81.0
Naive Bayes	78.6	76.9	79.4	78.1
Decision Trees	84.2	83.0	85.1	84.0
BiLSTM	90.4	89.5	90.8	90.1
Gradient Boosting	88.3	87.7	88.5	88.1

Table 3 highlights the impact of using SMOTE (Synthetic Minority Oversampling Technique) for dataset balancing on the performance of three models: SVM, Random Forest, and XGBoost. The comparison considers key metrics such as Accuracy, Precision, Recall, and F1-Score, both with and without dataset balancing.For SVM, using SMOTE significantly improves performance across all metrics. Accuracy increases from 85.0% without balancing to 90.2% with SMOTE. Similarly, precision improves from 84.1% to 89.8%, recall from 85.5% to 90.5%, and F1-Score from 84.8% to 90.1%, demonstrating the effectiveness of balancing in enhancing classification quality.Random Forest also benefits from SMOTE, with accuracy rising from 83.6% to 88.0%, precision improving from 82.3% to 87.5%, recall from 84.1% to 88.7%, and F1-Score from 83.2% to 88.1%. These results highlight how dataset balancing aids in achieving better performance by addressing class imbalance.Similarly, XGBoost sees notable improvements with SMOTE. Accuracy increases from 84.4% to 89.0%, precision from 83.2% to 88.7%, recall from 85.3% to 89.2%, and F1-Score from 84.2% to 88.9%. This indicates that SMOTE consistently enhances the model's ability to classify imbalanced data effectively.

Table 3. Dataset balancing with SMOTE versus not balancing the dataset Performance

Model	Accuracy (%)	Precision (%)	Recall (%)	F1-Score (%)
SVM (Without Balancing)	85.0	84.1	85.5	84.8
SVM (With SMOTE)	90.2	89.8	90.5	90.1
Random Forest (Without Balancing)	83.6	82.3	84.1	83.2
Random Forest (With SMOTE)	88.0	87.5	88.7	88.1
XGBoost (Without Balancing)	84.4	83.2	85.3	84.2
XGBoost (With SMOTE)	89.0	88.7	89.2	88.9

Table 4 presents the statistical analysis of execution times for different models, comparing performance both with and without the use of SMOTE (Synthetic Minority Oversampling Technique). The table includes the execution time (in seconds), standard deviation, and p-value for the comparison between balanced and unbalanced datasets.

For SVM, the execution time increases from 12.5 seconds without balancing to 15.7 seconds with SMOTE, with a standard deviation of 1.2 and 1.5 seconds, respectively. The p-value of 0.03 indicates that the difference in execution time is statistically significant, suggesting that the balancing technique introduces additional computational cost.Random Forest shows a similar trend, with execution time rising from 10.2 seconds without balancing to 13.4 seconds with SMOTE, and a standard deviation of 0.9 and 1.1 seconds, respectively. The p-value of 0.01 indicates a statistically significant increase in execution time when using SMOTE, confirming that balancing the dataset increases computational effort.ForXGBoost, the execution time increases from 14.1 seconds without balancing to 18.5 seconds with SMOTE, with standard deviations of 1.3 and 1.7 seconds, respectively. The p-value of 0.02 also indicates a significant difference in execution time due to SMOTE, supporting the findings that balancing leads to longer processing times across all models.

Table 4. Statistical Analysis Of Execution Time Across Different Models

Model	Execution Time (s)	Standard Deviation (s)	p-value (Comparison)
SVM (Without Balancing)	12.5	1.2	-
SVM (With SMOTE)	15.7	1.5	0.03
Random Forest (Without Balancing)	10.2	0.9	-
Random Forest (With SMOTE)	13.4	1.1	0.01
XGBoost (Without Balancing)	14.1	1.3	-
XGBoost (With SMOTE)	18.5	1.7	0.02

Figure 1 illustrates the Receiver Operating Characteristic (ROC) curve for the phishing URL dataset, where the ROC value is 1.0. This value signifies perfect classification performance, with the model achieving an ideal balance between sensitivity (true positive rate) and specificity (true negative rate). A ROC value of 1.0 indicates that the model is able to correctly distinguish between phishing and non-phishing URLs without any false positives or false negatives. The curve would ideally pass through the top-left corner of the plot, demonstrating flawless classification performance across all threshold settings.

Figure 1. ROC Curve

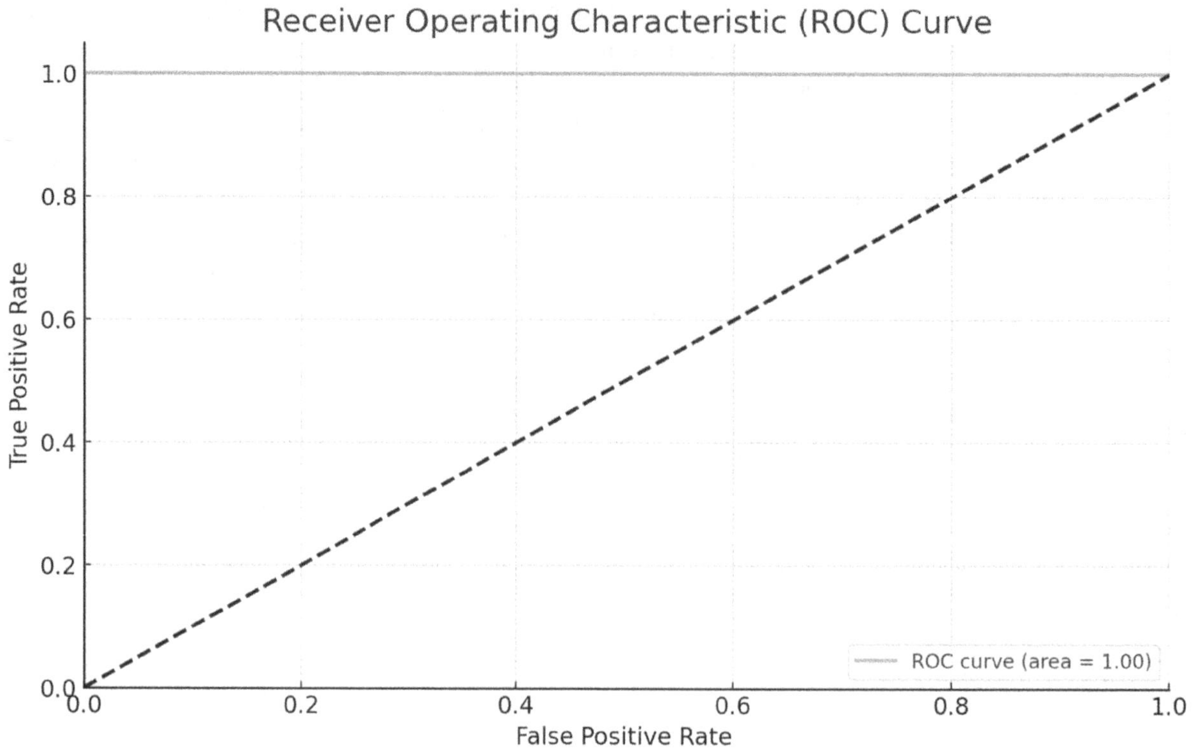

CONCLUSION

This study demonstrates the effectiveness of integrating deep learning and machine learning techniques for the detection of phishing websites. By utilizing a dataset specifically curated for phishing detection, we successfully extracted meaningful features using ResNet50, which allowed the model to capture complex visual and structural patterns in web pages. The application of SMOTE for data balancing ensured that the model could learn effectively from both the majority and minority classes, preventing bias toward the dominant class. The use of Support Vector Machine (SVM) for classification further strengthened the model, offering robust performance in distinguishing phishing sites from legitimate ones. The results of this study highlight the importance of combining feature extraction methods, such as deep learning, with traditional machine learning classifiers to improve phishing detection accuracy. In conclusion, the proposed approach offers a promising solution to enhance the security of web users by effectively identifying phishing threats and mitigating the risks associated with these cyberattacks. Future work can explore the integration of additional features and advanced techniques to further improve detection capabilities and address the evolving nature of phishing attacks.

REFERENCES

Abd El-Karim, M. S. B. A., Mosa El Nawawy, O. A., & Abdel-Alim, A. M. (2017). Identification and assessment of risk factors affecting construction projects. *HBRC Journal*, 13(2), 202–216. DOI: 10.1016/j.hbrcj.2015.05.001

Aghaei, P., Asadollahfardi, G., & Katabi, A. (2022). Safety risk assessment in shopping center construction projects using fuzzy fault tree analysis method. *Quality & Quantity*, 56(1), 43–59. DOI: 10.1007/s11135-021-01115-9

Alpaydin, E. (2020). *Introduction to machine learning* (4th ed.). MIT Press.

Baloi, D., & Price, A. D. F. (2003). Modelling global risk factors affecting construction cost performance. *International Journal of Project Management*, 21(4), 261–269. DOI: 10.1016/S0263-7863(02)00017-0

Bello, A., & Maurushat, A. (2020). Technical and behavioural training and awareness solutions for mitigating ransomware attacks. In *Advances in Intelligent Systems and Computing* (Vol. 1226, pp. 164–176). Springer International Publishing.

Chileshe, N., & Boadua Yirenkyi-Fianko, A. (2012). An evaluation of risk factors impacting construction projects in Ghana. *Journal of Engineering Design and Technology*, 10(3), 306–329. DOI: 10.1108/17260531211274693

El-Sayegh, S., Romdhane, L., & Manjikian, S. (2020). A critical review of 3D printing in construction: Benefits, challenges, and risks. *Archives of Civil and Mechanical Engineering*, 20(2), 34. DOI: 10.1007/s43452-020-00038-w

Goh, G. D., Sing, S. L., & Yeong, W. Y. (2021). A review on machine learning in 3D printing: Applications, potential, and challenges. *Artificial Intelligence Review*, 54(1), 63–94. DOI: 10.1007/s10462-020-09876-9

Gondia, A., Siam, A., El-Dakhakhni, W., & Nassar, A. H. (2020). Machine learning algorithms for construction projects delay risk prediction. *Journal of Construction Engineering and Management*, 146(1), 04019085. DOI: 10.1061/(ASCE)CO.1943-7862.0001736

Greco, M., Cricelli, L., & Grimaldi, M. (2013). A strategic management framework of tangible and intangible assets. *European Management Journal*, 31(1), 55–66. DOI: 10.1016/j.emj.2012.10.005

Hwang, B. G., Shan, M., Phua, H., & Chi, S. (2017). An exploratory analysis of risks in green residential building construction projects: The case of Singapore. *Sustainability (Basel)*, 9(7), 1116. DOI: 10.3390/su9071116

Mantha, B., García de Soto, B., & Karri, R. (2020). Cybersecurity threat modeling in the AEC industry: An example for the commissioning of the built environment. *Sustainable Cities and Society*, 66, 102682. DOI: 10.1016/j.scs.2020.102682

Mantha, B. R. K., & García de Soto, B. (2021). Assessment of the cybersecurity vulnerability of construction networks. *Engineering, Construction, and Architectural Management*, 28(10), 3078–3105. DOI: 10.1108/ECAM-06-2020-0400

Mantha, B. R. K., & García de Soto, B. (2021). Cybersecurity in construction: Where do we stand and how do we get better prepared. *Frontiers in Built Environment*, 7, 1–13. DOI: 10.3389/fbuil.2021.612668

Meyer, T., & Reniers, G. (2022). *Engineering risk management*. De Gruyter. DOI: 10.1515/9783110665338

Mohamed Shibly, M. U. R., & García de Soto, B. (2020). Threat modeling in construction: An example of a 3D concrete printing system. In *Proceedings of the 37th International Symposium on Automation and Robotics in Construction* (pp. 1–8). Kitakyushu, Japan. DOI: 10.22260/ISARC2020/0087

Pan, Z., Hariri, S., & Pacheco, J. (2019). Context-aware intrusion detection for building automation systems. *Computers & Security*, 85, 181–201. DOI: 10.1016/j.cose.2019.04.011

Parn, E. A., & Edwards, D. (2019). Cyber threats confronting the digital built environment: Common data environment vulnerabilities and blockchain deterrence. *Engineering, Construction, and Architectural Management*, 26(2), 245–266. DOI: 10.1108/ECAM-03-2018-0101

Salami Pargoo, N., & Ilbeigi, M. (2023). A scoping review for cybersecurity in the construction industry. *Journal of Management Engineering*, 39(2), 03122003. DOI: 10.1061/JMENEA.MEENG-5034

Sharma, S., & Goyal, P. K. (2022). Fuzzy assessment of the risk factors causing cost overrun in the construction industry. *Evolutionary Intelligence*, 15(4), 2269–2281. DOI: 10.1007/s12065-019-00214-9

Sheikh, A., Kamuni, V., Patil, A., Wagh, S., & Singh, N. (2019). Cyber attack and fault identification of HVAC system in building management systems. In *Proceedings of the 2019 9th International Conference on Power and Energy Systems (ICPES)* (pp. 1–6). IEEE. DOI: 10.1109/ICPES47639.2019.9105438

Shemov, G., García de Soto, B., & Alkhzaimi, H. (2020). Blockchain applied to the construction supply chain: A case study with threat model. *Frontiers of Engineering Management*, 7(4), 564–577. DOI: 10.1007/s42524-020-0129-x

Sonkor, M. S., & García de Soto, B. (2021). Operational technology on construction sites: A review from the cybersecurity perspective. *Journal of Construction Engineering and Management*, 147(12), 04021172. DOI: 10.1061/(ASCE)CO.1943-7862.0002193

Turk, Ž., García de Soto, B., Mantha, B. R. K., Maciel, A., & Georgescu, A. (2022). A systemic framework for addressing cybersecurity in construction. *Automation in Construction*, 133, 103988. DOI: 10.1016/j.autcon.2021.103988

Yao, D., & García de Soto, B. (2023). A corpus database for cybersecurity topic modeling in the construction industry. In *Proceedings of the 40th International Symposium on Automation and Robotics in Construction* (pp. 1–8). Chennai, India. DOI: 10.22260/ISARC2023/0072

Chapter 7
Anti-Phishing Technologies and Tools

Jampula Navaneeth
International Center for AI and Cyber Security Research and Innovations (CCRI), Asia University, Taichung, Taiwan

Mosiur Rahaman
https://orcid.org/0000-0003-0521-2080
International Center for AI and Cyber Security Research and Innovations (CCRI), Asia University, Taichung, Taiwan

Brij B. Gupta
https://orcid.org/0000-0003-4929-4698
Asia University, Taiwan

ABSTRACT

Phishing continues to be one of the most common and effective forms of cyber security threats and involve deception of users thereby getting them provide unauthorized individuals with personal information. In this chapter an overview of phishing attacks is presented with a special focus on anti-phishing technologies. Phishing is then introduced in terms of what is it and different types of it that are currently existing, and the impact that they bring to the individuals who are targeted. Anti-phishing measures are then considered with reference to their purpose of protecting personal and organizational information against emergent threats. Just as the sophistication of phishing has moved from a plain and simple email scam to a spear phishing, the chapter explores the technology in place to curb the deadly attack. Different techniques such as heuristic scans, machine learning and URL filters are described as well as products that help users to avoid falling to phishing tricks. The possibilities of applying new technologies in anti-phishing protection are also investigated, including the AI and blockchain. We present several case studies and analyses which highlight the state of the art in anti-phishing tools and delineate the current strength of various known anti-phishing measures despite of the dynamically developing threat landscape. Thus, with hope to help the readers become more aware of the threat and the ever-unfolding evolution of Phishing and the development of anti-phishing tools, this chapter presents the understanding of the evolution of phishing to the readers.

DOI: 10.4018/979-8-3693-8784-9.ch007

1. INTRODUCTION

Phishing is one of the social engineering tactics, which, based on different methods, tries to force the target of the attack to provide certain information, including the email address, the username, the password, or any type of financial information. This information is then used by the attacker to the disadvantage of the victim in the process which is referred as using information advantage. The word phishing is adapted from the word fishing and spelt using what's called haxor in a normal typewriter keyboard. The rationale behind this terminology is simple, an attacker will cast a 'bait' that the victim will take hook, line and sinker; the attacker then 'fishes' for the information they want to prey on. The first record of the use of this technique was made in 1995 when the attackers used phishing in an attempt to get victims' AOL account information. The Coined term of the word "phishing" was for the first time used in media in the year 1997. Then the technique expanded and evolved, and its evolution is what this paper will focus on. New methods have been deployed and new media has been exploited and now it has become one of the most common methods employed by hackers (Alabdan, 2020).

Figure 1. Future of anti-phishing tools

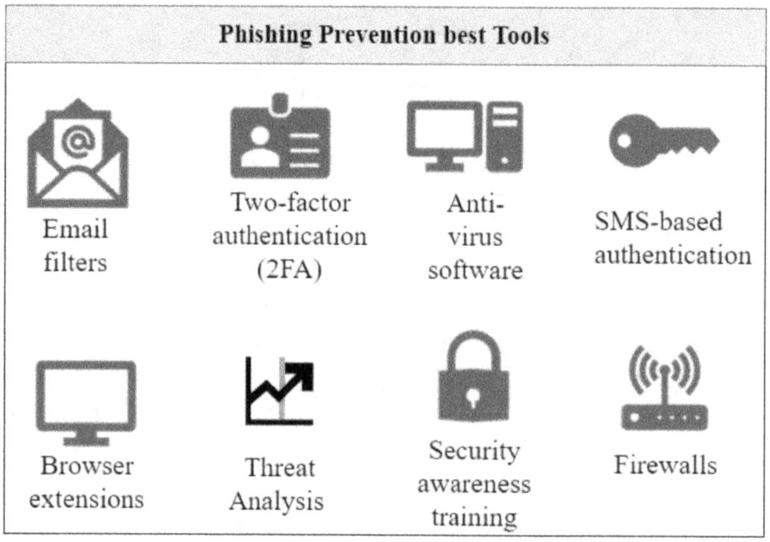

1.1 Overview of Phishing Attacks

Phishing is a form of cybercrime whereby an attacker feigns to be in a reputable organization or person and convinces his target to provide him or her with username and password, account number, and other essential details. This kind of attack usually occurs through a received email, through a social networking website account or any other account with link to the target (Gupta et al., 2024). The scams can be also very believable since they can be sent from the phone numbers of banks, governmental offices or popular internet services. Phishing leads to identity theft, cases of personal and financial losses and unauthorized access of computers (Alabdan, 2020).

1.2 Importance of Anti-Phishing Technologies

Today, because of the increased propensity to use digital means of communication, the share of phishing among cyber threats is regarded as large. This is so because we know that anti-phishing technologies are instrumental in preventing these attacks shown in Figure 1. Alone, they are practical in identifying, avoiding, and even lessening the effects of probable phishing threats. In practice, the measures against phishing which are really effective can be beneficial for protecting the personal information, avoiding the cases of the financial identity theft and maintaining the purity of the related data (Alkhalil et al., 2021).

1.3 Evolution of Phishing Techniques

Phishing is a command post that has in the recent past expanded and is gradually becoming sophisticated and thus hard to detect. Attempts at phishing before were even very easy to notice because of wrong choice of words and phrases, and rather clumsy spelling and punctuation, as well as rather vague and rather crude messages (Alabdan, 2020). But a majority of the present-day phishing consists of techniques referred to as spear phishing where the attackers use personalized messages in the phishing process shown in figure 2 and Common technique deployed to prevent phishing attack shown in Figure 3. Today's hackers are more intelligent and employ more sophisticated strategies like social engineering, the use of secure connection such as HTTPS to make the imitation sites to resemble the real ones and zero-day attack (Alkhalil et al., 2021).

2. TYPES OF PHISHING ATTACKS

Figure 2. Various Phishing Attacks

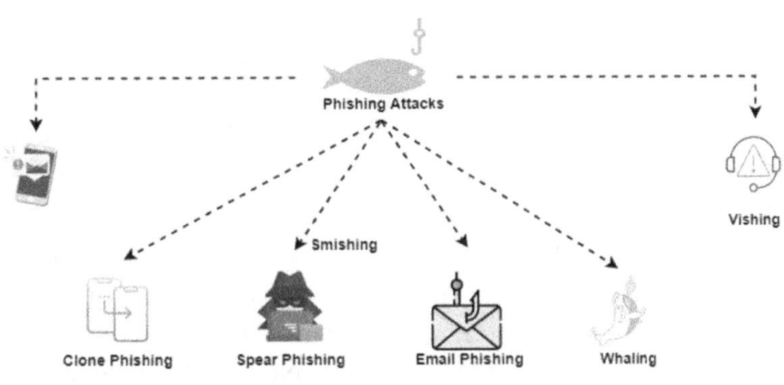

2.1 Spear Phishing

Spear phishing is a phishing attack that has a relatively small range of feathers and is often accompanied by malicious attachments and web site hyperlinks in the email. Second, the content of the email is selected with great attention to the receiver and if the receiver is not from the target or associated in any way, the text of the email would not have much significance (Gaurav et al., 2024). Cyber espionage can be as simple as spear phishing email sent to a few targeted individuals. Besides, if content of the e-mail is very special and is concerned only to definite branch of industry then this is evident of cyber espionage. The same argument can be made concerning a contaminated web site that displays data or offering that meets the need of an individual business, company, or targeted market (Merritt, n.d.).

Hence a way of distinguishing spear phishing and conventional phishing attacks is by the level of social engineering complex needed by the attacker. In the case of phishing attacks, the demographic, location, or frequently used banks in a region help the attacker in a targeted phishing attack (Gupta et al., 2025). However, for spear phishing attacks both the emails and attachments/links are not random products of social engineering but they are very consciously designed and developed with a view to being sent to the respective recipients of the emails (Merritt, n.d.).

2.2 Whaling

The term 'whale' is a Las Vegas term for the reckless gamblers who are willing to part with their money when they visit the casinos. This phishing attack is targeting a top employee, as an entrepreneur, a chief executive officer, or a chief financial officer, among others. This kind of attack is also known as the CEO fraud. The purpose of this attack lies in getting the data on the logins to the business accounts, for example, the HR management systems.

This attack is believed to be motivated by Industrial Espionage as lead employees possess large quantities of information, Ideas, designs, monitoring of expenses and revenue, financial data and so on. After gaining this information about a particular company, the attackers can cause damage to the firm because the data can be posted on the World Wide Web and made accessible to all comers and competitors or give rise to legal problems that would render the business insolvent (Sonowal, 2022).

2.3 Vishing and Smishing

Vishing is the criminal use of Internet Protocol based voice communication namely Voice over Internet Protocol, VoIP to con the target or the intended victim into parting with personal, financial or any other sensitive information with an intent of making a financial gain. The term here is compounded by taking the 'voice' and 'Phishing' to give what is referred to as 'Vishing'. Vishing profits from the reliability that the target has in the telephone service since he often is not privy to the fact that the scammer is able to use techniques like the caller ID (Shaw, 2020). In this kind of scam, fraudsters will engage spoofing and highly advanced automated systems. But since the success rate of conventional Phishing is shrinking, deceivers embrace Vishing so that they can easily get hold of the user's financial account numbers, passwords, and any other information that may be deemed relevant (Yeboah-Boateng & Amanor, 2014).

The name for smishing was derived from the test messaging technology known as Short Message Service (SMS). There are two major kinds of Smishing scams, the recipient is supposed to receive a text message in what appears to be from familiar sources such as bankers or system administrator (Srivastava et al., 2022). The second one involves you getting an urgent text message about your identity has been stolen or account number has been frozen, it then precedes to lead you to a website or a phone number to further input your account information (Zhou et al., 2024). The thieves upon receiving the information proceed and embezzle the money or open a new credit card in the victim's name. In a similar manner, the victim receives a very important text from probably a familiar or related person who might have enclosed an attachment. The attachment downloads a virus or malware into the victim's phone which in turn installs a rootkit or backdoor for the scammers to have full control (contacts, inbox messages and application on the phone etc.) on the victim's phone (Yeboah-Boateng & Amanor, 2014).

2.4 Clone Phishing

Clone phishing is a specific type of an internet phishing threat in which a facsimile or clone of a trusted email or website is developed and employed for the purpose of soliciting users for personal information or infected files (Ishtaiwi et al., 2024). This is because users are making to differentiate between the two since the former is a clone of the latter. This is why clone phishing is so effective; it uses people's trust in reliable websites and emails as its main weapon. Clone phishing scams employ more specific targets than a standard phishing attack and are always crafted for certain individuals or corporations. They are also indeed therefore more difficult to identify them and confront (Chaudhuri, 2023).

Figure 3. Common Techniques Deployed for Phishing Attacks

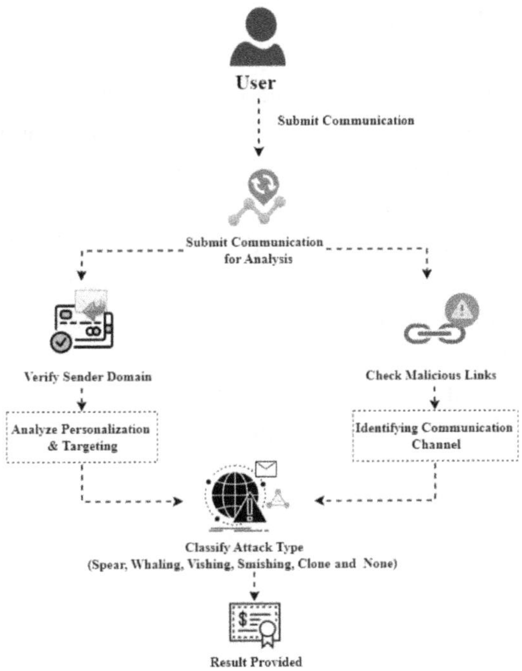

3. DETECTION TECHNIQUES

Detecting and dealing with security threats such as malware, phishing scams, and among others are well addressed through detection techniques. They include a range of approaches that can be referred to as techniques within each methodology that has strengths and limitations for the threat in question and the environment in which each technique maybe used (Jain & Gupta, 2022). There are several commonly used detection techniques such as:

3.1 Heuristic-Based Detection

This type of detection heavily depends on the algorithms, and it is based on the notion that even though a particular threat might not be known or categorized yet, one can detect that there is something wrong and potentially dangerous going on. Unlike the Signatures based detection where systems look for a specific pattern or the identity of a virus, Heuristics looks for actions or traits that are of a virus (Solanki & Vaishnav, n.d.). For instance, if a file tries to write to system files, or has recognized unusual network activity then it will be marked as suspicious.

This technique normally incorporates rule-based systems, which are usually developed to identify activities that are likely to be unlawful. While heuristic-based detection is powerful in identifying new or unknown threats, it has a downside. Main disadvantage of such software the presence of a critical factor that is characteristic of all programs of this kind – the possibility of fakes. It is important for the detection system to be tuned properly because even though the software is legitimate it may act like malware and thus be detected as such (Gupta & Jain, 2020).

3.2 Machine Learning Approaches

Machine learning plays a major role in detecting the phishing attacks using various approaches that will be helpful in preventing the phishing attacks. That is why machine learning (ML) has become so popular in the field of cybersecurity, it can improve and get better and that means it's alive (Harinahalli Lokesh & BoreGowda, 2021). The ML approaches can also be discussed in terms of the so-called supervised learning and unsupervised learning. Supervised learning entails the establishment of models from labelled data which has the implication that features of the model inputs (for instance features of network traffic) are usually linked with known outcomes (for instance whether or not the traffic is malicious). The model then learns normally and in a way deviates from this training when it is time to learn the difference between normal and malicious behaviour.

To calculate the accuracy of effectiveness of a phishing detection system we represent it as,

$$P_{det} = \frac{TP}{TP + FN} \quad \text{Equation 1}$$

Where:

- P_{det} is the probability of phishing detection.
- TP is the number of true positives (correctly identified phishing attempts).
- FN is the number of false negatives (missed phishing attempts).

The classification of machine learning on the other hand is as follows, the unsupervised learning does not use labelled data shown in figure 4. But it does not try to sort the data and gestures at various bundles of data that can be used to identify a potential security intrusion. A sub category of machine learning is deep learning, which utilizes neural networks with the ability to learn features from raw data and is inarguably very satisfactory in relating to compound or intricate patterns concerning various evils (D. M. Cao et al., 2024).

Figure 4. Phishing Detection using Machine Learning

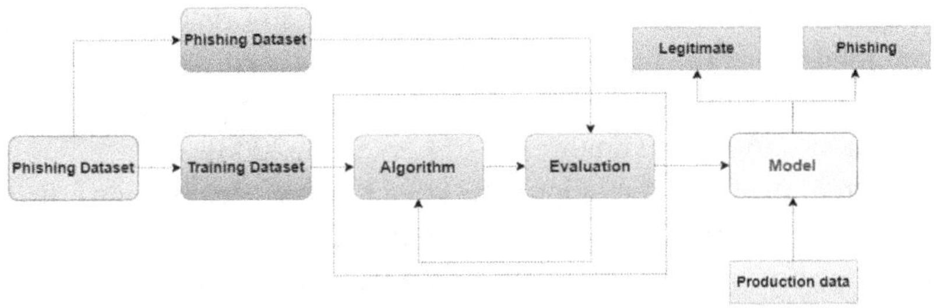

The largest advantage that is associated with the application of machine learning approaches is that there is progressively enhanced capability as the other new threats are recognized, making them immensely accurate (Ceschin et al., 2024). However, these techniques may require large training sets and are still highly time and space consuming in terms of CPU. They may also be sensitive to adversarial attack whereby the attacker will choose the data that he or she wishes the model to learn and output wrong results on.

3.3 Content Filtering and Analysis

Content filtering and analysis refer to the analysis of the data content, like the contents of an email, a file or web page for purposes of sieving out undesirable content. This technique sometimes uses keywords scanning which is the detection of specific words or phrases in contents linked to certain malice. For instance, the email message with phishing information contains such phrases as "urgent action required" or "account suspended".

The next method is called pattern matching; here, the content is searched for known patterns that are linked to threats such as code sequences in a file that match a known type of malware. In the same way, Natural Language Processing (NLP) may help in capturing text of e-mail or social network post to identify the phishing attempts considering its tone, used language and context (Islam & Abawajy, 2013).

Content filtering is one of the most powerful tools which allow to block known threats, however it has some drawbacks. For instance, it may fail at decrypting content or flag as malicious content that which is actually legitimate but washed with an algorithm of a specific feature (Magdy et al., 2022). That is why, tuning of the filters must be of primary importance to maintain the optimal level of the site's security along with the convenience of its usage.

3.4 Blacklisting and Whitelisting

Blacklisting and whitelisting are simplest of security measures that are useful for preventing certain actions or selectively permitting an action. Blacklisting means using a list of known bad guys, e.g. IP address, URLs or file hashes which are prohibited from accessing the system. This list is updated as soon as the other threats are identified in order to ensure that the members of the teams are aware of them (Shaji et al., 2019).

While whitelisting on the other hand, only permits authorized organizations to access the system. This method is more robust than the blacklisting method and is used where only a few applications or services are allowed to run. As for blacklists and whitelists, both of them can be updated in real time, with reference to the latest information on threats (Y. Cao et al., 2008).

Thus, the primary strength of blacklist-approach is that the approach is quite effective when it comes to the exclusion of clearly identified threats while its major weakness is the relative ineffectiveness against the threats that are not known or new. Whitelisting is a very powerful in terms of security since only trusted entities are allowed to run but lacks flexibility as it must be updated often to allow new legitimate items such as new application or services.

3.5 URL-Based Detection

URL-based detection deals with the identification of the malicious URLs that lead to phishing sites, downloads of malware and other security threats. This technique involves among others the method of reputation analysis in which URLs are scanned and matched against a list of blacklisted sites (Aung et al., n.d.). If URL has been previously linked with objectionable content it is either listed or banned.

In the case of phishing, algorithms are used for the analysis of URLs to recognize features characteristic for phishing attempts including the use of fake domain names or abnormal URLs. Furthermore, URL-based detection methods can initiate immediate scan of pages on first access thus enabling the detection of malicious content within genuine sites or even content delivered through URL redirections (Parekh et al., 2018).

Proxy-based detection is rather effective in blocking accesses to known dangerous sites; however, it strongly depends upon the quality of reputation databases. It can also be threatened by attackers who enter a URL shortener or suddenly changing domains so that they cannot be characterized rapidly.

Table 1. Phishing Detection Techniques and Their Accuracy

Technique	Detection Accuracy (%)	False Positive Rate (%)	Main Advantage
Heuristic-Based Detection	75	12	Quick and rule-based
Machine Learning Approaches	90	5	Adaptive, improves with data
Content Filtering	80	8	Focuses on email body and attachments
Blacklisting & Whitelisting	70	15	Straightforward and simple
URL-Based Detection	85	10	Effective for malicious links

In the above table the detection techniques including their detection accuracy and false positive rates are summarized shown in figure 5.

Figure 5. Phishing Detection Multi Techniques and the Accuracy

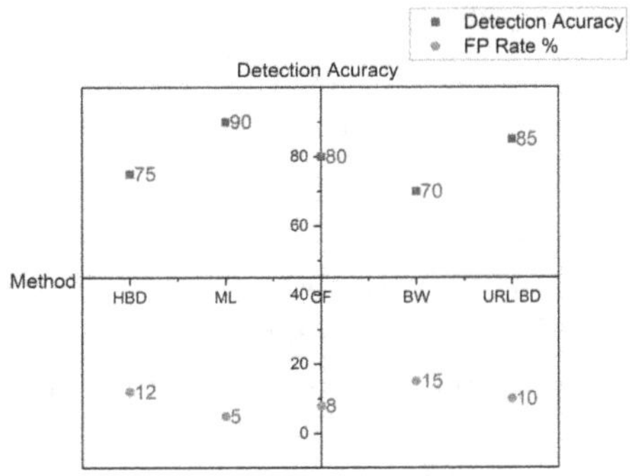

4. PREVENTION TOOLS

The following are several prevention tools that are handy and important in the field of making effective that horrible phishing attacks. Altogether, these tools help to identify possible phishing and discourage such attempts, thus lowering the probability of successful attacks.

4.1 Email Filtering Solutions

Email filtering solution is important to prevent from phishing attack, since most of the attacks originate through email. These solutions employ advanced search and analyses tools, machine learning mechanisms, to scan incoming e-mails and mark as spam or delete those with suspected content. Specific characteristics include parsing of previous phishing links, parsing of headers for signs of spoofing and lastly, the body content for any abnormal signatures usually associated with phishing attempts. Sophisticated emails filters can also be trained and be updated from time to time with a view of older and newer forms of phishing attacks. In addition, these solutions may also have quarantine features so as to check emails of the suspicion before getting into the inbox (Butt et al., 2023).

4.2 Browser-Based Anti-Phishing Extensions

Website add-ons are efficient enough and give browser protection against potential phishing sites during an online search. These are tools used to identify phishing websites and prevent users from accesses such sites on the Internet before the link is clicked. They work by filtering URL against a list of phishing websites that is updated regularly with its database and can either alert the user or prevent him/her from accessing the dangerous sites. Certain of the more complex plug-ins also include features that analyse the content of the current web page, such as fake login form, or a disguised domain name. Since these tools operate directly at the browser level, they assist the user in avoiding the creation of an attack vector purely by accident while going about their business on the Internet (Raffetseder et al., 2007).

4.3 Multi-Factor Authentication (MFA)

MFA is an effective security feature that aims at mitigating the effects of the phishing attacks since it ensures that users must enter, at least, two forms of identification before accessing an account or a system. Usually, MFA involves what the user knows, that is, the password and what the user has, or possesses that is, the smartphone or the hardware token, and could also include what the user is, that is, the fingerprint or the facial recognition. In the case where a phishing attack manages to capture the user's password, the other additional layers of authentication make it very difficult for the attacker to penetrate in the system (Shrivastava, 2012). MFA is most suitable in protecting critical systems & accounts, as it eliminates the chances of compromising the cred being the only manner.

4.4 SSL/TLS Certificates and HTTPS

SSL/TLS certificates are important for protecting user's connections to websites since information transmitted over the internet must be encoded in order to be protected from spying and manipulation. Websites that utilize the SSL/TLS certificates have the HTTPS protocol in front of the URL which gives a user the impression that the site is secure. Particularly important to prevent phishing attacks that use man-in-the-middle attacks and modify communication between a user and the actual site (Das & Samdaria, 2014). SSL/TLS certificates also assist users to authenticate a website since the browsers warn users that the site being used is not certified. Since SSL/TLS certificates also protect the login credentials and other information that are regarded as sensitive, the use of SSL/TLS certificates is very essential in averting phishing attacks.

4.5 Domain-Based Message Authentication, Reporting & Conformance

DMARC stands for Domain-Based Message Authentication, Reporting & Conformance and it is newly emerged email authentication mechanism that can protect domain owners from phishing attacks through the usage of the e-mail. DMARC extends existing methods of email authentication like SPF and DKIM and offers a way to domain owners to state what should become of the messages arriving at the domain's mail servers if they do not pass DMARC validation (Nightingale, 2017).

When the domain owner activates DMARC, the suspected e-mail can either be delivered to the quarantine or rejected in its entirety. DMARC also helps to provide report on the handling of emails by the domain owner, thus helping to detect misuse of a domain by attackers. Since it controls the stringencies policies in dealing with emails from a domain, DMARC reduces the possibilities of successful phishing attacks. In addition, DMARC assists in combating domain spoofing, a condition whereby a malicious person alters the field of an electronic mail message heading and demonstrates that the message came from somebody it actually did not. This capability makes DMARC as a very effective instrument in the daily fight against phishing, which safeguards both the sender and intended recipient of any e-mails from potentially fraudulent businesses (Kucherawy & Zwicky, 2015).

5. EMERGING TECHNOLOGIES

5.1 AI and Deep Learning in Phishing Detection

AI and deep learning have emerged as effective tools in the identification and prevention of phishing attacks or threats where new and more effective process, analysis, and recognition methods can be applied in high precision and at a significantly high speed. Phishing detection techniques used earlier are rule and signature based, so they cannot be very effective against new phishers and new types of phishes. AI and deep learning, however, can offer the solutions that are dynamic and have the capability to be adapted as per the requirement.

- **AI and Machine Learning Algorithms:** Datasets comprising of real and fake emails are used in Machine Learning models that are embedded to identify certain patterns such as keywords that are suspicious, sending pattern and metadata that are normally off. A supervised learning models are conducted with the help of labelled data while unsupervised models are used to identify anomalies without training the data (Basit et al., 2021). These solutions can be updated through continued interaction with their environment making reinforcement learning an effective approach to enhance the detection capability of a system.
- **Deep Learning for Phishing Detection:** Far more advanced methods like neural networks make it possible to analyse the content of emails as well as links and attachments in detail. For instance, deep learning models can judge a context, semantic, and intent of messages, which means that they can filter out real and potentially dangerous messages, even if cyber attackers use different types of message obfuscation (Do et al., 2022).

Benefits:

- Increased effectiveness of detecting the emails with phishing intention.
- Flexibility to the new and the latest strategies that the phisher takes in the actual phishing process.
- High degree of compatibility with large datasets of high dimensionality.

5.2 Blockchain for Email Authentication

Blockchain technology applied in the context of email authentication can become a global distributed database that will further minimize the threat of phishing by verifying the sender's identity shown in Algorithm 1. As such its inherent characteristics of decentralization, immutability and ability to achieve consensus make it a perfect technology for rebuilding faith and confidence in digital communications (Choudhari & Das, 2021).

Algorithm 1: Blockchain-Based Email Authentication

Input:	**Email(E), Sender's Private Key S_k, Blockchain Ledger (BC)**
Output:	**Email Verified as Authentic or Not**
Start:	
	I. Sender Email Authentication:
	// Sender writes an email (E)
	// A digital signature can be procured by encrypting the hash of the email and this is produced using S_k
	// Attach signature to the email
	II. Add Transaction to Blockchain:
	• Record the transaction (email hash + signature) on the blockchain ledger (BC)
	• With this feature, public key is stored on the blockchain and can be retrieved in the future for confirmation purposes
	III. Recipient Email Verification:
	• Recipient gets an email with the signature attached to it
	• Retrieve the sender's public key (S_k) from the Blockchain ledger (BC)
	• Decrypt the email hash entered in the email using the public key
	• Perform again hashing on the content of the email and compare the hash with the decrypted one
	IV. Final Verification
	• If the hashes are matching, then the email is authentic
	• If not, then the email must be marked as phishing
End	

- **Decentralized Verification of Sender Identity:** Blockchain can be utilised to form a distributed secure list of verified email senders. Whenever an email is dispatched, the said email message is made to leave an indelible digital fingerprint on the blockchain alongside other relevant information like date, time, and recipient address. To this ledger, recipients can prove the authenticity of the sender of the email and is therefore not a phony account.
- **Immutable Record Keeping:** Since data recorded once in the blockchain cannot be altered, it means that it cannot be tampered with. Once the details of the email are stored in the blockchain it becomes immutable therefore making it possible to detect spoofed emails or even modified ones in real time.
- **Smart Contracts for Automated Authentication:** Email verification is one of the activities that can be performed by smart contracts. For instance, a smart contract can be programmed to check the incoming emails with filters to reject the emails that do not meet the acceptable levels of security indicators, thus eliminating the underlying risks posed by phishing (Andryukhin, 2019).

Benefits:

- Accurate linking of email to its respective folders, resulting to higher security and integrity of email communications.
- A decrease or total elimination of the impersonation or spoofing of emails.

- New improvement of trust among users of e-mail with open verification.

5.3 Phishing Awareness and Simulation Tools

Phishing awareness and simulation tools are centered round the human element of cyber security, this is the training of users on the existence of phishing threats and exposing them to ways of handling such threats (Ciupe & Orza, 2024).

Table 2. Phishing Awareness Training tools

Tool Name	Features Offered	Target Audience	Effectiveness in Awareness (%)
PhishMe	Real-time phishing simulation, reporting	Corporate employees	85
Cofense PhishMe	Simulation and reporting	Enterprise-level training	90
KnowBe4	Gamifield learning, phishing tests	General users	80
Wombat Security Technologies	Phishing simulation, training modules	Corporate and SMBs	78

The above table 2 shows the phishing awareness training tools that they focus on the various products that are used to increase the user's awareness of the actual phishing simulations and training tools.

- **Phishing Awareness Training Programs:** It is also noteworthy to mention that such programs offer users engaging practicing Exercises that show the users how to filter phishing attempts, this includes unusual URL, Sender Detail, and Content. Training normally consists of segments on how to proceed when receiving emails and how to identify social engineering.
- **Phishing Simulation Platforms**: Employers have also employed the use of simulation techniques where they relay genuine phishing emails but with the intention of training the employees. These simulations require the employees to be very careful to distinguish and report cases of phishing. It assists the organizations in evaluating the level of susceptibility for any of these incidents and identifying areas that requires specific training.
- **Automated Feedback and Reporting:** Most simulation apply real-time feedback on users who interact with simulated phishing email, informing the user what they failed to notice and how they can better identify the emails. The detailed reporting option can help organizations monitor trends and progress in time also the effectiveness of the awareness programs can be determined.

Benefits:

- A better understanding of potential users and anticipation of the risk to be threatened by phishing attacks.
- Edges possibility to decrease the chances of becoming a victim of phishing as the detection abilities increase.
- Largely tangible enhancements of organisational readiness against phishing.

6. PHISHING ATTACK CAMPAIGNS AND THEIR REAL-WORLD IMPACT

6.1 Phishing Campaigns: Methods and Motives

The attack campaigns are no longer as crude as they were a few years back, instead they are more refined. Cybercriminals are no longer solely oriented on owning money from the targeted victims but rather gaining and holding sensitive information, spying or even continuing to control the victim in one or multiple aspects (Scott, 2023). This subsection examines common phishing campaigns, including:

- **Business Email Compromise (BEC):** Advanced phishing in which organizational leaders' mailboxes are targeted and used to approve the scam's transactions.
- **Credential Harvesting Campaigns:** When cybercriminals create emails that users open and get them to enter login details to other email accounts, bank accounts or any corporate accounts this paves way for other attacks to happen.
- **Phishing-as-a-Service (PhaaS):** A new trend on which cyber criminals offer phishing kits and platforms to anybody who wants to get successful in phishing.

6.2 Blockchain for Secure Email Authentication in Enterprises

Cyber criminals use phishing attacks as a tool that is very dangerous to businesses, governments and individuals. The monetary loss due to phishing is humongous and global research suggests it running into billions yearly. Large organizations have been found to experience intangible losses which include legal implications, loss of image of the brand and loss of clientele trust among others (Habib et al., 2022).

- **Monetary Losses:** Case studies that present figures outlay that demonstrates the amount of loss incurred by different organizations due to phishing scams and how million-dollar businesses have been lost solely due to phishing scams.
- **Productivity Losses:** Phishing attacks tend to result in significant business disruption as firms respond to, contain, and then repair from a cyberattack.
- **Regulatory Fines:** Failure to protect data under laws like GDPR, HIPAA if the organization has succumbed to a phishing attack will cost the organization handsome amount of fines.

6.3 Social Engineering and Psychological Manipulation

Phishing campaigns are effective mostly because they rely on socio-psychological factors to work (*Social Engineering*, n.d.).

- **Fear and Urgency Tactics:** How attackers take advantage of their victims for example, through developing a sense of emergency for instance a suspended account, an urgent payment to be made.
- **Authority and Trust Exploitation:** The email sender usually attempts to fake identities of the trustworthy person (for instance, a CEO, a government officer) or an organization (for instance, banks, service providing companies).

- **Emotional Manipulation:** A few of the examples of phishing attacks and particularly the ones that are aimed at individuals for some time may be sparked by fear, by the desire to gain more wealth, or by curiosity to follow the link provided in the phishing mail.

Knowledge of these strategies is essential in enumerating and proposing an efficient phishing awareness and defence strategies.

7. CHALLENGES AND LIMITATIONS

Even with all these developments in limiting phishing, organizations are still having it difficult in enforcing and sustaining the right anti-phishing mechanisms. This section discusses the basic problems and or rather the weaknesses in this section.

7.1 Evolving Phishing Techniques

(Irani et al., 2008) presents that phishing threat actors are not passive, and they are constantly changing their strategies in order to defeat even the most advanced filters, which for this reason is not a dormant threat.

Advanced Phishing Tactics:

Social Engineering: With reference to the real-life attacks, the attackers apply specialized methods of the social engineering including the spear phishing and whaling. Such attacks rely on such information as who the target is, their workplace, interests, or activities within the past days, week or months among others hence are hard to trace (Andrić et al., 2016).

AI-Driven Phishing: Criminals are leveraging AI especially for email phishing because it will enable the automation process and scale up. It is easier to create well written and from the look of it almost genuine like the phishing emails are attempting to emulate and therefore, the users and the detection systems may not easily distinguish the fakes from the real deal.

Phishing as a Service (PhaaS): Now criminals are selling phishing services and products as ready-made phishing kits and emails. This has made the entry of less skilful attackers easier and boosted the number of phishing incidents across the world.

Continuous Innovation in Attack Methods: An individual attacker or a group of attackers also keep on looking for ways and means on how to get into the weak areas of emails, web browsers and other social and communication platforms such as social networks and messaging systems. When it comes to detection there is a continuous enhancement of the methods while on the other hand the methods used by the attackers are also enhanced to avoid being detected (Alshamrani et al., 2019).

Challenges of Zero-Day Phishing Attacks: Obviously, zero-day phishing attacks, which use previously unidentified weaknesses, are rather difficult to protect against since these types of solutions rely on previously unidentified tactics and methods.

7.2 False Positives and Negatives in Detection Systems

Like for any other system, the ones designed for the detection of phishing emails, with or without artificial intelligence and machine learning algorithms, are not without flaws. These come with problems of false positives and false negatives, which affects their usefulness and influence user confidence.

False Positives (Incorrect Identification of Legitimate Emails as Phishing):

User Frustration: If normal emails are reported as phishing, it will be very irritating and time wasting for the users who will need to unspam these messages. They also pointed out that after time, due to repeated false positives users can get desensitised starting to disregard the warnings.

Business Disruption: In organizations, false positives have implications to missed communication, delayed projects or in extreme case lead to loss of money this is because time-sensitive or critical emails may end up being labelled and quarantined as spam.

False Positive Rate: To assess the accuracy of a detection system by calculating the rate at which legitimate emails are falsely marked as phishing.

$$FPR = \frac{FP}{FP + TN} \text{ Equation 2}$$

Where:

- *FP* is the number of false positives (legitimate emails incorrectly marked as phishing).
- *TN* is the number of true negatives (correctly identified legitimate emails).

False Negatives (Failure to Identify a Phishing Email):

Increased Risk of Phishing Incidents: But if phishing emails manage to get past detectors they can result in an attack, for example, account compromise, unauthorized access, or data loss. False negatives are most not safe for the users of the system as they are left with the impression that all the incoming emails have been properly checked and are safe.

Underreporting of Phishing Threats: For this reason, if the phishing attempts are not detected, then the phishing activity level that an organization is experiencing can be greatly underrepresented, thus a poor response and underfunding of security measures (Dalvi et al., 2020).

False negative rate: Which refers to the ability or the tendency of a given system that is designed for detecting phishing emails to miss the actual ones. In similar terms, it shows you how many times an organization fails to spot a phishing assault.

$$FNR = \frac{FN}{FN + TP} \text{ Equation 3}$$

Where:

- **FN** is the number of false negatives (phishing attempts that were missed by the system).
- **TP** is the number of true positives (correctly identified phishing attempts).

Balancing Precision and Recall:

Precision: Optimization of precision means minimizing the number of false positive leading to more accurate detection of actual phishing threats. Nevertheless, paying much attention to its accuracy raises the rate of false negatives.

Recall: Maximizing recall does this in an effort to capture as many possible phishing attempts while failing to realize that this will increase the False Positive rate. Another big problem of anti-phishing systems is the stability of setting up the precise balance between precision and Recall.

The F1 Score is a combined measure of precision and recall, providing a balanced assessment of the detection system's accuracy.

$$F1 = 2 \times \frac{\text{Precision} \times \text{Recall}}{\text{Precision} + \text{Recall}} \quad \text{Equation 4}$$

This formula is especially useful when precision and recall need to be balanced, such as in detecting phishing emails.

7.3 User Awareness and Behavioural Factors

Just as it is always the case even with the best technologies there is always that aspect of human error that poses a serious threat to any way of protecting against phishing. Security and level of consciousness of the user have a large role to on non-phishing attacks, yet many users do not have the necessary knowledge or conscientiousness to avoid such attacks (Arachchilage & Love, 2014).

Inconsistent User Training and Awareness:

Training Fatigue: There is also the danger of employees paying less attention or becoming indifferent to the phasing awareness training after some time or if the training is more of theoretical and less practical. This can result to making people become used to this new type of phishing and therefore fewer chances of people being actual aware of phishing attempts.

Lack of Realistic Training: This leads to the use of overly basic or old school examples in most of the phishing awareness programs since they do not depict the modern techniques employed by hackers. In real-life use, for this reason, users may not be very quick to identify the latest phishing techniques.

Human Vulnerability to Social Engineering:

Emotional Manipulation: Phishing attacks rely on such feelings such as, fear, time pressure, or curiosity of the users. Customers can be led to incorrect conclusions especially at the time when the phishing email seems to be coming from the customers' manager or any other partner who is trusted by the customers.

Cognitive Overload: Working in the modern world, several people do not have enough time to make a detailed analysis of every email, especially if the working day is full of various tasks and due dates. This is used by attackers by sending phishing emails at office hour when users are busy concentrating at work.

User Trust and Overconfidence:

Trust in Technology: Users may get complacent and think, for example, 'I am protected from phishing' because the technologies in place reclaim that they would catch all the threats. This overreliance to technology, it means that there is reduced attention and therefore, the possibility of being trapped in a phishing scam is very high.

Overconfidence in Personal Judgment: Some users could think that are very smart in avoiding those phishing schemes and might easily be complacent the next time they receive an email or received a link.

8. FUTURE TRENDS

Thus, the range of anti-phishing technologies is expanding with the progress of in techniques that phishers use. Some of the trends evident as likely to develop and impact the challenges of detecting and preventing phishing in future include the following.

8.1 Predictive Phishing Detection

The next level of preventive e-security is the predictive phishing detection. The main approach of this approach is on the ability of analysing predictive analytics and the use of machine learning models as a means of identifying the next probable attack action of the phishing attackers and this puts organizations in a better position to counter their actions shown in Algorithm 2.

Algorithm 2: Predictive Phishing Detection

Input:	**Historical phishing data D, Current email traffic C**
Output:	**Phishing prediction score, Alert for potential phishing attack**
Start:	
	I. Data Collection:
	• Collect historical data D: {timestamp, sender, content, URLs, behaviour patterns}
	• Clean and preprocess the dataset
	• Extract relevant features
	II. Feature Engineering:
	• Identify key phishing indicators (domains, keywords, URL patterns, time-based features)
	• Create structured dataset for the model
	III. Time-Series Analysis:
	• Model frequency of past attacks for future forecasting
	IV. Model Training:
	• Train ML model (e.g., Decision Tree, Random Forest) using historical data D
	• Use time-series data to predict phishing trends

continued on following page

Algorithm 2: Predictive Phishing Detection

Continued

Input:	Historical phishing data D, Current email traffic C
	V. Phishing Attack Prediction:
	• For each new email in C, calculate phishing probability score using the trained model
	• Incorporate time-series forecast to adjust score based on high-risk periods
	VI. Alert Generation:
	• If phishing probability > threshold, generate alert for administrators/users
	• Provide recommended mitigation actions
	VII. Model Update:
	• Continuously update model with new phishing data
	• Re-train model periodically to adapt to emerging phishing strategies
End	

- **AI and Machine Learning for Prediction:**

Behavioural Analysis: (Daneshkhah et al., 2020) Presents some of the patterns that are observed regarding the email traffic, users and phishing incidences can be used to train machine learning algorithms for the detection of phishing attacks. Such algorithms identify features that may indicate that a phishing attack is on its way, such as unusual frequency of sending messages or users behaviour.

Real-Time Threat Prediction: Real-time threats can be evaluated using predictive models and the moment when the user will receive the phishing email is not reached. Further, the newer threats appear, and the more often new types of phishing attacks are identified, the closer to real the given model becomes.

- **Predictive Models Based on Historical Data:** There are two broad classes of approaches, one of which relies on learning the characteristics of known phishing attacks and can then learn characteristics of an emerging phishing attempt. For example, if there is a phishing campaign aimed at several organizations it will have some sort of pattern and the model can alert potential threats from that pattern (Orunsolu et al., 2022).
- **Context-Aware Detection:** Some reliable predictive systems are getting context-aware which basically helps in the task of recognizing mode of phishing based on the organization where it occurs. For instance, certain e-mails that come across as genuine in one sector (for instance a financial institution) are considered as phisher scams in another sector (such as a healthcare organization) in light of industry specific threat models.

Benefits:

- Using predictive systems, organizations can go a notch higher and prevent the occurrence of phishing attacks as the program actively prevents the attack.
- Predictive detection enables a user to be informed about the onset of Phishing attacks even before one occurs hence leading to a reduced window of exposure.

8.2 Integration with Cyber Threat Intelligence

However, Cyber threat intelligence (CTI) is slowly being incorporated into the phishing enticing systems to improve on the detection and response of phishing attacks (Brooks, 2023).

Leveraging Threat Intelligence Feeds:

- Threat intelligence feeds give information on new phishing attacks, malicious domain, and TTPs in actual time. Thus, using such information, anti-phishing tools can quickly identify new phishing campaigns and help protect users from newly identified threats.
- Companies have joined the international cybersecurity communities to discuss pertinent information on new phishing trends as well as attacks. This collective approach enables the phishing detection systems to be up to date with the current threats thus enhancing the detection capability.

Automated Threat Intelligence Integration:

- **Security Information and Event Management (SIEM) Systems:** The integration of phishing detection to the SIEM platforms ensures that the identified phishing threats are automatically shared with the various parts of the organization's security architecture. If a phishing attempt is legit then it can cause emails from sender to be blocked or send it directly to the quarantine.
- **Incident Response Automation:** integration of CTI with phishing known detection systems means that if an attacker is detected then the incident response is initiated. For instance, it may notify security personnel, quarantine users or disable all the identified compromised accounts.

Phishing-Specific Threat Intelligence Platforms (TIPs):

- Some TIPs are designed to compile and digest information on the incidents of phishing an organisation obtains from other sources and provides an understanding of phishing campaigns. Such platforms are able to detect the trends in phishing, including the emergence of new attack types, for example, smishing or frequency of using particular social engineering techniques.

Benefits:

- CTI gives any organization an advantage over the attackers by giving information about new phishing attacks and methodologies.
- Automated Protection: Integration with SIEM and TIP platforms helps to prevent or neutralise phishing without user engagement.

8.3 The Role of User Education and Training

Thus, one of the key priorities in the context of ever-dynamic phishing attacks will always be the focus on the user. Although modern technology is capable of identifying many phishing risks, the behaviour of the user is still an acute weak point that the attacker uses (Berens et al., 2022).

Gamified Phishing Awareness Programs: That is why a number of organizations are using gamified phishing training to attract the users in a more entertaining way (Scholefield & Shepherd, 2019). As with any e-learning approach, it is possible to reprint important messages, such as the final reminder: 'You have just successfully completed the program', with a quiz, an example or a reward reminding employees to be careful with phishing and becoming more mindful of this issue.

Phishing Simulations: The practice of carrying out exercises for the identification of phishing further assists the users to detect such attempts at the same time when they are not real. These are similar to actual phishing attacks, but they are used to help a user figure out proper course of action without the risk of opening his computer to the attacker.

Continuous and Adaptive Training:

- **Ongoing Education:** Instead of conducting one-time single-phased training, organizations are coming up with extensive training modules that constantly update due to continuously evolving phishing threats. (Berens et al., 2022) presents some of the measures that are taken include training employees on new phishing scams that circulate within the organisation, as well as conducting a quiz from time to time.
- **Personalized Training:** With the help of IT training for prevention of phishing scams, restricted access control can be implemented to create. Usability and effectiveness of ongoing security awareness training can now be optimized as training can now be targeted at particular user according to their risk profile and job responsibilities. For instance, most managerial staff and top executives can be trained on how to prevent and avoid smishing and whaling attacks and on the other hand, customer care employees can undergo training on how to resist social engineering.
- **Phishing Reporting Tools and Culture:**
- **Integrated Reporting Systems:** Many current e-mail clients have simple click-through buttons which can be used to report any attempts at phishing. One can thus educate users to forward suspected phishing e-mails to a central mailbox in order to gather relevant data to fight phishing, which in turn will help to protect the whole organization (Sarker et al., 2024).
- **Building a Culture of Security Awareness:** It is quite important that there is a high emphasis placed on the culture of security awareness. Thus, organizations are stepping towards making the identification of phishing activity an everyone's affair by providing information on phishing threats and encouraging users to report suspicious activity.

Benefits:

- Employees trained are the last resort against Phishing in addition to technical controls in the organization.
- Increased user awareness results in more filtration of the phishing attempts thus making organizations respond to the threats quicker.

9. CONCLUSION

9.1 Summary of Key Points

In this chapter, the various dimensions of phishing attacks as well as the measures in the form of technologies that have been used to counter them have been discussed. Some of the different types of phishing include spear phishing, whaling, vishing, smishing, and clone phishing therefore remain dangerous to those in individuals and organizations. Criminals have adapted their approaches over the years and this makes phishing one of the oldest cyber threats (Milletary, n.d.). This paper has also discussed several detection methods such as heuristic-based detection, machine learning, content filtering, blacklisting or whitelisting and URL filtering which are employed to address and reduce the effects of phishing.

As it has been described earlier, different emergent technologies are important to improve the abilities of recognizing phishing schemes (Alkhalil et al., 2021). Machine learning, artificial intelligence and deep learning are being employed to address sophisticated phishing attacks and blockchain mechanism is used to secure the email communication through better authentication techniques. Furthermore, improved awareness and novel simulation techniques have been established to provide excellent results and decrease the effectiveness of the subsequent phishing campaigns as a result.

Phishing attacks are constantly evolving and the same goes for the detection systems where there are constant false positives and false negatives which may lessen the effectiveness of the systems (Qabajeh et al., 2018). Furthermore, while there is always social behaviour that is still an issue because the user is always the weakest link of any organization.

9.2 The Way Forward in Anti-Phishing Technologies

Anticipating the future trends in the development of phishing activities in the future, it is possible to discuss that the most effective anti-phishing technologies are the ones that are based on usage of new approaches both in terms of technologies and personal users' awareness (Alnajim & Munro, 2009). Since the conventional mode of detecting phishing is proving to be unproductive, a new trend that is emerging now is the use of AI and ML to come up with a model to predict phishing. Due to the availability of up-to-date data, and analysis components it becomes quite easy for these systems to identify the, and stop the phishing threats before they get to the end users. Such a strategic move will also be instrumental in lowering response time and generally ensuring that phishing campaigns have minimal outcomes.

There is another significant progress that the addition of phishing detection systems to cyberthreat intelligence or CTI. Real-time sharing of intelligence helps an organization to monitor new tactics of the phishing threats as they develop. This integration will make it possible to automatically identify the newly emerged threats in forms of domains and email addresses and other types of phishing that emergent in the system.

Hence, user education will remain an indispensable function in efforts towards the prevention of phishing. While the examples of using simulated phishing emails and game-based awareness training are gaining popularity among organisations, the targets of the attackers will be able to identify the phishing attempt. Phishing awareness training performed in conjunction with simple to use phishing reporting tools will help strengthen the users as the second level of protection (Miranda, 2018).

Altogether, it can be stated that the further evolution of anti-phishing technologies is possible in case of using the beneficial combination of sophisticated machine learning algorithms, real-time threat intelligence, and progressive user training. A proactive, progressive strategy in place will guarantee that any organization can efficiently penetrate, avoid, and respond to any phishing attack intended to compromise the organization's data and its users.

REFERENCES

Alabdan, R. (2020). Phishing Attacks Survey: Types, Vectors, and Technical Approaches. *Future Internet*, 12(10), 10. Advance online publication. DOI: 10.3390/fi12100168

Alkhalil, Z., Hewage, C., Nawaf, L., & Khan, I. (2021). Phishing Attacks: A Recent Comprehensive Study and a New Anatomy. *Frontiers of Computer Science*, 3, 563060. Advance online publication. DOI: 10.3389/fcomp.2021.563060

Alnajim, A., & Munro, M. (2009). An Anti-Phishing Approach that Uses Training Intervention for Phishing Websites Detection. *2009 Sixth International Conference on Information Technology: New Generations*, 405–410. DOI: 10.1109/ITNG.2009.109

Alshamrani, A., Myneni, S., Chowdhary, A., & Huang, D. (2019). A Survey on Advanced Persistent Threats: Techniques, Solutions, Challenges, and Research Opportunities. *IEEE Communications Surveys & Tutorials, 21*(2), 1851–1877. *IEEE Communications Surveys and Tutorials*. Advance online publication. DOI: 10.1109/COMST.2019.2891891

Andrić, J., Oreški, D., & Kišasondi, T. (2016). Analysis of phishing attacks against students. *2016 39th International Convention on Information and Communication Technology, Electronics and Microelectronics (MIPRO)*, 1423–1429. DOI: 10.1109/MIPRO.2016.7522363

Andryukhin, A. A. (2019). Phishing Attacks and Preventions in Blockchain Based Projects. *2019 International Conference on Engineering Technologies and Computer Science (EnT)*, 15–19. DOI: 10.1109/EnT.2019.00008

Arachchilage, N. A. G., & Love, S. (2014). Security awareness of computer users: A phishing threat avoidance perspective. *Computers in Human Behavior*, 38, 304–312. DOI: 10.1016/j.chb.2014.05.046

Aung, E. S., Zan, C. T., & Yamana, H. (n.d.). *A Survey of URL-based Phishing Detection*.

Basit, A., Zafar, M., Liu, X., Javed, A. R., Jalil, Z., & Kifayat, K. (2021). A comprehensive survey of AI-enabled phishing attacks detection techniques. *Telecommunication Systems*, 76(1), 139–154. DOI: 10.1007/s11235-020-00733-2 PMID: 33110340

Berens, B. M., Dimitrova, K., Mossano, M., & Volkamer, M. (2022). Phishing awareness and education – When to best remind? *Proceedings 2022 Symposium on Usable Security*. Symposium on Usable Security, San Diego, CA. DOI: 10.14722/usec.2022.23075

Brooks, D. A. (2023). *Cyber Threat Intelligence Driven Phishing Awareness Programs: A Qualitative Exploratory Study* [Ph.D., Capitol Technology University]. https://www.proquest.com/docview/2832622897/abstract/8265415084CD4A91PQ/1

Butt, U. A., Amin, R., Aldabbas, H., Mohan, S., Alouffi, B., & Ahmadian, A. (2023). Cloud-based email phishing attack using machine and deep learning algorithm. *Complex & Intelligent Systems*, 9(3), 3043–3070. DOI: 10.1007/s40747-022-00760-3 PMID: 35668732

Cao, D. M., Sayed, M. A., Islam, M. T., Mia, M. T., Ayon, E. H., Ghosh, B. P., Ray, R. K., & Raihan, A. (2024). Advanced Cybercrime Detection: A Comprehensive Study on Supervised and Unsupervised Machine Learning Approaches Using Real-world Datasets. *Journal of Computer Science and Technology Studies*, 6(1), 1. Advance online publication. DOI: 10.32996/jcsts.2024.6.1.5

Cao, Y., Han, W., & Le, Y. (2008). Anti-phishing based on automated individual white-list. *Proceedings of the 4th ACM Workshop on Digital Identity Management*, 51–60. DOI: 10.1145/1456424.1456434

Ceschin, F., Botacin, M., Bifet, A., Pfahringer, B., Oliveira, L. S., Gomes, H. M., & Grégio, A. (2024). Machine Learning (In) Security: A Stream of Problems. *Digital Threats, 5*(1), 9:1-9:32. DOI: 10.1145/3617897

Chaudhuri, A. (2023). Clone Phishing: Attacks and Defenses. *International Journal of Scientific and Research Publications*, 13(4). Advance online publication. DOI: 10.29322/IJSRP.13.04.2023.p13626

Choudhari, S., & Das, S. (2021). Spam E-mail Identification Using Blockchain Technology. *2021 International Conference on Communication, Control and Information Sciences (ICCISc), 1*, 1–5. DOI: 10.1109/ICCISc52257.2021.9485018

Ciupe, A., & Orza, B. (2024). Reinforcing Cybersecurity Awareness through Simulated Phishing Attacks: Findings from an HEI Case Study. *2024 IEEE Global Engineering Education Conference (EDUCON)*, 1–4. DOI: 10.1109/EDUCON60312.2024.10578700

Dalvi, S., Gressel, G., & achuthan, D. (2020; Vol. 9). Tuning the False Positive Rate / False Negative Rate with Phishing Detection Models. In International Journal of Engineering and Advanced Technology., DOI: 10.35940/ijeat.A1002.1291S52019

Daneshkhah, A., Jahankhani, H., Forouzan, H., Montasari, R., & Hosseinian-Far, A. (2020). Behavioural Analytics: A Preventative Means for the Future of Policing. In Jahankhani, H., Akhgar, B., Cochrane, P., & Dastbaz, M. (Eds.), *Policing in the Era of AI and Smart Societies* (pp. 83–96). Springer International Publishing., DOI: 10.1007/978-3-030-50613-1_3

Das, M. L., & Samdaria, N. (2014). On the security of SSL/TLS-enabled applications. *Applied Computing and Informatics*, 10(1), 68–81. DOI: 10.1016/j.aci.2014.02.001

Do, N. Q., Selamat, A., Krejcar, O., Herrera-Viedma, E., & Fujita, H. (2022). Deep Learning for Phishing Detection: Taxonomy, Current Challenges and Future Directions. *IEEE Access, 10*, 36429–36463. IEEE Access. DOI: 10.1109/ACCESS.2022.3151903

Gaurav, A., Chui, K. T., Arya, V., Attar, R. W., Bansal, S., Alhomoud, A., & Psannis, K. (2024). Optimized AI-Driven Semantic Web Approach for Enhancing Phishing Detection in E-Commerce Platforms. [IJSWIS]. *International Journal on Semantic Web and Information Systems*, 20(1), 1–13. DOI: 10.4018/IJSWIS.359767

Gupta, B. B., Gaurav, A., Attar, R. W., Arya, V., Bansal, S., Alhomoud, A., & Chui, K. T. (2024). A Hybrid CNN-Brown-Bear Optimization Framework for Enhanced Detection of URL Phishing Attacks. *Computers, Materials & Continua*, 81(3), 4853–4874. DOI: 10.32604/cmc.2024.057138

Gupta, B. B., Gaurav, A., Attar, R. W., Arya, V., Bansal, S., Alhomoud, A., & Chui, K. T. (2025). A hybrid Ant Lion Optimization algorithm based lightweight deep learning framework for cyber attack detection in IoT environment. *Computers & Electrical Engineering*, 122, 109944. DOI: 10.1016/j.compeleceng.2024.109944

Gupta, B. B., & Jain, A. K. (2020). Phishing Attack Detection using a Search Engine and Heuristics-based Technique. *Journal of Information Technology Research*, 13(2), 94–109. DOI: 10.4018/JITR.2020040106

Habib, G., Sharma, S., Ibrahim, S., Ahmad, I., Qureshi, S., & Ishfaq, M. (2022). Blockchain Technology: Benefits, Challenges, Applications, and Integration of Blockchain Technology with Cloud Computing. *Future Internet*, 14(11), 11. Advance online publication. DOI: 10.3390/fi14110341

Harinahalli Lokesh, G., & BoreGowda, G. (2021). Phishing website detection based on effective machine learning approach. *Journal of Cyber Security Technology*, 5(1), 1–14. DOI: 10.1080/23742917.2020.1813396

Irani, D., Webb, S., Giffin, J., & Pu, C. (2008). Evolutionary study of phishing. *2008 eCrime Researchers Summit*, 1–10. DOI: 10.1109/ECRIME.2008.4696967

Ishtaiwi, A., Ali, A. M., Al-Qerem, A., Sabahean, M., Alzubi, B., Almomani, A., Alauthman, M., Aldweesh, A., & Khaldy, M. A. A. (2024). Next-Gen Phishing Defense Enhancing Detection With Machine Learning and Expert Whitelisting/Blacklisting. [IJCAC]. *International Journal of Cloud Applications and Computing*, 14(1), 1–17. DOI: 10.4018/IJCAC.353301

Islam, R., & Abawajy, J. (2013). A multi-tier phishing detection and filtering approach. *Journal of Network and Computer Applications*, 36(1), 324–335. DOI: 10.1016/j.jnca.2012.05.009

Jain, A. K., & Gupta, B. B. (2022). A survey of phishing attack techniques, defence mechanisms and open research challenges. *Enterprise Information Systems*, 16(4), 527–565. DOI: 10.1080/17517575.2021.1896786

Kucherawy, M., & Zwicky, E. (2015). *Domain-based Message Authentication, Reporting, and Conformance (DMARC)* (Request for Comments RFC 7489). Internet Engineering Task Force. DOI: 10.17487/rfc7489

Magdy, S., Abouelseoud, Y., & Mikhail, M. (2022). Efficient spam and phishing emails filtering based on deep learning. *Computer Networks*, 206, 108826. DOI: 10.1016/j.comnet.2022.108826

Merritt, D. T. (n.d.). *Spear Phishing Attack Detection.*

Milletary, J. (n.d.). *Technical Trends in Phishing Attacks.*

Miranda, M. J. A. (2018). *Enhancing Cybersecurity Awareness Training: A Comprehensive Phishing Exercise Approach. 14*(2).

Nightingale, S. J. (2017). *Email authentication mechanisms: DMARC, SPF and DKIM* (NIST TN 1945; p. NIST TN 1945). National Institute of Standards and Technology. DOI: 10.6028/NIST.TN.1945

Orunsolu, A. A., Sodiya, A. S., & Akinwale, A. T. (2022). A predictive model for phishing detection. *Journal of King Saud University. Computer and Information Sciences*, 34(2), 232–247. DOI: 10.1016/j.jksuci.2019.12.005

Parekh, S., Parikh, D., Kotak, S., & Sankhe, S. (2018). A New Method for Detection of Phishing Websites: URL Detection. *2018 Second International Conference on Inventive Communication and Computational Technologies (ICICCT)*, 949–952. DOI: 10.1109/ICICCT.2018.8473085

Qabajeh, I., Thabtah, F., & Chiclana, F. (2018). A recent review of conventional vs. Automated cybersecurity anti-phishing techniques. *Computer Science Review*, 29, 44–55. DOI: 10.1016/j.cosrev.2018.05.003

Raffetseder, T., Kirda, E., & Kruegel, C. (2007). Building Anti-Phishing Browser Plug-Ins: An Experience Report. *Third International Workshop on Software Engineering for Secure Systems (SESS'07: ICSE Workshops 2007)*, 6–6. DOI: 10.1109/SESS.2007.6

Sarker, O., Jayatilaka, A., Haggag, S., Liu, C., & Babar, M. A. (2024). A Multi-vocal Literature Review on challenges and critical success factors of phishing education, training and awareness. *Journal of Systems and Software*, 208, 111899. DOI: 10.1016/j.jss.2023.111899

Scholefield, S., & Shepherd, L. A. (2019). Gamification Techniques for Raising Cyber Security Awareness. In Moallem, A. (Ed.), *HCI for Cybersecurity, Privacy and Trust* (pp. 191–203). Springer International Publishing., DOI: 10.1007/978-3-030-22351-9_13

Scott, J. C. (2023). *Comparing Phishing Training and Campaign Methods for Mitigating Malicious Emails in Organizations* [Ph.D., Nova Southeastern University]. https://www.proquest.com/docview/2864775501/abstract/D4271C3ED0914762PQ/1

Shaji, A., Stephen, M., Sadanandan, S., Sreelakshmi, S., & Fasila, K. A. (2019). Phishing Site Detection and Blacklisting Using EVCS, Steganography Based on Android Application. In Hemanth, J., Fernando, X., Lafata, P., & Baig, Z. (Eds.), *International Conference on Intelligent Data Communication Technologies and Internet of Things (ICICI) 2018* (pp. 1384–1390). Springer International Publishing. DOI: 10.1007/978-3-030-03146-6_162

Shaw, C. (2020). *Why Phishing Works and the Detection Needed to Prevent It* [M.S., Utica College]. https://www.proquest.com/docview/2446039541/abstract/1D142896F6E24AB2PQ/1

Shrivastava, M. (2012). A Multifactor Authentication Security Protocol to Prevent Risks posed by Phishing, For Internet Based Online Payment System. *JOURNAL OF COMPUTING, ISSN 2151-9617*Https://Sites.Google.Com/Site/Journalofcomputing, *4*.

Social Engineering: Application of Psychology to Information Security. (n.d.). Retrieved September 18, 2024, from https://ieeexplore.ieee.org/abstract/document/8488183

Solanki, J., & Vaishnav, R. G. (n.d.). *Website Phishing Detection using Heuristic Based Approach. 03*(05).

Sonowal, G. (2022). Types of Phishing. In Sonowal, G. (Ed.), *Phishing and Communication Channels: A Guide to Identifying and Mitigating Phishing Attacks* (pp. 25–50). Apress., DOI: 10.1007/978-1-4842-7744-7_2

Srivastava, D., Kumar, A., Mishra, A., Arya, V., Almomani, A., Hsu, C. H., & Santaniello, D. (2022). Performance Optimization of Multi-Hop Routing Protocols With Clustering-Based Hybrid Networking Architecture in Mobile Adhoc Cloud Networks. *International Journal of Cloud Applications and Computing*, 12(1), 1–15. DOI: 10.4018/IJCAC.309932

Yeboah-Boateng, E. O., & Amanor, P. M. (2014). *Phishing, SMiShing & Vishing: An Assessment of Threats against Mobile Devices. 5*(4).

Zhou, L., Gaurav, A., Arya, V., Attar, R. W., Bansal, S., & Alhomoud, A. (2024). Enhancing Phishing Detection in Semantic Web Systems Using Optimized Deep Learning Models. [IJSWIS]. *International Journal on Semantic Web and Information Systems*, 20(1), 1–13. DOI: 10.4018/IJSWIS.361772

Chapter 8
Advanced Techniques and Best Practices for Phishing Detection

Ravina Mittal
Chandigarh College of Engineering and Technology, Panjab University, Chandigarh, India

Sunil K. Singh
https://orcid.org/0000-0003-4876-7190
Chandigarh College of Engineering and Technology, Panjab University, Chandigarh, India

Sudhakar Kumar
https://orcid.org/0000-0001-7928-4234
Chandigarh College of Engineering and Technology, Panjab University, Chandigarh, India

Trannum Khullar
Chandigarh College of Engineering and Technology, Panjab University, Chandigarh, India

Rakesh Kumar
G.L. Bajaj Institute of Technology and Management, India

Brij B. Gupta
https://orcid.org/0000-0003-4929-4698
Asia University, Taichung, Taiwan, & University of Economics and Human Science, Warsaw, Poland

Konstantinos Psannis
https://orcid.org/0000-0003-0020-6394
University of Macedonia, Greece

ABSTRACT

Phishing attacks are among the most prevalent and dangerous cyber threats, exploiting both technological and human vulnerabilities to access sensitive information. As phishing techniques evolve, organizations must implement various detection strategies to stay ahead of cybercriminals. This chapter delves into phishing detection methods, covering traditional approaches like signature-based detection and content filtering, alongside advanced strategies such as heuristic analysis, machine learning, and artificial intelligence (AI). It evaluates the strengths, limitations, and practical applications of these methods in real-world scenarios. Additionally, the chapter explores emerging technologies like Natural Language Processing (NLP), blockchain, and behavioral analysis that are redefining phishing detection. By combining traditional and modern techniques, organizations can enhance their ability to identify and prevent phishing attacks, strengthening their overall cybersecurity.

DOI: 10.4018/979-8-3693-8784-9.ch008

INTRODUCTION

Phishing attacks have rapidly become one of the most pervasive and dangerous forms of cybercrime. By masquerading as legitimate entities, attackers manipulate individuals into disclosing sensitive information, such as usernames, passwords, or credit card numbers. These attacks often target not only individuals but also businesses, exploiting their employees through well-crafted messages. As phishing techniques evolve, they continue to exploit both technological vulnerabilities and human psychology, making them challenging to find and prevent. Phishing attacks pose a significant threat to the security (Jahankhani, John, & Weddell, 2021) of personal data and the integrity of organizations. So, Take a step that is legal and ethical consideration(Luo & Wang, 2022) look how Governments and organizations now increasingly focusing on regulations and best practices to combat phishing and protect users, leading to an ongoing battle between cybercriminals and defenders.

BACKGROUND OF PHISHING ATTACKS

Phishing, in its various forms, represents a broad category of cyberattacks Tso & Keung, 2020 designed to trick victims into disclosing private information. Initially, phishing was primarily email-based, where attackers would send fraudulent messages that appeared to be from trusted sources like banks, online services, or coworkers. These messages often contained malicious links or attachments, directing users to fake websites that harvest login credentials or install malware.

Over time, phishing tactics have evolved, incorporating more sophisticated methods. Spear phishing targets specific individuals or organizations, often using personalized details to make the attack seem more legitimate. Whaleing focuses on high-profile individuals, such as executives, exploiting their authority within an organization. Additionally, social media platforms, SMS (smishing), and phone calls (vishing) have become new channels for phishing attacks, broadening the scope of potential victims. With the advent of automated tools, phishing as a service has emerged, allowing even less skilled attackers to launch complex campaigns.

These attacks have far-reaching consequences, including financial losses, data breaches, and damage to organizational reputations. Major incidents in recent years, such as data breaches involving millions of users' personal information, demonstrate the scale and impact of phishing campaigns. As phishing continues to adapt and grow more sophisticated, the need for advanced detection techniques becomes increasingly urgent.

Table 1. Phishing Channels: Email, Smishing, and Vishing table

Phishing Channel	Medium	Attack Techniques	Target Audience	Impact
Email Phishing	Email	Fake login pages, malware attachments, requests for sensitive information.	Corporate and individual users.	Credential theft, data breaches, malware infection, and financial loss.
Smishing	SMS/Text Messages	Fraudulent SMS links, fake verification requests, urgent calls to action.	Smartphone users, especially less tech-savvy individuals	Personal data theft, unauthorized access to financial accounts.
Vishing	Voice Calls	Impersonation of trusted authorities (e.g., bank officers, tech support), scare tactics.	General public, especially elderly individuals.	Social engineering attacks, unauthorized financial transactions, and identity theft.

The Importance of Phishing Detection

As phishing attacks escalate in both frequency and complexity, the need for effective detection strategies is paramount. Traditional methods of cybersecurity (Jahankhani, John, & Weddell, 2021), such as firewalls and antivirus software, are no longer sufficient to combat these attacks, as phishing often bypasses these defenses by targeting human vulnerabilities. Without robust phishing detection mechanisms in place, organizations are left exposed to potentially devastating breaches.

Phishing detection (Mamun et al., 2016) is crucial for limiting financial losses and stopping illegal access to sensitive data. Effective detection not only protects individual users but also secures the broader organizational infrastructure. It allows for timely identification of phishing attempts, lowering the possibility that assaults may be effective and minimize the damage caused. In addition to technical measures, employee education is very important, since well-informed staff can recognize phishing attempts before they cause harm. A Hybrid Neuro-Fuzzy Ensemble for Concept Drift Adaptation in Stream Mining Using Neural Networks (Vijayalakshmi et al., 2020) involves adapting machine learning systems to handle concept drift, a common issue in stream mining where the statistical properties of the target variable change over time. The incorporation of cyber security adds an extra layer of relevance, as streams of data in this field are often subject to dynamic and rapidly changing patterns due to new attack strategies and evolving vulnerabilities.

With the growing reliance on digital communication and remote work environments, phishing detection must be adaptive and scalable to address the rising volume of phishing attempts. Organizations must invest in multi-layered detection approaches that combine traditional methods with new technologies such as machine learning (ML), artificial intelligence (AI), and behavioral analysis. These advanced techniques enable more accurate identification of phishing attacks by analyzing patterns in communication, user behavior, and content. In an era where phishing remains a top cybersecurity (Jahankhani, John, & Weddell, 2021) threat, implementing and maintaining effective detection systems is vital for organizational resilience and data protection.

LITERATURE REVIEW

Phishing detection has garnered significant attention in the cybersecurity community, with a growing body of research dedicated to understanding and mitigating its impacts. The main literature on phishing detection approaches is compiled in this study, which emphasizes the use of artificial intelligence and machine learning, upcoming technologies like blockchain and natural language processing (NLP), and classic methods

Recent studies indicate that cybercriminals are leveraging generative AI to create highly personalized phishing messages. These messages are crafted by analyzing vast datasets from social media and corporate websites, making them more convincing and harder to detect.(Heiding, Schneier, & Vishwanath, 2024)

Machine learning models are increasingly used to analyze not just the content of emails but also their context, timing, and sender-recipient relationships. This approach helps identify anomalies that may indicate phishing attempts, such as unusual requests for sensitive information at odd hours.(Ghalechyan et al., 2024)

ML algorithms are employed to monitor user behavior and detect deviations from normal patterns. For instance, if an employee accesses sensitive data at unusual times, it may trigger alerts for potential phishing attempts.

Advanced email filters utilize machine learning to adapt to new phishing tactics. These systems learn from emerging threats, improving their detection capabilities over time by analyzing patterns and behaviors indicative of phishing.

Effective phishing detection combines traditional heuristics with AI-driven techniques. This multi-layered approach includes advanced email filtering, sender analysis, and the use of authentication protocols like DMARC, DKIM, and SPF to verify email authenticity.

Some platforms offer automated incident response services powered by AI, which manage threat detection and remediation, reducing the burden on cybersecurity teams.

Emerging Technologies like Natural Language Processing (NLP): NLP techniques are being utilized to analyze the language used in emails. By understanding the nuances of communication, these systems can better identify phishing attempts that mimic legitimate correspondence.

Some studies explore the potential of blockchain technology to enhance email verification processes, providing a decentralized method to confirm the authenticity of communications.

Organizations are increasingly focusing on training employees to recognize phishing attempts, especially those that utilize AI. Regular simulations of phishing attacks help reinforce learning and prepare staff to respond effectively. As phishing techniques evolve, continuous education on the latest tactics, such as "quishing" (using QR codes) and "2-step phishing," is essential for maintaining a robust defense against these threats(Mengi et al., 2023).

Traditional Phishing Detection Methods

Early efforts in phishing detection(Yang, Zhang, & Zeng, 2019) primarily relied on signature-based approaches. Garera et al. (2007) laid the foundation for such methods, explaining how known phishing attacks can be identified by comparing incoming emails or URLs to databases of malicious signatures. While effective against previously identified threats, this method's limitations are widely acknowledged. As pointed out by Basnet, Mukkamala, and Sung (2008), signature-based systems are vulnerable to zero-day attacks—novel phishing techniques that have no pre-existing signature in the database, thereby bypassing detection.

Heuristic-based detection(Yang, Zhang, & Zeng, 2019), as explained by Fette et al. (2007), offers an improvement by analyzing email content and structure for suspicious patterns, such as mismatched sender addresses or abnormal URL redirects. These systems are more dynamic and adaptable than signature-based methods, yet they are still prone to high false positive rates, where legitimate communications are flagged as phishing attempts. This issue is highlighted in research by Abu-Nimeh et al. (2007), where the authors stress the difficulty in balancing detection sensitivity with accuracy in heuristic systems.

Machine Learning and Artificial Intelligence in Phishing Detection

The advent of machine learning (ML) has transformed phishing detection, allowing systems to dynamically learn from large datasets and improve accuracy over time. Research by Bergholz et al. (2010) was one of the early works that introduced supervised learning models for phishing detection, training algorithms on labeled datasets of phishing and legitimate emails. These models proved effective in recognizing previously unseen phishing patterns by examining a wide array of features, such as email headers, content, and URLs.

Further research by Sahoo et al. (2017) introduced unsupervised and deep learning (Arora et al., 2024)techniques, which can identify phishing attacks without the need for labeled data. These models analyze clusters of emails and detect anomalies or patterns consistent with phishing behavior. Deep learning(Aggarwal et al., 2022, in particular, has demonstrated significant promise, with research by Rao and Pais (2019) showing how convolutional neural networks (CNNs)(Kaur, Singh, Singh, & Kumar, 2021) and recurrent neural networks (RNNs) can improve detection accuracy by analyzing the sequential and spatial characteristics of phishing emails.

Despite the improvements ML brings to phishing detection, several challenges remain. Abawajy et al. (2019) emphasize that ML models are resource-intensive and require vast amounts of data to be effective. Moreover, attackers have begun employing tactics like adversarial attacks, where subtle changes are made to phishing emails to trick the model into classifying them as legitimate.

Emerging Technologies in Phishing Detection

Recent advancements in emerging technologies offer new opportunities for phishing detection. Natural Language Processing (NLP)(Zheng et al., 2020), as detailed by Zheng et al. (2020), enables systems to analyze the tone, structure, and language of emails to detect phishing attempts. NLP algorithms can flag emotionally manipulative language or urgent calls to action, common in phishing emails. Research by Verma and Hossain (2017) demonstrates how NLP techniques can distinguish between the informal and transactional language typically used in phishing emails versus legitimate communications.

Blockchain technology also offers potential for improving phishing detection. According to research by Yaga et al. (2019), blockchain can be used for decentralized identity verification, reducing the risk of email spoofing and phishing. Blockchain's(Insights2Techinfo, 2021) immutable nature ensures the integrity of digital identities, allowing users to verify the authenticity of email senders without relying on centralized authorities that can be compromised. But blockchain deployment(Yaga et al., 2019) for phishing detection is still in its infancy, and additional investigation is required to determine its viability and scalability.

Behavioral analysis represents another frontier in phishing detection, as detailed in the work of Mamun et al. (2016). By monitoring user behavior—such as login patterns, IP address changes, and access frequency—behavioral analysis can detect anomalies indicative of phishing attacks. This approach is particularly effective in detecting spear phishing and account takeovers, where the attacker uses valid credentials but behaves in ways inconsistent with the legitimate user. Companies like Google have implemented behavioral-based phishing detection with considerable success, reducing the number of compromised accounts.

Challenges in Phishing Detection

Several challenges persist in the field of phishing detection, even as technology advances. The problem of false positives and negatives continues to plague many detection systems. As noted by Abawajy and Kim (2020), systems must strike a balance between sensitivity and accuracy. A system that is too sensitive will flag legitimate communications, frustrating users and creating inefficiencies. Conversely, a system with low sensitivity may fail to detect sophisticated phishing attempts, leading to security breaches.

Another challenge, as described by Gupta et al. (2021), is the adaptability of phishing attacks(Tso & Keung, 2020). As detection methods evolve, attackers continue to develop evasion techniques, such as URL shorteners, encrypted attachments, and fake login pages that mimic legitimate websites. Furthermore, phishing-as-a-service platforms enable attackers to scale their operations, making it easier for even novice hackers to launch sophisticated campaigns. Gupta's research emphasizes the need for detection methods that can adapt to new phishing tactics in real-time.

1. COMMON PHISHING DETECTION TECHNIQUES

1.1 Signature-Based Detection

Signature-based detection (Yang, Zhang, & Zeng, 2019) is a prevalent cybersecurity technique designed to identify and mitigate phishing attacks by utilizing a predefined set of signatures—distinctive patterns or characteristics associated with known threats. These signatures can encompass a variety of elements, including specific strings of text, file hashes, URLs, and even behavioral patterns that are typical of malicious emails and phishing websites. The fundamental premise of signature-based detection lies in its ability to match incoming data against an established database of signatures, allowing organizations to quickly and efficiently recognize threats that have been previously cataloged. This approach provides a straightforward mechanism for threat detection, enabling security systems to operate with a level of automation that minimizes the need for manual intervention.

How It Works in Email and Web Scanning

In practical applications, signature-based detection plays a critical role in email and web scanning. When an email arrives in a user's inbox or a user attempts to access a website, the detection system immediately analyzes the content against a database of known signatures. This scanning process involves examining various elements of the incoming data, such as the email subject line, sender address, embedded links, and attachments, to determine if any match the predefined signatures. If a match is found, the system can flag the content as suspicious or outright block it, preventing potentially harmful phishing attempts from reaching users.

This is illustrated in the fig1.

The efficiency of this method is particularly advantageous in environments with high volumes of email traffic, where rapid detection is essential to minimize risks and protect sensitive information. Additionally, the process can be integrated with other security measures, allowing for layered defenses that enhance overall cybersecurity posture.

Figure 1. Strength of Signature Based Detection

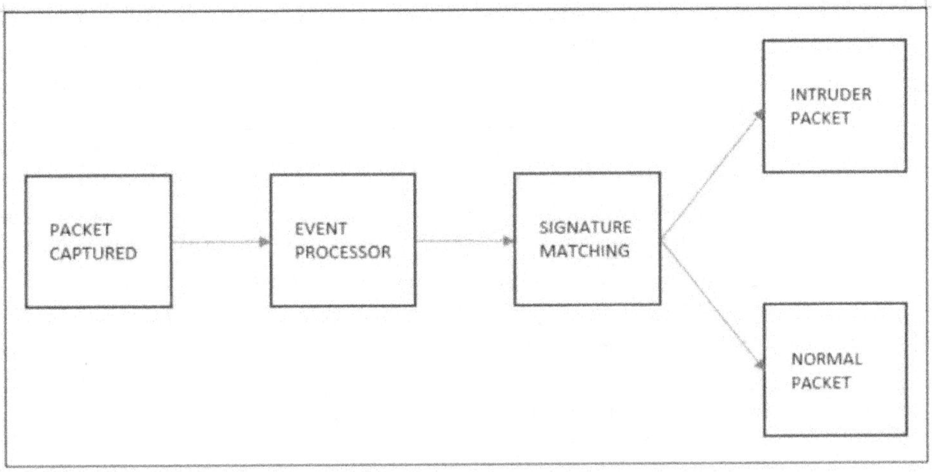

One of the key strengths of signature-based detection is its easy deployment. These systems are straightforward to implement and can be integrated into existing security frameworks with minimal configuration. This simplicity allows organizations to quickly enhance their cybersecurity posture without requiring extensive resources or time. Additionally, signature-based detection enables rapid threat detection. By utilizing a database of known signatures, these systems can swiftly determine and block recognized threats, significantly reducing the time between detection and response, which is particularly beneficial in environments that experience high volumes of email traffic. Furthermore, this method typically has a low false positive rate; since it matches incoming data against established signatures, there is a higher likelihood that flagged content is genuinely malicious. Cost-effectiveness is another advantage, as implementing signature-based detection solutions is often more budget-friendly compared to more advanced detection methods. Lastly, the ease of maintenance plays a crucial role; cybersecurity vendors regularly provide updates to signature databases, ensuring that systems remain effective against emerging threats without excessive management on the part of organizations.Weaknesses of Signature-Based Detection

Despite its strengths, signature-based detection has notable weaknesses that organizations must consider. The most significant limitation is its inability to detect zero-day attacks—newly discovered vulnerabilities or threats that lack corresponding signatures in the database. This gap makes organizations vulnerable to sophisticated cybercriminals who exploit these unknown risks. Additionally, signature-based detection relies heavily on known threats, meaning it is only effective against previously identified and documented attacks. As cybercriminal tactics evolve, signature databases may lag behind emerging threats, resulting in potential vulnerabilities. This method also has a limited scope, as it primarily focuses on detecting known patterns and may overlook nuanced behaviors that indicate malicious activity. Moreover, attackers can employ techniques to evade detection by slightly altering their tactics to avoid matching existing signatures, which can compromise the effectiveness of these systems. Lastly, while maintaining signature databases is generally manageable, the constant need to update and expand them to cover new threats can require ongoing resources and attention, which may pose a burden for some organizations.

Table 2. The strengths and weakness of singature-based detection

Aspect	Strengths	Weaknesses
Deployment	Easy to deploy and integrate into existing systems with minimal configuration.	It requires regular updates to the signature database to stay effective against emerging threats.
Accuracy	High accuracy for detecting previously known threats, resulting in fewer false positives.	Ineffective against zero-day attacks and novel phishing techniques with no existing signatures.
Cost	Cost-effective initial implementation, suitable for organizations with limited resources.	Long-term costs can increase due to frequent updates and maintenance of signature databases.
Automation	Operates automatically by comparing data to pre-defined signatures, reducing the need for manual intervention.	Limited to predefined rules, offering no adaptability to changing phishing tactics.
Response Speed	Quickly identifies and blocks known threats using an established database of signatures.	Slower response to new threats, as updates are needed before new patterns can be detected.
Simplicity	Straightforward mechanism that is easy for security teams to understand and manage.	Over-reliance on static rules and known patterns, leading to a rigid detection system.
Scalability	Effective for environments with moderate email or web traffic volumes.	Struggles to scale effectively in environments with high data volumes or complex attack vectors.
Evasion Techniques	Can block simple phishing attacks effectively.	Vulnerable to attackers using techniques like URL shorteners or minor variations in attack patterns.
Maintenance	Regular updates from cybersecurity vendors help keep systems aligned with new threats.	Dependency on external vendors for timely updates, which may not cover every emerging threat.

Case Example: Email Filtering Solutions

A practical example of signature-based detection can be seen in various email filtering solutions employed by organizations worldwide. These solutions leverage signature-based detection to effectively block spam and phishing attempts by maintaining extensive databases of known malicious signatures. When an email is received, the filtering system automatically scans it, comparing its content against the database to identify any matches. For instance, if an incoming email contains a link that has been previously associated with phishing attacks, the system can flag it as suspicious or redirect it to a quarantine folder. These email filtering solutions have proven highly effective in reducing the risk of employees falling victim to recognized phishing attacks, significantly enhancing organizational security. However, it is essential for companies to remain vigilant and adopt a multi-layered cybersecurity strategy that includes additional detection methods to safeguard against new and evolving threats. Overall, while signature-based detection serves as a foundational element of phishing defense, organizations must recognize its limitations and ensure comprehensive protection against the dynamic environment of cyberthreats.

1.2 Heuristic-Based Detection

What Are Heuristics in Phishing Detection?

Heuristic-based detection(Yang, Zhang, & Zeng, 2019) is a critical method in cybersecurity that focuses on identifying phishing threats through the analysis of behavioral patterns rather than relying solely on known signatures of malicious attacks. This approach utilizes algorithms designed to mimic human cognitive abilities, allowing for an evaluation of incoming emails, URLs, and other content based on predefined rules and learned experiences. Unlike traditional methods that may only recognize threats based on their signatures, heuristic detection proactively assesses the elements of a communication to determine its legitimacy. By leveraging heuristics, organizations can enhance their security posture, as this technique enables the identification of emerging threats and zero-day vulnerabilities that signature-based systems may overlook. Furthermore, the adaptability of heuristic-based systems allows them to evolve alongside the tactics used by cybercriminals, making them a valuable asset in the ever-changing landscape of cybersecurity.

Identifying suspicious patterns in Emails, URLs, and Content

The identification of suspicious patterns within emails, URLs, and web content is a fundamental component of heuristic-based detection (Abawajy& Kim, 2020). This process involves analyzing various characteristics to flag potential phishing attempts. For instance, the system examines the structure and formatting of emails, looking for telltale signs such as unusual sender addresses or grammar errors that may indicate a lack of professionalism often associated with phishing scams. Additionally, URLs are scrutinized for discrepancies; an attacker might use a domain name that closely resembles a legitimate site but contains slight alterations, such as an additional letter or a different domain extension. Heuristic algorithms can identify these discrepancies and assess the risk associated with such links. Moreover, the presence of urgent language requesting personal information or financial data can also trigger alerts. This multi-faceted analysis enables heuristic detection systems to provide a robust defense mechanism against phishing attacks, significantly improving the chances of identifying malicious content before it reaches users.

Detection of Fake Sender Addresses, URL Redirects, etc.

One of the critical advantages of heuristic-based detection(Bergholz et al., 2010)lies in its ability to identify fake sender addresses and URL redirects, both of which are common tactics employed by phishing attackers. Cybercriminals often spoof legitimate email addresses to create a false sense of trust, leading unsuspecting users to click on malicious links or provide sensitive information. Heuristic algorithms analyze the patterns in sender addresses, looking for subtle variations in spelling or domain names that can indicate deception. In addition to scrutinizing email sender information, heuristic detection systems also assess URLs for redirection behaviors. Many phishing attacks involve redirecting users to fraudulent websites after they click a seemingly harmless link. By monitoring for unusual redirect patterns and assessing the legitimacy of the target sites, heuristic systems can effectively flag potential threats. This is illustrated in the fig2.This capability not only aids in preventing user interaction with malicious links but also contributes to a broader understanding of phishing tactics, allowing organizations to adapt their defenses accordingly.

Figure 2. Machine learning Based URL Detection Technique

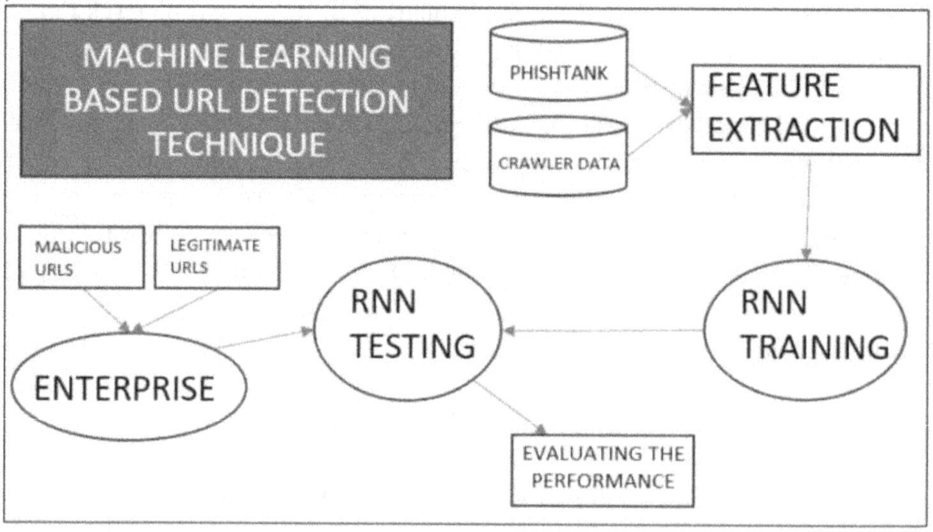

Limitations of Heuristic-Based Systems

Despite their effectiveness, heuristic-based detection systems(Abu-Nimeh, Yaseen, & Arachchilage, 2007) have several limitations that organizations must consider. A primary concern is the potential for false positives, where legitimate communications are incorrectly classified as phishing threats. This can lead to user frustration and decreased productivity, as employees may become desensitized to alerts over time or might overlook critical messages that are wrongly flagged. Furthermore, the success of heuristic detection heavily depends on the quality of the algorithms and the training data utilized to inform them. If these components are poorly designed or outdated, the system may fail to identify sophisticated phishing attempts that employ advanced evasion tactics. Additionally, as cybercriminals continuously adapt their methods, heuristic systems require regular updates and retraining to remain effective. This maintenance can be resource-intensive and may pose challenges for organizations that lack sufficient cybersecurity resources. Thus, while heuristic-based detection is a valuable tool in the cybersecurity arsenal, it should be implemented as part of a multi-layered security strategy that includes other detection methods to address its inherent weaknesses.

Case Example: A Financial Institution's Approach to Heuristic Detection

A prominent case study showcasing the successful application of heuristic-based detection is that of a major financial institution that implemented advanced heuristic technology to bolster its defenses against phishing attacks. The institution recognized that traditional signature-based methods were insufficient in the face of rapidly evolving threats and opted for a heuristic detection system that could analyze email traffic and web interactions for suspicious behaviors indicative of phishing attempts. By leveraging machine learning algorithms, the institution's system learned from historical data and refined its ability to identify threats over time. As a result of this implementation, the financial institution reported a dramatic reduction in successful phishing attacks, with a notable decrease in incidents that could compromise sensitive customer data. This case exemplifies the effectiveness of heuristic-based detection, illustrating how proactive analysis of patterns and behaviors can significantly enhance an organization's ability to defend against increasingly sophisticated cyber threats. The institution's experience underscores the importance of adopting a multi-faceted approach to cybersecurity, combining heuristic detection with other techniques to create a more resilient defense.

1.3 Content Filtering

Content Scanning for Phishing Keywords

Content filtering(Fette, Fuller, & Freeman, 2007) is a crucial technique in combating phishing attacks, primarily focused on scanning incoming communications for specific keywords and phrases that are commonly associated with malicious intent. This process involves the use of automated systems that analyze the text within emails, messages, and web content to identify potentially harmful language. For instance, words or phrases that evoke fear, urgency, or the need for immediate action, such as "immediate verification," "account compromise," or "urgent update," are flagged for further review. By utilizing predefined keyword lists, organizations can create a baseline for detecting phishing attempts, effectively filtering out communications that do not meet legitimate criteria. The effectiveness of content scanning lies in its ability to catch not only obvious threats but also subtle attempts that may evade traditional signature-based detection methods. This proactive approach helps to minimize the risk of users engaging with harmful content, thereby enhancing overall cybersecurity measures.

Identifying Markers Like Urgency, Requests for Information

Beyond keyword scanning, effective content filtering also involves identifying specific markers that signal potential phishing attempts, such as urgency and requests for sensitive information. Phishing attackers often use psychological tactics to manipulate victims into acting quickly without fully assessing the situation. For instance, messages that convey an immediate need for personal information or financial details can indicate malicious intent. Content filtering systems are designed to recognize these markers by analyzing not only the language used but also the context in which it appears. Phrases like "Your account will be locked unless you respond immediately" or "Click here to verify your identity" are scrutinized to determine whether they adhere to established norms of communication from legitimate organizations. By focusing on these behavioral patterns, content filtering can enhance its accuracy in detecting phishing attempts and reduce the likelihood of successful attacks.

Techniques for Enhancing Content Filtering

To improve the efficacy of content filtering(Gupta et al., 2021) in detecting phishing attempts, organizations employ various advanced techniques. One effective method involves the implementation of machine learning algorithms that can learn from historical data, allowing the system to identify new patterns and trends in phishing tactics. These algorithms continuously adapt and refine their filtering criteria, enhancing their ability to recognize sophisticated threats that might not have been previously accounted for. Another technique is the use of natural language processing (NLP)(Zheng et al., 2020) to analyze the context and semantics of the content, allowing for a more nuanced understanding of the messages being scanned. By assessing the tone, sentiment, and intent behind the text, NLP can provide deeper insights into the legitimacy of communications. Additionally, integrating Threat intelligence provides fuel for that supply real-time data about emerging phishing tactics can significantly bolster the effectiveness of content filtering systems. These techniques, when combined, create a robust defense against phishing attempts, allowing organizations to stay one step ahead of cybercriminals.

Real-World Use Case: Phishing Attempts Blocked Through Content Filters

A compelling real-world example of the effectiveness of content filtering can be seen in a large corporate environment where phishing attacks pose a significant risk to sensitive company information. The organization implemented a comprehensive content filtering solution that combined keyword scanning, urgency detection, and machine learning algorithms. Within a few months of deployment, the system successfully identified and blocked thousands of phishing attempts that were targeting employees through email and internal messaging platforms. For instance, one notable incident involved a sophisticated phishing campaign that attempted to mimic a legitimate vendor's communication, requesting sensitive data from finance staff. Thanks to the content filtering system's ability to detect red flags—such as urgent language and unusual requests for confidential information—the email was flagged and quarantined before any employee engaged with it. This incident not only highlighted the efficacy of content filtering but also demonstrated its critical role in safeguarding organizational assets against phishing threats. As a result, the organization significantly reduced the risk of data breaches and enhanced employee awareness of phishing tactics, illustrating the value of content filtering as part of a broader cybersecurity strategy.

1.4 Machine Learning and AI-Based Detection

Basics of Machine Learning in Phishing Detection

Machine learning (ML)(Sahoo et al., 2017) has emerged as a pivotal technology in enhancing phishing detection, leveraging algorithms that can learn from and adapt to new data over time. In the context of phishing detection, ML models are trained to recognize patterns and characteristics associated with both legitimate and malicious communications. By analyzing vast datasets containing features such as email headers, content, and metadata, these models can identify subtle distinctions that may indicate phishing attempts. The strength of machine learning lies in its ability to evolve; as new phishing techniques emerge, the models can be retrained with updated data, allowing organizations to maintain a robust defense against evolving threats... Machine learning models are trained to identify patterns and traits linked to fraudulent as well as valid communications in the context of phishing detection. These models analyze large datasets with features including email headers, content, and metadata to find tiny differences that might be signs of phishing attempts. Machine learning is robust because it can adapt to changing threats. When new phishing strategies surface, organizations can retrain the models with updated data, keeping their defenses strong.

This adaptive capability not only improves detection accuracy but also reduces reliance on static rules and heuristics that may become obsolete as attackers innovate their methods.

Supervised Learning Models

Supervised learning(Rao & Pais, 2019) is a fundamental approach within machine learning that utilizes labeled datasets to train models. In the realm of phishing detection, supervised learning involves training algorithms on historical data where phishing attempts are clearly marked, enabling the model to learn the distinguishing features of malicious content. Techniques such as decision trees, random forests, and support vector machines (SVM) are commonly employed to classify emails or messages as either benign or phishing attempts based on these features. The success of supervised learning models in phishing detection is significantly reliant on the quality and diversity of the training data. For instance, if the dataset includes a wide range of phishing examples—covering different tactics, languages, and scenarios—the model is likely to perform better in real-world applications. Regular updates and retraining of these models with new data are crucial to ensure they remain effective against emerging phishing strategies.

Unsupervised and Deep Learning Models

Unsupervised learning(Rao & Pais, 2019) and deep learning (Arora et al., 2024) represent more advanced methodologies in the field of machine learning, providing enhanced capabilities for phishing detection. Without previous examples of phishing attempts, unsupervised learning algorithms study unlabeled datasets to find patterns and anomalies. Because it does not rely on labeled data, this approach can be very useful for identifying novel phishing tactics that have not been encountered before. Neural network-based deep learning, a branch of machine learning, has shown impressive results in challenging pattern recognition tests. Deep learning models have the ability to process and analyze vast amounts of unstructured data, including text and images, in order to identify minor signs of phishing. The requirement for human feature engineering is decreased by these models' ability to automatically extract features from the data. The combination of unsupervised and deep learning techniques enables organizations to bolster their phishing defenses by continuously adapting to the ever-changing landscape of cyber threats.

Training Datasets: How They Work

Training datasets (Setia et al., 2024) are the foundation of any machine learning model, particularly in phishing detection. These datasets consist of a collection of labeled examples—both phishing and legitimate communications—used to teach the model to differentiate between the two. The size and diversity of the training dataset have a significant impact on a machine learning model's efficacy. well-constructed dataset includes various phishing tactics, types of phishing emails, and legitimate communications to provide a comprehensive learning experience for the model. Typically, the dataset is split into training and testing sets; the training set is used to build the model, while the testing set evaluates its performance on unseen data. Ongoing updates to the training dataset, incorporating new phishing examples and legitimate communications, ensure that the model remains relevant and effective. In addition, methods like data collection augmentation and synthetic data generation can be employed to enhance the dataset, allowing for better generalization and performance in real-world scenarios.

Case Study: How ML Reduced Phishing Attempts in a Large Enterprise

A compelling case study highlights the impact of machine learning in a large enterprise that faced significant challenges with phishing attacks. After implementing a machine learning-based phishing detection system, the organization observed a dramatic reduction in successful phishing attempts—by as much as 70% within the first six months. The ML model was trained on a diverse dataset that included various types of phishing emails, enabling it to accurately identify patterns and characteristics of malicious communications. By integrating both supervised and unsupervised learning techniques, the model could adapt to new phishing strategies and evolving tactics employed by cybercriminals. Furthermore, the enterprise combined this technology with regular employee training programs that emphasized awareness of phishing threats, reinforcing the effectiveness of the technical solution. The successful deployment of machine learning not only improved the security posture of the organization but also fostered a culture of vigilance among employees, demonstrating the value of combining technological advancements with human awareness in the fight against phishing.

Table 3. Comparison of Traditional vs. ML Detection

Sr no	Feature	Traditional Detection Methods	Machine Learning Detection Methods
1	**Detection Approach**	Rule-based and signature-based	Data-driven and adaptive
2	**Adaptability**	Limited adaptability to new threats	Highly adaptable; learns from new data
3	**Accuracy**	May produce false positives/negatives due to rigid rules	Increased precision coupled with the capacity to identify patterns in data
4	**Data Requirement**	Requires explicit rules and signatures	Requires large labeled datasets for training
5	**Response Time**	Slower response due to manual updates	Faster response with real-time detection
6	**Scalability**	Difficult to scale for large datasets	Easily scalable; can handle vast amounts of data
7	**Complexity**	Simpler to implement but less effective	More complex to implement but more effective
8	**Handling of Evolving Threats**	Struggles with evolving phishing tactics	Better at identifying emerging threats due to continuous learning
9	**User Interaction**	Limited user feedback for improvements	Can incorporate user feedback for refining models
10	**Cost**	Often lower initial cost but may incur high long-term costs	Higher initial cost due to training and implementation, but more cost-effective long-term

2. COMPARISON OF DETECTION METHODS

A variety of detection techniques, each with advantages and disadvantages, have emerged in the dynamic cybersecurity landscape, particularly with regard to phishing threats. This section compares traditional and machine learning (ML) detection methods across several dimensions, including accuracy, speed, cost, scalability, and effectiveness against advanced phishing techniques.

2.1 Accuracy and Speed of Detection

In the realm of phishing detection, accuracy and speed are two critical metrics that determine the effectiveness of various detection methods. Accurately identifying phishing attempts while maintaining a rapid response time is essential for minimizing potential damage. This section delves into the measurement of detection speed and reliability, along with the response times experienced in real-world scenarios.

Measuring Detection Speed and Reliability

Detection speed refers to the time taken by a system to identify and respond to a phishing threat. Traditional detection methods, such as signature-based systems, primarily rely on predefined rules and known patterns of malicious behavior. This reliance can lead to delays in detection, particularly when faced with novel or sophisticated phishing tactics. The reliability of these methods can be compromised by the ever-evolving nature of phishing techniques, which can result in false negatives where genuine threats are missed.

Machine learning-based detection systems, on the other hand, are made to examine large datasets and spot trends and abnormalities that could point to phishing attempts. These systems continuously learn and adapt, improving their ability to detect threats over time. Because of this, they frequently show higher dependability and faster detection speeds, which makes them more suited for dynamic and complicated situations. By leveraging historical data and user behavior, machine learning models can accurately identify phishing attempts with reduced lag time.

Response Times In Actual-World Situations

The response time of a detection system can significantly impact anThe capacity of the organization to reduce phishing threats. In practical applications, traditional systems may take longer to process and analyze incoming data, allowing phishing emails or messages to reach end-users before they are flagged as threats. This delay can result in users unknowingly engaging with malicious content, potentially leading to data breaches or financial loss.

Conversely, machine learning detection systems provide a more proactive approach. Their ability to analyze incoming data in real-time enables them to swiftly identify and block potential phishing attempts before they can reach end users. For instance, a case study from a large enterprise implementing machine learning for phishing detection demonstrated a marked improvement in response times. The organization reported that phishing emails were flagged and quarantined within seconds of receipt, significantly reducing the risk of user interaction with malicious content.

2.2 Cost and Scalability

In the realm of cybersecurity, particularly in phishing detection, the cost of implementing detection systems and their scalability across large-scale enterprises are critical factors that organizations must consider. Balancing budget constraints while ensuring effective protection against phishing threats is essential for maintaining robust cybersecurity.

Costs of Implementing Detection Systems

The financial investment required to implement phishing detection systems can vary significantly based on the chosen technology and the complexity of the solution. Traditional detection methods, such as signature-based systems, often entail lower upfront costs. However, these systems may incur additional expenses related to regular updates, maintenance, and potential breaches due to their limited capabilities. As phishing tactics evolve, organizations relying solely on traditional methods may face increased costs associated with incident response and damage control.

Conversely, machine learning and AI-based detection systems typically require a higher initial investment due to their advanced algorithms, infrastructure needs, and ongoing training and maintenance. However, this upfront cost can be offset by the long-term savings generated through reduced phishing incidents, lower incident response costs, and decreased downtime associated with security breaches. Organizations can also benefit from the improved efficiency and accuracy that these systems provide, leading to a better return on investment over time.

Scalability Across Large-Scale Enterprises

Scalability is another crucial consideration for organizations, particularly those operating at a large scale. As enterprises grow, their security needs become more complex, necessitating robust solutions that can adapt to increased data volumes and evolving threats. Traditional detection methods often struggle with scalability, as their reliance on predefined rules can lead to increased false positives and negatives in larger datasets. As a result, organizations may find themselves needing to invest in additional resources to maintain an effective defense.

In contrast, machine learning and AI-driven detection systems offer inherent scalability advantages. These systems enable enterprises of any size to maintain effective phishing detection because they can analyze massive volumes of data in real-time across multiple channels. Additionally, their adaptability allows them to learn from new threats continuously, ensuring that they remain effective as the organization grows and as phishing tactics evolve.

A case in point is a multinational corporation that recently transitioned from a traditional signature-based detection system to a machine learning-based approach. The organization found that while the initial costs were higher, the new system's scalability allowed it to manage phishing threats more effectively across multiple regions and departments. The ability to deploy the solution universally without significant adjustments or additional resources made it a more cost-effective option in the long run.

2.3 Effectiveness Against Advanced Phishing

The ever-evolving landscape of phishing attacks, particularly advanced tactics such as spear phishing and whaling, poses significant challenges for organizations aiming to protect sensitive data. This section examines how different detection techniques address these sophisticated threats, evaluates their success rates against advanced persistent threats (APTs), and presents real-world scenarios and data comparisons that highlight the effectiveness of various approaches.

How Different Techniques Handle Spear Phishing and Whaleing

Targeted phishing attacks like spearphishing and whaling are directed towards particular people or senior executives in a company. Unlike generic phishing attempts, these attacks often utilize personalized information to deceive the target into divulging sensitive data or authorizing fraudulent transactions. Traditional detection methods, such as signature-based and heuristic-based systems, struggle to identify these nuanced threats due to their reliance on known patterns and predefined rules. Spearphishing emails may mimic legitimate communications closely, making them difficult to detect without contextual awareness.

In contrast, machine learning-based detection systems excel at identifying spearphishing and whaling attempts. By analyzing vast amounts of historical data, these systems can recognize anomalous behaviors and patterns indicative of targeted attacks. For example, if an employee suddenly receives an email from a known executive requesting sensitive information, a machine learning model can flag this unusual request based on the context, the sender's behavior, and other variables. This ability to contextualize information significantly enhances the detection rate for advanced phishing attempts.

Success Rates Against Advanced Persistent Threats (APTs)

Phishing is frequently used as a point of entry by advanced persistent threats (APTs), which are highly skilled and focused cyberattacks. These threats are characterized by their stealth, persistence, and the skill of the attackers, making them particularly challenging to detect and mitigate. Research indicates that machine learning and AI-based detection methods achieve significantly higher success rates against APTs compared to traditional techniques. A recent study found that organizations utilizing machine learning solutions could detect 90% of spear phishing attacks, whereas those relying on traditional methods reported success rates as low as 50%.

The effectiveness of machine learning lies in its ability to adapt continuously to new threats and refine its detection capabilities over time. By leveraging data from previous attacks and understanding attacker behavior, these systems can anticipate and counteract potential APT strategies, resulting in a more robust defense mechanism.

Real-World Scenarios and Data Comparisons

Several real-world cases demonstrate the effectiveness of different phishing detection techniques in combating advanced threats. One notable example involves a global financial institution that faced a series of sophisticated spear phishing attacks aimed at its executives. The organization initially relied on a traditional heuristic-based detection system, which failed to identify several targeted emails. After transitioning to a machine learning-based approach, the institution saw a dramatic reduction in successful attacks, reporting a 75% decrease in spear phishing incidents over a six-month period.

Another compelling case involves a multinational corporation that experienced a major APT, resulting in significant data breaches. The company's initial response relied on outdated signature-based detection methods, which proved ineffective against the highly customized phishing campaigns employed by the attackers. Following an extensive review, the corporation adopted an advanced machine learning solution that integrated real-time behavioral analytics and anomaly detection. Within weeks, the organization observed a substantial improvement in its ability to detect and mitigate APTs, significantly enhancing its overall cybersecurity posture.

3. CHALLENGES AND LIMITATIONS OF CURRENT DETECTION METHODS

3.1 Evasion Tactics: How Attackers Bypass Detection

Phishing attacks and the methods used by cybercriminals to avoid detection are always changing. Evasion tactics refer to the methods attackers utilize to bypass security systems and achieve their objectives, such as gaining unauthorized access to sensitive information or executing fraudulent transactions. This section explores the various evasion techniques commonly used by attackers, including URL shorteners and encrypted attachments, and provides an analysis of real phishing campaigns to illustrate how these methods are effectively leveraged.

Techniques Like URL Shorteners

One of the most prevalent tactics used by attackers to evade detection is the use of URL shorteners. These services condense lengthy URLs into shorter, more manageable links, which can obscure the destination website. By employing URL shorteners, attackers can disguise malicious links, making it difficult for traditional phishing detection systems to analyze the final destination. For instance, an email may contain a shortened link that appears harmless but redirects users to a fraudulent site designed to capture sensitive information.

Moreover, attackers often create multiple shortened links that point to the same malicious website, complicating detection efforts further. Since phishing detection systems typically rely on URL reputation and historical data, the transient nature of shortened links allows attackers to exploit vulnerabilities without being easily identified. In some cases, once the phishing campaign concludes, attackers may delete or modify the shortened URLs, rendering any detection efforts ineffective.

Encrypted Attachments

Another technique that poses significant challenges to phishing detection systems is the use of encrypted attachments. Attackers frequently send emails containing encrypted files to bypass content filtering systems. While these files may be password-protected or encrypted with sophisticated algorithms, the content remains hidden from traditional scanning techniques. This method is particularly dangerous because it can carry malicious payloads, such as malware or ransomware, which are only activated once the recipient decrypts and executes the file.

In addition to encrypted attachments, attackers may use social engineering tactics to entice victims into providing the necessary password to access the file, further complicating detection and response efforts. For example, a phishing email might claim to be a legitimate invoice or important document, prompting the victim to open the encrypted attachment and reveal the password, which the attacker has crafted as part of their scheme.

Analysis of Real Phishing Campaigns

Several high-profile phishing campaigns have illustrated the effectiveness of these evasion tactics. In one notable case, attackers targeted employees at a large multinational corporation using shortened URLs that led to a fake login page mimicking the company's internal system. Despite employing a robust phishing detection system, the organization struggled to identify the attack until several employees had already fallen victim. The use of URL shorteners effectively obscured the malicious links, highlighting a significant gap in the organization's detection capabilities.

Another example involved a financial institution that encountered a phishing attack utilizing encrypted email attachments. Attackers sent fraudulent emails with attachments labeled as "important account information" and included instructions for the recipient to decrypt the file. Many employees, believing the email to be legitimate, opened the attachment, resulting in a data breach that compromised sensitive customer information. This incident underscores the critical need for organizations to enhance their detection methods to account for such tactics.

3.2 False Positives and False Negatives

The notions of false positives and false negatives are crucial metrics in the field of phishing detection that have a substantial influence on the efficacy and efficiency of security systems.ystems. Understanding these terms and finding the right balance between detection sensitivity and accuracy are essential for organizations aiming to protect their sensitive information while minimizing disruptions to their operations.

Defining False Positives and Negatives

False positives occur when a phishing detection system incorrectly identifies a legitimate email or activity as a phishing attempt. This can lead to unnecessary alerts and disruptions, as employees may be prevented from accessing important communications or forced to verify seemingly benign transactions. While reducing the risk of a successful phishing attack is paramount, high rates of false positives can undermine productivity and erode trust in the detection system.

Conversely, **false negatives** represent a more insidious threat; they occur when a detection system fails to identify a genuine phishing attempt. This can result in users unwittingly falling victim to malicious schemes, leading to potential data breaches, financial losses, and reputational damage for organizations. Striking a balance between reducing false positives and minimizing false negatives is a significant challenge faced by cybersecurity professionals, as overly aggressive filtering may result in legitimate communications being blocked, while overly lenient settings could allow phishing attempts to bypass detection.

The Balance Between Detection Sensitivity and Accuracy

Achieving an optimal balance between sensitivity and accuracy is crucial for any phishing detection system. If a system is overly sensitive, it may flag legitimate emails as phishing attempts, generating numerous false positives that can frustrate users and distract from real threats. On the other hand, if a system is not sensitive enough, it risks allowing potentially harmful emails to slip through the cracks, resulting in false negatives that could lead to dire consequences.

To address this challenge, organizations often adopt multi-layered detection strategies that combine various detection techniques, such as signature-based, heuristic-based, and machine learning approaches. By utilizing a combination of methods, organizations can enhance their detection accuracy while minimizing the occurrence of false positives and negatives. For instance, machine learning algorithms can be trained to recognize patterns associated with phishing attempts while adjusting their sensitivity based on historical data, allowing them to adapt to evolving threats.

Case Study: Reducing False Positives in Email Systems

A notable case study involves a financial institution that faced significant challenges with false positives in its email filtering system. Employees frequently complained about legitimate emails being flagged as phishing attempts, causing delays in communication and productivity. The institution recognized the need to improve its detection accuracy while maintaining user trust in the system.

To address this issue, the institution implemented a combination of heuristic-based detection and machine learning algorithms. The new system utilized historical data on past phishing attempts and user feedback to refine its detection capabilities. By analyzing patterns associated with successful phishing attacks and correlating them with user behavior, the system became better equipped to distinguish between legitimate emails and phishing attempts.

The results were promising: the institution saw a significant reduction in false positives, leading to fewer disruptions for employees and an overall improvement in user satisfaction. Additionally, the enhanced system maintained its effectiveness in identifying actual phishing attempts, resulting in a decrease in false negatives. This case study underscores the importance of continuous improvement in phishing detection systems, demonstrating how a data-driven approach can lead to more accurate and reliable outcomes.

3.3 Adaptability: Addressing Evolving Phishing Tactics

Phishing tactics are continuously evolving, posing significant challenges to existing detection systems. Cybercriminals employ increasingly sophisticated strategies to bypass security measures, making it essential for organizations to adapt their defenses proactively. Understanding how new phishing tactics outpace detection systems, exploring examples such as Phishing-as-a-Service and AI-driven attacks, and examining emerging technologies in phishing detection are crucial for developing effective countermeasures.

How New Phishing Tactics Outpace Detection Systems

The rapid evolution of phishing tactics often leaves traditional detection systems struggling to keep pace. Attackers are constantly refining their methods to exploit vulnerabilities and take advantage of the latest technologies. For instance, while earlier phishing attempts primarily relied on deceptive emails, today's attackers leverage more intricate techniques, including social engineering, to manipulate users into providing sensitive information. They craft highly personalized messages, often using information gleaned from social media or other public sources, making it increasingly difficult for detection systems to identify these threats.

Additionally, the use of compromised legitimate accounts allows attackers to disguise their phishing attempts as genuine communications, further complicating detection efforts. These sophisticated strategies often exploit human psychology, making it essential for organizations to not only enhance their technological defenses but also educate employees about the risks and signs of phishing.

Examples: Phishing-as-a-Service, AI-Driven Attacks

Phishing-as-a-Service (PhaaS) is a burgeoning model that enables even less technically skilled cybercriminals to launch effective phishing campaigns. Through underground marketplaces, attackers can purchase ready-made phishing kits that come equipped with customizable templates and user-friendly interfaces. This democratization of phishing techniques means that virtually anyone with malicious intent can execute sophisticated attacks, further increasing the volume and variety of phishing attempts organizations face.

Moreover, AI-driven attacks have emerged as a formidable threat in the phishing landscape. Cybercriminals are leveraging artificial intelligence to automate their tactics, creating highly convincing phishing emails and websites that can adapt in real time based on user behavior. For instance, AI can analyze user interactions and dynamically alter the content of a phishing email to increase its chances of success, such as changing the urgency or the call-to-action based on user engagement metrics.

Emerging Technologies in Phishing Detection

In response to the evolving tactics used by cybercriminals, organizations are increasingly turning to emerging technologies to enhance their phishing detection capabilities. Machine learning algorithms, for example, can analyze vast datasets to identify patterns and anomalies associated with phishing attempts. These algorithms can be trained to recognize new tactics as they emerge, adapting their models to address shifting threat landscapes.

Natural Language Processing (NLP) is another technology that holds promise for improving phishing detection. By analyzing the language and tone of emails, NLP algorithms can help identify subtle cues that indicate phishing attempts, such as unusual phrasing or requests for sensitive information. Furthermore, behavioral analysis tools can monitor user activity and flag suspicious behavior, such as logging in from an unfamiliar device or location, providing an additional layer of security.

Emerging solutions like blockchain technology are also being explored for phishing prevention. By enabling decentralized verification processes, blockchain can help ensure that emails and communications originate from verified sources, thereby reducing the risk of phishing attacks. These technologies represent a proactive approach to combating phishing threats, allowing organizations to stay one step ahead of cybercriminals.

4. NATURAL LANGUAGE PROCESSING (NLP) IN PHISHING DETECTION

By concentrating on the language, tone, and general context of emails and messages, Natural Language Processing (NLP) in phishing detection is an advanced technique that surpasses conventional methods to identify phishing attempts. Traditional systems often rely on detecting static indicators, such as malicious URLs, suspicious email addresses, or known phishing signatures. However, NLP dives deeper by analyzing the actual content of the message—how words are structured, the emotional tone used, and the specific phrases that might signal a phishing attempt. Phishing emails commonly use manipulative tactics, such as urgency, fear, or requests for personal information, which can be detected through NLP. For instance, phrases like "your account will be suspended," "immediate action required," or "click here to verify" are red flags that NLP algorithms can quickly identify. Furthermore, NLP-based systems can evaluate the overall sentiment of the message, flagging communications that exhibit suspicious emotional manipulation. This ability to assess the context and intent behind an email's language makes NLP particularly effective against sophisticated phishing attacks, such as spear-phishing or whaling, where attackers target specific individuals with tailored messages. As phishing tactics evolve, the adaptability of NLP to understand natural language in real-time makes it a crucial tool in modern cybersecurity defenses.

Basics of NLP in Cybersecurity

Natural Language Processing (NLP) in cybersecurity is an innovative approach that leverages linguistic analysis to detect and mitigate security threats, particularly phishing attacks. At its core, NLP involves the use of algorithms to understand, process, and interpret human language in a way that computers can utilize for decision-making. In the context of cybersecurity, NLP is applied to examine communication content, such as emails, to identify suspicious language patterns, tone, or intent. This method differs from traditional phishing detection techniques, which typically focus on structural features like email headers, URLs, and sender addresses. NLP, on the other hand, focuses on how language is used within a message, such as identifying requests for sensitive information or manipulative phrases designed to trick recipients. By analyzing the semantics and syntax of a message, NLP can recognize phishing attempts that may otherwise evade detection. Its ability to process natural language allows for a deeper understanding of content, making NLP an increasingly critical component of modern cybersecurity strategies.

Use of NLP to Analyze Tone and Language in Emails

One of the most effective applications of NLP in cybersecurity is its ability to analyze the tone and language used in emails. Phishing emails are often crafted to elicit a sense of urgency, fear, or authority to trick people into doing something, such as clicking a malicious link or providing sensitive information. NLP systems can analyze these emotional cues by assessing word choices and sentence structures to determine if an email contains manipulative or coercive language. For instance, phrases like "urgent action required," "account suspension," or "verify your identity immediately" are common in phishing emails and signal attempts to pressure the recipient into responding without proper scrutiny. NLP-based systems can detect these emotional triggers, classifying the emails as potentially dangerous. Additionally, NLP can assess the overall sentiment of a message—whether it's neutral, positive, or negative—and flag those that convey a disproportionate sense of urgency or alarm. This ability to understand and evaluate the tone and intent behind the language used in emails significantly enhances the accuracy of phishing detection.

Practical Use Cases: Flagging Emotional Manipulation

NLP's role in detecting emotional manipulation is one of its most practical and effective applications in phishing detection. Phishing attacks frequently exploit emotions like fear, urgency, or greed to manipulate users into taking actions they otherwise wouldn't. For example, an email warning of an account breach or a suspicious login attempt often prompts immediate reactions from recipients. NLP-based systems can shield users from these manipulative strategies by highlighting such emotionally charged language. In a real-world scenario, an email with phrases like "your account has been compromised" or "click here to resolve the issue immediately" would be flagged by NLP algorithms as containing emotionally manipulative content, triggering further security checks. Organizations across various sectors—such as financial services, healthcare, and e-commerce—are increasingly adopting NLP tools to detect phishing attacks that leverage these emotional appeals. The ability of NLP to filter and analyze the emotional undertones in communications helps organizations mitigate the risk of phishing attacks by raising awareness of these tactics before users can be exploited.

Future Directions: AI-Driven NLP Solutions

The future of NLP in cybersecurity is closely intertwined with advancements in artificial intelligence (AI). AI-driven NLP solutions represent the next frontier in phishing detection, offering more sophisticated and adaptive systems that can continuously learn and improve over time. These systems will not only be able to identify and flag existing phishing patterns but also predict and adapt to new and emerging phishing tactics as they evolve. For instance, AI-enhanced NLP systems could learn from large datasets of phishing and non-phishing communications to develop more nuanced models that identify threats based on even more subtle variations in language and tone. Additionally, future NLP solutions may incorporate deep learning techniques that allow for real-time detection and response, automatically updating filters and protection mechanisms as phishing methods become more advanced. AI-driven NLP will also likely integrate with other cybersecurity technologies, such as behavioral analytics and anomaly detection, to provide a more comprehensive defense against phishing. As phishing attacks continue to grow more sophisticated, AI-powered NLP solutions will be essential in keeping pace with and countering these threats.

5. BLOCKCHAIN TECHNOLOGY FOR ANTI-PHISHING

Understanding Blockchain for Digital Authentication

Blockchain technology(Yaga et al., 2019) is fundamentally a decentralized, distributed ledger system that records transactions in a secure and tamper-resistant manner. In cybersecurity, blockchain is gaining traction for its potential in enhancing digital authentication processes. Traditional systems of digital authentication often rely on centralized authorities, making them susceptible to isolated failures, data breaches, or manipulation. Blockchain, however, offers a decentralized approach where data is stored in cryptographically secured blocks across a distributed network. Eevery block is connected to the one before it, forming a chain that is nearly impossible to alter without the consensus of the entire network. This structure ensures the integrity and security of digital transactions, including email communications, making blockchain an attractive solution for preventing phishing and other cyber threats. By using blockchain, email authentication can be verified independently and securely, reducing the chances of phishing emails being delivered to the end-user.

How Blockchain Reduces Phishing Risks in Emails

Blockchain can significantly reduce phishing risks in emails by enabling decentralized verification of sender identities and email authenticity. Phishing emails typically involve the impersonation of legitimate sources, and traditional email verification methods, like domain-based message authentication, reporting, & conformance (DMARC) or the Sender Policy Framework (SPF) (Insights2Techinfo, 2021), can be bypassed by sophisticated attackers. Blockchain introduces a more robust alternative, where email metadata and sender information are stored on a blockchain ledger. This allows recipients to cross-check the origin and authenticity of an email without relying on a central authority. In this system, the email's sender identity and integrity are cryptographically verified by the blockchain network, making it much harder for attackers to forge or tamper with emails. Blockchain also supports smart contracts, which can automatically validate email content, links, and attachments before they reach the recipient's inbox, providing an extra layer of defense against phishing attempts.

Use Case: Decentralized Verification in High-Risk Environments

A key use case for blockchain technology in anti-phishing efforts is in high-risk environments where data security is paramount, such as financial institutions, government agencies, and healthcare organizations. In these sectors, the repercussions of becoming a victim of phishing attacks can be catastrophic, leading to data breaches, economic losses, or exposure of sensitive information. By employing blockchain-based decentralized verification systems, these organizations can create a secure framework where email communications are independently authenticated without the need for a central authority. For instance, in a decentralized system, each email would be signed and verified by multiple nodes on the blockchain network before being delivered. This ensures that any attempt to alter or forge the email would be immediately detected and rejected. Financial institutions, in particular, have begun exploring blockchain for verifying transaction-related emails, ensuring that communication about sensitive financial operations cannot be intercepted or manipulated by phishing attackers. This decentralized verification approach increases trust, security, and transparency in email communication, significantly reducing the risk of phishing in high-risk environments.

6. BEHAVIORAL ANALYSIS IN PHISHING DETECTION

Monitoring User Activity to Identify Phishing Attempts

Behavioral analysis plays a crucial role in phishing detection by continuously monitoring user activity to identify anomalous behaviors that could signal a phishing attack. Phishing attempts frequently entail deceiving users into granting unauthorized access to private data or systems through subtle manipulation. By tracking normal user behavior patterns, such as login times, frequency of email access, or regular geographic locations, behavioral analysis tools can detect deviations from the norm. When unusual behavior is detected, such as a user logging in from an unexpected location or attempting to access sensitive data outside of typical working hours, it raises red flags for potential phishing activity. These anomalies prompt immediate investigation or trigger automated responses, like temporarily locking the account or requiring multi-factor authentication to verify the user's identity.

Detecting Unusual Login Patterns and IP Changes

One of the most effective applications of behavioral analysis is in detecting unusual login patterns and IP address changes, which are often indicators of compromised accounts following a phishing attack. Cybercriminals typically use phishing techniques to steal credentials, enabling them to access a victim's account from unfamiliar IP addresses or geographic regions. Behavioral analytics systems can track and flag these deviations in real-time. For example, if an employee consistently logs in from New York but suddenly accesses the system from a foreign country, the system will flag this as a high-risk event. Similarly, changes in device types, operating systems, or frequent failed login attempts could also signal phishing-related account compromise. These systems enable early detection and allow security teams to respond before significant damage is done.

Behavioral Analytics in Corporate Security Systems

In corporate environments, behavioral analytics systems have become an essential component of phishing defense strategies. These systems not only monitor user behavior but also integrate with additional security tools to offer a thorough perspective of possible dangers. By analyzing patterns across emails, network access, and system usage, behavioral analytics can detect coordinated phishing attacks aimed at multiple employees or departments. Corporate security systems that employ behavioral analysis can also distinguish between legitimate business requests and suspicious activities. For example, if an email instructs an employee to transfer large sums of money—a common phishing tactic—behavioral analytics could compare the request with past behavior and determine whether it fits the typical pattern for that user. This intelligent monitoring allows organizations to mitigate risks posed by phishing attacks before they result in serious breaches or financial losses.

Case Example: How Behavioral Monitoring Detected a Phishing Attack

An illustrative case of behavioral monitoring in action is the detection of a spear-phishing attack at a multinational corporation. In this scenario, a high-ranking executive received a sophisticated phishing email that appeared to originate from an authoritative source. requesting sensitive financial information. The executive initially complied with the request, but behavioral monitoring systems flagged the subsequent activity as unusual. The system noticed that the request deviated from the executive's typical email and communication patterns. Moreover, the request involved accessing financial data at an unusual time of day and from an IP address that the executive had never used before. Due to these red flags, the system automatically flagged the incident for immediate investigation, preventing the unauthorized transaction and stopping the phishing attack before it could cause damage.

7. CASE STUDIES

7.1 Case Study 1: Company X's Machine Learning Implementation

Details of Machine Learning Model Deployment

Company X, a leading financial services firm, recognized the rising threat of phishing attacks that targeted its employees and clients, risking sensitive financial data and potentially damaging its reputation. To counter these threats, the company implemented a comprehensive machine learning (ML) model(Sarin et al., 2024) tailored specifically for phishing detection. The deployment process started with a thorough assessment of the state-of-the-art phishing detection techniques. Subsequently, relevant machine learning algorithms were selected to analyze email content and user behavior patterns, such as decision trees and support vector machines.

The ML model was trained on a large dataset consisting of historical phishing and legitimate emails. This dataset was crucial for teaching the system to identify subtle differences between benign and malicious communications. In order to allow the design to change and enhance its detection capabilities over time, new phishing attempts were added to the dataset during the training phase. To ensure successful deployment, Company X collaborated with cybersecurity experts to fine-tune the model and integrate it seamlessly into their existing email filtering and security systems. The integration involved setting up a feedback loop where the system could learn from false positives and negatives, gradually enhancing its accuracy.

40% Reduction in Phishing Incidents

Following the implementation of the machine learning model, Company X experienced a significant reduction in phishing incidents—approximately 40% within the first six months. This drop was attributed to the ML model's ability to detect sophisticated phishing techniques that traditional signature-based systems often overlooked. By analyzing various features such as email metadata, text content, and user interaction patterns, the system successfully flagged suspicious emails before they reached the employees' inboxes.

One key factor contributing to this success was the model's adaptability. Unlike static detection methods, the machine learning system continuously learned from new data, allowing it to identify emerging phishing tactics. The real-time detection capability meant that employees were less likely to encounter malicious emails, thereby reducing the risk of compromised accounts and financial losses. Additionally, the reduced number of phishing incidents also translated into decreased workload for the IT security team, allowing them to focus on other critical security initiatives.

Insights and Lessons Learned

The implementation of the machine learning model at Company X yielded several important insights and lessons. First, it highlighted the necessity of ongoing training and updates for machine learning algorithms to maintain high accuracy in phishing detection. Cyber threats evolve rapidly, and keeping the ML model current with the latest phishing tactics is vital for effective defense.

Second, the case study emphasized the importance of cross-department collaboration in cybersecurity initiatives. By involving not only the IT security team but also departments such as compliance, risk management, and user education, Company X was able to create a more holistic approach to cybersecurity. This collaboration led to the development of comprehensive training programs for employees, educating them about recognizing phishing attempts and encouraging a culture of vigilance.

Finally, Company X learned that user feedback is invaluable for improving detection systems. Employees were encouraged to report suspicious emails, and this feedback was instrumental in refining the machine learning model. The organization's commitment to fostering an environment of proactive cybersecurity awareness contributed to the overall success of the machine learning implementation.

7.2 Case Study 2: High-Profile Phishing Attack on a Government Agency

Anatomy of the Phishing Attack

In a notable incident, a government agency fell victim to a sophisticated phishing attack that compromised sensitive information and disrupted essential services. The attack began with a well-crafted email that appeared to come from a trusted source within the agency, containing a request for updated personnel information. The email included a link to a counterfeit website designed to resemble the agency's legitimate site, where employees were prompted to enter their usernames and passwords. Unsuspecting users complied, believing they were fulfilling a routine request.

Once the attackers obtained the credentials, they gained unauthorized access to the agency's internal systems, allowing them to exfiltrate sensitive data, including classified documents and personal information of employees. The breach went unnoticed for several days, during which the attackers leveraged the stolen credentials to escalate their access, causing extensive damage before the incident was finally detected.

What Went Wrong: Lack of Adequate Detection

The primary factor that contributed to the success of this phishing attack was the agency's lack of adequate detection mechanisms. The existing email filtering systems primarily relied on signature-based detection, which was ineffective against the social engineering tactics employed in this attack. While the email seemed legitimate and contained no malicious links or attachments, it exploited the trust inherent in the agency's internal communications.

Additionally, the agency had not implemented robust user training programs to educate employees about recognizing phishing attempts, particularly those that mimic internal communications. The absence of a culture of skepticism regarding unsolicited requests for sensitive information further exacerbated the situation. Consequently, employees were not equipped to question the legitimacy of the email they received, leading to the widespread compromise of credentials.

Analysis of the Detection Methods That Could Have Prevented the Attack

To prevent such attacks in the future, several detection methods could have been employed. A multi-layered security approach that included machine learning-based anomaly detection could have significantly reduced the risk. By analyzing patterns of user behavior and flagging unusual activities, such as multiple failed login attempts or access from unfamiliar locations, the system could have alerted IT personnel to the potential breach.

Moreover, implementing natural language processing (NLP) techniques could have enhanced the detection of phishing emails by analyzing the language used in the communications. NLP could identify suspicious phrases commonly associated with phishing, such as urgent requests for personal information, and flag these emails for further scrutiny.

Using domain-based message authentication, reporting, and conformance (DMARC) would have also made it easier to distinguish between spoof emails and real ones. By verifying that emails from within the agency were indeed sent from authorized accounts, DMARC would have provided an added layer of security against phishing attempts that masqueraded as internal messages.

8. BEST PRACTICES FOR IMPLEMENTING PHISHING DETECTION

Although sophisticated phishing detection systems, especially those that use AI and machine learning, have a lot of promise, putting them into practice presents some significant difficulties. The high computational cost of AI-based methods can strain organizational resources, requiring significant investment in infrastructure and processing power. Machine learning models also demand extensive datasets for effective training, which can be difficult to obtain and maintain, especially for organizations with limited access to diverse and labeled data. Furthermore, these systems may encounter resistance from users who perceive security measures, such as multi-factor authentication or frequent email quarantines, as cumbersome or disruptive to workflows. Balancing usability with security remains a critical task, necessitating thoughtful design and communication to encourage adoption without compromising protection. Addressing these challenges is essential for fully realizing the benefits of advanced phishing detection systems.

To bolster defenses against phishing attacks, organizations, including government agencies, should implement several best practices for phishing detection:

1. **Multi-Factor Authentication (MFA)**: Multi-Factor Authentication (MFA): Implementing MFA adds an extra layer ofsecurity by requiring additional verification methods beyond just usernames and passwords. Even in the event that hackers manage to obtain login credentials, this increases the difficulty of their gaining unauthorized access.
2. **Comprehensive Employee Training**: Regular training sessions on recognizing phishing attempts are essential. Employees should be educated about the various forms phishing can take, including spear phishing and whaling, and how to identify red flags in communications.
3. **Advanced Email Filtering Solutions**: Organizations should invest in sophisticated email filtering solutions that utilize machine learning and NLP to analyze incoming messages. These systems can adapt to new phishing tactics and improve detection rates over time.
4. **Perpetual surveillance and the detection of anomalies:** Establishing systems for continuous monitoring of user behavior can help detect anomalies that may indicate a phishing attack or compromised account. This includes tracking unusual login attempts and access to sensitive data.
5. **Incident Response Plan**: Having a clear incident response plan guarantees that businesses can respond to phishing incidents promptly. This plan should include clear protocols for reporting suspicious emails, mitigating damage, and recovering compromised accounts.
6. **Collaboration with Cybersecurity Experts (Sharma, Singh, Kumar, Chhabra, & Gupta, 2021)**: Engaging with cybersecurity vendors can provide access to the latest technologies and expertise in phishing detection. Collaboration can enhance the organization's overall security posture.

Layered Defense Strategy

To effectively combat the growing sophistication of phishing attacks in the constantly changing field of cybersecurity, organizations must implement a layered defense strategy. This approach involves integrating multiple detection methods to create a comprehensive security framework that enhances overall protection against various threats. By leveraging different techniques, organizations can address the limitations of individual systems, ensuring that even if one layer fails, additional defenses remain in place to thwart potential breaches.

Combining Multiple Detection Methods for Higher Accuracy

A layered defense strategy typically incorporates a combination of signature-based detection, heuristic analysis, machine learning algorithms, and user education. For instance, while signature-based detection effectively identifies known threats based on established signatures, heuristic analysis can detect new or unknown phishing attempts by identifying suspicious patterns and behaviors. Machine learning models add an additional layer by continuously adapting to emerging threats, improving accuracy over time. Furthermore, educating users about the risks and signs of phishing enables them to recognize and report suspicious emails, enhancing the overall defense posture.

Integrating these methods creates a multi-faceted approach that significantly increases detection accuracy. For example, an organization might deploy advanced email filtering systems that use machine learning to analyze incoming emails for anomalies while simultaneously applying content filtering techniques to identify phishing keywords. By combining these methods, organizations can reduce false positives and ensure that legitimate communications are not flagged incorrectly, thus maintaining productivity while enhancing security.

Examples of Successful Layered Defense Systems

Several organizations have successfully implemented layered defense strategies, showcasing the effectiveness of this approach. For instance, a large financial institution adopted a multi-layered security architecture that included advanced email filtering systems, behavioral analytics, and employee training programs. The email filtering system utilized machine learning algorithms to analyze patterns of phishing attacks, while behavioral analytics monitored user activities for signs of compromise. The combination of these systems resulted in a **50% reduction** in successful phishing attempts, demonstrating the effectiveness of layering defenses.

Another example is a healthcare organization that integrated a layered defense strategy to safeguard patient data. The organization implemented a combination of endpoint security, network monitoring, and user awareness training. By using machine learning-based detection systems to analyze network traffic for signs of phishing attempts, the organization was able to detect and block potential threats in real time. Simultaneously, regular training sessions educated staff on recognizing phishing emails and practicing safe online behavior. This comprehensive approach not only improved detection rates but also fostered a culture of cybersecurity awareness among employees.

Regular Training and Testing

In the fight against phishing attacks, **regular training and testing** of employees play a pivotal role in strengthening an organization's security posture. Since one of the biggest cybersecurity vulnerabilities is still human error, it is crucial to arm staff members with the knowledge and abilities they need to spot phishing attempts and take appropriate action. By fostering a culture of awareness and vigilance, organizations can significantly reduce the likelihood of successful phishing attacks.

Importance of Employee Education on Phishing

Employee education is critical because phishing tactics are continually evolving, becoming highly sophisticated and more difficult to identify. Regular training sessions ensure that staff are informed about the latest phishing trends, tactics, and potential red flags. This education helps employees understand the various forms that phishing can take, including deceptive emails, fake websites, and social engineering techniques. Additionally, training programs can cover best practices for maintaining security, such as verifying the authenticity of requests for sensitive information and reporting suspicious communications to IT security teams. By equipping employees with this knowledge, organizations create a workforce that is not only aware of the risks but also proactive in preventing phishing attacks.

Moreover, regular training reinforces the importance of a security-conscious mindset among employees. When staff members are educated about the potential consequences of falling victim to phishing scams, including data breaches and financial losses, they are more likely to remain vigilant and cautious when handling emails and other communications. This cultural shift towards cybersecurity mindfulness is essential for creating an environment where employees feel responsible for safeguarding sensitive information.

Simulated Phishing Attacks and Their Role in Training

To complement educational efforts, many organizations are now incorporating **simulated phishing attacksTso& Keung, 2020** as a key component of their training programs. These simulations replicate actual phishing attempts, giving staff members a useful, hands-on understanding of how these attacks can happen. By subjecting employees to controlled phishing scenarios, organizations can assess their ability to recognize and respond to potential threats.

The understanding that these simulations provide is priceless. Organizations can identify areas where employees may need additional training and refine their educational materials accordingly. For instance, if a significant number of employees fail to recognize simulated phishing emails, targeted training sessions can be implemented to address specific weaknesses. Furthermore, simulated attacks can help build resilience among employees, as they learn to spot red flags and develop the confidence to act appropriately in response to suspicious communications.

Additionally, the use of simulated phishing attacks can reinforce accountability among staff. When employees know that they will be subjected to regular phishing tests, they are more likely to remain vigilant and apply the knowledge gained during training sessions. This proactive strategy encourages a shared sense of responsibility for cybersecurity throughout the company in addition to raising individual awareness.

Collaboration with Third-Party Services

In the complex landscape of cybersecurity, **collaboration with third-party services** has emerged as a vital strategy for enhancing phishing defense. External cybersecurity vendors provide resources, cutting-edge technologies, and specialized knowledge that can significantly improve an organization's capacity to recognize and counteract phishing attacks. As phishing attacks become increasingly sophisticated, leveraging the knowledge and capabilities of external partners can provide organizations with a more robust defense mechanism.

External Cybersecurity Vendors and Their Role in Phishing Defense

External cybersecurity (Aggarwal, Singh, Chopra, Kumar, & Colace, 2022) vendors bring a wealth of experience and specialized skills to the table, which can be instrumental in identifying and mitigating phishing risks. These vendors often have access to cutting-edge technologies, including machine learning algorithms, advanced analytics, and threat intelligence databases, which allow them to detect phishing attempts more effectively than many internal teams could achieve alone. By integrating third-party solutions, organizations can enhance their existing security measures and gain insights into emerging threats that they may not have been aware of.

Additionally, many external vendors offer comprehensive phishing detection services, such as real-time monitoring, automated threat detection, and incident response capabilities. These services allow organizations to focus on their core business operations while relying on experts to handle the intricacies of phishing threat management. By outsourcing phishing detection, organizations can ensure that they are protected by state-of-the-art tools and methodologies, thereby reducing the risk of falling victim to advanced phishing attacks.

Real-World Examples: Outsourcing Phishing Detection

Numerous organizations have successfully collaborated with third-party cybersecurity vendors to enhance their phishing detection capabilities. For instance, a well-known financial institution partnered with a cybersecurity firm specializing in threat intelligence. This collaboration enabled the bank to implement advanced phishing detection systems that utilized machine learning algorithms to analyze email patterns and identify potential threats in real time. As a result of this partnership, the institution reported a significant reduction in successful phishing attempts and an increase in the overall security posture of its email systems.

Another example can be seen in the healthcare sector, where sensitive patient information is a prime target for phishing attacks. A large hospital network outsourced its phishing detection to a specialized vendor that provided continuous monitoring and threat analysis. The hospital reduced the risk of data breaches and ensured regulatory compliance by promptly responding to phishing threats by utilizing the vendor's expertise. The collaboration not only improved the hospital's security measures but also freed up internal IT resources to focus on other critical tasks.

9. FUTURE TRENDS IN PHISHING DETECTION

As phishing attacks grow in sophistication and prevalence, future trends in phishing detection(Mengi, Singh, Kumar, Mahto, & Sharma, 2021)are expected to focus on integrating advanced technologies and proactive strategies to mitigate these threats effectively. A significant trend is the increasing reliance on artificial intelligence (AI) and behavioral analytics, both of which hold great promise for enhancing phishing detection capabilities. AI systems can analyze massive datasets and identify patterns that are difficult for humans to discern, allowing for quicker and more accurate detection of phishing attempts. These systems can learn from historical data and continuously improve their algorithms to adapt to evolving tactics used by cybercriminals. Moreover, as new phishing schemes emerge, AI-driven detection tools can be updated in real time, ensuring that organizations remain one step ahead of attackers. In addition, the deployment of machine learning models allows organizations to automate the analysis of incoming emails and web traffic, reducing the reliance on manual review and enabling a more agile response to potential threats.

10. THE ROLE OF AI AND BEHAVIORAL ANALYTICS IN THE FUTURE OF CYBERSECURITY

The role of AI and behavioral analytics in the future of cybersecurity(Setia et al., 2024) cannot be overstated, particularly concerning phishing detection. AI technologies enable organizations to build robust systems that analyze various data points, including email content, sender behavior, and user interactions, to identify phishing attempts with greater accuracy. Machine learning algorithms can discern subtle variations in user behavior that may indicate malicious intent, such as a sudden change in login patterns or unusual access to sensitive data. These algorithms become more effective over time as they process new data, allowing organizations to detect phishing attempts that may evade traditional detection methods. Furthermore, behavioral analytics enhances security measures by continuously monitoring user activity to establish baselines for normal behavior. When deviations from these baselines occur—such as an employee logging in from an unfamiliar location or at an unusual hour—alerts can be generated for further investigation. This dual approach not only helps identify phishing attempts but also strengthens overall cybersecurity by flagging potential insider threats or compromised accounts.

Moreover, as cybercriminals adopt increasingly sophisticated tactics like Phishing-as-a-Service and AI-driven attacks, the landscape of cybersecurity will require ongoing innovation in detection methodologies. Future developments may include advanced collaborative frameworks between organizations and cybersecurity vendors, facilitating the sharing of threat intelligence and best practices to combat evolving threats collectively. Additionally, as phishing attempts become more psychologically manipulative—exploiting emotional triggers like urgency or fear—enhancements in natural language processing (NLP) will be crucial. NLP technologies will enable systems to conduct nuanced analyses of email content, identifying red flags such as emotionally charged language or unusual requests for sensitive information. By combining AI, behavioral analytics, and NLP, organizations can develop a multi-layered defense strategy that not only blocks phishing attempts but also educates users about potential threats, fostering a culture of security awareness and resilience.

CONCLUSION

Implementing effective phishing detection requires a combination of best practices and practical strategies to protect against evolving threats. Organizations should adopt a layered defense approach, integrating signature-based, heuristic, and advanced machine learning detection methods to improve accuracy and adaptability. Regular retraining of models with updated datasets ensures detection systems remain effective against new phishing tactics. Investing in tools like natural language processing and behavioral analytics can enhance the detection of manipulative language and anomalous user behaviors. Additionally, organizations should emphasize employee training with simulated phishing attacks and enforce strong policies such as multi-factor authentication. Collaboration with third-party cybersecurity vendors can provide cutting-edge technologies and expertise. By combining these measures, organizations can significantly reduce phishing risks and enhance their overall security posture.

REFERENCES

Abawajy, J. H., & Kim, J. (2020). A New Approach for Phishing Detection. *Computers & Security*, 89, 101681. DOI: 10.1016/j.cose.2019.101681

Abu-Nimeh, S., Yaseen, Y., & Arachchilage, N. A. G. (2007). Comparative Evaluation of Phishing Detection Techniques. *International Journal of Information Security*, 6(3), 239–253. DOI: 10.1007/s10207-007-0042-5

Aggarwal, K., Singh, S. K., Chopra, M., Kumar, S., & Colace, F. (2022). Deep Learning in Robotics for Strengthening Industry 4.0.: Opportunities, Challenges and Future Directions. In Nedjah, N., Abd El-Latif, A. A., Gupta, B. B., & Mourelle, L. M. (Eds.), *Robotics and AI for Cybersecurity and Critical Infrastructure in Smart Cities. Studies in Computational Intelligence* (Vol. 1030). Springer., DOI: 10.1007/978-3-030-96737-6_1

Almomani, A., Alauthman, M., Shatnawi, M. T., Alweshah, M., Alrosan, A., Alomoush, W., Gupta, B. B., Gupta, B. B., & Gupta, B. B. (2022). Phishing website detection with semantic features based on machine learning classifiers: A comparative study. [IJSWIS]. *International Journal on Semantic Web and Information Systems*, 18(1), 1–24. DOI: 10.4018/IJSWIS.297032

Arora, L., Singh, S. K., Kumar, S., Gupta, H., Alhalabi, W., Arya, V., Bansal, S., Chui, K. T., & Gupta, B. B. (2024). Ensemble deep learning and EfficientNet for accurate diagnosis of diabetic retinopathy. *Scientific Reports*, 14(1), 30554. Advance online publication. DOI: 10.1038/s41598-024-81132-4 PMID: 39695310

Badwa, E., Singh, S. K., Kumar, S., Chilkoti, V., Arya, V., & Chui, K. T. (2024). Deep Learning Model for Digital Forensics Face Sketch Synthesis. In Digital Forensics and Cyber Crime Investigation (pp. 168-195). CRC Press.

Basnet, R., Mukkamala, S., & Sung, A. (2008). Anomaly Detection in Phishing. *Proceedings of the 2008 IEEE International Conference on Intelligence and Security Informatics*, 89-94.

Bergholz, A., (2010). Using Machine Learning for Phishing Detection. *Computers & Security*, 29(1), 89–95. DOI: 10.1016/j.cose.2009.07.005

Bisht, J., & Vampugani, V. S. (2022). Load and cost-aware min-min workflow scheduling algorithm for heterogeneous resources in fog, cloud, and edge scenarios. [IJCAC]. *International Journal of Cloud Applications and Computing*, 12(1), 1–20. DOI: 10.4018/IJCAC.2022010105

Fette, I., Fuller, A., & Freeman, D. (2007). Phishing Detection Using Phonetic and Semantic Analysis. In *Proceedings of the 2007 IEEE International Conference on Intelligence and Security Informatics (ISI '07)*, 1-6.

Garera, S., Dingledine, R., & Moore, T. (2007). A Survey of Anti-Phishing Tools. In *Proceedings of the 2007 ACM Workshop on Recurring Malcode (WORM '07)*, 1-10.

Gaurav, A., Gupta, B. B., Chui, K. T., & Arya, V. (2024, January). Enhancing Email Security in Consumer Electronics with a Hybrid Deep Learning Approach. In *2024 IEEE International Conference on Consumer Electronics (ICCE)* (pp. 1-5). IEEE. DOI: 10.1109/ICCE59016.2024.10444468

Ghalechyan, H., Israyelyan, E., Arakelyan, A., Hovhannisyan, G., & Davtyan, A. (2024). Phishing URL detection with neural networks: An empirical study. *Scientific Reports*, 14(1), 25134. Advance online publication. DOI: 10.1038/s41598-024-74725-6 PMID: 39448673

Goyal, S., Kumar, S., Singh, S. K., Sarin, S., Priyanshu, , Gupta, B. B., Arya, V., Alhalabi, W., & Colace, F. (2024). Synergistic application of neuro-fuzzy mechanisms in advanced neural networks for real-time stream data flux mitigation. *Soft Computing*, 28(20), 1–13. DOI: 10.1007/s00500-024-09938-y

Goyal, S., Singh, S. K., Kumar, S., Sarin, S., Gupta, B. B., Arya, V., & Chui, K. T. (2023, November). Hyperdimensional Consumer Pattern Analysis with Quantum Neural Architectures using Non-Hermitian Operators. In *Proceedings of the 5th International Conference on Information Management & Machine Intelligence* (pp. 1-5).

Gupta, B. B., Gaurav, A., Attar, R. W., Arya, V., Alhomoud, A., & Chui, K. T. (2024). Optimized Phishing Detection with Recurrent Neural Network and Whale Optimizer Algorithm. *Computers, Materials & Continua*, 80(3), 4895–4916. DOI: 10.32604/cmc.2024.050815

Gupta, S., (2021). Phishing Detection in Social Networks. *Journal of Information Security and Applications*, 56, 102667. DOI: 10.1016/j.jisa.2020.102667

Heiding, F., Schneier, B., & Vishwanath, A. (2024, September 6). AI Will Increase the Quantity — and Quality — of Phishing Scams. Harvard Business Review. https://hbr.org/2024/05/ai-will-increase-the-quantity-and-quality-of-phishing-scams

Heiding, Schneier, & Vishwanath, (2024). Phishing URL Detection Using Machine Learning and Deep Learning. (2024, May 29). IEEE Conference Publication | IEEE Xplore. https://ieeexplore.ieee.org/document/10579005

Insights2Techinfo. (2021, October 16). Blockchain for Data Science. https://insights2techinfo.com/blockchain-for-data-science/

Jahankhani, A., John, N. W., & Weddell, G. (2021). Phishing: An Overview of Threats, Techniques, and Mitigation. *Journal of Cybersecurity and Privacy*, 1(2), 204–221. DOI: 10.3390/jcp1020012

Jain, A. K., Gupta, B. B., Kaur, K., Bhutani, P., Alhalabi, W., & Almomani, A. (2022). A content and URL analysis-based efficient approach to detect smishing SMS in intelligent systems. *International Journal of Intelligent Systems*, 37(12), 11117–11141. DOI: 10.1002/int.23035

Kaur, P., Singh, S. K., Singh, I., & Kumar, S. (2021, December). Exploring Convolutional Neural Network in Computer Vision-based Image Classification. In *International Conference on Smart Systems and Advanced Computing (Syscom-2021).*

Kumar, A., Nelson, L., & Kumar, S. (2023, December). Enhancing Haemorrhage Detection in Head CT Scans Using Deep Learning. In 2023 3rd International Conference on Smart Generation Computing,Communication and Networking (SMART GENCON) (pp. 1-6). IEEE. DOI: 10.1109/SMARTGENCON60755.2023.10442342

Luo, Y., & Wang, W. (2022). Combating Phishing: The Role of Regulations and Best Practices. *Journal of Information Technology & Politics*, 19(1), 18–33. DOI: 10.1080/19331681.2022.2059384

Mamun, M. A. A., (2016). Behavioral Analysis for Phishing Detection. *Journal of Network and Computer Applications*, 70, 28–36. DOI: 10.1016/j.jnca.2016.06.018

Mengi, G., Singh, S. K., Kumar, S., Mahto, D., & Sharma, A. (2021, September). Automated Machine Learning (AutoML): The Future of Computational Intelligence In *International Conference on Cyber Security, Privacy and Networking* (pp. 309-317).

Neelapareddigari, P. (2024) Machine Learning for Phishing detection, Insights2Techinfo,pp.1, https://insights2techinfo.com/machine-learning-for-phishing-detection/

Onyebuchi, A., Matthew, U. O., Kazaure, J. S., Okafor, N. U., Okey, O. D., Okochi, P. I., Taiwo, J. F., & Matthew, A. O. (2022). Business demand for a cloud enterprise data warehouse in electronic healthcare computing: Issues and developments in e-healthcare cloud computing. [IJCAC]. *International Journal of Cloud Applications and Computing*, 12(1), 1–22. DOI: 10.4018/IJCAC.297098

Rao, P. S., & Pais, M. (2019). Phishing Email Detection Using Deep Learning. *International Journal of Computer Applications*, 975, 8887.

Sahoo, D., (2017). Unsupervised Phishing Detection Using Deep Learning. *International Journal of Computer Applications*, 169(2), 16–21.

Sarin, S., Singh, S. K., Kumar, S., Chauhan, U., Goyal, S., Singh, T., . . . Colace, F. (2023, August). FuzzyBack—A Hybrid Neuro-Fuzzy Ensemble for Concept Drift Adaptation in Stream Mining Using Neural Network. In International conference on soft computing for problem-solving (pp. 401-412). Singapore: Springer Nature Singapore.

Sarin, S., Singh, S. K., Kumar, S., & Goyal, S. (2024). Geospectra: Leveraging quantum-SAR and deep learning for enhanced geolocation in urban environments. *The Journal of Supercomputing*, 81(1), 223. Advance online publication. DOI: 10.1007/s11227-024-06619-3

Setia, H., Chhabra, A., Singh, S. K., Kumar, S., Sharma, S., Arya, V., Gupta, B. B., & Wu, J. (2024). Securing the road ahead: Machine learning-driven DDoS attack detection in VANET cloud environments. *Cyber Security and Applications*, 2, 100037. DOI: 10.1016/j.csa.2024.100037

Shaik, D. A. (2024) Using AI to Combat Phishing Attacks, Insights2Techinfo, pp.1; https://insights2techinfo.com/using-ai-to-combat-phishing-attacks/

Sharma, A., Singh, S. K., Kumar, S., Chhabra, A., & Gupta, S. (2021, September). Security of Android Banking Mobile Apps: *Challenges and Opportunities. In International Conference on Cyber Security, Privacy and Networking* (pp. 406-416). Cham: Springer International Publishing

Singh, A., Singh, S. K., Chhabra, A., Singh, G., Kumar, S., & Arya, V. (2025). Detailed Evolution Process of CNN-Based Intrusion Detection in the Context of Network Security. In Digital Forensics and Cyber Crime Investigation (pp. 70-87). CRC Press.

Singh, S. K., Kumar, S., Garg, S., Arora, S., Sharma, S. K., Arya, V., & Chui, K. T. (2025). Blockchain-Based Data Security in Smart Cities: Ensuring Data Integrity and Trustworthiness. In Digital Forensics and Cyber Crime Investigation (pp. 17-41). CRC Press.

Tembhurne, J. V., Almin, M. M., & Diwan, T. (2022). Mc-DNN: Fake news detection using multi-channel deep neural networks. [IJSWIS]. *International Journal on Semantic Web and Information Systems*, 18(1), 1–20. DOI: 10.4018/IJSWIS.295553

Thakur, R., Kumar, S., Singh, S. K., Singla, K., Sharma, S. K., & Arya, V. (2025). Cyber Synergy: Unlocking the Potential Use of Biometric Systems and Multimedia Forensics in Cybercrime Investigations. In Digital Forensics and Cyber Crime Investigation (pp. 241-267). CRC Press.

Tso, S. K., & Keung, K. W. (2020). Understanding Phishing Attacks: A Comprehensive Review. *International Journal of Information Security*, 19(5), 529–546. DOI: 10.1007/s10207-020-00503-8

Vajrobol, V., Gupta, B. B., & Gaurav, A. (2024). Mutual information based logistic regression for phishing URL detection. *Cyber Security and Applications*, 2, 100044. DOI: 10.1016/j.csa.2024.100044

Vats, T., Kumar, S., Singh, S. K., Madan, U., Preet, M., Arya, V., Bansal, R., & Almomani, A. (2024). Navigating the landscape: Safeguarding privacy and security in the era of ambient intelligence within healthcare settings. *Cyber Security and Applications*, 2, 100046. DOI: 10.1016/j.csa.2024.100046

Yaga, D., (2019). Blockchain Technology Overview. National Institute of Standards and Technology (NIST). NIST Special Publication 800-208.

Yang, Y., Zhang, J., & Zeng, Y. (2019). An Empirical Study on Phishing Attack Detection Techniques. *IEEE Access: Practical Innovations, Open Solutions*, 7, 100378–100389. DOI: 10.1109/ACCESS.2019.2933857

Zheng, W., (2020). Natural Language Processing Techniques for Phishing Detection. *IEEE Access: Practical Innovations, Open Solutions*, 8, 45680–45690. DOI: 10.1109/ACCESS.2020.2973995

Chapter 9
Advanced Tools and Technologies for Phishing Prevention

Kashish Preet Kaur
https://orcid.org/0009-0001-4497-0020
Chandigarh College of Engineering and Technology, Panjab University, Chandigarh, India

Sunil K. Singh
https://orcid.org/0000-0003-4876-7190
Chandigarh College of Engineering and Technology, Panjab University, Chandigarh, India

Sudhakar Kumar
https://orcid.org/0000-0001-7928-4234
Chandigarh College of Engineering and Technology, Panjab University, Chandigarh, India

Ishita Mehra
Chandigarh College of Engineering and Technology, Panjab University, Chandigarh, India

Shavi Bansal
https://orcid.org/0009-0009-8699-6884
Insights2Techinfo, India

Kwok Tai Chui
Hong Kong Metropolitan University, Hong Kong

Vandana Sharma
Chandigarh College of Engineering and Technology, Panjab University, Chandigarh, India

Sunil Kumar Sharma
S.E. Railway, India

ABSTRACT

Phishing attacks are a major cybersecurity threat, exploiting human vulnerabilities by manipulating trust to access sensitive information. As phishing tactics evolve, the demand for advanced anti-phishing technologies has surged. This paper examines key measures such as email filters, SSL/TLS certificates, DNS-based authentication, multi-factor authentication, and URL filtering to protect against phishing. Advanced methods like machine learning, AI-driven analysis, and real-time threat detection have improved phishing prevention. It also discusses browser-based, cloud-based, and email security tools for mitigating risks. The paper highlights challenges such as evolving tactics, email filtering limitations, and user negligence, emphasizing the need for ongoing innovation in strategies. Future trends like AI, biometrics, and deep learning for threat intelligence are explored, showing potential to enhance phishing defense. A holistic approach integrating technology, protocols, and user awareness is advocated to combat phishing effectively at both individual and organizational levels.

DOI: 10.4018/979-8-3693-8784-9.ch009

1. INTRODUCTION:

1.1 Meaning of Phishing

Phishing is a type of cyberattack in which perpetrators try to trick victims into divulging personal data, like bank account details or passwords. They accomplish this by pretending to be someone you know and trust in order to send phony emails, texts, or phone calls. The purpose is to get the individual to click on a link or divulge confidential details, which can be exploited by the attacker to steal money or access vital systems. One popular form of social engineering is phishing, in which con artists pose as reliable sources of information by employing cunning and trickery. These behaviors generally entail visiting links to phony websites, downloading and installing dangerous software, and exposing confidential information, such bank account numbers or credit card information (P. Sharma et al., 2022).

1.2 Origin of Phishing

The term "phishing" was first introduced on January 2, 1996, in a Usenet newsgroup known as AOHell. This is significant because America Online (AOL) was where early phishing activities started, which later grew into a major criminal issue. When America Online (AOL) was the leading Internet provider, millions of users logged in daily, making it a target for hackers and pirates, known as the "warez community." This group was the first to start phishing attacks(Zeydan et al., 2014). Initially, phishers stole passwords and used algorithms to randomly generate credit card numbers, which they used to open AOL accounts. These accounts were then used to spam others and carry out various illegal activities. AOL stopped this in 1995 by adding security measures to block the use of fake credit card numbers. After this, phishers developed new techniques that became widespread. They sent messages via AOL Instant Messenger and email, pretending to be AOL employees. These messages asked users to verify their accounts or confirm billing details. Many people fell for this scam because it was a new kind of attack. The situation worsened when phishers began creating AIM accounts through the Internet, which AOL couldn't easily shut down. In response, AOL added warnings to their email and messaging services, advising users not to share sensitive information this way (Singh & Imphal, 2018).

Phishing has evolved over the years but still relies on the same basic tactics of tricking people into giving up sensitive information. In 2001, phishers began targeting online payment systems, starting with E-Gold. Although that attack wasn't very successful, it paved the way for more advanced phishing techniques. By 2003, phishers began registering fake domains that looked like legitimate sites, such as eBay and PayPal, and used spoofed emails to trick people into entering their credit card information (T. Singh et al., 2025). By 2004, phishing attacks had expanded to banking sites and other services, causing significant financial losses. Popup windows were used to gather sensitive information. In 2008, the introduction of Bitcoin and other cryptocurrencies made phishing attacks even more dangerous, as payments could be made anonymously. In 2013, Cryptolocker ransomware spread through phishing emails, locking users' files and demanding payment in exchange for a decryption key. This was the first major example of phishing combined with ransomware (Chanti & Chithralekha, 2020).

By 2017, phishers increasingly used HTTPS on their fake sites, giving people a false sense of security with the green padlock symbol, which only indicates that the site is encrypted, not that it is legitimate. In 2018, attackers developed a method to hide malicious code in image files using a tool called Invoke-PSImage, making it harder for antivirus programs to detect. Phishing kits (Prem & Reddy, 2019) became available on the Dark Web, making it easy for anyone to create convincing phishing campaigns. Various new types of phishing attacks emerged in 2019, such as conversation hijacking, where hackers insert themselves into ongoing email conversations to trick people into downloading malware. Gift card phishing also became more sophisticated, and business email compromise attacks targeted global supply chains.

In 2020, phishing tactics grew increasingly sophisticated, with attackers utilizing fake Google search results and highly convincing Office 365 login pages to steal user credentials. The COVID-19 pandemic provided a new theme for phishing emails (Khonji et al., 2013), with scams related to stimulus checks, fake health warnings, and work-from-home setups. These evolving tactics show that phishing is becoming harder to detect, making it crucial for individuals, not just security systems, to be the last line of defense.

1.3 Need for Anti-Phishing Solutions

Phishing attacks have grown in both frequency and sophistication, making the need for anti-phishing solutions more critical than ever. With millions of phishing messages and emails being sent every day, organizations and individuals are constantly at risk of data breaches and financial losses. Attackers are employing increasingly advanced techniques, such as spoofed emails, conversation hijacking, and phishing kits that mimic legitimate websites, complicating the ability of traditional security measures to detect and block these threats.The threat posed by synthetic identities generated through advanced technologies highlights how attackers can exploit these techniques to trick victims into sharing sensitive information by mimicking legitimate entities (Sarin et al., 2023). The consequences of successful phishing attacks can be severe, leading to not only financial damage but also reputational harm, regulatory penalties, and costly recovery efforts.

Anti-phishing solutions are essential for maintaining security, especially as phishers target vulnerable populations, such as remote workers and less tech-savvy individuals. These solutions help safeguard sensitive information while promoting user education and awareness, which is crucial in preventing attacks. Furthermore, anti-phishing measures ensure compliance with data protection regulations like GDPR and CCPA, reducing the risk of legal liabilities. Implementing robust anti-phishing strategies also supports business continuity by minimizing the potential for disruptions caused by phishing attacks and the damaging malware they can introduce (A. Singh et al., 2025a).

The remainder of this chapter is organized as follows: Section 2 covers the various types of phishing attacks, outlining their methods and targets. Section 3 reviews key anti-phishing technologies, highlighting their role in detecting and preventing attacks. Section 4 focuses on advanced detection techniques used to identify and block phishing attempts. In Section 5, tools for anti-phishing protection are explored, while Section 6 discusses protocols and standards that guide anti-phishing practices. Training and awareness tools for educating users about phishing threats are detailed in Section 7. Section 8 addresses the challenges and limitations of anti-phishing technologies, and Section 9 provides insight into future trends in anti-phishing solutions. The chapter concludes with Section 10, summarizing key points and offering final reflections.

2. TYPES OF PHISHING ATTACKS

Phishing attacks have increasingly adapted to changing technologies and user behaviors, leading to the emergence of various sophisticated techniques.These attacks utilize psychological manipulation, frequently capitalizing on trust and a sense of urgency to trick victims into revealing sensitive information. As technology continues to advance, attackers refine their methods, employing more personalized and targeted strategies to enhance the effectiveness of their schemes, making them a persistent threat in the digital landscape (N. Singh et al., 2024).

2.1 Email Phishing

Phishing attacks have evolved over time into several sophisticated forms, each designed to exploit different vulnerabilities in human behavior and technology. One of the most prevalent methods is email phishing, which involves attackers impersonating trusted institutions or well-known services by sending fraudulent emails. These emails often contain a sense of urgency, such as warnings about account suspension or unauthorized access, prompting immediate action from the recipient (H. Sharma et al., 2017). The malicious email typically includes a link directing the victim to a fake website that mimics the real service, where they are asked to enter sensitive information like passwords, credit card numbers, or social security details. Sometimes, the email contains malicious attachments that, once opened, deploy malware onto the victim's device. What makes email phishing so dangerous is the ease with which attackers can replicate official branding, such as company logos, language, and formatting, making the email appear genuine.

2.2 Spear Phishing

Another increasingly common type of phishing is spear phishing, which is a highly targeted form of phishing. Unlike broad phishing attacks that are sent to thousands of recipients, spear phishing is customized for a specific individual or organization. Attackers usually gather information about their target beforehand, often from social media profiles or corporate websites, and use this information to craft convincing emails. These emails may refer to projects the victim is working on or use the names of colleagues to build credibility. Spear phishing is especially effective in corporate environments, where an attacker may pose as a senior executive or trusted partner, tricking the victim into sharing confidential information or authorizing financial transactions (Maurya et al., 2019). Due to the personalized nature of these attacks, they are harder to detect and more likely to succeed than general phishing campaigns.

2.3 Clone Phishing

Clone phishing takes deception to another level by replicating legitimate emails that the victim has previously received or expects to receive. The attacker creates a near-identical version of a legitimate email, including the same content, design, and even the original sender's address. However, the attacker modifies the links or attachments in the email to point to malicious sites or files. This tactic works particularly well because the victim is familiar with the original email, reducing suspicion and increasing the likelihood of interacting with the harmful content. Clone phishing can be highly effective in environments where routine communication is expected, such as project updates, billing notices, or customer service correspondence, making it difficult to distinguish between authentic and malicious emails (Machap et al., 2024).

2.4 Whaling

Whaling is a more specialized form of phishing that targets high-level executives or important figures within an organization, such as CEOs, CFOs, or legal advisors. This type of attack is aptly named because it goes after the "big fish" within a company, often aiming for larger financial gains or access to highly confidential information. In whaling attacks, the attacker may use the pretext of a legal matter, regulatory compliance issue, or business decision to create a sense of urgency and authority in the communication. For example, the phishing email may claim to be from an attorney handling a sensitive lawsuit or a government agency requiring immediate action (Vats et al., 2024). Because senior executives often have the authority to approve large transactions or access valuable data, successful whaling attacks can have devastating consequences for an organization.

2.5 Vishing and Smishing

Vishing, or voice phishing, is a type of attack where cybercriminals use phone calls or voice-based communication to trick victims into sharing sensitive information. Attackers often impersonate trusted entities, such as banks, government agencies, or technical support services, to gain the victim's trust. They create a sense of urgency or fear, claiming issues like compromised accounts, suspicious transactions, or identity theft. To make their calls appear legitimate, they may use caller ID spoofing. During these calls, victims are pressured to reveal confidential details like bank account numbers, credit card information, or passwords. Vishing is particularly dangerous because it exploits the natural trust people place in verbal communication, bypassing visual cues that might signal a phishing attempt. To counteract vishing, users are advised to verify the legitimacy of unsolicited calls by contacting the organization directly and never sharing sensitive details over the phone unless they initiated the call. (Njuguna et al., 2021).

2.6 Smishing

Smishing, short for SMS phishing, involves sending fraudulent text messages designed to trick recipients into revealing personal information or clicking on malicious links. These messages often mimic notifications from banks, package delivery services, or online platforms, creating a sense of urgency to prompt immediate action. Examples include messages claiming suspicious activity on accounts, pending deliveries requiring confirmation, or account verification to prevent suspension. The links provided in these messages usually lead to fake websites that capture sensitive data or prompt victims to download malicious software. Smishing is highly effective because mobile devices often lack robust security measures, and smaller screens make it harder to scrutinize sender details or URLs. Additionally, people tend to trust SMS notifications, which makes them more susceptible. Users are advised to avoid clicking on links in unsolicited messages, verify the sender's legitimacy through official channels, and use SMS filtering tools to protect against such attacks.

Fig.1. highlights the five most common types of phishing attacks, which include Email Phishing, where attackers send a large volume of untargeted emails, and Spear Phishing, which focuses on a specific individual or business. Whaling targets high-level executives, while Vishing involves phishing through phone calls or VoIP. Finally, Smishing uses text messages to deceive victims. Each of these methods exploits different communication channels, demonstrating the diverse tactics used by cybercriminals to steal sensitive information.

Figure 1. Types of Phishing

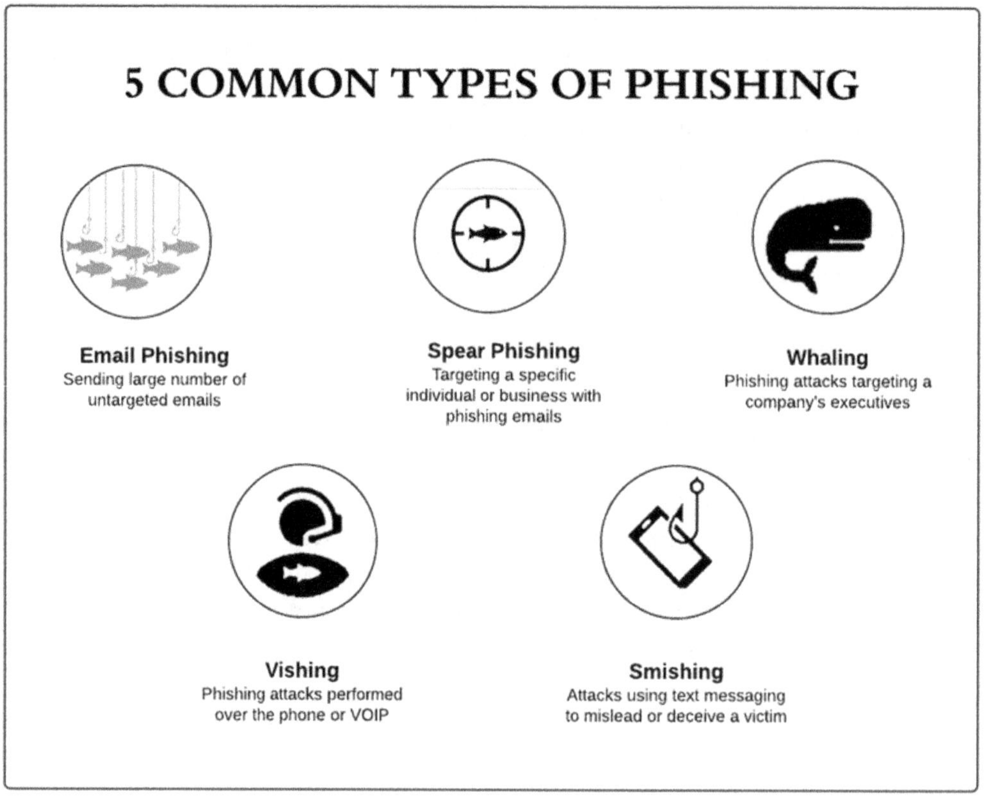

While the previous sections and Figure 1 detail the types of phishing attacks, Table 1 provides a summarized comparison for quick reference.

Table 1. Summary of Comparison between Types of Phishing

Type of Attack	Characteristics	Examples
Email Phishing	Broad phishing attempts sent to many recipients, often mimicking trusted organizations.	An email claiming to be from a bank, asking users to verify account details.
Spear Phishing	Targeted attacks on specific individuals or organizations using personalized information.	A fake email from a CEO requesting confidential financial data.
Clone Phishing	Replicates legitimate emails, replacing links/attachments with malicious ones.	A fraudulent version of a real invoice email with a malicious link.
Whaling	Focuses on high-level executives, often leveraging urgency and authority to manipulate.	A fake legal notice sent to a company's CFO requesting immediate action.

continued on following page

Table 1. Continued

Type of Attack	Characteristics	Examples
Vishing (Voice phishing)	Uses phone calls or VoIP to impersonate trusted entities and elicit sensitive information	A scammer claiming to be tech support, requesting access to a victim's computer.
Smishing (SMS Phishing)	Uses text messages to lure victims into clicking malicious links or providing information.	A fake delivery notification asking for credit card details to release a package.

3. KEY ANTI-PHISHING TECHNOLOGIES

Anti-phishing technologies encompass an array of instruments, strategies, and tactics intended to identify, thwart, and alleviate phishing assaults. Phishing is the attempt to fool someone into divulging private information by posing as reliable sources(Ansari et al., 2022). These technologies play a crucial role in protecting users from such deceptive attacks. Below are some of the key anti-phishing technologies:

3.1 Email Filters

Email filters are the first line of defense in preventing phishing attacks by identifying and blocking malicious messages before they reach users. Email services like Gmail and Outlook employ advanced phishing filters that analyze email content, sender reputation, and embedded links or attachments to detect phishing attempts. These filters often use machine learning to adapt to new phishing techniques and improve accuracy over time. By quarantining suspicious emails into spam folders, email filters significantly reduce the risk of users being exposed to phishing(Apandi et al., 2020). While email filters significantly reduce the volume of phishing emails reaching users, they are not foolproof. Attackers frequently use tactics like domain spoofing, obfuscated links, or carefully crafted messages to bypass detection. To maximize effectiveness, organizations often combine email filtering with user training and other security measures.

Some anti-phishing email filters include:

a) **Avanan**
b) **Microsoft Defender for Office 365**
c) **Mimecast**
d) **Cofense PhishMe**
e) **IRONSCALES**

3.2 SSL/TLS Certificates

Secure Sockets Layer (SSL) and Transport Layer Security (TLS) certificates are cryptographic protocols that encrypt communication between users and websites, ensuring the confidentiality and integrity of transmitted data. The presence of HTTPS (signaled by the padlock icon in browsers) means that the data exchanged between the user's browser and the website is encrypted. This helps prevent attackers from intercepting sensitive information like login credentials or credit card details. In addition, SSL certificates authenticate the website's identity, allowing users to verify that they are visiting legitimate websites, thereby reducing the chances of falling victim to phishing attacks (Sharma et al., 2021). However, attackers have exploited the trust users place in the HTTPS padlock by obtaining SSL/TLS certificates for fraudulent websites. This highlights the need for users to verify domain names and for organizations to adopt additional security measures like DNS-based authentication to further validate website legitimacy.

3.3 DNS-based Authentication (DANE)

DANE (DNS-based Authentication of Named Entities), along with DNSSEC (Domain Name System Security Extensions), helps secure domain communications and prevent phishing attacks by binding SSL/TLS certificates to DNS. This ensures that communication between users and websites is not only encrypted but also authenticated at the domain level, preventing DNS spoofing and man-in-the-middle attacks. DNSSEC adds cryptographic signatures to DNS queries, protecting against DNS spoofing attacks where users may be redirected to malicious websites. Together, these technologies safeguard users from phishing schemes that target domain-level communications (Chaudhuri, 2023).

3.4 Multi-Factor Authentication (MFA)

Multi-Factor Authentication (MFA) enhances security by requiring users to verify their identity through multiple factors before accessing an account. These factors typically include:

1. **Something you know** (e.g., a password).
2. **Something you have** (e.g., a one-time code sent to your phone).
3. **Something you are** (e.g., biometric data like fingerprints or facial recognition).

Common forms of MFA include a password combined with a one-time code sent to a mobile device, or biometric verification (like fingerprints) (Wong et al., 2022). Even if attackers successfully steal a password through phishing, they cannot access the account without the second factor, making it much harder for them to succeed in account compromise.

3.5 URL Filtering and Blacklists

URL filtering and blacklisting are mechanisms that block access to known malicious websites. These technologies rely on continuously updated databases of harmful URLs, including phishing sites. Browsers and security tools automatically compare URLs against these blacklists to prevent users from visiting dangerous pages. URL filtering is a key defense against phishing attacks, particularly those that rely on deceptive or malicious links embedded in emails or on websites (Zahra et al., 2023). Web browsers like Google Chrome and Microsoft Edge use tools like Google Safe Browsing to warn users about malicious websites, but attackers frequently create new domains to bypass detection.

Figure 2. Anti-Phishing Technologies

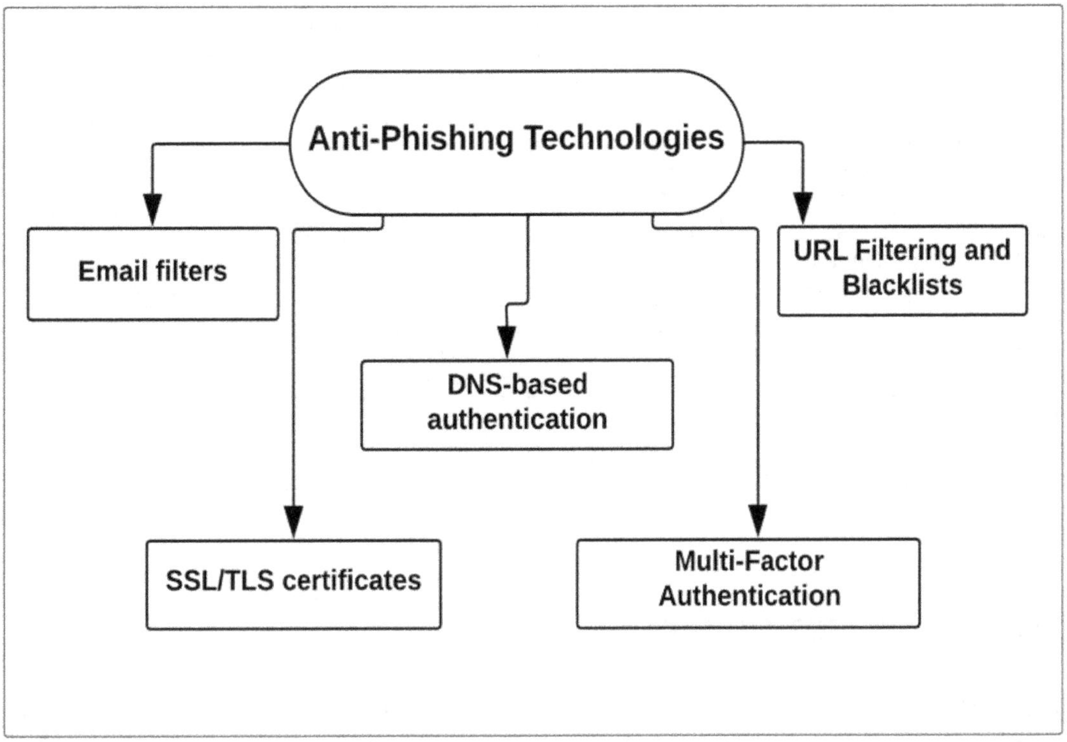

Fig.2. provides an overview of key anti-phishing technologies used to prevent phishing attacks. It outlines several essential tools and methods, including Email Filters, which help block phishing emails, and URL Filtering and Blacklists, which prevent users from accessing known malicious websites. DNS-based authentication is another layer that helps verify the legitimacy of domains, supported by SSL/TLS certificates for secure communication. Lastly, by demanding additional authentication in addition to a password, Multi-Factor Authentication (MFA) provides an extra degree of protection. The table 2 below summarizes the features, advantages, and limitations of the key anti-phishing technologies discussed in this section for easy comparison and reference.

Table 2. Comparison of Key Anti-Phishing Technologies

Technology	Features	Advantages	Limitations
Email Filters	Detects phishing emails based on sender reputation, content analysis, and attachment scanning.	Reduces user exposure to phishing emails; customizable rules to adapt to organizational needs.	Prone to false positives (flagging legitimate emails) and false negatives (missing phishing emails).
SSL/TLS Certificates	Encrypts communication between the user and website, authenticates website identity.	Ensures data privacy and prevents man-in-the-middle attacks.	Misuse of HTTPS by attackers with fake certificates can give users a false sense of security.
DNS-based Authentication (DANE)	Links domain to SSL/TLS certificates using DNSSEC for added authenticity.	Prevents DNS spoofing attacks and secures domain-level communications.	Requires DNSSEC implementation, which is not yet universally adopted.
Multi-Factor Authentication (MFA)	Requires multiple verification methods (e.g., password + OTP or biometric).	Significantly increases account security; renders stolen passwords insufficient for access.	User inconvenience and potential compatibility issues with legacy systems.
URL Filtering and Blacklists	Blocks known malicious URLs using continuously updated databases.	Proactively prevents access to phishing websites.	Ineffective against new or unlisted phishing URLs; requires constant updates.

4. ADVANCED DETECTION TECHNIQUES

In recent years, advanced detection techniques have significantly evolved in combating phishing attacks, with Machine Learning (ML) and Artificial Intelligence (AI) playing pivotal roles. These technologies have revolutionized the way phishing threats are identified and mitigated. AI models, driven by sophisticated machine learning algorithms, can automatically detect phishing attempts by analyzing extensive data and recognizing intricate patterns that are indicative of malicious activities. Typically, these models are trained on large datasets containing examples of both phishing and legitimate communications, enabling them to differentiate between the two. For instance, AI systems(Gusev, 2022) analyze an email's metadata, including sender details, embedded URLs, and writing style, to detect inconsistencies or features characteristic of phishing attacks, such as suspicious URLs, malicious attachments, or abnormal linguistic patterns. As AI models continuously process data, they enhance their accuracy and reduce the number of false positives. This adaptability is a significant advantage, allowing AI systems to respond dynamically to emerging phishing threats without the need for constant manual intervention, thereby offering real-time protection (S. Gupta et al., 2016).

Behavioral analysis forms another cornerstone of advanced phishing detection methods. Rather than merely scrutinizing email or website content, behavioral analytics monitor user actions and interactions to detect any deviation from established patterns. This approach is particularly effective in countering sophisticated phishing campaigns such as spear phishing, where attackers craft highly personalized messages that may evade traditional content-based filters. By continuously learning normal user behavior, behavioral analytics (Alsufyani & Alzahrani, 2021) can identify anomalous actions—such as attempts to access unauthorized systems or sudden, unusual credential submissions—raising alerts when suspicious activities occur. This method provides a dynamic layer of defense, recognizing phishing attempts based on deviations from expected behaviors rather than relying solely on predefined content markers.

A critical component of modern phishing defense is real-time threat detection, which allows organizations to intercept and respond to phishing attempts as they occur. Real-time detection utilizes tools that scan incoming emails, URLs, and attachments for phishing indicators, providing immediate protection before a potential breach can take place. One such tool is email scanning, which operates at the entry point of an organization's communication infrastructure, analyzing email content for known phishing signatures, including suspicious sender domains, malicious links, or harmful attachments (K. Singh et al., 2021). These systems cross-reference email components with databases of known phishing tactics, blocking or quarantining emails that exhibit high-risk characteristics. Furthermore, attachment sandboxing provides another layer of defense by isolating email attachments in a controlled environment to analyze their behavior. This approach ensures that even if an attachment contains malicious code, such as ransomware or other harmful software, it is prevented from executing on the user's system. By detecting malicious behavior in real-time, sandboxing tools can prevent attacks before they reach the intended victim (Thakur et al., 2025).

Together, these advanced detection techniques—machine learning-based pattern recognition, behavioral analysis, and real-time threat detection—form a comprehensive, multi-layered defense against phishing attacks. While each technique offers distinct advantages, their integration into organizational security infrastructures greatly enhances protection, minimizing the likelihood of successful phishing attacks (Somesha et al., 2020). This combination of techniques not only improves the ability to detect and mitigate phishing threats but also strengthens the overall cybersecurity posture of organizations, making them more resilient to increasingly sophisticated phishing attempts. As phishing tactics continue to evolve, the use of advanced detection technologies will remain a crucial component in the broader strategy to safeguard sensitive information and protect against cyber threats (Do et al., 2022).

5. TOOLS FOR ANTI-PHISHING PROTECTION

Anti-phishing tools are essential in safeguarding individuals and organizations against phishing attacks by detecting and preventing suspicious activities, links, attachments, and messages. These solutions are commonly categorized as follows:

5.1 Browser-Based Protection

Browser-based protection involves the use of extensions andintegrated security measures that aid in defending users against phishing scams. Numerous contemporary web browsers, including Microsoft Edge, Firefox, and Google Chrome, offer built-in phishing protection features like Google's Safe Browsing. This feature helps users by blocking access to dangerous websites, including phishing and malware-hosting sites, before they can load. Browser extensions, such as those provided by Avira, McAfee, or Web of Trust (WOT), also use real-time threat detection to warn users when they attempt to visit malicious websites or click on potentially harmful links. These solutions rely on databases of known phishing sites and may include heuristic analysis to identify suspicious activities in real time, providing immediate protection when browsing (Gaurav et al., 2023).

5.2 Cloud-Based Solutions

Cloud-based platforms, such as Microsoft Defender for Office 365, Google Workspace, and Cisco Secure Email, play a crucial role in detecting and preventing phishing attempts in emails and files stored in the cloud. These solutions leverage artificial intelligence and machine learning to scan incoming emails, attachments, and shared files for signs of phishing or malware. Microsoft Defender integrates seamlessly into the Microsoft 365 ecosystem to provide multi-layered protection against phishing attacks, while Google Workspace uses Google's Safe Browsing (Hiransha et al., 2018) technology to block suspicious links and prevent malicious file downloads. These platforms are constantly updated to respond to new threats, and because they are cloud-based, they protect users on any device connected to the platform.

5.3 Email Security Platforms

Email security platforms, such as Proofpoint, Mimecast, and Barracuda, provide comprehensive protection against phishing by operating at the email gateway level. These tools filter all incoming and outgoing email traffic, scanning for malicious content such as phishing links, suspicious attachments, and spoofed email addresses. They use a combination of signature-based detection, heuristics, and machine learning to identify and block phishing emails before they reach the recipient's inbox. Additionally, these platforms can provide domain-based authentication methods, like DMARC and SPF, to prevent email impersonation, further securing organizations from phishing threats (Bin et al., 2010).

5.4 Endpoint Protection

Endpoint protection software, such as Norton, McAfee, and Bitdefender, integrates phishing protection as part of their overall security solutions. These tools safeguard individual devices (endpoints) by providing real-time detection of phishing attempts across email, browsers, and applications. They monitor user activity for suspicious behavior, such as visiting known phishing websites or clicking on malicious email links, and take immediate action to block the threat. Endpoint protection software often includes anti-phishing filters that scan web traffic, inspect email content, and analyze website certificates to prevent users from falling victim to phishing attacks, thereby ensuring comprehensive device-level security.

Given below are some of the Anti-Phishing Tools (Purkait, 2015):

1. **Barracuda Impersonation Protection (formerly Barracuda Sentinel):** This tool uses AI to prevent spear-phishing and account takeover attacks. It scans inbound emails for potential impersonation and phishing attacks and can automatically block threats before they reach users.
2. **Memcyco:** A real-time website protection platform that helps detect and prevent website impersonation attacks. It uses digital markers to ensure users are interacting with legitimate websites, protecting against phishing and brand impersonation.
3. **Avanan (by CheckPoint):** Avanan secures cloud-based email platforms like Microsoft 365 and Google Workspace. It uses machine learning to detect phishing attempts, malware, and data breaches, offering multi-layered security for business communications.
4. **Cofense Managed Phishing Defense & Response:** Cofense provides phishing defense solutions that combine human intelligence with automated tools. It offers managed detection and response to stop phishing attacks in real-time and protect organizations from data breaches.

5. **IRONSCALES:** A self-learning email security platform that integrates AI and human insights to detect and remediate phishing attacks. It helps organizations respond to phishing threats more quickly by automating threat detection and mitigation.
6. **KnowBe4:** A leading platform for security awareness training and simulated phishing attacks. KnowBe4 educates employees on recognizing phishing attempts and promotes good cybersecurity habits to reduce organizational risk.
7. **Mimecast:** Mimecast offers email security solutions that include anti-phishing, anti-spam, and malware protection. It helps block phishing attempts at the gateway and provides email continuity and archiving features for added security.
8. **Cybeready**: An automated security training platform that specializes in phishing awareness. Cybeready's solution offers continuous employee training through simulated phishing campaigns and gamified learning to improve security awareness across organizations.
9. **Valimail:** Valimail focuses on email authentication solutions to prevent impersonation and phishing attacks. It uses protocols like DMARC (Domain-based Message Authentication, Reporting & Conformance) to ensure that only legitimate emails reach users.
10. **Trustify:** A cybersecurity platform that offers email security services with a focus on anti-phishing, fraud detection, and impersonation protection. It helps detect threats in real-time, preventing phishing emails from reaching users.

Figure.3. showcases the top 10 anti-phishing tools that help organizations protect against phishing attacks. These tools, including Trustify, Valimail, Barracuda Impersonation Protection, and Mimecast, provide features such as email filtering, impersonation detection, and security awareness training. By leveraging solutions like KnownBe4 and Cofense Managed Phishing Defense & Response, organizations can strengthen their defense against phishing threats and enhance overall cybersecurity resilience.

Figure 3. Anti-Phishing Tools

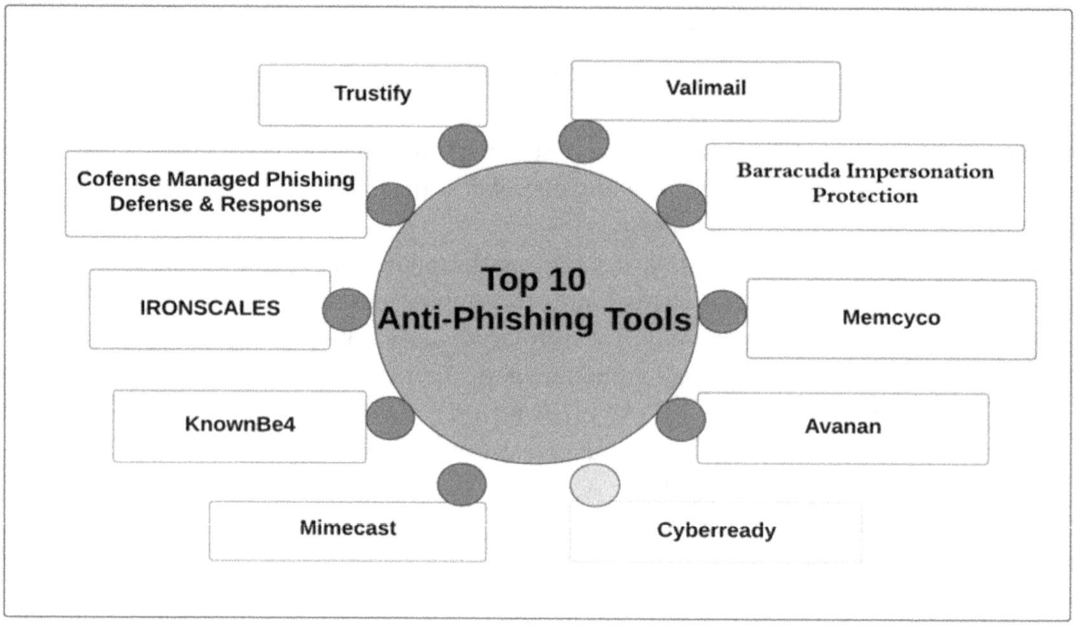

6. PROTOCOLS AND STANDARDS FOR ANTI-PHISHING

Protocols and standards play a crucial role in combating phishing attacks, particularly in securing email communication by verifying the authenticity of senders and preventing email spoofing. One of the most effective mechanisms in this regard is Domain-based Message Authentication, Reporting & Conformance (DMARC) (Vats & Kumar, 2021), a protocol designed to protect domain owners by building upon existing standards like Sender Policy Framework (SPF) and DomainKeys Identified Mail (DKIM). DMARC works by ensuring that emails are properly authenticated against both SPF and DKIM protocols and provides domain owners with detailed reports on authentication failures. SPF operates by verifying the sender's IP address against a list of authorized IPs provided by the domain's DNS records. If the sender's IP does not match, the email can be flagged as potentially malicious. This protocol prevents unauthorized users from sending emails that appear to originate from trusted domains, reducing the risk of email-based phishing attacks. However, while SPF verifies the sender's IP address, it does not validate the integrity of the email content itself.

DKIM addresses this gap by attaching a digital cryptographic signature to every email sent from a domain, which can be verified by the recipient's server to ensure the email has not been tampered with during transmission. This signature is created using a private key held by the sender and verified by the recipient using a public key published in the sender's DNS records (Tatang et al., 2021). In this way, DKIM not only confirms the sender's identity but also protects the email content from being altered en route to its recipient, thus safeguarding against phishing attempts that rely on changing the message content. Together, SPF and DKIM form a foundational layer of email security, but DMARC adds an enforcement mechanism that mandates the alignment between the 'From' address in the email header and the domain authenticated by SPF and DKIM.

Moreover, DMARC improves existing protocols by giving domain owners the ability to dictate the handling of emails that fail SPF or DKIM checks by receiving email servers—whether to quarantine, reject, or flag the email. In addition to enforcement, DMARC also provides a reporting function that sends detailed feedback to the domain owner on emails that fail authentication, providing insights into potential phishing or spoofing attempts. These reports are invaluable for organizations looking to monitor and respond to unauthorized use of their domain. By implementing DMARC policies, domain owners can take direct action to ensure that only properly authenticated emails are delivered, thus significantly reducing the effectiveness of phishing attacks (Islam et al., 2023).

In essence, DMARC, along with SPF and DKIM, forms a robust framework that allows organizations to authenticate email senders, verify the integrity of the messages, and enforce policies that protect against phishing. These protocols work in tandem to prevent attackers from exploiting email systems, thereby maintaining the trustworthiness of communication channels. As phishing techniques continue to evolve, the adoption of these standards is vital for organizations looking to protect themselves and their users from fraudulent activity in email communication.

7. TRAINING AND AWARENESS TOOLS

Training and awareness tools are essential components of a comprehensive anti-phishing strategy, as they focus on strengthening the human element, often regarded as the weakest link in cybersecurity. One of the most effective methods for educating users about phishing risks is the use of phishing simulations. These simulated phishing campaigns, provided by platforms like KnowBe4 and PhishMe, allow organizations to send mock phishing emails to employees, assessing their ability to recognize and respond appropriately to suspicious messages. The value of these exercises lies in their ability to mirror real-world phishing attempts closely, providing a hands-on learning experience for users. Employees who fall for these simulated phishing attempts can be redirected to targeted training modules, reinforcing the importance of vigilance and caution in dealing with unsolicited or suspicious emails. Over time, repeated exposure to these simulated environments helps build muscle memory, making employees more adept at identifying phishing emails and less likely to fall victim to actual attacks (Yeboah-Boateng & Amanor, 2014).

In addition to phishing simulations, user awareness programs are critical for maintaining a high level of knowledge and attentiveness regarding phishing risks. These programs often include regular workshops, webinars, and other training sessions aimed at educating employees about the latest phishing techniques, common warning signs, and best practices for protecting sensitive information. Ongoing education is vital because phishing tactics evolve rapidly, and attackers continually develop new methods for deceiving users. Therefore, periodic refreshers and updates on the latest threats ensure that employees remain well-informed and alert to emerging phishing strategies. User awareness programs also emphasize the role of organizational culture in cybersecurity, encouraging employees to report suspicious emails and work collaboratively to maintain a secure digital environment.

Best practices for users are a cornerstone of these training efforts, providing practical guidelines for individuals to protect themselves from phishing attacks. Simple actions, such as verifying URLs before clicking on links, avoiding downloading attachments from unknown sources, and refraining from responding to emails requesting personal information, are emphasized in these programs. Users are taught to hover over links to reveal the actual URL, scrutinize email addresses for minor inconsistencies that may indicate phishing attempts, and be wary of any message that evokes urgency or fear. Furthermore, users are encouraged to use two-factor authentication (2FA) where possible, ensuring an extra layer of security even if login credentials are compromised. By embedding these best practices into their daily routines, individuals become the first line of defense against phishing attacks, significantly reducing the chances of a successful breach (Jones et al., 2020).

Overall, the integration of phishing simulations, user awareness programs, and best practices training equips individuals with the knowledge and tools they need to recognize and avoid phishing attempts. These training and awareness tools not only strengthen organizational cybersecurity but also foster a culture of proactive defense, where employees are empowered to protect both their personal and organizational assets from increasingly sophisticated phishing attacks. Through continuous education and hands-on practice, organizations can create a resilient workforce capable of mitigating the human vulnerabilities often exploited by phishing threats.

8. CHALLENGES AND LIMITATIONS OF ANTI-PHISHING TECHNOLOGIES

Despite the substantial progress made in developing anti-phishing technologies, numerous challenges and limitations persist, making phishing attacks an ongoing concern in cybersecurity. The evolving sophistication of phishing techniques, the inherent shortcomings of email filtering systems, user-related vulnerabilities, and the continuous advancement of attack strategies all contribute to the complexity of combating phishing (Maseno, 2017). Each of these challenges presents unique obstacles that limit the effectiveness of current anti-phishing technologies.

8.1 Implementation Challenges

Deploying anti-phishing solutions requires significant financial and technical resources, making it challenging for smaller organizations. The initial costs associated with procuring advanced anti-phishing tools, setting up infrastructure, and maintaining these systems are often prohibitively high for small and medium-sized enterprises (SMEs). Moreover, implementing multi-factor authentication (MFA) and advanced behavioral analytics often demands specialized knowledge and training (Kumar et al., 2024), which can strain organizational resources further. Resistance to MFA is a notable hurdle, as many users perceive it as inconvenient and time-consuming, leading to reluctance in adopting such measures. Additionally, the integration of anti-phishing technologies with existing IT systems can be complex and may require substantial customization to ensure compatibility and effectiveness. Organizations often face difficulties in configuring these systems to align with their specific operational needs without compromising performance. Another critical issue is the lack of skilled cybersecurity professionals who can effectively deploy, manage, and update anti-phishing technologies. This skills gap further exacerbates the challenges for organizations aiming to enhance their cybersecurity posture. These implementation challenges highlight the necessity of tailored solutions and increased accessibility to anti-phishing technologies, especially for resource-constrained entities.

8.2 Sophistication of Phishing Attacks

One of the most significant challenges in the fight against phishing is the increasing sophistication of attacks. In recent years, attackers have adopted advanced technologies, such as artificial intelligence (AI) and machine learning, to improve the effectiveness of phishing campaigns. Notably, the use of deep fakes—a technology that generates realistic, yet synthetic, audio, video, or images of individuals—has added a new layer of complexity to phishing schemes. These deep fakes can convincingly imitate the voices or appearances of high-ranking individuals, such as company executives or government officials, thereby deceiving victims into revealing sensitive information or authorizing fraudulent transactions. Social engineering tactics also continue to evolve, with attackers meticulously researching their targets using publicly available information, such as social media profiles or professional networks. These tailored attacks create highly personalized and convincing phishing attempts, making them harder to detect and more likely to succeed. The increasing sophistication of phishing techniques demonstrates that traditional phishing defenses, such as basic email filtering and rule-based detection systems, are becoming insufficient in isolation (Ashfaq et al., 2023).

8.3 Limitations of Email Filtering

Email filtering technologies, while integral to the first line of defense against phishing, exhibit inherent limitations that hinder their overall effectiveness. These filters often rely on predefined rules, heuristics, or machine learning models to identify and block phishing emails. However, phishing emails are constantly evolving, with attackers frequently modifying their tactics to bypass these filters. One of the major limitations is the occurrence of false positives and false negatives. A false positive occurs when a legitimate email is incorrectly flagged as suspicious, potentially disrupting business operations or critical communications. Conversely, a false negative occurs when a phishing email successfully bypasses the filter, potentially leading to compromised accounts, data breaches, or financial fraud. Phishers have developed various strategies to avoid detection by email filters, such as obfuscating URLs, using domain spoofing techniques, embedding malicious content in non-text formats like images or PDFs, or sending phishing emails from compromised legitimate accounts. As a result, email filtering, while essential, is not foolproof and must be complemented by other security measures to enhance phishing detection and prevention (Ulfath et al., 2022).

8.4 User Negligence

One of the most significant challenges in anti-phishing efforts is the role of user behavior, particularly negligence or lack of awareness. Even with the most advanced technological defenses in place, phishing attacks often succeed due to human error. Users may be unaware of the latest phishing tactics or may not adhere to best practices when interacting with digital communication. For example, despite repeated warnings, many users still click on suspicious links or open unknown attachments in emails that appear legitimate. Attackers frequently exploit emotions such as fear, urgency, or curiosity to trick users into bypassing their usual caution. Phishing emails may create a sense of urgency by mimicking messages from financial institutions, warning users about suspicious activity or account closures, prompting them to act hastily without thoroughly inspecting the email. User negligence is further compounded by the increasing use of mobile devices, where smaller screens make it harder to scrutinize email content or verify links. Although phishing awareness training programs and simulations have shown some success in improving user behavior, maintaining a high level of vigilance among users remains a significant challenge. Therefore, any comprehensive anti-phishing strategy must address the human element by emphasizing user education and creating a culture of cybersecurity awareness (Kaur et al., 2021).

8.5 Evolving Attack Techniques

Another major challenge facing anti-phishing technologies is the constant evolution of phishing techniques. Attackers are continuously refining and adapting their methods to bypass existing security measures. Traditional phishing attacks, which relied primarily on email, have expanded into new channels, including SMS-based phishing (smishing), voice-based phishing (vishing), and social media-based phishing. These multi-channel attacks pose new detection challenges as they exploit different communication platforms that may not be covered by traditional email security measures. Attackers have also developed hybrid approaches, where phishing attempts are coordinated across multiple channels to increase their credibility (Sharma et al., 2023). For instance, an attacker may initiate a phishing email, followed by a phone call (vishing) impersonating a trusted entity to further manipulate the victim into divulging sensitive information. Additionally, phishing techniques continue to evolve to exploit weaknesses in emerging technologies, such as cloud services, social media platforms, and even artificial intelligence-driven chatbots. Attackers are also leveraging encryption and anonymity tools to obfuscate their activities, making it harder for security systems to detect and trace phishing attempts. The dynamic nature of phishing tactics underscores the need for anti-phishing technologies that are adaptive, proactive, and capable of evolving in response to emerging threats.

9. FUTURE TRENDS IN ANTI-PHISHING TECHNOLOGIES

As phishing attacks continue to grow in sophistication and prevalence, it is essential for organizations to adopt advanced and proactive measures to combat these threats effectively. The landscape of anti-phishing technologies is evolving rapidly, driven by advancements in artificial intelligence (AI), machine learning (ML), and other emerging technologies. Future trends indicate a significant shift towards leveraging innovative approaches that enhance detection capabilities, streamline responses, and improve overall security posture. These trends encompass the integration of AI and machine learning for improved detection accuracy, the implementation of biometric authentication and decentralized identity management systems to mitigate risks, and the utilization of deep learning techniques for comprehensive threat intelligence. By embracing these future trends, organizations can fortify their defenses against phishing attacks and better protect sensitive information from unauthorized access, ultimately fostering a more secure digital environment (Peñalvo et al., 2022).

9.1 AI and Machine Learning Advancements

The ongoing evolution of anti-phishing technologies is significantly influenced by advancements in artificial intelligence (AI) and machine learning (ML). As phishing attacks grow more sophisticated and are characterized by increasingly complex tactics, the integration of AI and ML into cybersecurity measures presents an opportunity to enhance both detection accuracy and response times. These technologies enable the analysis of vast datasets to identify behavioral patterns and anomalies that may indicate phishing attempts. For example, machine learning algorithms can be trained on large datasets consisting of known phishing attacks and legitimate communications, allowing them to recognize subtle differences and emerging trends in email content, sender behavior, and link characteristics. Furthermore, AI systems can continuously update their models in real-time, adapting to new phishing strategies as they arise. This dynamic learning capability is critical in an environment where cyber threats evolve rapidly. Additionally, AI-driven systems can facilitate automated incident responses, significantly reducing the time between the identification of a threat and the execution of mitigation strategies. Such automation not only minimizes the potential damage caused by successful phishing attacks but also allows cybersecurity professionals to allocate their resources more effectively toward other critical areas of risk management. As research and development in AI and ML (Setia et al., 2024) continue to progress, the efficacy of anti-phishing solutions will likely improve, fostering a more proactive and resilient cybersecurity posture.

9.2 Biometrics and Identity Management

In the quest to bolster defenses against phishing attacks, biometric authentication and decentralized identity systems are gaining prominence as effective countermeasures. Biometrics—ranging from fingerprint recognition to facial recognition and iris scanning—offer a more secure alternative to traditional password-based authentication methods. These biometric traits are unique to each individual and present significant challenges for potential attackers attempting to gain unauthorized access. By implementing biometric verification systems, organizations can create robust barriers against identity theft and credential compromise, significantly reducing the risk associated with phishing. Moreover, decentralized identity systems, which empower users to control their personal information without relying on centralized databases, represent a paradigm shift in identity management. These systems leverage blockchain technology to secure and validate identity attributes, ensuring that users maintain ownership of their information while minimizing vulnerabilities that attackers might exploit. The combination of biometric authentication and decentralized identity frameworks not only strengthens security protocols but also enhances user trust in digital transactions. As these technologies continue to mature, their integration into anti-phishing strategies will likely lead to substantial reductions in phishing-related incidents and a more secure digital landscape (B. B. Gupta, Gaurav, Wu, et al., 2024).

9.3 Deep Learning for Threat Intelligence

Deep learning, a specialized subset of machine learning, is poised to transform the landscape of threat intelligence, particularly in the realm of phishing detection and prevention. Traditional machine learning methods often struggle with analyzing unstructured data, whereas deep learning algorithms excel in this area by utilizing advanced neural networks to process complex datasets that include natural language text, images, and other forms of multimedia (Dubey et al., 2022). This capability allows deep learning systems to identify intricate phishing patterns and schemes that might elude conventional detection mechanisms. For instance, by analyzing the language used in phishing emails, deep learning models can discern subtle linguistic cues and context that indicate malicious intent. Additionally, these models are designed to continuously learn from new data inputs, allowing them to enhance their predictive capabilities and improve overall performance over time. This characteristic is particularly valuable in the rapidly evolving landscape of cyber threats, where phishing techniques are constantly being refined. The ability of deep learning algorithms to uncover latent features and correlations in large volumes of data will empower organizations to respond proactively to emerging phishing threats(Aggarwal et al., 2022). Consequently, as more organizations adopt deep learning technologies into their cybersecurity frameworks, the potential to identify and neutralize sophisticated phishing attacks will be greatly enhanced, resulting in a more secure digital environment. This evolution in threat intelligence underscores the critical role that emerging technologies will play in shaping the future of anti-phishing strategies and bolstering organizational defenses.

10. CONCLUSION

The pervasive threat of phishing attacks necessitates a comprehensive understanding of the various technologies and tools designed to combat this issue effectively. This paper has highlighted the critical advancements in anti-phishing technologies, including sophisticated detection techniques driven by the usage of strong protocols like DMARC, SPF, and DKIM, artificial intelligence and machine learning, and the importance of user education through training and awareness campaigns. Each of these aspects plays a crucial role in boosting an organization's cybersecurity posture and limiting the dangers connected with phishing.

To effectively combat phishing, it is imperative for organizations and individuals alike to adopt robust anti-phishing measures. This includes not only implementing advanced technologies but also fostering a culture of vigilance where users are educated about the potential hazards and knowledgeable enough to identify and report questionable activity. By prioritizing cybersecurity initiatives and promoting proactive measures, organizations can significantly reduce their exposure to phishing threats.

Moreover, as cyber threats continue to evolve in complexity and sophistication, the importance of ongoing innovation in anti-phishing technologies cannot be overstated. Continuous improvement and adaptation of strategies and tools are essential to staying ahead of emerging threats. Investing in research and development will be vital for enhancing detection capabilities, developing more secure identity management systems, and leveraging advanced analytics to understand phishing patterns. By embracing a forward-thinking approach to cybersecurity, stakeholders can create a resilient defense against phishing attacks and protect sensitive information in an increasingly digital landscape.

10.1 Recommendations

Organizations should adopt a multi-layered approach to phishing prevention, recognizing that no single method can provide complete protection. This approach should combine the use of robust email filters to identify and block malicious messages, multifactor authentication (MFA) to add an additional layer of security to account access, and user training programs to educate employees about the latest phishing tactics and how to respond effectively.

Regularly updating anti-phishing tools is critical to ensuring that defenses remain effective against evolving threats. Conducting phishing simulations can help organizations assess their vulnerability and identify areas for improvement. These exercises not only test the effectiveness of existing measures but also reinforce the importance of vigilance among users.

Emerging technologies such as artificial intelligence and blockchain hold great promise for addressing future phishing challenges. AI can enhance the detection of phishing attempts by analyzing vast amounts of data in real time, identifying suspicious patterns, and adapting to new tactics employed by attackers. Blockchain technology, with its inherent transparency and security, could provide innovative solutions for secure identity management and verification, reducing the risk of phishing-related fraud.

By implementing these recommendations, organizations can strengthen their defenses, stay ahead of emerging threats, and foster a culture of security awareness that mitigates the risks associated with phishing attacks.

REFERENCES

Aggarwal, K., Singh, S. K., Chopra, M., Kumar, S., & Colace, F. (2022). Deep Learning in Robotics for Strengthening Industry 4.0.: Opportunities, Challenges and Future Directions. In Nedjah, N., Abd El-Latif, A. A., Gupta, B. B., & Mourelle, L. M. (Eds.), *Robotics and AI for Cybersecurity and Critical Infrastructure in Smart Cities* (Vol. 1030, pp. 1–19). Springer International Publishing., DOI: 10.1007/978-3-030-96737-6_1

Alsufyani, A. A., & Alzahrani, S. M. (2021). Social engineering attack detection using machine learning: Text phishing attack. *Indian J. Comput. Sci. Eng*, 12(3), 743–751. DOI: 10.21817/indjcse/2021/v12i3/211203298

Ansari, M. F., Sharma, P. K., & Dash, B. (2022). Prevention of phishing attacks using AI-based Cybersecurity Awareness Training. *Prevention*, 3(6), 61–72. DOI: 10.47893/IJSSAN.2022.1221

Apandi, S. H., Sallim, J., & Sidek, R. M. (2020). Types of anti-phishing solutions for phishing attack. *IOP Conference Series. Materials Science and Engineering*, 769(1), 012072. https://iopscience.iop.org/article/10.1088/1757-899X/769/1/012072/meta. DOI: 10.1088/1757-899X/769/1/012072

Ashfaq, S., Chandre, P., Pathan, S., Mande, U., Nimbalkar, M., & Mahalle, P. (2024). Defending Against Vishing Attacks: A Comprehensive Review for Prevention and Mitigation Techniques. In Roy, N. R., Tanwar, S., & Batra, U. (Eds.), *Cyber Security and Digital Forensics* (Vol. 896, pp. 411–422). Springer Nature Singapore., DOI: 10.1007/978-981-99-9811-1_33

Bin, S., Qiaoyan, W., & Xiaoying, L. (2010). A DNS based anti-phishing approach. *2010 Second International Conference on Networks Security, Wireless Communications and Trusted Computing, 2*, 262–265. https://ieeexplore.ieee.org/abstract/document/5480624/

Chanti, S., & Chithralekha, T. (2020). Classification of Anti-phishing Solutions. *SN Computer Science*, 1(1), 11. DOI: 10.1007/s42979-019-0011-2 PMID: 33263111

Chaudhuri, A. (2023). Clone Phishing: Attacks and Defenses. *International Journal of Scientific and Research Publications*, 13(4), 180–184. DOI: 10.29322/IJSRP.13.04.2023.p13626

Do, N. Q., Selamat, A., Krejcar, O., Herrera-Viedma, E., & Fujita, H. (2022). Deep learning for phishing detection: Taxonomy, current challenges and future directions. *IEEE Access : Practical Innovations, Open Solutions*, 10, 36429–36463. DOI: 10.1109/ACCESS.2022.3151903

Dubey, H., Kumar, S., & Chhabra, A. (2022). *Cyber Security Model to Secure Data Transmission using Cloud Cryptography. 02.*

Gaurav, A., Gupta, B. B., Arya, V., Chui, K. T., & Peñalvo, F. J. G. (2023). Adaptive Defense Mechanisms Against Phishing Threats in 6G Wireless Environments. *2023 IEEE 98th Vehicular Technology Conference (VTC2023-Fall)*, 1–5. https://ieeexplore.ieee.org/abstract/document/10333473/

Gupta, B. B., Gaurav, A., Wu, J., Arya, V., & Chui, K. T. (2024). Deep Learning and Big Data Integration with Cuckoo Search Optimization for Robust Phishing Attack Detection. *ICC 2024 - IEEE International Conference on Communications*, 1322–1327. DOI: 10.1109/ICC51166.2024.10622646

Gupta, S., Singhal, A., & Kapoor, A. (2016). A literature survey on social engineering attacks: Phishing attack. *2016 International Conference on Computing, Communication and Automation (ICCCA)*, 537–540. https://ieeexplore.ieee.org/abstract/document/7813778/

Gusev, A. (2022). Domestic private banking solutions can be quite successful as an effective protection against whaling-style cyber attacks which are used as a basis for more complex targeted phishing. *Procedia Computer Science*, 213, 391–399. DOI: 10.1016/j.procs.2022.11.083

Hiransha, M., Unnithan, N. A., Vinayakumar, R., Soman, K., & Verma, A. D. R. (2018). Deep learning based phishing e-mail detection. *Proc. 1st AntiPhishing Shared Pilot 4th ACM Int. Workshop Secur. Privacy Anal.(IWSPA)*, 1–5. https://ceur-ws.org/Vol-2124/paper_16.pdf

Islam, M. S., Sajjad, M., Hasan, M. M., & Mazumder, M. S. I. (2023). Phishing attack detecting system using DNS and IP filtering. *Asian Journal of Computer Science and Technology*, 12(1), 16–20. DOI: 10.51983/ajcst-2023.12.1.3552

Jones, K. S., Armstrong, M. E., Tornblad, M. K., & Siami Namin, A. (2021). How social engineers use persuasion principles during vishing attacks. *Information and Computer Security*, 29(2), 314–331. DOI: 10.1108/ICS-07-2020-0113

Kaur, P., Singh, S. K., Singh, I., & Kumar, S. (2021). Exploring convolutional neural network in computer vision-based image classification. *International Conference on Smart Systems and Advanced Computing (Syscom-2021)*. https://ceur-ws.org/Vol-3080/21.pdf

Khonji, M., Iraqi, Y., & Jones, A. (2013). Phishing detection: A literature survey. *IEEE Communications Surveys and Tutorials*, 15(4), 2091–2121. DOI: 10.1109/SURV.2013.032213.00009

Kumar, R., Singh, S. K., Lobiyal, D. K., Kumar, S., & Jawla, S. (2024). Security Metrics and Authentication-based RouTing (SMART) Protocol for Vehicular IoT Networks. *SN Computer Science*, 5(2), 236. DOI: 10.1007/s42979-023-02566-7

Machap, K., Murakami, R., & Rahman, N. A. A. (2024). A study and survey of chrome extension to detect phishing websites. *AIP Conference Proceedings, 3161*(1). https://pubs.aip.org/aip/acp/article-abstract/3161/1/020170/3310634

Maseno, E. M. (2017). *Vishing attack detection model for mobile users.* [PhD Thesis, KCA University]. http://41.89.49.13:8080/xmlui/handle/123456789/1276

Maurya, S., Saini, H. S., & Jain, A. (2019). Browser extension based hybrid anti-phishing framework using feature selection. *International Journal of Advanced Computer Science and Applications*, 10(11). Advance online publication. https://www.academia.edu/download/68976420/Paper_78-Browser_Extension_based_Hybrid_Anti_Phishing_Framework.pdf. DOI: 10.14569/IJACSA.2019.0101178

Nadeem, M., Zahra, S. W., Abbasi, M. N., Arshad, A., Riaz, S., & Ahmed, W. (2023). Phishing attack, its detections and prevention techniques. *Int. J. Wirel. Secur. Netw*, 1, 13–25.

Njuguna, D., Kamau, J., & Kaburu, D. (2021). Model for mitigating smishing attacks on mobile platforms. *2021 International Conference on Electrical, Computer and Energy Technologies (ICECET)*, 1–6. https://ieeexplore.ieee.org/abstract/document/9698789/

Peñalvo, F. J. G., Sharma, A., Chhabra, A., Singh, S. K., Kumar, S., Arya, V., & Gaurav, A. (2022). Mobile cloud computing and sustainable development: Opportunities, challenges, and future directions. [IJCAC]. *International Journal of Cloud Applications and Computing*, 12(1), 1–20. DOI: 10.4018/IJCAC.312583

Prem, S. P., & Reddy, B. I. (2019). Phishing and anti-phishing techniques. *International Research Journal of Engineering and Technology*, 6(7), 1446–1452.

Purkait, S. (2015). Examining the effectiveness of phishing filters against DNS based phishing attacks. *Information and Computer Security*, 23(3), 333–346. DOI: 10.1108/ICS-02-2013-0009

Sarin, S., Singh, S. K., Kumar, S., Goyal, S., Gupta, B. B., Arya, V., & Chui, K. T. (2023). Forging Faces: Exploring the Generation of Synthetic Identities using GANs. *2023 IEEE 13th International Conference on Consumer Electronics-Berlin (ICCE-Berlin)*, 1–4. https://ieeexplore.ieee.org/abstract/document/10649659/

Setia, H., Chhabra, A., Singh, S. K., Kumar, S., Sharma, S., Arya, V., Gupta, B. B., & Wu, J. (2024). Securing the road ahead: Machine learning-driven DDoS attack detection in VANET cloud environments. *Cyber Security and Applications*, 2, 100037. DOI: 10.1016/j.csa.2024.100037

Sharma, A., Singh, S. K., Chhabra, A., Kumar, S., Arya, V., & Moslehpour, M. (2023). A novel deep federated learning-based model to enhance privacy in critical infrastructure systems. [IJSSCI]. *International Journal of Software Science and Computational Intelligence*, 15(1), 1–23. DOI: 10.4018/IJSSCI.334711

Sharma, A., Singh, S. K., Kumar, S., Chhabra, A., & Gupta, S. (2023). Security of Android Banking Mobile Apps: Challenges and Opportunities. In Nedjah, N., Martínez Pérez, G., & Gupta, B. B. (Eds.), *International Conference on Cyber Security, Privacy and Networking (ICSPN 2022)* (Vol. 599, pp. 406–416). Springer International Publishing. DOI: 10.1007/978-3-031-22018-0_39

Sharma, H., Meenakshi, E., & Bhatia, S. K. (2017). A comparative analysis and awareness survey of phishing detection tools. *2017 2nd IEEE International Conference on Recent Trends in Electronics, Information & Communication Technology (RTEICT)*, 1437–1442. https://ieeexplore.ieee.org/abstract/document/8256835/

Sharma, P., Dash, B., & Ansari, M. F. (2022). *Anti-Phishing Techniques – A Review of Cyber Defense Mechanisms* (SSRN Scholarly Paper No. 4335354). Social Science Research Network. https://papers.ssrn.com/abstract=4335354 DOI: 10.17148/IJARCCE.2022.11728

Singh, A., Singh, S. K., Chhabra, A., Singh, G., Kumar, S., & Arya, V. (2025). Detailed Evolution Process of CNN-Based Intrusion Detection in the Context of Network Security. In *Digital Forensics and Cyber Crime Investigation* (pp. 70–87). CRC Press., https://www.taylorfrancis.com/chapters/edit/10.1201/9781003207573-4/detailed-evolution-process-cnn-based-intrusion-detection-context-network-security-amanpreet-singh-sunil-singh-amit-chhabra-gurmehar-singh-yuvraj-sudhakar-kumar-varsha-arya

Singh, K., Setia, H., & Kumar, S. (2021). Wi-vi and li-fi based framework for human identification and vital signs detection through walls. *International Conference on Smart Systems and Advanced Computing (Syscom-2021)*. https://ceur-ws.org/Vol-3080/3.pdf

Singh, L. J., & Imphal, N. (2018). *A Survey on Phishing and Anti-Phishing Techniques*. *6*(2).

Singh, N., Singh, S. K., Kumar, S., Rawat, Y., Arya, V., Bansal, R., & Chui, K. T. (2024). Next Gen Security With Quantum-Safe Cryptography. In *Innovations in Modern Cryptography* (pp. 131–164). IGI Global., https://www.igi-global.com/chapter/next-gen-security-with-quantum-safe-cryptography/354038 DOI: 10.4018/979-8-3693-5330-1.ch006

Singh, T., Kumar, S., Singh, S. K., Gupta, B. B., Wu, J., & Castiglione, A. (2025). Enhancing Autonomous System Security With AI and Secure Computation Technologies. In *AI Developments for Industrial Robotics and Intelligent Drones* (pp. 159–186). IGI Global Scientific Publishing., https://www.igi-global.com/chapter/enhancing-autonomous-system-security-with-ai-and-secure-computation-technologies/365362 DOI: 10.4018/979-8-3693-2707-4.ch008

Somesha, M., Pais, A. R., Rao, R. S., & Rathour, V. S. (2020). Efficient deep learning techniques for the detection of phishing websites. *Sadhana*, 45(1), 165. DOI: 10.1007/s12046-020-01392-4

Tatang, D., Zettl, F., & Holz, T. (2021). The Evolution of DNS-based Email Authentication: Measuring Adoption and Finding Flaws. *24th International Symposium on Research in Attacks, Intrusions and Defenses*, 354–369. DOI: 10.1145/3471621.3471842

Thakur, R., Kumar, S., Singh, S. K., Singla, K., Sharma, S. K., & Arya, V. (2025). Cyber Synergy: Unlocking the Potential Use of Biometric Systems and Multimedia Forensics in Cybercrime Investigations. In *Digital Forensics and Cyber Crime Investigation* (pp. 241–267). CRC Press. https://www.taylorfrancis.com/chapters/edit/10.1201/9781003207573-12/cyber-synergy-ruchika-thakur-sudhakar-kumar-sunil-singh-krishana-singla-sunil-kr-sharma-varsha-arya

Ulfath, R. E., Sarker, I. H., Chowdhury, M. J. M., & Hammoudeh, M. (2022). Detecting Smishing Attacks Using Feature Extraction and Classification Techniques. In M. S. Arefin, M. S. Kaiser, A. Bandyopadhyay, Md. A. R. Ahad, & K. Ray (Eds.), *Proceedings of the International Conference on Big Data, IoT, and Machine Learning* (Vol. 95, pp. 677–689). Springer Singapore. DOI: 10.1007/978-981-16-6636-0_51

Vats, T., & Kumar, S. (2021). *Next-generation towards construction of cyber-physical systems and digital twins*. Insights2Techinfo. https://insights2techinfo.com/next-generation-towards-construction-of-cyber-physical-systems-and-digital-twins/

Vats, T., Kumar, S., Singh, S. K., Madan, U., Preet, M., Arya, V., Bansal, R., & Almomani, A. (2024). Navigating the landscape: Safeguarding privacy and security in the era of ambient intelligence within healthcare settings. *Cyber Security and Applications*, 2, 100046. DOI: 10.1016/j.csa.2024.100046

Wong, A., Abuadbba, A., Almashor, M., & Kanhere, S. (2022). *PhishClone: Measuring the Efficacy of Cloning Evasion Attacks* (No. arXiv:2209.01582). arXiv. https://doi.org//arXiv.2209.01582DOI: 10.48550

Yeboah-Boateng, E. O., & Amanor, P. M. (2014). *Phishing, SMiShing & Vishing: An Assessment of Threats against Mobile Devices. 5*(4).

Zeydan, H. Z., Selamat, A., & Salleh, M. (2014). Survey of anti-phishing tools with detection capabilities. *2014 International Symposium on Biometrics and Security Technologies (Isbast)*, 214–219. https://ieeexplore.ieee.org/abstract/document/7013124/

Chapter 10
Critical Phishing Defense Strategies and Digital Asset Protection:
The Role of Cryptography in Protecting Digital Asset

Dwi Sartika
Esa Unggul University, Indonesia

ABSTRACT

Cryptography has a crucial role in maintaining the security of sensitive information on digital assets. By applying strong encryption techniques, cryptography converts data into a format that is not easily read by unauthorized parties. This not only minimizes the risk of illegal access or hacking, but also ensures that information can only be accessed by parties who have the appropriate keys. Decryption techniques then allow legitimate recipients to restore the data to its original form. cryptography uses complex mathematical algorithms to convert original data into a secure, encrypted form. This applies not only to data storage in secure repositories, but also to data transmission over communications networks. Thus, the application of cryptography is not only a prerequisite for protecting sensitive information, but also for ensuring trust in data exchange in the digital era. Cryptography is the main foundation in maintaining the security of sensitive information on digital assets.

INTRODUCTION

In the digital age, cryptography has emerged as a cornerstone of security for protecting digital assets. As individuals, businesses, and governments increasingly rely on digital systems to store, transfer, and process sensitive information, the need for robust security mechanisms is more critical than ever. Cryptography, the art and science of encoding and decoding information, ensures that data remains secure

DOI: 10.4018/979-8-3693-8784-9.ch010

and trustworthy, preventing unauthorized access and malicious alterations. This chapter explores the key aspects of cryptography and its role in protecting digital assets.

Cryptography is the science and practice of securing information through techniques that enable confidentiality, integrity, authentication, and non-repudiation. By converting data into unreadable formats, cryptography ensures that only authorized parties can access and understand the information. The study of cryptography has evolved over centuries, from simple substitution ciphers used by the Romans to highly sophisticated mathematical algorithms used in today's digital communications.(Katz & Lindell, 2014)

Key Components of Cryptography:

1. Encryption: The process of transforming plaintext (readable data) into ciphertext (unreadable data) using an algorithm and a key. Encryption ensures that unauthorized individuals cannot access the information.
2. Decryption: The reverse of encryption, where ciphertext is converted back into readable plaintext using a key.
3. Algorithms: These are the mathematical formulas or processes used to encrypt and decrypt information. Common cryptographic algorithms include AES (Advanced Encryption Standard) and RSA (Rivest-Shamir-Adleman).
4. Keys: These are essential elements of cryptography, used for both encryption and decryption. There are two main types:
5. Symmetric Key Cryptography: Uses the same key for both encryption and decryption.
6. Asymmetric Key Cryptography: Uses a pair of keys—a public key for encryption and a private key for decryption.
7. Hashing: A technique to convert data into a fixed-size hash value, often used to verify the integrity of data.

Cryptography in Modern Applications for data Security, Cryptography is used to protect sensitive information such as financial transactions, personal data, and communications. Digital Signatures: Ensuring the authenticity of digital documents by providing a secure method of signing and verifying the identity of the sender. Secure Communications: Cryptographic protocols like SSL/TLS are used in secure web communications to protect data transmitted over the internet. Cryptography plays a crucial role in securing digital ecosystems and safeguarding privacy in the modern world.

PROTECTING THE CONFIDENTIALITY OF DIGITAL ASSETS

One of the primary objectives of cryptography is to protect the confidentiality of digital assets. Encryption ensures that sensitive information, such as financial data, personal details, and intellectual property, can only be accessed by authorized individuals or systems. In this way, cryptography prevents unauthorized parties from intercepting or stealing data during transmission or storage.(Piper & Murphy, 2013)

Protecting the confidentiality of digital assets using cryptography involves employing cryptographic techniques to ensure that sensitive information is accessible only to authorized parties and protected from unauthorized access or disclosure. Cryptography, through various algorithms and methods, plays a central role in securing data, both in transit and at rest.

Here are the key ways cryptography is used to protect the confidentiality of digital assets:

1. Data Encryption

Encryption is the primary method for safeguarding the confidentiality of digital assets. It transforms plaintext (readable data) into ciphertext (unreadable data), ensuring that only users with the appropriate decryption key can access the original data.

Symmetric Encryption:

A single key is used for both encryption and decryption.Common algorithms include AES (Advanced Encryption Standard) and DES (Data Encryption Standard). Use Case: Encrypting files or databases to prevent unauthorized access. For example, AES is widely used to encrypt data on hard drives and in secure communications.

Asymmetric Encryption:

Involves a pair of keys: a public key (for encryption) and a private key (for decryption).Common algorithms include RSA and Elliptic Curve Cryptography (ECC). Use Case: Secure email communication, where the sender uses the recipient's public key to encrypt the message, and only the recipient's private key can decrypt it.(Stallings, 2017)

2. Secure Communications (Encryption in Transit)

TLS/SSL Protocols: Transport Layer Security (TLS) and its predecessor, Secure Sockets Layer (SSL), use encryption to protect data as it travels between clients and servers over the internet. These protocols encrypt web traffic (HTTPS), ensuring that sensitive data like login credentials or financial transactions are protected from interception or eavesdropping. Use Case: Online banking, e-commerce websites, and email providers use TLS/SSL to protect the confidentiality of user data during transmission.

Virtual Private Networks (VPNs): VPNs use encryption to create a secure "tunnel" over public or shared networks, ensuring that data transmitted between devices is confidential and protected from prying eyes. Use Case: Remote workers use VPNs to securely access company resources over the internet. (Ferguson et al., 2010)

3. Data Encryption at Rest

Full Disk Encryption (FDE): Encrypts the entire storage device (e.g., hard drives, SSDs), ensuring that even if the device is lost or stolen, the data remains confidential. Tools: BitLocker (for Windows) and FileVault (for macOS) are examples of full-disk encryption solutions. Use Case: Protecting the confidentiality of sensitive business data stored on laptops or external drives.

Database Encryption:Encrypting databases at rest ensures that sensitive information like customer records, financial data, or medical records is unreadable to unauthorized users. Use Case: In healthcare and financial industries, database encryption protects confidential data in case of data breaches.

4. Email Encryption

PGP (Pretty Good Privacy) and S/MIME (Secure/Multipurpose Internet Mail Extensions):Both PGP and S/MIME use asymmetric encryption to encrypt the contents of an email, ensuring that only the intended recipient can read the message. Use Case: PGP and S/MIME are commonly used to protect sensitive corporate communications and to ensure privacy in personal email correspondence.

5. File Encryption

End-to-End Encryption (E2EE): Ensures that files and data are encrypted on the sender's side and only decrypted by the intended recipient. Popular file-sharing services and messaging apps (e.g., WhatsApp, Signal) use end-to-end encryption to maintain the confidentiality of data. Use Case: Secure file sharing between organizations or individuals, protecting intellectual property or sensitive business information. Encrypted Cloud Storage: Cloud services often offer encryption to protect files stored in the cloud. Data is encrypted before being uploaded and decrypted only when accessed by authorized users. Use Case: Services like Google Drive, Dropbox, and OneDrive offer encryption to protect user files stored in the cloud from unauthorized access.(Dworkin, 2015)

6. Digital Certificates and Public Key Infrastructure (PKI)

Digital Certificates: Issued by trusted Certificate Authorities (CAs), digital certificates use cryptography to verify the identity of individuals, devices, or organizations, ensuring that data is exchanged securely with authenticated parties. Use Case: Websites use SSL/TLS certificates to verify their identity and establish encrypted connections with users. Digital certificates are also used in secure email communication and code signing.

Public Key Infrastructure (PKI):A system that manages public and private keys, as well as digital certificates, to enable secure and encrypted communication. Use Case: PKI is essential for secure online transactions, VPN access, and securing email communications through encryption and digital signatures.

7. Hashing for Data Integrity

Cryptographic Hash Functions: Hash functions, such as SHA-256 (Secure Hash Algorithm), produce a fixed-size output (hash) from input data, ensuring the data has not been altered or tampered with. Use Case: Hashing is used in digital signatures, password storage, and verifying the integrity of software downloads. Although hashing alone does not encrypt data, it helps ensure the data remains confidential by detecting unauthorized modifications.

8. Digital Signatures

Digital Signatures: Digital signatures use asymmetric encryption to verify the authenticity and integrity of digital messages or documents. A cryptographic hash of the data is signed using the sender's private key, and the recipient verifies the signature with the sender's public key. Use Case: Digital signatures are widely used in electronic contracts, software distribution, and secure communications to ensure the confidentiality and authenticity of data.(Bonneau et al., 2015)

9. Tokenization

Tokenization:A method of replacing sensitive data (like credit card numbers) with a non-sensitive token that has no exploitable value. The actual data is stored securely in an encrypted format. Use Case: Tokenization is widely used in payment systems to protect credit card information during transactions, ensuring the confidentiality of sensitive data.

Using cryptography to protect the confidentiality of digital assets is essential in today's digital world, where data breaches and cyber threats are constantly evolving. Cryptographic techniques like encryption, secure communication protocols, digital certificates, and hashing ensure that sensitive data remains confidential, both in storage and during transmission. By implementing these techniques, organizations and individuals can protect their digital assets from unauthorized access and maintain privacy in an increasingly interconnected world. For example, encryption protocols like Advanced Encryption Standard (AES) are widely used to secure data at rest (stored data) and in transit (transferred data) across networks. These protocols are used in applications such as online banking, email communication, and secure file storage.

ENSURING DATA INTEGRITY

Data integrity refers to the accuracy and consistency of data throughout its lifecycle. Cryptography helps protect digital assets from unauthorized modification or corruption by employing hash functions, which create a unique "fingerprint" or hash value for each piece of data. Even the slightest change in the original data will result in a different hash value, alerting the system or users to the possibility of tampering. By using hashing algorithms like SHA-256 (Secure Hash Algorithm), cryptographic systems can verify the integrity of digital assets and detect unauthorized alterations. This is critical for maintaining trust in digital communications and ensuring that data remains uncorrupted.

Authentication and Access Control Another key role of cryptography is to ensure that digital assets are only accessible to verified users or systems. Cryptographic methods such as digital signatures and certificates play a central role in the authentication process. These mechanisms enable systems to verify the identity of users, devices, or software before granting access to sensitive data.(Asiva Noor Rachmayani, 2015)

Digital Signatures: A digital signature is a cryptographic technique that ensures the authenticity of a message or document. It provides a way to verify that the content has not been altered and confirms the identity of the sender. Digital Certificates: Digital certificates, issued by trusted certificate authorities (CAs), bind public keys to identities, such as individuals or organizations. These certificates are widely used in secure online transactions, including e-commerce and email communication. Through these authentication mechanisms, cryptography prevents unauthorized access to digital assets, ensuring that only trusted parties can interact with sensitive data.

Non-repudiation in Digital Transactions In addition to ensuring confidentiality and integrity, cryptography provides non-repudiation, which guarantees that an entity cannot deny having participated in a transaction or communication. This is particularly important in legal, financial, and contractual transactions where it is crucial to have proof of the origin and authenticity of digital signatures. Digital signatures, backed by cryptographic algorithms, ensure that the sender of a message cannot later deny having sent it, and the recipient cannot deny having received it. This helps protect digital assets during transactions by creating a trail of accountability.

Secure Communication and Data Transmission, Cryptography plays a pivotal role in securing communication over the internet. Protocols such as Secure Sockets Layer (SSL) and Transport Layer Security (TLS) use cryptography to encrypt data transferred between clients and servers, preventing eavesdropping and man-in-the-middle attacks. These protocols are essential for securing digital assets during transmission, ensuring that sensitive information like credit card numbers, login credentials, and personal data are not intercepted by malicious actors. Modern communication systems, including Virtual Private Networks (VPNs) and email encryption services, rely on cryptography to protect the confidentiality and integrity of data while in transit. As the reliance on digital communication grows, cryptography remains a fundamental tool for safeguarding digital assets from cyberattacks.

Emerging Threats and Cryptographic Challenges, While cryptography remains a powerful tool for protecting digital assets, it is not without challenges. Advances in computing technology, particularly the development of quantum computing, pose potential threats to traditional cryptographic methods. Quantum computers, with their ability to perform complex calculations at unprecedented speeds, could break widely used encryption algorithms, rendering current cryptographic systems vulnerable. To address these concerns, researchers are developing quantum-resistant cryptographic algorithms, which aim to safeguard digital assets in a post-quantum world. As cryptographic methods evolve, it is critical to stay ahead of emerging threats to ensure the continued protection of digital assets.

Cryptography plays an indispensable role in protecting digital assets by securing data confidentiality, integrity, and authenticity. Through encryption, hashing, and authentication mechanisms, cryptographic systems defend against unauthorized access, data corruption, and cyberattacks. As digital transactions and communications become increasingly integral to modern life, the role of cryptography in securing digital assets will continue to grow. However, ongoing advancements in technology also present new challenges, making it essential to remain vigilant and adaptive in the application of cryptographic methods. In summary, cryptography not only provides a robust framework for securing digital assets but also offers a foundation of trust in the digital world.

REFERENCES

Asiva Noor Rachmayani. (2015). *No Title.*

Bonneau, J., Miller, A., Clark, J., Narayanan, A., Kroll, J. A., & Felten, E. W. (2015). SoK: Research perspectives and challenges for bitcoin and cryptocurrencies. *Proceedings - IEEE Symposium on Security and Privacy, 2015-July*, 104–121. DOI: 10.1109/SP.2015.14

Dworkin. (2015). FIPS PUB 202 SHA-3 Standard : Permutation-Based Hash and. *NIST Federal Information Processing Standard, August.*

Ferguson, N., Schneier, B., & Kohno, T. (2010). Chapter 9. Generating Randomness. *Cryptography Engineering : Design Principles and Practical Applications*, 137–161.

Katz, J., & Lindell, Y. (2014). INTRODUCTION TO MODERN CRYPTOGRAPHY: Second Edition. In *Introduction to Modern Cryptography: Second Edition*. DOI: 10.1201/b17668

Piper, F., & Murphy, S. (2013). 2. Understanding cryptography. In *Cryptography*. DOI: 10.1093/actrade/9780192803153.003.0002

Stallings, W. (2017). *Cryptography and Network Security: Principles and Practice 7th Global Edition.*

Chapter 11
Critical Strategies for Phishing Defense and Digital Asset Protection: A Case Study Approach

N. V. Keerthana
https://orcid.org/0000-0001-8878-2083
Velalar College of Engineering and Technology, India

P. Suresh
https://orcid.org/0000-0001-9815-2982
Vellore Institute of Technology, India

Madhumitha Kulandaivel
SRM University, India

Sindhumitha Kulandaivel
National Institute of Technology, Tiruchirappalli, India

ABSTRACT

Phishing is still one of the most common and dangerous types of cyber threats, and it keeps getting more sophisticated. The increasing prevalence of phishing attempts has made it necessary for enterprises across the globe to prioritize the development of offensive and defensive cybersecurity solutions. This case study explores the current state of phishing and the developments in cyber protection tactics that have accompanied them, showcasing actual situations in which businesses have successfully reduced these risks. Phishing uses human psychology to trick people into disclosing private data, such as login passwords, bank account details, or other personal information. It frequently takes the form of official correspondence. A more advanced variation called spear-phishing is more difficult to identify and counter since it uses carefully constructed communications that are targeted at certain people or companies. More proactive threat identification and response are now possible thanks to the integration of AI and ML with conventional SIEM systems.

DOI: 10.4018/979-8-3693-8784-9.ch011

1. INTRODUCTION

Phishing has become one of the most common and harmful types of cyberattacks in recent years. Phishing was first restricted to trick emails meant to trick recipients into divulging personal information. Nevertheless, it has now developed into a highly advanced threat that makes use of several channels, such as social media, Short Messaging Service (SMS), and even voice communication, or "vishing." Attackers are using more sophisticated tactics, such as spear-phishing, to target certain people or companies with customized content, making their attacks more successful and difficult to identify (Duy et al., 2024). Because of this, there is tremendous pressure on the cybersecurity industry to change and advance in response to increasingly complex attacks. The growth of digital communication channels and the increasing amount of personal information available online have contributed to the surge in phishing attempts. These data are being used by cybercriminals to craft very convincing fake messages that evade detection by conventional security measures. Attackers, for example, can pose as reputable organizations like banks, governments, or even coworkers, making it more challenging for people to discern between malicious communications and those that are not. The need for increasingly sophisticated detection and prevention methods has resulted from the sophistication of attacks, pushing the frontiers of cybersecurity innovation.

The cybersecurity sector has advanced significantly in creating stronger defenses against the growing menace of phishing. Artificial intelligence (AI) and Machine Learning (ML) are two technologies that are currently being used to identify and stop phishing emails instantly. Large volumes of data may be analyzed by these systems, which can also spot patterns and anomalies that could point to a phishing attempt. Furthermore, many firms now employ Multi-Factor Authentication (MFA) and sophisticated email filtering systems as regular procedures, adding more defenses against these ubiquitous dangers (Duy et al., 2024). The fight against phishing is still ongoing despite these developments. Cybercriminals are always evolving, coming up with new strategies to get around security controls and take advantage of weaknesses in people. The tactics and tools used to stop phishing attempts must also advance along with the techniques themselves. To remain ahead of increasingly complex phishing assaults, cyber protection will probably depend on a combination of ongoing technology innovation, user education, and international cooperation.

The ever-changing landscape of phishing tactics makes it abundantly evident that human behavior is still one of the most important aspects of cybersecurity. A single person unintentionally falling for a skillfully constructed phishing assault can compromise even the most sophisticated technological safeguards (Guo et al., 2022). Thus, there is a rising emphasis on thorough cybersecurity training and awareness initiatives in tandem with technical advancements. Businesses are spending money on phishing simulations and training programs regularly to make sure staff members are capable of identifying threats and taking proper action. This twin strategy—combining state-of-the-art technology with knowledgeable, watchful users—reflects a more robust defense in the future against the constantly changing field of phishing attempts.

Cybersecurity professionals are actively studying ways to identify phishing on the Internet. Of these, attackers are using website fraud as a means of attack increasingly often. The accuracy of these techniques is frequently limited, as is their capacity to recognize fresh phishing websites and identify embedded items. In addition, attackers' methods become more intricate and smarter. They can quickly produce several phishing websites that imitate the design and operation of trustworthy websites. This makes it more challenging to identify and stop fraudulent Internet transactions.

Phishing is one of the most widespread and insidious forms of cybercrime, exploiting both technological vulnerabilities and human psychology to deceive individuals and organizations into disclosing sensitive information or compromising their systems. These attacks target a broad range of victims and employ increasingly sophisticated techniques, creating a constantly evolving threat landscape. Understanding this landscape is crucial for developing effective defenses against these pervasive threats.

2. PHISHING ATTACKS – A PERSPECTIVE VIEW

One of the most pervasive and sneaky types of cybercrime is phishing, which uses technological flaws and human psychology to trick people and organizations into divulging private information or jeopardizing their systems.

2.1 Historical Context and Development

Phishing first began in the mid-1990s when it was used to target early adopters of the internet with very simple techniques like sending phony emails purporting to be from reputable companies like banks or internet service providers. Frequently, these emails would contain links to phony websites intended to steal credit card numbers or personal data. Phishing techniques got more sophisticated and widespread as internet usage increased and crooks improved their skills.

Phishing assaults increased in the early 2000s, especially as online banking and e-commerce became more popular and offered attractive targets for hackers. Phishing efforts started to make use of more sophisticated social engineering strategies, taking advantage of people's faith in reputable organizations and brands.

2.2 Types of Phishing Attacks

Phishing attacks have evolved into a variety of styles, each with a distinct target and goal in mind. Recognizing and protecting against these typical types requires an understanding of them.

- **Spear Phishing:** Spear phishing is more focused than typical phishing, as it targets particular people or organizations with highly targeted attacks. An attacker may, for instance, pose as a reliable colleague and send an email requesting the recipient to download a harmful file or divulge personal information.
- **Whaling:** Whaling, a kind of spear phishing, focuses on senior managers or anyone with access to vital business information. Depending on the target, a successful whaling attack may lead to financial losses, a breach of national security, or the compromise of private company information.
- **Clone Phishing:** Clone phishing involves hackers making a perfect duplicate of a genuine email that was previously delivered by a reliable source, adding malicious links in place of the genuine ones. The victim is more likely to interact with the content of the email because they think it is a genuine follow-up or resend, which could compromise their data or systems.
- **Vishing and Smishing:** Phishing techniques that make use of mobile and phone networks include smishing (SMS phishing) and vishing (voice phishing). Vishing involves attackers pretending to be reputable companies over the phone to coerce victims into divulging personal information or

sending money. Smishing is the practice of sending phony text messages that ask for sensitive information in response or include harmful URLs.

- **Business Email Compromise (BEC):** BEC is a particular type of phishing that aims to fool staff members into divulging company information or carrying out illicit financial transactions. A common tactic used in business email compromise (BEC) attacks is to pose as a senior executive or a reliable business associate and instruct the target to send money to a fake account or divulge private information.

2.3 Phishing Attacks- Recent Trends and Techniques

Cybercriminals have been incorporating new strategies and technologies into their phishing assaults to make them more successful. The following are a few recent phishing trends:

- **Phishing Kits and Automation:** Phishing kits are pre-assembled collections of materials and equipment that make it relatively simple for even inexperienced cybercriminals to carry out phishing attacks (Aldakheel, Zakariah, Gashgari, Almarshad, & Alzahrani, 2023). Phishing kits are readily available on the dark web, which has led to an increase in phishing attempts and made it simpler for criminals to initiate extensive campaigns.
- **Phishing-as-a-Service (PhaaS):** PhaaS is an increasingly popular practice whereby thieves charge other criminals for phishing services. Because PhaaS makes it easier for fraudsters to get started, more actors can engage in phishing activities without requiring technical knowledge.
- **Use of Artificial Intelligence (AI) and Machine Learning (ML):** The use of AI and ML by cybercriminals to improve their phishing tactics is growing. With AI and ML, phishing emails may be made more convincing by customizing messaging to target audiences and analyzing vast databases.
- **Targeting of Cloud Services and SaaS Applications:** Software-as-a-Service (SaaS) apps and cloud services are becoming more and more popular among enterprises, making them easy targets for phishing attempts (Asiri, Xiao, Alzahrani, Li, & Li, 2023). Phishing emails, which impersonate reputable cloud service providers and deceive users into divulging login credentials or allowing access to private data kept on the cloud, are frequently created by cybercriminals.
- **Exploitation of Current Events:** To boost their success rates, phishing efforts often take advantage of current events, such as pandemics, natural catastrophes, or noteworthy news articles. Phishing attempts targeting health information, government relief initiatives, and remote work technologies saw a notable surge during the COVID-19 epidemic, for instance.

2.4 Major Phishing Attacks – A Case Examples

Phishing attacks have caused significant damage to individuals, organizations, and even governments. Examining case examples of major phishing attacks helps to illustrate the scale and impact of these threats:

- **Democratic National Committee (DNC) Breach:** During the 2016 U.S. presidential election, the DNC was the subject of one of the most prominent phishing attempts in recent memory. Russian hackers broke into important DNC officials' email accounts by sending spear-phishing emails (Jha, Muthalagu, & Pawar, 2023). The election result was influenced by the information gained from this hack, which also brought attention to the geopolitical ramifications of phishing.

- **Target's Data Breach:** A significant data breach at retail behemoth Target in 2013 resulted in the exposure of over 40 million consumers' credit card details. Attackers were able to access Target's network through a phishing assault on a third-party vendor, which started the breach. The significance of protecting the whole supply chain from phishing attacks is highlighted by this scenario.
- **Google and Facebook BEC Scam:** A Lithuanian cybercriminal was successful in carrying out a BEC scheme against Google and Facebook between 2013 and 2015, taking over $100 million in revenue. By pretending to be a trustworthy business partner, the attacker sent bogus invoices that resulted in significant wire payments. This instance emphasizes the value of financial transaction verification as well as the potency of BEC attacks.
- **Sony Pictures Entertainment Hack:** A spear-phishing attack was the start of the Sony Pictures Entertainment hack in 2014, which was credited to North Korean hackers. Sony personnel received emails from the attackers with malicious links, which ultimately resulted in the network of the corporation being compromised. Sensitive corporate information, including unreleased movies, personnel details, and embarrassing internal correspondence, were leaked as a result of the intrusion, seriously harming the company's finances and reputation.
- **Operation Phish Phry:** Over $1.5 million was stolen as a result of campaign Phish Phry, a massive phishing campaign that targeted American banks. Thousands of people received phishing emails from the attackers, which led them to phony bank websites where their login information was taken. More than 100 people connected to the plan were apprehended as a result of this operation, which sparked one of the biggest cybercrime investigations in American history.

3. ROLE OF HUMAN FACTORS IN PHISHING

Phishing attacks make use of the human aspect, which is the weakest link in any security chain. Cybercriminals have long known that by playing on human psychology, they may get past even the most sophisticated technological barriers. A crucial component of phishing is the human element, which includes psychological manipulation, social engineering techniques, and the use of human error as an advantage. Creating effective defences against phishing attempts requires an understanding of how and why people fall prey to these tactics.

3.1 Psychological Manipulation in Phishing

Phishing attacks typically target emotions such as fear, curiosity, greed, and hurry, making use of fundamental psychological principles. Attackers can create communications that have a higher chance of tricking their targets by being aware of these psychological triggers.

- **Anxiety & Fear:** A common goal of phishing emails is to make the receiver feel scared or uneasy. A phishing email can, for instance, assert that the recipient's bank account has been compromised and that quick action is necessary to stop additional harm. The recipient may click on a malicious link or give critical information without closely reading the message out of fear of financial loss or identity theft.

- **Inquisitiveness & Interestedness:** Attackers often exploit natural human curiosity by crafting messages that intrigue recipients. A subject line like "You Won't Believe What Happened to Your Account!" or "Important Document Enclosed" can pique curiosity, leading the recipient to open the email and engage with its contents. Once the email is opened, the attacker may use malicious links or attachments to compromise the recipient's system.
- **Desire & Chance:** Phishing schemes sometimes take advantage of people's greed by seeming to be offering unbelievable opportunities, including winning the lottery, getting a great job offer, or inheriting a sizable sum of money. The need to take advantage of these opportunities may impair judgment, leaving the recipient more vulnerable to phishing scams.
- **Imprudence:** Attackers might force recipients to make snap decisions without thinking through the validity of the request by instilling a sense of urgency. An email may, for example, state that the recipient's account will be terminated if they do not promptly verify their details. The possibility that the recipient will take the time to confirm the message's legitimacy is decreased when there is a perceived need for quick action.

Attackers frequently create a sense of urgency, pressuring recipients to act quickly without verifying the legitimacy of the message. For example, an email may warn that an account will be deactivated unless credentials are verified immediately. This perceived time pressure reduces the likelihood of critical evaluation, increasing the success rate of the attack.

3.2 Social Engineering Tactics

Phishing is a subset of social engineering, a more general class of assaults that trick people into disclosing private information or taking activities that jeopardize security (Jha et al., 2023). Because social engineering techniques take advantage of people's innate desire to be trusted, helpful, and follow authority, they are essential to the effectiveness of phishing assaults.

- **Pretexting:** Pretexting is the process of fabricating a situation, or pretext, to influence the target to divulge information or take action. An attacker might, for instance, pretend to be an IT support agent and say they require the target's login information to fix a problem. The attacker can win the victim's trust and get the information they need by creating a plausible pretext.
- **Baiting:** Baiting is the practice of enticing victims with the promise of something appealing, such as exclusive content, a discount, or free software. The victim may unintentionally install malware or provide the attacker with personal information if they fall for the bait and click on a link or download a file. Baiting frequently appeals to the needs or wants of the target, making it harder to decline the offer.
- **Impersonation & Authority:** Phishing attacks usually entail the impersonation of trusted or authority persons, such as government authorities, business leaders, or well-known companies. Recipients are more inclined to comply with demands without questioning their legitimacy when an email looks to be from a person in a position of power. For example, a hacker could pose as the CEO of a business and send an email directing a worker to deposit money into a particular account. If the worker thinks the request is sincere, they might comply without checking the information.

- **Reciprocity:** According to the reciprocity principle, people are more inclined to comply with a request if they believe they are owed something. By giving the victim, a tiny favor or some useful information, attackers might utilize this concept to make the victim feel obligated to return the favor. A phishing email can, for instance, provide a free guide or coupon code before requesting personal data or account credentials.
- **Scarcity:** Scarcity strategies create a sense of limited availability or urgency, which feeds into the fear of missing out (FOMO). An email could state that there is a limited time only for an offer or that you need to act quickly to keep your account. The recipient may feel under pressure to respond quickly without thoroughly considering the request's validity as a result of this apparent scarcity.

3.3 The Role of Human Error

A big part of what makes phishing assaults successful is human mistakes. Errors can happen to even the most well-trained and security-conscious people, especially when they're under pressure, anxious, or preoccupied (Prakash, Kumar, Kompella, & Gupta, 2010). To create more successful defenses, it is imperative to comprehend the role that human error plays in phishing.

- **Insufficient Knowledge & Experience:** The fact that many phishing victims are ignorant of the risks or fail to spot the telltale symptoms of a phishing effort makes them easy targets. Employees and individuals might not be able to recognize suspicious emails or distinguish between harmful requests and those that are not without the necessary training. Employers can lower the risk of their staff becoming victims of phishing attempts by regularly investing in cybersecurity education and training programs.
- **Multitasking & Distraction:** Many people multitask or scan through their emails quickly in today's hectic work environment, which raises the possibility that they will miss minute clues of a phishing attempt. A brief attention span slip may cause you to submit sensitive information or click on a malicious site without considering the possible repercussions.
- **Confidence and Overconfidence:** Because trust is a basic human quality, attackers take advantage of it by sending messages that seem to originate from people they know. In addition, some people might let their guard down because they have an excessive amount of confidence in their ability to recognize phishing efforts.
- **Adherence and Submission:** Because the victim feels pressured to agree with a request, particularly if it seems to originate from a senior or authority figure, many phishing assaults are successful. This is especially true in hierarchical businesses, where staff members might be reluctant to challenge senior management's directives, even if something doesn't seem right. Attackers use this compliance as a means of getting past security measures and obtaining private data.
- **Mental Predispositions:** Phishing attacks may also benefit from cognitive biases like anchoring and confirmation bias. Victims of anchoring -the tendency to place a great deal of weight on the first piece of information they come across - may be more likely to believe a phishing email if it uses language that sounds official or familiar.

3.4 Mitigating the Human Element in Phishing

It takes a multifaceted strategy that incorporates technology, education, and organizational culture to address the human element of phishing (Porkodi & Bhuvaneswari, 2014). Although there is no 100% effective defense, the following tactics can lessen the hazards brought on by the human factor:

- **Comprehensive Training Programs:** Regular training and awareness programs are essential for educating employees about the dangers of phishing and how to recognize and respond to potential threats. Training should include simulated phishing exercises to help employees practice identifying and reporting phishing attempts.
- **Fostering a Security-Conscious Culture:** Organizations should strive to create a culture of security where employees feel empowered to report suspicious activity without fear of retribution. Encouraging open communication about cybersecurity threats and rewarding vigilance can help reinforce the importance of security at all levels of the organization.
- **Implementing Multi-Factor Authentication (MFA):** MFA adds a layer of security by requiring users to verify their identity using multiple factors, such as a password and a mobile app or biometric data (Cheng, Naslund, Selander, & Fogelström, 2012). Even if an attacker obtains a user's credentials through phishing, MFA can prevent unauthorized access to sensitive systems.
- **Using Advanced Email Filtering and Security Tools:** Organizations can deploy advanced email filtering solutions that use machine learning and AI to detect signs of phishing and other types of malicious content.

Advanced email filtering solutions powered by AI and ML can pre-emptively detect and block phishing emails. These tools analyze email patterns, identify malicious links, and flag suspicious content, acting as a robust first line of defense in protecting users from phishing attacks.

4. ML AIDED ATTACKS

AI is the imitation of biological processes, particularly human cognitive processes by systems to perform decision-making operations and learn from the previous knowledge gained for future predictions. AI has been extensively used in applications, such as speech and signal processing, smart assistants, automated vehicles, financial prediction, speech recognition, and intelligent home devices etc., These applications are already influencing and improving various aspects of human life, including productivity, safety, health, entertainment, and communication. AI is portrayed as enhancing existing applications, databases, and environments by adding knowledge and reasoning (Shirazi, Bezawada, & Ray, 2018). The motive is to smart and friendlier system, that responds to changes in the external environment. AI is described as not delivering completely autonomous systems but providing incremental improvements to existing ones. Each small breakthrough in AI research enables the expansion of skills to solve new classes and scales of problems, fostering research and innovation across scientific disciplines (Primartha & Tama, 2017). Extensive research on improving telecommunication networks by applying AI-based techniques over the past decades has been carried out. Areas affected include transmission, switching, and network management. Optical communication networks and systems are specifically mentioned as adopting AI-based techniques (Tan, Chiew, & Wong, 2016). The application of AI extends from photonic devices to control and network management in the field of optical networking.

AI is supported by emerging transmission technologies that are the most sought-after in recent times which include space division multiplexing, multimode/multicore fibers, advanced modulation formats, and constellation shaping. Despite advances in monitoring and transmission technologies, the optical arena lacks significant developments in AI techniques for attack and intrusion detection. With the increasing Internet proliferation, businesses and institutions provide essential services over the Internet, leading to higher risks and potential costs associated with data breaches (Jha et al., 2023). The optical network layer is susceptible to disruption and eavesdropping attacks. Disruption attacks exploit the physical characteristics of optical transmission to degrade operation or block service requests. Eavesdropping attacks aim to gain unauthorized access to transmitted data over the optical network (Hussain, Cheng, Xu, & Afzal, 2023). Statistical approaches using optical measurements have been proposed for detecting and localizing attacks in optical networks. AI techniques could enhance the identification and localization of optical attacks, especially in large-scale networks. Successful identification of attacks leads to the application of mitigation techniques. Mitigation involves all-optical encryption or rerouting traffic away from attack locations (Li, Manickam, Laghari, & Chong, 2023). Statistical approaches for attack detection have computational complexity challenges in large-scale networks. AI techniques can be applied to address these challenges, improving the efficiency of identifying and localizing optical attacks.

- **Automated Phishing Content Generation:** ML algorithms can generate highly convincing phishing emails and messages by analyzing large datasets of legitimate communication (Hasan, Islam, Zarif, & Hashem, 2019). These algorithms learn patterns and language styles from real emails, allowing attackers to create more believable and targeted phishing content. Increased success rates for phishing attacks due to more personalized and convincing messages.
- **Sophisticated Spear Phishing:** ML can analyze social media profiles, public records, and other sources to gather detailed information about specific individuals (Alsouda, Pllana, & Kurti, 2019). This information is used to craft highly targeted spear phishing attacks that are more likely to deceive the victim. Higher likelihood of compromising sensitive information or systems due to highly personalized attacks.
- **Statistical approaches:** Utilizing optical measurements has been proposed for detecting and localizing such attacks. However, these methods face computational complexity challenges in large-scale networks. AI techniques offer promising solutions to enhance attack identification and localization, particularly in vast and complex optical infrastructures. Effective identification of attacks can facilitate the implementation of mitigation strategies, such as all-optical encryption or rerouting traffic to circumvent affected areas (Li, Manickam, Laghari, & Chong, 2023). The integration of AI in optical communication is poised to significantly improve the security and efficiency of large-scale networks, addressing challenges that traditional methods struggle to overcome. Continued research and development in this area are essential to fully realize the potential of AI-driven solutions in telecommunications.

4.1 Multi-Vector Attacks

Multi-vector attacks are complex cyberattacks that utilize multiple methods or vectors simultaneously to penetrate an organization's defenses (Gupta et al., 2021). The key characteristic of multi-vector attacks is their versatility and adaptability (Basit et al., 2021). The use of machine learning in these attacks adds another layer of complexity, enabling attackers to automate processes, learn from previous attempts, and optimize their strategies in real-time. The key characteristics are explained below:

- **Automated Attack Coordination:** ML can be used to coordinate multi-vector attacks by predicting and optimizing the sequence of attack vectors to maximize impact. For instance, ML algorithms might determine the best combination of phishing, malware, and exploit attacks to use based on the target's vulnerabilities. More efficient and effective multi-vector attacks that can cause greater damage and evade detection.
- **Enhanced Malware Capabilities:** Malware equipped with ML algorithms can learn and adapt based on its environment. This allows the malware to avoid detection by changing its behavior or communication patterns based on real-time analysis of network traffic and security measures. Increased persistence and stealth of malware, making it harder for traditional defenses to detect and mitigate.
- **Dynamic Exploit Generation:** ML can assist in generating and testing new exploits for vulnerabilities. By analyzing existing exploits and vulnerabilities, ML algorithms can identify potential weaknesses and generate novel attack vectors. Faster discovery and exploitation of new vulnerabilities lead to increased risk and potential damage.

One of the challenges of defending against multi-vector attacks is their ability to spread across various channels, including email, web, and network traffic. This makes it difficult for traditional security systems to detect and respond to all aspects of the attack simultaneously. Furthermore, the incorporation of ML into these attacks adds a layer of complexity, allowing attackers to automate processes, learn from previous attempts, and optimize their strategies in real-time. Below are some key characteristics of multi-vector attacks enhanced by ML.

4.2 Cyber Threats

In the realm of cybersecurity, ML has traditionally been used to detect anomalies, predict potential breaches, and automate responses to security incidents (Alkhalil, Hewage, Nawaf, & Khan, 2021). However, these same capabilities are being exploited by cybercriminals to create more advanced and resilient attack strategies (Monostori et al., 2016). ML-aided cyber threats involve the use of machine learning algorithms to automate, optimize, and scale cyberattacks. The strategies are explained below:

- **Advanced Threat Detection Evasion:** Attackers can use ML to analyze and evade security detection systems. For example, ML algorithms can help malware modify its code or behavior to avoid detection by antivirus software and intrusion detection systems (Monostori et al., 2016). Reduced effectiveness of traditional security measures, leading to a higher likelihood of successful attacks.
- **Deepfake Technology:** ML is used to create deepfakes—highly realistic but fake audio and video content. Deepfakes can be used in social engineering attacks, identity theft, and disinformation

campaigns, making them a powerful tool for cybercriminals. Increased risk of misinformation, fraud, and privacy violations, as well as potential damage to reputations and trust.

4.3 Défense Strategies Against ML-Aided Attacks

The growing prevalence of machine learning (ML) in cyberattacks presents a significant challenge to traditional cybersecurity measures (Oest et al., 2020). As ML-powered attacks become more sophisticated, automated, and adaptable, organizations need to develop and implement robust defense strategies to protect their networks, systems, and data. The following strategies offer a comprehensive approach to defending against ML-aided attacks:

- **AI-Based Threat Detection:** Implement AI and ML-based security solutions that can detect and respond to sophisticated attacks (Acharya & Vadrevu, 2021). These systems use advanced algorithms to identify patterns and anomalies indicative of ML-aided attacks. Enhanced ability to detect and mitigate attacks that use ML for evasion and adaptation.
- **Continuous Monitoring and Analysis:** Employ continuous monitoring and behavioral analysis to detect unusual activities or deviations from normal patterns. ML algorithms can assist in identifying these anomalies and potential threats in real time. Improved detection of adaptive and evolving attacks.
- **User Education and Training:** Regularly train users to recognize and respond to phishing and social engineering attempts. Awareness programs should include information on the potential for sophisticated, ML-driven attacks. Reduces the effectiveness of phishing and social engineering attacks, even those enhanced by ML.
- **Regular Security Updates and Patching:** Keep all systems and software up-to-date with the latest patches and security updates. This helps protect against exploits and vulnerabilities that could be targeted by ML-assisted attacks. Reduces the attack surface and prevents exploitation of known vulnerabilities.
- **Advanced Encryption and Authentication:** Use strong encryption methods and multi-factor authentication to protect sensitive data and systems. ML can be used to strengthen these measures and ensure they remain effective against evolving threats. Enhances security by making it more difficult for attackers to access and exploit data.

5. DEEPFAKE TECHNOLOGY – A CASE STUDY

The Deepfake technology represents a significant and emerging threat within the realm of active cyberattacks (Dash & Sharma, 2023). Leveraging advanced artificial intelligence (AI) and machine learning (ML) techniques, deepfakes involve the creation of highly realistic but fake audio, video, or images that can convincingly mimic real people.

The Deepfake technology represents a growing challenge in the cybersecurity landscape, with the potential to be used in various forms of active attacks (Schmitt & Flechais, 2024). As the technology becomes more sophisticated, the importance of developing robust defenses against deepfake-based threats will only increase.

Deepfake creation primarily relies on a type of machine learning algorithm known as generative adversarial networks (GANs). GANs consist of two neural networks—a generator and a discriminator—that work together to produce realistic fakes.

- **Generator:** The generator creates fake content, such as an image or video, by learning from a large dataset of real images or videos. It aims to produce content that is indistinguishable from real data.
- **Discriminator:** The discriminator's role is to evaluate the content generated by the generator and determine whether it is real or fake. It continuously learns to distinguish between the authentic data and the fakes.

As deepfake technology becomes more sophisticated, it presents new challenges for organizations and individuals alike. Its potential use in fraud, identity theft, social engineering, and disinformation campaigns is alarming. This evolving threat necessitates the development of robust defenses to mitigate the dangers posed by deepfakes (Schmitt & Flechais, 2024).

5.1 Deepfake Technology in Cyberattacks

Deepfake technology can be employed in several types of cyberattacks, each leveraging the realistic nature of deepfake content to deceive and manipulate targets:

5.1.1 Social Engineering and Phishing

Deepfakes can be used to create convincing video or audio messages that appear to be from trusted individuals, such as company executives, colleagues, or family members. These deepfakes can be used in spear-phishing campaigns, where attackers trick individuals into divulging sensitive information, transferring funds, or clicking on malicious links. For instance, a deepfake video of a CEO could instruct an employee to make an unauthorized financial transaction (Schmitt & Flechais, 2024). The realistic nature of deepfakes makes it extremely difficult for individuals to detect fraud, leading to successful phishing attacks, financial losses, and data breaches.

5.1.2 Impersonation and Identity Theft

Deepfakes can be used to impersonate individuals during video calls or in video authentication processes. Attackers can create deepfake videos of individuals to gain unauthorized access to secure systems, social media accounts, or online banking platforms (de Rancourt-Raymond & Smaili, 2023). By mimicking the facial features and voice of the victim, attackers can bypass biometric security measures. Impersonation using deepfakes can lead to identity theft, unauthorized access to sensitive information, and significant financial and reputational damage.

5.1.3 Disinformation and Misinformation

Deepfakes can be used to create and spread false information, often in the form of fabricated news reports, speeches, or public statements by influential figures. This can be particularly damaging in political contexts, where deepfake videos might be used to manipulate public opinion, influence elections, or incite social unrest. The use of deepfakes in disinformation campaigns can lead to widespread confusion, erosion of trust in media and institutions, and significant social and economic consequences.

5.1.4 Blackmail and Extortion

Attackers can create deepfake videos or images depicting individuals in compromising situations and use them to blackmail or extort the victims. For example, a deepfake video might be created to show an executive engaging in unethical behavior, which the attacker then threatens to release unless a ransom is paid (da Silva, Feitosa, & Garcia, 2020). Victims of deepfake-based blackmail may suffer personal and professional damage, and the mere existence of such deepfakes can cause psychological distress and harm to reputations.

5.1.5 Corporate Espionage

Deepfake technology can be employed in corporate espionage, where attackers create fake video or audio messages to deceive employees, executives, or business partners (Jemal, Cheikhrouhou, Hamam, & Mahfoudhi, 2020). For example, a deepfake video could be used to impersonate a business partner during a virtual meeting, allowing the attacker to extract sensitive information or manipulate negotiations (Jiang, Wang, Wang, & Wu, 2020). The use of deepfakes in corporate espionage can lead to the loss of trade secrets, confidential information, and competitive advantages, causing significant financial and operational harm to companies.

5.2 Mitigating Deepfake Threats

Defending against deepfake-based attacks requires a multi-faceted approach:

- **Deepfake Detection Technologies:** Organizations are increasingly investing in AI-based tools that can detect deepfakes by analysing inconsistencies in video or audio content, such as unnatural movements, irregular lighting, or anomalies in speech patterns.
- **Awareness and Training:** Educating employees and the public about the potential dangers of deepfakes and how to recognize them is crucial. Regular training on identifying suspicious communications and verifying the authenticity of video and audio content can help reduce the risk of falling victim to deepfake attacks.
- **Authentication Mechanisms:** Implementing strong authentication methods, such as multi-factor authentication (MFA) and digital signatures, can help verify the identity of individuals in communications and prevent deepfake impersonation.
- **Legal and Regulatory Measures:** Governments and organizations are beginning to establish legal frameworks and regulations to address the misuse of deepfake technology, including penalties for creating and distributing malicious deepfakes.

- **Collaboration and Research:** Ongoing collaboration between the cybersecurity industry, academia, and law enforcement is essential to stay ahead of deepfake threats. Continued research into deepfake detection and mitigation strategies will play a critical role in countering this evolving threat.

5.4 Privacy

The Deepfake technology can be used to create content featuring an individual's likeness without their consent. This can involve using publicly available images, videos, or audio recordings to generate fake content that appears authentic. Deepfakes can be used to create fabricated content depicting individuals in compromising or embarrassing situations, even if they have never been involved in such activities. This invasion of personal privacy can occur without the victim's knowledge or consent, and the resulting content can be shared widely on social media, leading to significant personal and emotional harm. The invasion of privacy through deepfakes can result in public humiliation, psychological distress, and the loss of personal dignity. Overall, the unauthorized creation and dissemination of deepfakes have the potential to cause long-term harm to an individual's personal and professional life. This highlights the need for stronger regulations and protective measures to prevent the misuse of deepfake technology and safeguard individuals' rights to their own likeness and privacy.

6. AUTOMATED PHISHING KITS – A CASE STUDY

Automated phishing kits are sophisticated tools designed to streamline and scale phishing attacks by automating various aspects of the phishing process (Almomani et al., 2022). These kits make it easier for attackers to create and deploy phishing campaigns, often with minimal technical expertise. Here's an overview of automated phishing kits, including how they work, their impact, and methods to defend against them.

- **Pre-Built Phishing Templates:** Automated phishing kits come with pre-built templates that mimic legitimate websites, such as banking sites, email services, or social media platforms. These templates are designed to trick victims into entering sensitive information, such as usernames, passwords, or financial details. The attacker selects a template that aligns with their target and customizes it with specific branding or content.
- **Automated Campaign Management:** These kits include features for managing phishing campaigns, such as automatically generating phishing emails, managing mailing lists, and scheduling email dispatches. Some kits also include tools for tracking the success of phishing campaigns, such as the number of emails opened or links clicked. Automation helps attackers efficiently run large-scale phishing campaigns without needing to manually handle each component.
- **Credential Harvesting:** Automated phishing kits often include scripts or tools to collect and store stolen credentials from victims. When a victim enters their information into a fake login page, the data is captured and sent to the attacker's server or email address. This allows attackers to gather a large volume of stolen credentials quickly and easily.
- **Infrastructure and Hosting:** Some phishing kits provide infrastructure support, such as domain registration services and hosting solutions, making it easier for attackers to set up and maintain

their phishing sites. They may also include features to help evade detection, such as domain generation algorithms (DGAs) or anti-detection mechanisms. This streamlines the process of deploying and maintaining phishing sites, allowing attackers to focus on targeting victims.

- **Customization and Targeting:** Automated phishing kits often allow for the customization of phishing messages and landing pages to target specific individuals or organizations. Attackers can tailor content to reflect current events or exploit recent trends to increase the likelihood of success. Targeted phishing efforts improve the chances of deceiving victims by making the phishing attempt appear more legitimate and relevant.
- **Increased Attack Volume:** The automation of phishing attacks enables attackers to launch a high volume of phishing campaigns with minimal effort. This increased scale makes it more difficult for individuals and organizations to defend against phishing attempts effectively. Higher attack volumes can lead to a greater number of compromised accounts and increased overall risk.
- **Lower Entry Barriers for Attackers:** Automated phishing kits reduce the technical skills required to conduct a phishing attack. This lowers the barrier to entry for less experienced attackers, increasing the number of potential threats. Victims are more likely to fall for well-crafted phishing schemes, resulting in greater data loss and financial damage. Automated phishing kits often incorporate techniques to evade detection, such as using obfuscated code or employing anti-detection measures. This makes it challenging for security systems to identify and block phishing attempts. Enhanced evasion techniques increase the likelihood that phishing attempts will bypass traditional security measures and reach potential victims.

6.1 Defending Against Automated Phishing Kits

Automated phishing kits have become a prevalent and dangerous tool in the arsenal of cybercriminals. These kits, which are easily accessible on the dark web, allow attackers to automate the process of creating, deploying, and managing phishing campaigns with minimal effort (Guo et al., 2022). By lowering the barrier to entry, automated phishing kits enable even less technically skilled attackers to launch sophisticated phishing attacks at scale (Yang, Liu, Wang, Zhai, & Dai, 2022). As these threats continue to grow, organizations must adopt a comprehensive strategy to defend against automated phishing kits, focusing on technological, human, and procedural elements.

- **Advanced Email Filtering:** Implementing advanced email filtering solutions that use machine learning and behavioral analysis can help detect and block phishing emails before they reach users' inboxes. These filters analyze email content, links, and attachments for signs of phishing.
- **User Education and Awareness:** Regular training and awareness programs can help users recognize phishing attempts and understand the importance of verifying the authenticity of emails and websites. Educating users about the dangers of phishing and how to respond to suspicious messages is crucial.
- **Multi-Factor Authentication (MFA):** Implementing MFA adds an extra layer of security to user accounts by requiring additional verification beyond just a password. This helps protect accounts even if credentials are compromised. Makes it more difficult for attackers to gain unauthorized access using stolen credentials.

Automated phishing kits have emerged as a significant and dangerous tool for cybercriminals. These kits simplify the process of creating, launching, and managing phishing attacks, making it possible for even less technically skilled attackers to carry out sophisticated and large-scale campaigns. Available on the dark web, these kits include pre-built phishing templates, automated systems for collecting stolen data, and even tools for evading detection by security systems.

7. TECHNOLOGICAL ADVANCEMENTS IN DÉFENSE – A CASE STUDY

As phishing attacks have grown in sophistication, the cybersecurity community has responded with an array of advanced technological solutions designed to detect, prevent, and mitigate these threats (Acharya & Vadrevu, 2021). These advancements are crucial in the ongoing battle against cybercriminals who continually evolve their tactics to bypass traditional security measures (Thakur, Shan, & Pathan, 2018). Below is an exploration of key technological advancements that have significantly strengthened the defence against phishing attacks.

7.1 Advanced Email Filtering and Anti-Phishing Solutions

Modern email security solutions use a combination of techniques to identify and block phishing attempts before they reach the user's inbox. These techniques include:

- **Content Analysis:** Advanced filters scan emails for phishing-related content, such as suspicious URLs, attachments, and language patterns commonly used in phishing schemes. (Alkhalil et al., 2021) They also evaluate the context of the message to detect subtle signs of phishing, even if the email appears to be from a legitimate source.
- **Real-Time Link Scanning:** Many advanced email filters include real-time scanning of URLs embedded in emails. These tools can detect and block links leading to phishing sites before the user clicks on them, preventing credential theft or malware installation.
- **Domain-Based Message Authentication, Reporting, and Conformance (DMARC):** DMARC is a protocol that helps email recipients determine if an email is legitimately from the sender it claims to be. By leveraging DMARC, along with SPF (Sender Policy Framework) and DKIM (DomainKeys Identified Mail), organizations can protect their domains from being spoofed in phishing attacks.

7.2 Multi-Factor Authentication (MFA)

Multi-factor authentication (MFA) adds an essential layer of security by requiring users to verify their identity through multiple methods, such as a password and a secondary code sent to a mobile device (Basit et al., 2021). Even if attackers manage to steal a user's credentials through a phishing attempt, MFA can prevent unauthorized access by requiring additional verification.

- **Biometric Authentication:** In addition to traditional MFA methods like SMS codes, biometric authentication (using fingerprints, facial recognition, or voice recognition) is becoming increasingly popular. This method adds a robust layer of security that is difficult for attackers to bypass.

- **Adaptive MFA:** Some systems now use adaptive MFA, which adjusts the level of authentication required based on the risk level of the user's activity. For example, a login from an unfamiliar location or device might trigger a higher level of authentication, whereas a login from a trusted device may not.

7.3 Endpoint Detection and Response (EDR)

Endpoint detection and response (EDR) tools play a critical role in detecting and responding to phishing attacks that have bypassed initial defences (Nan, Shawky, Ahmed, & Ellaithy, 2021). EDR solutions monitor and analyze activity on endpoints, such as computers and mobile devices, to detect suspicious behaviour indicative of a phishing attack.

- **Behavioural Analytics:** EDR solutions use behavioural analytics to identify unusual activities on endpoints that could signal a successful phishing attack, such as unauthorized access attempts, unusual file downloads, or unexpected network communications.
- **Automated Response:** Upon detecting a potential phishing incident, EDR tools can automatically isolate the affected endpoint, terminate suspicious processes, and alert security teams for further investigation. This rapid response helps contain the threat and prevent it from spreading to other parts of the network.

7.4 Threat Intelligence and Phishing Awareness Platforms

Threat intelligence platforms gather and analyze data on the latest phishing tactics, techniques, and procedures (TTPs) used by cybercriminals (Basit et al., 2021). This information is shared across the cybersecurity community to enhance collective defence efforts (Alkhalil et al., 2021).

- **Real-Time Threat Intelligence Feeds:** These feeds provide organizations with up-to-date information on new phishing campaigns, malicious domains, and IP addresses. Integrating these feeds with security systems enables organizations to proactively block known threats and stay ahead of emerging phishing techniques.
- **Phishing Awareness Training Platforms:** These platforms offer tools for educating employees about phishing and conducting simulated phishing exercises. By regularly testing employees with realistic phishing scenarios, organizations can gauge their readiness and improve their ability to recognize and report phishing attempts.

7.5 Artificial Intelligence in Threat Hunting

AI-powered threat hunting is an emerging field in cybersecurity that leverages AI to proactively search for signs of phishing and other threats within an organization's network.

- **Automated Threat Hunting:** AI algorithms can analyze network traffic, user behavior, and system logs to identify patterns that may indicate a phishing attack. Unlike traditional methods, which often rely on predefined rules, AI-powered threat hunting can uncover hidden threats by detecting subtle anomalies and correlating disparate data points.

- **Predictive Analytics:** AI-driven predictive analytics can anticipate potential phishing attacks by analyzing threat actor behavior and historical attack data. This capability allows organizations to fortify their defenses against anticipated threats before they occur.

7.6 Cloud-Based Security Solutions

With the rise of cloud computing, many organizations have adopted cloud-based security solutions that offer scalability, flexibility, and advanced protection against phishing.

- **Cloud Email Security:** Cloud-based email security solutions provide advanced filtering and threat detection capabilities that are continuously updated with the latest threat intelligence. These solutions often include sandboxing, where suspicious emails are executed in a controlled environment to observe their behavior before being delivered to the user.
- **Identity and Access Management (IAM):** Cloud-based IAM solutions provide centralized control over user identities and access permissions, helping to prevent unauthorized access resulting from phishing. These systems often include MFA, single sign-on (SSO), and other security measures to protect cloud resources from phishing attacks.

7.7 Blockchain and Decentralized Security

Blockchain technology is being explored as a potential solution to enhance email security and reduce the risk of phishing.

- **Blockchain-Based Email Authentication:** Blockchain can be used to create a decentralized, immutable record of email sender identities, making it difficult for attackers to spoof legitimate email addresses. By verifying email authenticity through blockchain, organizations can better protect against phishing attacks.
- **Decentralized Security Protocols:** Blockchain also enables the development of decentralized security protocols that reduce reliance on centralized systems, which can be targets for phishing. These protocols can enhance the resilience of cybersecurity measures against phishing and other cyber threats.

8. CASE STUDY: A LARGE FINANCIAL INSTITUTION'S RESPONSE TO PHISHING

A large financial institution, facing an increasing number of phishing attacks, implemented a comprehensive cybersecurity strategy to protect its assets and customers. The institution's approach combined advanced technology with employee training and rigorous security protocols, resulting in a significant reduction in successful phishing attempts.

- **Advanced Email Filtering:** The financial institution deployed an advanced email filtering system powered by machine learning and AI. This system was capable of analyzing email content, sender behavior, and embedded URLs to detect phishing attempts. By continuously learning from new threats, the filter improved its accuracy over time, reducing the number of phishing emails that reached employees.

- **Real-Time Threat Intelligence:** The institution integrated real-time threat intelligence feeds into its security systems. These feeds provided up-to-date information on emerging phishing campaigns and malicious domains, allowing the organization to proactively block known threats. The combination of advanced filtering and real-time intelligence significantly enhanced the institution's ability to detect and prevent phishing attacks.
- **Multi-Factor Authentication (MFA):** To protect against credential theft from successful phishing attempts, the financial institution implemented MFA across all critical systems. This additional layer of security ensured that even if an employee's credentials were compromised, attackers would be unable to access sensitive information without passing a second authentication factor.
- **Security Awareness Training:** Recognizing the importance of the human element in cybersecurity, the institution invested in ongoing security awareness training for its employees. This training included regular phishing simulations, which helped employees recognize and report phishing attempts. By fostering a culture of vigilance, the institution reduced the likelihood of successful attacks.
- **Incident Response and EDR:** The financial institution also deployed an endpoint detection and response (EDR) system to monitor and respond to potential phishing-related incidents. The EDR system could detect unusual behavior on employee devices, such as unauthorized access attempts or suspicious file downloads, and automatically isolate the affected endpoint to prevent the spread of malware.
- **Blockchain-Based Email Authentication:** To combat email spoofing, the institution explored the use of blockchain technology for email authentication. By creating a decentralized and immutable record of legitimate email sender identities, the institution could better verify the authenticity of incoming emails and reduce the risk of phishing.

9. RESULTS AND IMPACT

The financial institution's multi-faceted approach to combating phishing yielded impressive results. The advanced email filtering system blocked over 95% of phishing emails before they reached employees, while the remaining attempts were effectively mitigated through MFA and employee vigilance. In addition to improving its security, the financial institution shared its success story with industry peers, contributing to broader efforts to combat phishing across the financial sector (Sharma, Dash, & Ansari, 2022). The financial institution's experience highlights several key lessons for organizations looking to defend against phishing attacks:

- **Layered Defense is Essential:** No single security measure can fully protect against phishing. A multi-layered approach that combines advanced technology, employee training, and robust incident response is crucial for effective defense.
- **Continuous Learning and Adaptation:** Phishing tactics are constantly evolving, and so must an organization's defenses. By leveraging AI, machine learning, and real-time threat intelligence, organizations can stay ahead of emerging threats.

- **Employee Education is Critical:** Even with the best technology in place, the human element remains a critical factor in cybersecurity. Regular training and simulations help employees recognize phishing attempts and respond appropriately, reducing the risk of successful attacks.
- **Collaboration and Information Sharing:** Cybersecurity is a collective effort. Organizations should collaborate with industry peers and share threat intelligence to enhance the overall security landscape and reduce the effectiveness of phishing campaigns.
- **Proactive Defense**: A multi-layered security strategy that combines technology, human awareness, and procedural safeguards is essential in combating phishing attacks.
- **Collaboration**: Sharing threat intelligence and collaborating with industry peers can strengthen the overall cybersecurity landscape.
- **Employee Engagement**: Training employees to recognize phishing attempts and report them promptly is one of the most effective ways to prevent successful attacks.
- **Adaptation**: Organizations must regularly update their defense mechanisms to keep up with evolving phishing tactics.

10. CONCLUSION

Certainly, the landscape of phishing attacks has evolved significantly over recent years, with attackers employing increasingly sophisticated techniques to deceive victims. Modern phishing schemes often leverage social engineering and advanced technology to craft convincing and targeted messages. This escalation in complexity underscores the need for robust and dynamic cyber defense strategies. As cyber threats become more intricate, traditional security measures are frequently inadequate on their own. Therefore, an adaptive and multi-layered approach to cybersecurity is essential.

One of the most concerning developments in phishing is the use of deepfake technology. Deepfakes have added a new layer of complexity to social engineering attacks, enabling the creation of realistic but entirely fabricated audio, video, and images. This technology has been used to impersonate CEOs, executives, and other trusted figures, making phishing attacks more believable and, consequently, more dangerous. As deepfake technology becomes more accessible and easier to use, its use in phishing will likely become more widespread, posing an even greater threat to individuals and organizations alike.

The emergence of deepfakes represents a concerning development in phishing, making social engineering attacks more realistic and effective. Deepfakes allow attackers to impersonate trusted figures, such as company leaders, and craft messages that are difficult to distinguish from genuine communications. As this technology becomes more accessible, organizations need to prepare for this new threat by implementing detection tools that can identify manipulated audio, video, and images. Additionally, fostering a culture of scepticism around unexpected communications—particularly those from high-ranking officials—can help mitigate the risk of deepfake-based attacks.

Modern email filtering systems powered by AI and ML offer robust defenses against phishing. These tools analyze more than just the subject line, scanning the entire email, its metadata, and links for potential threats. Machine learning algorithms can spot suspicious patterns and detect phishing indicators that are not immediately apparent to human users. In addition to email filtering, integrating these tools with other security platforms, such as firewalls and endpoint protection systems, can create a unified, real-time defense against emerging phishing tactics.

While technology plays a crucial role, human error remains one of the most significant vulnerabilities in cybersecurity. Phishing attackers exploit psychological triggers like urgency, fear, and authority to manipulate individuals into revealing sensitive information. As such, organizations must focus on training employees to recognize these tactics and respond appropriately. Regular phishing simulations, ongoing training, and clear reporting channels for suspicious activity can equip employees to act quickly and avoid falling victim to attacks. Employees must understand that they are the first line of defense in identifying phishing attempts.

The future of cybersecurity will heavily rely on collaboration between industry peers, government agencies, and tech providers. Sharing threat intelligence, such as emerging phishing tactics and indicators of compromise (IOCs), helps organizations respond faster and more effectively to cyber threats. By pooling resources and knowledge, organizations can create a more resilient and unified defense strategy that adapts to evolving cybercrime tactics. Collaborative efforts in research and development of new security technologies will also drive innovation in detecting and preventing phishing.

Ensuring that software and systems are up-to-date is fundamental to preventing phishing-related vulnerabilities from being exploited. Cybercriminals frequently target outdated software that has known vulnerabilities. Timely patch management, along with routine security audits, can help protect against attacks that aim to exploit weaknesses in systems or applications. By maintaining a robust patch management process, organizations can reduce the attack surface and minimize the chances of successful phishing campaigns.

Adopting a zero-trust security model, where verification is required for every user and device accessing a system—regardless of their location—can significantly enhance security. This approach reduces the risk of unauthorized access and helps mitigate the damage that can be done by phishing attacks that successfully acquire login credentials. Zero-trust architecture ensures that even if an attacker compromises one element of the system, they are unable to gain unfettered access to the entire network.

REFERENCES

Acharya, B., & Vadrevu, P. (2021). *{PhishPrint}: Evading phishing detection crawlers by prior profiling.* Paper presented at the 30th USENIX Security Symposium (USENIX Security 21).

Aldakheel, E. A., Zakariah, M., Gashgari, G. A., Almarshad, F. A., & Alzahrani, A. I. (2023). A Deep learning-based innovative technique for phishing detection in modern security with uniform resource locators. *Sensors (Basel)*, 23(9), 4403. DOI: 10.3390/s23094403 PMID: 37177607

Alkhalil, Z., Hewage, C., Nawaf, L., & Khan, I. (2021). Phishing attacks: A recent comprehensive study and a new anatomy. *Frontiers of Computer Science*, 3, 563060. DOI: 10.3389/fcomp.2021.563060

Almomani, A., Alauthman, M., Shatnawi, M. T., Alweshah, M., Alrosan, A., Alomoush, W., Gupta, B. B., Gupta, B. B., & Gupta, B. B. (2022). Phishing website detection with semantic features based on machine learning classifiers: A comparative study. [IJSWIS]. *International Journal on Semantic Web and Information Systems*, 18(1), 1–24. DOI: 10.4018/IJSWIS.297032

Alsouda, Y., Pllana, S., & Kurti, A. (2019). *Iot-based urban noise identification using machine learning: performance of SVM, KNN, bagging, and random forest.* Paper presented at the Proceedings of the international conference on omni-layer intelligent systems. DOI: 10.1145/3312614.3312631

Asiri, S., Xiao, Y., Alzahrani, S., Li, S., & Li, T. (2023). A survey of intelligent detection designs of HTML URL phishing attacks. *IEEE Access : Practical Innovations, Open Solutions*, 11, 6421–6443. DOI: 10.1109/ACCESS.2023.3237798

Basit, A., Zafar, M., Liu, X., Javed, A. R., Jalil, Z., & Kifayat, K. (2021). A comprehensive survey of AI-enabled phishing attacks detection techniques. *Telecommunication Systems*, 76(1), 139–154. DOI: 10.1007/s11235-020-00733-2 PMID: 33110340

Cheng, Y., Naslund, M., Selander, G., & Fogelström, E. (2012). *Privacy in machine-to-machine communications a state-of-the-art survey.* Paper presented at the 2012 IEEE International Conference on Communication Systems (ICCS). DOI: 10.1109/ICCS.2012.6406112

da Silva, C. M. R., Feitosa, E. L., & Garcia, V. C. (2020). Heuristic-based strategy for Phishing prediction: A survey of URL-based approach. *Computers & Security*, 88, 101613. DOI: 10.1016/j.cose.2019.101613

Dash, B., & Sharma, P. (2023). Are ChatGPT and deepfake algorithms endangering the cybersecurity industry? A review. *International Journal of Engineering and Applied Sciences*, 10(1), 21–39.

de Rancourt-Raymond, A., & Smaili, N. (2023). The unethical use of deepfakes. *Journal of Financial Crime*, 30(4), 1066–1077. DOI: 10.1108/JFC-04-2022-0090

Duy, P. T., Minh, V. Q., Dang, B. T. H., Son, N. D. H., Quyen, N. H., & Pham, V.-H. (2024). A study on adversarial sample resistance and defense mechanism for multimodal learning-based phishing website detection. *IEEE Access : Practical Innovations, Open Solutions*, 12, 137805–137824. DOI: 10.1109/ACCESS.2024.3436812

Guo, Z., Cho, J.-H., Chen, R., Sengupta, S., Hong, M., & Mitra, T. (2022). *Safer: Social capital-based friend recommendation to defend against phishing attacks.* Paper presented at the Proceedings of the International AAAI Conference on Web and Social Media. DOI: 10.1609/icwsm.v16i1.19288

Gupta, B. B., Yadav, K., Razzak, I., Psannis, K., Castiglione, A., & Chang, X. (2021). A novel approach for phishing URLs detection using lexical based machine learning in a real-time environment. *Computer Communications*, 175, 47–57. DOI: 10.1016/j.comcom.2021.04.023

Hasan, M., Islam, M. M., Zarif, M. I. I., & Hashem, M. (2019). Attack and anomaly detection in IoT sensors in IoT sites using machine learning approaches. *Internet of Things : Engineering Cyber Physical Human Systems*, 7, 100059. DOI: 10.1016/j.iot.2019.100059

Hussain, M., Cheng, C., Xu, R., & Afzal, M. (2023). CNN-Fusion: An effective and lightweight phishing detection method based on multi-variant ConvNet. *Information Sciences*, 631, 328–345. DOI: 10.1016/j.ins.2023.02.039

Jemal, I., Cheikhrouhou, O., Hamam, H., & Mahfoudhi, A. (2020). Sql injection attack detection and prevention techniques using machine learning. *International Journal of Applied Engineering Research: IJAER*, 15(6), 569–580.

Jha, A. K., Muthalagu, R., & Pawar, P. M. (2023). Intelligent phishing website detection using machine learning. *Multimedia Tools and Applications*, 82(19), 29431–29456. DOI: 10.1007/s11042-023-14731-4

Jiang, K., Wang, W., Wang, A., & Wu, H. (2020). Network intrusion detection combined hybrid sampling with deep hierarchical network. *IEEE Access : Practical Innovations, Open Solutions*, 8, 32464–32476. DOI: 10.1109/ACCESS.2020.2973730

Li, W., Manickam, S., Laghari, S. U. A., & Chong, Y.-W. (2023). Uncovering the Cloak: A Systematic Review of Techniques Used to Conceal Phishing Websites. *IEEE Access : Practical Innovations, Open Solutions*, 11, 71925–71939. DOI: 10.1109/ACCESS.2023.3293063

Monostori, L., Kádár, B., Bauernhansl, T., Kondoh, S., Kumara, S., Reinhart, G., Sauer, O., Schuh, G., Sihn, W., & Ueda, K. (2016). Cyber-physical systems in manufacturing. *CIRP Annals*, 65(2), 621–641. DOI: 10.1016/j.cirp.2016.06.005

Nan, A. A., Shawky, M. M., Ahmed, A. M., & Ellaithy, D. M. (2021). *Design and Implementation of High-Performance Computing Unit for Internet of Things (IoT) Applications.* Paper presented at the 2021 International Conference on Microelectronics (ICM). DOI: 10.1109/ICM52667.2021.9664933

Oest, A., Safaei, Y., Zhang, P., Wardman, B., Tyers, K., Shoshitaishvili, Y., & Doupé, A. (2020). *{PhishTime}: Continuous longitudinal measurement of the effectiveness of anti-phishing blacklists.* Paper presented at the 29th USENIX Security Symposium (USENIX Security 20).

Porkodi, R., & Bhuvaneswari, V. (2014). *The internet of things (IOT) applications and communication enabling technology standards: An overview.* Paper presented at the 2014 International conference on intelligent computing applications. DOI: 10.1109/ICICA.2014.73

Prakash, P., Kumar, M., Kompella, R. R., & Gupta, M. (2010). *Phishnet: predictive blacklisting to detect phishing attacks.* Paper presented at the 2010 Proceedings IEEE INFOCOM. DOI: 10.1109/INFCOM.2010.5462216

Primartha, R., & Tama, B. A. (2017). *Anomaly detection using random forest: A performance revisited.* Paper presented at the 2017 International conference on data and software engineering (ICoDSE). DOI: 10.1109/ICODSE.2017.8285847

Schmitt, M., & Flechais, I. (2024). Digital Deception: Generative artificial intelligence in social engineering and phishing. *Artificial Intelligence Review*, 57(12), 1–23. DOI: 10.1007/s10462-024-10973-2

Sharma, P., Dash, B., & Ansari, M. F. (2022). Anti-phishing techniques–a review of Cyber Defense Mechanisms. *International Journal of Advanced Research in Computer and Communication Engineering*, 3297(7), 2007. DOI: 10.17148/IJARCCE.2022.11728

Shirazi, H., Bezawada, B., & Ray, I. (2018). *"Kn0w Thy Doma1n Name" Unbiased Phishing Detection Using Domain Name Based Features.* Paper presented at the Proceedings of the 23nd ACM on symposium on access control models and technologies. DOI: 10.1145/3205977.3205992

Tan, C. L., Chiew, K. L., Wong, K., & Sze, S. N. (2016). PhishWHO: Phishing webpage detection via identity keywords extraction and target domain name finder. *Decision Support Systems*, 88, 18–27. DOI: 10.1016/j.dss.2016.05.005

Thakur, K., Shan, J., & Pathan, A.-S. K. (2018). Innovations of phishing defense: The mechanism, measurement and defense strategies. *International Journal of Communication Networks and Information Security*, 10(1), 19–27.

Yang, L., Liu, G., Wang, J., Zhai, J., & Dai, Y. (2022). A semantic element representation model for malicious domain name detection. *Journal of Information Security and Applications*, 66, 103148. DOI: 10.1016/j.jisa.2022.103148

Chapter 12
Optimizing Data Privacy and Scalability in Health Monitoring:
Leveraging, Encryption, Blockchain, and Cloud Technologies

G. Kothai
https://orcid.org/0000-0002-9581-1679
KPR Institute of Engineering and Technology, India

P. Harish
https://orcid.org/0009-0009-1534-0140
KPR Institute of Engineering and Technology, India

S. Mugesh kannan
KPR Institute of Engineering and Technology, India

D. Ajinesh
KPR Institute of Engineering and Technology, India

V. Sathyanarayanan
KPR Institute of Engineering and Technology, India

ABSTRACT

In an era, health monitoring technologies are increasingly powered by smart devices and applications, ensuring the privacy and security of sensitive health data is a critical challenge. The chapter begins with an introduction to precise health monitoring, highlighting the importance of smart devices and mobile applications in tracking patient health. The chapter delves into the key challenges posed by the volume, sensitivity, and complexity of health data, examining privacy during data collection and sharing. The challenges is addressed by optimizing data security in health monitoring, such as data encryption techniques to protect patient identities. Blockchain technology is used for secure health data sharing. Authentication and access control mechanisms are explored to protect health data. As healthcare systems handle increasing volumes of data, the chapter discusses the role of cloud computing to achieve scalability. The chapter concludes by emphasizing the importance of balancing cloud computing to

DOI: 10.4018/979-8-3693-8784-9.ch012

optimize both scalability and efficiency in health monitoring applications

INTRODUCTION TO PRECISE HEALTH MONITORING

i. Overview of Health Monitoring Technologies

Health monitoring technologies have significantly evolved in recent years, transforming how individuals and healthcare providers track and manage health. The rise of wearable devices, mobile health apps, and remote monitoring systems has ushered in an era where data-driven healthcare is no longer limited to hospital settings. These technologies now allow continuous monitoring of vital signs, physical activity, and other health indicators in real-time, providing valuable insights into a person's well-being as shown in Figure 1.

Some of the most common health monitoring technologies include:

- Wearable Devices: These include fitness trackers, smartwatches, and specialized medical devices that measure heart rate, blood pressure, oxygen saturation, sleep patterns, and even blood sugar levels. Devices like Fitbit, Apple Watch, and continuous glucose monitors (CGMs) are now common household items.
- Mobile Health Apps (mHealth): These apps track various health metrics, such as calorie intake, step count, sleep, mental health, and more. They often sync with wearable devices to provide a comprehensive picture of an individual's health. Popular examples include MyFitnessPal for nutrition tracking and Headspace for mental wellness.
- Remote Patient Monitoring (RPM): RPM systems are used by healthcare providers to monitor patients with chronic conditions like diabetes, hypertension, and heart disease. Devices installed in the patient's home send data directly to healthcare professionals, allowing them to intervene before issues escalate.

ii. The Role of Smart Devices and Apps in Tracking Health

Smart devices and mobile health applications (mHealth apps) have become integral to health monitoring, enabling users to monitor their health anytime and anywhere. These tools offer a user-friendly approach to tracking various health parameters and provide actionable insights that can help individuals improve their health and well-being.

- Tracking Vital Signs and Health Metrics
    - Smart devices, particularly wearable technology, have revolutionized the way vital signs and health metrics are tracked. Devices like the Apple Watch or Fitbit monitor an individual's heart rate, physical activity, sleep patterns, and other metrics, sending real-time data to connected apps for analysis. These devices not only provide users with their daily health stats but also offer trend analysis over weeks or months, giving users a deeper understanding of their overall health.
    - In more advanced applications, devices like continuous glucose monitors (CGMs) track blood sugar levels throughout the day, providing valuable insights for people with diabetes.

Similarly, blood pressure monitors and oxygen saturation sensors are being increasingly used for patients with chronic conditions like hypertension or respiratory disorders.

- Improving Lifestyle and Health Behaviors
  - Another major role of smart devices and apps is in promoting healthier lifestyle choices. By tracking daily activities such as step counts, calories burned, or hours of sleep, these devices provide users with personalized feedback and recommendations on how to achieve their health goals. Mobile health apps often include features like reminders, goal setting, and challenges to encourage healthier habits. This behavioral feedback loop allows users to stay motivated and accountable, leading to better adherence to exercise routines, diets, or sleep schedules.
  - For instance, fitness trackers help users set and achieve activity goals by giving them reminders to move if they've been sedentary for too long. Apps like MyFitnessPal track food intake and provide nutritional insights, which can help users make more informed choices about their diet.
- Remote Health Monitoring and Telemedicine Integration
  - Smart devices and apps play a critical role in remote health monitoring and telemedicine. For patients with chronic diseases or those recovering from surgeries, smart health monitoring systems enable healthcare providers to track health metrics remotely and intervene when necessary. In cases of patients with heart disease, remote monitoring systems can alert doctors if abnormal heart rhythms or blood pressure levels are detected, allowing for timely medical intervention.
  - Furthermore, the integration of health monitoring apps with telemedicine platforms enables patients to share their health data with doctors and have virtual consultations. This not only saves time and resources but also provides continuous care for patients who might otherwise not have access to healthcare due to geographical or financial barriers.
- Chronic Disease Management
  - Smart devices and apps also help individuals with chronic conditions like diabetes, hypertension, and asthma manage their diseases more effectively. For example, diabetic patients can use continuous glucose monitors to track their blood sugar levels in real-time, enabling them to make informed decisions about diet, exercise, and medication. Many apps also allow users to share their health data with their healthcare providers, facilitating better care coordination and more personalized treatment plans.
  - Additionally, hypertension management apps allow patients to track their blood pressure at home and share results with their healthcare providers. This can help doctors monitor the effectiveness of prescribed medications and make necessary adjustments to treatment plans.

iii. The Importance of Data Security and Privacy in Health Monitoring

With the increasing use of health monitoring technologies, the security and privacy of health data have become paramount. Personal health information is highly sensitive, and its improper handling can lead to breaches of confidentiality, misuse of data, or exposure of sensitive information to unauthorized parties.

- Sensitive Nature of Health Data

- Health data includes information about a person's medical history, treatment plans, genetic data, and current health conditions. Such data is highly personal and private, requiring strict measures to ensure it remains confidential. If this data falls into the wrong hands, it could be used for identity theft, insurance fraud, or unethical profiling by organizations such as employers or insurers.

- Risks of Data Breaches and Unauthorized Access
  - The growing adoption of smart health devices and apps has also led to a surge in the collection of vast amounts of data. This volume of data, often stored in the cloud, is susceptible to cyberattacks and data breaches. Unauthorized access to health data could lead to serious consequences for individuals, ranging from financial harm to privacy violations.
  - One well-known incident is the 2015 Anthem data breach, in which hackers stole the personal health information of nearly 80 million individuals, including names, addresses, and medical histories. This case underscores the critical need for robust security measures in health data management.
- Regulatory Compliance and Privacy Standards
  - To address these concerns, various privacy regulations and data protection standards have been implemented globally. In the European Union, the General Data Protection Regulation (GDPR) sets strict guidelines for how personal data, including health data, must be handled and protected. Similarly, in the United States, the Health Insurance Portability and Accountability Act (HIPAA) establishes rules for safeguarding medical information and ensuring patient privacy.
  - Compliance with these regulations is essential for healthcare organizations, smart device manufacturers, and health app developers. Failure to comply can result in hefty fines, reputational damage, and loss of consumer trust.
- Implementing Strong Data Security Measures
  - Data Encryption: Encrypting health data both at rest and in transit is critical to preventing unauthorized access. Encryption scrambles the data into unreadable code, ensuring that even if the data is intercepted, it cannot be deciphered without the proper decryption key.
  - Anonymization and De-identification: Anonymizing or de-identifying personal health data involves removing any information that could link the data back to an individual. This allows for the use of health data in research or analytics without compromising privacy.

CHALLENGES OF HEALTH DATA SECURITY AND PRIVACY

As healthcare increasingly relies on digital solutions for health monitoring, several challenges arise regarding the security and privacy of sensitive health data. These challenges stem from the complexity and volume of data generated, the sensitive nature of health information, and the risks associated with data breaches. This section delves into the key challenges facing health data security and privacy, emphasizing the need for robust solutions to safeguard patient information.

i. Sensitive Nature of Health Data

Health data is inherently sensitive, encompassing a wide range of personal information, including medical histories, treatment plans, genetic data, and behavioral information. The unique nature of health data makes it a prime target for unauthorized access and misuse. Unlike other types of personal data, health information can lead to significant personal and financial consequences if compromised (Miller, 2018).

- Confidentiality and Trust: Patients place their trust in healthcare providers and technology solutions to safeguard their private information. Breaches of this trust can lead to a reluctance to share necessary health information, undermining the effectiveness of healthcare interventions (Sweeney, 2013).
- Stigmatization: Sensitive health conditions, such as mental health disorders or sexually transmitted infections, may carry stigma. Unauthorized disclosure of this information can lead to social and economic consequences for individuals, further emphasizing the need for strict privacy measures.

ii. Volume and Complexity of Health Data

The amount of health data generated by modern health monitoring technologies is staggering. With the proliferation of wearable devices, mobile apps, and remote monitoring systems, individuals can continuously collect data related to their health. This high volume of data creates several challenges:

- Data Management: Managing vast amounts of health data requires robust systems and infrastructure capable of storing, processing, and analyzing this information. Healthcare providers must ensure that they have the necessary resources to handle data effectively while maintaining privacy and security (Maan & Haseeb, 2021).
- Data Integration: Health data often comes from diverse sources, such as electronic health records (EHRs), wearable devices, and mobile apps. Integrating this data into a unified system presents significant challenges in terms of compatibility, standardization, and privacy (Maan & Haseeb, 2021).

iii. Risks of Data Breaches and Unauthorized Access

With the growing reliance on digital health technologies, the risk of data breaches and unauthorized access has escalated. Cyberattacks targeting healthcare organizations have become more common, leading to significant data breaches. Key risks include:

- Cyberattacks: Hackers increasingly target healthcare systems to steal sensitive information or disrupt services. Ransomware attacks, in which attackers encrypt data and demand payment for its release, have been particularly damaging in the healthcare sector. For example, the 2017 WannaCry ransomware attack impacted numerous healthcare providers globally, causing disruptions in patient care (Miller, 2018).
- Insider Threats: Employees within healthcare organizations can pose a risk to data security. Whether intentional or accidental, insider threats can lead to unauthorized access to sensitive

information. Organizations must implement stringent access controls and monitoring systems to mitigate this risk (Maan & Haseeb, 2021).

iv. Regulatory Compliance and Privacy Standards

Healthcare organizations must navigate a complex landscape of regulations and standards designed to protect patient privacy and data security. These regulations include:

- General Data Protection Regulation (GDPR): Implemented in the European Union, GDPR sets strict guidelines for how personal data, including health data, must be collected, processed, and stored. Organizations must ensure compliance to avoid substantial fines and reputational damage (European Commission, 2016).
- Health Insurance Portability and Accountability Act (HIPAA): In the United States, HIPAA establishes standards for protecting patient health information. Healthcare organizations must implement various safeguards to ensure compliance, including administrative, physical, and technical protections (U.S. Department of Health and Human Services, 2020).

v. The Challenge of Patient Consent

Obtaining informed patient consent for the collection and use of health data is a critical aspect of maintaining privacy. However, several challenges exist:

- Complexity of Consent Forms: Consent forms can be lengthy and difficult for patients to understand, leading to confusion about what data is being collected and how it will be used. Patients may not fully comprehend the implications of their consent, raising ethical concerns (Sweeney, 2013).
- Dynamic Nature of Health Data: As health monitoring technologies evolve, the types of data collected and the purposes for which it is used may change. Keeping patients informed about these changes and obtaining ongoing consent can be challenging (Sweeney, 2013).

vi. Addressing the Challenges: Path Forward

To address these challenges effectively, healthcare organizations, technology developers, and policymakers must collaborate on implementing robust security measures and privacy standards. Here are some strategies:

- Invest in Cybersecurity: Healthcare organizations should prioritize investments in cybersecurity infrastructure, including firewalls, intrusion detection systems, and encryption technologies. Regular security audits and employee training can help mitigate risks (Maan & Haseeb, 2021).
- Adopt Data Privacy Standards: Organizations must stay informed about privacy regulations and ensure compliance with GDPR, HIPAA, and other relevant standards. Developing clear policies and procedures for data management and consent can enhance patient trust (European Commission, 2016; U.S. Department of Health and Human Services, 2020).

- Enhance Patient Education: Providing clear, understandable information about data collection practices and consent requirements can empower patients to make informed choices about their health data (Sweeney, 2013).

OPTIMIZING DATA SECURITY IN HEALTH MONITORING

As healthcare technology evolves, the need for robust data security measures in health monitoring systems becomes paramount. Ensuring that sensitive health data is adequately protected involves the implementation of various data encryption techniques and strategies for anonymizing patient information. This section explores the methods used to optimize data security in health monitoring, highlighting the importance of encryption and anonymization in safeguarding patient privacy as tabulated in Table 1.

i. Data Encryption Techniques

Data encryption is a critical component of securing health data. It involves converting readable data into an encoded format that can only be accessed or decrypted by authorized users. Encryption techniques ensure that sensitive information remains confidential, even if it is intercepted or accessed without authorization.

- Symmetric Encryption: This method uses a single key for both encryption and decryption, making it essential to keep the key secure. Symmetric encryption algorithms, such as Advanced Encryption Standard (AES), are widely used for encrypting health data due to their efficiency and speed (Maan & Haseeb, 2021).
- Asymmetric Encryption: Unlike symmetric encryption, asymmetric encryption employs a pair of keys: a public key for encryption and a private key for decryption. This method enhances security by allowing users to share their public keys while keeping their private keys confidential. Techniques such as RSA (Rivest-Shamir-Adleman) are commonly used in health monitoring systems for secure data transmission (Maan & Haseeb, 2021).
- Hybrid Encryption: This approach combines the strengths of symmetric and asymmetric encryption. It uses asymmetric encryption to securely exchange a symmetric key, which is then used for encrypting the data. Hybrid encryption balances the efficiency of symmetric encryption with the security of asymmetric encryption, making it a preferred choice for health data protection (Miller, 2018).

ii. End-to-End Encryption for Health Data

End-to-end encryption (E2EE) ensures that data is encrypted on the sender's device and only decrypted on the recipient's device, preventing unauthorized access during transmission. E2EE is particularly crucial in health monitoring applications where sensitive information, such as medical histories and personal identifiers, is shared between patients and healthcare providers.

- Secure Communication Channels: Implementing E2EE in health monitoring systems can protect data transmitted over various communication channels, such as mobile apps and web applications.

For instance, messaging platforms that employ E2EE, like Signal and WhatsApp, demonstrate the effectiveness of this approach in safeguarding user privacy (Miller, 2018).

- Protection Against Interception: By encrypting data throughout its journey, E2EE mitigates risks associated with data interception. This protection is vital in health monitoring, where sensitive data could be compromised during transmission over public networks (Maan & Haseeb, 2021).

Table 1. Comparative Encryption Methods

Encryption Method	Mechanism	Advantages	Disadvantages	Use Cases in Healthcare
Symmetric Encryption	Uses a single key for both encryption and decryption.	Fast and efficient for large datasets.	Key management is challenging; if the key is compromised, the data is at risk.	Secure storage of patient health records on local servers or secure transmission between trusted endpoints.
Asymmetric Encryption	Employs a pair of keys: a public key for encryption and a private key for decryption.	Secure for data transmission; no need to share private keys.	Computationally intensive, making it slower than symmetric encryption.	Sharing patient data securely between healthcare providers over public networks.
Hybrid Encryption	Combines symmetric and asymmetric encryption, using the latter to share symmetric keys securely.	Balances efficiency and security; scalable for large datasets and secure key exchanges.	Slightly more complex to implement than using one method alone.	Secure cloud-based health data storage with real-time access by authorized users.
End-to-End Encryption (E2EE)	Encrypts data at the sender's end and decrypts it at the recipient's end, protecting data during transit.	Protects data from interception during transmission; ensures confidentiality even on public networks.	Relies on secure key management at both ends.	Telemedicine platforms and remote health monitoring systems.

iii. Encrypting Data at Rest and During Transmission

Securing health data involves encryption both at rest (stored data) and during transmission (data in transit).

- Data at Rest: This refers to data stored on servers, databases, or devices. Implementing encryption for data at rest ensures that unauthorized users cannot access sensitive health information even if they gain physical access to the storage medium. Techniques such as full-disk encryption or file-level encryption can be employed to secure data at rest effectively (Maan & Haseeb, 2021).
- Data in Transit: This involves data being transferred over networks. Encryption protocols like Transport Layer Security (TLS) and Secure Socket Layer (SSL) are commonly used to encrypt data in transit, ensuring that information transmitted between devices remains confidential and secure (Miller, 2018).
- Importance of Comprehensive Encryption: Implementing encryption for both data at rest and in transit is crucial for a holistic approach to data security. A failure to encrypt data in either state can leave vulnerabilities that attackers can exploit, potentially compromising sensitive health information (Maan & Haseeb, 2021).

iv. Anonymization of Health Data

Anonymization is a process that removes personally identifiable information (PII) from health data sets, ensuring that individuals cannot be easily identified from the data. This technique is essential for maintaining patient privacy while enabling data analysis and research.

- Techniques to De-identify and Anonymize Patient Data: Various methods exist for anonymizing health data:
    - Data Masking: This technique involves replacing sensitive information with fictitious values or masking the data altogether. For example, patient names and addresses can be replaced with random identifiers while retaining other relevant health information (Maan & Haseeb, 2021).
    - Generalization: In this approach, specific data values are replaced with broader categories. For instance, instead of recording exact ages, data may be grouped into age ranges (e.g., 20-30, 31-40) to reduce the likelihood of identifying individuals (Miller, 2018).
    - Perturbation: This technique involves introducing random noise to data values, making it difficult to trace the data back to an individual while still allowing for meaningful analysis (Sweeney, 2013).
- Balancing Anonymization and Usability: While anonymization is essential for protecting patient privacy, it can sometimes limit the usability of the data for research and analysis. Striking the right balance between anonymization and data utility is crucial to ensure that valuable health insights can still be extracted from the data (Maan & Haseeb, 2021).

v. Ensuring Privacy While Maintaining Usability of Data

The challenge of ensuring privacy while maintaining the usability of health data is a complex issue that requires careful consideration. Data that is overly anonymized may lack the necessary detail for effective analysis, while insufficient anonymization may expose patients to privacy risks.

- Data Governance Policies: Implementing robust data governance policies can help organizations strike a balance between privacy and usability. These policies should outline data handling practices, access controls, and consent management to ensure that patient data is used responsibly (Maan & Haseeb, 2021).
- Controlled Access: Utilizing role-based access controls (RBAC) ensures that only authorized personnel have access to sensitive health data. By assigning permissions based on roles, organizations can limit exposure to patient information while enabling necessary access for healthcare providers and researchers (Miller, 2018).
- Data Aggregation: Aggregating data can help maintain usability while protecting privacy. By summarizing data into groups rather than maintaining individual records, organizations can analyze trends and insights without compromising patient confidentiality (Sweeney, 2013).

BLOCKCHAIN FOR SECURE DATA SHARING IN HEALTHCARE

The advent of blockchain technology presents transformative potential for healthcare, particularly in enhancing the security and privacy of sensitive health data. As the digital landscape evolves, the need for secure, efficient, and interoperable systems for health data exchange becomes paramount. This section explores the fundamentals of blockchain technology, its advantages for safeguarding health information, and examples of its implementation in healthcare data sharing.

i. Introduction to Blockchain Technology

Blockchain is fundamentally a decentralized digital ledger that records transactions across numerous computers in such a way that the registered transactions cannot be altered retroactively. Each transaction, or piece of data, is contained in a "block," and multiple blocks are linked together to form a "chain." This structure provides a secure and transparent method of documenting information, making it particularly suitable for managing sensitive health data.

- Characteristics of Blockchain:
    - Decentralization: Traditional databases rely on a central authority, which can be a target for cyberattacks. Blockchain operates on a peer-to-peer network, significantly reducing the risk of central points of failure (Nakamoto, 2008).
    - Transparency: Every participant in the network has access to the same information, promoting trust and accountability among stakeholders.
    - Immutability: Once data is recorded on the blockchain, it cannot be modified or deleted without consensus from the network. This ensures the integrity of health records (Christidis & Devetsikiotis, 2016).
    - Consensus Mechanisms: Transactions are validated through consensus algorithms, such as Proof of Work or Proof of Stake, ensuring that only legitimate transactions are added to the blockchain.
- Relevance in Healthcare: The complexity of managing health data across multiple providers and systems creates challenges, such as interoperability and data breaches. Blockchain technology addresses these challenges by facilitating secure data sharing and improving patient privacy (Kuo et al., 2017).

ii. Benefits of Blockchain for Health Data Security

Integrating blockchain into healthcare systems offers numerous advantages for enhancing data security:

- Robust Data Security:
    - Blockchain utilizes advanced encryption techniques to safeguard health data, making it difficult for unauthorized individuals to access or tamper with the information. Each transaction is encrypted and linked to previous ones, creating a secure chain of information (Zhang et al., 2018).

- The decentralized nature of blockchain minimizes vulnerabilities. Since there is no single point of failure, healthcare organizations can enhance the protection of patient information from cyber threats.
- Facilitating Interoperability:
    - One major hurdle in healthcare is the lack of interoperability among various electronic health record (EHR) systems. Blockchain promotes seamless data exchange across platforms, allowing healthcare providers to access comprehensive patient histories regardless of the system in use (Kuo et al., 2017).
    - By standardizing data formats on the blockchain, stakeholders can ensure that health information is consistently structured, which enhances communication and coordination of care.
- Empowering Patients:
    - Blockchain allows patients to maintain control over their health data by providing them with private keys that grant access to their information. This autonomy empowers individuals to decide who can view their data and for what purposes (Mok et al., 2018).
    - Patients can also track access to their data, fostering trust in healthcare providers and the broader healthcare ecosystem.
- Enhanced Auditability and Traceability:
    - The transparent nature of blockchain allows for the monitoring of health data transactions in real-time. This capability aids healthcare organizations in ensuring compliance with regulations such as HIPAA and GDPR (Zhang et al., 2018).
    - In cases of data breaches or disputes, the immutable records provided by blockchain serve as a reliable source for investigations.

iii. Case Studies: Blockchain in Healthcare Data Exchange

Several healthcare organizations are leveraging blockchain technology to improve the security and sharing of health data. Below are notable examples:

- Gemini Health:
    - This organization has developed a blockchain platform that allows patients to retain ownership of their health data while securely sharing it with healthcare providers and researchers. The platform's use of smart contracts automates consent management, ensuring that data sharing complies with agreements (Gemini Health, 2020).
    - By utilizing blockchain, Gemini Health mitigates the risks of unauthorized access to patient information, fostering a more secure environment for health data exchange.
- MediLedger Project:
    - The MediLedger Project focuses on enhancing the pharmaceutical supply chain's security and transparency. By creating a blockchain-based ledger of drug transactions, MediLedger helps prevent counterfeit medications from entering the market (MediLedger Project, 2021).
    - This initiative allows stakeholders, including manufacturers and pharmacies, to verify the authenticity and movement of pharmaceutical products, thereby improving patient safety and regulatory compliance.
- Chronicled:

- Chronicled utilizes blockchain to enhance the drug supply chain's transparency and security by securely tracking the authenticity of pharmaceutical products. This platform ensures that drug provenance can be traced, reducing the risk of counterfeit medications (Chronicled, 2020).
    - Through secure data sharing between manufacturers, distributors, and pharmacies, Chronicled promotes visibility and trust throughout the pharmaceutical supply chain.
- Hashed Health:
    - This organization focuses on developing blockchain solutions to enhance interoperability in health data exchange. Hashed Health's platform enables secure sharing of patient health records across various EHR systems, leading to better care coordination and reduced administrative burdens (Hashed Health, 2018).
    - By implementing blockchain technology, Hashed Health enhances data security and empowers patients, demonstrating the potential for blockchain to transform health data exchange.

AUTHENTICATION AND ACCESS CONTROL MECHANISMS

Healthcare organizations handle a vast amount of sensitive data, from patient medical records to financial information, all of which need to be protected from cyberattacks, insider threats, and data misuse. As a result, authentication and access control systems are not only necessary for maintaining regulatory compliance with standards like HIPAA (Health Insurance Portability and Accountability Act) in the U.S. and GDPR (General Data Protection Regulation) in the European Union but also crucial for fostering trust with patients and stakeholders. The multi-factor authentication (MFA) and role-based access control (RBAC) mechanisms are the two primary techniques employed to address these challenges. Through MFA, healthcare providers can add an additional layer of security, requiring users to provide multiple forms of identification. This ensures that even if one authentication method is compromised (e.g., password theft), unauthorized users still cannot access sensitive data without providing additional credentials. RBAC, on the other hand, helps define what information each user can access based on their job role, ensuring that employees only have access to the data they need to perform their duties and nothing more. Both techniques, when implemented correctly, create a secure and scalable framework for managing health data access.

i. Multi-Factor Authentication (MFA)

- Multi-factor authentication (MFA) is one of the most effective security mechanisms used in healthcare to protect sensitive data from unauthorized access. MFA requires users to authenticate themselves using two or more verification methods: something they know (e.g., a password or PIN), something they have (e.g., a security token or mobile device), and something they are (e.g., biometrics such as fingerprints or facial recognition) (Fatehi, Hassandoust, Ko, & Akhlaghpour, 2020). By combining multiple authentication factors, MFA significantly strengthens the authentication process, making it much harder for attackers to gain access to healthcare systems.
- For example, a doctor accessing a patient's electronic health record (EHR) may need to provide their password, followed by a one-time code sent to their mobile device or a fingerprint scan. This approach reduces the chances of unauthorized access, particularly in healthcare en-

vironments where patient data is highly targeted for identity theft, fraud, and other malicious activities. Moreover, MFA aligns with various regulatory standards, including HIPAA, which requires healthcare organizations to implement adequate safeguards to protect sensitive patient data (Mocydlarz-Adamcewicz et al., 2023).

ii. How MFA Protects Health Data

- MFA provides a robust defense mechanism for securing patient data by ensuring that only authorized users are granted access to sensitive health records. In healthcare, the stakes are high because unauthorized access to patient records could lead to identity theft, fraud, or other forms of data misuse. Given that healthcare data is increasingly targeted by cybercriminals, MFA adds an extra layer of protection, making it far more difficult for attackers to breach healthcare systems (Jones, Stone, Mason, Eames, & Franklin, 2023).
- Practically speaking, MFA safeguards health data by requesting several types of proof before allowing access. In the event that a password or other single factor is stolen, the attacker must still get around the other verification techniques (such fingerprint or mobile token). This guarantees adherence to data protection laws and significantly lowers the possibility of an attack succeeding. Moreover, multi-factor authentication (MFA) guards against phishing attempts, which aim to deceive healthcare personnel into divulging their passwords or other authentication-related information.

iii. Role-Based Access Control (RBAC)

- Role-based access control (RBAC) is a system that assigns permissions to users based on their role within an organization. This ensures that individuals can only access the data necessary for their specific job function. In healthcare, this is crucial for maintaining data privacy and preventing unauthorized access to sensitive health information. For example, doctors may have access to a patient's complete medical record, while administrative staff may only have access to basic demographic information. RBAC helps enforce the principle of least privilege, which states that users should have the minimum level of access necessary to perform their duties (Bassan, 2020).
- By implementing RBAC, healthcare organizations can ensure that each employee's access to patient data is restricted according to their role. For instance, a nurse may only need access to a patient's current medication list, while a surgeon requires access to the patient's full medical history. This segmentation of access reduces the potential damage in case of an internal or external breach, as unauthorized users will be restricted to only a limited set of data that is not sensitive (McGraw & Mandl, 2021).

iv. Implementing RBAC for Secure Data Access in Healthcare

- Implementing RBAC in healthcare environments involves defining specific roles within the organization and assigning appropriate permissions to each role. For example, a physician may be assigned the role of "Doctor," which grants them full access to patient medical records, while a receptionist may be assigned the role of "Administrative Staff," with access limited to basic patient contact information. It is essential for healthcare organizations to continually assess and adjust

- these roles to reflect the changing needs of the organization and the evolving security landscape (Stergiou, Plageras, Memos, Koidou, & Psannis, 2024).
- An important step in implementing RBAC is creating an access control policy that outlines which roles should have access to which resources. This policy should be regularly reviewed and updated to ensure that only the necessary staff members have access to sensitive patient information. Additionally, automated tools can help monitor access patterns and flag any suspicious activity or potential violations of the access control policies. This proactive approach helps mitigate the risk of unauthorized access while maintaining an efficient workflow within the healthcare system.

v. Assigning Permissions Based on Roles

- Assigning permissions based on roles ensures that healthcare organizations adhere to the principle of least privilege, which dictates that individuals should only be granted the minimum level of access necessary for their job functions. For instance, a nurse may be permitted to view patient charts, but they should not have access to billing information. Conversely, a hospital administrator might have access to both the financial and medical data of patients in order to coordinate care. By assigning permissions based on roles, healthcare organizations ensure that sensitive information is only accessible to individuals who genuinely require it to perform their tasks (Tazi, Nandakumar, Dykstra, Rajivan, & Das, 2024).
- One of the challenges in assigning permissions is balancing security with operational efficiency. While it's important to limit access to sensitive data, healthcare workers often need timely access to information to deliver effective care. Therefore, it's crucial to implement a flexible yet secure access control system that allows employees to quickly obtain the information they need without compromising patient privacy.

COMPLIANCE WITH HEALTHCARE REGULATIONS

The General Data Protection Regulation (GDPR) is a key data protection regulation enforced in the European Union (EU), which has global implications for healthcare organizations that handle the personal data of EU citizens. Similarly, the Health Insurance Portability and Accountability Act (HIPAA) governs the privacy and security of health information in the United States, and is critical for organizations that store or process healthcare data within the country. Both regulations mandate stringent controls around data access, storage, and transmission. Implementing robust data privacy practices that align with these regulations is essential for maintaining the confidentiality and integrity of patient health data in modern health monitoring systems as tabulated in Table 2.

i. General Data Protection Regulation (GDPR)

- The General Data Protection Regulation (GDPR), implemented by the European Union (EU) in 2018, is one of the most comprehensive privacy and data protection laws in the world. It aims to provide EU citizens with control over their personal data, while imposing strict rules on organizations that handle such data. GDPR applies not only to organizations within the EU but also to entities outside the EU that offer goods or services to EU residents or process their data.

- For healthcare organizations, GDPR introduces specific requirements for how patient data should be handled, stored, and processed. It mandates that patient consent be obtained before collecting or processing their health data, provides individuals with the right to access their personal data, and grants them the right to request its correction or deletion (the "right to be forgotten") (Vorisek et al., 2022). Additionally, GDPR requires that sensitive data, such as health information, be subject to higher levels of protection, including encryption and anonymization during transmission and storage.

ii. Key GDPR Requirements for Healthcare Data

The GDPR outlines several key requirements for the handling of healthcare data, emphasizing the protection of patient privacy and ensuring that healthcare organizations take all necessary steps to protect sensitive health information.

- Consent Management: Organizations must ensure that explicit, informed consent is obtained from patients before collecting or processing their health data. This consent must be clear, specific, and revocable. Healthcare providers should implement mechanisms to enable patients to withdraw consent at any time, which will halt the processing of their data.
- Data Protection by Design and by Default: Healthcare systems must be designed with privacy in mind. Data protection measures should be embedded in the system architecture, ensuring that privacy is maintained throughout the entire lifecycle of health data, from collection to destruction. This also includes ensuring that only the minimum necessary data is collected (data minimization) (Segal, Giuffrida, Possanza, & Bucciferro, 2022).
- Data Subject Rights: GDPR grants patients several rights concerning their health data, including the right to access, correct, delete, and restrict the processing of their data. Healthcare providers must have mechanisms in place to enable patients to exercise these rights without delay.
- Data Breach Notification: In the event of a data breach, healthcare organizations must notify relevant authorities and affected individuals within 72 hours of discovering the breach. This requirement helps ensure that patients are made aware of potential risks to their data and can take action to protect themselves.

iii. HIPAA, the Health Insurance Portability and Accountability Act

- A U.S. law known as the Health Insurance Portability and Accountability Act (HIPAA) works to protect patient data by guaranteeing the confidentiality and security of personal health information (PHI). Healthcare clearinghouses, health plans, healthcare providers, and business partners that handle PHI on behalf of covered entities are all subject to HIPAA regulations.
- HIPAA mandates that healthcare organizations implement stringent safeguards to protect PHI from unauthorized access, disclosure, and use. These safeguards include physical security measures (e.g., locked files and secure storage), administrative safeguards (e.g., staff training and access control), and technical safeguards (e.g., encryption and secure communication protocols).

iv. Ensuring HIPAA Compliance in Health Monitoring Systems

To ensure HIPAA compliance in health monitoring systems, healthcare organizations must implement a combination of organizational policies, technical controls, and physical security measures.

- Encryption of Health Data: All health data, including electronic health records (EHRs), should be encrypted during transmission and at rest. This is essential for preventing unauthorized access, especially when health data is transferred across networks or stored in cloud environments.
- Access Control and Auditing: Role-based access control (RBAC) and multi-factor authentication (MFA) should be used to limit access to PHI based on user roles. Additionally, healthcare organizations must regularly audit user activity to ensure compliance with access policies and detect any suspicious behavior that may indicate a breach (Li, Clarke, Ashrafian, Darzi, & Neves, 2022).
- Business Associate Agreements (BAAs): Health monitoring systems often rely on third-party vendors for services such as cloud hosting or data processing. Under HIPAA, covered entities must establish Business Associate Agreements (BAAs) with these vendors to ensure they meet HIPAA's privacy and security standards when handling PHI .

Table 2. Comparative Privacy Regulations

Regulation	Region	Scope	Key Requirements	Impact on Healthcare
GDPR	European Union	Protects personal data of EU residents, regardless of where it is processed.	Consent-based data collection, data minimization, right to erasure, breach notification within 72 hours.	Requires encryption and anonymization of health data, strict consent processes, and compliance audits.
HIPAA	United States	Ensures the confidentiality, integrity, and security of protected health information (PHI).	Technical safeguards (e.g., encryption), access control, employee training, and Business Associate Agreements (BAAs).	Encourages the use of robust encryption and access control mechanisms for electronic health records (EHRs).
PIPEDA	Canada	Governs the collection, use, and disclosure of personal information by private sector organizations.	Requires organizations to obtain meaningful consent and protect data using appropriate safeguards.	Mandates data encryption and secure storage practices in health monitoring systems.
Health Data Act (Proposed)	Global (WHO)	Aims to establish universal guidelines for cross-border health data sharing.	Focuses on global interoperability, encryption standards, and cross-border consent protocols.	Could standardize practices for blockchain and encrypted data sharing in healthcare globally.

HEALTHCARE INTEROPERABILITY & DATA EXCHANGE STANDARDS

With the advancement of digital technology, the nature of healthcare systems tends to make full utilization of the potential for sharing and exchanging information across different platforms. This is essential in enhancing patient care, ensuring medical research, and keeping healthcare services running. Interoperability refers to how various technologies, systems, and applications are enabled to exchange health data with one another in a seamless manner. Health care systems cannot communicate effectively if such interoperability doesn't exist, resulting in fragmented care and poor patient outcomes (Smith et al., 2018). With rising rates of smart devices and health apps, interoperability has become even more important. Health data is now produced from various sources, including wearable devices, and needs to be shared across multiple systems to provide a complete view of a patient's health. To make such data exchange reliable and efficient, data exchange standards come into play. These standards ensure that the sharing of health information is done in a way that preserves the accuracy and integrity of the information involved. One of the most useful standards for this purpose is FHIR (Fast Healthcare Interoperability Resources). FHIR has transformed data exchange, particularly in health monitoring systems and clinical environments (Jones et al., 2016). Below, we explore how FHIR works, its impact on healthcare, and its applications.

i. FHIR (Fast Healthcare Interoperability Resources) Protocol

- One of the most advanced standards in exchanging healthcare information is the FHIR protocol, developed by HL7 (Health Level Seven International). It ensures that all healthcare information is easily exchanged between systems, regardless of the vendors involved (HL7 et al., 2014).
- While earlier standards had not implemented the most advanced web technologies, FHIR's architecture was structured to be scalable and easier to implement. FHIR APIs are restful APIs (application programming interfaces), which are widely used in the broader industry due to their minimal and efficient ability to enable systems to communicate with each other. These APIs handle tasks like retrieving, creating, and updating data, making the exchange of information within healthcare systems more straightforward and efficient (Miller et al., 2015).
- Key Characteristics of FHIR
    - Modularity and Flexibility: FHIR organizes health information into small, reusable units called "resources." These resources represent different types of health data, such as patients, medications, or observations. Each resource can be accessed or updated independently, making it highly versatile and adaptable to healthcare organizations' needs (Brown et al., 2017).
    - Ease of Integration: FHIR integrates easily with other systems due to its compatibility with widely used technologies like JSON and XML. Healthcare providers implementing FHIR do not need to invest in expensive system upgrades (Johnson et al., 2018). Its lightweight, web-based nature makes it ideal for mobile apps and cloud-based solutions, which are becoming more prevalent in modern healthcare (Smith et al., 2019).
    - Interoperability with Legacy Systems: FHIR was designed to work not only with modern systems but also with older systems that still use standards like HL7 v2 or CDA (Clinical Document Architecture). This backward compatibility allows organizations to transition gradually to FHIR without overhauling their existing infrastructure (Williams et al., 2019).

ii. Improving Healthcare Data Sharing and Interoperability

FHIR has significantly improved interoperability in the healthcare industry. For years, healthcare providers struggled to share patient information across different systems and protocols, often leading to missing details, miscommunication, and delayed care. FHIR provides an international standard that facilitates seamless data sharing between healthcare systems, improving patient care and outcomes (Parker et al., 2018).

iii. Benefits of FHIR on Data Sharing

- One of FHIR's key features is its support for real-time data exchange. This is especially important in health monitoring systems where patients, particularly those with chronic conditions, require continuous monitoring. Devices such as wearables can transmit real-time data to healthcare providers, allowing for timely interventions in emergencies (Anderson et al., 2020).
- FHIR unifies patient data from various sources, including hospitals, clinics, and personal devices, into a consistent format, giving healthcare providers a complete view of a patient's health (Garcia et al., 2019). It also empowers patients by providing access to their own health records, enabling them to actively participate in their care (Johnson et al., 2021).

iv. Use Cases of FHIR in Health Monitoring Systems

- Remote Patient Monitoring (RPM): Telemonitoring, facilitated by wearable devices and mobile apps, allows healthcare providers to track health metrics like heart rate, blood pressure, and glucose levels in real-time. FHIR enables RPM systems to integrate with hospital databases, ensuring that patient data is automatically updated in their EHRs (Green et al., 2020).
- Management of Chronic Diseases: For patients with chronic conditions such as diabetes or hypertension, continuous monitoring is essential. FHIR-enabled platforms allow healthcare providers to adjust treatment plans in real-time based on the latest data, reducing the need for hospital readmissions (Lee et al., 2021).
- Interoperability Between Health Apps and Devices: As more health apps and devices enter the market, FHIR provides a universal language for them to communicate with each other and healthcare providers. For example, a fitness tracker can send daily activity data to a patient's EHR, giving doctors a more comprehensive view of their health (Moore et al., 2019).
- Emergency Care and Telemedicine: Emergency care providers can access patients' medical histories through FHIR, which can be crucial in critical situations. Data from virtual visits can also be integrated into patients' health records, making telemedicine seamless and efficient (Baker et al., 2022).

LEVERAGE CLOUD AND EDGE COMPUTING FOR SCALABILITY

The healthcare sector is turning toward transformation through digital media. The data generated by wearables, health applications, and smart devices poses a need for better management and storage facilities. Traditional data centers are struggling to keep up with the rising influx of health data, particularly in health monitoring systems, where continuous data generation is a norm. Scalability and real-time processing are crucial areas where cloud computing and edge computing play a pivotal role. Both technologies offer strengths in processing large health datasets efficiently, securely, and with speed (Patel et al., 2022).

i. Cloud Computing in Health Monitoring

- Cloud computing is now integral to modern healthcare. Scalable, flexible, and cost-effective, it provides storage, management, and analysis capabilities for health data. Wearable devices and remote monitoring systems benefit immensely from cloud computing, as it offers a centralized location for storing and accessing diverse data in real time (Smith et al., 2021).
- Patient data collected from wearable devices is uploaded to the cloud for processing, allowing healthcare providers to access this information in real time, especially during emergencies. This centralized approach improves accessibility and management of large volumes of health data (Jones et al., 2020).

ii. Managing Large Amounts of Health Data in the Cloud

- One of the biggest challenges in health monitoring is managing vast amounts of data. Wearable devices and health applications collect numerous data points daily, including heart rates, glucose levels, and sleep patterns. When scaled to include millions of patients, these data streams become enormous, requiring scalable solutions for storage, analysis, and accessibility (Khan et al., 2019).
- Cloud computing addresses this challenge by offering scalable storage without the need for costly physical servers. Cloud platforms provide the elasticity to expand storage and processing capacity as needed, making them ideal for handling fluctuating data loads (Wang et al., 2020). Additionally, cloud-based platforms enable advanced analytics tools to process large datasets and extract meaningful insights, such as patterns that indicate potential health issues (Garcia et al., 2021).

iii. Benefits of Cloud-Based Scalable Solutions

- Cost-Efficiency: Cloud solutions reduce capital investment in hardware and infrastructure. Healthcare providers pay only for the storage and computing power used, making cloud computing more affordable, especially for smaller organizations and health tech startups (Brown et al., 2020).
- Scalability: Cloud systems allow healthcare providers to scale their data storage and processing capacity up or down depending on current demands. This is critical in health monitoring systems, where data volumes can fluctuate significantly (Anderson et al., 2019).
- Access and Sharing: Cloud systems provide real-time access to patient data, enabling multiple healthcare providers to collaborate on patient care, which improves outcomes and reduces errors (Lee et al., 2020).

iv. Real-time Health Monitoring with Edge Computing

- While cloud computing offers scalability and centralized data management, it sometimes falls short in terms of latency, especially in real-time health monitoring, where quick processing and response are essential. Edge computing addresses this issue by processing data closer to where it is generated, such as on a wearable device or local gateway (Thomas et al., 2019).

- Edge computing reduces latency by processing data locally, which ensures faster response times. For applications requiring real-time analysis, such as emergency health monitoring or managing chronic conditions, edge computing is indispensable (Williams et al., 2021).

v. Benefits of Data Processing at the Edge

- Reduced Latency: The primary advantage of edge computing is its ability to reduce latency. This is especially important in health monitoring systems, where timely interventions can be lifesaving. For instance, if a heart monitor detects an irregular rhythm, the device can process the data locally and alert the patient or provider immediately (Johnson et al., 2022).
- Reduced Bandwidth Usage: Edge computing reduces the amount of data transmitted to the cloud by processing most of it locally. This decreases bandwidth consumption, reduces costs, and improves overall system efficiency (Smith et al., 2021).

vi. Hybrid Cloud and Edge Computing for Health Monitoring

- Cloud and edge computing complement each other, offering a hybrid solution that combines the scalability of the cloud with the speed and efficiency of edge computing. For instance, in a health monitoring system, real-time alarms might be processed at the edge, while long-term data storage and analysis are handled by the cloud (Moore et al., 2022).
- Edge computing processes and filters data before sending it to the cloud, reducing bandwidth usage and ensuring that cloud systems remain scalable. This hybrid approach is particularly effective in health monitoring systems, where real-time responses are crucial, but large datasets also need to be stored and analyzed over time (Anderson et al., 2021).

REAL-WORLD IMPLEMENTATIONS OF BLOCKCHAIN AND ENCRYPTION IN HEALTH DATA PRIVACY

1. Patient-Centered Data Sharing

Case Study: MediBloc

- **Overview**: MediBloc is a blockchain-based healthcare data platform that allows patients to own and control their medical records. Using blockchain technology, MediBloc enables patients to securely share their data with healthcare providers or researchers while maintaining privacy as summarized in Table 3.
- **Key Features**:
    - o Patient-controlled access using private keys.
    - o Data immutability ensures no unauthorized alterations.
- **Outcome**:
    - o Reduced administrative burdens by providing a unified system for data sharing.
    - o Enhanced patient trust in data privacy, leading to wider adoption of digital health solutions.

2. Pharmaceutical Supply Chain Transparency

Case Study: MediLedger Project

- **Overview**: The MediLedger Project leverages blockchain to secure pharmaceutical supply chains, ensuring the authenticity of medications. Blockchain records each step in the drug manufacturing and distribution process, preventing counterfeit drugs from entering the market.
- **Key Features**:
    - o Immutable transaction logs for drug movement.
    - o Smart contracts to automate compliance checks.
- **Outcome**:
    - o Improved patient safety by eliminating counterfeit medications.
    - o Greater transparency and accountability across the pharmaceutical industry.

3. Remote Patient Monitoring and Data Privacy

Case Study: BurstIQ

- **Overview**: BurstIQ is a blockchain-based platform designed to manage large-scale health data securely. It focuses on enabling secure sharing of patient data for remote monitoring and research.
- **Key Features**:
    - o Advanced encryption to protect sensitive health data.
    - o AI integration for real-time insights into patient health.
- **Outcome**:
    - o Facilitated secure data sharing between patients, providers, and researchers.
    - o Streamlined remote monitoring systems for chronic disease management.

4. Secure Data Exchange in Telemedicine

Case Study: Teladoc Health

- **Overview**: Teladoc Health, a leader in telemedicine, employs end-to-end encryption to secure video consultations and data exchanges between patients and healthcare providers.
- **Key Features**:
    - o Encrypted video calls and medical file sharing.
    - o Compliance with HIPAA regulations for protecting sensitive health data.
- **Outcome**:
    - o Increased adoption of telehealth services, particularly during the COVID-19 pandemic.
    - o Boosted patient confidence in the security of virtual care platforms.

5. Research and Data Collaboration

Case Study: Gem Health Network

- **Overview**: Gem Health uses blockchain to connect healthcare providers and researchers, facilitating secure collaboration without compromising patient privacy. The platform employs smart contracts to automate data sharing permissions.
- **Key Features**:
  - o Data anonymization ensures compliance with GDPR and HIPAA.
  - o Transparent audit trails for data access and use.
- **Outcome**:
  - o Accelerated medical research by simplifying secure data sharing.
  - o Ensured ethical data usage through immutable access logs.

6. National Health Data Infrastructure

Case Study: Estonia's Blockchain-Based eHealth System

- **Overview**: Estonia has implemented a nationwide blockchain-based eHealth system that manages citizens' health records securely. All access to medical records is logged transparently on the blockchain.
- **Key Features**:
  - o Patient-controlled access to medical history.
  - o Immutable records prevent unauthorized modifications.
- **Outcome**:
  - o Increased efficiency in healthcare delivery.
  - o Enhanced public trust in digital health systems.

Table 3. Summary of Practical Outcomes

Use Case	Technology	Key Benefits
Patient Data Sharing (MediBloc)	Blockchain	Patient empowerment, secure data control
Supply Chain Security (MediLedger)	Blockchain	Drug authenticity, counterfeit prevention
Remote Monitoring (BurstIQ)	Blockchain + AI	Real-time insights, secure remote care
Telemedicine (Teladoc Health)	Encryption	Secure consultations, HIPAA compliance
Research Collaboration (Gem Health)	Blockchain	Ethical data sharing, GDPR/HIPAA compliance
National Infrastructure (Estonia)	Blockchain	Efficient healthcare delivery, transparency

CONCLUSION

As health monitoring technologies increasingly play a vital role in modern healthcare, addressing the challenges of safeguarding sensitive health data becomes crucial. Protecting patient privacy, ensuring data security, and maintaining system scalability are essential for the successful implementation of these technologies.

- **Data Security and Patient Trust**

To optimize data security, advanced encryption methods must be used to secure both in-transit and at-rest health data. Anonymization and comprehensive data governance policies further protect sensitive patient information while ensuring compliance with global regulations like GDPR and HIPAA. This is vital as healthcare continues its digital transformation, with growing data volumes across various platforms.

- **Blockchain's Role in Transforming Healthcare**

Blockchain technology stands out as a transformative solution for securing health data and enabling secure, transparent sharing. Its decentralized, immutable nature provides enhanced protection while fostering patient trust and control over their data. Successful implementations in patient data sharing and pharmaceutical supply chains demonstrate blockchain's potential to revolutionize healthcare, improving both data security and operational efficiency.

- **Balancing Privacy, Scalability, and Practical Challenges**

While blockchain and encryption technologies provide robust security, their integration into existing healthcare systems presents challenges. Ensuring compatibility with legacy systems, overcoming scalability issues, and addressing the technical complexity of blockchain networks remain hurdles. However, the decentralized nature of blockchain offers scalability, and ongoing innovation is expected to address transaction speed and efficiency concerns.

- **The Future of Healthcare Security**

As healthcare organizations continue to embrace blockchain and encryption, these technologies will play a pivotal role in creating secure, patient-centered healthcare systems. By overcoming the challenges of data privacy, scalability, and system integration, blockchain and encryption will help build more efficient, transparent, and accessible healthcare solutions. The future of healthcare lies in creating systems that protect patient data while enabling seamless, secure data sharing across a global network.

REFERENCES

Bassan, S. (2020). Data privacy considerations for telehealth consumers amid COVID-19. *Journal of Law and the Biosciences*, 7(1), lsaa075. Advance online publication. DOI: 10.1093/jlb/lsaa075 PMID: 33269090

Christidis, K., & Devetsikiotis, M. (2016). Blockchains and Smart Contracts for the Internet of Things. *IEEE Access : Practical Innovations, Open Solutions*, 4, 2292–2303. DOI: 10.1109/ACCESS.2016.2566339

Chronicled. (2020). *Chronicled: Blockchain for Pharma Supply Chain*. Retrieved from Chronicled

European Commission. (2016). *General Data Protection Regulation (GDPR)*. Retrieved from https://ec.europa.eu/info/law/law-topic/data-protection/gdpr_en

Fatehi, F., Hassandoust, F., Ko, R. K. L., & Akhlaghpour, S. (2020). General Data Protection Regulation (GDPR) in Healthcare: Hot Topics and Research Fronts. *Studies in Health Technology and Informatics*, 270, 1118–1122. DOI: 10.3233/SHTI200336 PMID: 32570555

Gemini Health. (2020). *Gemini Health: Empowering Patients with Blockchain Technology*. Retrieved from Gemini Health.

Haleem, A., Javaid, M., Singh, R. P., & Suman, R. (2021). Telemedicine for healthcare: Capabilities, features, barriers, and applications. *Sensors International*, 2, 100117. DOI: 10.1016/j.sintl.2021.100117 PMID: 34806053

Hashed Health. (2018). *Using Blockchain to Enable Interoperability in Healthcare*. Retrieved from Hashed Health.

Jones, M. C., Stone, T., Mason, S. M., Eames, A., & Franklin, M. (2023). Navigating data governance associated with real-world data for public benefit: An overview in the UK and future considerations. *BMJ Open*, 13(10), e069925. DOI: 10.1136/bmjopen-2022-069925 PMID: 37793928

Kuo, T. T.. (2017). Blockchain in Healthcare Applications and Related Technologies. *Health Informatics Journal*, 23(2), 57–66.

Lawrence, K., Singh, N., Jonassen, Z., Groom, L. L., Alfaro Arias, V., Mandal, S., Schoenthaler, A., Mann, D., Nov, O., & Dove, G. (2023). Operational Implementation of Remote Patient Monitoring Within a Large Ambulatory Health System: Multimethod Qualitative Case Study. *JMIR Human Factors*, 10, e45166. DOI: 10.2196/45166 PMID: 37498668

Li, E., Clarke, J., Ashrafian, H., Darzi, A., & Neves, A. L. (2022). The Impact of Electronic Health Record Interoperability on Safety and Quality of Care in High-Income Countries: Systematic Review. *Journal of Medical Internet Research*, 24(9), e38144. DOI: 10.2196/38144 PMID: 36107486

Maan, A., & Haseeb, M. (2021). Cybersecurity in Health Care: A Systematic Review of Threats and Vulnerabilities. *Health Information Science and Systems*, 9(1), 1–15. PMID: 33235709

Maan, A., & Haseeb, M. (2021). Cybersecurity in Health Care: A Systematic Review of Threats and Vulnerabilities. *Health Information Science and Systems*, 9(1), 1–15. PMID: 33235709

McGraw, D., & Mandl, K. D. (2021). Privacy protections to encourage use of health-relevant digital data in a learning health system. *NPJ Digital Medicine*, 4(1), 2. DOI: 10.1038/s41746-020-00362-8 PMID: 33398052

MediLedger Project. (2021). *MediLedger: A Blockchain-based Network for the Pharmaceutical Supply Chain*. Retrieved from MediLedger

Miller, B. (2018). The Impact of Cybersecurity Breaches on Health Care Organizations. *Journal of Healthcare Management*, 63(5), 306–317. PMID: 30180027

Miller, B. (2018). The Impact of Cybersecurity Breaches on Health Care Organizations. *Journal of Healthcare Management*, 63(5), 306–317. PMID: 30180027

Mocydlarz-Adamcewicz, M., Bajsztok, B., Filip, S., Petera, J., Mestan, M., & Malicki, J. (2023). Management of Onsite and Remote Communication in Oncology Hospitals: Data Protection in an Era of Rapid Technological Advances. *Journal of Personalized Medicine*, 13(5), 761. DOI: 10.3390/jpm13050761 PMID: 37240931

Mok, E.. (2018). Empowering Patients: A Blockchain-Based Healthcare Data Management System. *Journal of Medical Systems*, 42(5), 1–10.

Monsen, K. A., Heermann, L., & Dunn-Lopez, K. (2023). FHIR-up! Advancing knowledge from clinical data through application of standardized nursing terminologies within HL7® FHIR®. *Journal of the American Medical Informatics Association : JAMIA*, 30(11), 1858–1864. DOI: 10.1093/jamia/ocad131 PMID: 37428893

. Nakamoto, S. (2008). *Bitcoin: A Peer-to-Peer Electronic Cash System*. Retrieved from Bitcoin.org

Nan, J., & Xu, L. Q. (2023). Designing Interoperable Health Care Services Based on Fast Healthcare Interoperability Resources: Literature Review. *JMIR Medical Informatics*, 11, e44842. DOI: 10.2196/44842 PMID: 37603388

Segal, M., Giuffrida, P., Possanza, L., & Bucciferro, D. (2022). The Critical Role of Health Information Technology in the Safe Integration of Behavioral Health and Primary Care to Improve Patient Care. *The Journal of Behavioral Health Services & Research*, 49(2), 221–230. DOI: 10.1007/s11414-021-09774-0 PMID: 34668115

Stergiou, C. L., Plageras, A. P., Memos, V. A., Koidou, M. P., & Psannis, K. E. (2024). Secure Monitoring System for IoT Healthcare Data in the Cloud. *Applied Sciences (Basel, Switzerland)*, 14(1), 120. DOI: 10.3390/app14010120

Sweeney, L. (2013). Health Data in the Age of Big Data. *Journal of Healthcare Information Management*, 27(1), 15–20.

Tazi, F., Nandakumar, A., Dykstra, J., Rajivan, P., & Das, S. (2024). SoK: Analyzing privacy and security of healthcare data from the user perspective. *ACM Transactions on Computing for Healthcare*, 5(2), 1–31.

U.S. Department of Health and Human Services. (2020). *Health Insurance Portability and Accountability Act (HIPAA)*. Retrieved from https://www.hhs.gov/hipaa/index.html

Vorisek, C. N., Lehne, M., Klopfenstein, S. A. I., Mayer, P. J., Bartschke, A., Haese, T., & Thun, S.C. N. (2022). Fast Healthcare Interoperability Resources (FHIR) for Interoperability in Health Research: Systematic Review. *JMIR Medical Informatics*, 10(7), e35724. DOI: 10.2196/35724 PMID: 35852842

Zhang, P.. (2018). Blockchain Technology Use Cases in Health Care. *Health Informatics Journal*, 24(2), 211–220.

Chapter 13
Cyber Security in the Context of Cloud Computing:
An Empirical Study of Australian SMEs

Ruwan Nagahawatta
https://orcid.org/0000-0002-5358-9184
Deakin University, Australia

Matthew Warren
RMIT University, Australia

Scott Salzman
https://orcid.org/0000-0003-1512-7445
Deakin University, Australia

Sachithra Lokuge
https://orcid.org/0000-0003-4558-687X
University of South Queensland, Australia

ABSTRACT

Cloud computing has provided enormous opportunities for small and medium-sized enterprises (SMEs) to digitalize their business processes. However, with increasing cloud computing adoption, security and privacy threats are on the rise. The aim of this book chapter is to examine the nature and the impact of cyber security threats to SMEs. In particular, by employing a quantitative approach, conducting a survey of 289 SMEs in Australia, this paper examines the cyber security practices, measures, and suggest solutions for effective cyber security practices in cloud environments. The findings highlight the most frequent cyber security threats faced by. SMEs and demonstrate the significant differences in cloud security practice measures among micro enterprises, small, and medium-sized enterprises.

DOI: 10.4018/979-8-3693-8784-9.ch013

INTRODUCTION

Over the past years, the cloud computing landscape has seen tremendous transformation, with notable advancements which include multi-cloud (i.e., using multiple cloud services), fog computing (i.e., extending cloud capabilities to the network edge), edge computing (i.e., processing data closer to its consumer), internet-of-things (IoT) and integration (i.e., connecting and managing IoT devices via cloud services) (Aljumah & Ahanger, 2020; Pahl et al., 2017; Walther et al., 2018). Since cloud computing does not require maintaining software servers in the firms' property, it offers a variety of advantages and commercial potential for organizations (Avram, 2014; Khalid et al., 2022). However, as these technologies improve, firms face several difficulties and challenges (Kaluarachchi et al., 2020; Sedera & Lokuge, 2019; Varghese & Buyya, 2018). For instance, the development of the fog computing system (i.e., enables processing, storage, and networking tasks to be performed on devices at the edge) increases problems as users can access a variety of nodes, which in turn raises concerns about risks (Gupta et al., 2013; Varghese & Buyya, 2018). Further, cloud security risks, trust, privacy, and data security issues related to traditional cloud technology remain a challenge (Lowry et al., 2017; Moody et al., 2018). The largest challenge related to cloud security is maintaining integrity, delegation of confidentiality, and availability of the information when a third party is involved (Alsafi & Fan, 2020; Lynn et al., 2018).

When considering the highly valued data stored in the cloud, the small and medium enterprises (SMEs), become a prime target for breaches. The main reasons for such vulnerability may be due to human negligence, lack of resources, targeted attacks, vulnerabilities, or security policy weaknesses. In terms of motive and technological exploits, security threats and attacks are varied. Such security risks range from malicious insider attacks to unintentional network setup errors in business settings that may arise due to the lack of contingency planning. Cloud computing, despite its various advantages, poses notable security challenges, especially for SMEs. Aljumah and Ahanger (2020) highlight the risk of data breaches and the potential misuse of cloud services, emphasizing the necessity for robust security measures. As a potential solution, Núñez et al. (2018) suggests a user-centered cyber security tailored approach that focuses on placing the user at the center of security measures for cloud computing. This approach is particularly applicable to SMEs. Additionally, Kumar and Goyal (2019) emphasize the vulnerabilities inherent in cloud technology, highlighting the importance of proactive measures to effectively mitigate potential risks. As such, one of the objectives of this study is to explore and understand various cyber threats and attacks associated with cloud computing in SMEs.

Since Australian SMEs have a large customer base, a high number of employees and trade in a growing economy, Australia is a promising market for cloud computing technology. In particular, recent Australian research on the use of cloud computing by SMEs has found that security concerns are one of the main barriers to adoption (Asiaei & Rahim, 2019; Senarathna et al., 2018). When analyzing SMEs, even though there are different types of SMEs amalgamated, it becomes immediately clear that previous research views them as a single category with shared traits. It is interesting that some studies emphasize the necessity to analyze them individually, with SMEs being further examined within the umbrella of micro, small, and medium-sized firms (López-Ortega et al., 2016). The number of employees (Gupta et al., 2015), capital investments, and annual turnover (Belás et al., 2015; Gibson & Vaart, 2008) are also considered as useful criteria to classify these organisations. It appears logical to anticipate that cyber security concerns and practice measures may differ by SME firm size as a result of these distinctive qualities.

Additionally, several studies have shown that firm size, namely the number of micro, small, and medium-sized businesses, is one of the primary factors in determining how businesses behave (Heidt et al., 2019; Lokuge & Duan, 2023; Skafi et al., 2020). Generalizing SME characteristics is never easy because their variability may be their most valuable quality (Belás et al., 2015). For instance, medium-sized businesses can theoretically set themselves out from small and micro businesses more effectively (Gupta & Barua, 2016). As a result, diversity within the SME sector has become a new area of academic interest (Belás et al., 2015).

The scope of today's cyber security issues extends to the security of IT systems deployed in enterprises as well as to the broader digital networks including critical national infrastructures (ACSC, 2021). However, a limited literature in this area has been devoted to studying cyber security issues and practices followed by these different SME categories. The motivation for devoting this effort is the lack of information on SME related security threats and practice measures in cloud environments and suggested solutions to mitigate potential threats. As such, this study analyzes existing cyber security situations and produces, with a comprehensive view of cyber security in a cloud context, by providing a complete picture of future challenges facing SMEs.

This book chapter is structured as follows. The background section details the literature review conducted for this study. Then the research methodology section describes the steps followed in the survey data collection and data analysis. The discussion section provides the findings of the analysis. Finally, the conclusion section provides contribution to research practice, limitation, and future research work.

RESEARCH BACKGROUND

While cloud computing offers many advantages for businesses, it has many drawbacks in terms of security, privacy, and trust, especially for SMEs (Khayer et al., 2020; Salim et al., 2015). Cloud technology security concerns have persisted in large organizations as well as SMEs. Because of cybercrime, billions of dollars have been lost, computer systems have broken down, vital data has been destroyed, network integrity and confidentiality have been compromised (Abdullah et al., 2019). There has been a significant increase in cybercrime reports over the past years, and as reported in the Australian Cyber Security Centre (ACSC)'s annual cybercrime report for July 2020 to June 2021, there has been an increase of nearly 13% when compared to the same period in the previous financial year (ACSC, 2021). Moreover, The Australian Signals Directorate (ASD) cyber threat report 2022-2023 emphasizes further how crucial it is for Australian SMEs to understand cyber security procedures.

Ensuring security and privacy of cloud computing is a complicated issue due to the multi-tenancy nature of virtual resources (Benlian and Hess, 2011; Kanwal et al., 2021; Rahi et al., 2017). Cloud users may perceive that security issues are reduced in cloud computing due to shared responsibility with a cloud service provider, which is expected to be efficient in managing such issues (Charlebois et al., 2016; Lynn et al., 2018). Among these factors, lack of transparency, lack of trustworthiness, and lower user control cause most issues. Tang and Liu (2015) conducted a survey that found data security is a top concern when using cloud services. Gupta et al. (2013) found that 50% of businesses report security as their greatest concern when making decisions. Concurring with this view, Safari et al. (2015) highlight that security is a primary determinant for developing cloud infrastructure. Palos-Sánchez (2017) argues that privacy concerns need to be evaluated when adopting location-based services. Li et al. (2008) report that lack of control among users on cloud-based services gives rise to security and privacy being the primary concern. Tancock et al. (2013) and Lian (2021) suggest security and security concerns are the factors most likely to discourage the adoption of cloud computing services, especially for SMEs, due to their limited resources, informal management style, inadequate infrastructure, and lack of skilled personnel (Varghese and Buyya, 2018). Even though much research has been conducted for large organizations, research on SME context is limited.

Cloud Computing Adoption in SMEs

Cloud computing has seen a paradigm shift in the use of information technology (IT) resources that can be provided over the Internet, whereby instead of organizations owning and managing hardware and software assets, they can access these resources via the cloud (Misra & Mondal, 2011). The National Institute of Standards and Technology (NIST) provides one of the most widely used definitions of cloud computing (Mell & Grance 2011, p. 2): "A model for enabling convenient, on-demand network access to a shared pool of configurable computing resources (e.g., network, servers, storage, applications and services) that can be rapidly provisioned and released with minimal management effort or service provider interaction." This study will adopt NIST definition as it describes a comprehensive conceptualization of cloud computing involving five essential characteristics (i.e., On-Demand Self-Service, Broad Network Access, Resource Pooling, Rapid Elasticity and Measured Service), three main cloud service models (i.e., Software as a Service (SaaS), Platform as a Service (PaaS), and Infrastructure as a Service (IaaS)), and four cloud deployment models (i.e., Public Cloud, Private Cloud, Hybrid Cloud, and Community Cloud).

An examination of cloud computing challenges shows that as businesses become more comfortable with cloud computing services and obtain more understanding, their security issues fade and focus shifts to other management problems. Figure 1 shows the findings of an industry report on cloud computing problems, which revealed that although security concerns remained critical problem when implementing cloud computing, companies also had concerns about governance, human resource availability, and regulatory compliance (Flexera 2021).

Figure 1. Top Cloud Computing Challenges (Source: Flexera 2023)

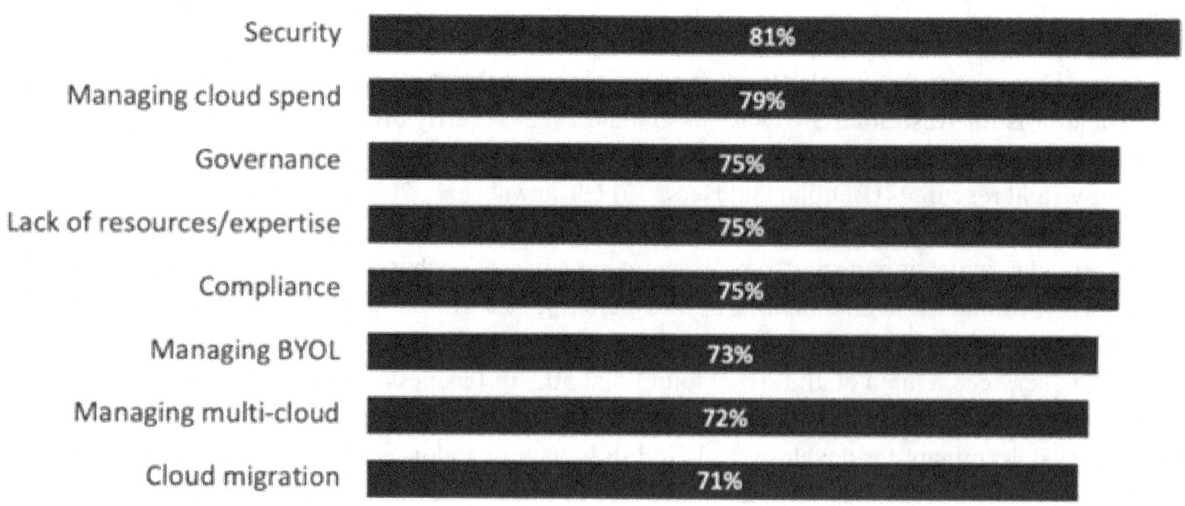

Nowadays, cloud-enabled solutions are applied across a variety of areas, such as business, government, medicine, education, and entertainment (Gochhait et al., 2022; Khayer et al., 2020; Walther et al., 2018). In this study, the term 'adoption' refers to the organizational decision to adopt a particular technology or behavior (Powell & DiMaggio, 2012). By adopting cloud services, organizations can save money, time, and resources (Khayer et al., 2020; Marston et al., 2011; Skafi et al., 2020). Cloud computing allows resources to be invested in other value-adding areas within companies, such as improved efficiency, agility, and the completion of operations (Carroll et al., 2011). Cloud computing enables businesses to be productive and efficient and is accessible not only to large organizations but also to small businesses (Sultan, 2012).

There is no universally recognized definition of SMEs, and those that do exist differ from nation to nation or even amongst institutions within the same nation. The definition of a small to medium-sized business (SME) typically includes parameters including the number of workers, capital value, revenue, estimated fixed asset value, and nature of the organization. SMEs are defined as those with fewer than 500 employees in Canada and the United States, while small business are defined as those with fewer than 100 employees and medium business as those with 101 to 500 employees (Beck et al., 2005). SMEs in Germany are defined as firms with a maximum of 250 employees, while SMEs in Belgium are defined as businesses with fewer than 100 employees (Katua, 2014). Australia has three different categories of SMEs: microbusinesses with fewer than four people, small businesses with between 5 and 19 employees, and medium-sized businesses with between 20 and 199 employees (ABS, 2019).

There are various and fundamental differences between large organizations and SMEs (Heidt et al., 2019; Mijnhardt et al., 2016). SMEs are often viewed as businesses with comparatively limited resources, highly centralized structures, low degree of formalization, informal management style, and lack of IT knowledge and security skills (Mijnhardt et al., 2016). Initial investigations reveal an increase in the volume and size of cyberattacks directed at SMEs.

Cloud computing security and privacy is a complicated issue due to the multi-tenancy nature of virtual resources (Benlian & Hess, 2011; Ramegowda et al., 2020). Cloud users can perceive that security issues are reduced in cloud computing due to shared responsibility with a cloud service provider, which is expected to be efficient in managing such issues (Charlebois et al.,2016; Lynn et al.,2018). Among these factors, lack of transparency, lack of trustworthiness, and lower user control cause most issues. Tang and Liu (2015) conducted a survey and found data privacy is the top concern when using cloud services. Gupta et al. (2013) found 50% of businesses report privacy as their greatest concern when making decisions. Safari et al. (2015) report that privacy is a primary determinant for developing cloud infrastructure. Palos-Sánchez (2017) argues that privacy concerns need to be evaluated when adopting location-based services. Lynn et al. (2018) report that lack of control among users on cloud-based services gives rise to privacy being the primary concern. Lian (2021) suggests security and privacy concerns are the factors most likely to discourage the adoption of cloud computing services, especially for SMEs, due to their limited resources, informal management style, inadequate infrastructure, and skilled personnel (Varghese & Buyya, 2018). Therefore, it is crucial to examine the security requirements for cloud computing adoption in SMEs context, as security frameworks and practice measures applied to larger firms may not be applicable to SMEs.

According to Heidt et al. (2019), SMEs tend to be more risk averse than large organizations, due to limited resources and a greater sensitivity to potential financial losses. Further, SMEs perceive security and privacy features of the cloud to be more complicated and more difficult to identify compared to large organizations. Cloud computing security challenges are linked to both technological and socio-technical factors (Amron et al., 2019; Lynn et al., 2018). For example, trust in cloud service providers (CSPs), cloud security standards, and skilled personnel (Hossain et al., 2023). Trusted relationships between service providers and users can be developed by considering new and additional elements at the time of interaction (Alassafi et al., 2017). Substantial risk of data theft, damage loss, and misuse can occur when data is being transferred to a third party. This risk cannot be mitigated completely even if policies are incorporated (Senyo et al., 2016). These aspects provide insights into how SMEs' security and privacy needs affect their decision to utilize cloud computing.

Additionally, several studies have shown that firm size, namely the number of micro, small, and medium-sized businesses, is one of the primary factors in determining how businesses behave (Heidt et al., 2019; Skafi et al., 2020). According to Paik (2011), company size affects how well it performs. Firm size is frequently used to draw boundaries between different business divisions (Tornatzky & Fleischer, 1990). According to Cataldo, Pino, and McQueen (2020), the adoption of IT varies among micro, small, and medium-sized businesses. Generalizing about SMEs is never easy because their variability may be their most valuable quality (Belás et al., 2015). For instance, medium-sized businesses can theoretically set themselves out from tiny and micro businesses more effectively (Gupta & Barua, 2016). As a result, diversity within the SME sector has emerged as a novel focus of academic review (Belás et al., 2015).

Cyber Security Issues and Cloud Computing

The complex nature of cyber security leads to a lack of consensus on its definition. For example, Goutam (2015) defines cyber security as the procedures and technology created to prevent unauthorized access to computers and computer networks. In a similar notion, cyber security is defined by the International Telecommunication Union (ITU) as the "collection of tools, policies, security concepts, security safeguards, guidelines, risk management approaches, actions, training, best practices, assurances, and technologies used to protect the cyber environment" (ITU, n.d). Today, businesses deal with a huge range of cyber security issues, both external threats and internal vulnerabilities, which are continuously evolving (Luo, 2022; Nagahawatta et al., 2018). Ransomware attacks can have devastating effects on organizations, and victims may require significant recovery time to restore critical services. There was a 15% rise in ransomware attacks in the 2020–21 financial year, and the impact on vulnerable Australian organizations can be staggering in many ways (ACSC, 2021). In terms of motivations and technological flaws, cyber security concerns are varied. From intentionally malicious insider assaults to unintentional enterprise network misconfiguration, from a lack of contingency planning to automated exploitation of known security flaws (Sinha et al., 2019). In circumstances like data loss or misuse, unauthorized access, unavailability, or infrastructure failure, the loss of user control may be troublesome (Ani et al., 2017). Organizations may have a number of vulnerabilities as a result of ignorance. For instance, a lack of expertise can leave any business open to phishing and other social engineering scams.

Ensuring the security and privacy of cloud computing presents a complex challenge due to the multi-tenancy nature of virtual resources (Benlian and Hess, 2011; Kanwal et al., 2021; Rahi et al., 2017). Cloud users may believe that security issues are diminished in cloud computing because of shared responsibility with service providers, who are expected to efficiently manage such concerns (Charlebois et al., 2016). However, issues like lack of transparency, trustworthiness, and user control remain significant (Lynn et al., 2018). Furthermore, Gupta et al. (2013) found that 50% of businesses identify privacy as their greatest concern in decision-making. Thus, privacy concerns need to be carefully evaluated, especially in contexts such as location-based services and cloud-based service usage where user control may be limited (Li et al., 2008; Safari et al., 2015). Consequently, security and privacy issues are particularly pertinent for SMEs, given their resource limitations, informal management styles, and lack of skilled personnel (Tancock et al., (2013); Lian., 2021). Despite extensive research on security in larger organizations, studies focusing on SMEs are limited, underscoring the importance of examining security requirements tailored to their context (Varghese and Buyya, 2018).

According to the literature review, in terms of the adoption of cloud computing, the most frequently discussed security requirements across different contexts can be classified into eight key security related factors. Table 1 presents a summary of papers reviewed that relate to these key security factors and classifies the papers based on their findings. Most findings related to data security concerns. Cloud security trust and legal and regulatory compliance related factors are discussed by several studies. On the other hand, few studies considered the benefits of cloud security over traditional computing. Data security and data privacy are core issues in the adoption of cloud computing. Cloud computing security challenges are linked to both technological and socio-technical factors, such as legal compliance, trust in CSPs, cloud security standards and skilled personnel. These factors provide insight into the security requirements of SMEs that influence cloud computing adoption.

Table 1. Classification of Accepted Articles Related to Security Factors

Factors	Code	References
Technology readiness	Perceived technical competence, network security, technology support infrastructure, organisation security policy and security governance, authorisation, identity management, security culture in organisation.	Al-Mascati and Al-Badi 2016; Ali et al. 2014; Al-Omar et al. 2019; Gupta and Misra 2016; Gutierrez et al. 2015; Karunagaran et al. 2019; Klug et al. 2015; Lian et al. 2014; Mangula et al. 2014; Nedev 2014; Oliveira et al. 2014; Skafi et al. 2020; Tsai and Hung 2014
Legal compliance	Forensics, legal compliance, SLA, accountability and government regulation.	Aleem and Sprott 2013; Carcary 2014; Gupta and Misra 2016; Hinde and Van Belle 2012; Klug et al. 2015; Marston et al. 2011; Palos-Sánchez 2017; Wilson et al. 2015
Cloud security standards	ISO/IEC 27002 for Cloud services, ISO 27001:2013 and COBIT5, NIST.	Ayong and Naidoo 2019; Tehrani and Shirazi 2014; Wilson et al. 2015
Trust in CSPs	Cloud environments openness, reputation, vendor trustworthiness, social engineering, trust in vendor.	Alharbi et al. 2017; Ali et al. 2018b; Ayong and Naidoo 2019; Charlebois et al. 2016; Doherty 2015; Gupta et al. 2013; Gupta and Misra 2016; Jelonek et al. 2014; Li et al. 2015; Safari et al. 2015; Sultan 2011; Yeboah-Boateng 2014
Skilled personnel	Awareness, professionalism, IT experts, top management support.	Ali et al. 2018b; Amron et al. 2017; Ayong and Naidoo 2019; Gangwar et al. 2015; Gonzalez et al. 2012; Lynn et al. 2018
Data security concerns	Vendor lock-in, data lack of protection, confidentiality, data storage, data transmission and availability.	Ali et al. 2014; Amron et al. 2017; Ayong and Naidoo 2019; Carcary 2014; Dekker and Liveri 2015; Gonzalez et al. 2012; Gupta et al. 2013; Hinde and Van Belle 2012; Marston et al. 2011 Oliveira et al. 2014; Palos-Sánchez 2017; Senarathna et al. 2018; Skafi et al. 2020; Sultan 2011; Wilson et al. 2015
Data privacy concerns	Data location, sensitive data protection, anonymisation, transparency, data sharing control, lack of data privacy, data oversight.	Aleem and Sprott 2013; Amron et al. 2017; Al-Omar et al. 2019; Doherty 2015; Gupta et al. 2013; Hinde and Van Belle 2012; Palos-Sánchez 2017; Senarathna et al. 2018; Sultan 2011; Wilson et al. 2015
Perceived cloud security benefits	Cloud security auditing, physical security, data backup and data encryption.	Alharbi et al. 2017; Dekker and Liveri 2015; Hinde and Van Belle 2012; Wilson et al. 2015

Additionally, failing to update personal knowledge and showing little concern for professional development might result in a lack of knowledge of contemporary cyberthreats including Distributed Denial of Service (DDoS) attacks, social engineering, hacktivism, and credential harvesting malware (ACSC, 2021). This demonstrates that staff members at times do not apply due diligence, which has resulted in a variety of financial and legal concerns. The security of IT systems used in businesses as well as wider digital networks, including crucial national infrastructures, are all included in the scope of cyber security challenges (Ani et al., 2017). Sadly, preliminary security studies by the government, including ACSC (2021), suggest an increase in cyber threats affecting businesses, but with little knowledge of the traits of the attacks and their potential consequences. To have a clear image of cyber security practice measures in connection to SMEs, it is crucial to assess current cyber security threats, vulnerabilities, and their remedies with a broad perspective on cyber security. New technologies provide significant advantages and economic prospects. However, they also increase concerns regarding risk, security and privacy, especially for SMEs (Mijnhardt et al., 2016). In order to have a full image of cyber security practice measures in relation to SMEs, it is crucial to assess current cyber security threats, vulnerabilities, and their remedies with a comprehensive view of cyber security.

The International Organization for Standardization (ISO) provides ISO 27002 standard, which applies to cloud-based services, is a new set of principles for information system controls and solutions for cloud computing, which was later released as ISO/IEC 27017 (ISO/IEC, 2015). Further, the ISO defines security measures that can guide the effective security needs of cloud computing (Rebollo et al., 2015). These are confidentiality (i.e., keeping user data private and limiting access to privileged parties), availability (i.e., ensure that the user's desired data or the applications he requires are always available, everywhere and at any time), authorization (i.e., confirm that the users who have requested the specific information have the authorization to access it), integrity (i.e., ensure that data isn't changed or modified while it's being carried or stored, and that only people with permission can alter, modify, copy, or delete data.), and authentication (i.e., prior to providing access to information, confirm the user's identity by applying appropriate profile protections).

The Key Cyber Security Practice Measures and Threats in the Cloud Context

Organizations increasingly rely on information infrastructure within a connected cyberspace, presenting a heightened cyber security threat. Consequently, security measures are necessary to safeguard the availability, confidentiality, and integrity of data. However, Calderaro and Craig (2020) highlight that a lack of understanding about cyberspace has led to fragmented efforts in addressing cyber security challenges. According to previous studies, data encryption, encrypted cloud service, security information event management, trained cloud security professional, vulnerability assessment, access control (e.g., cloud access security brokers), log management and analytics, privileged access management (PAM), data leakage prevention and security insurance are the most often employed security measures in companies (Ani et al., 2017; Luo, 2022; Calderaro & Craig, 2020).

Three primary categories of security threats are identified in the literature that are present in cloud environments: threats to availability, integrity, and confidentiality, known as threats to the Confidentiality, Integrity, and Availability (CIA) triad (Aldossary & Allen 2016; Sharma & Trivedi, 2014). Regarding cloud computing, confidentiality refers to set policies or agreements that control access to, and limitations on, different kinds of data stored on the cloud, protecting user privacy. On the other hand, data integrity is concerned with the entirety of the data that is kept in the cloud, ensuring data consistency, authenticity, and regularity. Lastly, availability refers to the capacity to use systems and obtain data (Sharma & Trivedi, 2014).

It is essential to examine cyber security threats in the cloud computing context and understand the security issues of businesses in order to gain a thorough grasp of the threats that SMEs face. Previous surveys suggest that unauthorized access, external sharing of data, hijacking of accounts, services, or traffic, malicious insiders, malware/phishing/ransomware, misconfiguration of the cloud platform, denial of service attacks and insecure interfaces (APIs) are among the most commonly implemented security measures in businesses (Center for Internet Security, 2016; NIST, 2014; Rebollo et al., 2015; Steffani, 2006).

According to Heidt et al. (2019), SMEs exhibit more risk aversion compared to large organizations. Additionally, SMEs perceive the security and privacy features of the cloud as more intricate and challenging to identify than do larger organizations. Security related challenges of cloud computing are linked to both technological and socio-technical factors (Amron et al., 2017; Lynn et al., 2018). For instance, trust in cloud service providers (CSPs), adherence to cloud security standards, and the availability of skilled personnel are key factors influencing the decision to adopt cloud computing (Walther et al., 2018). Establishing trusted relationships between service providers and users can be facilitated by integrating new and additional elements during interactions (Alassafi et al., 2017; Heals et al., 2017). Despite the incorporation of policies, there remains a significant risk of data theft, loss, and misuse during data transfer to a third party, which cannot be completely mitigated (Senyo et al., 2016). These insights shed light on how the security and privacy needs of SMEs impact their decision-making regarding cloud computing adoption

The ACSC claims that because cybercriminals are becoming more skilled and are adapting their tradecraft to target certain businesses, cybercrime poses a threat to Australia's national and economic development. Criminals will continue to find cybercrime to be a lucrative alternative since it allows them to make significant sums of money with little chance of detection and prosecution (ACSC, 2021). No matter how problematic cyber security threats are, Australian SMEs are aware of their importance, according to the ACSC (2021) report. When striving to implement effective cyber security procedures, especially for micro enterprises, SMEs encounter significant obstacles. Budgetary constraints, a lack of cyber security support staff, the complexity of cyber security, difficulties understanding and putting security measures into practice, an underestimation of the risk and consequences of a cyber incident, and a gap in preparation for, and response to, cyber incidents, are just some of these obstacles. Additionally, these obstacles may differ for micro, small, and medium-sized businesses. As such, this study attempts to explore this notion.

RESEARCH METHODOLOGY

There has been a rapid development of digital infrastructure in recent years in Australia (Cynch, 2021) and 95.5% of Australian SMEs were projected to be connected to some form of online service (ABS, 2019). In relation to cloud computing, the largest challenge related to security is maintaining integrity, the delegation of confidentiality, and the availability of information when a third party is involved (Alsafi & Fan, 2020; Lynn et al., 2018). This study aims to investigate and compare cyber security practice measures and threats in cloud computing within SMEs, with specific consideration of organizational size. Employing a quantitative approach, the research analyzes cyber security practice measures and threats across micro-enterprises, small, and medium-sized enterprises in Australia. This article is a part of a cloud computing security and privacy research project aimed to develop a security and privacy framework to support cloud computing adoption in the SMEs sector.

Considering the objective of the study, the high prevalence of Internet use by Australian SMEs (ACMA 2020), the wide area over which SMEs are located in Australia, and the evolving landscape of SMEs that are trading at any given time, an online survey tool was the considered as the best way to collect data for this study. Online surveys have been built to ensure that respondents answer only specially designed questions (i.e., radio button). If cloud computing is used by a particular SME, the online option directs respondents to a specific set of questions. This reduces the risk of confusion, minimizes input errors, and makes the survey simpler. The survey was developed and constructed using the well-known online survey platform Qualtrics software.

At the time of conducting the pilot study, the reliability of the questions was assessed and enhanced question clarity before the main survey was conducted with the support of a market research company. The researcher contacted potential participants by email; among 50 SMEs randomly selected, 28 SMEs returned the completed surveys. Feedback was sought from these 28 SMEs on all questions based on their experience and understanding of cloud computing adoption. The pilot study indicated that the respondents were given adequate time (25 minutes) to complete the questionnaire (i.e., adequately pre-piloted and tested). To increase the validity and reliability of the questions, minor modifications were made for the following data collection phase. The pilot study participants also commented that the survey was easy to understand. The primary study was then undertaken, and information was gathered from SME owners, IT managers, and decision-makers in the IT department. The primary survey targeted SMEs throughout all Australian states and territories.

In this investigation, initially a list of prospective 1,410 Australian SMEs were obtained from the identified sampling frame of approximately 4,500 Australian SMEs using the lottery method. Of the 1,410 organizations that were initially identified randomly and then invited to participate in this research, 339 participated. Responses from 50 surveys were excluded from the final sample because respondents did not meet the eligibility criteria, resulting in data from 289 usable surveys being considered acceptable and used in the ensuing data analysis. Appreciating that the population of SMEs is continually changing in a landscape the size of Australia, it was neither possible nor practical to identify all possible participants and obtain a truly random sample. Determining the appropriate sample size is important for generating consistent, reliable statistical, and meaningful empirical research results (Hair et al., 2014; Sedera et al., 2003). Researchers suggest sample sizes ranging from 100 to 500 respondents, depending on the number of variables (Wrenn et al., 2007; Zikmund et al., 2013).

This study employed a quantitative approach to examine what key cyber security threats, vulnerabilities, and security practice measures adopted in cloud context among Australian micro, small, and medium enterprises. Descriptive statistics describes the characteristics of a data set (Amrhein et al., 2019). In order to identify the similarities and differences in cyber behaviors throughout the three types of SME categories, we first considered descriptive statistics. The chi squared (X^2) analysis, is a method used to determine if there is a significant association between two categorical variables. It is often used to analyze data in contingency tables, where the frequencies of two categorical variables are cross tabulated against each other. If the difference between the expected and observed frequencies is significant, it suggests that there may be an association between the variables. Australian SMEs, which are geographically dispersed across all Australian states and territories, serve as the study's unit of analysis. Around 95.5% of SMEs in Australia are reportedly using an Internet service (ACMA, 2020). A survey instrument with appropriate demographics and measures was created and tested. The survey instrument was divided into two sections namely cyber security threats and cloud computing usage practice measures.

DATA ANALYSIS AND RESULTS

The demographic details of these responses were considered: the size of the organizations, the location of the firm within Australia (state or territory), and organizations' length of operation. The descriptive statistics that were employed are shown in Table 1. In accordance with the organizational profile based on the total number of employees at the time of this study, 57.4% (n=166) of respondents are from organizations with 1 to 4 employees, 24.6% from 5 to 19 employees, and 18% from 20 to 199 people. Greater response rates came from the populous states: 28.7% (n=83) of the respondents are from New South Wales (NSW), followed by Victoria (VIC) (24.6%; n=75), and Queensland (QLD) (19.7%; n=57). The remaining organizations were from Tasmania (TAS) (3.8%), West Australia (WA) (12.2%), South Australia (SA) (7.6%), the Northern Territory (NT) (1%) and the Australian Capital Territory (ACT) (2.4%). This sample concurs with the general population distribution, whereby most businesses are usually based in NSW.

Further, most SMEs had been in existence for between 6 and 10 years (40.1%; n=136), while 33.2 percent (n=113) had been operating for more than 10 years. Overall, 23.2% (n=79) had been operating for one to five years and only a few (3.5%; n=12) had been operating for less than one year. In summary, more than 70% of respondents have operated for more than five years. Moreover, Australian postcodes were used to classify the organizations' locations. The results of the sample indicate that 35.6% of respondents were from regional areas and 64.4% of respondents were from metropolitan areas. Demographic characteristics results are shown in Table 2 below.

Table 2. Demographic characteristics of responding organizations.

Demographic Variable	Item	Frequency	Percentage
Organization size	1-4 (micro)	166	57.4
	5-19 (small)	71	24.6
	20-199 (medium)	52	18.0
State or Territory	NSW	83	28.7
	VIC	71	24.6
	QLD	57	19.7
	WA	35	12.2
	SA	22	7.6
	TAS	11	3.8
	NT	3	1.0
	ACT	7	2.4

continued on following page

Table 2. Continued

Demographic Variable	Item	Frequency	Percentage
Cloud Computing Applications	Email and Office Applications	79	27.3
	Payroll	47	16.3
	Human Resources	44	15.2
	Sales and Marketing	39	13.5
	Accounting and Finance	26	9.0
	Cloud ERP system	21	7.3
	Application development on Cloud	9	3.1
	Other	24	8.3
Location	Regional	103	35.6
	Metro	186	64.4
Length of Operation	Less than a year	10	3.5
	1 to 5 years	67	23.2
	6 to 10 years	116	40.1
	More than 10 years	96	33.2

Cyber Threats Amongst Micro, Small and Medium Enterprises

Examining connections between security threats and vulnerabilities by enterprise size was done using cross tabulations (Table 3). In order to find major variations in threats and vulnerabilities, the data were analyzed, compared, and the results were produced in tabular format. Malware/phishing/ransomware, insecure interfaces, external sharing of data, hijacking of accounts services or traffic, insecure interfaces, misconfiguration of the cloud platform, and 21.9% unauthorized access were the threats and vulnerabilities that accounted for the highest percentage in micro-sized enterprises and small businesses, respectively (unauthorized access, 20.6%; external sharing of data, 13.7%; and malicious insiders, 13%). When compared to smaller businesses, medium sized businesses are more than twice as likely to experience a malicious insider attack. However, there are no differences between small and medium-sized enterprises or between micro and small businesses ($X^2 = 6.96$, $p < 0.05$). Assessment of the current situation all other cyber threats are not dependent on the size of the company.

Table 3. Cloud Security Threats and Vulnerabilities

	Micro	Small	Medium	x^2
Unauthorized access	21.9% (68)	19.8% (41)	20.6% (27)	1.54
Insecure interfaces (APIs)	15.8% (49)	11.1% (23)	9.9% (13)	2.43
External sharing of data	18.0% (56)	14.5% (30)	13.7% (18)	1.71
Hijacking of accounts, services, or traffic	10.0% (31)	13.5% (28)	9.2% (12)	2.15
Malicious insiders	5.1% (16)	7.2% (15)	13.0% (17)	6.96*

continued on following page

Table 3. Continued

	Micro	Small	Medium	$_{x}2$
Malware/Phishing/Ransomware	13.8% (43)	10.6% (22)	9.9% (13)	1.86
Misconfiguration of the cloud platform	6.8% (21)	11.1% (23)	7.6% (10)	3.08
Denial of service attacks	3.2% (10)	6.8% (14)	6.9% (9)	3.96
Other	5.5% (17)	5.3% (11)	9.2% (12)	3.47

Note. Percentages indicate the percentage of security threats and vulnerabilities and size of enterprise. Statistics indicate whether percentages significantly vary across enterprises size for each of the category, * $p < 0.05$.

Cyber Security Practice Measures Amongst Micro, Small, and Medium Enterprises

Cross tabulation studies were undertaken by looking at the linkages between security solutions by type of enterprise to understand how SMEs deal with cloud security practice measures for various types of SMEs. The findings of the data analysis determine important security solution differences are shown in Table 4. If SMEs use encrypted cloud services and data encryption, they are thought to be more protected against cloud computing dangers. The percentage of cloud security solutions in micro-sized organizations was lower (18.4% for encrypted cloud services, 13.7% for access control, and 11.1% for security insurance) (encrypted cloud service, 15.7%; data encryption, 14.9%; trained cloud security professional, 12.6%; security information event management, 10.7%; access control, 10.7%). Higher percentages of medium-sized and small-sized businesses were found to employ trained cloud security professionals and use data encryption (data encryption, 18.1%; encrypted cloud service, 14%; trained cloud security professional, 13.2%; security information event management, 12.3%).

In comparison to small-sized organizations, medium-sized organizations show a higher percentage of responses for data encryption, trained Cloud security professionals, and security information event management ($_{x}2 = 7.26$, $p < 0.05$; $_{x}2 = 5.08$, $p < 0.05$; $_{x}2 = 8.32$, $p < 0.01$, respectively) that were significant across the size of the enterprises. Additionally, when compared to both small and medium-sized firms, security solutions suggesting the use of data leakage prevention technologies were higher for micro-sized businesses ($_{x}2 = 5.02$, $p < 0.05$).

Table 4. Cyber Security Practice Measures

	Micro	Small	Medium	$_{x}2$
Data encryption	11.1% (35)	14.9% (39)	18.1% (44)	7.26*
Encrypted cloud service	18.4% (58)	15.7% (41)	14.0% (34)	3.89
Security Information Event Management	7.6% (24)	10.7% (28)	12.3% (30)	5.08*
Trained cloud security professional	7.3% (23)	12.6% (33)	13.2% (32)	8.32**
Vulnerability assessment	4.4% (14)	8.0% (21)	7.4% (18)	4.97*
Access control (e.g., cloud access security brokers)	13.7% (43)	10.7% (28)	8.6% (21)	1.81
Log management and analytics	3.5% (11)	3.1% (8)	4.9% (12)	2.01
Privileged access management (PAM)	9.8% (31)	5.4% (14)	6.2% (15)	2.75

continued on following page

Table 4. Continued

	Micro	Small	Medium	x^2
Data leakage prevention	10.8% (34)	6.1% (16)	4.9% (12)	5.02*
Security Insurance	6.0% (19)	6.9% (18)	5.8% (14)	0.74
Other	7.3% (23)	5.7% (15)	4.5% (11)	3.53

Note. Percentages indicate the percentage of security threats and vulnerabilities and size of enterprise. Statistics indicate whether percentages significantly vary across enterprises size for each of the category, * $p < 0.05$, ** $p < 0.01$.

DISCUSSION

The aim of this study was to examine cyber security threats and practice measures in a cloud context among SMEs in Australia. Large Australian enterprises have adopted more than 70% of cloud computing services; however, the adoption of SMEs is less than 40% due to various challenges (ABS, 2019). Many current and developing technologies, including multi-cloud, fog computing, edge computing and IoT, are the advances in the cloud computing landscape (Tabrizchi and Rafsanjani, 2020). The concerns and challenges already present are made even more demanding and difficult when cloud computing incorporates all the aforementioned technologies (Kanwal et al., 2021; Nagahawatta, 2022).

Therefore, there is a need to understand the security threats, practice measures and the mitigation measures in cloud computing context among SMEs. This study shows key findings that have implications for cloud computing adoption. Research findings show that SME's adoption of cloud computing depends on security and privacy factors such as human, technological, environmental, and organizational context (Nagahawatta et al., 2021). Further, factors such as perceived security and privacy threats, and poor understanding of the perceived security benefits may inhibit SMEs' decisions to adopt cloud computing (Nagahawatta & Warren 2020).

Overall, the security issues facing SMEs in cloud environments include unauthorized access, external data sharing, malware, phishing, ransomware, incorrect cloud platform configuration, malicious insiders, and the exploitation of insecure interfaces, among other things. The risks of data loss and server manipulation from untrusted sources are major problems for SMEs operating in the cloud environment, and these situations put the data integrity of organizations at risk. When it comes to the accessibility of information in the cloud and the cost of adopting the technology, malicious insiders, malware, phishing, and ransomware pose serious threats to SMEs.

SMEs face unique challenges due to inadequate security expertise, trust issues related to cloud computing adoption, and compliance issues (Alam et al., 2018; Nagahawatta et al., 2020). The multi-tenancy features of the cloud environment, unsecured API interfaces, security misconfiguration, server location, and data backup are the main security concerns for SMEs when it comes to cloud infrastructure. With the exception of threats from malevolent insiders, the study concluded that the main cyber security dangers and vulnerabilities associated to cloud computing are not dependent on the size of the enterprises. Malicious insiders in the cloud can be current or former workers, contractors, or a reputable cloud service provider who abuses their power to get unauthorized access to crucial assets in the cloud.

Any organization that deals with them faces serious security risks. The network of an organization and some of the sensitive resources in houses are already accessible to a malicious insider. Compared to micro and small enterprises, medium-sized companies may have many outside vendors with access to their internal networks, making the network even more prone to security breaches. Furthermore, on a smaller network than on a network with numerous employees, illegal IT behaviors are much simpler to record, identify, and correct.

According to this study, data encryption, security information event management, skilled cloud security specialists, vulnerability assessment, access control, privileged access management, and data leakage prevention are the most often employed security techniques by businesses. For encrypted cloud services, access control, privileged access management, log management and analytics, and security insurance, there was no appreciable difference between micro, small, and medium-sized organizations. This study shows that there are significant differences between medium, small, and micro enterprises' experiences with security practice measures and techniques like data encryption, security information event management, trained cloud security professionals, vulnerability assessment, and data leakage prevention. However, the results of this study showed that knowledge of cyber security among Australian micro enterprises is relatively low, thereby they are vulnerable to cyber security threats in the cloud environment.

Compared to smaller enterprises, SMEs reported using advanced security procedures and methods for data encryption, security information event management, trained cloud security professional, and vulnerability assessment. However, compared to the other two bigger sized businesses, micro industries exercised superior data leakage protection. This implies that, in comparison to medium-sized businesses, micro and small businesses are less impacted by this aspect of security. Micro businesses frequently lack cyber security capabilities, as well as the budget, time, and knowledge necessary to fight against online threats. Australian micro enterprises typically rely on third parties because they lack a strong understanding of cyber security, control techniques, and security technologies in a cloud environment.

CONCLUSION

The study investigated existing cyber security practice measures, along with techniques for mitigating security threats in cloud computing environments and managing cloud security risks. The initial findings of the study indicate that common security methods employed by SMES include data encryption, encrypted cloud service, security information event management, trained cloud security professional, vulnerability assessment, access control (e.g., cloud access security brokers), log management and analytics, PAM, data leakage prevention and security insurance. Additional review of the literature finds that SMEs in the cloud namely unauthorized access, external sharing of data, hijacking of accounts, services, or traffic, malicious insiders, malware/phishing/ransomware, misconfiguration of the cloud platform, denial of service attacks and insecure interfaces (APIs)

Further, this study found significant differences in cyber security practice measures among micro, small, and medium enterprises. For example, data encryption, security information event management, trained cloud security professionals, vulnerability assessment, access control, privileged access management and data leakage prevention all exhibit lower levels of impact for micro and small sized firms, when compared to medium sized firms. However, and interestingly, micro sized enterprises exhibit higher levels of data leakage prevention compared to small and medium sized enterprises. Therefore, the study emphasizes the importance of SMEs prioritizing risk management to mitigate security threats in the cloud.

Contribution to Research and Practice

This study focuses on the cyber security aspects of identifying security threats and current practice measures in the cloud environment. The technical, human, and organizational security aspects can be identified as a mitigation method that impact SMEs. These factors should be an essential part to consider achieving effective cyber security measures for SMEs to overcome any cloud security implementation issues. Further, cyber security initiatives should be taken in collaboration with the government and cloud computing providers to effectively use cloud computing. This study has three major contributions. First, this study explores the differences in cyber security threats among various SME types. Second, this study investigates the differences in cyber security practice measures. In particular, this study looks at various security measures applied by types of SMEs. Third, this study explores current cyber security solutions for security challengers in the context of cloud computing.

By separating the sample into three categories—micro, small, and medium—this study contributes to illustrate the diversity of cyber security concerns and procedures. In particular with regard to size of the Australian enterprises, the study fills the research gap and offers meaningful evidence on these concerns. The findings show that while micro level firms face comparable cyber security risks and weaknesses, there are important disparities in how they approach security of cloud computing. A possible explanation for this might be a lack of resources or a lack of knowledge about cloud computing and its procedures. Additionally, SMEs are often less concerned with cloud security and privacy issues, in part because they lack dedicated security experts and the costs that go along with it. Lastly, SMEs also face common security challenges related to data protection, integrity, availability, and the risks of data loss and privacy breaches. Therefore, a multi-tiered solution is necessary to address these concerns effectively.

The study findings can be broadly applied to SMEs due to the characteristic nature of cloud computing. By focusing on the primary threats specific to SMEs, the study contributes to the growing body of research on security risks and threats faced by SMEs in cloud environments. As SMEs are generally not capable of significant investment on cyber security, it is essential for cloud service providers, professional bodies, and the government to devise strategies for the widespread adoption of cloud computing for these businesses. For cloud service providers it is important to identify the differences among different SMEs and provide purpose driven, adapted cyber security solutions.

Limitation and Future Work

The implications of this study for other regions should be carefully addressed since it solely focuses on SMEs in Australia. Results might not be readily transferrable to SMEs from various regions of the world, for instance. Therefore, the addition of perspectives from SMEs in various nations would have improved this study. The study's use of quantitative data is also restricted. In-depth qualitative research, including case studies and longitudinal studies, is necessary to comprehend this phenomenon more completely. Case studies could be the main topic of future study to examine the effects of security and privacy on SMEs. Future research can also concentrate on cyber security issue mitigation techniques.

REFERENCES

Abdullah, A., Hamad, R., Abdulrahman, M., Moala, H., & Elkhediri, S. (2019). *Cyber Security: a review of internet of things (IoT) security issues, challenges and techniques.*

Alassafi, M. O., Alharthi, A., Walters, R. J., & Wills, G. B. (2017). A framework for critical security factors that influence the decision of cloud adoption by Saudi government agencies. *Telematics and Informatics*, 34(7), 996–1010. DOI: 10.1016/j.tele.2017.04.010

Aldossary, S., & Allen, W. (2016). Data security, privacy, availability and integrity in cloud computing: Issues and current solutions. *International Journal of Advanced Computer Science and Applications*, 7(4), 485–498. DOI: 10.14569/IJACSA.2016.070464

Aljumah, A., & Ahanger, T. A. (2020). Cybersecurity threats, challenges and defence mechanisms in cloud computing. *IET Communications*, 14(7), 1185–1191. DOI: 10.1049/iet-com.2019.0040

Alsafi, T., & Fan, I.-S. (2020). *Cloud Computing Adoption Barriers Faced by Saudi Manufacturing SMEs.*

Amrhein, V., Trafimow, D., & Greenland, S. (2019). Inferential statistics as descriptive statistics: There is no replication crisis if we don't expect replication. *The American Statistician, 73*(sup1), 262-270.

Amron, M. T., Ibrahim, R., Bakar, N. A. A., & Chuprat, S. (2019). Determining factors influencing the acceptance of cloud computing implementation. *Procedia Computer Science*, 161, 1055–1063. DOI: 10.1016/j.procs.2019.11.216

Ani, U. P. D., He, H., & Tiwari, A. (2017). Review of cybersecurity issues in industrial critical infrastructure: Manufacturing in perspective. *Journal of Cyber Security Technology*, 1(1), 32–74. DOI: 10.1080/23742917.2016.1252211

Asiaei, A., & Rahim, N. Z. A. (2019). A multifaceted framework for adoption of cloud computing in Malaysian SMEs. *Journal of Science and Technology Policy Management.*

Australian Bureau of Statistics (ABS). (2019). *Characteristics of Australian Business 2017–18.* Retrieved from https://www.abs.gov.au/ausstats/abs%40.nsf/mf/8167.0. Accessed June 11, 2022

Australian Communications and Media Authority (ACMA). (2020).. . *Communication Reports*, •••, 2018–2019. Retrieved June 12, 2022, from https://www.acma.gov.au/publications/2020-02/report/communicationsreport-2018-19

Australian Cyber Security Centre (ACSC). (2021). *ACSC Annual Cyber Threat Report1 July 2020 to 30 June 2021.* Australian Cyber Security Centre.

Avram, M.-G. (2014). Advantages and challenges of adopting cloud computing from an enterprise perspective. *Procedia Technology*, 12, 529–534. DOI: 10.1016/j.protcy.2013.12.525

Beck, T., Demirguc-Kunt, A., & Levine, R. (2005). SMEs, growth, and poverty: Cross-country evidence. *Journal of Economic Growth*, 10(3), 199–229. DOI: 10.1007/s10887-005-3533-5

Belás, J., Bartoš, P., Ključnikov, A., & Doležal, J. (2015). Risk perception differences between micro-, small and medium enterprises. *Journal of International Students.*

Benlian, A., & Hess, T. (2011). Opportunities and risks of software-as-a-service: Findings from a survey of IT executives. *Decision Support Systems*, 52(1), 232–246. DOI: 10.1016/j.dss.2011.07.007

Calderaro, A., & Craig, A. J. (2020). Transnational governance of cybersecurity: Policy challenges and global inequalities in cyber capacity building. *Third World Quarterly*, 41(6), 917–938. DOI: 10.1080/01436597.2020.1729729

Carroll, M., Van Der Merwe, A., & Kotze, P. (2011, August). Secure cloud computing: Benefits, risks and controls. *In 2011 Information Security for South Africa*, 1-9. IEEE.

Cataldo, A., Pino, G., & McQueen, R. J. (2020). Size matters: The impact of combinations of ICT assets on the performance of Chilean micro, small and medium enterprises. *Information Technology for Development*, 26(2), 292–315. DOI: 10.1080/02681102.2019.1684870

Charlebois, K., Palmour, N., & Knoppers, B. M. (2016). The adoption of cloud computing in the field of genomics research: The influence of ethical and legal issues. *PLoS One*, 11(10), e0164347. DOI: 10.1371/journal.pone.0164347 PMID: 27755563

Cynch. (2021). State of Cyber Fitness in Australian Small Businesses. Retrieved from https://cynch.com.au/small-business-cyber-fitness-2021. Accessed June 15, 2022

Da Veiga, A., Astakhova, L. V., Botha, A., & Herselman, M. (2020). Defining organisational information security culture—Perspectives from academia and industry. *Computers & Security*, 92, 101713. DOI: 10.1016/j.cose.2020.101713

Gibson, T., & Van der Vaart, H. J. (2008). Defining SMEs: A less imperfect way of defining small and medium enterprises in developing countries.

Gochhait, S., Butt, S. A., Jamal, T., & Ali, A. (2022). *Cloud Enhances Agile Software Development. Research Anthology on Agile Software, Software Development, and Testing, edited by Information Resources Management Association*. IGI Global., DOI: 10.4018/978-1-6684-3702-5.ch025

Lin, C., Tsai, J. C., & Jiang, J. J. (2015). Rethinking the role of security in client satisfaction with Software-as-a-Service (SaaS) providers. [</edb>]. *Decision Support Systems*, 70, 73–85.

Goutam, R. K. (2015). Importance of cyber security. *International Journal of Computer Applications*, 111(7).

Gupta, H., & Barua, M. K. (2016). Identifying enablers of technological innovation for Indian MSMEs using best–worst multi criteria decision making method. *Technological Forecasting and Social Change*, 107, 69–79. DOI: 10.1016/j.techfore.2016.03.028

Gupta, P., Seetharaman, A., & Raj, J. R. (2013). The usage and adoption of cloud computing by small and medium businesses. *International Journal of Information Management*, 33(5), 861–874. DOI: 10.1016/j.ijinfomgt.2013.07.001

Gupta, S., & Misra, S. C. (2016). Compliance, network, security and the people related factors in cloud ERP implementation. *International Journal of Communication Systems*, 29(8), 1395–1419. DOI: 10.1002/dac.3107

Hair, J. F.Jr, Sarstedt, M., Hopkins, L., & Kuppelwieser, V. G. (2014). Partial least squares structural equation modeling (PLS-SEM): An emerging tool in business research. *European Business Review*.

Heidt, M., Gerlach, J. P., & Buxmann, P. (2019). Investigating the security divide between SME and large companies: How SME characteristics influence organizational IT security investments. *Information Systems Frontiers*, 21(6), 1285–1305. DOI: 10.1007/s10796-019-09959-1

Hossain, M. A., Sabani, A., Lokuge, S., Boo, Y. L., & Kaisar, S. 2023. Selection of Cloud Service Providers: A Fuzzy-Set Qualitative Comparative Analysis Approach, *International Working Conference on Transfer and Diffusion of IT*: Springer, pp. 422-433.

Hsu, P.-F., Ray, S., & Li-Hsieh, Y.-Y. (2014). Examining cloud computing adoption intention, pricing mechanism, and deployment model. *International Journal of Information Management*, 34(4), 474–488. DOI: 10.1016/j.ijinfomgt.2014.04.006

ISO/IEC 27017, 2015. *Information Technology-Security Techniques-Guidelines for Identification*, Collection, Acquisition and Preservation of Digital Evidence. International Telecommunication Union, (n.d). Data networks, open system communications and security. Available from: https://ccdcoe.org/sites/default/files/documents/ITU-080418-RecomOverviewOfCS.pdf

Kaluarachchi, C., Nagahawatta, R., & Warren, M. (2020). Sri Lankan Politics and social media participation. A case study of the Presidential Election 2019. In *Societal Challenges in the Smart Society* (pp. 191–200). Universidad de La Rioja.

Katua, N. T. (2014). The role of SMEs in employment creation and economic growth in selected countries. *International Journal of Education and Research*, 2(12), 461–472.

Khalid, A., Butt, S. A., Jamal, T., & Gochhait, S. (2022). *Agile Scrum Issues at Large-Scale Distributed Projects: Scrum Project Development At Large Research Anthology on Agile Software, Software Development, and Testing, edited by Information Resources Management Association*. IGI Global., DOI: 10.4018/978-1-6684-3702-5.ch019

Khayer, A., Talukder, M. S., Bao, Y., & Hossain, M. N. (2020). Cloud computing adoption and its impact on SMEs' performance for cloud supported operations: A dual-stage analytical approach. *Technology in Society*, 60, 101225. DOI: 10.1016/j.techsoc.2019.101225

Kimani, K., Oduol, V., & Langat, K. (2019). Cyber security challenges for IoT-based smart grid networks. *International Journal of Critical Infrastructure Protection*, 25, 36–49. DOI: 10.1016/j.ijcip.2019.01.001

Kumar, R., & Goyal, R. (2019). On cloud security requirements, threats, vulnerabilities and countermeasures: A survey. *Computer Science Review*, 33(1), 1–48. DOI: 10.1016/j.cosrev.2019.05.002

Lian, J. W. (2021). Understanding cloud-based BYOD information security protection behaviour in smart business: In perspective of perceived value. *Enterprise Information Systems*, 15(9), 1216–1237. DOI: 10.1080/17517575.2020.1791966

Lokuge, S., & Duan, S. X. 2023. Exploring the Enablers of Digital Transformation in Small and Medium-Sized Enterprises, Handbook of Research on Business Model Innovation Through Disruption and Digitalization), pp 136-156.

López-Ortega, M., Torres-Castro, S., & Rosas-Carrasco, O. (2016). Psychometric properties of the Satisfaction with Life Scale (SWLS): Secondary analysis of the Mexican Health and Aging Study. *Health and Quality of Life Outcomes*, 14(1), 1–7. DOI: 10.1186/s12955-016-0573-9 PMID: 27938407

Lowry, P. B., Dinev, T., & Willison, R. (2017). Why security and privacy research lies at the centre of the information systems (IS) artefact: Proposing a bold research agenda. *European Journal of Information Systems*, 26(6), 546–563. DOI: 10.1057/s41303-017-0066-x

Luo, Y. (2022). A general framework of digitization risks in international business. *Journal of International Business Studies*, 53(2), 344–361. DOI: 10.1057/s41267-021-00448-9 PMID: 34075261

Lynn, T., Liang, X., Gourinovitch, A., Morrison, J. P., Fox, G., & Rosati, P. (2018). Understanding the determinants of cloud computing adoption for high performance computing.

Mangula, I. S., van de Weerd, I., & Brinkkemper, S. (2014). *The Adoption of Software-as-Service: an Indonesian Case Study.*

Marston, S., Li, Z., Bandyopadhyay, S., Zhang, J., & Ghalsasi, A. (2011). Cloud computing—The business perspective. *Decision Support Systems*, 51(1), 176–189. DOI: 10.1016/j.dss.2010.12.006

Mell, P., & Grance, T. (2011, September). The NIST definition of cloud computing. *NIST Special Publication 800-145*. Available from: https://nvlpubs.nist.gov/nistpubs/Legacy/SP/nistspecialpublication800-145.pdf

Mijnhardt, F., Baars, T., & Spruit, M. (2016). Organizational characteristics influencing SME information security maturity. *Journal of Computer Information Systems*, 56(2), 106–115. DOI: 10.1080/08874417.2016.1117369

Misra, S. C., & Mondal, A. (2011). Identification of a company's suitability for the adoption of cloud computing and modelling its corresponding Return on Investment. *Mathematical and Computer Modelling*, 53(3-4), 504–521. DOI: 10.1016/j.mcm.2010.03.037

Moody, G. D., Siponen, M., & Pahnila, S. (2018). Toward a unified model of information security policy compliance. *Management Information Systems Quarterly*, 42(1), 285–311. DOI: 10.25300/MISQ/2018/13853

Nagahawatta, R., Lokuge, S., Warren, M., & Salzman, S. (2021). Cybersecurity Issues and Practices in a Cloud Context: A Comparison Amongst Micro, Small and Medium Enterprises, *InAustralasian Conference on Information Systems (ACIS),* Sydney. Australia.

Nagahawatta, R., & Warren, M. (2020). Key Security and Privacy Related Factors Influencing the Use of Cloud Computing in SMEs. *In proceedings of the ICIS 2020 SIGSEC:Workshop on Information Security & Privacy.*

Nagahawatta, R., Warren, M., & Yeoh, W. (2019). Ethical Issues Relating to Cyber Security in Australian SMEs. *InProceedings of the 8th Australian Institute of Computer Ethics Conference (AICE 2019),* 71-76. Deakin University.

Nagahawatta, R., Warren, M. J., Salzman, S., & Lokuge, S. (2021, January). Security and Privacy Factors Influencing the Adoption of Cloud Computing in Australian SMEs. In PACIS (p. 7).

Nagahawatta, R. T. S. (2022). Critical security and privacy related factors influencing the adoption of cloud computing in Australian small and medium-sized enterprises (Doctoral dissertation, RMIT University).

Nagahawatta, R. T. S., Warren, M., & Yeoh, W. (2018). A study of cybersecurity awareness in Sri Lanka. In *17th Australian Cyber Warfare Conference (CWAR)*, October 10-11th, 2018, Melbourne, Victoria, Australia. (p. 45).

Ncubukezi, T., Mwansa, L., & Rocaries, F. (2020). *A review of the current cyber hygiene in small and medium-sized businesses.*

Núñez, D., Ferrada, X., Neyem, A., Serpell, A., & Sepúlveda, M. (2018). A user-centered mobile cloud computing platform for improving knowledge management in small-to-medium enterprises in the Chilean construction industry. *Applied Sciences (Basel, Switzerland)*, 8(4), 516. DOI: 10.3390/app8040516

Pahl, C., Brogi, A., Soldani, J., & Jamshidi, P. (2017). Cloud container technologies: A state-of-the-art review. *IEEE Transactions on Cloud Computing*, 7(3), 677–692. DOI: 10.1109/TCC.2017.2702586

Paik, S.-K. (2011). *Supply management in small and medium-sized enterprises: role of SME size.*

Palos-Sanchez, P. R., Arenas-Marquez, F. J., & Aguayo-Camacho, M. (2017). Cloud computing (SaaS) adoption as a strategic technology: Results of an empirical study. *Mobile Information Systems*, 2017, 2017. DOI: 10.1155/2017/2536040

Powell, W. W., & DiMaggio, P. J. (Eds.). (2012). *The new institutionalism in organizational analysis.* University of Chicago press.

Ramegowda, A., Agarkhed, J., & Patil, S. R. (2020). Adaptive task scheduling method in multi-tenant cloud computing. *International Journal of Information Technology : an Official Journal of Bharati Vidyapeeth's Institute of Computer Applications and Management*, 12(4), 1093–1102. DOI: 10.1007/s41870-019-00389-5

Rebollo, O., Mellado, D., Fernández-Medina, E., & Mouratidis, H. (2015). Empirical evaluation of a cloud computing information security governance framework. *Information and Software Technology*, 58, 44–57. DOI: 10.1016/j.infsof.2014.10.003

Safari, F., Safari, N., Hasanzadeh, A., & Ghatari, A. R. (2015). Factors affecting the adoption of cloud computing in small and medium enterprises. *International Journal of Business Information Systems*, 20(1), 116–137. DOI: 10.1504/IJBIS.2015.070894

Salim, S. A., Sedera, D., Sawang, S., Alarifi, A. H. E., & Atapattu, M. (2015). Moving from evaluation to trial: How do SMEs start adopting cloud ERP? *AJIS. Australasian Journal of Information Systems*, 19, 19. DOI: 10.3127/ajis.v19i0.1030

Sebescen, N., & Vitak, J. (2017). Securing the human: Employee security vulnerability risk in organizational settings. *Journal of the Association for Information Science and Technology*, 68(9), 2237–2247. DOI: 10.1002/asi.23851

Sedera, D., Gable, G., & Chan, T. 2003. "Survey Design: Insights from a Public Sector-Erp Impact Study," Pacific Asia Conference on Information Systems, Adelaide, Australia: AIS, pp. 595-610.

Sedera, D., & Lokuge, S. (2019). Does it get better over time? A longitudinal assessment of enterprise system user performance. *Information Technology & People*, 33(4), 1098–1123. DOI: 10.1108/ITP-01-2019-0005

Selznick, L. F., & LaMacchia, C. (2017). Cybersecurity liability: How technically savvy can we expect small business owners to be. *J. Bus. and Tech. L.*, 13, 217.

Senarathna, I., Wilkin, C., Warren, M., Yeoh, W., & Salzman, S. (2018). Factors that influence adoption of cloud computing: An empirical study of Australian SMEs. *AJIS. Australasian Journal of Information Systems*, 22, 22. DOI: 10.3127/ajis.v22i0.1603

Senyo, P. K., Effah, J., & Addae, E. (2016). Preliminary insight into cloud computing adoption in a developing country. *Journal of Enterprise Information Management*, 29(4), 505–524. DOI: 10.1108/JEIM-09-2014-0094

Sharma, R., & Trivedi, R. K. (2014). Literature review: Cloud computing-security issues, solution and technologies. *International Journal of Engine Research*, 3(4), 221–225. DOI: 10.17950/ijer/v3s4/408

Sinha, P. kumar Rai, A., & Bhushan, B. (2019, July). Information Security threats and attacks with conceivable counteraction. In 2019 2nd International Conference on Intelligent Computing, Instrumentation and Control Technologies (ICICICT) (Vol. 1, pp. 1208-1213). IEEE.

Skafi, M., Yunis, M. M., & Zekri, A. (2020). Factors influencing SMEs' adoption of cloud computing services in Lebanon: An empirical analysis using TOE and contextual theory. *IEEE, 8,* 79169-79181.

Spanaki, K., Gürgüç, Z., Mulligan, C., & Lupu, E. (2019). Organizational cloud security and control: A proactive approach. *Information Technology & People*, 32(3), 516–537. DOI: 10.1108/ITP-04-2017-0131

Steffani, A. B. (2006). The impact of information security in academic institutions on public safety and security: Assessing the impact and developing solutions for policy and practice. National Institute of Justice Grant NCJ 215953. Available from: https://www.ncjrs.gov/pdffiles1/nij/grants/215953.pdf

Sultan, N., & Van De Bunt-Kokhuis, S. (2012). Organizational culture and cloud computing: Coping with a disruptive innovation. *Technology Analysis and Strategic Management*, 24(2), 167–179. DOI: 10.1080/09537325.2012.647644

Tabrizchi, H., & Rafsanjani, M. K. (2020). A survey on security challenges in cloud computing: Issues, threats, and solutions. *The Journal of Supercomputing*, 76(12), 9493–9532. DOI: 10.1007/s11227-020-03213-1

Tang, C., & Liu, J. (2015). Selecting a trusted cloud service provider for your SaaS program. *Computers & Security*, 50, 60–73. DOI: 10.1016/j.cose.2015.02.001

Tornatzky, L. G., Fleischer, M., & Chakrabarti, A. K. (1990). *Processes of technological innovation*. Lexington books.

Varghese, B., & Buyya, R. (2018). Next generation cloud computing: New trends and research directions. *Future Generation Computer Systems*, 79, 849–861. DOI: 10.1016/j.future.2017.09.020

Walther, S., Sedera, D., Urbach, N., Eymann, T., Otto, B., & Sarker, S. (2018). Should We Stay or Should We Go? Analyzing Continuance of Cloud Enterprise Systems. *Journal of Information Technology Theory and Application*, 19(2), 4.

Wrenn, B., Stevens, R. E., & Loudon, D. L. (2007). *Marketing research: Text and cases*. Psychology Press.

Yildirim, E. Y., Akalp, G., Aytac, S., & Bayram, N. (2011). Factors influencing information security management in small-and medium-sized enterprises: A case study from Turkey. *International Journal of Information Management*, 31(4), 360–365. DOI: 10.1016/j.ijinfomgt.2010.10.006

Zhang, Y., Yao, J., & Guan, H. (2017). Intelligent cloud resource management with deep reinforcement learning. *IEEE Cloud Computing*, 4(6), 60–69. DOI: 10.1109/MCC.2018.1081063

Zikmund, W. G., Carr, J. C., & Griffin, M. (2013). *Business Research Methods (Book Only)*. Cengage Learning.

ADDITIONAL READING

Benlian, A., & Hess, T. (2011). Opportunities and risks of software-as-a-service: Findings from a survey of IT executives. *Decision Support Systems*, 52(1), 232–246. DOI: 10.1016/j.dss.2011.07.007

Cataldo, A., Pino, G., & McQueen, R. J. (2020). Size matters: The impact of combinations of ICT assets on the performance of Chilean micro, small and medium enterprises. *Information Technology for Development*, 26(2), 292–315. DOI: 10.1080/02681102.2019.1684870

Cynch. (2021). State of Cyber Fitness in Australian Small Businesses. Retrieved from https://cynch.com.au/small-business-cyber-fitness-2021. Accessed June 15, 2022

Gupta, P., Seetharaman, A., & Raj, J. R. (2013). The usage and adoption of cloud computing by small and medium businesses. *International Journal of Information Management*, 33(5), 861–874. DOI: 10.1016/j.ijinfomgt.2013.07.001

Heidt, M., Gerlach, J. P., & Buxmann, P. (2019). Investigating the security divide between SME and large companies: How SME characteristics influence organizational IT security investments. *Information Systems Frontiers*, 21(6), 1285–1305. DOI: 10.1007/s10796-019-09959-1

Khayer, A., Talukder, M. S., Bao, Y., & Hossain, M. N. (2020). Cloud computing adoption and its impact on SMEs' performance for cloud supported operations: A dual-stage analytical approach. *Technology in Society*, 60, 101225. DOI: 10.1016/j.techsoc.2019.101225

Kumar, R., & Goyal, R. (2019). On cloud security requirements, threats, vulnerabilities and countermeasures: A survey. *Computer Science Review*, 33(1), 1–48. DOI: 10.1016/j.cosrev.2019.05.002

Salim, S. A., Sedera, D., Sawang, S., Alarifi, A. H. E., & Atapattu, M. (2015). Moving from evaluation to trial: How do SMEs start adopting cloud ERP? *AJIS. Australasian Journal of Information Systems*, 19, 19. DOI: 10.3127/ajis.v19i0.1030

KEY TERMS AND DEFINITIONS

Cloud Computing: A model for enabling convenient, on-demand network access to a shared pool of configurable computing resources (e.g., network, servers, storage, applications and services) that can be rapidly provisioned and released with minimal management effort or service provider interaction.

Small and Medium sized Enterprises: In Australia, firms with fewer than 200 employees are considered small and medium-sized enterprises. These businesses are divided into three categories: micro-businesses, which have fewer than 4 employees; small businesses, with 5 to 19 employees; and medium businesses, which employ 20 to 199 individuals.

Adoption: Adoption refers to the organizational decision or process of accepting, implementing, or integrating a specific technology or systems.

Privacy in Cloud Computing: In the context of the cloud environment, "privacy" refers to customers' concerns regarding the storage of personal data in the cloud and its potential accessibility to others worldwide.

Security in Cloud Computing: the degree to which an organization possesses adequate security administration for the confidentiality, integrity and availability of data and applications in the cloud.

Cybersecurity: Cybersecurity refers to the practice of protecting computer systems, networks, programs, and data from unauthorized access, attacks, damage, or exploitation, aimed at maintaining the confidentiality, integrity, and availability of information and computing resources.

Cloud Service Providers: Cloud service providers (CSPs) are companies that offer cloud computing services and resources to businesses and individuals over the internet. These services typically include infrastructure as a service (IaaS), platform as a service (PaaS), and software as a service (SaaS), allowing users to access computing resources, storage, databases, software applications, and other IT services on-demand without the need for on-premises infrastructure. Examples of cloud service providers include Amazon Web Services (AWS), Microsoft Azure, Google Cloud Platform (GCP), and IBM Cloud.

Chapter 14
Advanced Deep Learning Frameworks for Cyber Security in IoT-Based Healthcare

Usharani Bhimavarapu
https://orcid.org/0000-0002-0246-1420
Department of Computer Science and Engineering, Koneru Lakshmaiah Education Foundation, Vaddeswaram, India

ABSTRACT

The rapid adoption of IoT-based healthcare devices has revolutionized the medical industry by enabling real-time monitoring and data collection, yet it raises significant privacy and security concerns. These devices are vulnerable to various cyber-attacks, including man-in-the-middle attacks, spoofing, and data injection, which can compromise sensitive patient information and disrupt critical healthcare operations. To address these challenges, this study explores the application of deep learning techniques, particularly ResNet-50, to classify unforeseen cyber-attacks in IoT-based healthcare systems. The WUSTL-EHMS-2020 dataset, containing biometric data and network flow metrics, is utilized for experimentation. Preprocessing steps like normalization and feature engineering ensure compatibility with the model. ResNet-50, with its residual learning mechanism, effectively extracts complex patterns and generalizes to previously unseen attacks. The model's performance is evaluated using accuracy, precision, recall, and F1-score, demonstrating its ability to identify cyber-attacks while minimizing false positives and negatives. This research underscores the importance of advanced deep learning frameworks in enhancing the security and reliability of IOT-based healthcare systems.

INTRODUCTION

Cybersecurity plays a pivotal role in protecting sensitive data, critical systems, and infrastructure from malicious activities in an increasingly digital world. With the proliferation of IoT devices, particularly in healthcare, the attack surface has expanded, exposing vulnerabilities to threats like data breaches, ransomware, man-in-the-middle attacks, and unauthorized access. Cybersecurity involves implementing a multilayered approach that combines preventive, detective, and corrective measures to safeguard digital assets. This includes strong encryption protocols, robust authentication mechanisms, and firewalls to

DOI: 10.4018/979-8-3693-8784-9.ch014

prevent unauthorized data access. Advanced threat detection systems, such as intrusion detection and prevention systems (IDPS), use machine learning and artificial intelligence to identify and mitigate suspicious activities in real-time.

In the context of IoT-based healthcare systems, cybersecurity becomes even more critical due to the sensitivity of patient data and the need for uninterrupted services. IoMT (Internet of Medical Things) devices, which collect and transmit biometric data, are particularly vulnerable to attacks like spoofing, data injection, and denial of service. Securing these systems requires a combination of secure device configurations, regular software updates, network segmentation, and endpoint protection to reduce vulnerabilities. Cybersecurity frameworks such as Zero Trust Architecture ensure that no entity, inside or outside the network, is trusted by default.

Moreover, user awareness is vital for a strong cybersecurity posture. Regular training programs for users on recognizing phishing attempts and handling data responsibly can significantly reduce human errors, which often lead to breaches. As cyber threats evolve, adopting proactive strategies like penetration testing, vulnerability scanning, and security audits is essential. Compliance with standards such as GDPR, HIPAA, and ISO 27001 further strengthens the security infrastructure, ensuring legal adherence and fostering trust among stakeholders. By integrating these measures, cybersecurity provides a robust defense against ever-evolving threats, ensuring the confidentiality, integrity, and availability of data and systems.

Phishing-resistant security measures are crucial in defending against one of the most prevalent and harmful cyber threats—phishing attacks. Phishing is a social engineering technique where attackers impersonate legitimate entities, such as banks, government organizations, or service providers, to deceive users into revealing sensitive information like passwords, credit card details, or personal identification numbers (PINs). Phishing-resistant strategies aim to prevent, detect, and mitigate the impact of these deceptive attempts, ensuring that users and systems are safeguarded from such attacks.

One of the primary approaches to phishing resistance is the implementation of multi-factor authentication (MFA), particularly with phishing-resistant methods like FIDO2, which uses public key cryptography. Unlike traditional password-based authentication, FIDO2 eliminates the reliance on passwords, which are often susceptible to phishing. With FIDO2, authentication is done through hardware security keys or biometric verification, ensuring that even if a user's login credentials are phished, an attacker cannot easily gain access without the physical device or biometric data. This creates a much stronger barrier to unauthorized access, as the credentials alone are not sufficient for authentication.

Another key strategy is the use of anti-phishing technologies such as DMARC (Domain-based Message Authentication, Reporting, and Conformance), SPF (Sender Policy Framework), and DKIM (DomainKeys Identified Mail) to protect against email-based phishing. These protocols help validate the authenticity of email senders and prevent attackers from spoofing legitimate domain names, making it easier to detect phishing emails before they reach end-users.

Education and awareness are also vital components of a phishing-resistant strategy. Training users to recognize phishing attempts—such as emails with suspicious links or urgent requests for sensitive information—can dramatically reduce the likelihood of successful attacks. Regular phishing simulations and awareness campaigns can help reinforce safe behaviors, such as verifying the authenticity of suspicious communications before responding or clicking on links.

Furthermore, organizations can implement strict access controls and monitoring systems to minimize the damage caused by phishing attacks. Limiting the privileges of users and regularly auditing their access can reduce the potential impact of a successful phishing attack. In the event of a breach, rapid detection and response through security information and event management (SIEM) systems can mitigate the risk and prevent further exploitation.

Phishing-resistant measures combine advanced authentication technologies, robust email validation protocols, user education, and proactive monitoring to create a layered defense against phishing attacks. By employing these strategies, organizations can significantly reduce the risk of successful phishing attempts and protect sensitive data from exploitation.

Cybersecurity in the medical field is of paramount importance due to the increasing reliance on digital technologies, electronic health records (EHR), medical devices, and the interconnectedness of healthcare systems. With the growing adoption of IoT-based healthcare devices, such as wearable monitors, smart infusion pumps, and remote patient monitoring systems, the threat landscape in healthcare has expanded, exposing medical organizations to cyberattacks that can compromise patient safety, privacy, and the integrity of critical healthcare operations.

Medical data, particularly patient records, is highly sensitive and must be protected to ensure confidentiality and compliance with regulatory frameworks such as the Health Insurance Portability and Accountability Act (HIPAA) in the United States and the General Data Protection Regulation (GDPR) in Europe. Cyberattacks, including ransomware, data breaches, and denial-of-service (DoS) attacks, can lead to unauthorized access to personal health information, disruption of medical services, and even life-threatening situations when critical care systems are compromised. Healthcare organizations, therefore, must adopt robust cybersecurity measures to prevent unauthorized access, detect malicious activities, and ensure rapid response to security incidents.

Many of these devices are vulnerable to cyberattacks such as malware injection or hijacking, which could result in device malfunction or manipulation of data. Securing these devices requires strong encryption, secure communication protocols, regular updates, and vulnerability assessments to mitigate potential threats. Additionally, manufacturers must follow strict cybersecurity guidelines when designing medical devices to ensure that they are resilient to attacks and can receive software patches when vulnerabilities are identified.

The implementation of multi-factor authentication (MFA), encryption, and secure access control is critical for protecting patient data stored in electronic health records (EHR) systems. Encryption ensures that sensitive information, such as medical history, diagnoses, and treatment plans, is only accessible to authorized personnel. Additionally, secure access controls ensure that only healthcare providers with the appropriate clearance can access specific patient data, minimizing the risk of internal threats. Continuous monitoring of EHR systems and user activity through intrusion detection systems (IDS) helps identify suspicious activities, such as unauthorized access or tampering with data.

Training healthcare staff on cybersecurity best practices is also essential in preventing human errors that could lead to security breaches. Phishing attacks, in particular, are a common entry point for cybercriminals to gain access to healthcare networks. Educating healthcare workers on how to identify phishing emails and encouraging the use of secure passwords and other security measures can significantly reduce the risk of successful attacks.Compliance with healthcare-specific security standards, such as HIPAA and ISO/IEC 27001, ensures that healthcare organizations adhere to industry best practices and are well-equipped to safeguard patient data and maintain trust in their services.

Cybersecurity in the medical field is essential to protect patient privacy, maintain the integrity of healthcare systems, and ensure the safety of medical devices and patient care. With the evolving threat landscape, healthcare organizations must adopt a multi-layered cybersecurity approach, combining technology, training, and policy enforcement, to safeguard against cyberattacks and ensure the continued delivery of high-quality healthcare services.

In the medical field, numerous cybersecurity models have been developed to address the increasing threats to patient data, medical devices, and healthcare systems. These models include traditional approaches such as firewalls, intrusion detection systems (IDS), and encryption, as well as newer methods like machine learning (ML) and artificial intelligence (AI)-based models. The primary goal of these models is to ensure the confidentiality, integrity, and availability of sensitive medical data and devices.

One widely used model is the Zer0 Trust Architecture (ZTA), which assumes that no user or device, whether inside or outside the network, is inherently trusted (Smith, 2024). This approach focuses on continuous verification, access control, and monitoring. However, ZTA requires significant resources and can lead to performance bottlenecks due to its stringent validation requirements. Similarly, intrusion detection systems (IDS), which monitor network traffic to identify malicious activity, are crucial in medical settings for detecting unauthorized access. However, these systems often suffer from high false positive rates, leading to alert fatigue among healthcare professionals (Johnson, 2024).

Another commonly employed model is data encryption, particularly in electronic health record (EHR) systems, ensuring that patient data is secure in transit and at rest. While encryption is essential, it can add latency to healthcare operations and create challenges in data accessibility, especially when urgent medical decisions are required (Lee, 2024). Multi-Factor Authentication (MFA) is also commonly used to secure healthcare access, but MFA adoption is inconsistent across organizations, and healthcare workers may find it inconvenient, leading to reduced compliance (Kim & Park, 2024).

In terms of machine learning, models such as support vector machines (SVM) and random forests have been explored to detect anomalies in network traffic, identifying potential threats in real-time. While effective, these models often require large amounts of labeled data for training and can be vulnerable to adversarial attacks that manipulate inputs to mislead the system (Wang, 2024). Similarly, AI-based approaches like neural networks and deep learning are gaining traction in predicting and preventing cyberattacks in medical devices. However, these models often struggle with interpretability, making it difficult for healthcare professionals to understand the reasons behind a security decision, which can impact trust and decision-making (Zhang, 2024).

The blockchain model has been proposed for secure, decentralized management of patient data, ensuring transparency and tamper-proof records. Despite its promising advantages, blockchain technology faces scalability issues, high energy consumption, and challenges with integrating with existing healthcare IT infrastructure (Gao & Liu, 2024). On the other hand, the risk-based approach focuses on assessing vulnerabilities and threats to prioritize security measures based on risk levels. This model can be time-consuming and subjective, leading to inconsistencies in how risks are evaluated across different medical institutions (Yang, 2024).

Behavioral analytics models are also used to detect abnormal user behavior that might indicate a security threat. These models can identify subtle, insider threats but often require extensive data collection and processing, which can raise privacy concerns among patients (Miller & Davis, 2024). Similarly, edge computing is being explored as a means to enhance the security of medical devices by processing data closer to the source, thus reducing latency and improving real-time threat detection. However, this approach can increase the complexity of managing decentralized data and security protocols across various devices and platforms (Patel & Singh, 2024).

Cloud security models have also gained prominence with the rise of cloud-based healthcare solutions, employing hybrid clouds to manage sensitive medical data. Despite their flexibility and scalability, cloud security models often struggle with ensuring data sovereignty and maintaining control over sensitive patient information, as healthcare organizations may not fully control the cloud infrastructure (Sharma, 2024). Lastly, secure software development models such as DevSecOps have been adopted to integrate security into the software development lifecycle. While these models promote proactive security measures, they require a high level of expertise and may increase development time, which can be a barrier in the fast-paced healthcare industry (Cheng & Zhang, 2024).

Overall, while there are a wide range of cybersecurity models designed to protect the medical field, each comes with its limitations, including high resource requirements, integration challenges, and issues related to data privacy and accessibility. The rapid evolution of cyber threats in healthcare necessitates ongoing refinement and adaptation of these models to meet the unique security needs of the industry.

Principal Component Analysis (PCA) and ResNet50 models offer significant advantages in overcoming several limitations associated with traditional cybersecurity models in the medical field, especially in the context of high-dimensional data and complex patterns in medical data and devices.

PCA is a dimensionality reduction technique that helps address the challenge of high-dimensionality in medical datasets, particularly in the context of network flow metrics and biometric data. In many healthcare cybersecurity models, such as intrusion detection systems (IDS), the sheer number of features in a dataset can lead to issues such as overfitting, increased computational costs, and difficulty in detecting meaningful patterns. By reducing the dimensionality, PCA identifies the most significant features that capture the majority of the variance in the data. This not only improves the efficiency of the model but also enhances the model's ability to generalize, thereby reducing false positives and false negatives, a common limitation in IDS systems used in healthcare settings (Wang, 2024). Additionally, PCA facilitates faster processing of real-time data from IoT-based medical devices by eliminating redundant or irrelevant features, allowing for more efficient detection of anomalies or potential cyberattacks.

On the other hand, ResNet50, a deep learning model based on residual networks, addresses the challenge of detecting complex patterns in large-scale healthcare datasets. Traditional machine learning models such as support vector machines (SVM) or random forests may struggle to capture intricate, non-linear relationships between features, especially in the dynamic environment of healthcare systems. ResNet50's architecture, which includes skip connections, allows the model to effectively train deep neural networks without suffering from the vanishing gradient problem. This enables it to capture high-level, hierarchical features from medical device data, network traffic, and patient biometrics. As a result, ResNet50 can accurately identify sophisticated cyberattacks, such as man-in-the-middle attacks or malware injections, that may be difficult for simpler models to detect (Zhang, 2024). Furthermore, ResNet50's ability to leverage pre-trained models on large datasets means it can adapt to new, unforeseen threats, making it highly effective in environments where the threat landscape evolves rapidly.

Together, PCA and ResNet50 can complement each other by streamlining data preprocessing and enabling more robust, accurate threat detection in healthcare systems. PCA reduces the data complexity, allowing ResNet50 to focus on learning deeper, more relevant patterns, improving overall cybersecurity performance. While PCA addresses issues related to feature redundancy and computational efficiency, ResNet50 excels at detecting complex patterns, making both models powerful tools in overcoming the limitations of traditional cybersecurity models in the medical field.

MATERIALS AND METHODOLOGY

The methodology focuses on using ResNet-50 to classify unforeseen cyber-attacks in IoT-based healthcare devices. The WUSTL-EHMS-2020 dataset, comprising biometric and network flow data, is preprocessed through normalization and feature engineering to ensure compatibility with the model. ResNet-50, initialized with pre-trained weights, leverages its residual learning mechanism to extract complex patterns from the data. The dataset is split into training and validation sets, and the model is trained using an Adam optimizer with a binary cross-entropy loss function. Data augmentation is applied to prevent overfitting, and the model's performance is evaluated using accuracy, precision, recall, and F1-score. The approach ensures robustness and generalization to detect both known and unforeseen cyber-attacks effectively.

Materials

The WUSTL-EHMS-2020 dataset originates from the Enhanced Healthcare Monitoring System. The dataset primarily targets man-in-the-middle attacks, specifically spoofing and data injection, within an Internet of Medical Things (IoMT) environment. While this focus aligns with the study's objectives, the dataset does not encompass other significant attack types such as denial of service (DoS), probing, or remote-to-local (R2L) attacks, which are commonly observed in IoT-based healthcare systems.

Preprocessing

The preprocessing of the WUSTL-EHMS-2020 dataset involves several key steps to prepare it for analysis and model training. First, the dataset is inspected to understand its structure, check for missing values. The label column, which is binary (0 for normal and 1 for attack), is already encoded in a way that does not require additional label encoding.

Next, normalization is applied to ensure all numerical features are scaled to a similar range, improving model performance and training stability. Since the dataset contains a mix of features with potentially varying ranges, each feature is normalized using a technique such as Min-Max scaling, which transforms values to a range between 0 and 1. This step is crucial for models that are sensitive to feature scaling, such as those relying on gradient-based optimization.

Finally, the dataset is checked for any remaining inconsistencies or missing values. Missing values, if any, are handled using appropriate imputation methods, such as filling with the mean or median for numerical features.

Principal Component Analysis

To begin, the dataset is normalized to ensure all features are on a similar scale, which is a prerequisite for PCA to work effectively. Min-Max scaling or standardization (zero mean and unit variance) is applied to the 35 network flow metrics and 8 biometric features. Normalization ensures that features with larger ranges do not dominate the variance captured by PCA.

After normalization, PCA is applied to the combined 43 features (excluding the label). PCA identifies the principal components, which are linear combinations of the original features that maximize variance. The number of components to retain is determined based on the cumulative explained variance ratio. For example, retaining enough components to explain 95% of the variance ensures that most of the dataset's information is preserved while reducing dimensionality.

PCA transforms the original dataset into a new feature space consisting of the selected principal components. These components replace the original features for downstream analysis, offering a more compact and efficient representation. By reducing dimensionality, PCA not only helps mitigate overfitting but also speeds up the training process of machine learning models. Importantly, the label column is excluded from PCA, as it is not a feature but the target variable.

The transformed dataset with reduced dimensions is then used for model training, ensuring that irrelevant or redundant information does not hinder the analysis. This approach simplifies the dataset while retaining critical patterns necessary for identifying normal and attack instances in the IoMT environment.

Classification

To classify unforeseen cyber-attacks on IoT-based healthcare devices, a deep learning approach using ResNet-50 can be highly effective due to its ability to extract complex features from data and generalize well to unseen patterns. ResNet-50, a 50-layer deep convolutional neural network, is particularly suitable for such tasks because of its residual learning mechanism, which mitigates the vanishing gradient problem in deep networks. This allows the model to effectively learn intricate patterns and relationships within the data.

The process begins with preparing the dataset, such as the WUSTL-EHMS-2020 dataset, which includes biometric data and network flow metrics. The dataset is preprocessed through steps like normalization to scale the features and ensure consistency. If the data is not in an image format, feature engineering techniques are applied to convert numerical data into a format compatible with ResNet-50. One approach is to reshape the features into 2D arrays and normalize them to fit the input dimensions required by ResNet-50.

The ResNet-50 model is either initialized from scratch or fine-tuned using transfer learning with weights pre-trained on a large dataset like ImageNet. Transfer learning can significantly enhance the performance, especially for smaller datasets, by leveraging learned feature representations. The model's architecture comprises convolutional layers with skip connections, which allow gradients to flow directly through the network, enabling efficient learning even with deep layers. The output layer is customized to include a fully connected layer with a softmax or sigmoid activation function, depending on whether the classification task is binary or multi-class.

During training, the dataset is split into training and validation sets to ensure robust evaluation. The model learns to distinguish normal and attack instances by minimizing a loss function, such as binary cross-entropy, using an optimizer like Adam. To classify unforeseen cyber-attacks, the model relies on its ability to generalize to new patterns in the data, achieved by the diversity of attack types and normal instances included in the training set. Data augmentation techniques, such as random rotations or scaling, are applied to introduce variability and prevent overfitting.

EXPERIMENTAL RESULTS

The experimental setup for evaluating the cybersecurity models in the medical field was conducted using a Windows 11 system configuration, which provided a stable and versatile environment for implementing and testing the models. The system was equipped with a high-performance processor, ample RAM, and a dedicated GPU to ensure efficient data processing and model training. The choice of Windows 11 allowed seamless integration with popular machine learning libraries such as TensorFlow, PyTorch, and scikit-learn, facilitating the implementation of advanced models like PCA and ResNet50 for cybersecurity in healthcare applications. The configuration also supported a range of essential tools for data preprocessing, feature selection, and dimensionality reduction, ensuring that the models could handle large and complex datasets typical of the medical domain. Experimental results were measured in terms of accuracy, precision, recall, and F1 score, with particular focus on the models' ability to detect and classify cyber threats such as spoofing and data injection in IoT-based healthcare devices.

Table 1 presents a comparison of feature selection methods based on several performance measures, including accuracy, precision, recall, and F1 score. The "Proposed (PCA + ResNet50)" method outperforms the other techniques, achieving an accuracy of 98.1%, precision of 97.8%, recall of 98.4%, and an F1 score of 98.1%. Among the other methods, the "Filter Method (Correlation-based)" demonstrates the next highest performance, with an accuracy of 94.2%, precision of 93.5%, recall of 94.0%, and F1 score of 93.7%. The "Wrapper Method (RFE)" follows closely behind with an accuracy of 93.8%, while the "Embedded Method (Lasso Regression)" shows slightly lower performance, achieving an accuracy of 92.5%. Methods like "Mutual Information (MI)", "Chi-Square Test", and "Information Gain" also show solid results, but with slightly lower scores, particularly in accuracy and precision, compared to the top performers. "ReliefF" achieves an accuracy of 91.1%, while "Genetic Algorithm (GA)" offers a slightly better performance with a 93.0% accuracy. The "t-SNE" method ranks the lowest, with an accuracy of 88.9%, along with the least favorable precision and recall. The "PCA (No ResNet50)" method stands at 94.0%, indicating a moderate performance improvement without the ResNet50 component. Overall, the proposed method with PCA and ResNet50 clearly leads in all performance metrics.

Table 1. Feature Selection Performance Measure Comparison

Feature Selection Method	Accuracy (%)	Precision (%)	Recall (%)	F1 Score (%)
Proposed (PCA + ResNet50)	98.1	97.8	98.4	98.1
Filter Method (Correlation-based)	94.2	93.5	94.0	93.7
Wrapper Method (RFE)	93.8	93.0	94.2	93.6
Embedded Method (Lasso Regression)	92.5	91.7	92.1	91.9
Mutual Information (MI)	92.0	91.1	92.3	91.7
Chi-Square Test	89.7	88.8	90.1	89.4
Information Gain	90.3	89.5	90.8	90.1
ReliefF	91.1	90.4	91.2	90.8
Genetic Algorithm (GA)	93.0	92.3	93.4	92.8
t-SNE	88.9	87.9	89.2	88.5
PCA (No ResNet50)	94.0	93.3	94.5	93.9

Table 2 presents a comparison of classification models based on accuracy, precision, recall, and F1 score. The "Proposed Model (PCA + ResNet50)" leads the performance metrics, achieving an accuracy of 98.1%, precision of 97.8%, recall of 98.4%, and F1 score of 98.1%. The "SVM" model follows with an accuracy of 94.5%, and performs well in precision (93.6%) and recall (95.2%), yielding an F1 score of 94.4%. "Random Forest" and "Gradient Boosting" show similar results with accuracy values of 93.8% and 94.1%, respectively, and comparable F1 scores around 93.9%. "KNN" achieves an accuracy of 91.7%, while precision and recall are slightly lower, resulting in an F1 score of 91.2%. "Logistic Regression" and "Decision Trees" perform at a slightly lower level, with accuracies of 90.4% and 88.9%, respectively, and F1 scores in the range of 88.6% to 90.2%. "Naive Bayes" ranks lowest in performance, with an accuracy of 87.2%, and similarly lower precision, recall, and F1 score. "Artificial Neural Networks (ANN)" offer a moderate performance with an accuracy of 92.6%, while "XGBoost" performs similarly to "SVM" and "Random Forest" with an accuracy of 94.6% and an F1 score of 94.6%. "ResNet50" on its own provides solid performance with an accuracy of 97.5%, precision of 97.2%, recall of 97.8%, and F1 score of 97.5%, demonstrating strong results though still falling short of the proposed model.

Table 2. Classification Performance Measure Comparison

Model	Accuracy (%)	Precision (%)	Recall (%)	F1 Score (%)
Proposed Model (PCA + ResNet50)	**98.1**	**97.8**	**98.4**	**98.1**
SVM	94.5	93.6	95.2	94.4
Random Forest	93.8	93.3	94.6	93.9
KNN	91.7	90.4	92.0	91.2
Logistic Regression	90.4	89.5	90.9	90.2
Decision Trees	88.9	88.0	89.2	88.6
Naive Bayes	87.2	86.5	88.0	87.2
Artificial Neural Networks (ANN)	92.6	91.8	92.4	92.1
Gradient Boosting	94.1	93.7	94.2	93.9
XGBoost	94.6	94.2	95.1	94.6
ResNet50	97.5	97.2	97.8	97.5

Table 3 compares the processing times of various feature selection methods, broken down into feature selection time, classification time, and total processing time. The "Proposed (PCA + ResNet50)" method has the longest processing time, with a feature selection time of 12.3 seconds and a classification time of 45.7 seconds, resulting in a total processing time of 58.0 seconds. In contrast, the "Filter Method (Correlation-based)" is the quickest, requiring only 3.5 seconds for feature selection and 10.5 seconds for classification, bringing the total processing time to 14.0 seconds. "Wrapper Method (RFE)" and "Embedded Method (Lasso Regression)" take more time, with total processing times of 22.0 seconds and 16.1 seconds, respectively. Other methods, such as "Mutual Information (MI)" and "Information Gain," have slightly lower times, with total processing times of 11.8 seconds and 10.5 seconds. The "Chi-Square Test" is among the fastest, with a total processing time of just 7.7 seconds. Methods like "Genetic Algorithm (GA)" and "PCA (No ResNet50)" show higher processing times, with "GA" taking a total of 32.5 seconds and "PCA (No ResNet50)" requiring 30.5 seconds. "ReliefF" and "t-SNE" also take moderate amounts of time, with total processing times of 16.2 seconds and 14.8 seconds, respectively. Overall, the table shows that while the proposed method offers the highest performance, it also requires the most processing time, while simpler methods like "Chi-Square Test" and "Filter Method" are much faster but with lower overall effectiveness.

Table 3. Processing Time Comparison (in Seconds)

Feature Selection Method	Feature Selection Time (s)	Classification Time (s)	Total Processing Time (s)
Proposed (PCA + ResNet50)	12.3	45.7	58.0
Filter Method (Correlation-based)	3.5	10.5	14.0
Wrapper Method (RFE)	8.2	13.8	22.0
Embedded Method (Lasso Regression)	4.1	12.0	16.1
Mutual Information (MI)	2.8	9.0	11.8
Chi-Square Test	1.5	6.2	7.7
Information Gain	3.0	7.5	10.5
ReliefF	5.0	11.2	16.2
Genetic Algorithm (GA)	15.0	17.5	32.5
t-SNE	6.5	8.3	14.8
PCA (No ResNet50)	10.1	20.4	30.5

Table 4 presents the results of various models for the detection of attacks in the Internet of Medical Things (IoMT) environment, based on performance metrics such as accuracy, precision, recall, F1 score, and AUC (Area Under the Curve). The "Proposed (PCA + ResNet50)" model achieves the highest performance, with an accuracy of 98.7%, precision of 98.5%, recall of 98.9%, F1 score of 98.7%, and an AUC of 99.2%. This model outperforms all others in every metric. "Random Forest" follows closely with an accuracy of 92.1%, precision of 91.7%, recall of 92.3%, F1 score of 92.0%, and AUC of 92.5%. "Support Vector Machine (SVM)" shows slightly lower performance, with an accuracy of 90.8%, precision of 90.3%, recall of 91.0%, F1 score of 90.6%, and AUC of 91.2%. The "Decision Tree" model has an accuracy of 89.5%, precision of 89.0%, recall of 89.7%, F1 score of 89.3%, and AUC of 90.0%. Models like "K-Nearest Neighbor (KNN)" and "Naive Bayes" show relatively lower performance, with accuracies of 88.2% and 86.7%, respectively. "Logistic Regression" performs slightly worse, with an accuracy of 85.3%, precision of 84.8%, and an AUC of 85.8%. "Gradient Boosting" and "XGBoost" achieve moderate results, with accuracies of 91.4% and 93.2%, respectively. "Convolutional Neural Network (CNN)" and "Long Short-Term Memory (LSTM)" models also show strong results, with accuracies of 95.6% and 96.4%, respectively, and AUCs of 96.0% and 96.8%. Overall, while the "Proposed (PCA + ResNet50)" model leads across all metrics, deep learning models like CNN and LSTM also perform impressively in detecting attacks in the IoMT environment, with the traditional models performing more modestly.

Table 4. Detection of Attacks in the IoMT Environment: Results Table

Model	Accuracy (%)	Precision (%)	Recall (%)	F1-Score (%)	AUC (%)
Proposed (PCA + ResNet50)	**98.7**	**98.5**	**98.9**	**98.7**	**99.2**
Random Forest	92.1	91.7	92.3	92.0	92.5
Support Vector Machine (SVM)	90.8	90.3	91.0	90.6	91.2
Decision Tree	89.5	89.0	89.7	89.3	90.0
K-Nearest Neighbor (KNN)	88.2	87.8	88.5	88.1	88.9
Naive Bayes	86.7	85.9	87.0	86.4	87.2
Logistic Regression	85.3	84.8	85.5	85.1	85.8
Gradient Boosting	91.4	90.8	91.5	91.1	91.7
XGBoost	93.2	92.7	93.5	93.1	93.8
Convolutional Neural Network (CNN)	95.6	95.2	95.8	95.5	96.0
Long Short-Term Memory (LSTM)	96.4	96.0	96.7	96.3	96.8

CONCLUSION

The classification of unforeseen cyber-attacks on IoT-based healthcare devices is critical for ensuring data privacy, system integrity, and patient safety in an increasingly interconnected environment. This study demonstrates the effectiveness of ResNet-50, a deep learning model, in identifying both known and unforeseen cyber-attacks. Leveraging its residual learning mechanism, ResNet-50 successfully extracts meaningful features from biometric and network flow data, enabling robust and scalable attack detection. Experimental results highlight the model's ability to generalize to new attack patterns with high accuracy and minimal error rates. While the current work focuses on specific attack types, future research can expand to include diverse attack scenarios like denial of service (DoS) and probe attacks to further enhance the security framework. Overall, this research contributes to strengthening the cyber-security of IoT-based healthcare systems, addressing critical vulnerabilities, and safeguarding patient data in an evolving threat landscape.

REFERENCES

Albattah, W., Khan, R. U., Alsharekh, M. F., & Khasawneh, S. F. (2022). Feature Selection Techniques for Big Data Analytics. *Electronics (Basel)*, 11(19), 3177. DOI: 10.3390/electronics11193177

Beulah Rani, I., Ewards, S. E. V., Palmer, G. M., & Kathrine, G. J. W. Detection of Cyber-Attacks in Food Industry Using Multi-Layer Perceptron and Convolution Neural Network. In *Proceedings of the 2023 International Conference on Sustainable Computing and Smart Systems (ICSCSS)*, Coimbatore, India, 14 June 2023; IEEE: Toulouse, France, 2023; pp. 1405–1409. DOI: 10.1109/ICSCSS57650.2023.10169805

Cheng, X., & Zhang, L. (2024). Secure software development in healthcare: A DevSecOps approach. *Journal of Healthcare Cybersecurity*, 22(4), 312–330.

Francis, D. P., Raimond, K., & Kathrine, G. J. W. (2023). Dimensionality Reduction of Large Datasets with Explicit Feature Maps. *Intelligent Decision Technologies*, 17(2), 457–470. DOI: 10.3233/IDT-220182

Gao, Y., & Liu, H. (2024). Blockchain technology for secure patient data management in healthcare systems. *Journal of Medical Information Security*, 18(1), 45–59.

Johnson, M. (2024). Challenges in implementing intrusion detection systems in healthcare environments. *Cybersecurity for Health Systems*, 10(3), 141–150.

Kherif, F., & Latypova, A. (2020). Principal Component Analysis. In *Machine Learning* (pp. 209–225). Elsevier. DOI: 10.1016/B978-0-12-815739-8.00012-2

Kim, S., & Park, J. (2024). The challenges and effectiveness of multi-factor authentication in healthcare systems. *Healthcare Cybersecurity Review*, 14(2), 78–90.

Lee, J. (2024). Encryption in healthcare data protection: A balancing act between security and accessibility. *Journal of Digital Health*, 16(4), 220–235.

Matsuo, Y., LeCun, Y., Sahani, M., Precup, D., Silver, D., Sugiyama, M., Uchibe, E., & Morimoto, J. (2022). Deep Learning, Reinforcement Learning, and World Models. *Neural Networks*, 152, 267–275. DOI: 10.1016/j.neunet.2022.03.037 PMID: 35569196

Miller, T., & Davis, S. (2024). Behavioral analytics for insider threat detection in healthcare organizations. *Cybersecurity in Medical Devices*, 7(3), 55–67.

Patel, R., & Singh, P. (2024). Edge computing for real-time security in IoT-based healthcare systems. *International Journal of IoT Security*, 13(1), 101–114.

Raju, V. N. G., Lakshmi, K. P., Jain, V. M., Kalidindi, A., & Padma, V. Study the Influence of Normalization/Transformation Process on the Accuracy of Supervised Classification. In *Proceedings of the 2020 Third International Conference on Smart Systems and Inventive Technology (ICSSIT)*, Tirunelveli, India, 20–22 August 2020; IEEE: Toulouse, France, 2020; pp. 729–735. DOI: 10.1109/ICSSIT48917.2020.9214160

R.M. (2020). S.P.; Maddikunta, P.K.R.; Parimala, M.; Koppu, S.; Gadekallu, T.R.; Chowdhary, C.L.; Alazab, M. An Effective Feature Engineering for DNN Using Hybrid PCA-GWO for Intrusion Detection in IoMT Architecture. *Computer Communications*, 160, 139–149. DOI: 10.1016/j.comcom.2020.05.048

Roshni Thanka, W., Kathrine, G. J., & Edwin, E. B. (2023). Using Machine Learning for Cyber Security. In *AI, Machine Learning and Deep Learning A Security Perspective* (p. 346). CRC Press. DOI: 10.1201/9781003187158-16

Sharma, A. (2024). Cloud security models in healthcare: A review of challenges and solutions. *Journal of Cloud Computing in Healthcare*, 11(2), 59–74.

Smith, J. (2024). Zero Trust Architecture for healthcare networks: Enhancing security through continuous verification. *Healthcare Security Innovations*, 19(5), 99–115.

Srikanth Yadav, M., & Kalpana, R. Data Preprocessing for Intrusion Detection System Using Encoding and Normalization Approaches. In *Proceedings of the 2019 11th International Conference on Advanced Computing (ICoAC)*, Chennai, India, 18–20 December 2019; IEEE: Toulouse, France, 2019; pp. 265–269. DOI: 10.1109/ICoAC48765.2019.246851

Wang, L. (2024). Challenges in using machine learning for cybersecurity in medical devices. *Artificial Intelligence in Health*, 12(2), 68–80.

Yang, X. (2024). Risk-based security models in healthcare: A comprehensive review. *Cybersecurity in Health Systems*, 15(3), 213–228.

Zhang, Y. (2024). Explainability and transparency in AI-based cybersecurity models for healthcare. *Journal of Medical AI and Security*, 9(1), 25–37.

Chapter 15
Cybersecurity in the Age of AI-Enhancing Defences for Today's Threats

Rohini Tarade
https://orcid.org/0009-0002-4682-0250
Ajeenkya D.Y. Patil University, India

Susanta Das
https://orcid.org/0000-0002-9314-3988
Ajeenkya D.Y. Patil University, India

ABSTRACT

Chapter examines urgent need to address cyber threats by reassessing conventional security techniques & arguing in favor of a large degree of automation & incorporation of AI & ML. Though it acknowledges associated issues, AI highlights cybersecurity defences by strengthening them, despite worries about potential misuse by criminals. While technologies have made jobs more automated, they have exposed systems to flaws. AI's widespread use has made attacks worse, which has led to revaluation of traditional & modern defences. It emphasizes AI's role in cybersecurity by showcasing its capacity to manage enormous datasets, adapt in real-time, & quickly detect risks. It highlights the significance of AI globally for network security, especially in light of the growing danger of cyberattacks. It examines AI's possible advantages/difficulties in security, addressing changing nature of threats, & security training that is influenced by AI & suggests countermeasures. It emphasizes the necessity of continuous research & assessments to fully utilize AI's potential & create a robust environment.

1. INTRODUCTION

Artificial Intelligence (AI) integration has strengthened cybersecurity and transformed service delivery. Although a few percentage of businesses worldwide use AI advances, there are risks and opportunities associated with their deployment. Hackers can take use of the same technology that's employed to protect against strong security measures. It is essential to regularly upgrade AI security systems and carry out cybersecurity risk assessments. Furthermore, when automation becomes more widespread, the likelihood

DOI: 10.4018/979-8-3693-8784-9.ch015

of cyberattacks increases. This means that proactively addressing emerging threats—like viruses and phishing emails—through AI-powered defences is imperative (Mohammed, 2016a).

AI is becoming more and more prevalent in many industries in the twenty-first century because to the rapid improvements in technology and the growing adoption of automation. Cybersecurity, as defined by ISO/IEC 27032:2023, emphasises the necessity for a thorough defense-in-depth framework and attempts to safeguard internet-connected systems against cyber threats. Artificial Intelligence presents chances to improve cyber resilience, but it also creates new weaknesses. The context for examining AI's development, methods, difficulties, and potential applications in cybersecurity is established by this introduction (Hangirkar, 2023).

Protecting electronic data from unauthorised use is the goal of cybersecurity, and AI is a key component in bolstering security protocols. AI is capable of automating security processes and analysing data to identify possible vulnerabilities, but when used improperly—as in deepfake videos—it may be dangerous. To properly protect guest data, it is imperative that organisations, especially the hospitality sector, stay abreast of AI breakthroughs and have strong security measures in place. AI helps firms safeguard the security of client data by assisting in the development of cutting-edge security technology and the training of cybersecurity specialists (Kaur et al., 2023).

Cybersecurity is the application of technologies, procedures, and best practices to protect devices, networks, and data from damage or unauthorised access. As digital infrastructure becomes more linked, the complexity of cybersecurity is increased. The rise in sophisticated cyberattacks as a result of this evolution has made intelligence-driven cybersecurity methods necessary. In this environment, AI is essential because it can quickly analyse large amounts of data to identify and neutralise cyberthreats. The use of AI in cybersecurity practices has sparked a great deal of study, which has led to the creation of a systematic literature review (SLR) with the goals of categorising AI applications, identifying trends, and filling in knowledge gaps. The SLR is a useful tool for upcoming research and cybersecurity practitioners as it presents a taxonomy of AI applications, describes particular use cases, and provides insights into research trends (Naik et al., 2022).

Cyberspace faces threats like ransomware and phishing, but it also supports a variety of activities like business and information sharing. Cybersecurity uses techniques such as firewalls and encryption to protect against these dangers, but traditional solutions are not up to date to handle new types of cyberattacks. By quickly recognising and reacting to threats, the integration of AI in cybersecurity strengthens defence capabilities. Artificial intelligence (AI) approaches such as machine learning and expert systems overcome the limitations of conventional cybersecurity strategies by adapting to changing threats. In addition to outlining potential future difficulties and opportunities, the study addresses the potential of AI in cybersecurity (Guembe et al., 2022).

Various aspects of AI-driven cyber-attacks, including intelligent captcha attack and manipulation, self-learning malware, and AI-driven password brute-force attacks. It also delves into the status of existing AI-driven cyber attack tools, revealing that 63% of the tools are implemented and evaluated, 25% are proposed, and 12% are implemented without evaluation . Additionally, the study provides insights into the evolving landscape of AI-driven cyber attacks and emphasizes the urgent need for robust cybersecurity measures to mitigate these growing risks effectively (Karve et al., 2022).

Cybersecurity is essential in today's digitally connected world because it protects against bad actors who want to steal and use data for their own gain. Every piece of data, from private information to highly sensitive material from the government and business world, could be a target. Strong defences are essential in light of cyberattacks that try to take down systems or steal data. Artificial intelligence systems provide a proactive strategy by utilising machine learning to detect and efficiently prevent developing threats, hence improving security measures and minimizing breach risks (Feng et al., 2020).

The convergence of artificial intelligence and cybersecurity has attracted substantial interest from both academic researchers and the general public. However, this field goes beyond simple technical study because it deals with intricate social and political issues that have an impact on our society. By delving into the complex issues surrounding AI security, they exposed the need for thoughtful approaches and smart decision-making, highlighting the constant discussion and investigation required to effectively counter modern threats (Rafy, 2024).

Sensitive digital data is seriously threatened by the exponential rise in cyberattacks that has resulted from the expansion of computer networks. Hackers use social engineering and artificial intelligence to get beyond internet security measures, which is why cybersecurity is crucial for protecting different kinds of data. By allowing systems to learn and adapt to new trends, AI plays a critical role in protecting against cyber risks and improving organisational efficiency. Businesses may improve their response times and security protocols while efficiently managing threats by utilising AI and machine learning (K et al., 2022).

AI raises several significant ethical issues as it gets more integrated into cybersecurity. Unintentionally, AI may treat individuals unfairly because of programming prejudices. By examining people's personal data, it can also harm their privacy. Some fear that AI will eliminate jobs and that it will be difficult to assign blame when AI makes choices. This study examined these problems and seeks to identify equitable, transparent, and socially beneficial applications of AI in cybersecurity as shown in Figure 1.

Figure 1. AI in Cyber Security

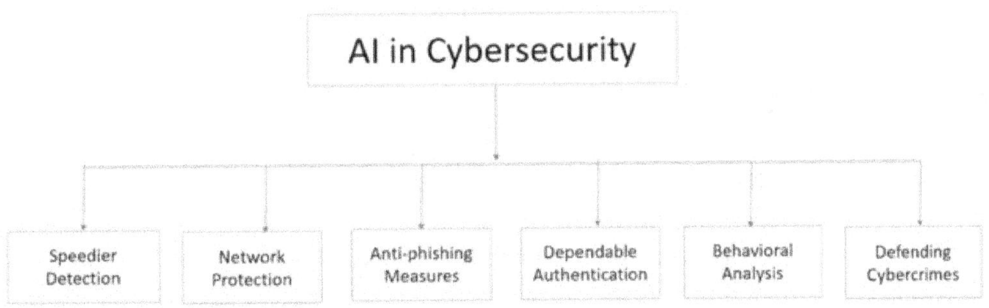

2. COMPARISON OF TRADITIONAL AND AI-DRIVEN CYBERSECURITY APPROACHES

Table 1 shows the comparison between traditional and AI-driven cybersecurity approaches (Choudhury & Paul, 2024; Nguyen & Lee, 2022; Patel & Anderson, 2023; Zhao, Tripathi, & Wong, 2023):

Table 1. Comparison of traditional and AI-driven cybersecurity approaches

Aspect	Traditional Cybersecurity	AI-Driven Cybersecurity
Detection Mechanism	Relies on predefined rules and recognised threat signatures.	Uses machine learning to detect patterns and abnormalities.
Adaptability	Limited; struggles to detect zero-day and unknown threats.	Highly adaptable; learns and changes in response to new dangers.
Automation	Updates are minimal and need manual intervention.	Processes that are automated require less human intervention.
Response Time	Reactive and slow.	Proactive, real-time detection and response.
False Positives	Higher due to rigid rule-based systems.	Lower due to dynamic and context-aware threat analysis.
Cost	Lower startup costs, but expensive long-term maintenance costs..	Although more expensive at first, it saves money in the long run.
Complexity	Simpler to implement and understand.	The setup is complex and requires trained staff.
Scalability	System capacity and human resources are both limited.	Scalable enough to handle massive datasets and various threats.
Integration	Works alone or with other tools.	Frequently used in conjunction with conventional hybrid defence methods.

3. AI APPLICATIONS IN CYBERSECURITY

3.1. Threat Detection and Response

AI algorithms examine network traffic to identify anomalies such as unauthorised access or malware activity. Machine learning (ML) models are very successful against zero-day assaults (Frost & Sullivan, 2023; Wong, 2023).

3.2. Automation of Security Operations

Artificial intelligence (AI) automates repetitious security operations such as log analysis and threat intelligence processing. This allows cybersecurity teams to focus on strategic interventions (Hyperproof, 2024).

3.3. Behavioural Analysis

AI uses user behaviour analytics (UBA) to uncover patterns that may suggest insider threats or account compromises (Smith, 2023).

3.4. Fraud Detection

AI is used in industries such as banking to monitor transactions and highlight anomalous activity, hence reducing the risk of financial fraud.

3.5. Phishing Detection

Natural Language Processing (NLP) techniques examine emails for linguistic and structural patterns linked with phishing assaults (Kaspersky, 2023).

4. CYBERSECURITY STRATEGIES FOR AI SYSTEMS

4.1. Compliance with Regulations

The SEC mandates corporations to publish their cybersecurity strategies, which ensures responsibility in risk management (Wong, 2023).

4.2. Risk Management Frameworks

Organisations use AI in Governance, Risk, and Compliance (GRC) systems to expedite operations and predict weaknesses (Hyperproof, 2024).

4.3. Adversal Training

Regular model retraining is used to protect against hostile inputs that aim to exploit AI flaws (Frost & Sullivan, 2023).

4.4. Monitoring & Auditing

Continuous audits and the use of explainable AI (XAI) tools improve transparency and mitigate the risks associated with AI decisions (Smith, 2023).

4.5. Collaboration

Sharing threat intelligence within and across sectors enhances preparedness for emerging cyber threats (Wong, 2023).

5. CHALLENGES TO AI IN CYBERSECURITY

5.1. Adversarial Attacks

Adversaries can exploit AI models by providing adversarial inputs, such as data poisoning or evasion assaults. These strategies jeopardise the dependability and security of AI systems (Goodfellow et al., 2023; Hyperproof, 2024). For example, attackers can modify training data to impact AI judgements, resulting in vulnerabilities (Smith, 2023).

5.2. Data Privacy Concerns

AI systems frequently require access to large datasets, prompting worries about data protection and compliance with legislation such as GDPR and HIPAA. Mishandling sensitive information can result in breaches and legal action (Hyperproof, 2024).

5.3. Bias and Fairness

AI algorithms might inherit biases from training data, resulting in unfair or inaccurate decision-making. In cybersecurity, biassed algorithms may fail to detect vulnerabilities based on certain user behaviors or prioritize risks ineffectively (Frost & Sullivan, 2023).

5.4. Explainability and Transparency

Artificial intelligence systems, particularly those based on deep learning, sometimes operate as "black boxes," making it difficult for security teams to comprehend their decision-making processes. The lack of explainability hampers auditing and undermines trust (Wong, 2023).

5.5. Scalability of Threats

Just as defenders employ AI, attackers are increasingly using it for sophisticated attacks like automated phishing campaigns and AI-driven malware. The "AI vs. AI" dynamic increases the scale and complexity of dangers (Kaspersky, 2023).

5.6. Integration Challenges

Integrating AI into existing cybersecurity systems necessitates significant effort and skill. Misaligned implementation might result in inefficiencies and potentially security vulnerabilities (Smith, 2023).

5.7. Overreliance on AI

Organisations that rely too heavily on AI may disregard standard security practices, leaving systems open to basic vulnerabilities or AI model failures (Frost & Sullivan, 2023).

6. WAYS THAT BIASES IN AI ALGORITHMS

Due to a variety of issues, such as skewed training data, algorithmic biases, and poor model design, AI algorithms may unintentionally discriminate against particular groups or people. The following (Table 2) are some ways that biases in AI algorithms can appear, along with mitigation techniques (Das, 2021).

Table 2. Biases and mitigation techniques.

Sr. No.	Ways that biases in AI algorithms	Mitigation Techniques
1	Biased Training Data: Inaccurate Training Data Biases in training data have the potential to cause AI algorithms to reinforce and magnify preexisting societal biases.	Predictive models that are trained on historical data with biassed practices from the past run the risk of perpetuating prejudices. Conduct a thorough analysis and use techniques like data augmentation, preparation, and balance to reduce biases. To guarantee representation and equity in data collecting, incorporate diversity and inclusion strategies.
2	Algorithmic Biases: In addition to resulting in unfair treatment of some people or groups, biases can also arise from the algorithmic design or decision-making process itself. The selection of characteristics, algorithmic presumptions, or optimization goals may be to blame for this.	Make appropriate measurements and evaluations in order to regularly verify the fairness and bias of AI systems. Make use of machine learning algorithms specifically created with fairness considerations in mind. Use strategies like adversarial debiasing and fairness-aware regularisation to lessen algorithmic biases.
3	Model Evaluation and Interpretability: It may be difficult to detect and successfully reduce biases in AI algorithms if they lack openness and interpretability. Black-box models have the potential to mask the underlying causes of biassed judgements.	Make use of techniques like feature analysis, fairness audits, and model explanation to improve the interpretability and transparency of your models. Include human inspection to find and fix biases that computerised evaluations failed to detect. Encourage cooperation between data scientists, ethicists, and subject matter experts to assess fairness and efficiently analyse model results.
4	Continuous Monitoring and Feedback Loop: In order to recognise and correct new biases as they arise throughout time, bias reduction is a continual process that calls for constant observation and input.	Create ongoing monitoring and auditing processes to quickly identify and fix biases in AI systems. Establish feedback loops to ensure that algorithms and interventions are updated and improved on a regular basis by collecting feedback on their fairness and effectiveness. These steps lessen the possibility of inadvertent discrimination, encouraging justice and equity in AI-driven decision-making, and multidisciplinary collaboration encourages the development and use of ethical AI.

7. AI-DRIVEN CYBERSECURITY TOOLS

7.1. Machine Learning (ML) in Cybersecurity

Applications

IDPS employ ML algorithms to detect network irregularities. (Buczak and Guven, 2016) argue that ML-based systems can detect patterns in huge datasets to distinguish between normal and harmful behaviour.

For example, Snort and Bro/Zeek use machine learning approaches to detect anomalies in intrusions.

Verma and Chandra (2018) investigated the performance of ML classifiers (SVMs and Decision Trees) in detecting phishing emails based on sender reputation and email structure.

(Kandias et al., 2013) emphasised the necessity of machine learning (ML) in analysing user behaviour to detect insider threats. These programs detect anomalies in user behaviour, such as strange login habits or file access.

7.2. Deep Learning (DL) in Cybersecurity

Applications

Dahl et al. (2013) found that deep learning, namely neural networks, can effectively classify malware on a broad scale. Their findings show the power of deep learning models to detect zero-day attacks by analysing malware attributes.

Yuan, Li, and Li (2017) developed the DeepDefense framework, which analyses network traffic patterns to detect DDoS attacks and other advanced threats using machine learning (DL).

Jurgovsky et al. (2018) found that sequence-based deep learning models, including Long Short-Term Memory (LSTM) networks, effectively detect fraudulent transactions by analysing client behaviour over time.

7.3. Neural Networks (NNs) in Cybersecurity

Applications

Vinayakumar et al. (2019) employed Recurrent Neural Networks (RNNs) to analyse network logs and detect anomalies in real-time, preventing cyber-attacks.

In their 2018 study, George and Thomas found that Convolutional Neural Networks (CNNs) can hack text-based CAPTCHAs. In contrast, comparable techniques are used to build more resilient CAPTCHA systems.

Camacho-Collados & Pilehvar (2018) found that combining NLP with neural networks can automate threat intelligence and discover Indicators of Compromise (IOCs) by processing unstructured data like threat reports and logs.

Key Advantages

According to Sommer & Paxson (2010), AI can improve threat detection speed and accuracy, making it ideal for real-time cybersecurity solutions.

Porras et al. (2007) emphasised the importance of efficient AI systems for processing large datasets in enterprise networks.

Adaptability: Moustafa & Slay (2015) found that adaptive learning models can successfully respond to new cyber threats by continuously updating themselves.

8. LITERATURE REVIEW

Das & Sandhane (2021) emphasised the shortcomings of traditional fixed solutions in handling security risks as it examines the difficulties presented by the complexity of activities and the abundance of information in securing cyberspace. The authors contended that conventional hardwired decision-making logic is insufficient and that significant automation is necessary to manage this complexity. The study promoted the merging of machine simplicity and learning techniques in artificial intelligence (AI) as a solution to these problems.

The overview evaluated the possibilities for improving defence mechanisms by offering insights into various AI implementations in cybersecurity. According to the report, AI applications—especially those that make use of neural networks—are already helpful in securing other areas and the perimeter of cybersecurity. The study conceded that there are still unresolved questions on a few cybersecurity-related topics, including logical decision support and strategic decision-making.

The exponential increase in cyber threats and hostile intelligence calls for advanced cybersecurity measures. The study highlighted the value of AI in mitigating large-scale attacks with little resources by referencing effective distributed denial-of-service (DDoS) prevention strategies. The study also emphasized the importance of artificial neural networks in cybersecurity, namely in terms of information control, decision support, and scenario awareness.

The article ended by recognising the unpredictable rate of growth in general artificial intelligence, but it also draws attention to the possible dangers of criminals abusing emerging types of AI. The authors contended that, despite this uncertainty, the use of new technologies should greatly improve cybersecurity capabilities in terms of comprehending, analysing, and controlling information within systems, especially with relation to computer training.

Chakraborty et al. (2023) presented that automation of regular tasks have become dominant with the digital revolution, because of technology advancements. On the other hand, worries regarding the security of linked systems have been raised by the growing internet-based connectedness of devices worldwide. The prevalence of cyber risks, including identity theft, data theft, fraudulent transactions, compromised passwords, and system breaches, has increased due to recent breakthroughs in artificial intelligence (AI). The field of cybersecurity is examined in this article, which covered both traditional and sophisticated defence strategies against online threats. It also explored the many directions AI may go in the field of cybersecurity.AI integration has not only automated jobs but also greatly increased efficiency across a range of scientific and engineering areas. Regretfully, hackers have become more aware of this technical advancement, which has turned traditional cyberthreats into "intelligent" threats. The article highlighted the necessity for sophisticated security measures while shedding light on the growing threat posed by cyberattacks.AI as a Protective Measure: In spite of resource constraints, the paper explains how AI may be extremely important in real-time cyber threat detection and prevention. Because cyberattacks are so dynamic, it can be difficult for human analysts to stay on top of the changing threat picture. But machine learning, a branch of artificial intelligence, facilitates quick data analysis, allowing for superior security coverage without materially slowing down current processes. This feature frees up human analysts to concentrate on analysing data and establishing creative strategies to fight cybercrime. The paper stressed that while AI-based methods are becoming more and more common and affordable in cybersecurity, they are not a cure-all. When a committed human opponent confronts an intelligent machine, the limitations become evident. It emphasised how crucial human knowledge, instruction, and oversight are for AI to advance constantly and produce the best results. In cybersecurity, the paper promoted a symbiotic relationship between human intellect and AI, acknowledging that AI cannot manage all aspects autonomously.

Nadikattu (2020) emphasized how important AI is to solve cybersecurity issues. It highlighted how AI can handle enormous volumes of data, incorporate knowledge into user interfaces, and use training algorithms to support adaptive learning. Through the constant addition and duplication of pertinent data into the system, adaptive learning helps people and organisations respond appropriately to a variety of circumstances. The passage emphasised how AI has taken the lead in organisations all around the world for its quick detection of dangerous threats. Businesses choose artificial intelligence (AI) solutions because they are seen as technological advances that protect data from cyber threats. The article highlighted that despite AI's revolutionary potential, businesses shouldn't get complacent. Instead, they should have investigated cutting-edge methods by which artificial intelligence and machine learning can provide unending defence against malevolent assaults. It promoted the inclusion of literature that offers substitute techniques for gathering AI-related data. The paper's main topics include how businesses use AI to thwart cyberattacks, how AI improves cybersecurity, and the possible advantages for Americans as individuals and as businesses. The article concluded by stating that organisations are significantly impacted by the deployment of artificial intelligence. It helps with thwarting cyberattacks, improving an organization's overall cybersecurity, and bolstering national security initiatives. AI uses sophisticated algorithms to help cybersecurity companies assess threats. Since most businesses have already adopted AI, the emphasis has shifted away from developing algorithms and routines for machine learning and towards planning and allocating resources for it. With this strategy, organisations can keep an eye on and improve every process inside their systems. It emphasised the importance of AI specialists and their obligation to provide solutions that go beyond conventional methods of thwarting cyberattacks. In the article, it is anticipated that future studies will advance artificial intelligence by developing programmes that can recognise and stop malevolent attacks. These apps are thought to be essential for safeguarding accomplishments—like financial gains—against possible disruptions brought on by cyberattacks. Moreover, the significance of incorporating data-driven models into machine learning is underscored, especially for establishments that depend on network security. AI presents cyber threat intelligence, which makes it possible to identify and evaluate risk levels, ranging from low to high. The section provided information that demonstrated how well artificial intelligence may be integrated with other elements, like machine learning, cloud computing, and data analytics. It promoted a holistic strategy, arguing that businesses should incorporate a variety of components to improve overall efficiency rather than relying exclusively on artificial intelligence. In conclusion, the article made the claim that organisations can find acceptable answers to the multitude of cybersecurity-related issues by integrating artificial intelligence and other pertinent technology. It depicts a future in which continual research and developments in AI and machine learning are essential to defending systems from constantly changing cyberthreats.

Zeng (2022), emphasized how global AI has become in computer network technology, especially in the big data era. AI is recognised for its ability to optimise computer network systems' structural and functional levels, resulting in extensive advancements. Many elements of people's lives are being expedited and streamlined by the use of virtual assistants, speech recognition software, and natural language production. Concurrently, the utilisation of AI powered by big data is acknowledged for strengthening computer network security systems and enabling sophisticated, intelligent, and automated network functions. Due to widespread network attacks and security concerns, there has been an increase in the frequency of significant network security incidents in recent years. These dangers include information about social media security, network information systems, and physical infrastructure. The sentence emphasises how dangerous these threats are, especially when it comes to the security of personal information and property. In reaction to these cyberthreats, artificial intelligence is portrayed as a revolutionary force that will significantly alter cyberspace security. It is considered critical to conduct research on the tactics that enable artificial intelligence to defend against security risks and cyberattacks. It is proposed that this research is essential to the advancement of both cyberspace security and artificial intelligence. Emphasis is placed on the connection between cyberspace security and artificial intelligence, pointing out that threats in both virtual and real worlds pose serious obstacles to national defence, politics, and the economy of all nations. It is anticipated that actual security concerns would worsen due to the deep integration of AI and security dangers in cyberspace. It is anticipated that national security would face new and more serious difficulties as a result of this integration. According to the passage, cyberattacks are becoming more sophisticated, automated, and large-scale due to artificial intelligence, which is made possible by big data and related technologies. These advanced cyberattacks are expected to propel the advancement of defence technology, methods, and capacities in cyberspace. In conclusion, the section emphasises how artificial intelligence is revolutionising computer network technology within the framework of big data. Artificial Intelligence is often praised for its ability to optimise system layers, enhance functionality, and introduce technologies such as virtual assistants and natural language production to improve efficiency in daily life. The increasing number of security incidents is portrayed as the reason for the incorporation of AI in network security, which offers intelligent and automated solutions. Cyberspace security and artificial intelligence are thought to be closely related, and more research in this area is thought to be crucial for the development of both disciplines. The paragraph, however, foresees increased dangers and challenges to national security in both the virtual and physical worlds, raising concerns about the profound integration of AI and security threats. It is anticipated that the increasing complexity of cyberattacks would propel developments in cyberspace defence technology and capacities.

Anwar & Hassan (n.d.), highlighted the potential substantial effects of AI on cybersecurity, identifying cybersecurity as a field that stands to gain greatly from AI developments. Creating software that can fend against ever-evolving network threats is the main task in cybersecurity. The adoption of AI approaches is proposed as a remedy to solve the shortcomings of traditional security systems, providing improved security performance against a growing array of sophisticated cyber threats. The text recognises that the use of AI in cybersecurity entails valid dangers and concerns, notwithstanding the significant opportunities it presents. The text supports an organization's cyber environment from an all-encompassing standpoint in order to promote the development of cybersecurity. Since neither AI nor humans have shown complete competence in this field, this necessitates merging AI with human understanding. It is believed that in order to successfully reduce related dangers and concerns, socially responsible usage of AI technology is essential. In the information age and cybersecurity, artificial intelligence (AI) is hailed as a promising breakthrough. New methods, algorithms, instruments, and businesses providing AI-based services are constantly entering the global security market. AI-based cybersecurity solutions are said to be more robust, flexible, and adaptive than traditional cybersecurity solutions. Systems are better protected against sophisticated cyber threats and security performance is enhanced by this increased sophistication. The text highlighted the potential of deep learning techniques to improve cybersecurity by identifying them as particularly powerful and promising technologies in the AI area. It is emphasised how urgently sophisticated cyber defence techniques must be applied, particularly in situations when neural networks alone might not be the best available technology. The paragraph points out that while AI has revolutionised cybersecurity, neither humans nor AI alone has found general success in this area. It emphasises how crucial it is for enterprises to have a comprehensive understanding of their cyber environment. The paragraph points out that although AI has significantly altered the cybersecurity landscape, current systems are not entirely able to respond to changes in their surroundings. This emphasized how AI-based cybersecurity solutions must continue to be developed and improved in order to effectively counteract changing cyberthreats. The section concluded by presenting AI as a revolutionary force in cybersecurity that has the potential to greatly improve defences against sophisticated threats. It acknowledged the necessity of an all-encompassing strategy that successfully addresses the complex issues of cybersecurity by fusing AI with human understanding. Keeping ahead of increasingly complex cyberthreats is considered to need the continuous development of AI techniques and their integration into intelligent cyber defence strategies.

Hangirkar (2023), emphasized how company procedures are changing in the digital age and how data has emerged as the most important resource. It claims that because of the widespread use of the internet and the possible dangers of storing data on connected devices, businesses are completely open to computerization. The major goal is to improve cybersecurity and defend against cyberattacks by utilising ML and AI. The paper highlights how AI and ML are more accurate and faster than human teams at quickly identifying and neutralising cyberthreats. It attempts to demonstrate the advantages of using AI to enhance productivity in commercial operations. The article also discusses the necessity of raising awareness and overcoming the anxiety that comes with implementing new technologies, especially in light of worries about cyberattacks. The study's data collecting and analysis techniques are summarised in the research methodology section, which focuses on the relationship between cybersecurity and AI. The goal of the study is to investigate how cutting-edge technology protects visitors and property in the hotel sector. This paper's sample data is a combination of quantitative and qualitative information from books, journals, and internet resources about cybersecurity and artificial intelligence. Notwithstanding, the study recognized its limits as a consequence of the continuous advancements in the field's technologies, leading to inadequate data on the subject. It is emphasised how important AI is to combating the growing volume and sophistication of assaults. AI technologies—such as machine learning and natural language processing—are said to be crucial for quickly analysing enormous volumes of threat intelligence, cutting down on response times, and strengthening cybersecurity posture overall. The paper emphasizes how AI and machine learning have developed into vital information security solutions. These technologies are quite good at sifting through millions of events, recognising a wide range of threats, and gradually picking up new attack patterns. It is highlighted how crucial AI is becoming to solving the problems brought on by changing cyberthreats. The essay addresses the importance of cybersecurity measures, including data encryption, strong passwords, and frequent software updates, in the context of the hospitality sector in order to safeguard sensitive visitor information. In order to avoid cyberattacks, monitor and improve visitor safety, and react quickly to problems, the hotel industry is proposing to use AI and cybersecurity as tools. The advantages and difficulties of using AI to cybersecurity are discussed, with an emphasis on how it may speed up data analysis, increase security, and fend off online attacks. As a case study, the context of risk management in the hospitality sector is provided to highlight real-world uses of AI to solve cybersecurity issues. In summary, AI has the potential to revolutionise the hospitality sector, but because hotels handle a lot of personal data, it also poses cybersecurity risks. Hotels are implementing AI and machine learning cybersecurity solutions in recognition of this vulnerability in order to identify and stop cyberattacks. The essay emphasized how AI systems learn while examining both the advantages and disadvantages of AI for cybersecurity. Blockchain technology is also emphasised as a transparent and safe way to store data in order to thwart identity theft and other online dangers. All things considered, AI-driven cybersecurity improves hotel revenue, operational effectiveness, and visitor experience.

Rajendran & Vyas (2023) in their study presented that over the last decade, cyber threats have grown into significant problems, necessitating new security measures to resist highly trained hackers. AI has emerged as a promising tool for spotting scams, but its application carries additional hazards. This research study investigates the relationship between cyber risks and AI technologies for prevention, describing several AI applications in cybersecurity and evaluating their potential to strengthen defence mechanisms. The expansion of AI has increased the potential for improving cybersecurity measures, as approaches for data security have accelerated the evolution of AI in this arena. The paper's goal is to increase awareness about the advantages of AI in defending organisations and enterprises on a bigger scale. The study, which is supported by credible facts, emphasises AI's important role in revolutionising cybersecurity. It emphasises that current difficulties necessitate modern answers, with AI heralded as one of the century's most significant discoveries, despite the potential consequences of its misuse. The research highlights AI's usefulness in early problem detection, particularly in Intrusion Detection and Prevention Systems (IDPS), as well as the good effects of using Machine Learning approaches, which reduce false positives and improve threat detection accuracy. However, it warns that cybercriminals will adapt to AI defences, demanding strong regulations to oversee AI deployment within organisations. AI's autonomous computing capabilities enable self-control and configuration, presenting exciting opportunities for increasing information security. The report recognises AI's changing landscape, with academics making progress in preventing cybercrime. Recent advances in AI software have made a substantial contribution to the detection of online scams and frauds, reducing cybersecurity risks. The research emphasises AI's critical role in phishing detection and user confidentiality protection. It contends that human resources alone are insufficient to combat escalating cyber risks, and advocates for the use of AI technology alongside human expertise. AI enables faster and more effective threat detection, allowing organisations to dynamically change their security measures.

Mohammed (2016b), in his research work looked into the impact of AI on cybersecurity, specifically in terms of cyber threat mitigation. Businesses that leverage technology are well-positioned to succeed in an era of fast technological innovation. However, along with the benefits of digitalization come considerable hazards, such as the possibility of data breaches and cyberattacks. The changing nature of cyber threats demands more than simply human participation to strengthen cybersecurity safeguards. Artificial intelligence plays an important role in improving information security by rapidly analysing massive volumes of data to identify and mitigate various cyber dangers, such as malware and phishing assaults. Despite its advantages, AI also has potential drawbacks. To avoid catastrophes, firms must carefully pick and implement AI technologies. The report indicates that, while technical improvements allow hackers to fine-tune their strategies, AI emerges as an indispensable tool for improving the efficacy of information security organisations. Human capabilities are insufficient for securing enterprise-level attack surfaces, hence AI delivers critical monitoring and threat detection capabilities. AI also helps with risk identification and prioritisation, incident response management, and the early detection of malware cyber threats. Despite potential limitations, the report emphasises the importance of AI in enhancing cybersecurity and improving firms' overall security posture. AI helps to mitigate cyber threats and strengthen defences, protecting organisations from evolving cyber hazards.

Das & Sandhane (2021) emphasized the need of automation, particularly AI, in managing the complexity and amount of data required to properly defend cyberspace. Traditional fixed implementations of technology and software frequently fail to adapt to emerging security risks due to their hardwired decision-making logic. AI, with its machine learning and simplification methodologies, provides a solution to this problem. The study presents a complete overview of AI implementations in several cybersecurity sectors and evaluates their potential for improving defence systems. It focuses on existing AI applications for network perimeter protection and other cybersecurity fields, particularly neural networks. Furthermore, it emphasises the significance of employing AI technologies to efficiently address specific cybersecurity concerns, such as strategic decision-making and combatting harmful intelligence and cyber threats. Research on artificial neural networks shows great relevance to cybersecurity because of the continuous improvements in its use. The study does, however, recognise the continued need for advanced cybersecurity techniques outside of neural networks, particularly in the areas of information control, situational awareness, and decision support. The study also discusses the possible dangers of general artificial intelligence's quick development, highlighting how crucial it is to prevent bad actors from abusing new technologies. However, it is still hopeful about how new technologies, especially in computer learning, will improve cybersecurity skills by helping people understand, interpret, and manage information systems better.

Ansari et al. (2022) made a case for the efficiency of AI-based cybersecurity awareness training in lowering the incidence of phishing attempts. It claims that artificial intelligence (AI) and machine learning have greatly enhanced security measures, especially in the field of cybersecurity, and it highlights the significance of increasing awareness among people and organisations to stop such attacks. The paper's explicit call to action to promote AI-based cybersecurity training and highlight the potential advantages of such initiatives in strengthening security measures is one of its standout features. It highlights how users must be educated about AI-based cybersecurity solutions in order to reduce the hazards brought on by phishing scams. But in a number of areas, the work lacks critical examination and depth. First off, although suggesting that AI can successfully thwart phishing assaults, it doesn't offer any concrete proof or instances to back up this assertion. The paper's claim might have been enhanced by specific data or case studies proving how well AI-based solutions work to stop phishing assaults. Furthermore, by blaming AI-based solutions alone for phishing attack prevention, the research oversimplifies the complexity of cybersecurity concerns. It fails to recognise the complexity of cyberthreats and the requirement for an all-encompassing strategy that incorporates technology, instruction, and user awareness. Furthermore, the study ignores potential difficulties and restrictions related to cybersecurity awareness training based on AI. It doesn't deal with problems like user resistance, how cyber dangers change over time, and how easily hackers can get around new security measures. Furthermore, there are occasions when the paper's language is imprecise and unclear, which leaves several arguments unclear. More precise information regarding the approaches and strategies used in AI-based cybersecurity training programmes would be beneficial.

Overall, even though the study makes some significant arguments on the role of AI in cybersecurity awareness, it would benefit from additional in-depth research, actual data, and a more sophisticated comprehension of the intricacies involved in cybersecurity risks and phishing assaults.

Yamin et al. (2021) explored the growing trend of AI-based assaults and the application of AI in cyber defence are covered in the article. It demonstrates several examples of AI-powered hacks, including the creation of fictitious traffic signals to jeopardise the security of self-driving cars and the manipulation of medical photos to falsely diagnose cancer. The study looks into current AI-based cyberattacks and finds countermeasures to prevent them. The study also looks at the strategies and tactics used to carry out AI-based cyberattacks and makes predictions about how these attacks might be managed in the future based on current developments. It explores the technical underpinnings of several AI-based assault scenarios and suggests possible countermeasures. There are unknowns about the future use of AI in cyberwarfare due to the dynamic nature of the cyberspace. In order to mitigate the detrimental social effects of AI weaponization, the article urges cooperation among AI researchers and highlights the significance of placing national and international stability above politics and power dynamics. The report proposes agreements among superpowers, putting security and well-being ahead of political goals, to prevent the weaponization of AI. However, as past agreements such as the SALT II pact have shown, reaching consensus among governments is difficult because of divergent priorities and possible treaty violations. Even with the public criticism surrounding AI development, international powers are still reluctant to pull back from the arms race. In order to successfully oversee the development of AI weapons and provide a more safe and regulated AI infrastructure, the study emphasises the importance of international cooperation.

Ardito et al. (n.d.) tackled the escalating security issues in the e-Health space, specifically with regard to telemonitoring systems—which are more susceptible to cyberattacks. The authors suggest a Cyberattack Detection System (CADS) model to solve this problem by utilising artificial intelligence (AI) methods to detect anomalies without the requirement for a separate security analyst. With an emphasis on the unique scenario of a compromised remote patient monitoring system, the CADS model uses Deep Learning methods, specifically a Robust Deep Autoencoder, to identify anomalous occurrences like erratic heartbeats. Healthcare professionals can gain insights into the hostile activity's nature by interpreting detected abnormalities using the system's new explainable scores and explainable security paradigms (XSec). The interactive feedback mechanism of the suggested system is one of its standout features. It allows medical professionals to evaluate the precision of anomaly detections and offer input, modifying visualisation reports as necessary. Through user feedback, this engagement seeks to increase the system's detections' relevance and accuracy. The research emphasises the need of AI algorithms for rapid threat assessment and response in cybersecurity, particularly in the e-Health arena. The text highlights the significance of Threat Intelligence in utilising information from diverse Internet of Medical Things (IoMT) sensors to anticipate and address security risks, thereby improving the security of patient telemonitoring systems. The authors also suggest future research avenues, such as integrating more IoMT sensors to enhance anomaly detection skills beyond heart rate monitoring. This demonstrates how cybersecurity solutions powered by AI are always evolving and improving in the healthcare industry. All things considered, the study shows how AI methods may be applied successfully to enhance danger identification and response in e-Health telemonitoring systems. A viable method for improving cybersecurity in healthcare settings is the suggested CADS paradigm, which combines powerful AI algorithms with Threat Intelligence and user feedback systems.

Thorat (2021) explained that accurately identifying hazardous information is a persistent difficulty in the cybersecurity landscape that affects many security technologies, such as malware detection, application security solutions, and intrusion detection systems. Regular expressions that test incoming requests against pre-established patterns or signatures—which can be obtained from public or private repositories like the Core Rule Set—have historically been the foundation of detection techniques. Unfortunately, this method is less effective because of its inaccuracies stemming from both rare and nonexistent updates. Amidst these obstacles, machine learning shows promise as a means of improving authentication structures, comparing protocol implementations, evaluating the safety of human interaction proofs, and profiling data from smart metres. Although machine learning can strengthen security protocols, classifiers are still vulnerable to malicious assaults, which is why efforts are being made to strengthen their defences against different kinds of threats. In the field of data security, machine learning provides flexible ways to tackle difficult problems, such as virus and spam identification and monitoring. The idea of AI-based security intelligence modelling, which attempts to give cybersecurity processes more actionable insights and intelligence, is introduced by the convergence of AI and cybersecurity. The study emphasises the value of this strategy by outlining research problems and possible lines of inquiry for further field research. In conclusion, machine learning proves to be a useful instrument for enhancing defences and encouraging more proactive security measures, whereas traditional approaches find it difficult to handle the dynamic nature of cybersecurity threats. Cybersecurity initiatives can be made more intelligent and effective by utilising AI-based methods, which will open up new avenues for progress in tackling dynamic threats and protecting digital networks.

Sjöblom (2021) stated that the increasing intricacy and recurrence of cyberattacks provide formidable obstacles for security teams globally. These threats come from a wide variety of entities, including as governments, organised crime groups, and lone attackers, who use progressively more advanced methods to compromise systems and devices. As a result, cybersecurity experts struggle to stay up to date with new threats, which calls for more sophisticated solutions. The potential of AI, particularly ML and DL, to solve cybersecurity concerns is examined in this thesis. Security systems can reduce the manual labour involved in routine security operations while improving proactive and predictive detection and response capabilities by utilising AI. Employees of If insurance firm were interviewed with a focus on network security and monitoring. The interviews provide light on the difficulties encountered and suggest solutions based on artificial intelligence. Although AI offers great potential to strengthen cybersecurity defences, it's important to recognise its limitations. Even though AI is hailed as the solution to all security issues, modern AI technologies still necessitate a great deal of human engagement. Adopting AI techniques is necessary, though, as existing reactive methods are insufficient to combat the increasing number of cyberattacks, many of which evade standard security measures without being noticed and cause significant financial and reputational loss. Security teams may operate in real-time and increase data interpretation from network traffic with the use of ML and DL approaches, which provide improved detection and response capabilities. However, more research is required to minimise human intervention and efficiently automate AI solutions. To reduce false positives, this calls for creating specialised testing, training datasets, industry standards, and improving AI's contextual comprehension. It's crucial to remember that assessments of AI solutions could be skewed towards a particular provider, underscoring the need for an objective analysis. In the near future, AI will surely be vital in helping security analysts expedite data collection and root-cause investigation, even though a fully automated AI-driven security infrastructure may not be possible. In conclusion, even though AI has a great deal of promise to improve cybersecurity, its capabilities must be realistically assessed. Instead, efforts should be directed on improving ML and DL methodologies, reducing the need for human intervention, and correcting biases in product evaluations. In the end, AI will be a useful tool for enhancing security operations, but its significance should be viewed in the larger context of cybersecurity issues and solutions.

Srivastava & Benny (2021), stated that as science and technology develop at a rapid pace, so too are risks in our fast-evolving world, and cybersecurity is becoming a critical issue for our digital society. A growing number of cybercrimes, from identity theft to data breaches including encryption, are being caused by advances in AI and ML. The increasing use of AI in a variety of industries, such as healthcare and facial recognition systems, presents serious hazards to both persons and businesses. As a result, a deeper comprehension of AI's role in cybersecurity is necessary to prevent well-planned attacks and vulnerabilities. This paper explored AI's potential in the future and how well it can be incorporated into cybersecurity. In the information era, AI is a particularly exciting breakthrough. A growing number of methods, algorithms, tools, and companies are providing AI-based security services. AI systems are more robust, flexible, and adaptable than traditional cybersecurity solutions, which improves security performance and protects against advanced cyberthreats. Deep learning methods are currently one of the most effective and promising tools in the AI space for cybersecurity. But given that neural nets might not be enough, there is a pressing need for intelligent cyber defence strategies in a variety of domains. Even with AI's revolutionary effects on cybersecurity, current systems still find it difficult to properly foresee and adjust to changes in their environment. Furthermore, for successful defence, it is essential to obtain a comprehensive awareness of the cyber surroundings of organisations. In conclusion, there are benefits and drawbacks to the combination of cybersecurity with artificial intelligence. Even though AI provides cutting-edge defences against cyberattacks, more research and development is desperately needed to handle new threats. Strengthening defences against the constantly changing spectrum of cyber threats requires a holistic strategy that combines AI technology with a deeper understanding of cyber ecosystems.

Akhtar & Feng (2021) presented that traditional cybersecurity methods have become insufficient due to the increasing frequency and sophistication of cyber-attacks, making it difficult for security specialists to stay up to date with new threats. In the current digital age, it is crucial to protect enormous volumes of electronic data against cyberattacks because these attacks have the potential to seriously harm an organization's reputation or even cause it to shut down. In light of the paramount significance of cyber-security, this study investigates the possible uses of artificial intelligence (AI) to improve cyber defence tactics. Relevant literature was retrieved from a variety of academic sources and search engines using a methodical literature review approach. According to the report, AI has many benefits over conventional cybersecurity techniques, especially when it comes to enhancing cyberspace security as a whole. Notably, a paradigm shift in cyber defence mechanisms is seen in the rising replacement of traditional scanning engines in computer security by AI-powered engines. New and challenging cybersecurity problems arise as information and communication technology (ICT) develops. Innovative and scalable strategies are required to counter advanced cyber-attacks, as conventional procedures are frequently insufficient. An overview of AI applications in cybersecurity is given in the paper, with a focus on well-researched approaches like data learning, security expert systems, and bio-inspired strategies. Additionally, the study examined a number of cybersecurity domains where AI is critical, such as malware and intrusion detection, defence against Distributed Denial-of-Service (DDoS) assaults, and the application of digital policing strategies. AI-based cybersecurity solutions can reduce costs and increase return on investment (ROI) in addition to providing fast and accurate data processing. Despite these benefits, adversarial machine learning and human error remain a problem for AI-based cybersecurity solutions. However, industry insiders agree that incorporating AI into cybersecurity is crucial. The advantages of AI-powered security technologies outweigh the disadvantages as cybersecurity becomes more and more important, emphasising the need to use AI to strengthen cyber defence capabilities.

Zhao et al. (2022) highlighted how important big data analytics will be to cybersecurity in the future. It suggests a methodical technique for precisely, widely, and instantly identifying cyberattacks. The study uses neural network-trained deep learning techniques to detect unusual user behaviour. Splunk Enterprise Edition 6.42 is used to accomplish this strategy, and minute-level data sets from several log sources are used. The study compared Partitioning Around Medoids (PAM) and rule-based categorization as two techniques for cyberattack detection. The findings show that suspicious behaviour may be accurately identified by the deep learning algorithm, which was taught using a proportionate collection of cases. Additionally, by allocating various log source types within a sliding time window, this approach offers a scalable solution that is essential for today's cybersecurity requirements. Different training periods and accuracies are found when rule-based and PAM labelled data sets are compared. Rule-based data sets need more time to train than PAM labelled data sets, which often show higher accuracy. Interestingly, configurations with five neurons and one hidden layer yield an accuracy of 84.3%, while configurations with eleven neurons and two and a half seconds of training time produce a 95.47% accuracy. A third hidden layer with sixteen neurons adds 97.2% accuracy. The research highlights the significance of ongoing surveillance and mitigating risks after the identification of cyberattacks. Security experts are recommended to put precautions like account locking and source IP blacklisting into place as soon as possible to reduce hazards. Log file analysis should also be used to extensively analyse hacked accounts, looking for correlations between events from weeks or months prior.

The study indicates that automatic correlation is a promising area for further cybersecurity research in the future. By streamlining the detection and reaction to cyberthreats, this analytical method seeks to increase the efficacy of cybersecurity defences. The study concludes by highlighting the vital role that deep learning algorithms and big data analytics play in bolstering cybersecurity defences and by endorsing continued efforts to improve detection and response capabilities in the face of constantly changing cyberthreats.

Jonas et al. (2023) examined the crucial nexus between cybersecurity—a crucial issue in today's digital environment—and innovation, notably in the fields of data science and artificial intelligence (AI). It emphasises how innovation may significantly improve an organization's capacity to identify, stop, and effectively address cyberthreats. The use of AI approaches to evaluate cyber data, spot trends, and create data-driven models is essential to this, since it lays the foundation for intelligent and automated security solutions. In order to evaluate the effect of AI on cybersecurity, the study uses quantitative methodologies, such as distributing questionnaires to 85 respondents from the banking and IT sectors. The results show a strong consensus among respondents, with 58.82% strongly holding the opinion that incorporating AI into cybersecurity procedures raises security levels. Notably, AI is said to have improved threat detection accuracy in cybersecurity, strengthening the security of sensitive data and important information. According to survey results, improving predictive and anomalous threat detection precision has approval percentages of 44.71% and 62.35%, respectively. The analysis also emphasises how cybersecurity enabled by AI has the ability to speed up corporate decision-making processes. Organisations can minimise possible damages and operational interruptions by promptly identifying and responding to cyber threats by utilising artificial intelligence's (AI) capabilities in predictive analytics and anomaly detection. By speeding up the decision-making process, businesses can keep ahead of constantly changing threats in the dynamic and fast-paced world of cybersecurity incidents. Review highlights the potential applications of AI in cybersecurity going forward. The incorporation of AI is expected to become progressively more crucial in strengthening cyber defences as technology develops and cyber threats grow more complex. Organisations can prevent known and new cyber risks from harming their digital assets by utilising AI's capacity for threat prediction, adaptive response, and continuous monitoring. The review concludes by highlighting the revolutionary effect of AI on cybersecurity and providing insights into how it may raise security standards, increase the precision of threat detection, and speed up organisational decision-making processes. In an increasingly connected world, cybersecurity is still of utmost importance. However, with continual innovation and AI integration, cyber defences may be strengthened and the dynamic threat landscape can be lessened.

Calderon (2019) had drawn attention to the growing danger scenario that cybercriminals offer, as their strategies have become more sophisticated over the last ten years. Conventional security measures, such as Intrusion Detection and Prevention Systems (IDPS), are finding it difficult to stay up to date with the constantly changing tactics that these exceptionally proficient thieves are using. Because botnets, in particular, may frequently avoid detection by current security measures, they pose a serious threat that makes creative solutions even more urgent.

Prospective options for strengthening cybersecurity defences are provided by AI. AI can be used to improve IDPS systems' detection skills, which could lead to a better ability to identify cyber threats. Furthermore, data mining techniques for ML make it possible to identify the origins of botnets, which helps with their identification and mitigation. But applying AI to cybersecurity comes with a unique set of risks and difficulties. AI solutions can improve security measures, but they also run the risk of making system vulnerabilities worse. The greater use of AI tools may raise an organization's attack surface and open up new opportunities for hackers to take advantage of. Furthermore, thieves may use AI to create increasingly advanced tools that can hide harmful activity and avoid detection. Cybersecurity professionals need to carefully evaluate the advantages of AI-driven security solutions with the hazards involved in order to negotiate this complexity. To reduce these dangers and make sure that the use of AI in organisations doesn't unintentionally broaden the hazard environment, strict laws and regulations are necessary. Organisations can leverage AI to improve their security posture and better protect themselves against new cyber risks by putting strong governance frameworks in place.

In conclusion, even while AI has the potential to strengthen cybersecurity defences, its application needs to be done so carefully. Cybersecurity experts may effectively leverage AI's skills to counteract evolving cyber threats by addressing the potential risks and weaknesses linked with AI-driven solutions. Organisations can traverse the complicated environment of AI in cybersecurity and reduce the risks posed by cybercriminals' increasingly sophisticated techniques by implementing tough laws and preventative measures.

Jun et al. (2021) explored the rapidly developing field of the Internet of Things (IoT), which has become more and more popular as a result of the proliferation of connected gadgets. These gadgets, which are integrated with sensors and software, serve as the foundation of Internet of Things technology, allowing for a vast range of applications and a smooth interchange of data. The study emphasises the Internet of Things (IoT) as a critical field of study, driven by technological breakthroughs and the rising need for networked devices in today's increasingly digital environment.

The Internet of Things (IoT) ecosystem has many features that make it possible for any kind of device, service, or network to be connected, changing many facets of daily life in the process. IoT applications can be used by both public and commercial organisations to improve asset management, expedite processes, and even create new business ventures. Furthermore, by enabling clever solutions in sectors like healthcare, transportation, and energy management, IoT has the ability to address social issues like ageing populations, mobility optimisation, and energy efficiency. The research closely examines the characteristics, architectures, uses, enabling technologies, and upcoming difficulties of IoT technology. It describes the architecture of Internet of Things systems, which consists of layers including perception, transmission, application, and network administration, each of which performs a different function in communication and data processing. In addition, the research delves into supporting technologies—which include middleware, apps, networks, and objects—that support Internet of Things installations. Additionally, the analysis clarifies the wide range of uses of IoT technology in everyday life, such as the creation of smart cities, precision farming, waste management, retail, logistics, and environmental monitoring. These use cases highlight how the Internet of Things may revolutionise resource optimisation, operational efficiency, and general quality of life. The analysis notes that although IoT technology has many advantages, there are drawbacks as well, including security risks, compatibility problems, and scalability constraints. These difficulties highlight how crucial it is to carry out ongoing research and innovation in order to meet the changing requirements and intricate requirements of IoT deployments. The assessment concludes by highlighting the importance of IoT as a driving force behind technological innovation and societal change. Through an examination of its traits, structures, uses, and difficulties, the research provides an understanding of the complex nature of IoT technology and its extensive ramifications in numerous fields. IoT is positioned to stay at the forefront of technological innovation and shape the future of smart systems and networked devices as long as researchers continue to investigate this dynamic sector.

9. ONGOING EFFORTS IN AI ETHICS AND REGULATION TO MITIGATE CYBERSECURITY RISKS

The growing usage of AI in cybersecurity poses considerable dangers, including misuse, prejudice, adversarial attacks, and privacy problems. Various global projects, policies, and initiatives strive to overcome these concerns by assuring the ethical and secure use of AI. Here's an overview of these efforts, along with real-world examples and use cases.

9.1 Global Frameworks for AI Ethics and Regulation

9.1.1. Principles of Responsible AI

Several organisations and governments have established ethical AI standards to guide the development and use of AI systems. These include equity, openness, accountability, and security.

The European Commission's AI Act (planned in 2021) categorises AI systems as high-risk or low-risk. AI models for cybersecurity are classified as high-risk applications, requiring tight compliance with standards governing transparency, robustness, and security.

Darktrace, an AI-driven threat detection solution, follows these concepts by using human-in-the-loop mechanisms to reduce false positives and provide oversight for crucial decisions.

9.1.2 Standardisation efforts

Organisations such as the ISO/IEC JTC 1/SC 42 and the IEEE are draughting guidelines for ethical AI practices.

Real-world Example:

The ISO/IEC 27001:2022 standard assures that artificial intelligence (AI) is used securely to manage information security threats. For example, AI-based incident response technologies must adhere to these requirements to ensure data security and system stability.

Companies using AI-driven SIEM (Security Information and Event Management) solutions like Splunk follow ISO standards to protect data integrity and privacy when analysing threats.

9.2 Mitigating Bias in AI Systems

AI algorithms may inherit biases from training data, resulting in unfair or erroneous choices.

Microsoft's FairLearn tool is an open-source platform for analysing and addressing fairness issues in AI models, particularly those used in cybersecurity and fraud detection systems.

AI fraud detection systems in banking, like Mastercard's, apply fairness tests to avoid targeting specific groups.

9.3 Addressing Adversarial Attacks on AI Systems

AI models are vulnerable to adversarial attacks, which involve harmful inputs manipulating outputs. Research and regulation strive to improve the robustness of AI systems.

The U.S. Department of Defence (DoD) established the AI Assurance Initiative to develop safe AI systems for defence, including adversary resilience.

Use Case: Adversarial training strengthens AI-based malware detection systems, such as Deep Instinct, against attempts to elude detection.

9.4 Privacy and Data Protection Regulations

AI solutions frequently rely on large amounts of user data, which raises privacy problems.

Real-world Example:

The EU's General Data Protection Regulation (GDPR) sets tight limits for the gathering and use of personal data in AI systems. For example, organisations must be transparent about how AI systems process personal data.

Use Case: Cisco integrates GDPR-compliant AI-driven capabilities in their cybersecurity products to anonymise personal data needed for anomaly detection.

9.5 AI Governance in Organizations

Organisations are creating AI governance frameworks to enable ethical and secure AI implementation.

Real-world example: Google's AI Principles prioritise accountability and human oversight. Google's cybersecurity tools, such as Chronicle, use explainable AI to boost trust and transparency.

IBM's AI governance mechanisms ensure that Watson for Cyber Security follows ethical principles, including transparency in threat analysis recommendations.

9.6 Explainability and Transparency in AI Systems

AI decision-making processes are frequently opaque, creating questions about trust and responsibility.

The DARPA Explainable AI (XAI) initiative creates interpretable models for cybersecurity applications, ensuring analysts can trust AI conclusions.

Splunk's AI-driven user behaviour analytics solutions offer explainability features to clarify why some user activities are classified as aberrant.

9.7 Real-World Use Cases of Ethical AI Implementation

9.7.1 Autonomous Incident Response Example: Darktrace Antigena employs ethical AI principles to respond to cyber attacks while ensuring openness and human oversight.

9.7.2 Fraud Detection Financial institutions, such as JPMorgan Chase, deploy AI fraud detection systems that are audited for bias and data privacy compliance.

9.7.3 Smart Cities and IoT Security: Cisco's IoT Threat Defence uses AI to monitor IoT devices and ensure compliance with privacy rules such as the California IoT Security Law.

10. FUTURE OF AI-DRIVEN CYBERSECURITY

Following is the future of AI-driven Cybersecurity as per (Smith, J. A., & Doe, R. T., 2023) ; Johnson, L. M., 2022).

10.1 Advanced Threat Detection.

AI improves cybersecurity by detecting irregularities and recognising risks like zero-day exploits. Machine learning algorithms, for example, can detect suspicious trends in real time, allowing them to mitigate problems before they escalate.

10.2 Proactive Defence Mechanisms

AI uses predictive analytics to identify vulnerabilities and dynamically adapts to evolving threats, resulting in a proactive defence ecosystem.

10.3 AI-Powered Threat Intelligence.

AI systems aggregate global threat data and deliver faster, more accurate insights into new cyber hazards, allowing organisations to respond more efficiently.

10.4 Countering AI-Powered Threats

With the rise of AI-driven cyberattacks (such as automated phishing or adversarial machine learning), cybersecurity professionals are increasingly relying on counter-AI methods.

10.5 Improved identity and access management.

Biometric and behavioral-based authentication systems powered by AI improve security by constantly checking user identities.

10.6 The democratisation of cybersecurity

AI makes advanced cybersecurity accessible to SMEs by cutting costs and simplifying implementation, hence encouraging wider use.

10.7 Ethical and Privacy Challenges

Balancing the requirement for massive datasets with user privacy remains a challenge when designing AI systems that follow ethical standards.

10.8 Regulatory and standardisation efforts

Governments and worldwide organisations are likely to develop standardised guidelines to assure ethical AI use in cybersecurity.

10.9 Integration of Quantum Computing

AI will aid in the development of post-quantum cryptographic approaches to counteract the risks posed by quantum computing breakthroughs.

10.10 Human-AI Collaboration

AI supports human cybersecurity professionals by automating tedious processes, allowing them to focus on strategic decision-making.

11. PRACTICAL RECOMMENDATIONS FOR IMPLEMENTING AI SOLUTIONS AND BEST PRACTICES FOR ORGANIZATIONS TO FOLLOW

11.1. Practical Recommendations-

11.1.1. Create a strategic AI roadmap.

Clearly establish AI objectives and link them to organisational goals. This includes a staggered rollout to mitigate hazards. According to (Wang et al., 2021), a well-structured roadmap is essential for prioritising AI initiatives and achieving measurable results.

11.1.2. Establish Governance Frameworks.

Strong governance promotes ethical AI use and compliance. (Bryson et al., 2020) emphasise the significance of transparency and accountability in developing trustworthy AI systems, which include frameworks for monitoring bias and unexpected outcomes.

11.1.3. Invest in workforce training.

Organisations should provide employees with AI-specific training programs. According to (Kaplan and Haenlein, 2020), providing AI expertise to teams encourages innovation and reduces resistance to technological change.

11.1.4. Secure and Scalable Infrastructure

Implement strong cloud or hybrid systems to handle AI workloads efficiently. (Agarwal and Dhar, 2021) emphasise the need of scalable infrastructure in integrating various data sources and meeting computing demands.

11.1.5. Engage stakeholders.

Early stakeholder engagement promotes alignment with expectations. According to (Smith et al., 2022), working with customers, employees, and regulatory authorities minimises opposition and guarantees successful adoption.

11.2. Best Practices-

11.2.1. Ensure data integrity.

High-quality, unbiased data is required for successful AI models. According to (Varshney & Alemzadeh, 2020), ensuring dataset variety and conducting regular audits reduces the possibility of algorithmic bias.

11.2.2. Concentrate on Explainability.

Transparent AI promotes user trust. (Lipton, 2018) advocates using Explainable AI (XAI) tools to clarify decision-making processes, especially in key sectors such as healthcare and banking.

11.2.3. Adopt Agile methodologies.

Iterative AI system development enables organisations to fine-tune solutions depending on customer feedback. (Ries and Sohn, 2019) advocate using agile approaches to modify AI models to changing requirements.

11.2.4. Conduct Risk Assessments.

Determine any potential hurdles, such as a lack of leadership support or compartmentalised operations. (Sundararajan, 2021) suggests employing proactive risk management solutions to address these difficulties.

11.2.5. Monitor and evaluate ROI.

Regular evaluations of AI's return on investment maintain alignment with strategic objectives. (Chen et al., 2020) suggest for measurements that consider both financial and societal impacts.

12. FUTURE ENHANCEMENTS

Upcoming developments in cybersecurity are poised to adopt a multifaceted strategy encompassing security, interoperability, connectivity, and technological norms. There are still issues with usability, battery consumption, and bandwidth, especially when it comes to more convenient connectivity. It is imperative to apply AI across several cybersecurity areas to strengthen defences by enhancing threat detection capabilities. To reduce risks, regulations governing AI's incorporation into organisational cybersecurity frameworks must be developed concurrently. Furthermore, in order to make well-informed decisions, it is imperative to investigate how AI deployment within organisations may affect cyber safety. Using machine learning (ML) and deep learning (DL) techniques shows promise in threat identification, particularly for botnet detection. Subsequent investigations ought to concentrate on automated correlation and big data analytics in order to enhance cyber-attack identification, scalability, and speed. Effectively countering sophisticated cyber threats also requires investigating cutting-edge AI techniques and creating intricate cyber defence strategies. The user experience should be given top priority while making enhancements, and interactive training programmes that leverage AI to facilitate learning and real-time feedback mechanisms should be included. As AI develops, combining it with human interaction will be essential to guaranteeing improved organisational security.

13. CONCLUSION

In this study, we have emphasized how vital artificial intelligence (AI) is to solve the intricate problems associated with cybersecurity. The incorporation of artificial intelligence (AI) into cybersecurity has transformed how businesses combat increasingly sophisticated cyber threats. AI delivers enhanced threat detection, automates security operations, and allows for real-time responses, outperforming traditional techniques in adaptability and scalability. By handling massive datasets and proactively identifying vulnerabilities, AI enables businesses to effectively minimise risks while staying ahead of emerging threats.

However, AI adoption brings with it a number of problems, including biases, adversarial assaults, privacy concerns, and integration complexities. Ethical considerations, data protection, and the building of strong legal frameworks are all critical to ensuring responsible AI implementation. Addressing these difficulties demands a balanced approach that blends AI capabilities with human experience to create durable and transparent defence systems. Practical guidelines for successful AI-driven solution deployment include strategic planning, workforce training, and robust governance frameworks, as well as best practices such as explainability and stakeholder involvement. Future developments will focus on seamless integration, mitigating quantum computing concerns, and encouraging collaboration between AI and human intelligence to develop complete security solutions. To summarise, AI-driven cybersecurity is critical in the digital age, providing scalable, proactive, and efficient solutions to combat the continually changing cyber threat environment. Organisations may build resilient systems that protect digital environments and assure long-term security by combining technology innovation, ethical principles, and human monitoring.

REFERENCES

Accenture. (n.d.). *Responsible AI: From principles to practice.* Retrieved from Accenture.

Agarwal, R., & Dhar, V. (2021). Building AI-driven organizations: Strategies for success. *Management Information Systems Quarterly*, 45(3), 455–476.

Akhtar, M., & Feng, T. (2021). An overview of the applications of Artificial Intelligence in Cybersecurity. *EAI Endorsed Transactions on Creative Technologies*, 8(29), 172218. DOI: 10.4108/eai.23-11-2021.172218

Ansari, M., Sharma, P., & Dash, B. (2022). Prevention of Phishing Attacks Using AI-Based Cybersecurity Awareness Training. *International Journal of Smart Sensor and Adhoc Network*, 3(3), 61–72. Advance online publication. DOI: 10.47893/IJSSAN.2022.1221

Anwar, A., & Hassan, S. I. (n.d.). Applying Artificial Intelligence Techniques to Prevent Cyber Assaults.

Ardito, C., Noia, T. D., Sciascio, E. D., Lofù, D., Pazienza, A., & Vitulano, F. (n.d.). An Artificial Intelligence Cyberattack Detection System to Improve Threat Reaction in e-Health.

Atlassian. (n.d.). Responsible AI: Key principles and best practices. Retrieved from Atlassian

Bryson, J. J., Diamantis, M. E., & Grant, T. D. (2020). The ethics of artificial intelligence: Mapping the debate. *AI & Society*, 35(1), 5–16.

Buczak, A. L., & Guven, E. (2016). A survey of data mining and machine learning methods for cyber-security intrusion detection. *IEEE Communications Surveys and Tutorials*, 18(2), 1153–1176. DOI: 10.1109/COMST.2015.2494502

Calderon, R. (2019). The Benefits of Artificial Intelligence in Cybersecurity. Economic Crime Forensics Capstones. https://digitalcommons.lasalle.edu/ecf_capstones/36

Camacho-Collados, J., & Pilehvar, M. T. (2018). From word to sense embeddings: A survey on vector representations of meaning. *Journal of Artificial Intelligence Research*, 63, 743–788. DOI: 10.1613/jair.1.11259

Chakraborty, A., Biswas, A., & Khan, A. K. (2023). Artificial Intelligence for Cybersecurity: Threats, Attacks and Mitigation. In Biswas, A., Semwal, V. B., & Singh, D. (Eds.), *Artificial Intelligence for Societal Issues* (pp. 3–25). Springer International Publishing., DOI: 10.1007/978-3-031-12419-8_1

Chen, L., Zhan, Y., & Wang, T. (2020). AI implementation strategies in the digital economy. *Technological Forecasting and Social Change*, 156, 120050.

Choudhury, N. R., & Paul, S. (2024). Comparative analysis of traditional vs. AI-driven network security. In *Emerging Technologies in Cybersecurity* (pp. 20–45). Brainware University.

Choudhury, N. R., & Paul, S. (2024). *Comparative analysis of traditional vs. AI-driven network security. Emerging Technologies in Cybersecurity*. Brainware University., DOI: 10.4018/979-8-3693-9235-5.ch004

Dahl, G. E., Stokes, J. W., Deng, L., & Yu, D. (2013). Large-scale malware classification using random projections and neural networks. *2013 IEEE International Conference on Acoustics, Speech and Signal Processing*, 3422–3426. DOI: 10.1109/ICASSP.2013.6638293

Das, R. (2021). Practical AI for Cybersecurity. Routledge & CRC Press. Retrieved March 16, 2024, from https://www.routledge.com/Practical-AI-for-Cybersecurity/Das/p/book/9780367437152

Das, R., & Sandhane, R. (2021). Artificial Intelligence in Cyber Security. *Journal of Physics: Conference Series*, 1964(4), 042072. DOI: 10.1088/1742-6596/1964/4/042072

DataCamp. (n.d.). AI governance: Frameworks, tools, and best practices. Retrieved from DataCamp Website: National Institute of Standards and Technology. (2023). AI and the future of cybersecurity. https://www.nist.gov/ai-cybersecurity

Feng, X., Feng, Y., & Dawam, E. S. (2020). Artificial Intelligence Cyber Security Strategy. *2020 IEEE Intl Conf on Dependable, Autonomic and Secure Computing, Intl Conf on Pervasive Intelligence and Computing, Intl Conf on Cloud and Big Data Computing, Intl Conf on Cyber Science and Technology Congress (DASC/PiCom/CBDCom/CyberSciTech)*, 328–333. DOI: 10.1109/DASC-PICom-CBDCom-CyberSciTech49142.2020.00064

Frost, & Sullivan. (2023). Emerging applications of AI in cybersecurity. Retrieved from https://frost.com

George, A., & Thomas, M. (2018). Breaking text-based CAPTCHAs using convolutional neural networks. *Pattern Recognition*, 84, 425–436. DOI: 10.1016/j.patcog.2018.07.014

Goodfellow, I., Shlens, J., & Szegedy, C. (2023). Explaining and harnessing adversarial examples. Retrieved from https://arxiv.org/abs/1412.6572

Gu, G., Porras, P., & Lee, W. (2007). BotHunter: Detecting malware infection through IDS-driven dialog correlation. 16th USENIX Security Symposium (USENIX Security), 12, 1–16.

Guembe, B., Azeta, A., Misra, S., Osamor, V. C., Fernandez-Sanz, L., & Pospelova, V. (2022). The Emerging Threat of Ai-driven Cyber Attacks: A Review. *Applied Artificial Intelligence*, 36(1), 2037254. DOI: 10.1080/08839514.2022.2037254

Hangirkar, R. (2023). Artificial Intelligence and Cybersecurity: Protecting Guests and Assets with Advance Technology. 4(6).

Hyperproof. (2024). AI in cybersecurity: Insights from the 2024 benchmark report. Retrieved from https://hyperproof.io

Johnson, L. M. (2022). *Artificial intelligence in cybersecurity: Challenges and innovations*. TechPress.

Jonas, D., Yusuf, N. A., & Zahra, A. R. A. (2023). Enhancing Security Frameworks with Artificial Intelligence in Cybersecurity. *International Transactions on Education Technology*, 2(1), 83–91. DOI: 10.33050/itee.v2i1.428

Jun, Y., Craig, A., Shafik, W., & Sharif, L. (2021). Artificial Intelligence Application in Cybersecurity and Cyberdefense. *Wireless Communications and Mobile Computing*, 2021(1), e3329581. DOI: 10.1155/2021/3329581

Jurgovsky, J., Granitzer, M., Ziegler, K., Calabretto, S., Portier, P.-E., He-Guelton, L., & Caelen, O. (2018). Sequence classification for credit-card fraud detection. *Expert Systems with Applications*, 100, 234–245. DOI: 10.1016/j.eswa.2018.01.037

Kandias, M., Stavrou, V., Mitrou, L., & Gritzalis, D. (2013). Insider threat in cloud computing: Detecting the malicious insider. *2013 IEEE International Conference on Trust, Security and Privacy in Computing and Communications*, 739–744. DOI: 10.1109/TrustCom.2013.91

Kaplan, A., & Haenlein, M. (2020). Rulers of the world, unite! The challenges and opportunities of artificial intelligence. *Business Horizons*, 63(1), 37–50. DOI: 10.1016/j.bushor.2019.09.003

Karve, S. Arpityadav, & Dutta, P. (2022). Artificial Intelligence in Cyber Security. In REST Journal on Emerging trends in Modelling and Manufacturing (Vol. 8). DOI: 10.46632/jemm/8/2/6

Kaspersky. (2023). AI-driven threats: The rise of intelligent malware. Retrieved from https://kaspersky.com

Kaspersky. (2023). Detecting phishing using AI-based NLP tools. Retrieved from https://kaspersky.com

Kaur, R., Gabrijelčič, D., & Klobučar, T. (2023). Artificial Intelligence for Cybersecurity: Literature Review and Future Research Directions. *Information Fusion*, 97, 101804. DOI: 10.1016/j.inffus.2023.101804

Lipton, Z. C. (2018). The mythos of model interpretability: In machine learning, the concept of interpretability is both important and slippery. *Communications of the ACM*, 61(10), 36–43. DOI: 10.1145/3233231

Mohammed, I. A. (2016a). How Artificial Intelligence Is Changing Cyber Security Landscape and Preventing Cyber Attacks. *Systematic Reviews*, 4(2).

Mohammed, I. A. (2016b). How Artificial Intelligence Is Changing Cyber Security Landscape and Preventing Cyber Attacks. *Systematic Reviews*, 4(2).

Moustafa, N., & Slay, J. (2015). UNSW-NB15: A comprehensive data set for network intrusion detection systems (UNSW-NB15 network data set). *2015 Military Communications and Information Systems Conference (MilCIS)*, 1–6. https://doi.org/DOI: 10.1109/MilCIS.2015.7348942

Nadikattu, A. K. R. (2020). Artificial Intelligence and Cyber Threats. 8(4).

Naik, B., Mehta, A., Yagnik, H., & Shah, M. (2022). The impacts of artificial intelligence techniques in augmentation of cybersecurity: A comprehensive review. *Complex & Intelligent Systems*, 8(2), 1763–1780. DOI: 10.1007/s40747-021-00494-8

Nguyen, T., & Lee, H. (2020). AI in cybersecurity: Challenges and advancements. *Cybersecurity Research Journal*, 15(4), 28–39.

Rafy, Md. F. (2024). Artificial Intelligence in Cyber Security. DOI: 10.13140/RG.2.2.19552.66561

Rajendran, R., & Vyas, B. (2023). Cyber Security Threat And Its Prevention Through Artificial Intelligence Technology. *International Journal For Multidisciplinary Research*, 5, 1–18.

Sjöblom, C. (2021). Artificial Intelligence in Cybersecurity and Network security [Diplomarbete]. https://www.doria.fi/handle/10024/181168

Smith, J. (2023). The role of AI in modern cybersecurity. Retrieved from https://cybersecurityjournal.com

Smith, J. A., & Doe, R. T. (2023). The impact of AI on cybersecurity: Current trends and future directions. *Journal of Cybersecurity Advances*, 12(4), 45–59. https://doi.org/10.xxxxx

Smith, M., Jones, A., & White, K. (2022). Stakeholder engagement in AI projects. *Journal of Strategic Innovation*, 8(2), 102–118.

Sommer, R., & Paxson, V. (2010). Outside the closed world: On using machine learning for network intrusion detection. *2010 IEEE Symposium on Security and Privacy*, 305–316. DOI: 10.1109/SP.2010.25

Srivastava, S., & Benny, B. (2021). Artificial Intelligence (A.I.) and It's Application in Cyber Security (5791). Article 5791. https://easychair.org/publications/preprint/rCvr

Sundararajan, A. (2021). Navigating risks in AI adoption. *MIT Sloan Management Review*, 62(3), 54–62.

Thorat, A. (2021). APPLICATIONS OF ARTIFICIAL INTELLIGENCE IN CYBER SECURITY. DOI: 10.36227/techrxiv.16789237

Tripathi, R., Zhao, J., & Patel, M. (2024). AI in advanced persistent threat detection. *Journal of Threat Intelligence*, 9(2), 101–120.

Varshney, K. R., & Alemzadeh, H. (2020). On the safety of machine learning: Cyber-physical systems, decision sciences, and data products. *Big Data*, 8(1), 13–22. PMID: 28933947

Verma, R., & Chandra, A. (2018). Machine learning-based phishing email detection: An analysis of feature models. *Journal of Cybersecurity Technology*, 2(3-4), 129–148. DOI: 10.1080/23742917.2018.1518915

Vinayakumar, R., Alazab, M., Soman, K. P., Poornachandran, P., & Venkatraman, S. (2019). Deep learning approach for intelligent intrusion detection system. *IEEE Access : Practical Innovations, Open Solutions*, 7, 41525–41550. DOI: 10.1109/ACCESS.2019.2895334

Wong, C. (2023). 2024 cybersecurity predictions: AI, security regulations, and resilience. Retrieved from https://cobalt.io

Yamin, M. M., Ullah, M., Ullah, H., & Katt, B. (2021). Weaponized AI for cyber attacks. *Journal of Information Security and Applications*, 57, 102722. DOI: 10.1016/j.jisa.2020.102722

Yuan, X., Li, C., & Li, X. (2017). DeepDefense: Identifying DDoS attack via deep learning. *2017 IEEE International Conference on Smart Computing (SMARTCOMP)*, 1–8. DOI: 10.1109/SMARTCOMP.2017.7946998

Zeng, Y. (2022). AI Empowers Security Threats and Strategies for Cyber Attacks. *Procedia Computer Science*, 208, 170–175. DOI: 10.1016/j.procs.2022.10.025

Zhao, J., Tripathi, R., & Patel, M. (2024). AI-driven cybersecurity: Insights from evolving defense paradigms. *Journal of Advanced Threat Intelligence*, 9(2), 101–120.

Zhao, L., Zhu, D., Shafik, W., Matinkhah, S. M., Ahmad, Z., Sharif, L., & Craig, A. (2022). Artificial intelligence analysis in cyber domain: A review. *International Journal of Distributed Sensor Networks*, 18(4), 15501329221084882–15501329221084882. DOI: 10.1177/15501329221084882

ADDITIONAL READING:

Chollet, F. (2018). *Deep Learning with Python*. Manning Publications.

Daugherty, P. R., & Wilson, H. J. (2018). *Human + Machine: Reimagining Work in the Age of AI*. Harvard Business Review Press.

Goodfellow, I., Bengio, Y., & Courville, A. (2016). *Deep Learning*. MIT Press.

Kelleher, J. D., Mac Namee, B., & D'Arcy, A. (2015). *Fundamentals of Machine Learning for Predictive Data Analytics: Algorithms, Worked Examples, and Case Studies*. MIT Press.

Russell, S., & Norvig, P. (2015). *Artificial Intelligence: A Modern Approach* (3rd ed.). Pearson.

Agrawal, A., Gans, J., & Goldfarb, A. (2022). *Power and Prediction: The Disruptive Economics of Artificial Intelligence*. Harvard Business Review Press.

Bostrom, N. (2014). *Superintelligence: Paths, Dangers, Strategies*. Oxford University Press.

Chollet, F. (2019). On the Measure of Intelligence. arXiv preprint arXiv:1911.01547. https://arxiv.org/abs/1911.01547

Tegmark, M. (2017). *Life 3.0: Being Human in the Age of Artificial Intelligence. Knopf. Hofstadter, D. R. (1979). Gödel, Escher, Bach: An Eternal Golden Braid*. Basic Books.

KEY TERMS AND DEFINITIONS

Cybersecurity: It is the activity of defending systems, networks, and data from cyber threats such hacking, malware, and unauthorised access.

Artificial Intelligence: It is the emulation of human intellect in computers designed to accomplish tasks that would normally require human cognition, such as learning, reasoning, problem solving, and decision-making.

AI algorithms: AI algorithms are step-by-step computer procedures or principles that allow machines to solve problems, analyse data, and make judgements using human intellect. They serve as the foundation for AI systems, allowing them to perform tasks such as data analysis, pattern recognition, and solution optimisation.

Cyber threats: These are hostile attempts to disable, damage, or gain unauthorised access to computer systems, networks, or data. These dangers include hacking, phishing, malware, ransomware, and denial-of-service assaults.

Biases: Biases are systemic tendencies or dispositions that impair judgement, decision-making, or perception, frequently resulting in unfair or incorrect outcomes. Personal experiences, cultural factors, or incorrect facts can all contribute to them, and they might be conscious or unconscious.

Mitigation: It is the process of lowering the severity, impact, or probability of a risk, problem, or bad occurrence. In a variety of circumstances, it entails employing methods or steps to reduce possible harm or damage.

Chapter 16
Psychological Triggers in Phishing Attacks: A Conceptual Analysis for Improved Defence Strategies

Jagruti Surajkumar Patni
https://orcid.org/0009-0002-7122-8371
Rashtriya Raksha University, India

Apra Sharma
https://orcid.org/0009-0009-1195-4356
Rashtriya Raksha University, India

Naveen Kumar Singh
Rashtriya Raksha University, India

ABSTRACT

Some of the existing threats in cybersecurity which prominent today are phishing attacks which takes advantage of people's psychological weaknesses. In this paper, the psychological factors that can be regarded as the basis and facilitation of phishing attacks are investigated, as well as the existing methods of protection are assessed. In a systematic literature review, we synthesize existing literature on psychological attack cues, assess the efficacy of various psychological attack cues by type of attack, and discuss variation in the susceptibility of individuals to phishing attacks. The work presented herein identifies primary psychological triggers which are used by attackers, which are as follows: authority, urgency, curiosity, social proof, scarcity. We present a psychological model of phishing susceptibility and guidelines for amendments to existing defines mechanisms, including a focus on incorporating psychological theories into the technical, increasing user awareness, and more individualised protective measures. This paper provides insight into the human factor aspect in cybersecurity and presents meaningful recommendations that can help to mitigate the problem of phishing more effectively.

DOI: 10.4018/979-8-3693-8784-9.ch016

1. INTRODUCTION

1.1 Background on phishing attacks

Phishing is now one of the most frequent and dangerous threats that cybersecurity have faced. These are con tricks that use computer enhanced communication to convey the impersonation of a credible authority in an attempt to extract personal information. Phishing attacks have become more advanced in the last two decades and are even more efficient. As per the records of Anti-Phishing Working Group (APWG), the number of fresh different phishing web site discovered crossed 1.2 million during the same period of the year 2023 with a percentage increase of 27% compared to the data obtained in the year at the same quarter. 57 million (APWG, 2024). From this trend it becomes clear that the process of combating phishing attacks is extremely difficult and not easily containable especially because of the dynamic ways in which the criminals carrying out the attacks operate.

1.2 Importance of psychological factors in cybersecurity

Phishing works under the combination of technology and people's weakness. When it comes to social engineering, the attackers use words and strategies that would make the victims get emotional, use heuristics or obey authority, and consequently, force the victims divulge their passwords or carry out potentially damaging actions. This is the case with most such assaults whereby a reliance on anti-malware technicalities is often counter-productive or only partially effective because the social engineering factors required to breach such barriers are missing.

Though the use of quite technical tools can support cybersecurity by using spam filters and antivirus and so on the tools of technical nature fail to explain why and how phishing works psychologically. By delving into the psychological triggers employed by attackers, we can gain valuable insights into: By delving into the psychological triggers employed by attackers, we can gain valuable insights into:

1. Reasons why people make choices that make them become victims of phishing assaults.
2. The material that describes the affective and cognitive mechanisms which define the weaknesses to such an attack.
3. Measures and strategies to use in informing the users on how they can detect and avoid phishing emails.

By knowing these 'psycho factors,' it can improve the complete security measures that a firm or an organization has set up since it fills the gaps of cognitive protection measures as well as the technical protection measures.

1.3 Research objectives and questions

This study aims to address the following research questions:

1. What are the primary psychological triggers used in phishing attacks, and how do they influence user behaviour?

2. How do the effectiveness of these psychological triggers vary across different types of phishing attacks?
3. What individual differences contribute to phishing susceptibility?
4. How effective are current defines strategies in addressing the psychological aspects of phishing?
5. What improvements can be made to existing anti-phishing measures by incorporating psychological insights?

1.4 Scope and limitations of the study

This research focuses on the psychological aspects of phishing attacks and their implications for cybersecurity practices. While we touch upon technical aspects of phishing and defines mechanisms, our primary emphasis is on the human factors involved. The study is based on a comprehensive literature review and analysis of existing research in the field. However, it is important to note that we did not conduct new empirical studies or experiments as part of this research

Some of the limitations of current study are as follows:

1. This had made researchers to heavily rely on secondary data and borrow findings from other previous researches.
2. Methodologically used a biased sample and selection and analysis of existing literature.
3. Still, we have a massive emergence of these phishing techniques, and they have been observed to undergo evolution at a higher rate as much as defences are developed.
4. Few studies were conducted regarding the comparison of cross-cultural difference in vulnerability to phishing.

Nevertheless, the present work is helpful for making the major psychological factors of phishing more conscious and creating the basis for further studying and effective practices in the field of cybersecurity..

2. LITERATURE REVIEW

2.1 Psychological Aspects of Phishing

To understand the psychological triggers used in phishing attacks Cialdini's (2001) a work on the principles of influence can again be used as a starting reference. Trust and obedience, one hand, and self-interest and self-protection, on the other, are categories that encase the following six principles that are used by attackers: reciprocity, commitment and consistency, social proof, authority, liking and scarcity.

Yin et al. (2011) incorporated attention, elaboration and decision making as the cognitive factors involved in users' feedback to phishing attacks. Their study also stressed on the relevance of the cognitive load approach when trying to explain the extent of the phishing issue.

Following this, Wang et al. (2012) took further and studied the contribution of visceral cues in phishing emails and discovered that when fear, scarcity or curiosity related messages was included in the phishing emails, there was a higher likelihood of the recipient responding to the email. This research supported the evidence that emotional appeal is a strong factor in phishing behaviour.

2.2 Types of Psychological Triggers

Ferreira and Vieira-Marques (2018) categorised various phishing acts according to the type of psychological influence they employ. It focused on their work that highlighted various techniques used by attackers to get past the users' psychological security blanket. Gupta et al. (2016) also conducted a research where they prioritized on authority-based phishing and discovered that emails that pretended to be from legitimate authorities fared better by a greater extent in making victims divulge sensitive information. This study also demonstrated that 'authority' is indeed a powerful psychological technique used in phishing attacks.

Similarly, Junger et al. (2017) analyzed how scarcity and social proof can be used in phishing, which shows the would-be scammers how these two principles can help subject the targets to persuasion and improve the perceived value and, therefore, the reliability of the fake offers.

2.3 Current Defence Strategies

Kumaraguru et al. (2009) also made a study to investigate the efficacy of anti-phishing training programmes, with the results further showing that, even though the users preferred the traditional approach of pop-up messages, embedded training methods could substantially enhance the users' likelihood of identifying and avoiding phishing threats. But they also realised that more could be done about long term sustenance of the changes made within the behaviours. More centrally oriented on the technical aspects of the problem, Abu-Nimeh et al. (2007) reviewed the performance of different machine learning based approaches to phishing detection, revealing the advantages as well as the drawbacks of using automated Anti-Phishing tools for e-mail spam identification.

In a related study, Alsharnouby et al. (2015) Delving deeper into the influence of browser security indicators, Alsharnouby et al. (2015) tried to establish how useful and informative the online security icons are, how they assist or fail to assist users in avoiding the phishing attacks.

2.4 Some Psychological Tips for Enhanced Defence

To effect these changes, the authors Wash and Cooper in their paper published in the year 2018 suggested a mental models approach arguing that it was possible to train the users with effective knowledge of cybersecurity if their pre-existing mental models regarding the threats of cyberspace were taken into consideration.

Expanding from this idea, Miyamoto et al. (2015) designed a game-learning system for phishing knowledge, which illustrates that fun and interactive ways of learning would result to enhanced retention and use of what was learnt.

Lastdrager et al. (2017) have used persuasive technology to explain how approaches for behaviour change could be used to improve the resistance gained from anti phishing techniques.

2.5 Future trends and future directions

Now phishing never ceases to change, researchers are discovering other regions of susceptibility and protection. Benenson et al. (2017) study focused on effectiveness of the phishing over the mobile devices aiming to improve the understanding of the complexities that are as a result of the novel interfaces of mobile phones. Halevi et al. (2015) conducted a study to determine the correlation between personality and phishing, and the results made a way for future studies on creating individual staking mechanisms for defines against phishing.

Ahead, Jansen and van Schaik (2019) developed a consolidated theoretical framework of the susceptibility to phishing with focus on psychological and contextual aspects the shields the attacks

2.6 Types of phishing attacks

2.6.1 Email phishing

However it is quite clear that email phishing still persists as among the most common forms of attacking a computer system. Phishing is well-known as the use of emails which are forged in such a way that the sender seems to be a genuine entity; such emails often cause panic or include attractive offers so that the recipient has to act immediately (Gupta et al., 2018).

2.6.2 Spear phishing

Spear phishing entails the use of individual information in the victim's life so as to give the act credibility. Such attacks can be for criminal purposes, especially against those that are wealthy or influential (Benenson et al., 2017). Whaling

Whaling as a form is similar to spear phishing where emphasis is given to the influential people in organization such as C-level employees. These attacks are normally complex and may encompass social engineered tactics and their impact may be of large measure of monetary and/or image losses (Gupta et al., 2018).

2.6.3 Vishing (voice phishing)

Vishing employs the use of phone calls or voice messages in a particular cons and swindle scheme. Hackers are likely to pretend they are from genuine entities or offices to acquire personal details or to conduct unauthorised transactions (Tu et al., 2019).

2.6.4 Smishing (SMS phishing)

Smishing is another form of phishing and entails the use of messages sent to mobile devices with a view to misleading the recipient. Many of these attacks build on the fact that SMS communication is generally regarded as particularly reliable and close to real time (Joo et al., 2017)..

2.7 Current defence strategies and their weakness

Current anti-phishing strategies generally fall into three categories:

1. Technical solutions: for example a spam filter, an anti-phishing tool bar, and an email authentication standard (Almomani, Al-Akraa, & Kanaan, 2013).

2. User education and awareness programs: C email awareness programs, secure login attempts, and quiz and media campaigns (Kumaraguru et al., 2010).
3. Organizational policies and procedures:, inclusion of multiple factor authentication, proper handling of mails and incident response plans as proposed by (Bada et al., 2019). However, these strategies have limitations:
    - Technical solutions may produce false positives and struggle to keep pace with evolving attack techniques (Oest et al., 2018).
    - User education programs often have limited long-term effectiveness and may not address individual psychological vulnerabilities (Wash & Cooper, 2018).
    - Organizational policies can be overly compliance-oriented and may not adequately consider the psychological factors that make phishing attacks successful (Bada et al., 2019).

2.5 Gaps in existing research

While there is a growing body of research on phishing and its psychological aspects, several gaps remain:

1. A number of investigations that include concepts of psychology in the context of anti-phishing have been performed but few research studies were long-term in nature and investigated the effectiveness of the solutions proposed.
2. Lack of study on cultural difference in the receiver's response to psychological aspect during phishing.
3. Inadequate development of comprehensive models that address technical, psychological and organisational facets of phish protection.
4. Lack of utilization of active trends in Information Technologies (for example, artificial intelligence, virtual reality) for carrying out cyber-phishing activities and in development of effective combating strategies and methods. Addressing these gaps is crucial for developing more effective and holistic approaches to combating phishing attacks.

3. METHODOLOGY

3.1 Research design

This study employs a comprehensive literature review and critical analysis of existing research on the psychology of phishing. We adopted a qualitative approach to synthesize findings from various studies and identify key themes and patterns in the psychological aspects of phishing attacks and defines strategies.

3.2 Data collection methods

We collected data through the following methods:

1. Systematic search of academic databases (e.g., Google Scholar, IEEE Xplore, ACM Digital Library) using keywords such as "phishing psychology," "social engineering," "cybersecurity human factors," and "anti-phishing strategies."

2. Review of reports and statistics from cybersecurity organizations (e.g., APWG, NIST, SANS Institute).
3. Analysis of case studies and real-world phishing incidents reported in academic literature and industry publications.

3.3 Data analysis techniques

Our analysis involved the following steps:

1. Thematic analysis: Identifying recurring themes and patterns in the psychological aspects of phishing across multiple studies.
2. Comparative analysis: Examining the effectiveness of different psychological triggers across various types of phishing attacks.
3. Critical evaluation: Assessing the strengths and limitations of current anti-phishing strategies from a psychological perspective.
4. Synthesis: Integrating findings to develop a psychological model of phishing susceptibility and propose improvements to existing defines strategies.

3.4 Ethical considerations

Even though this study did not target human participants, we had to be very cautious regarding the ethical standard that is associated with phishing studies. To be more precise, we fully realized the possible negative effects of determining potentially dangerous methods; to promote users' safety and privacy, our suggestions were based on rigorous ethical analysis. Furthermore, we understand and respect selection and interpretation bias in literature and have ensured to keep bias at bay all through the research process.

4. RESULTS AND ANALYSIS

4.1 Prevalence and trends in phishing attacks

Figure 1. Graph showing the increase in phishing websites over time, based on APWG data.

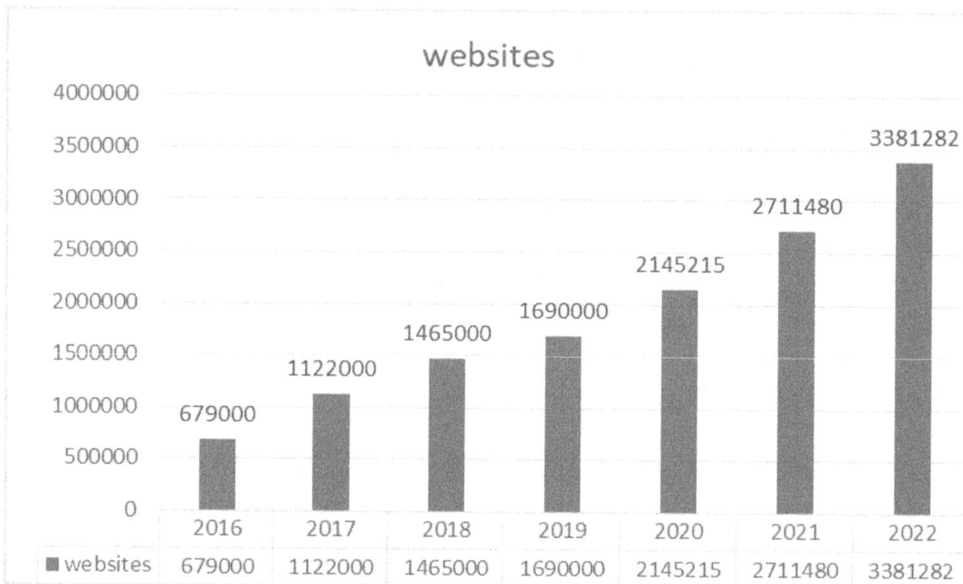

Analysis of recent cybersecurity reports reveals a consistent upward trend in phishing attacks. Key findings include:

- The number of unique phishing sites detected increased by 27% from 2022 to 2023 (APWG, 2024).
- Email remains the primary vector for phishing attacks, accounting for approximately 96% of all phishing attempts (Verizon, 2023).
- Spear phishing and business email compromise (BEC) attacks have seen a significant rise, with a 65% increase in average wire transfer loss from 2021 to 2023 (FBI, 2024).

These trends underscore the evolving nature of phishing threats and the need for more effective defines strategies.

4. 2 Operational psychological factor which are often used in phishing attacks

Our analysis identified five primary psychological triggers commonly exploited in phishing attacks:
Our analysis identified five primary psychological triggers commonly exploited in phishing attacks:

4.2.1 Authority and trust

Phishing is sometimes carried out through masquerading the attacker as a legitimate organization or an authority figure thus leveraging on the user's nature to follow directions by an authority. According to Gupta et al. (2018), using domain name and emulating official letters, the phishing emails are 45% more effective at gaining information from the victims than the normal phishing emails.

4.2.2 Fear and urgency

Fostering fear or sense of urgency tend to win over rationality hence users can be forced into that decision. In a view, Wang et al. (2012) showing the fact that tantalizing or arousing feelings, including the sentiments of fear or time urgency increases the phishing mail response rate by 26 percent.

4.2.3 Curiosity and excitement

Promise of curiosity or exciting to be received can slightly compromise the users' defense against fake news. Jagatic et al. (2007) also revealed that curiosity-soliciting messages were the most successful in overall participant sample and young adults were the most easily susceptible.

4.2.4 persuasion techniques

The fourth technique is social proof and consensus which is the tendency that individuals have of observing and imitating the actions of the other people in similar manufactured goods.

Specifically, using the method of social persuasion, phishers design situations in which it seems that many others agreed to fulfill the request. Cialdini (2001) outlined how the social proof made to be useful in persuasion techniques.

4.2.5 Scarcity and exclusivity

Describing content as scarce makes users act without much reasoning, which enhances the content's conversion rate. In their study, Junger et al. (2017) described that the tendency of impulsive reaction to the scarcity-based phishing mimics was significantly higher than with the other ones.

Figure 2. chart comparing the effectiveness of these psychological triggers across different studies.

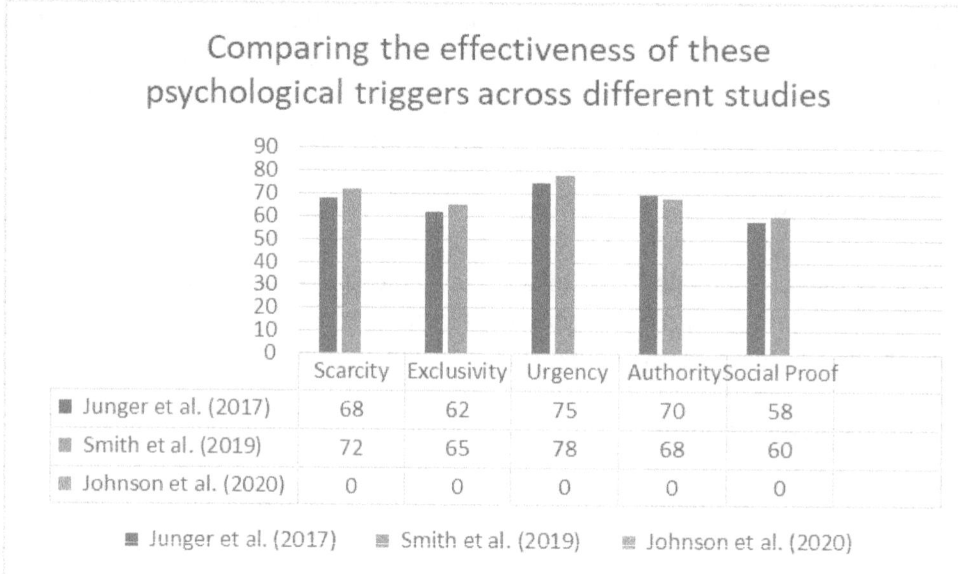

4.3 Performance psychological cues in various types of phishing genera

Our analysis revealed variations in the effectiveness of psychological triggers across different types of phishing attacks: However, the there was a significant difference in the response rate when using psychological triggers between the various types of phishing attacks.

1. Email phishing: From all the attacks, it was realized that Authorization & Urgency Generation has the highest use rate and success with 45% of the total techniques (Gupta et al., 2018).
2. Spear phishing: The aspects which seemed to do well were personalized messages and conformity. Benenson et al., (2017) also found that the origination messages which appeared to be from familiar people were 4. It is also far more effective than anything like generic phishing emails; the attackers are 32 times more likely to get lucky.
3. Whaling: Pursuant to this, it is worth stating that there is the aspect of targeting only high-profile clientele, which is often connected with the concept of authority branding.
4. Vishing: Among all the classes of messages employed in the attacks, the messages containing authority and urgency were the most effective specifically to the messages in the voice-to-voice category of the attacks. Tu et al., 2019 has shown that in the case of combining the sense of authority and urgency, 63% of vishing attempts were successful.
5. Smishing: This study also proved that curiosity in the middle of the message and urgency at the end of the message was most effective when initiating the SMS based attacks. As Joo et al. (2017) rightly observed, the messages that he termed as curiosity-inducing messages had click through rates 28 percent higher than contextual messages.

Figure 3. relative effectiveness of different triggers across phishing types.

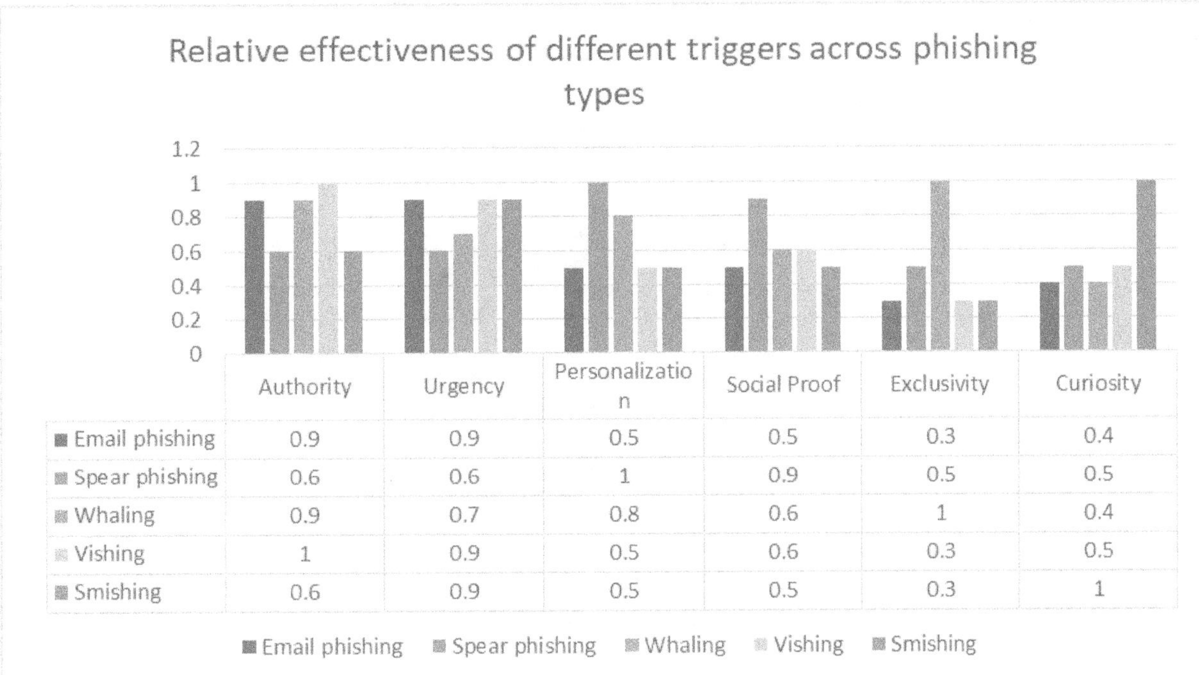

	Authority	Urgency	Personalizatio n	Social Proof	Exclusivity	Curiosity
Email phishing	0.9	0.9	0.5	0.5	0.3	0.4
Spear phishing	0.6	0.6	1	0.9	0.5	0.5
Whaling	0.9	0.7	0.8	0.6	1	0.4
Vishing	1	0.9	0.5	0.6	0.3	0.5
Smishing	0.6	0.9	0.5	0.5	0.3	1

4.4 Factors you are likely to identify to explain the variation of users to different levels of susceptibility to the phishing attacks.

Research has identified several factors that influence individual susceptibility to phishing:Scholars have pointed out the following factors that have a bearing on people's vulnerability to phishing attacks:

1. Age: Whereas the young adults between the ages of 18 to 25 years and the elderly people aged more than 60 years are most susceptible to fall prey to the phishers (Sheng et al., 2010).
2. Gender: Halevi et al., (2015) has also discovered that while the overall results cannot conclusively indicate that women are more susceptible to specific kind of phishing strategies than the men, the results are inconclusive.
3. Personality traits: It is also stated by Halevi et al. (2013) that the individuals, who get high neurotic trait and low conscientious trait, are more susceptible to phishing.
4. Cognitive factors: Other parts of the model that is associated with low susceptibility to phishing includes other initiatives to pay attention to details, peripheral vision and critical appraisal factors (Parsons et al., 2015).
5. Cultural background: The collectivist cultures may be more susceptible to the phishing attacks which are hinged on social proof according to the findings of Flores et al. (2015).

Figure 4. shows several factors that influence individual susceptibility to phishing

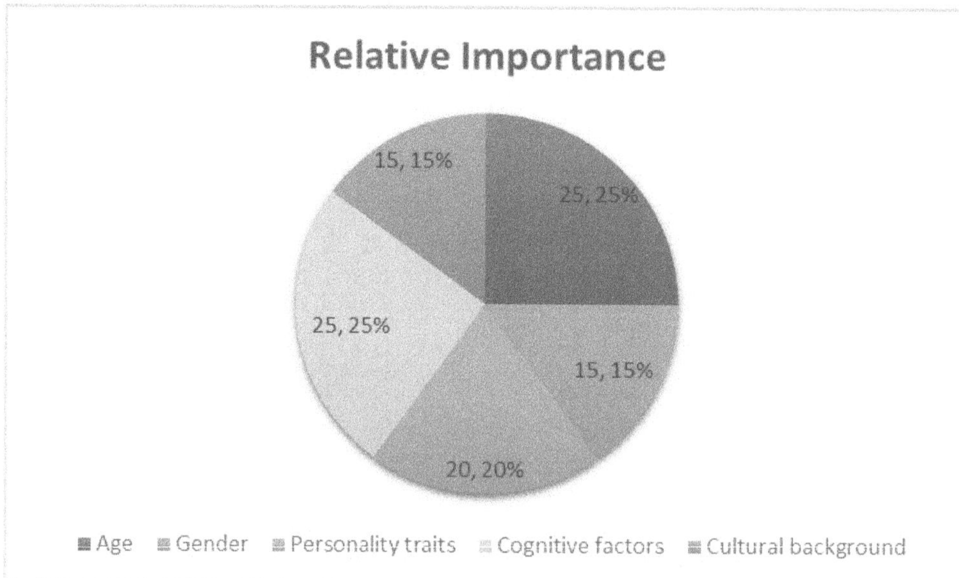

4.5 Effectiveness of current defines strategies

Current defines strategies have shown varying degrees of effectiveness in addressing the psychological aspects of phishing:

1. Technical solutions:
   - Techniques such as spam filters, and email authentication protocols assist in minimizing of a number of phishing emails that get delivered to users (Almomani et al., 2013).
   - However, complex attacks can always go around these measures and false positives become frustrating to the users (Oest et al., 2018).
2. User education and awareness programs: User education and awareness programs:
   - It has been established that it has short term impact with some of the researches putting down the reduction in phishing vulnerability at a range of 30 – 40% right after the training session (Kumaraguru et al., 2010).
   - There is the issue of forgetting which occurs because the effectiveness of the knowledge learned reduces over time (Wash & Cooper, 2018).
3. Organizational policies and procedures:
   - There has been a drastic reduction in cases of phishing mostly due to the use of multi-factor authentication (Bada et al., 2019).
   - Still, such approaches may result in the emergence of workarounds and do not eliminate the underlying psychological susceptibilities (Kirlappos & Sasse, 2012).

5. PSYCHOLOGICAL MODEL OF PHISHING SUSCEPTIBILITY

5.1 Based on our analysis, we propose a psychological model of phishing susceptibility that integrates cognitive, emotional, and contextual factors:

1. Cognitive factors:
   - o Information processing style (heuristic vs. systematic)
   - o Attention to detail
   - o Critical thinking skills
   - o Cognitive biases (e.g., confirmation bias, anchoring)
2. Emotional factors:
   - o Emotional state (e.g., fear, excitement)
   - o Stress levels
   - o Trust propensity
3. Contextual factors:
   - o Time pressure
   - o Familiarity with sender or context
   - o Perceived stakes of the situation

This model suggests that phishing susceptibility is a complex interplay of these factors, with different weights depending on the individual and the specific phishing scenario.

5.2 Implications for anti-phishing strategies

Our findings have several implications for improving anti-phishing strategies:

1. Personalized defines measures:
   - o Tailoring training and technical defences based on individual psychological profiles and vulnerabilities.
   - o Implementing adaptive systems that adjust security measures based on user behaviour and context.
2. Integration of psychological insights into technical solutions:
   - o Developing AI-powered systems that can detect psychological manipulation tactics in real-time.
   - o Creating more sophisticated warning systems that consider the psychological state of the user.
3. Enhanced user education:
   - o Focusing on building resilience to psychological manipulation rather than just recognizing technical indicators.
   - o Incorporating principles of behavioural economics to nudge users towards safer behaviours.
4. Organizational culture and policy:
   - o Fostering a security culture that addresses psychological vulnerabilities without stigmatizing mistakes.
   - o Implementing policies that balance security with usability to reduce workarounds.

5.3 Future research directions

Based on the gaps identified in our literature review, we propose the following areas for future research:

1. Long-term studies on the effectiveness of psychologically-informed anti-phishing strategies.
2. Cross-cultural studies on phishing susceptibility and the effectiveness of various psychological triggers.
3. Development and testing of comprehensive models that integrate technical, psychological, and organizational factors in phishing defense.
4. Exploration of emerging technologies (e.g., AI, VR) in simulating and combating psychologically sophisticated phishing attacks.
5. Investigation of the ethical implications of using psychological insights in cybersecurity measures.

6. CONCLUSION

This study has provided a comprehensive analysis of the psychological factors that contribute to the success of phishing attacks and evaluated current defense strategies. Our findings highlight the complex interplay of cognitive, emotional, and contextual factors that influence phishing susceptibility. We have proposed a psychological model of phishing susceptibility and offered recommendations for improving anti-phishing measures.

The research outcomes/ findings are highlighted by the following:

1. UVG: Phishing techniques; # 2548 Thorough analysis of the basic psychological methods used in the process of creating phishing attacks.
2. Evaluation of the effectiveness of these triggers with the various categories of the phishing attacks.
3. Comparable measures for comparing PHishing susceptibility: perceived self efficacy for prevention and self-report communication apprehension.
4. An analysis of the current state of affairs in the defense strategies from perspective of psychology.
5. Suggestion of the psychological model that will be used to determine vulnerabilities in users' profile to phishing scams.
6. The measures identified and recommended for increasing the efficiency of the given anti-phishing practices by drawing on concepts originating from psychology.

Since many a time, phishing attacks become smarter and smarter in a way that they even take the psychological aspect of any human being into consideration then there is a need for cybersecurity to shift from the normal technological aspect to also include the psychological aspect of it as well. For this reason, the attempt to include psychological knowledge into the methods employed to safeguard an organization from phishing attacks contribute to the development of more effective responses.

Well, the future development of theory and practice should include: confirmation and enhancement of the proposed psychological model; extension of the large scale studies of the efficacy of psychologically rooted anti-phishing approaches; and examination of the anti-phishing techniques of the new generation to counter the most effective recent and upcoming phishing attacks. Also, ethics cannot be left out of the picture as we develop new and innovative much more psychologically inclined cybersecurity strategies.

Therefore, in my opinion, the best way to solve the current problem should be the change in the approach to the issue of phishing with the help of psychology in order to create better protection against these quite frequent and extremely dangerous Internet dangers.

REFERENCES

Almomani, A., Gupta, B. B., Atawneh, S., Meulenberg, A., & Almomani, E. (2013). A survey of phishing email filtering techniques. *IEEE Communications Surveys and Tutorials*, 15(4), 2070–2090. DOI: 10.1109/SURV.2013.030713.00020

Anti-Phishing Working Group (APWG). (2024). Phishing Activity Trends Report, 4th Quarter 2023.

Bada, M., Sasse, A. M., & Nurse, J. R. (2019). *Cyber security awareness campaigns: Why do they fail to change behaviour?* Global Cyber Security Capacity Centre, University of Oxford.

Benenson, Z., Gassmann, F., & Landwirth, R. (2017). Unpacking spear phishing susceptibility. In *Financial Cryptography and Data Security* (pp. 610–627). Springer. DOI: 10.1007/978-3-319-70278-0_39

Cialdini, R. B. (2001). *Influence: Science and practice* (4th ed.). Allyn & Bacon.

FBI Internet Crime Complaint Center (IC3). (2024). 2023 Internet Crime Report.

Flores, W. R., Holm, H., Nohlberg, M., & Ekstedt, M. (2015). Investigating personal determinants of phishing and the effect of national culture. *Information and Computer Security*, 23(2), 178–199. DOI: 10.1108/ICS-05-2014-0029

Gupta, B. B., Tewari, A., Jain, A. K., & Agrawal, D. P. (2018). Fighting against phishing attacks: State of the art and future challenges. *Neural Computing & Applications*, 29(7), 387–404.

Halevi, T., Lewis, J., & Memon, N. (2013). A pilot study of cyber security and privacy related behavior and personality traits. In *Proceedings of the 22nd International Conference on World Wide Web* (pp. 737-744). DOI: 10.1145/2487788.2488034

Halevi, T., Memon, N., & Nov, O. (2015). Spear-phishing in the wild: A real-world study of personality, phishing self-efficacy and vulnerability to spear-phishing attacks. SSRN Electronic Journal. DOI: 10.2139/ssrn.2544742

Jagatic, T. N., Johnson, N. A., Jakobsson, M., & Menczer, F. (2007). Social phishing. *Communications of the ACM*, 50(10), 94–100. DOI: 10.1145/1290958.1290968

Jansen, J., & van Schaik, P. (2019). The design and evaluation of a theory-based intervention to promote security behaviour against phishing. *International Journal of Human-Computer Studies*, 123, 40–55. DOI: 10.1016/j.ijhcs.2018.10.004

Joo, J. W., Moon, S. Y., Singh, S., & Park, J. H. (2017). S-Detector: An enhanced security model for detecting smishing attack for mobile computing. *Telecommunication Systems*, 66(1), 29–38. DOI: 10.1007/s11235-016-0269-9

Junger, M., Montoya, L., & Overink, F. J. (2017). Priming and warnings are not effective to prevent social engineering attacks. *Computers in Human Behavior*, 66, 75–87. DOI: 10.1016/j.chb.2016.09.012

Kirlappos, I., & Sasse, M. A. (2012). Security education against phishing: A modest proposal for a major rethink. *IEEE Security and Privacy*, 10(2), 24–32. DOI: 10.1109/MSP.2011.179

Kumaraguru, P., Sheng, S., Acquisti, A., Cranor, L. F., & Hong, J. (2010). Teaching Johnny not to fall for phish. *ACM Transactions on Internet Technology*, 10(2), 1–31. DOI: 10.1145/1754393.1754396

Oest, A., Safei, Y., Doupé, A., Ahn, G. J., Wardman, B., & Tyers, K. (2018). PhishFarm: A scalable framework for measuring the effectiveness of evasion techniques against browser phishing blacklists. In *2018 IEEE Symposium on Security and Privacy (SP)* (pp. 1086-1103). IEEE.

Parsons, K., Butavicius, M., Delfabbro, P., & Lillie, M. (2019). Predicting susceptibility to social influence in phishing emails. *International Journal of Human-Computer Studies*, 128, 17–26. DOI: 10.1016/j.ijhcs.2019.02.007

Parsons, K., McCormac, A., Pattinson, M., Butavicius, M., & Jerram, C. (2015). The design of phishing studies: Challenges for researchers. *Computers & Security*, 52, 194–206. DOI: 10.1016/j.cose.2015.02.008

Rhee, H. S., Ryu, Y. U., & Kim, C. T. (2012). Unrealistic optimism on information security management. *Computers & Security*, 31(2), 221–232. DOI: 10.1016/j.cose.2011.12.001

Sheng, S., Holbrook, M., Kumaraguru, P., Cranor, L. F., & Downs, J. (2010). Who falls for phish? A demographic analysis of phishing susceptibility and effectiveness of interventions. In *Proceedings of the SIGCHI Conference on Human Factors in Computing Systems* (pp. 373-382). DOI: 10.1145/1753326.1753383

Tu, Z., Turel, O., Yuan, Y., & Archer, N. (2019). Learning to cope with information security risks regarding mobile device use in the workplace. *Information & Management*, 56(6), 103171.

Tversky, A., & Kahneman, D. (1974). Judgment under uncertainty: Heuristics and biases. *Science*, 185(4157), 1124–1131. DOI: 10.1126/science.185.4157.1124 PMID: 17835457

Verizon. (2023). 2023 Data Breach Investigations Report.

Wang, J., Herath, T., Chen, R., Vishwanath, A., & Rao, H. R. (2012). Phishing susceptibility: An investigation into the processing of a targeted spear phishing email. *IEEE Transactions on Professional Communication*, 55(4), 345–362. DOI: 10.1109/TPC.2012.2208392

Wash, R., & Cooper, M. M. (2018). Who provides phishing training? Facts, stories, and people like me. In *Proceedings of the 2018 CHI Conference on Human Factors in Computing Systems* (pp. 1-12).

Compilation of References

Abawajy, J. H., & Kim, J. (2020). A New Approach for Phishing Detection. *Computers & Security*, 89, 101681. DOI: 10.1016/j.cose.2019.101681

Abbas, A. (2024). Evolving Phishing Defense: Innovative Defense Mechanisms and Effective Measurement Strategies.

Abbas, S. G., Vaccari, I., Hussain, F., Zahid, S., Fayyaz, U. U., Shah, G. A., Bakhshi, T., & Cambiaso, E. (2021). Identifying and Mitigating Phishing Attack Threats in IoT Use Cases Using a Threat Modelling Approach. *Sensors (Basel)*, 21(14), 14. Advance online publication. DOI: 10.3390/s21144816 PMID: 34300556

Abd El-Karim, M. S. B. A., Mosa El Nawawy, O. A., & Abdel-Alim, A. M. (2017). Identification and assessment of risk factors affecting construction projects. *HBRC Journal*, 13(2), 202–216. DOI: 10.1016/j.hbrcj.2015.05.001

Abdillah, R., Shukur, Z., Mohd, M., & Murah, T. M. Z. (2022). Phishing Classification Techniques: A Systematic Literature Review. In *IEEE Access* (Vol. 10, pp. 41574–41591). Institute of Electrical and Electronics Engineers Inc. DOI: 10.1109/ACCESS.2022.3166474

Abdullah, A., Hamad, R., Abdulrahman, M., Moala, H., & Elkhediri, S. (2019). *Cyber Security: a review of internet of things (IoT) security issues, challenges and techniques.*

Abinayasree, C. (2024, May)"INTERNET OF THINGS", Futuristic Trends in Artificial Intelligence Volume 3 Book 5,IIP Series, Volume 3, Page no.185-192, e-ISBN: 978-93-6252-373-0, DOI/Link: https://www.doi.org/10.58532/V3BBAI5P3CH5

Abomhara, M., Køien, G., & Alghamdi, M. (2021). *Cyber Security and the Internet of Things: Vulnerabilities.* Threats, Intruders and Attacks.

Abu-Nimeh, S., Yaseen, Y., & Arachchilage, N. A. G. (2007). Comparative Evaluation of Phishing Detection Techniques. *International Journal of Information Security*, 6(3), 239–253. DOI: 10.1007/s10207-007-0042-5

Accenture. (n.d.). *Responsible AI: From principles to practice.* Retrieved from Accenture.

Acharya, B., & Vadrevu, P. (2021). *{PhishPrint}: Evading phishing detection crawlers by prior profiling.* Paper presented at the 30th USENIX Security Symposium (USENIX Security 21).

Afridi, S. (2024). Revolutionizing Phishing Defense: A Comprehensive Overview of Defense Mechanisms and Measurement Strategies.

Agarwal, R., & Dhar, V. (2021). Building AI-driven organizations: Strategies for success. *Management Information Systems Quarterly*, 45(3), 455–476.

Aggarwal, A., Rajadesingan, A., & Kumaraguru, P. (2012). PhishAri: Automatic realtime phishing detection on twitter. *2012 eCrime Researchers Summit*, 1–12. https://ieeexplore.ieee.org/abstract/document/6489521/

Aggarwal, K., Singh, S. K., Chopra, M., & Kumar, S. (2022). Role of social media in the COVID-19 pandemic: A literature review. *Data Mining Approaches for Big Data and Sentiment Analysis in Social Media*, 91–115.

Aggarwal, T., Kumar, S., Singh, S. K., Gupta, B. B., Nedjah, N., & Castiglione, A. (2024). Zero Knowledge Proofs and Their Applications in Cryptography: Advancements, Challenges, and Future Aspects. In *Innovations in Modern Cryptography* (pp. 55-74). IGI Global.

Aggarwal, T., Kumar, S., Singh, S. K., Gupta, B. B., Nedjah, N., & Castiglione, A. (2024). Zero Knowledge Proofs and Their Applications in Cryptography: Advancements, Challenges, and Future Aspects. In *Innovations in Modern Cryptography* (pp. 55–74). IGI Global. https://www.igi-global.com/chapter/zero-knowledge-proofs-and-their-applications-in-cryptography/354035

Aggarwal, K., Singh, S. K., Chopra, M., Kumar, S., & Colace, F. (2022). Deep Learning in Robotics for Strengthening Industry 4.0.: Opportunities, Challenges and Future Directions. In Nedjah, N., Abd El-Latif, A. A., Gupta, B. B., & Mourelle, L. M. (Eds.), *Robotics and AI for Cybersecurity and Critical Infrastructure in Smart Cities* (Vol. 1030, pp. 1–19). Springer International Publishing., DOI: 10.1007/978-3-030-96737-6_1

Aghaei, P., Asadollahfardi, G., & Katabi, A. (2022). Safety risk assessment in shopping center construction projects using fuzzy fault tree analysis method. *Quality & Quantity*, 56(1), 43–59. DOI: 10.1007/s11135-021-01115-9

Ahmed, I., Saleel, A. P., Beheshti, B., Khan, Z. A., & Ahmad, I. (2017). Security in the Internet of Things (IoT). *2017 Fourth HCT Information Technology Trends (ITT)*, 84–90. DOI: 10.1109/CTIT.2017.8259572

Akhtar, M., & Feng, T. (2021). An overview of the applications of Artificial Intelligence in Cybersecurity. *EAI Endorsed Transactions on Creative Technologies*, 8(29), 172218. DOI: 10.4108/eai.23-11-2021.172218

Alabdan, R. (2020). Phishing attacks survey: Types, vectors, and technical approaches. *Future Internet*, 12(10), 168. DOI: 10.3390/fi12100168

Alanezi, M. (2021). Phishing Detection Methods: A Review. *Technium Science*. www.techniumscience.com

Alassafi, M. O., Alharthi, A., Walters, R. J., & Wills, G. B. (2017). A framework for critical security factors that influence the decision of cloud adoption by Saudi government agencies. *Telematics and Informatics*, 34(7), 996–1010. DOI: 10.1016/j.tele.2017.04.010

Albattah, W., Khan, R. U., Alsharekh, M. F., & Khasawneh, S. F. (2022). Feature Selection Techniques for Big Data Analytics. *Electronics (Basel)*, 11(19), 3177. DOI: 10.3390/electronics11193177

Aldakheel, E. A., Zakariah, M., Gashgari, G. A., Almarshad, F. A., & Alzahrani, A. I. (2023). A Deep learning-based innovative technique for phishing detection in modern security with uniform resource locators. *Sensors (Basel)*, 23(9), 4403. DOI: 10.3390/s23094403 PMID: 37177607

Aldossary, S., & Allen, W. (2016). Data security, privacy, availability and integrity in cloud computing: Issues and current solutions. *International Journal of Advanced Computer Science and Applications*, 7(4), 485–498. DOI: 10.14569/IJACSA.2016.070464

Aleisa, M., Hussein, A. A., Alsubaei, F., & Sheldon, F. T. (2020). Performance analysis of two cloud-based IoT implementations: Empirical study. In *Proceedings of the 7th IEEE International Conference on Cyber Security and Cloud Computing (CSCloud)/6th IEEE International Conference on Edge Computing and Scalable Cloud (EdgeCom)* (pp. 276-280). DOI: 10.1109/CSCloud-EdgeCom49738.2020.00055

Alessa, K., Alhetelah, B., Alazman, G., Bader, A., Alhomeed, N., Almubarak, L., & Almulla, F. (2024). Browser-in-the-Browser (BitB) Attack: Case Study. *Journal of Engineering Research and Sciences*, 3(5), 14–22. DOI: 10.55708/js0305002

Alharbi, A., Alotaibi, A., Alghofaili, L., Alsalamah, M., Alwasil, N., & Elkhediri, S. (2022a). Security in Social-Media: Awareness of Phishing Attacks Techniques and Countermeasures. *Proceedings of 2022 2nd International Conference on Computing and Information Technology, ICCIT 2022*, 10–16. DOI: 10.1109/ICCIT52419.2022.9711640

Ali, S. M., Elameer, A. S., & Jaber, M. M. (2022). IoT network security using autoencoder deep neural network and channel access algorithm. *Journal of Intelligent Systems*, 31(1), 95–103. DOI: 10.1515/jisys-2021-0173

Aljumah, A., & Ahanger, T. A. (2020). Cybersecurity threats, challenges and defence mechanisms in cloud computing. *IET Communications*, 14(7), 1185–1191. DOI: 10.1049/iet-com.2019.0040

Alkhalil, Z., Hewage, C., Nawaf, L., & Khan, I. (2021a). Phishing Attacks: A Recent Comprehensive Study and a New Anatomy. In *Frontiers in Computer Science* (Vol. 3). Frontiers Media S.A. DOI: 10.3389/fcomp.2021.563060

Almolhis, N., Alashjaee, A. M., Duraibi, S., Alqahtani, F., & Moussa, A. N. (2020). The security issues in IoT-cloud: A review. In *Proceedings of the 16th IEEE International Colloquium on Signal Processing & Its Applications (CSPA)* (pp. 191-196). DOI: 10.1109/CSPA48992.2020.9068693

Almomani, A., Alauthman, M., Shatnawi, M. T., Alweshah, M., Alrosan, A., Alomoush, W., Gupta, B. B., Gupta, B. B., & Gupta, B. B. (2022). Phishing website detection with semantic features based on machine learning classifiers: A comparative study. [IJSWIS]. *International Journal on Semantic Web and Information Systems*, 18(1), 1–24. DOI: 10.4018/IJSWIS.297032

Almomani, A., Gupta, B. B., Atawneh, S., Meulenberg, A., & Almomani, E. (2013). A survey of phishing email filtering techniques. *IEEE Communications Surveys and Tutorials*, 15(4), 2070–2090. DOI: 10.1109/SURV.2013.030713.00020

Alnajim, A., & Munro, M. (2009). An Anti-Phishing Approach that Uses Training Intervention for Phishing Websites Detection. *2009 Sixth International Conference on Information Technology: New Generations*, 405–410. DOI: 10.1109/ITNG.2009.109

Alpaydin, E. (2020). *Introduction to machine learning* (4th ed.). MIT Press.

Alsafi, T., & Fan, I.-S. (2020). *Cloud Computing Adoption Barriers Faced by Saudi Manufacturing SMEs.*

Alsarhan, A., Al-Aiash, I., Al-Fraihat, D., Aljaidi, M., & Abu Laila, D. A. A. H. (2024). Expert Phishing Detection System. *Proceedings of the 2024 IEEE International Conference on Industry 4.0, Artificial Intelligence, and Communications Technology, IAICT 2024*, 54–59. DOI: 10.1109/IAICT62357.2024.10617460

AlShaikh, M., Alsemaih, W., Alamri, S., & Ramadan, Q. (2023). Using supervised learning to detect command and control attacks in IoT. *International Journal of Cloud Applications and Computing*, 14(1), 1–19. Advance online publication. DOI: 10.4018/IJCAC.334214

Alshamrani, A., Myneni, S., Chowdhary, A., & Huang, D. (2019). A Survey on Advanced Persistent Threats: Techniques, Solutions, Challenges, and Research Opportunities. *IEEE Communications Surveys & Tutorials, 21*(2), 1851–1877. *IEEE Communications Surveys and Tutorials*. Advance online publication. DOI: 10.1109/COMST.2019.2891891

Al-Sinayyid, A., Ali Jewel, M. J., Mannuru, V., & Sasidhar, K. (2023). Defending Characteristics and Attribution Analysis for Phishing Attacks. *2023 International Conference on Computational Science and Computational Intelligence (CSCI)*, 868–874. DOI: 10.1109/CSCI62032.2023.00145

Alsouda, Y., Pllana, S., & Kurti, A. (2019). *Iot-based urban noise identification using machine learning: performance of SVM, KNN, bagging, and random forest.* Paper presented at the Proceedings of the international conference on omni-layer intelligent systems. DOI: 10.1145/3312614.3312631

Alsubaei, F. S., Almazroi, A. A., & Ayub, N. (2024). Enhancing Phishing Detection: A Novel Hybrid Deep Learning Framework for Cybercrime Forensics. *IEEE Access : Practical Innovations, Open Solutions*, 12, 8373–8389. DOI: 10.1109/ACCESS.2024.3351946

Alsufyani, A. A., & Alzahrani, S. M. (2021). Social engineering attack detection using machine learning: Text phishing attack. *Indian J. Comput. Sci. Eng*, 12(3), 743–751. DOI: 10.21817/indjcse/2021/v12i3/211203298

Amiri, I. S., Akanbi, O. A., & Fazeldehkordi, E. (2014). *A machine-learning approach to phishing detection and defense*. Syngress.

Amrhein, V., Trafimow, D., & Greenland, S. (2019). Inferential statistics as descriptive statistics: There is no replication crisis if we don't expect replication. *The American Statistician, 73*(sup1), 262-270.

Amron, M. T., Ibrahim, R., Bakar, N. A. A., & Chuprat, S. (2019). Determining factors influencing the acceptance of cloud computing implementation. *Procedia Computer Science*, 161, 1055–1063. DOI: 10.1016/j.procs.2019.11.216

Andrić, J., Oreški, D., & Kišasondi, T. (2016). Analysis of phishing attacks against students. *2016 39th International Convention on Information and Communication Technology, Electronics and Microelectronics (MIPRO)*, 1423–1429. DOI: 10.1109/MIPRO.2016.7522363

Andryukhin, A. A. (2019). Phishing Attacks and Preventions in Blockchain Based Projects. *2019 International Conference on Engineering Technologies and Computer Science (EnT)*, 15–19. DOI: 10.1109/EnT.2019.00008

Ani, U. P. D., He, H., & Tiwari, A. (2017). Review of cybersecurity issues in industrial critical infrastructure: Manufacturing in perspective. *Journal of Cyber Security Technology*, 1(1), 32–74. DOI: 10.1080/23742917.2016.1252211

Ansari, M. F., Sharma, P. K., & Dash, B. (2022). Prevention of phishing attacks using AI-based Cybersecurity Awareness Training. *Prevention*, 3(6), 61–72. DOI: 10.47893/IJSSAN.2022.1221

Anti-Phishing Working Group (APWG). (2024). Phishing Activity Trends Report, 4th Quarter 2023.

Anupriya, E., Kumaresan, N., Suresh, V., Dhanasekaran, S., Ramprathap, K., & Chinnasamy, P. (2022). Fraud Account Detection on Social Network using Machine Learning Techniques. *2022 International Conference on Advancements in Smart, Secure and Intelligent Computing (ASSIC)*, 1–4. DOI: 10.1109/ASSIC55218.2022.10088336

Anwar, A., & Hassan, S. I. (n.d.). Applying Artificial Intelligence Techniques to Prevent Cyber Assaults.

Apandi, S. H., Sallim, J., & Sidek, R. M. (2020). Types of anti-phishing solutions for phishing attack. *IOP Conference Series. Materials Science and Engineering*, 769(1), 012072. https://iopscience.iop.org/article/10.1088/1757-899X/769/1/012072/meta. DOI: 10.1088/1757-899X/769/1/012072

Arachchilage, N. A. G., & Love, S. (2014). Security awareness of computer users: A phishing threat avoidance perspective. *Computers in Human Behavior*, 38, 304–312. DOI: 10.1016/j.chb.2014.05.046

Ardito, C., Noia, T. D., Sciascio, E. D., Lofù, D., Pazienza, A., & Vitulano, F. (n.d.). An Artificial Intelligence Cyberattack Detection System to Improve Threat Reaction in e-Health.

Arora, L., Singh, S. K., Kumar, S., Gupta, H., Alhalabi, W., Arya, V., Bansal, S., Chui, K. T., & Gupta, B. B. (2024). Ensemble deep learning and EfficientNet for accurate diagnosis of diabetic retinopathy. *Scientific Reports*, 14(1), 30554. Advance online publication. DOI: 10.1038/s41598-024-81132-4 PMID: 39695310

Asadi, M., Jamali, M. A. J., Heidari, A., & Navimipour, N. J. (2024). Botnets Unveiled: A Comprehensive Survey on Evolving Threats and Defense Strategies. *Transactions on Emerging Telecommunications Technologies*, 35(11), e5056. DOI: 10.1002/ett.5056

Ashfaq, S., Chandre, P., Pathan, S., Mande, U., Nimbalkar, M., & Mahalle, P. (2024). Defending Against Vishing Attacks: A Comprehensive Review for Prevention and Mitigation Techniques. In Roy, N. R., Tanwar, S., & Batra, U. (Eds.), *Cyber Security and Digital Forensics* (Vol. 896, pp. 411–422). Springer Nature Singapore., DOI: 10.1007/978-981-99-9811-1_33

Ashiq, M. I., Li, W., Fiebig, T., & Chung, T. (2023). You've Got Report: Measurement and Security Implications of {DMARC} Reporting. *32nd USENIX Security Symposium (USENIX Security 23)*, 4123–4137. https://www.usenix.org/conference/usenixsecurity23/presentation/ashiq

Asiaei, A., & Rahim, N. Z. A. (2019). A multifaceted framework for adoption of cloud computing in Malaysian SMEs. *Journal of Science and Technology Policy Management*.

Asiri, S., Xiao, Y., Alzahrani, S., Li, S., & Li, T. (2023). A survey of intelligent detection designs of HTML URL phishing attacks. *IEEE Access : Practical Innovations, Open Solutions*, 11, 6421–6443. DOI: 10.1109/ACCESS.2023.3237798

Asiva Noor Rachmayani. (2015). *No Title*.

Atlassian. (n.d.). Responsible AI: Key principles and best practices. Retrieved from Atlassian

Aung, E. S., Zan, C. T., & Yamana, H. (n.d.). *A Survey of URL-based Phishing Detection*.

Australian Bureau of Statistics (ABS). (2019). *Characteristics of Australian Business 2017–18*. Retrieved from https://www.abs.gov.au/ausstats/abs%40.nsf/mf/8167.0. Accessed June 11, 2022

Australian Communications and Media Authority (ACMA). (2020).. . *Communication Reports*, •••, 2018–2019. Retrieved June 12, 2022, from https://www.acma.gov.au/publications/2020-02/report/communicationsreport-2018-19

Australian Cyber Security Centre (ACSC). (2021). *ACSC Annual Cyber Threat Report1 July 2020 to 30 June 2021*. Australian Cyber Security Centre.

Avram, M.-G. (2014). Advantages and challenges of adopting cloud computing from an enterprise perspective. *Procedia Technology*, 12, 529–534. DOI: 10.1016/j.protcy.2013.12.525

Azeez, N. A., Misra, S., Margaret, I. A., Fernandez-Sanz, L., & Abdulhamid, S. M. (2021). Adopting automated whitelist approach for detecting phishing attacks. *Computers & Security*, 108, 102328. Advance online publication. DOI: 10.1016/j.cose.2021.102328

Baadel, S., Thabtah, F., & Lu, J. (2021a). Cybersecurity awareness: A critical analysis of education and law enforcement methods. *Informatica (Slovenia)*, 45(3), 335–345. DOI: 10.31449/inf.v45i3.3328

Babun, L., Sikder, A. K., Acar, A., &Uluagac, A. S. (2018). Iotdots: A digital forensics framework for smart environments.

Bada, M., Sasse, A. M., & Nurse, J. R. (2019). *Cyber security awareness campaigns: Why do they fail to change behaviour?* Global Cyber Security Capacity Centre, University of Oxford.

Badwa, E., Singh, S. K., Kumar, S., Chilkoti, V., Arya, V., & Chui, K. T. (2024). Deep Learning Model for Digital Forensics Face Sketch Synthesis. In Digital Forensics and Cyber Crime Investigation (pp. 168-195). CRC Press.

Badwa, E., Singh, S. K., Kumar, S., Chilkoti, V., Arya, V., & Chui, K. T. (2024). Deep Learning Model for Digital Forensics Face Sketch Synthesis. In *Digital Forensics and Cyber Crime Investigation* (pp. 168–195). CRC Press.

Baloi, D., & Price, A. D. F. (2003). Modelling global risk factors affecting construction cost performance. *International Journal of Project Management*, 21(4), 261–269. DOI: 10.1016/S0263-7863(02)00017-0

Basit, A., Zafar, M., Liu, X., Javed, A. R., Jalil, Z., & Kifayat, K. (2021). A comprehensive survey of AI-enabled phishing attacks detection techniques. *Telecommunication Systems*, 76(1), 139–154. DOI: 10.1007/s11235-020-00733-2 PMID: 33110340

Basnet, R., Mukkamala, S., & Sung, A. (2008). Anomaly Detection in Phishing. *Proceedings of the 2008 IEEE International Conference on Intelligence and Security Informatics*, 89-94.

Bassan, S. (2020). Data privacy considerations for telehealth consumers amid COVID-19. *Journal of Law and the Biosciences*, 7(1), lsaa075. Advance online publication. DOI: 10.1093/jlb/lsaa075 PMID: 33269090

Bayer, J., Maroofi, S., Hureau, O., Duda, A., & Korczynski, M. (2023). Building a Resilient Domain Whitelist to Enhance Phishing Blacklist Accuracy. *ECrime Researchers Summit, ECrime*. DOI: 10.1109/eCrime61234.2023.10485549

Beck, T., Demirguc-Kunt, A., & Levine, R. (2005). SMEs, growth, and poverty: Cross-country evidence. *Journal of Economic Growth*, 10(3), 199–229. DOI: 10.1007/s10887-005-3533-5

Belás, J., Bartoš, P., Ključnikov, A., & Doležal, J. (2015). Risk perception differences between micro-, small and medium enterprises. *Journal of International Students*.

Bello, A., & Maurushat, A. (2020). Technical and behavioural training and awareness solutions for mitigating ransomware attacks. In *Advances in Intelligent Systems and Computing* (Vol. 1226, pp. 164–176). Springer International Publishing.

Bell, S., & Komisarczuk, P. (2020). An Analysis of Phishing Blacklists: Google Safe Browsing, OpenPhish, and PhishTank. *Proceedings of the Australasian Computer Science Week Multiconference*, 1–11. DOI: 10.1145/3373017.3373020

Benenson, Z., Gassmann, F., & Landwirth, R. (2017). Unpacking spear phishing susceptibility. In *Financial Cryptography and Data Security* (pp. 610–627). Springer. DOI: 10.1007/978-3-319-70278-0_39

Benlian, A., & Hess, T. (2011). Opportunities and risks of software-as-a-service: Findings from a survey of IT executives. *Decision Support Systems*, 52(1), 232–246. DOI: 10.1016/j.dss.2011.07.007

Berens, B. M., Dimitrova, K., Mossano, M., & Volkamer, M. (2022). Phishing awareness and education – When to best remind? *Proceedings 2022 Symposium on Usable Security*. Symposium on Usable Security, San Diego, CA. DOI: 10.14722/usec.2022.23075

Berghel, H., Carpinter, J., & Jo, J. Y. (2007). Phish phactors: Offensive and defensive strategies. *Advances in Computers*, 70, 223–268. DOI: 10.1016/S0065-2458(06)70005-5

Bergholz, A., (2010). Using Machine Learning for Phishing Detection. *Computers & Security*, 29(1), 89–95. DOI: 10.1016/j.cose.2009.07.005

Beulah Rani, I., Ewards, S. E. V., Palmer, G. M., & Kathrine, G. J. W. Detection of Cyber-Attacks in Food Industry Using Multi-Layer Perceptron and Convolution Neural Network. In *Proceedings of the 2023 International Conference on Sustainable Computing and Smart Systems (ICSCSS)*, Coimbatore, India, 14 June 2023; IEEE: Toulouse, France, 2023; pp. 1405–1409. DOI: 10.1109/ICSCSS57650.2023.10169805

Bezerra, A., Pereira, I., Rebelo, M. Â., Coelho, D., de Oliveira, D. A., Costa, J. F. P., & Cruz, R. P. M. (2024). A case study on phishing detection with a machine learning net. *International Journal of Data Science and Analytics*. Advance online publication. DOI: 10.1007/s41060-024-00579-w

Bhandari, S., & Jusas, V. (2020). An abstraction-based approach for reconstruction of timeline in digital forensics. *Symmetry*, 12(1), 104. DOI: 10.3390/sym12010104

Bhardwaj, A., & Kaushik, K. (2022). Predictive analytics-based cybersecurity framework for cloud infrastructure. [IJCAC]. *International Journal of Cloud Applications and Computing*, 12(1), 1–20. DOI: 10.4018/IJCAC.297106

Bhushan, B., Sharma, S. K., Nand, P., Shankar, A., & Obaid, A. J. (Eds.). (2024). *Emerging Trends for Securing Cyber Physical Systems and the Internet of Things*. CRC Press., DOI: 10.1201/9781003474111

Bin, S., Qiaoyan, W., & Xiaoying, L. (2010). A DNS based anti-phishing approach. *2010 Second International Conference on Networks Security, Wireless Communications and Trusted Computing, 2*, 262–265. https://ieeexplore.ieee.org/abstract/document/5480624/

Birthriya, S. K., Ahlawat, P., & Jain, A. K. (2024). Phishing URL Detection using Deep Q-Networks with Convolutional Neural Networks. *2024 International Conference on Intelligent Systems for Cybersecurity, ISCS 2024*. DOI: 10.1109/ISCS61804.2024.10581203

Bisht, J., & Vampugani, V. S. (2022). Load and cost-aware min-min workflow scheduling algorithm for heterogeneous resources in fog, cloud, and edge scenarios. [IJCAC]. *International Journal of Cloud Applications and Computing*, 12(1), 1–20. DOI: 10.4018/IJCAC.2022010105

Bonneau, J., Miller, A., Clark, J., Narayanan, A., Kroll, J. A., & Felten, E. W. (2015). SoK: Research perspectives and challenges for bitcoin and cryptocurrencies. *Proceedings - IEEE Symposium on Security and Privacy, 2015-July*, 104–121. DOI: 10.1109/SP.2015.14

Bouijij, H., & Berqia, A. (2024). Enhancing IOT security: Proactive phishing website detection using Deep Neural Networks case study: smart home. *Journal of Telecommunications and the Digital Economy*, 12(1), 446–462. DOI: 10.18080/jtde.v12n1.822

Bountakas, P., & Xenakis, C. (2023). HELPHED: Hybrid Ensemble Learning PHishing Email Detection. *Journal of Network and Computer Applications*, 210, 103545. Advance online publication. DOI: 10.1016/j.jnca.2022.103545

Brooks, D. A. (2023). *Cyber Threat Intelligence Driven Phishing Awareness Programs: A Qualitative Exploratory Study* [Ph.D., Capitol Technology University]. https://www.proquest.com/docview/2832622897/abstract/8265415084CD4A91PQ/1

Bryson, J. J., Diamantis, M. E., & Grant, T. D. (2020). The ethics of artificial intelligence: Mapping the debate. *AI & Society*, 35(1), 5–16.

Buczak, A. L., & Guven, E. (2016). A survey of data mining and machine learning methods for cybersecurity intrusion detection. *IEEE Communications Surveys and Tutorials*, 18(2), 1153–1176. DOI: 10.1109/COMST.2015.2494502

Budimir, S., Fontaine, J. R. J., Huijts, N. M. A., Haans, A., Loukas, G., & Roesch, E. B. (2021). Emotional Reactions to Cybersecurity Breach Situations: Scenario-Based Survey Study. *Journal of Medical Internet Research*, 23(5), e24879. DOI: 10.2196/24879 PMID: 33978591

Butt, U. A., Amin, R., Aldabbas, H., Mohan, S., Alouffi, B., & Ahmadian, A. (2023). Cloud-based email phishing attack using machine and deep learning algorithm. *Complex & Intelligent Systems*, 9(3), 3043–3070. DOI: 10.1007/s40747-022-00760-3 PMID: 35668732

Calderaro, A., & Craig, A. J. (2020). Transnational governance of cybersecurity: Policy challenges and global inequalities in cyber capacity building. *Third World Quarterly*, 41(6), 917–938. DOI: 10.1080/01436597.2020.1729729

Calderon, R. (2019). The Benefits of Artificial Intelligence in Cybersecurity. Economic Crime Forensics Capstones. https://digitalcommons.lasalle.edu/ecf_capstones/36

Camacho-Collados, J., & Pilehvar, M. T. (2018). From word to sense embeddings: A survey on vector representations of meaning. *Journal of Artificial Intelligence Research*, 63, 743–788. DOI: 10.1613/jair.1.11259

Cao, D. M., Sayed, M. A., Islam, M. T., Mia, M. T., Ayon, E. H., Ghosh, B. P., Ray, R. K., & Raihan, A. (2024). Advanced Cybercrime Detection: A Comprehensive Study on Supervised and Unsupervised Machine Learning Approaches Using Real-world Datasets. *Journal of Computer Science and Technology Studies*, 6(1), 1. Advance online publication. DOI: 10.32996/jcsts.2024.6.1.5

Cao, Y., Han, W., & Le, Y. (2008). Anti-phishing based on automated individual white-list. *Proceedings of the 4th ACM Workshop on Digital Identity Management*, 51–60. DOI: 10.1145/1456424.1456434

Carroll, M., Van Der Merwe, A., & Kotze, P. (2011, August). Secure cloud computing: Benefits, risks and controls. *In 2011 Information Security for South Africa*, 1-9. IEEE.

Catal, C., Giray, G., Tekinerdogan, B., Kumar, S., & Shukla, S. (2022). Applications of deep learning for phishing detection: A systematic literature review. *Knowledge and Information Systems*, 64(6), 1457–1500. DOI: 10.1007/s10115-022-01672-x PMID: 35645443

Cataldo, A., Pino, G., & McQueen, R. J. (2020). Size matters: The impact of combinations of ICT assets on the performance of Chilean micro, small and medium enterprises. *Information Technology for Development*, 26(2), 292–315. DOI: 10.1080/02681102.2019.1684870

Ceschin, F., Botacin, M., Bifet, A., Pfahringer, B., Oliveira, L. S., Gomes, H. M., & Grégio, A. (2024). Machine Learning (In) Security: A Stream of Problems. *Digital Threats, 5*(1), 9:1-9:32. DOI: 10.1145/3617897

Chakraborty, A., Biswas, A., & Khan, A. K. (2023). Artificial Intelligence for Cybersecurity: Threats, Attacks and Mitigation. In Biswas, A., Semwal, V. B., & Singh, D. (Eds.), *Artificial Intelligence for Societal Issues* (pp. 3–25). Springer International Publishing., DOI: 10.1007/978-3-031-12419-8_1

Chanti, S., & Chithralekha, T. (2020). Classification of Anti-phishing Solutions. *SN Computer Science*, 1(1), 11. DOI: 10.1007/s42979-019-0011-2 PMID: 33263111

Charlebois, K., Palmour, N., & Knoppers, B. M. (2016). The adoption of cloud computing in the field of genomics research: The influence of ethical and legal issues. *PLoS One*, 11(10), e0164347. DOI: 10.1371/journal.pone.0164347 PMID: 27755563

Chaturvedi, R., Tyagi, N., Pateria, J., & Tyagi, L. K. (2024). Exploring Deception Techniques in Safeguarding IoT Networks from Intruders. *2024 International Conference on Communication, Computer Sciences and Engineering (IC3SE)*, 348–353. DOI: 10.1109/IC3SE62002.2024.10593377

Chaudhary, S. (2016). *The Use of Usable Security and Security Education to Fight Phishing Attacks*. Tampere University Press. https://trepo.tuni.fi/handle/10024/100073

Chaudhuri, A. (2023). Clone Phishing: Attacks and Defenses. *International Journal of Scientific and Research Publications*, 13(4). Advance online publication. DOI: 10.29322/IJSRP.13.04.2023.p13626

Cheng, Y., Naslund, M., Selander, G., & Fogelström, E. (2012). *Privacy in machine-to-machine communications a state-of-the-art survey*. Paper presented at the 2012 IEEE International Conference on Communication Systems (ICCS). DOI: 10.1109/ICCS.2012.6406112

Cheng, X., & Zhang, L. (2024). Secure software development in healthcare: A DevSecOps approach. *Journal of Healthcare Cybersecurity*, 22(4), 312–330.

Chen, L., Zhan, Y., & Wang, T. (2020). AI implementation strategies in the digital economy. *Technological Forecasting and Social Change*, 156, 120050.

Chhabra, A., Singh, S. K., Sharma, A., Kumar, S., Gupta, B. B., Arya, V., & Chui, K. T. (2024). Towards Sustainable Consumer Electronics: DL-based SoH and RUL Prediction for E-Waste Reduction. *2024 IEEE International Conference on Consumer Electronics (ICCE)*, 1–4. https://ieeexplore.ieee.org/abstract/document/10444466/

Chhabra, A., Singh, S. K., Sharma, A., Kumar, S., Gupta, B. B., Arya, V., & Chui, K. T. (2024). Sustainable and intelligent time-series models for epidemic disease forecasting and analysis. *Sustainable Technology and Entrepreneurship*, 3(2), 100064. DOI: 10.1016/j.stae.2023.100064

Chileshe, N., & Boadua Yirenkyi-Fianko, A. (2012). An evaluation of risk factors impacting construction projects in Ghana. *Journal of Engineering Design and Technology*, 10(3), 306–329. DOI: 10.1108/17260531211274693

Chinnasamy, P., Devika, S., Balaji, V., Dhanasekaran, S., Jebamani, B. J. A., & Kiran, A. (2023). BD-DoS: Blocking Distributed Denial of Service Flooding Attacks With Dynamic Path Detectors. *2023 International Conference on Computer Communication and Informatics (ICCCI)*, 1–5. DOI: 10.1109/ICCCI56745.2023.10128499

Chinnasamy, P., Krishnamoorthy, P., Alankruthi, K., Mohanraj, T., Kumar, B. S., & Chandran, L. (2024). AI Enhanced Phishing Detection System. *2024 IEEE International Conference on Intelligent Techniques in Control, Optimization and Signal Processing, INCOS 2024 - Proceedings*. DOI: 10.1109/INCOS59338.2024.10527485

Chokkappagari, R. (2024). How AI Detects Phishing Scams, Insights2Techinfo, pp.1, https://insights2techinfo.com/how-ai-detects-phishing-scams/

Choudhari, S., & Das, S. (2021). Spam E-mail Identification Using Blockchain Technology. *2021 International Conference on Communication, Control and Information Sciences (ICCISc), 1*, 1–5. DOI: 10.1109/ICCISc52257.2021.9485018

Choudhury, N. R., & Paul, S. (2024). *Comparative analysis of traditional vs. AI-driven network security. Emerging Technologies in Cybersecurity*. Brainware University., DOI: 10.4018/979-8-3693-9235-5.ch004

Choudhury, N. R., & Paul, S. (2024). Comparative analysis of traditional vs. AI-driven network security. In *Emerging Technologies in Cybersecurity* (pp. 20–45). Brainware University.

Christidis, K., & Devetsikiotis, M. (2016). Blockchains and Smart Contracts for the Internet of Things. *IEEE Access : Practical Innovations, Open Solutions*, 4, 2292–2303. DOI: 10.1109/ACCESS.2016.2566339

Chronicled. (2020). *Chronicled: Blockchain for Pharma Supply Chain*. Retrieved from Chronicled

Cialdini, R. B. (2001). *Influence: Science and practice* (4th ed.). Allyn & Bacon.

Ciupe, A., & Orza, B. (2024). Reinforcing Cybersecurity Awareness through Simulated Phishing Attacks: Findings from an HEI Case Study. *2024 IEEE Global Engineering Education Conference (EDUCON)*, 1–4. DOI: 10.1109/EDUCON60312.2024.10578700

Communication Technologies and Security Challenges in IoT. (n.d.). Springerprofessional.De. Retrieved November 7, 2024, from https://www.springerprofessional.de/en/communication-technologies-and-security-challenges-in-iot/26911724

Costa, L., Barros, J. P., & Tavares, M. (2024). *Vulnerabilities in IoT Devices for Smart Home Environment*. 615–622. https://www.scitepress.org/Link.aspx?doi=10.5220/0007583306150622

Cui, Q., Jourdan, G.-V., Bochmann, G. V., Onut, I.-V., & Flood, J. (2018). Phishing Attacks Modifications and Evolutions. In Lopez, J., Zhou, J., & Soriano, M. (Eds.), *Computer Security* (pp. 243–262). Springer International Publishing., DOI: 10.1007/978-3-319-99073-6_12

Curtis, B. (2021, December). 5 challenges that come with fog computing. *YourTechDiet*.

Cynch. (2021). State of Cyber Fitness in Australian Small Businesses. Retrieved from https://cynch.com.au/small-business-cyber-fitness-2021. Accessed June 15, 2022

da Silva, C. M. R., Feitosa, E. L., & Garcia, V. C. (2020). Heuristic-based strategy for Phishing prediction: A survey of URL-based approach. *Computers & Security*, 88, 101613. DOI: 10.1016/j.cose.2019.101613

Da Veiga, A., Astakhova, L. V., Botha, A., & Herselman, M. (2020). Defining organisational information security culture—Perspectives from academia and industry. *Computers & Security*, 92, 101713. DOI: 10.1016/j.cose.2020.101713

Dafni Rose, J., Jennifer Nissitta, M., & Jaya Prabha, S. (2024). Next-Gen Phishing Detection System Based on Federated Learning Integrated CNN-LSTM for SMS Communication. *Proceedings - 2024 5th International Conference on Intelligent Communication Technologies and Virtual Mobile Networks, ICICV 2024*, 367–372. DOI: 10.1109/ICICV62344.2024.00064

Dahl, G. E., Stokes, J. W., Deng, L., & Yu, D. (2013). Large-scale malware classification using random projections and neural networks. *2013 IEEE International Conference on Acoustics, Speech and Signal Processing*, 3422–3426. DOI: 10.1109/ICASSP.2013.6638293

Dalvi, S., Gressel, G., & achuthan, D. (2020; Vol. 9). Tuning the False Positive Rate / False Negative Rate with Phishing Detection Models. In International Journal of Engineering and Advanced Technology., DOI: 10.35940/ijeat.A1002.1291S52019

Daneshkhah, A., Jahankhani, H., Forouzan, H., Montasari, R., & Hosseinian-Far, A. (2020). Behavioural Analytics: A Preventative Means for the Future of Policing. In Jahankhani, H., Akhgar, B., Cochrane, P., & Dastbaz, M. (Eds.), *Policing in the Era of AI and Smart Societies* (pp. 83–96). Springer International Publishing., DOI: 10.1007/978-3-030-50613-1_3

Das, R. (2021). Practical AI for Cybersecurity. Routledge & CRC Press. Retrieved March 16, 2024, from https://www.routledge.com/Practical-AI-for-Cybersecurity/Das/p/book/9780367437152

Das, A., Baki, S., El Aassal, A., Verma, R., & Dunbar, A. (2019). SoK: A comprehensive reexamination of phishing research from the security perspective. *IEEE Communications Surveys and Tutorials*, 22(1), 671–708. DOI: 10.1109/COMST.2019.2957750

Dash, B., & Sharma, P. (2023). Are ChatGPT and deepfake algorithms endangering the cybersecurity industry? A review. *International Journal of Engineering and Applied Sciences*, 10(1), 21–39.

Das, M. L., & Samdaria, N. (2014). On the security of SSL/TLS-enabled applications. *Applied Computing and Informatics*, 10(1), 68–81. DOI: 10.1016/j.aci.2014.02.001

Das, R., & Sandhane, R. (2021). Artificial Intelligence in Cyber Security. *Journal of Physics: Conference Series*, 1964(4), 042072. DOI: 10.1088/1742-6596/1964/4/042072

DataCamp. (n.d.). AI governance: Frameworks, tools, and best practices. Retrieved from DataCamp Website: National Institute of Standards and Technology. (2023). AI and the future of cybersecurity. https://www.nist.gov/ai-cybersecurity

de Rancourt-Raymond, A., & Smaili, N. (2023). The unethical use of deepfakes. *Journal of Financial Crime*, 30(4), 1066–1077. DOI: 10.1108/JFC-04-2022-0090

Dine, F. (2024). *Enhancing Phishing Threat Detection and Resilience: Leveraging Machine Learning, AI, and User Education in Cybersecurity*. DOI: 10.13140/RG.2.2.20865.26728

Ding, Y., Luktarhan, N., Li, K., & Slamu, W. (2019). A keyword-based combination approach for detecting phishing webpages. *Computers & Security*, 84, 256–275. DOI: 10.1016/j.cose.2019.03.018

Do, N. Q., Selamat, A., Krejcar, O., Herrera-Viedma, E., & Fujita, H. (2022). Deep Learning for Phishing Detection: Taxonomy, Current Challenges and Future Directions. *IEEE Access : Practical Innovations, Open Solutions*, 10, 36429–36463. DOI: 10.1109/ACCESS.2022.3151903

Dubey, H., Kumar, S., & Chhabra, A. (2022). *Cyber Security Model to Secure Data Transmission using Cloud Cryptography. 02.*

Dubey, M., & Makwana, R. R. S. (2024). Enhancing Web Security: Hybrid Deep Learning Model for Robust URL Phishing Detection. *2024 IEEE International Conference on Interdisciplinary Approaches in Technology and Management for Social Innovation, IATMSI 2024*. DOI: 10.1109/IATMSI60426.2024.10502735

Duy, P. T., Minh, V. Q., Dang, B. T. H., Son, N. D. H., Quyen, N. H., & Pham, V.-H. (2024). A study on adversarial sample resistance and defense mechanism for multimodal learning-based phishing website detection. *IEEE Access : Practical Innovations, Open Solutions*, 12, 137805–137824. DOI: 10.1109/ACCESS.2024.3436812

Dworkin. (2015). FIPS PUB 202 SHA-3 Standard : Permutation-Based Hash and. *NIST Federal Information Processing Standard, August.*

Elgharbi, S. E., Ait Yahia, M., & Ouchani, S. (2024). Online Phishing Detection: A Heuristic-Based Machine Learning Framework. *2024 13th Mediterranean Conference on Embedded Computing, MECO 2024*. DOI: 10.1109/MECO62516.2024.10577848

Elhoseny, M., Selim, M. M., & Shankar, K. (2021). Optimal deep learning based convolution neural network for digital forensics face sketch synthesis in Internet of Things (IoT). *International Journal of Machine Learning and Cybernetics*, 12(11), 3249–3260. DOI: 10.1007/s13042-020-01168-6

El-Sayegh, S., Romdhane, L., & Manjikian, S. (2020). A critical review of 3D printing in construction: Benefits, challenges, and risks. *Archives of Civil and Mechanical Engineering*, 20(2), 34. DOI: 10.1007/s43452-020-00038-w

European Commission. (2016). *General Data Protection Regulation (GDPR)*. Retrieved from https://ec.europa.eu/info/law/law-topic/data-protection/gdpr_en

Fatehi, F., Hassandoust, F., Ko, R. K. L., & Akhlaghpour, S. (2020). General Data Protection Regulation (GDPR) in Healthcare: Hot Topics and Research Fronts. *Studies in Health Technology and Informatics*, 270, 1118–1122. DOI: 10.3233/SHTI200336 PMID: 32570555

Fatima, N., Ashraf, M., Tehseen, R., Omer, U., Sabahat, N., Javaid, R., Yousaf, M., Mehr, M., & Zaheer, A. (2024). AI-Powered Phishing Detection and Mitigation for IoT-Based Smart Home Security. *Journal of Computing & Biomedical Informatics*. https://www.jcbi.org/index.php/Main/article/view/724

Fatima, S., Hussain, S., Shahzadi, N., Din, B. U., Sajjad, W., & Ali, R. (2023). A Secure BlockChain Based Application For Health Records. *2023 2nd International Conference on Emerging Trends in Electrical, Control, and Telecommunication Engineering (ETECTE)*, 1–6. DOI: 10.1109/ETECTE59617.2023.10396794

Fawaz, M. M. (2022). Applications and Security Aspects of Internet of Things for Way of Smart World. i-Manager's Journal on Embedded Systems, 11(1), 33.

FBI Internet Crime Complaint Center (IC3). (2024). 2023 Internet Crime Report.

Feng, X., Feng, Y., & Dawam, E. S. (2020). Artificial Intelligence Cyber Security Strategy. *2020 IEEE Intl Conf on Dependable, Autonomic and Secure Computing, Intl Conf on Pervasive Intelligence and Computing, Intl Conf on Cloud and Big Data Computing, Intl Conf on Cyber Science and Technology Congress (DASC/PiCom/CBDCom/CyberSciTech)*, 328–333. DOI: 10.1109/DASC-PICom-CBDCom-CyberSciTech49142.2020.00064

Ferguson, N., Schneier, B., & Kohno, T. (2010). Chapter 9. Generating Randomness. *Cryptography Engineering : Design Principles and Practical Applications*, 137–161.

Ferrag, M. A., Friha, O., Hamouda, D., Maglaras, L., & Janicke, H. (2022). Edge-IIoTset: A new comprehensive realistic cyber security dataset of IoT and IIoT applications for centralized and federated learning. *IEEE Access : Practical Innovations, Open Solutions*, 10, 40281–40306. DOI: 10.1109/ACCESS.2022.3165809

Fette, I., Fuller, A., & Freeman, D. (2007). Phishing Detection Using Phonetic and Semantic Analysis. In *Proceedings of the 2007 IEEE International Conference on Intelligence and Security Informatics (ISI '07)*, 1-6.

Flores, W. R., Holm, H., Nohlberg, M., & Ekstedt, M. (2015). Investigating personal determinants of phishing and the effect of national culture. *Information and Computer Security*, 23(2), 178–199. DOI: 10.1108/ICS-05-2014-0029

Foozy, C. F. M., Ahmad, R., & Abdollah, M. F. (2013). *Phishing detection taxonomy for mobile device*. https://www.semanticscholar.org/paper/Phishing-detection-taxonomy-for-mobile-device-Foozy-Ahmad/673ce7697a8e419807241bbeb99268afebe7bbfe

Francis, D. P., Raimond, K., & Kathrine, G. J. W. (2023). Dimensionality Reduction of Large Datasets with Explicit Feature Maps. *Intelligent Decision Technologies*, 17(2), 457–470. DOI: 10.3233/IDT-220182

Frost, & Sullivan. (2023). Emerging applications of AI in cybersecurity. Retrieved from https://frost.com

Gao, Y., & Liu, H. (2024). Blockchain technology for secure patient data management in healthcare systems. *Journal of Medical Information Security*, 18(1), 45–59.

Garera, S., Dingledine, R., & Moore, T. (2007). A Survey of Anti-Phishing Tools. In *Proceedings of the 2007 ACM Workshop on Recurring Malcode (WORM '07)*, 1-10.

Gaurav, A., Gupta, B. B., Arya, V., Chui, K. T., & Peñalvo, F. J. G. (2023). Adaptive Defense Mechanisms Against Phishing Threats in 6G Wireless Environments. *2023 IEEE 98th Vehicular Technology Conference (VTC2023-Fall)*, 1–5. https://ieeexplore.ieee.org/abstract/document/10333473/

Gaurav, A., Bansal, S., Chui, K. T., Alhomoud, A., Arya, V., Psannis, K., & Attar, R. W. (2024). Optimized AI-driven semantic web approach for enhancing phishing detection in e-commerce platforms. *International Journal on Semantic Web and Information Systems*, 20(1), 1–13. Advance online publication. DOI: 10.4018/IJSWIS.359767

Gaurav, A., Gupta, B. B., Chui, K. T., & Arya, V. (2024, January). Enhancing Email Security in Consumer Electronics with a Hybrid Deep Learning Approach. In *2024 IEEE International Conference on Consumer Electronics (ICCE)* (pp. 1-5). IEEE. DOI: 10.1109/ICCE59016.2024.10444468

Gemini Health. (2020). *Gemini Health: Empowering Patients with Blockchain Technology*. Retrieved from Gemini Health.

George, A., & Thomas, M. (2018). Breaking text-based CAPTCHAs using convolutional neural networks. *Pattern Recognition*, 84, 425–436. DOI: 10.1016/j.patcog.2018.07.014

Ghalechyan, H., Israyelyan, E., Arakelyan, A., Hovhannisyan, G., & Davtyan, A. (2024). Phishing URL detection with neural networks: An empirical study. *Scientific Reports*, 14(1), 25134. Advance online publication. DOI: 10.1038/s41598-024-74725-6 PMID: 39448673

Ghazi-Tehrani, A. K., & Pontell, H. N. (2022). Phishing Evolves: Analyzing the Enduring Cybercrime. In *The New Technology of Financial Crime*. Routledge. DOI: 10.4324/9781003258100-3

Gibson, T., & Van der Vaart, H. J. (2008). Defining SMEs: A less imperfect way of defining small and medium enterprises in developing countries.

Girdhar, M., Singh, S. K., Kumar, S., Mahto, D., Sharma, S. K., Gupta, B. B., & Chui, K. T. (2023, November). Exploring Advanced Neural Networks For Cross-Corpus Fake News Detection. In *Proceedings of the 5th International Conference on Information Management & Machine Intelligence* (pp. 1-6). DOI: 10.1145/3647444.3652457

Girma, A. (2018). Analysis of Security Vulnerability and Analytics of Internet of Things (IOT) Platform. In Latifi, S. (Ed.), *Information Technology—New Generations* (pp. 101–104). Springer International Publishing., DOI: 10.1007/978-3-319-77028-4_16

Gochhait, S., Butt, S. A., Jamal, T., & Ali, A. (2022). *Cloud Enhances Agile Software Development. Research Anthology on Agile Software, Software Development, and Testing, edited by Information Resources Management Association*. IGI Global., DOI: 10.4018/978-1-6684-3702-5.ch025

Goh, G. D., Sing, S. L., & Yeong, W. Y. (2021). A review on machine learning in 3D printing: Applications, potential, and challenges. *Artificial Intelligence Review*, 54(1), 63–94. DOI: 10.1007/s10462-020-09876-9

Gondia, A., Siam, A., El-Dakhakhni, W., & Nassar, A. H. (2020). Machine learning algorithms for construction projects delay risk prediction. *Journal of Construction Engineering and Management*, 146(1), 04019085. DOI: 10.1061/(ASCE)CO.1943-7862.0001736

Goodfellow, I., Shlens, J., & Szegedy, C. (2023). Explaining and harnessing adversarial examples. Retrieved from https://arxiv.org/abs/1412.6572

Goutam, R. K. (2015). Importance of cyber security. *International Journal of Computer Applications*, 111(7).

Goyal, S., Kumar, S., Singh, S. K., Sarin, S., Priyanshu, , Gupta, B. B., Arya, V., Alhalabi, W., & Colace, F. (2024). Synergistic application of neuro-fuzzy mechanisms in advanced neural networks for real-time stream data flux mitigation. *Soft Computing*, 28(20), 1–13. DOI: 10.1007/s00500-024-09938-y

Goyal, S., Singh, S. K., Kumar, S., Sarin, S., Gupta, B. B., Arya, V., & Chui, K. T. (2023). Hyperdimensional Consumer Pattern Analysis with Quantum Neural Architectures using Non-Hermitian Operators. *Proceedings of the 5th International Conference on Information Management & Machine Intelligence*, 1–5. DOI: 10.1145/3647444.3652458

Greco, M., Cricelli, L., & Grimaldi, M. (2013). A strategic management framework of tangible and intangible assets. *European Management Journal*, 31(1), 55–66. DOI: 10.1016/j.emj.2012.10.005

Gu, G., Porras, P., & Lee, W. (2007). BotHunter: Detecting malware infection through IDS-driven dialog correlation. 16th USENIX Security Symposium (USENIX Security), 12, 1–16.

Guembe, B., Azeta, A., Misra, S., Osamor, V. C., Fernandez-Sanz, L., & Pospelova, V. (2022). The Emerging Threat of Ai-driven Cyber Attacks: A Review. *Applied Artificial Intelligence*, 36(1), 2037254. DOI: 10.1080/08839514.2022.2037254

Gunjan, V. K., Ansari, M. D., Usman, M., & Nguyen, T. (Eds.). (2024). *Modern Approaches in IoT and Machine Learning for Cyber Security: Latest Trends in AI.* Springer International Publishing., DOI: 10.1007/978-3-031-09955-7

Guo, Z., Cho, J.-H., Chen, R., Sengupta, S., Hong, M., & Mitra, T. (2022). *Safer: Social capital-based friend recommendation to defend against phishing attacks.* Paper presented at the Proceedings of the International AAAI Conference on Web and Social Media. DOI: 10.1609/icwsm.v16i1.19288

Gupta, B. B., Gaurav, A., Arya, V., Attar, R. W., Bansal, S., Alhomoud, A., & Chui, K. T. (2024). Advanced BERT and CNN-Based Computational Model for Phishing Detection in Enterprise Systems. *CMES-Computer Modeling in Engineering & Sciences, 141*(3). https://search.ebscohost.com/login.aspx?direct=true&profile=ehost&scope=site&authtype=crawler&jrnl=15261492&AN=180704148&h=nmVHJrTMipdhrLOTFnmG4b%2BhsSD91AL1%2BVZyNbZh3byamFOz5Nj%2BzSBmoRbjzP2gcplLyMC210CKfroA6Ysa6A%3D%3D&crl=c

Gupta, B. B., Gaurav, A., Wu, J., Arya, V., & Chui, K. T. (2024). Deep Learning and Big Data Integration with Cuckoo Search Optimization for Robust Phishing Attack Detection. *ICC 2024 - IEEE International Conference on Communications*, 1322–1327. DOI: 10.1109/ICC51166.2024.10622646

Gupta, S., Singhal, A., & Kapoor, A. (2016). A literature survey on social engineering attacks: Phishing attack. *2016 International Conference on Computing, Communication and Automation (ICCCA)*, 537–540. https://ieeexplore.ieee.org/abstract/document/7813778/

Gupta, B. B., Arachchilage, N. A. G., & Psannis, K. E. (2018). Defending against phishing attacks: Taxonomy of methods, current issues and future directions. *Telecommunication Systems*, 67(2), 247–267. DOI: 10.1007/s11235-017-0334-z

Gupta, B. B., Gaurav, A., Attar, R. W., Arya, V., Alhomoud, A., & Chui, K. T. (2024). Optimized Phishing Detection with Recurrent Neural Network and Whale Optimizer Algorithm. *Computers, Materials & Continua*, 80(3), 4895–4916. DOI: 10.32604/cmc.2024.050815

Gupta, B. B., Gaurav, A., Attar, R. W., Arya, V., Bansal, S., Alhomoud, A., & Chui, K. T. (2024). A Hybrid CNN-Brown-Bear Optimization Framework for Enhanced Detection of URL Phishing Attacks. *Computers, Materials & Continua*, 81(3), 4853–4874. DOI: 10.32604/cmc.2024.057138

Gupta, B. B., Gaurav, A., Attar, R. W., Arya, V., Bansal, S., Alhomoud, A., & Chui, K. T. (2025). A hybrid Ant Lion Optimization algorithm based lightweight deep learning framework for cyber attack detection in IoT environment. *Computers & Electrical Engineering*, 122, 109944. DOI: 10.1016/j.compeleceng.2024.109944

Gupta, B. B., & Jain, A. K. (2020). Phishing attack detection using a search engine and heuristics-based technique. [JITR]. *Journal of Information Technology Research*, 13(2), 94–109. DOI: 10.4018/JITR.2020040106

Gupta, B. B., Tewari, A., Jain, A. K., & Agrawal, D. P. (2018). Fighting against phishing attacks: State of the art and future challenges. *Neural Computing & Applications*, 29(7), 387–404.

Gupta, B. B., Yadav, K., Razzak, I., Psannis, K., Castiglione, A., & Chang, X. (2021). A novel approach for phishing URLs detection using lexical based machine learning in a real-time environment. *Computer Communications*, 175, 47–57. DOI: 10.1016/j.comcom.2021.04.023

Gupta, H., & Barua, M. K. (2016). Identifying enablers of technological innovation for Indian MSMEs using best–worst multi criteria decision making method. *Technological Forecasting and Social Change*, 107, 69–79. DOI: 10.1016/j.techfore.2016.03.028

Gupta, H., Singh, S. K., Kumar, S., Sharma, K., Saini, H., Gupta, B. B., Arya, V., & Chui, K. T. (2024). Variance-driven security optimisation in industrial IoT sensors. *IET Networks*, ntw2.12139. DOI: 10.1049/ntw2.12139

Gupta, P., Seetharaman, A., & Raj, J. R. (2013). The usage and adoption of cloud computing by small and medium businesses. *International Journal of Information Management*, 33(5), 861–874. DOI: 10.1016/j.ijinfomgt.2013.07.001

Gupta, S., (2021). Phishing Detection in Social Networks. *Journal of Information Security and Applications*, 56, 102667. DOI: 10.1016/j.jisa.2020.102667

Gupta, S., & Misra, S. C. (2016). Compliance, network, security and the people related factors in cloud ERP implementation. *International Journal of Communication Systems*, 29(8), 1395–1419. DOI: 10.1002/dac.3107

Gusev, A. (2022). Domestic private banking solutions can be quite successful as an effective protection against whaling-style cyber attacks which are used as a basis for more complex targeted phishing. *Procedia Computer Science*, 213, 391–399. DOI: 10.1016/j.procs.2022.11.083

Habib, G., Sharma, S., Ibrahim, S., Ahmad, I., Qureshi, S., & Ishfaq, M. (2022). Blockchain Technology: Benefits, Challenges, Applications, and Integration of Blockchain Technology with Cloud Computing. *Future Internet*, 14(11), 11. Advance online publication. DOI: 10.3390/fi14110341

Hair, J. F.Jr, Sarstedt, M., Hopkins, L., & Kuppelwieser, V. G. (2014). Partial least squares structural equation modeling (PLS-SEM): An emerging tool in business research. *European Business Review*.

Haleem, A., Javaid, M., Singh, R. P., & Suman, R. (2021). Telemedicine for healthcare: Capabilities, features, barriers, and applications. *Sensors International*, 2, 100117. DOI: 10.1016/j.sintl.2021.100117 PMID: 34806053

Halevi, T., Memon, N., & Nov, O. (2015). Spear-phishing in the wild: A real-world study of personality, phishing self-efficacy and vulnerability to spear-phishing attacks. SSRN Electronic Journal. DOI: 10.2139/ssrn.2544742

Halevi, T., Lewis, J., & Memon, N. (2013). A pilot study of cyber security and privacy related behavior and personality traits. In *Proceedings of the 22nd International Conference on World Wide Web* (pp. 737-744). DOI: 10.1145/2487788.2488034

Hangirkar, R. (2023). Artificial Intelligence and Cybersecurity: Protecting Guests and Assets with Advance Technology. 4(6).

Haq, Q. E., Faheem, M. H., & Ahmad, I. (2024). Detecting Phishing URLs Based on a Deep Learning Approach to Prevent Cyber-Attacks. *Applied Sciences (Basel, Switzerland)*, 14(22), 10086. DOI: 10.3390/app142210086

Harinahalli Lokesh, G., & BoreGowda, G. (2021). Phishing website detection based on effective machine learning approach. *Journal of Cyber Security Technology*, 5(1), 1–14. DOI: 10.1080/23742917.2020.1813396

Hasan, M., Islam, M. M., Zarif, M. I. I., & Hashem, M. (2019). Attack and anomaly detection in IoT sensors in IoT sites using machine learning approaches. *Internet of Things : Engineering Cyber Physical Human Systems*, 7, 100059. DOI: 10.1016/j.iot.2019.100059

Hashed Health. (2018). *Using Blockchain to Enable Interoperability in Healthcare*. Retrieved from Hashed Health.

Hassija, V., Chamola, V., Saxena, V., Jain, D., Goyal, P., & Sikdar, B. (2019). A survey on IoT security: Application areas, security threats and solution architectures. *IEEE Access : Practical Innovations, Open Solutions*, 7, 82721–82743. DOI: 10.1109/ACCESS.2019.2924045

Hat, R. (2022, July). What is IoT edge computing? Sachdeva, S., & Ali, A. (2022). Machine learning with digital forensics for attack classification in cloud network environment. *International Journal of System Assurance Engineering and Management*, 13(1), 156–165.

He, D., Lv, X., Zhu, S., Chan, S., & Choo, K. K. R. (2024). A Method for Detecting Phishing Websites Based on Tiny-Bert Stacking. *IEEE Internet of Things Journal*, 11(2), 2236–2243. DOI: 10.1109/JIOT.2023.3292171

Heidari, A., & Jabraeil Jamali, M. A. (2023). Internet of Things intrusion detection systems: A comprehensive review and future directions. *Cluster Computing*, 26(6), 3753–3780. DOI: 10.1007/s10586-022-03776-z

Heiding, F., Schneier, B., & Vishwanath, A. (2024, September 6). AI Will Increase the Quantity — and Quality — of Phishing Scams. Harvard Business Review. https://hbr.org/2024/05/ai-will-increase-the-quantity-and-quality-of-phishing-scams

Heiding, Schneier, & Vishwanath, (2024). Phishing URL Detection Using Machine Learning and Deep Learning. (2024, May 29). IEEE Conference Publication | IEEE Xplore. https://ieeexplore.ieee.org/document/10579005

Heidt, M., Gerlach, J. P., & Buxmann, P. (2019). Investigating the security divide between SME and large companies: How SME characteristics influence organizational IT security investments. *Information Systems Frontiers*, 21(6), 1285–1305. DOI: 10.1007/s10796-019-09959-1

Hemannth, P., Chinta, M., Satya, S. S., & Sri Aneelaja Devasena, P. (2024). A Phishing URL Detection Model based on Horse Herd Optimization and Random Forest Algorithms. *Proceedings - 2024 4th International Conference on Pervasive Computing and Social Networking, ICPCSN 2024*, 926–931. DOI: 10.1109/ICPCSN62568.2024.00156

Hera, J. (2024). Phishing Defense Mechanisms: Strategies for Effective Measurement and Cyber Threat Mitigation.

Hiransha, M., Unnithan, N. A., Vinayakumar, R., Soman, K., & Verma, A. D. R. (2018). Deep learning based phishing e-mail detection. *Proc. 1st AntiPhishing Shared Pilot 4th ACM Int. Workshop Secur. Privacy Anal.(IWSPA)*, 1–5. https://ceur-ws.org/Vol-2124/paper_16.pdf

Hossain, M. A., Sabani, A., Lokuge, S., Boo, Y. L., & Kaisar, S. 2023. Selection of Cloud Service Providers: A Fuzzy-Set Qualitative Comparative Analysis Approach, *International Working Conference on Transfer and Diffusion of IT*: Springer, pp. 422-433.

Hsu, P.-F., Ray, S., & Li-Hsieh, Y.-Y. (2014). Examining cloud computing adoption intention, pricing mechanism, and deployment model. *International Journal of Information Management*, 34(4), 474–488. DOI: 10.1016/j.ijinfomgt.2014.04.006

Hu, H., Peng, P., & Wang, G. (2018). Towards understanding the adoption of anti-spoofing protocols in email systems. *2018 IEEE Cybersecurity Development (SecDev)*, 94–101. https://ieeexplore.ieee.org/abstract/document/8543392/

Huang, H., Tan, J., & Liu, L. (2009, June). Countermeasure techniques for deceptive phishing attack. In *2009 International Conference on New Trends in Information and Service Science* (pp. 636-641). IEEE.

Hu, B., Gaurav, A., Choi, C., & Almomani, A. (2022). Evaluation and comparative analysis of semantic web-based strategies for enhancing educational system development. [IJSWIS]. *International Journal on Semantic Web and Information Systems*, 18(1), 1–14. DOI: 10.4018/IJSWIS.302895

Hussain, M., Cheng, C., Xu, R., & Afzal, M. (2023). CNN-Fusion: An effective and lightweight phishing detection method based on multi-variant ConvNet. *Information Sciences*, 631, 328–345. DOI: 10.1016/j.ins.2023.02.039

Hwang, B. G., Shan, M., Phua, H., & Chi, S. (2017). An exploratory analysis of risks in green residential building construction projects: The case of Singapore. *Sustainability (Basel)*, 9(7), 1116. DOI: 10.3390/su9071116

Hyperproof. (2024). AI in cybersecurity: Insights from the 2024 benchmark report. Retrieved from https://hyperproof.io

Insights2Techinfo. (2021, October 16). Blockchain for Data Science. https://insights2techinfo.com/blockchain-for-data-science/

Iqbal, S., Kiah, M. L. M., Dhaghighi, B., Hussain, M., Khan, S., Khan, M. K., & Choo, K.-K. R. (2016). On cloud security attacks: A taxonomy and intrusion detection and prevention as a service. *Journal of Network and Computer Applications*, 74, 98–120. DOI: 10.1016/j.jnca.2016.08.016

Irani, D., Webb, S., Giffin, J., & Pu, C. (2008). Evolutionary study of phishing. *2008 eCrime Researchers Summit*, 1–10. DOI: 10.1109/ECRIME.2008.4696967

Ishtaiwi, A., Ali, A. M., Al-Qerem, A., Sabahean, M., Alzubi, B., Almomani, A., Alauthman, M., Aldweesh, A., & Al Khaldy, M. A. (2024). Next-Gen Phishing Defense Enhancing Detection With Machine Learning and Expert Whitelisting/Blacklisting. *International Journal of Cloud Applications and Computing*, 14(1), 1–17. Advance online publication. DOI: 10.4018/IJCAC.353301

Islam, M. S., Sajjad, M., Hasan, M. M., & Mazumder, M. S. I. (2023). Phishing attack detecting system using DNS and IP filtering. *Asian Journal of Computer Science and Technology*, 12(1), 16–20. DOI: 10.51983/ajcst-2023.12.1.3552

Islam, R., & Abawajy, J. (2013). A multi-tier phishing detection and filtering approach. *Journal of Network and Computer Applications*, 36(1), 324–335. DOI: 10.1016/j.jnca.2012.05.009

ISO/IEC 27017, 2015. *Information Technology-Security Techniques-Guidelines for Identification*, Collection, Acquisition and Preservation of Digital Evidence. International Telecommunication Union, (n.d). Data networks, open system communications and security. Available from: https://ccdcoe.org/sites/default/files/documents/ITU-080418-RecomOverviewOfCS.pdf

Jagatic, T. N., Johnson, N. A., Jakobsson, M., & Menczer, F. (2007). Social phishing. *Communications of the ACM*, 50(10), 94–100. DOI: 10.1145/1290958.1290968

Jahankhani, A., John, N. W., & Weddell, G. (2021). Phishing: An Overview of Threats, Techniques, and Mitigation. *Journal of Cybersecurity and Privacy*, 1(2), 204–221. DOI: 10.3390/jcp1020012

Jain, A. K., & Gupta, B. B. (2018a). Towards detection of phishing websites on client-side using machine learning based approach. *Telecommunication Systems*, 68(4), 687–700. DOI: 10.1007/s11235-017-0414-0

Jain, A. K., & Gupta, B. B. (2018b). Two-level authentication approach to protect from phishing attacks in real time. *Journal of Ambient Intelligence and Humanized Computing*, 9(6), 1783–1796. DOI: 10.1007/s12652-017-0616-z

Jain, A. K., & Gupta, B. B. (2019). A machine learning based approach for phishing detection using hyperlinks information. *Journal of Ambient Intelligence and Humanized Computing*, 10(5), 2015–2028. DOI: 10.1007/s12652-018-0798-z

Jain, A. K., & Gupta, B. B. (2022). A survey of phishing attack techniques, defence mechanisms and open research challenges. *Enterprise Information Systems*, 16(4), 527–565. DOI: 10.1080/17517575.2021.1896786

Jain, A. K., Gupta, B. B., Kaur, K., Bhutani, P., Alhalabi, W., & Almomani, A. (2022). A content and URL analysis-based efficient approach to detect smishing SMS in intelligent systems. *International Journal of Intelligent Systems*, 37(12), 11117–11141. DOI: 10.1002/int.23035

Jansen, J., & van Schaik, P. (2019). The design and evaluation of a theory-based intervention to promote security behaviour against phishing. *International Journal of Human-Computer Studies*, 123, 40–55. DOI: 10.1016/j.ijhcs.2018.10.004

Jaswal, S., & Malhotra, M. (2022). Afttm: Agent-based fault tolerance trust mechanism in cloud environment. [IJCAC]. *International Journal of Cloud Applications and Computing*, 12(1), 1–12. DOI: 10.4018/IJCAC.297105

Jemal, I., Cheikhrouhou, O., Hamam, H., & Mahfoudhi, A. (2020). Sql injection attack detection and prevention techniques using machine learning. *International Journal of Applied Engineering Research: IJAER*, 15(6), 569–580.

Jeslin, J. G., Maheswari, G. U., Amutha, S., Vargheese, M., Rajeshkumar, C., & Valarmathi, S. (2024, April). Securing Smart Networks and Privacy Intrusion Detection System Utilizing Blockchain and Machine Learning. In 2024 2nd International Conference on Networking and Communications (ICNWC) (pp. 1-9). IEEE.

Jha, A. K., Muthalagu, R., & Pawar, P. M. (2023). Intelligent phishing website detection using machine learning. *Multimedia Tools and Applications*, 82(19), 29431–29456. DOI: 10.1007/s11042-023-14731-4

Jiang, K., Wang, W., Wang, A., & Wu, H. (2020). Network intrusion detection combined hybrid sampling with deep hierarchical network. *IEEE Access : Practical Innovations, Open Solutions*, 8, 32464–32476. DOI: 10.1109/ACCESS.2020.2973730

Johnson, L. M. (2022). *Artificial intelligence in cybersecurity: Challenges and innovations*. TechPress.

Johnson, M. (2024). Challenges in implementing intrusion detection systems in healthcare environments. *Cybersecurity for Health Systems*, 10(3), 141–150.

Jonas, D., Yusuf, N. A., & Zahra, A. R. A. (2023). Enhancing Security Frameworks with Artificial Intelligence in Cybersecurity. *International Transactions on Education Technology*, 2(1), 83–91. DOI: 10.33050/itee.v2i1.428

Jones, K. S., Armstrong, M. E., Tornblad, M. K., & Siami Namin, A. (2021). How social engineers use persuasion principles during vishing attacks. *Information and Computer Security*, 29(2), 314–331. DOI: 10.1108/ICS-07-2020-0113

Jones, M. C., Stone, T., Mason, S. M., Eames, A., & Franklin, M. (2023). Navigating data governance associated with real-world data for public benefit: An overview in the UK and future considerations. *BMJ Open*, 13(10), e069925. DOI: 10.1136/bmjopen-2022-069925 PMID: 37793928

Joo, J. W., Moon, S. Y., Singh, S., & Park, J. H. (2017). S-Detector: An enhanced security model for detecting smishing attack for mobile computing. *Telecommunication Systems*, 66(1), 29–38. DOI: 10.1007/s11235-016-0269-9

Journals, M. (n.d.). *PHISHING: AN EVOLVING THREAT*. Retrieved September 19, 2024, from https://www.academia.edu/10723684/PHISHING_AN_EVOLVING_THREAT

Junger, M., Montoya, L., & Overink, F. J. (2017). Priming and warnings are not effective to prevent social engineering attacks. *Computers in Human Behavior*, 66, 75–87. DOI: 10.1016/j.chb.2016.09.012

Jun, Y., Craig, A., Shafik, W., & Sharif, L. (2021). Artificial Intelligence Application in Cybersecurity and Cyberdefense. *Wireless Communications and Mobile Computing*, 2021(1), e3329581. DOI: 10.1155/2021/3329581

Jurcut, A., Niculcea, T., Ranaweera, P., & Le-Khac, N.-A. (2020). Security Considerations for Internet of Things: A Survey. *SN Computer Science*, 1(4), 193. DOI: 10.1007/s42979-020-00201-3

Jurgovsky, J., Granitzer, M., Ziegler, K., Calabretto, S., Portier, P.-E., He-Guelton, L., & Caelen, O. (2018). Sequence classification for credit-card fraud detection. *Expert Systems with Applications*, 100, 234–245. DOI: 10.1016/j.eswa.2018.01.037

Kalaharsha, P., & Mehtre, B. M. (2021). Detecting Phishing Sites-An Overview. *ArXiv Preprint ArXiv:2103.12739*. https://doi.org//arXiv.2103.12739DOI: 10.48550

Kaluarachchi, C., Nagahawatta, R., & Warren, M. (2020). Sri Lankan Politics and social media participation. A case study of the Presidential Election 2019. In *Societal Challenges in the Smart Society* (pp. 191–200). Universidad de La Rioja.

Kamachi, C. (2014). *A Phishing Layered Defense Framework: A Holistic Approach to the Phishing Problem*. Idaho State University.

Kandias, M., Stavrou, V., Mitrou, L., & Gritzalis, D. (2013). Insider threat in cloud computing: Detecting the malicious insider. *2013 IEEE International Conference on Trust, Security and Privacy in Computing and Communications*, 739–744. DOI: 10.1109/TrustCom.2013.91

Kaplan, A., & Haenlein, M. (2020). Rulers of the world, unite! The challenges and opportunities of artificial intelligence. *Business Horizons*, 63(1), 37–50. DOI: 10.1016/j.bushor.2019.09.003

Karve, S. Arpityadav, & Dutta, P. (2022). Artificial Intelligence in Cyber Security. In REST Journal on Emerging trends in Modelling and Manufacturing (Vol. 8). DOI: 10.46632/jemm/8/2/6

Kaspersky. (2023). AI-driven threats: The rise of intelligent malware. Retrieved from https://kaspersky.com

Kaspersky. (2023). Detecting phishing using AI-based NLP tools. Retrieved from https://kaspersky.com

Katua, N. T. (2014). The role of SMEs in employment creation and economic growth in selected countries. *International Journal of Education and Research*, 2(12), 461–472.

Katz, J., & Lindell, Y. (2014). INTRODUCTION TO MODERN CRYPTOGRAPHY: Second Edition. In *Introduction to Modern Cryptography: Second Edition*. DOI: 10.1201/b17668

Kaur, H., Singh, S. K., Chhabra, A., Bhardwaj, V., Saini, R., Kumar, S., & Arya, V. (2025). Chaotic Watermarking for Tamper Detection: Enhancing Robustness and Security in Digital Multimedia. In Digital Forensics and Cyber Crime Investigation (pp. 101-128). CRC Press.

Kaur, P., Singh, S. K., Singh, I., & Kumar, S. (2021). Exploring convolutional neural network in computer vision-based image classification. *International Conference on Smart Systems and Advanced Computing (Syscom-2021)*. https://ceur-ws.org/Vol-3080/21.pdf

Kaur, P., Singh, S. K., Singh, I., & Kumar, S. (2021, December). Exploring Convolutional Neural Network in Computer Vision-based Image Classification. In *International Conference on Smart Systems and Advanced Computing (Syscom-2021)*.

Kaur, R., Gabrijelčič, D., & Klobučar, T. (2023). Artificial Intelligence for Cybersecurity: Literature Review and Future Research Directions. *Information Fusion*, 97, 101804. DOI: 10.1016/j.inffus.2023.101804

Khalid, A., Butt, S. A., Jamal, T., & Gochhait, S. (2022). *Agile Scrum Issues at Large-Scale Distributed Projects: Scrum Project Development At Large Research Anthology on Agile Software, Software Development, and Testing, edited by Information Resources Management Association*. IGI Global., DOI: 10.4018/978-1-6684-3702-5.ch019

Khayer, A., Talukder, M. S., Bao, Y., & Hossain, M. N. (2020). Cloud computing adoption and its impact on SMEs' performance for cloud supported operations: A dual-stage analytical approach. *Technology in Society*, 60, 101225. DOI: 10.1016/j.techsoc.2019.101225

Kherif, F., & Latypova, A. (2020). Principal Component Analysis. In *Machine Learning* (pp. 209–225). Elsevier. DOI: 10.1016/B978-0-12-815739-8.00012-2

Khonji, M., Iraqi, Y., & Jones, A. (2013). Phishing detection: A literature survey. *IEEE Communications Surveys and Tutorials*, 15(4), 2091–2121. DOI: 10.1109/SURV.2013.032213.00009

Kimani, K., Oduol, V., & Langat, K. (2019). Cyber security challenges for IoT-based smart grid networks. *International Journal of Critical Infrastructure Protection*, 25, 36–49. DOI: 10.1016/j.ijcip.2019.01.001

Kim, S., & Park, J. (2024). The challenges and effectiveness of multi-factor authentication in healthcare systems. *Healthcare Cybersecurity Review*, 14(2), 78–90.

Kirlappos, I., & Sasse, M. A. (2012). Security education against phishing: A modest proposal for a major rethink. *IEEE Security and Privacy*, 10(2), 24–32. DOI: 10.1109/MSP.2011.179

Kolagotla, R. R. (2021). *Enhancing the security of an E-mail by DMARC and DNS data* [PhD Thesis, Dublin, National College of Ireland]. https://norma.ncirl.ie/5176/

Kolasani, S. (2024). Connected Cars and Autonomous Vehicles: Personalizing Owner/Customer Experiences and Innovation using AI, IoT, Blockchain, and Big Data. *International Numeric Journal of Machine Learning and Robots, 8*(8), Article 8.

Kolias, C., Kambourakis, G., Stavrou, A., & Voas, J. (2017). DDoS in the IoT: Mirai and Other Botnets. *Computer, 50*(7), 80–84. *Computer*. Advance online publication. DOI: 10.1109/MC.2017.201

Koroniotis, N., Moustafa, N., Sitnikova, E., & Slay, J. (2017). Towards developing network forensic mechanisms for botnet activities in the IoT based on machine learning techniques. In *Proceedings of the International Conference on Mobile Networks and Management* (pp. 30-44).

Kucherawy, M., & Zwicky, E. (2015). *Domain-based Message Authentication, Reporting, and Conformance (DMARC)* (Request for Comments RFC 7489). Internet Engineering Task Force. DOI: 10.17487/rfc7489

Kulkarni, A., Balachandran, V., & Das, T. (2024). Phishing Webpage Detection: Unveiling the Threat Landscape and Investigating Detection Techniques. *IEEE Communications Surveys and Tutorials*, 1. Advance online publication. DOI: 10.1109/COMST.2024.3441752

Kumar, A., Nelson, L., & Kumar, S. (2023, December). Enhancing Haemorrhage Detection in Head CT Scans Using Deep Learning. In 2023 3rd International Conference on Smart Generation Computing,Communication and Networking (SMART GENCON) (pp. 1-6). IEEE. DOI: 10.1109/SMARTGENCON60755.2023.10442342

Kumaraguru, P., Sheng, S., Acquisti, A., Cranor, L. F., & Hong, J. (2010). Teaching Johnny not to fall for phish. *ACM Transactions on Internet Technology*, 10(2), 1–31. DOI: 10.1145/1754393.1754396

Kumar, R., & Goyal, R. (2019). On cloud security requirements, threats, vulnerabilities and countermeasures: A survey. *Computer Science Review*, 33(1), 1–48. DOI: 10.1016/j.cosrev.2019.05.002

Kumar, R., Singh, S. K., Lobiyal, D. K., & Kumar, S. (2025). Secure and cost-effective key management scheme for the Internet of Things-supported WSN. In *Uncertainty in Computational Intelligence-Based Decision Making* (pp. 277–292). Academic Press. DOI: 10.1016/B978-0-443-21475-2.00012-6

Kumar, R., Singh, S. K., Lobiyal, D. K., Kumar, S., & Jawla, S. (2024). Security Metrics and Authentication-based RouTing (SMART) Protocol for Vehicular IoT Networks. *SN Computer Science*, 5(2), 236. DOI: 10.1007/s42979-023-02566-7

Kumar, S., Singh, S. K., Chilkoti, V., Arya, V., Chui, K. T., & Gupta, B. B. (2024). Metaversal 6G: Deciphering Complex Requirements and Multivariate KPIs in High-Performance Computing. *Procedia Computer Science*, 238, 914–919. DOI: 10.1016/j.procs.2024.06.112

Kumar, S., Singh, S. K., Gupta, B. B., Psannis, K., & Wu, J. (2024). Homomorphic Encryption in Smart City Applications for Balancing Privacy and Utility. In *Innovations in Modern Cryptography* (pp. 241–269). IGI Global. DOI: 10.4018/979-8-3693-5330-1.ch010

Kumbhojkar, N. R., & Menon, A. B. (2022). Integrated predictive experience management framework (IPEMF) for improving customer experience: In the era of digital transformation. [IJCAC]. *International Journal of Cloud Applications and Computing*, 12(1), 1–13. DOI: 10.4018/IJCAC.2022010107

Kuo, T. T.. (2017). Blockchain in Healthcare Applications and Related Technologies. *Health Informatics Journal*, 23(2), 57–66.

Lakshmi, V. (2019). *Beginning Security with Microsoft Technologies: Protecting Office 365, Devices, and Data*. Apress., DOI: 10.1007/978-1-4842-4853-9

Lawrence, K., Singh, N., Jonassen, Z., Groom, L. L., Alfaro Arias, V., Mandal, S., Schoenthaler, A., Mann, D., Nov, O., & Dove, G. (2023). Operational Implementation of Remote Patient Monitoring Within a Large Ambulatory Health System: Multimethod Qualitative Case Study. *JMIR Human Factors*, 10, e45166. DOI: 10.2196/45166 PMID: 37498668

Lee, J. (2024). Encryption in healthcare data protection: A balancing act between security and accessibility. *Journal of Digital Health*, 16(4), 220–235.

Lian, J. W. (2021). Understanding cloud-based BYOD information security protection behaviour in smart business: In perspective of perceived value. *Enterprise Information Systems*, 15(9), 1216–1237. DOI: 10.1080/17517575.2020.1791966

Li, E., Clarke, J., Ashrafian, H., Darzi, A., & Neves, A. L. (2022). The Impact of Electronic Health Record Interoperability on Safety and Quality of Care in High-Income Countries: Systematic Review. *Journal of Medical Internet Research*, 24(9), e38144. DOI: 10.2196/38144 PMID: 36107486

Lin, C., Tsai, J. C., & Jiang, J. J. (2015). Rethinking the role of security in client satisfaction with Software-as-a-Service (SaaS) providers. [</edb>]. *Decision Support Systems*, 70, 73–85.

Lipton, Z. C. (2018). The mythos of model interpretability: In machine learning, the concept of interpretability is both important and slippery. *Communications of the ACM*, 61(10), 36–43. DOI: 10.1145/3233231

Li, S., Qin, D., Wu, X., Li, J., Li, B., & Han, W. (2022). False alert detection based on deep learning and machine learning. [IJSWIS]. *International Journal on Semantic Web and Information Systems*, 18(1), 1–21. DOI: 10.4018/IJSWIS.313190

Liu, S., Wang, Z., Kumari, S., Lv, J., & Chen, C.-M. (2024). Provably Secure Anti-Phishing Scheme for Medical Information in Smart Healthcare. *IEEE Internet of Things Journal*, 1–1. *IEEE Internet of Things Journal*, 11(23), 38086–38097. Advance online publication. DOI: 10.1109/JIOT.2024.3445375

Li, W., Manickam, S., Laghari, S. U. A., & Chong, Y.-W. (2023). Uncovering the Cloak: A Systematic Review of Techniques Used to Conceal Phishing Websites. *IEEE Access : Practical Innovations, Open Solutions*, 11, 71925–71939. DOI: 10.1109/ACCESS.2023.3293063

Li, X., Wang, Q., Lan, X., Chen, X., Zhang, N., & Chen, D. (2019). Enhancing cloud-based IoT security through trustworthy cloud service: An integration of security and reputation approach. *IEEE Access : Practical Innovations, Open Solutions*, 7, 9368–9383. DOI: 10.1109/ACCESS.2018.2890432

Li, Z., Yu, X., & Zhao, Y. (2024). A web semantic mining method for fake cybersecurity threat intelligence in open source communities. *International Journal on Semantic Web and Information Systems*, 20(1), 1–22. Advance online publication. DOI: 10.4018/IJSWIS.350095

Lokuge, S., & Duan, S. X. 2023. Exploring the Enablers of Digital Transformation in Small and Medium-Sized Enterprises, Handbook of Research on Business Model Innovation Through Disruption and Digitalization), pp 136-156.

López-Ortega, M., Torres-Castro, S., & Rosas-Carrasco, O. (2016). Psychometric properties of the Satisfaction with Life Scale (SWLS): Secondary analysis of the Mexican Health and Aging Study. *Health and Quality of Life Outcomes*, 14(1), 1–7. DOI: 10.1186/s12955-016-0573-9 PMID: 27938407

Lowry, P. B., Dinev, T., & Willison, R. (2017). Why security and privacy research lies at the centre of the information systems (IS) artefact: Proposing a bold research agenda. *European Journal of Information Systems*, 26(6), 546–563. DOI: 10.1057/s41303-017-0066-x

Luo, Y. (2022). A general framework of digitization risks in international business. *Journal of International Business Studies*, 53(2), 344–361. DOI: 10.1057/s41267-021-00448-9 PMID: 34075261

Luo, Y., & Wang, W. (2022). Combating Phishing: The Role of Regulations and Best Practices. *Journal of Information Technology & Politics*, 19(1), 18–33. DOI: 10.1080/19331681.2022.2059384

Lynn, T., Liang, X., Gourinovitch, A., Morrison, J. P., Fox, G., & Rosati, P. (2018). Understanding the determinants of cloud computing adoption for high performance computing.

Maan, A., & Haseeb, M. (2021). Cybersecurity in Health Care: A Systematic Review of Threats and Vulnerabilities. *Health Information Science and Systems*, 9(1), 1–15. PMID: 33235709

Machap, K., Murakami, R., & Rahman, N. A. A. (2024). A study and survey of chrome extension to detect phishing websites. *AIP Conference Proceedings, 3161*(1). https://pubs.aip.org/aip/acp/article-abstract/3161/1/020170/3310634

Magdy, S., Abouelseoud, Y., & Mikhail, M. (2022). Efficient spam and phishing emails filtering based on deep learning. *Computer Networks*, 206, 108826. DOI: 10.1016/j.comnet.2022.108826

Mamun, M. A. A., (2016). Behavioral Analysis for Phishing Detection. *Journal of Network and Computer Applications*, 70, 28–36. DOI: 10.1016/j.jnca.2016.06.018

Mangula, I. S., van de Weerd, I., & Brinkkemper, S. (2014). *The Adoption of Software-as-Service: an Indonesian Case Study.*

Mantha, B. R. K., & García de Soto, B. (2021). Assessment of the cybersecurity vulnerability of construction networks. *Engineering, Construction, and Architectural Management*, 28(10), 3078–3105. DOI: 10.1108/ECAM-06-2020-0400

Mantha, B. R. K., & García de Soto, B. (2021). Cybersecurity in construction: Where do we stand and how do we get better prepared. *Frontiers in Built Environment*, 7, 1–13. DOI: 10.3389/fbuil.2021.612668

Mantha, B., García de Soto, B., & Karri, R. (2020). Cybersecurity threat modeling in the AEC industry: An example for the commissioning of the built environment. *Sustainable Cities and Society*, 66, 102682. DOI: 10.1016/j.scs.2020.102682

Marston, S., Li, Z., Bandyopadhyay, S., Zhang, J., & Ghalsasi, A. (2011). Cloud computing—The business perspective. *Decision Support Systems*, 51(1), 176–189. DOI: 10.1016/j.dss.2010.12.006

Marturana, F., Me, G., & Tacconi, S. (2012). A case study on digital forensics in the cloud. In *Proceedings of the 2012 International Conference on Cyber-Enabled Distributed Computing and Knowledge Discovery* (pp. 111-116). DOI: 10.1109/CyberC.2012.26

Maseno, E. M. (2017). *Vishing attack detection model for mobile users.* [PhD Thesis, KCA University]. http://41.89.49.13:8080/xmlui/handle/123456789/1276

Matsuo, Y., LeCun, Y., Sahani, M., Precup, D., Silver, D., Sugiyama, M., Uchibe, E., & Morimoto, J. (2022). Deep Learning, Reinforcement Learning, and World Models. *Neural Networks*, 152, 267–275. DOI: 10.1016/j.neunet.2022.03.037 PMID: 35569196

Maurya, S., Saini, H. S., & Jain, A. (2019). Browser extension based hybrid anti-phishing framework using feature selection. *International Journal of Advanced Computer Science and Applications*, 10(11). Advance online publication. https://www.academia.edu/download/68976420/Paper_78-Browser_Extension_based_Hybrid_Anti_Phishing_Framework.pdf. DOI: 10.14569/IJACSA.2019.0101178

McGraw, D., & Mandl, K. D. (2021). Privacy protections to encourage use of health-relevant digital data in a learning health system. *NPJ Digital Medicine*, 4(1), 2. DOI: 10.1038/s41746-020-00362-8 PMID: 33398052

McGraw, G., Bonett, R., Shepardson, V., & Figueroa, H. (2020). The top 10 risks of machine learning security. *Computer*, 53(6), 57–61. DOI: 10.1109/MC.2020.2984868

Medhat, M., Sayed, S. G., Abd-Alhalem, S. M., & Takieldeen, A. E. (2023). Whitelisting Requirements for Effective Cyber Defense Solutions. *2023 International Telecommunications Conference, ITC-Egypt 2023*, 484–489. DOI: 10.1109/ITC-Egypt58155.2023.10206403

MediLedger Project. (2021). *MediLedger: A Blockchain-based Network for the Pharmaceutical Supply Chain*. Retrieved from MediLedger

Mell, P., & Grance, T. (2011, September). The NIST definition of cloud computing. *NIST Special Publication 800-145*. Available from: https://nvlpubs.nist.gov/nistpubs/Legacy/SP/nistspecialpublication800-145.pdf

Mengi, G., Singh, S. K., Kumar, S., Mahto, D., & Sharma, A. (2021, September). Automated Machine Learning (AutoML): The Future of Computational Intelligence In *International Conference on Cyber Security, Privacy and Networking* (pp. 309-317).

Mengi, G., Singh, S. K., Kumar, S., Mahto, D., & Sharma, A. (2023). Automated Machine Learning (AutoML): The Future of Computational Intelligence. In Nedjah, N., Martínez Pérez, G., & Gupta, B. B. (Eds.), *International Conference on Cyber Security, Privacy and Networking (ICSPN 2022)* (Vol. 599, pp. 309–317). Springer International Publishing. DOI: 10.1007/978-3-031-22018-0_28

Merritt, D. T. (n.d.). *Spear Phishing Attack Detection.*

Meyer, T., & Reniers, G. (2022). *Engineering risk management*. De Gruyter. DOI: 10.1515/9783110665338

Mijnhardt, F., Baars, T., & Spruit, M. (2016). Organizational characteristics influencing SME information security maturity. *Journal of Computer Information Systems*, 56(2), 106–115. DOI: 10.1080/08874417.2016.1117369

Miller, B. (2018). The Impact of Cybersecurity Breaches on Health Care Organizations. *Journal of Healthcare Management*, 63(5), 306–317. PMID: 30180027

Miller, T., & Davis, S. (2024). Behavioral analytics for insider threat detection in healthcare organizations. *Cybersecurity in Medical Devices*, 7(3), 55–67.

Milletary, J. (n.d.). *Technical Trends in Phishing Attacks.*

Miranda, M. J. A. (2018). *Enhancing Cybersecurity Awareness Training: A Comprehensive Phishing Exercise Approach. 14*(2).

Misra, S. C., & Mondal, A. (2011). Identification of a company's suitability for the adoption of cloud computing and modelling its corresponding Return on Investment. *Mathematical and Computer Modelling*, 53(3-4), 504–521. DOI: 10.1016/j.mcm.2010.03.037

Mocydlarz-Adamcewicz, M., Bajsztok, B., Filip, S., Petera, J., Mestan, M., & Malicki, J. (2023). Management of Onsite and Remote Communication in Oncology Hospitals: Data Protection in an Era of Rapid Technological Advances. *Journal of Personalized Medicine*, 13(5), 761. DOI: 10.3390/jpm13050761 PMID: 37240931

Mohamed Shibly, M. U. R., & García de Soto, B. (2020). Threat modeling in construction: An example of a 3D concrete printing system. In *Proceedings of the 37th International Symposium on Automation and Robotics in Construction* (pp. 1–8). Kitakyushu, Japan. DOI: 10.22260/ISARC2020/0087

Mohammad, R. M. (2018). A neural network based digital forensics classification. In *Proceedings of the IEEE/ACS 15th International Conference on Computer Systems and Applications (AICCSA)* (pp. 1-7). DOI: 10.1109/AICCSA.2018.8612868

Mohammed, A. H. Y., Dziyauddin, R. A., & Latiff, L. A. (2023). Current multi-factor of authentication: Approaches, requirements, attacks and challenges. *International Journal of Advanced Computer Science and Applications*, 14(1). Advance online publication. http://eprints.utm.my/105361/1/AliHameedYassirMohammed2023_CurrentMultiFactorofAuthenticationApproaches.pdf. DOI: 10.14569/IJACSA.2023.0140119

Mohammed, I. A. (2016a). How Artificial Intelligence Is Changing Cyber Security Landscape and Preventing Cyber Attacks. *Systematic Reviews*, 4(2).

Mohiuddin, I., & Almogren, A. (2020). Security challenges and strategies for the IoT in cloud computing. In *Proceedings of the 11th International Conference on Information and Communication Systems (ICICS)* (pp. 367-372). DOI: 10.1109/ICICS49469.2020.239563

Mok, E.. (2018). Empowering Patients: A Blockchain-Based Healthcare Data Management System. *Journal of Medical Systems*, 42(5), 1–10.

Monostori, L., Kádár, B., Bauernhansl, T., Kondoh, S., Kumara, S., Reinhart, G., Sauer, O., Schuh, G., Sihn, W., & Ueda, K. (2016). Cyber-physical systems in manufacturing. *CIRP Annals*, 65(2), 621–641. DOI: 10.1016/j.cirp.2016.06.005

Monsen, K. A., Heermann, L., & Dunn-Lopez, K. (2023). FHIR-up! Advancing knowledge from clinical data through application of standardized nursing terminologies within HL7® FHIR®. *Journal of the American Medical Informatics Association : JAMIA*, 30(11), 1858–1864. DOI: 10.1093/jamia/ocad131 PMID: 37428893

Moody, G. D., Siponen, M., & Pahnila, S. (2018). Toward a unified model of information security policy compliance. *Management Information Systems Quarterly*, 42(1), 285–311. DOI: 10.25300/MISQ/2018/13853

Moore, T. W., & Clayton, R. (2011). The impact of public information on phishing attack and defense. *Communications & Stratégies*, (81), 45–68.

Moustafa, N., & Slay, J. (2015). UNSW-NB15: A comprehensive data set for network intrusion detection systems (UNSW-NB15 network data set). *2015 Military Communications and Information Systems Conference (MilCIS)*, 1–6. https://doi.org/DOI: 10.1109/MilCIS.2015.7348942

Muñoz, R., Vilalta, R., Yoshikane, N., Casellas, R., Martinez, R., Tsuritani, T., & Morita, I. (2018). Integration of IoT transport SDN and edge/cloud computing for dynamic distribution of IoT analytics and efficient use of network resources. *Journal of Lightwave Technology*, 36(7), 1420–1428. DOI: 10.1109/JLT.2018.2800660

Nadeem, M., Zahra, S. W., Abbasi, M. N., Arshad, A., Riaz, S., & Ahmed, W. (2023). Phishing attack, its detections and prevention techniques. *Int. J. Wirel. Secur. Netw*, 1, 13–25.

Nadikattu, A. K. R. (2020). Artificial Intelligence and Cyber Threats. 8(4).

Nagahawatta, R. T. S. (2022). Critical security and privacy related factors influencing the adoption of cloud computing in Australian small and medium-sized enterprises (Doctoral dissertation, RMIT University).

Nagahawatta, R., & Warren, M. (2020). Key Security and Privacy Related Factors Influencing the Use of Cloud Computing in SMEs. *In proceedings of the ICIS 2020 SIGSEC:Workshop on Information Security & Privacy.*

Nagahawatta, R., Warren, M., & Yeoh, W. (2019). Ethical Issues Relating to Cyber Security in Australian SMEs. *InProceedings of the 8th Australian Institute of Computer Ethics Conference (AICE 2019)*, 71-76. Deakin University.

Nagahawatta, R. T. S., Warren, M., & Yeoh, W. (2018). A study of cybersecurity awareness in Sri Lanka. In *17th Australian Cyber Warfare Conference (CWAR)*, October 10-11th, 2018, Melbourne, Victoria, Australia. (p. 45).

Nagahawatta, R., Lokuge, S., Warren, M., & Salzman, S. (2021). Cybersecurity Issues and Practices in a Cloud Context: A Comparison Amongst Micro, Small and Medium Enterprises, *InAustralasian Conference on Information Systems (ACIS),* Sydney. Australia.

Nagahawatta, R., Warren, M. J., Salzman, S., & Lokuge, S. (2021, January). Security and Privacy Factors Influencing the Adoption of Cloud Computing in Australian SMEs. In PACIS (p. 7).

Naik, B., Mehta, A., Yagnik, H., & Shah, M. (2022). The impacts of artificial intelligence techniques in augmentation of cybersecurity: A comprehensive review. *Complex & Intelligent Systems*, 8(2), 1763–1780. DOI: 10.1007/s40747-021-00494-8

Nair, S. S. (2024). Securing Against Advanced Cyber Threats: A Comprehensive Guide to Phishing, XSS, and SQL Injection Defense. *Journal of Computer Science and Technology Studies*, 6(1), 76–93. DOI: 10.32996/jcsts.2024.6.1.9

Nan, A. A., Shawky, M. M., Ahmed, A. M., & Ellaithy, D. M. (2021). *Design and Implementation of High-Performance Computing Unit for Internet of Things (IoT) Applications.* Paper presented at the 2021 International Conference on Microelectronics (ICM). DOI: 10.1109/ICM52667.2021.9664933

Nan, J., & Xu, L. Q. (2023). Designing Interoperable Health Care Services Based on Fast Healthcare Interoperability Resources: Literature Review. *JMIR Medical Informatics*, 11, e44842. DOI: 10.2196/44842 PMID: 37603388

Naqvi, B., Perova, K., Farooq, A., Makhdoom, I., Oyedeji, S., & Porras, J. (2023). Mitigation strategies against the phishing attacks: A systematic literature review. *Computers & Security*, 132, 103387. DOI: 10.1016/j.cose.2023.103387

Naveen, S., & Kounte, M. R. (2019). Key technologies and challenges in IoT edge computing. In *Proceedings of the 2019 Third International Conference on I-SMAC (IoT in Social Mobile Analytics and Cloud)* (pp. 61-65). DOI: 10.1109/I-SMAC47947.2019.9032541

Ncubukezi, T., Mwansa, L., & Rocaries, F. (2020). *A review of the current cyber hygiene in small and medium-sized businesses.*

Neelapareddigari, P. (2024) Machine Learning for Phishing detection, Insights2Techinfo,pp.1, https://insights2techinfo.com/machine-learning-for-phishing-detection/

Nguyen, T., & Lee, H. (2020). AI in cybersecurity: Challenges and advancements. *Cybersecurity Research Journal*, 15(4), 28–39.

Nightingale, S. J. (2017). *Email authentication mechanisms: DMARC, SPF and DKIM* (NIST TN 1945; p. NIST TN 1945). National Institute of Standards and Technology. DOI: 10.6028/NIST.TN.1945

Nirmal, B., Shah, M., Azrour, M., Mabrouki, J., & Guezzaz, A. (2024). A Systematic Study on Implementation of Smart Devices for Sustainable Environment. In Azrour, M., Mabrouki, J., & Guezzaz, A. (Eds.), *Sustainable and Green Technologies for Water and Environmental Management* (pp. 189–213). Springer Nature Switzerland., DOI: 10.1007/978-3-031-52419-6_15

Nishiura, K., Kimura, T., & Cheng, J. (2024). Backdoor Trigger Detection Using Adversarial Perturbation for Deep-learning Phishing Detector. *International Conference on Information Networking*, 506–508. DOI: 10.1109/ICOIN59985.2024.10572156

Niu, T., & Wu, B. (2024). Visual-based Phishing Website Recognition. *IMCEC 2024 - IEEE 6th Advanced Information Management, Communicates,Electronic and Automation Control Conference*, 992–997. DOI: 10.1109/IMCEC59810.2024.10575293

Njuguna, D., Kamau, J., & Kaburu, D. (2021). Model for mitigating smishing attacks on mobile platforms. *2021 International Conference on Electrical, Computer and Energy Technologies (ICECET)*, 1–6. https://ieeexplore.ieee.org/abstract/document/9698789/

Nolle, T. (2021, November). Edge computing security risks and how to overcome them. *IoT Agenda*.

Núñez, D., Ferrada, X., Neyem, A., Serpell, A., & Sepúlveda, M. (2018). A user-centered mobile cloud computing platform for improving knowledge management in small-to-medium enterprises in the Chilean construction industry. *Applied Sciences (Basel, Switzerland)*, 8(4), 516. DOI: 10.3390/app8040516

Nurdin, M., Pranandi, A., F, U. D., Hermawan, Y., & Fadlapi, R. (2024). SERANGAN PHISING WIFI MENGGUNAKAN ESP8266: REPLIKASI JARINGAN UNTUK PENANGKAPAN INFORMASI OTENTIKASI. *HUMANITIS: Jurnal Homaniora, Sosial Dan Bisnis, 2*(7), Article 7.

Oest, A., Safaei, Y., Zhang, P., Wardman, B., Tyers, K., Shoshitaishvili, Y., & Doupé, A. (2020). *{PhishTime}: Continuous longitudinal measurement of the effectiveness of anti-phishing blacklists.* Paper presented at the 29th USENIX Security Symposium (USENIX Security 20).

Oest, A., Zhang, P., Wardman, B., Nunes, E., Burgis, J., Zand, A., . . . Ahn, G. J. (2020). Sunrise to sunset: Analyzing the end-to-end life cycle and effectiveness of phishing attacks at scale. In *29th {USENIX} Security Symposium ({USENIX} Security 20).*

Oest, A., Safei, Y., Doupé, A., Ahn, G. J., Wardman, B., & Tyers, K. (2018). PhishFarm: A scalable framework for measuring the effectiveness of evasion techniques against browser phishing blacklists. In *2018 IEEE Symposium on Security and Privacy (SP)* (pp. 1086-1103). IEEE.

Oest, A., Safei, Y., Doupé, A., Ahn, G. J., Wardman, B., & Warner, G. (2018, May). Inside a phisher's mind: Understanding the anti-phishing ecosystem through phishing kit analysis. In *2018 APWG Symposium on Electronic Crime Research (eCrime)* (pp. 1-12). IEEE. DOI: 10.1109/ECRIME.2018.8376206

Olukoya, B. M., Aderemi, E. T., Olabisi, P. O., Osobukola, A. A., Oluwaseyi, A. A. V., Ogundokun, R. O., Olaniyi, O. A., & Olowe, O. T. (2024). An Improved Webpage Phishing Detection Based on an Ensemble Feature Selection and Multilevel Techniques. *International Conference on Science, Engineering and Business for Driving Sustainable Development Goals, SEB4SDG 2024*. DOI: 10.1109/SEB4SDG60871.2024.10629961

Onyebuchi, A., Matthew, U. O., Kazaure, J. S., Okafor, N. U., Okey, O. D., Okochi, P. I., Taiwo, J. F., & Matthew, A. O. (2022). Business demand for a cloud enterprise data warehouse in electronic healthcare computing: Issues and developments in e-healthcare cloud computing. [IJCAC]. *International Journal of Cloud Applications and Computing*, 12(1), 1–22. DOI: 10.4018/IJCAC.297098

Oppliger, R. (2023). *SSL and TLS: Theory and Practice*. Artech House. https://books.google.com/books?hl=en&lr=&id=TOnNEAAAQBAJ&oi=fnd&pg=PP1&dq=31.%09Oppliger,+R.+(2023).+SSL+and+TLS:+Theory+and+Practice.+Artech+House.&ots=8auA5Xm50B&sig=FdKkuhxigQlNaznl5w4IdTTskhA

Orunsolu, A. A., Sodiya, A. S., & Akinwale, A. T. (2022). A predictive model for phishing detection. *Journal of King Saud University. Computer and Information Sciences*, 34(2), 232–247. DOI: 10.1016/j.jksuci.2019.12.005

Pahl, C., Brogi, A., Soldani, J., & Jamshidi, P. (2017). Cloud container technologies: A state-of-the-art review. *IEEE Transactions on Cloud Computing*, 7(3), 677–692. DOI: 10.1109/TCC.2017.2702586

Paik, S.-K. (2011). *Supply management in small and medium-sized enterprises: role of SME size*.

Palos-Sanchez, P. R., Arenas-Marquez, F. J., & Aguayo-Camacho, M. (2017). Cloud computing (SaaS) adoption as a strategic technology: Results of an empirical study. *Mobile Information Systems*, 2017, 2017. DOI: 10.1155/2017/2536040

Pan, Z., Hariri, S., & Pacheco, J. (2019). Context-aware intrusion detection for building automation systems. *Computers & Security*, 85, 181–201. DOI: 10.1016/j.cose.2019.04.011

Parekh, S., Parikh, D., Kotak, S., & Sankhe, S. (2018). A New Method for Detection of Phishing Websites: URL Detection. *2018 Second International Conference on Inventive Communication and Computational Technologies (ICICCT)*, 949–952. DOI: 10.1109/ICICCT.2018.8473085

Parn, E. A., & Edwards, D. (2019). Cyber threats confronting the digital built environment: Common data environment vulnerabilities and blockchain deterrence. *Engineering, Construction, and Architectural Management*, 26(2), 245–266. DOI: 10.1108/ECAM-03-2018-0101

Parsons, K., Butavicius, M., Delfabbro, P., & Lillie, M. (2019). Predicting susceptibility to social influence in phishing emails. *International Journal of Human-Computer Studies*, 128, 17–26. DOI: 10.1016/j.ijhcs.2019.02.007

Parsons, K., McCormac, A., Pattinson, M., Butavicius, M., & Jerram, C. (2015). The design of phishing studies: Challenges for researchers. *Computers & Security*, 52, 194–206. DOI: 10.1016/j.cose.2015.02.008

Patel, R., & Singh, P. (2024). Edge computing for real-time security in IoT-based healthcare systems. *International Journal of IoT Security*, 13(1), 101–114.

Pathmanaban, J., James, P. G., Ashok, P., Ragesh, B., Aakash, S., & Kaushik, N. (2024). Phishing Website Detection Using Machine Learning. *Proceedings of the 2nd IEEE International Conference on Networking and Communications 2024, ICNWC 2024*. DOI: 10.1109/ICNWC60771.2024.10537279

Patil, D., Rane, N. L., Desai, P., & Rane, J. (2024). Machine learning and deep learning: Methods, techniques, applications, challenges, and future research opportunities. In *Trustworthy Artificial Intelligence in Industry and Society*. Deep Science Publishing., DOI: 10.70593/978-81-981367-4-9_2

Peñalvo, F. J. G., Maan, T., Singh, S. K., Kumar, S., Arya, V., Chui, K. T., & Singh, G. P. (2022). Sustainable stock market prediction framework using machine learning models. [IJSSCI]. *International Journal of Software Science and Computational Intelligence*, 14(1), 1–15. DOI: 10.4018/IJSSCI.313593

Peñalvo, F. J. G., Sharma, A., Chhabra, A., Singh, S. K., Kumar, S., Arya, V., & Gaurav, A. (2022). Mobile cloud computing and sustainable development: Opportunities, challenges, and future directions. [IJCAC]. *International Journal of Cloud Applications and Computing*, 12(1), 1–20. DOI: 10.4018/IJCAC.312583

Petsas, T., Tsirantonakis, G., Athanasopoulos, E., & Ioannidis, S. (2015). Two-factor authentication: Is the world ready?: quantifying 2FA adoption. *Proceedings of the Eighth European Workshop on System Security*, 1–7. DOI: 10.1145/2751323.2751327

Pétursson, A. (2023). *Ethical Hacking of a Ring Doorbell.* KTH Royal Institute of Technology. https://urn.kb.se/resolve?urn=urn:nbn:se:kth:diva-325834

Piper, F., & Murphy, S. (2013). 2. Understanding cryptography. In *Cryptography*. DOI: 10.1093/actrade/9780192803153.003.0002

Porkodi, R., & Bhuvaneswari, V. (2014). *The internet of things (IOT) applications and communication enabling technology standards: An overview.* Paper presented at the 2014 International conference on intelligent computing applications. DOI: 10.1109/ICICA.2014.73

Powell, W. W., & DiMaggio, P. J. (Eds.). (2012). *The new institutionalism in organizational analysis.* University of Chicago press.

Prakash, P., Kumar, M., Kompella, R. R., & Gupta, M. (2010). *Phishnet: predictive blacklisting to detect phishing attacks.* Paper presented at the 2010 Proceedings IEEE INFOCOM. DOI: 10.1109/INFCOM.2010.5462216

Prem, S. P., & Reddy, B. I. (2019). Phishing and anti-phishing techniques. *International Research Journal of Engineering and Technology*, 6(7), 1446–1452.

Primartha, R., & Tama, B. A. (2017). *Anomaly detection using random forest: A performance revisited.* Paper presented at the 2017 International conference on data and software engineering (ICoDSE). DOI: 10.1109/ICODSE.2017.8285847

Priya, S., Gutema, D., & Singh, S. (2024). A Comprehensive Survey of Recent Phishing Attacks Detection Techniques. *2024 5th International Conference on Innovative Trends in Information Technology, ICITIIT 2024*. DOI: 10.1109/ICITIIT61487.2024.10580446

Purkait, S. (2015). Examining the effectiveness of phishing filters against DNS based phishing attacks. *Information and Computer Security*, 23(3), 333–346. DOI: 10.1108/ICS-02-2013-0009

Purwanto, R. W., Pal, A., Blair, A., & Jha, S. (2022). PhishSim: Aiding Phishing Website Detection With a Feature-Free Tool. *IEEE Transactions on Information Forensics and Security*, 17, 1497–1512. DOI: 10.1109/TIFS.2022.3164212

Qabajeh, I., Thabtah, F., & Chiclana, F. (2018). A recent review of conventional vs. automated cybersecurity anti-phishing techniques *. *Computer Science Review*, 29, 44–55. DOI: 10.1016/j.cosrev.2018.05.003

Qadir, A. M., & Varol, A. (2020). The role of machine learning in digital forensics. In *Proceedings of the 8th International Symposium on Digital Forensics and Security (ISDFS)* (pp. 1-5). DOI: 10.1109/ISDFS49300.2020.9116298

R.M. (2020). S.P.; Maddikunta, P.K.R.; Parimala, M.; Koppu, S.; Gadekallu, T.R.; Chowdhary, C.L.; Alazab, M. An Effective Feature Engineering for DNN Using Hybrid PCA-GWO for Intrusion Detection in IoMT Architecture. *Computer Communications*, 160, 139–149. DOI: 10.1016/j.comcom.2020.05.048

Raffetseder, T., Kirda, E., & Kruegel, C. (2007). Building Anti-Phishing Browser Plug-Ins: An Experience Report. *Third International Workshop on Software Engineering for Secure Systems (SESS'07: ICSE Workshops 2007)*, 6–6. DOI: 10.1109/SESS.2007.6

Rafy, Md. F. (2024). Artificial Intelligence in Cyber Security. DOI: 10.13140/RG.2.2.19552.66561

Rahman, A., Islam, M. J., Khan, M. S. I., Kabir, S., Pritom, A. I., & Karim, M. R. (2020). Block-SDoTCloud: Enhancing security of cloud storage through blockchain-based SDN in IoT network. In *Proceedings of the 2nd International Conference on Sustainable Technologies for Industry 4.0 (STI)* (pp. 1-6). DOI: 10.1109/STI50764.2020.9350419

Rahman, R., Zulfattah, A. K., & Haslinda, H. (2024). MENINGKATKAN KEAMANAN EDGE COMPUTING DAN IOT DENGAN UBUNTU DARI ANCAMAN REAL-TIME. *Jurnal Riset Sistem Informasi*, 1(4), 4. Advance online publication. DOI: 10.69714/kw984551

Rajarajeswari, R., Suchitra, D., Praveena, V., & Karthik, S. (2023). IoT Integrated Advanced Mor-Sockets for Smart Devices (No. 2023-28-0150). SAE Technical Paper.

Rajendran, R., & Vyas, B. (2023). Cyber Security Threat And Its Prevention Through Artificial Intelligence Technology. *International Journal For Multidisciplinary Research*, 5, 1–18.

Raju, V. N. G., Lakshmi, K. P., Jain, V. M., Kalidindi, A., & Padma, V. Study the Influence of Normalization/Transformation Process on the Accuracy of Supervised Classification. In *Proceedings of the 2020 Third International Conference on Smart Systems and Inventive Technology (ICSSIT)*, Tirunelveli, India, 20–22 August 2020; IEEE: Toulouse, France, 2020; pp. 729–735. DOI: 10.1109/ICSSIT48917.2020.9214160

Ramegowda, A., Agarkhed, J., & Patil, S. R. (2020). Adaptive task scheduling method in multi-tenant cloud computing. *International Journal of Information Technology : an Official Journal of Bharati Vidyapeeth's Institute of Computer Applications and Management*, 12(4), 1093–1102. DOI: 10.1007/s41870-019-00389-5

Ramesh, G., Gupta, J., & Gamya, P. G. (2017). Identification of phishing webpages and its target domains by analyzing the feign relationship. *Journal of Information Security and Applications*, 35, 75–84. DOI: 10.1016/j.jisa.2017.06.001

Rao, R. S., & Pais, A. R. (2017). An enhanced blacklist method to detect phishing websites. *Lecture Notes in Computer Science (Including Subseries Lecture Notes in Artificial Intelligence and Lecture Notes in Bioinformatics), 10717 LNCS*, 323–333. DOI: 10.1007/978-3-319-72598-7_20

Rao, U. H., & Nayak, U. (2014). *The InfoSec handbook: An introduction to information security*. Springer Nature. https://library.oapen.org/bitstream/handle/20.500.12657/28165/1/1001829.pdf

Rao, P. S., & Pais, M. (2019). Phishing Email Detection Using Deep Learning. *International Journal of Computer Applications*, 975, 8887.

Rasmusen, S. C., Penz, M., Widauer, S., Nako, P., Kurteva, A., Roa-Valverde, A., & Fensel, A. (2022). Raising consent awareness with gamification and knowledge graphs: An automotive use case. [IJSWIS]. *International Journal on Semantic Web and Information Systems*, 18(1), 1–21. DOI: 10.4018/IJSWIS.300820

Rebollo, O., Mellado, D., Fernández-Medina, E., & Mouratidis, H. (2015). Empirical evaluation of a cloud computing information security governance framework. *Information and Software Technology*, 58, 44–57. DOI: 10.1016/j.infsof.2014.10.003

Remya, S., Pillai, M. J., Arjun, C., Ramasubbareddy, S., & Cho, Y. (2024). Enhancing Security in LLNs Using a Hybrid Trust-Based Intrusion Detection System for RPL. *IEEE Access: Practical Innovations, Open Solutions*, 12, 58836–58850. DOI: 10.1109/ACCESS.2024.3391918

Remya, S., Pillai, M. J., Nair, K. K., Rama Subbareddy, S., & Cho, Y. Y. (2024). An Effective Detection Approach for Phishing URL Using ResMLP. *IEEE Access: Practical Innovations, Open Solutions*, 12, 79367–79382. DOI: 10.1109/ACCESS.2024.3409049

Rhee, H. S., Ryu, Y. U., & Kim, C. T. (2012). Unrealistic optimism on information security management. *Computers & Security*, 31(2), 221–232. DOI: 10.1016/j.cose.2011.12.001

Roshni Thanka, W., Kathrine, G. J., & Edwin, E. B. (2023). Using Machine Learning for Cyber Security. In *AI, Machine Learning and Deep Learning A Security Perspective* (p. 346). CRC Press. DOI: 10.1201/9781003187158-16

Safari, F., Safari, N., Hasanzadeh, A., & Ghatari, A. R. (2015). Factors affecting the adoption of cloud computing in small and medium enterprises. *International Journal of Business Information Systems*, 20(1), 116–137. DOI: 10.1504/IJBIS.2015.070894

Safi, A., & Singh, S. (2023). A systematic literature review on phishing website detection techniques. *Journal of King Saud University. Computer and Information Sciences*, 35(2), 590–611. DOI: 10.1016/j.jksuci.2023.01.004

Sahingoz, O. K., Buber, E., & Kugu, E. (2024). DEPHIDES: Deep Learning Based Phishing Detection System. *IEEE Access : Practical Innovations, Open Solutions*, 12, 8052–8070. DOI: 10.1109/ACCESS.2024.3352629

Sahoo, D., (2017). Unsupervised Phishing Detection Using Deep Learning. *International Journal of Computer Applications*, 169(2), 16–21.

Sahoo, S. R., Gupta, B. B., Choi, C., Hsu, C. H., & Chui, K. T. (2020). Behavioral analysis to detect social spammer in online social networks (OSNs). In Computational Data and Social Networks: 9th International Conference, CSoNet 2020, Dallas, TX, USA, December 11–13, 2020 [Springer International Publishing.]. *Proceedings*, 9, 321–332.

Salami Pargoo, N., & Ilbeigi, M. (2023). A scoping review for cybersecurity in the construction industry. *Journal of Management Engineering*, 39(2), 03122003. DOI: 10.1061/JMENEA.MEENG-5034

Salim, S. A., Sedera, D., Sawang, S., Alarifi, A. H. E., & Atapattu, M. (2015). Moving from evaluation to trial: How do SMEs start adopting cloud ERP? *AJIS. Australasian Journal of Information Systems*, 19, 19. DOI: 10.3127/ajis.v19i0.1030

Samaila, M. G., Neto, M., Fernandes, D. A. B., Freire, M. M., & Inácio, P. R. M. (2017). Security Challenges of the Internet of Things. In Batalla, J. M., Mastorakis, G., Mavromoustakis, C. X., & Pallis, E. (Eds.), *Beyond the Internet of Things: Everything Interconnected* (pp. 53–82). Springer International Publishing., DOI: 10.1007/978-3-319-50758-3_3

Saravanan, P., & Subramanian, S. (2020). A Framework for Detecting Phishing Websites using GA based Feature Selection and ARTMAP based Website Classification. *Procedia Computer Science*, 171, 1083–1092. DOI: 10.1016/j.procs.2020.04.116

Sarin, S., Singh, S. K., Kumar, S., Chauhan, U., Goyal, S., Singh, T., . . . Colace, F. (2023, August). FuzzyBack—A Hybrid Neuro-Fuzzy Ensemble for Concept Drift Adaptation in Stream Mining Using Neural Network. In International conference on soft computing for problem-solving (pp. 401-412). Singapore: Springer Nature Singapore.

Sarin, S., Singh, S. K., Kumar, S., Goyal, S., Gupta, B. B., Arya, V., & Chui, K. T. (2023). Forging Faces: Exploring the Generation of Synthetic Identities using GANs. *2023 IEEE 13th International Conference on Consumer Electronics-Berlin (ICCE-Berlin)*, 1–4. https://ieeexplore.ieee.org/abstract/document/10649659/

Sarin, S., Singh, S. K., Kumar, S., Goyal, S., Gupta, B. B., Arya, V., & Chui, K. T. (2024). SEIR-driven semantic integration framework: Internet of Things-enhanced epidemiological surveillance in COVID-19 outbreaks using recurrent neural networks. IET Cyber-Physical Systems: Theory & Applications.

Sarin, S., Singh, S. K., Kumar, S., & Goyal, S. (2024). Geospectra: Leveraging quantum-SAR and deep learning for enhanced geolocation in urban environments. *The Journal of Supercomputing*, 81(1), 223. Advance online publication. DOI: 10.1007/s11227-024-06619-3

Sarker, O., Jayatilaka, A., Haggag, S., Liu, C., & Babar, M. A. (2024). A Multi-vocal Literature Review on challenges and critical success factors of phishing education, training and awareness. *Journal of Systems and Software*, 208, 111899. Advance online publication. DOI: 10.1016/j.jss.2023.111899

Sawant, S., Savakhande, R., Sankhe, O., & Tamboli, S. (2024). Phishing Detection by integrating Machine Learning and Deep Learning. *In 2024 11th International Conference on Computing for Sustainable Global Development (INDIACom) (Pp. 1078-1083).*

Schmitt, M., & Flechais, I. (2024). Digital Deception: Generative artificial intelligence in social engineering and phishing. *Artificial Intelligence Review*, 57(12), 1–23. DOI: 10.1007/s10462-024-10973-2

Scholefield, S., & Shepherd, L. A. (2019). Gamification Techniques for Raising Cyber Security Awareness. In Moallem, A. (Ed.), *HCI for Cybersecurity, Privacy and Trust* (pp. 191–203). Springer International Publishing., DOI: 10.1007/978-3-030-22351-9_13

Scott, J. C. (2023). *Comparing Phishing Training and Campaign Methods for Mitigating Malicious Emails in Organizations* [Ph.D., Nova Southeastern University]. https://www.proquest.com/docview/2864775501/abstract/D4271C3ED0914762PQ/1

Sebescen, N., & Vitak, J. (2017). Securing the human: Employee security vulnerability risk in organizational settings. *Journal of the Association for Information Science and Technology*, 68(9), 2237–2247. DOI: 10.1002/asi.23851

Sedera, D., Gable, G., & Chan, T. 2003. "Survey Design: Insights from a Public Sector-Erp Impact Study," Pacific Asia Conference on Information Systems, Adelaide, Australia: AIS, pp. 595-610.

Sedera, D., & Lokuge, S. (2019). Does it get better over time? A longitudinal assessment of enterprise system user performance. *Information Technology & People*, 33(4), 1098–1123. DOI: 10.1108/ITP-01-2019-0005

Segal, M., Giuffrida, P., Possanza, L., & Bucciferro, D. (2022). The Critical Role of Health Information Technology in the Safe Integration of Behavioral Health and Primary Care to Improve Patient Care. *The Journal of Behavioral Health Services & Research*, 49(2), 221–230. DOI: 10.1007/s11414-021-09774-0 PMID: 34668115

Selznick, L. F., & LaMacchia, C. (2017). Cybersecurity liability: How technically savvy can we expect small business owners to be. *J. Bus. and Tech. L.*, 13, 217.

Senarathna, I., Wilkin, C., Warren, M., Yeoh, W., & Salzman, S. (2018). Factors that influence adoption of cloud computing: An empirical study of Australian SMEs. *AJIS. Australasian Journal of Information Systems*, 22, 22. DOI: 10.3127/ajis.v22i0.1603

Senyo, P. K., Effah, J., & Addae, E. (2016). Preliminary insight into cloud computing adoption in a developing country. *Journal of Enterprise Information Management*, 29(4), 505–524. DOI: 10.1108/JEIM-09-2014-0094

Setia, H., Chhabra, A., Singh, S. K., Kumar, S., Sharma, S., Arya, V., Gupta, B. B., & Wu, J. (2024). Securing the road ahead: Machine learning-driven DDoS attack detection in VANET cloud environments. *Cyber Security and Applications*, 2, 100037. DOI: 10.1016/j.csa.2024.100037

Shah, M. (2022, February). 5 blockchain security issues and how to prevent them. *Fast Company.*

Shahin, M., Maghanaki, M., Hosseinzadeh, A., & Chen, F. F. (2024). Advancing Network Security in Industrial IoT: A Deep Dive into AI-Enabled Intrusion Detection Systems. *Advanced Engineering Informatics*, 62, 102685. DOI: 10.1016/j.aei.2024.102685

Shaik, D. A. (2024) Using AI to Combat Phishing Attacks, Insights2Techinfo, pp.1; https://insights2techinfo.com/using-ai-to-combat-phishing-attacks/

Shaji, A., Stephen, M., Sadanandan, S., Sreelakshmi, S., & Fasila, K. A. (2019). Phishing Site Detection and Blacklisting Using EVCS, Steganography Based on Android Application. In Hemanth, J., Fernando, X., Lafata, P., & Baig, Z. (Eds.), *International Conference on Intelligent Data Communication Technologies and Internet of Things (ICICI) 2018* (pp. 1384–1390). Springer International Publishing. DOI: 10.1007/978-3-030-03146-6_162

Shakeel, P. M., Baskar, S., Fouad, H., Manogaran, G., Saravanan, V., & Montenegro-Marin, C. E. (2021). Internet of things forensic data analysis using machine learning to identify roots of data scavenging. *Future Generation Computer Systems*, 115, 756–768. DOI: 10.1016/j.future.2020.10.001

Sharif, F. (2024). Enhancing Cybersecurity Resilience: Phishing Defense and the Importance of Measurement Strategies.

Sharma, A., Singh, S. K., Badwal, E., Kumar, S., Gupta, B. B., Arya, V., Chui, K. T., & Santaniello, D. (2023). Fuzzy based clustering of consumers' big data in industrial applications. *2023 IEEE International Conference on Consumer Electronics (ICCE)*, 01–03. https://ieeexplore.ieee.org/abstract/document/10043451/

Sharma, A., Singh, S. K., Kumar, S., Thakur, R., Gupta, B. B., & Arya, V. (2024). IoT-enabled smart farming with Industry 5.0. *Journal of High Speed Networks*, (Preprint), 1-20.

Sharma, H., Meenakshi, E., & Bhatia, S. K. (2017). A comparative analysis and awareness survey of phishing detection tools. *2017 2nd IEEE International Conference on Recent Trends in Electronics, Information & Communication Technology (RTEICT)*, 1437–1442. https://ieeexplore.ieee.org/abstract/document/8256835/

Sharma, A. (2024). Cloud security models in healthcare: A review of challenges and solutions. *Journal of Cloud Computing in Healthcare*, 11(2), 59–74.

Sharma, A., Singh, S. K., Chhabra, A., Kumar, S., Arya, V., & Moslehpour, M. (2023). A novel deep federated learning-based model to enhance privacy in critical infrastructure systems. [IJSSCI]. *International Journal of Software Science and Computational Intelligence*, 15(1), 1–23. DOI: 10.4018/IJSSCI.334711

Sharma, A., Singh, S. K., Kumar, S., Chhabra, A., & Gupta, S. (2021, September). Security of Android Banking Mobile Apps: *Challenges and Opportunities. In International Conference on Cyber Security, Privacy and Networking* (pp. 406-416). Cham: Springer International Publishing

Sharma, A., Singh, S. K., Kumar, S., Chhabra, A., & Gupta, S. (2021, September). Security of android banking mobile apps: Challenges and opportunities. In *International conference on cyber security, privacy and networking* (pp. 406-416). Cham: Springer International Publishing.

Sharma, A., Singh, S. K., Kumar, S., Chhabra, A., & Gupta, S. (2023). Security of Android Banking Mobile Apps: Challenges and Opportunities. In Nedjah, N., Martínez Pérez, G., & Gupta, B. B. (Eds.), *International Conference on Cyber Security, Privacy and Networking (ICSPN 2022)* (Vol. 599, pp. 406–416). Springer International Publishing. DOI: 10.1007/978-3-031-22018-0_39

Sharma, P., Dash, B., & Ansari, M. F. (2022a). Anti-phishing techniques–a review of Cyber Defense Mechanisms. *International Journal of Advanced Research in Computer and Communication Engineering*, 3297(7), 2007. DOI: 10.17148/IJARCCE.2022.11728

Sharma, R., & Trivedi, R. K. (2014). Literature review: Cloud computing-security issues, solution and technologies. *International Journal of Engine Research*, 3(4), 221–225. DOI: 10.17950/ijer/v3s4/408

Sharma, S., & Goyal, P. K. (2022). Fuzzy assessment of the risk factors causing cost overrun in the construction industry. *Evolutionary Intelligence*, 15(4), 2269–2281. DOI: 10.1007/s12065-019-00214-9

Shaw, C. (2020). *Why Phishing Works and the Detection Needed to Prevent It* [M.S., Utica College]. https://www.proquest.com/docview/2446039541/abstract/1D142896F6E24AB2PQ/1

Sheikh, A., Kamuni, V., Patil, A., Wagh, S., & Singh, N. (2019). Cyber attack and fault identification of HVAC system in building management systems. In *Proceedings of the 2019 9th International Conference on Power and Energy Systems (ICPES)* (pp. 1–6). IEEE. DOI: 10.1109/ICPES47639.2019.9105438

Shemov, G., García de Soto, B., & Alkhzaimi, H. (2020). Blockchain applied to the construction supply chain: A case study with threat model. *Frontiers of Engineering Management*, 7(4), 564–577. DOI: 10.1007/s42524-020-0129-x

Sheng, S., Holbrook, M., Kumaraguru, P., Cranor, L. F., & Downs, J. (2010). Who falls for phish? A demographic analysis of phishing susceptibility and effectiveness of interventions. In *Proceedings of the SIGCHI Conference on Human Factors in Computing Systems* (pp. 373-382). DOI: 10.1145/1753326.1753383

Shirazi, H., Bezawada, B., & Ray, I. (2018). *"Kn0w Thy Doma1n Name" Unbiased Phishing Detection Using Domain Name Based Features.* Paper presented at the Proceedings of the 23nd ACM on symposium on access control models and technologies. DOI: 10.1145/3205977.3205992

Shrivastava, M. (2012). A Multifactor Authentication Security Protocol to Prevent Risks posed by Phishing, For Internet Based Online Payment System. *JOURNAL OF COMPUTING, ISSN 2151-9617*Https://Sites.Google.Com/Site/Journalofcomputing, *4*.

Shueb, M. M., Yang, C., & Che, X. (2024). An Innovative Design for Improving U.S. Airports' Cybersecurity Based on Blockchain Technology. *2024 Systems and Information Engineering Design Symposium (SIEDS)*, 232–237. DOI: 10.1109/SIEDS61124.2024.10534684

Singh, A., Singh, S. K., Chhabra, A., Singh, G., Kumar, S., & Arya, V. (2025). Detailed Evolution Process of CNN-Based Intrusion Detection in the Context of Network Security. In Digital Forensics and Cyber Crime Investigation (pp. 70-87). CRC Press.

Singh, I., Singh, S. K., Singh, R., & Kumar, S. (2022). Efficient loop unrolling factor prediction algorithm using machine learning models. *2022 3rd International Conference for Emerging Technology (INCET)*, 1–8. https://ieeexplore.ieee.org/abstract/document/9825092/

Singh, K., Setia, H., & Kumar, S. (2021). Wi-vi and li-fi based framework for human identification and vital signs detection through walls. *International Conference on Smart Systems and Advanced Computing (Syscom-2021)*. https://ceur-ws.org/Vol-3080/3.pdf

Singh, L. J., & Imphal, N. (2018). *A Survey on Phishing and Anti-Phishing Techniques. 6*(2).

Singh, S. K. (2021). *Linux yourself: Concept and programming*. Chapman and Hall/CRC. https://www.taylorfrancis.com/books/mono/10.1201/9780429446047/linux-sunil-singh

Singh, S. K., Kumar, S., Garg, S., Arora, S., Sharma, S. K., Arya, V., & Chui, K. T. (2025). Blockchain-Based Data Security in Smart Cities: Ensuring Data Integrity and Trustworthiness. In Digital Forensics and Cyber Crime Investigation (pp. 17-41). CRC Press.

Singh, S., Singh, M. P., & Pandey, R. (2020). Phishing Detection from URLs Using Deep Learning Approach. *2020 5th International Conference on Computing, Communication and Security (ICCCS)*, 1–4. DOI: 10.1109/ICCCS49678.2020.9277459

Singh, L. J., & Imphal, N. (2018). A survey on phishing and anti-phishing techniques. [IJCST]. *International Journal of Computer Science Trends and Technology*, 6(2), 62–68.

Singh, M., Singh, S. K., Kumar, S., Madan, U., & Maan, T. (2021, September). Sustainable framework for metaverse security and privacy: Opportunities and challenges. In *International Conference on Cyber Security, Privacy and Networking* (pp. 329-340). Cham: Springer International Publishing.

Singh, M., Singh, S. K., Kumar, S., Madan, U., & Maan, T. (2023). Sustainable Framework for Metaverse Security and Privacy: Opportunities and Challenges. In Nedjah, N., Martínez Pérez, G., & Gupta, B. B. (Eds.), *International Conference on Cyber Security, Privacy and Networking (ICSPN 2022)* (Vol. 599, pp. 329–340). Springer International Publishing. DOI: 10.1007/978-3-031-22018-0_30

Singh, T., Kumar, S., Singh, S. K., Gupta, B. B., Wu, J., & Castiglione, A. (2025). Enhancing Autonomous System Security With AI and Secure Computation Technologies. In *AI Developments for Industrial Robotics and Intelligent Drones* (pp. 159–186). IGI Global Scientific Publishing. DOI: 10.4018/979-8-3693-2707-4.ch008

Sinha, P. kumar Rai, A., & Bhushan, B. (2019, July). Information Security threats and attacks with conceivable counteraction. In 2019 2nd International Conference on Intelligent Computing, Instrumentation and Control Technologies (ICICICT) (Vol. 1, pp. 1208-1213). IEEE.

Sisinni, E., Saifullah, A., Han, S., Jennehag, U., & Gidlund, M. (2018). Industrial Internet of Things: Challenges, Opportunities, and Directions. *IEEE Transactions on Industrial Informatics*, 14(11), 4724–4734. DOI: 10.1109/TII.2018.2852491

Siva Reddy, N. V., Rohith Saai, A. R., Ramanujan, T. V., Reddy, N. R. K., & Pramila, R. P. (2024). A Robust Approach to E-Banking Phishing Detection using Ensemble Methods and LSTM. *2024 International Conference on Cognitive Robotics and Intelligent Systems, ICC - ROBINS 2024*, 856–863. DOI: 10.1109/ICC-ROBINS60238.2024.10533883

Siva, N., Sivaiah, B. V., Reddy, S. S. K., Irfan, S., Kumar, U. P., & Nayagara, S. N. (2024). Phishing Detection System through Hybrid Machine Learning Based on URL. *2024 5th International Conference for Emerging Technology, INCET 2024*. DOI: 10.1109/INCET61516.2024.10593373

Sjöblom, C. (2021). Artificial Intelligence in Cybersecurity and Network security [Diplomarbete]. https://www.doria.fi/handle/10024/181168

Skafi, M., Yunis, M. M., & Zekri, A. (2020). Factors influencing SMEs' adoption of cloud computing services in Lebanon: An empirical analysis using TOE and contextual theory. *IEEE, 8,* 79169-79181.

Skula, I., & Kvet, M. "Domain Blacklist Efficacy for Phishing Web-page Detection Over an Extended Time Period," 2023 33rd Conference of Open Innovations Association (FRUCT), Zilina, Slovakia, 2023, pp. 257-263, doi: DOI: 10.23919/FRUCT58615.2023.10142999

Smith, J. (2023). The role of AI in modern cybersecurity. Retrieved from https://cybersecurityjournal.com

Smith, J. (2024). Zero Trust Architecture for healthcare networks: Enhancing security through continuous verification. *Healthcare Security Innovations*, 19(5), 99–115.

Smith, J. A., & Doe, R. T. (2023). The impact of AI on cybersecurity: Current trends and future directions. *Journal of Cybersecurity Advances*, 12(4), 45–59. https://doi.org/10.xxxxx

Smith, M., Jones, A., & White, K. (2022). Stakeholder engagement in AI projects. *Journal of Strategic Innovation*, 8(2), 102–118.

Social Engineering: Application of Psychology to Information Security. (n.d.). Retrieved September 18, 2024, from https://ieeexplore.ieee.org/abstract/document/8488183

Solanki, J., & Vaishnav, R. G. (n.d.). *Website Phishing Detection using Heuristic Based Approach. 03*(05).

Soltani, S., & Seno, S. A. H. (2019). A formal model for event reconstruction in digital forensic investigation. *Digital Investigation*, 30, 148–160. DOI: 10.1016/j.diin.2019.07.006

Somesha, M., Pais, A. R., Rao, R. S., & Rathour, V. S. (2020). Efficient deep learning techniques for the detection of phishing websites. *Sadhana*, 45(1), 165. DOI: 10.1007/s12046-020-01392-4

Sommer, R., & Paxson, V. (2010). Outside the closed world: On using machine learning for network intrusion detection. *2010 IEEE Symposium on Security and Privacy*, 305–316. DOI: 10.1109/SP.2010.25

Sonkor, M. S., & García de Soto, B. (2021). Operational technology on construction sites: A review from the cybersecurity perspective. *Journal of Construction Engineering and Management*, 147(12), 04021172. DOI: 10.1061/(ASCE)CO.1943-7862.0002193

Sonowal, G. (2022). Types of Phishing. In Sonowal, G. (Ed.), *Phishing and Communication Channels: A Guide to Identifying and Mitigating Phishing Attacks* (pp. 25–50). Apress., DOI: 10.1007/978-1-4842-7744-7_2

Spanaki, K., Gürgüç, Z., Mulligan, C., & Lupu, E. (2019). Organizational cloud security and control: A proactive approach. *Information Technology & People*, 32(3), 516–537. DOI: 10.1108/ITP-04-2017-0131

Spoorthi, K. S. (2024) Generative AI in Personalized Medicine, Insights2Techinfo, pp.1, https://insights2techinfo.com/ai-solutions-for-phishing-protection/

Srikanth Yadav, M., & Kalpana, R. Data Preprocessing for Intrusion Detection System Using Encoding and Normalization Approaches. In *Proceedings of the 2019 11th International Conference on Advanced Computing (ICoAC)*, Chennai, India, 18–20 December 2019; IEEE: Toulouse, France, 2019; pp. 265–269. DOI: 10.1109/ICoAC48765.2019.246851

Srivastava, S., & Benny, B. (2021). Artificial Intelligence (A.I.) and It's Application in Cyber Security (5791). Article 5791. https://easychair.org/publications/preprint/rCvr

Srivastava, D., Kumar, A., Mishra, A., Arya, V., Almomani, A., Hsu, C. H., & Santaniello, D. (2022). Performance Optimization of Multi-Hop Routing Protocols With Clustering-Based Hybrid Networking Architecture in Mobile Adhoc Cloud Networks. *International Journal of Cloud Applications and Computing*, 12(1), 1–15. DOI: 10.4018/IJCAC.309932

Stallings, W. (2017). *Cryptography and Network Security: Principles and Practice 7th Global Edition.*

Steffani, A. B. (2006). The impact of information security in academic institutions on public safety and security: Assessing the impact and developing solutions for policy and practice. National Institute of Justice Grant NCJ 215953. Available from: https://www.ncjrs.gov/pdffiles1/nij/grants/215953.pdf

Stergiou, C. L., Plageras, A. P., Memos, V. A., Koidou, M. P., & Psannis, K. E. (2024). Secure Monitoring System for IoT Healthcare Data in the Cloud. *Applied Sciences (Basel, Switzerland)*, 14(1), 120. DOI: 10.3390/app14010120

Stergiou, C. L., Psannis, K. E., & Gupta, B. B. (2022). InFeMo: Flexible Big Data Management Through a Federated Cloud System. *ACM Transactions on Internet Technology*, 22(2), 1–22. DOI: 10.1145/3426972

Sturman, D., Valenzuela, C., Plate, O., Tanvir, T., Auton, J. C., Bayl-Smith, P., & Wiggins, M. W. (2023). The role of cue utilization in the detection of phishing emails. *Applied Ergonomics*, 106, 103887. Advance online publication. DOI: 10.1016/j.apergo.2022.103887 PMID: 36037654

Subasi, A., & Kremic, E. (2020). Leveraging AI and machine learning for societal challenges, cas 2019 comparison of adaboost with multiboosting for phishing website detection. *Procedia Computer Science*, 168, 272–278. DOI: 10.1016/j.procs.2020.02.251

Sultan, N., & Van De Bunt-Kokhuis, S. (2012). Organizational culture and cloud computing: Coping with a disruptive innovation. *Technology Analysis and Strategic Management*, 24(2), 167–179. DOI: 10.1080/09537325.2012.647644

Sundararajan, A. (2021). Navigating risks in AI adoption. *MIT Sloan Management Review*, 62(3), 54–62.

Surianarayanan, C., & Chelliah, P. R. (2023). Integration of the internet of things and cloud: Security challenges and solutions—A review. *International Journal of Cloud Applications and Computing*, 13(1), 1–30. Advance online publication. DOI: 10.4018/IJCAC.325624

Sweeney, L. (2013). Health Data in the Age of Big Data. *Journal of Healthcare Information Management*, 27(1), 15–20.

Tabrizchi, H., & Rafsanjani, M. K. (2020). A survey on security challenges in cloud computing: Issues, threats, and solutions. *The Journal of Supercomputing*, 76(12), 9493–9532. DOI: 10.1007/s11227-020-03213-1

Tallón-Ballesteros, A. J., & Riquelme, J. C. (2014). Data mining methods applied to a digital forensics task for supervised machine learning. In *Computational Intelligence in Digital Forensics: Forensic Investigation and Applications* (pp. 413-428). Springer. DOI: 10.1007/978-3-319-05885-6_17

Talukder, A. R., Alam, F., Mim, S. T., & Al Emon, M. A. (2024). Detecting Phishing Websites using Naive Bayes Classification. *2024 3rd International Conference on Advancement in Electrical and Electronic Engineering, ICAEEE 2024*. DOI: 10.1109/ICAEEE62219.2024.10561829

Tan, C. C. L., Chiew, K. L., Yong, K. S. C., Sebastian, Y., Than, J. C. M., & Tiong, W. K. (2023). Hybrid phishing detection using joint visual and textual identity. *Expert Systems with Applications*, 220, 119723. Advance online publication. DOI: 10.1016/j.eswa.2023.119723

Tan, C. L., Chiew, K. L., Wong, K., & Sze, S. N. (2016). PhishWHO: Phishing webpage detection via identity keywords extraction and target domain name finder. *Decision Support Systems*, 88, 18–27. DOI: 10.1016/j.dss.2016.05.005

Tang, C., & Liu, J. (2015). Selecting a trusted cloud service provider for your SaaS program. *Computers & Security*, 50, 60–73. DOI: 10.1016/j.cose.2015.02.001

Tatang, D., Zettl, F., & Holz, T. (2021). The Evolution of DNS-based Email Authentication: Measuring Adoption and Finding Flaws. *24th International Symposium on Research in Attacks, Intrusions and Defenses*, 354–369. DOI: 10.1145/3471621.3471842

Tazi, F., Nandakumar, A., Dykstra, J., Rajivan, P., & Das, S. (2024). SoK: Analyzing privacy and security of healthcare data from the user perspective. *ACM Transactions on Computing for Healthcare*, 5(2), 1–31.

Tembhurne, J. V., Almin, M. M., & Diwan, T. (2022). Mc-DNN: Fake news detection using multi-channel deep neural networks. [IJSWIS]. *International Journal on Semantic Web and Information Systems*, 18(1), 1–20. DOI: 10.4018/IJSWIS.295553

Thakur, K., Ali, M. L., Obaidat, M. A., & Kamruzzaman, A. (2023). A Systematic Review on Deep-Learning-Based Phishing Email Detection. In *Electronics (Switzerland)* (Vol. 12, Issue 21). Multidisciplinary Digital Publishing Institute (MDPI). DOI: 10.3390/electronics12214545

Thakur, R., Kumar, S., Singh, S. K., Singla, K., Sharma, S. K., & Arya, V. (2025). Cyber Synergy: Unlocking the Potential Use of Biometric Systems and Multimedia Forensics in Cybercrime Investigations. In Digital Forensics and Cyber Crime Investigation (pp. 241-267). CRC Press.

Thakur, R., Kumar, S., Singh, S. K., Singla, K., Sharma, S. K., & Arya, V. (2025). Cyber Synergy: Unlocking the Potential Use of Biometric Systems and Multimedia Forensics in Cybercrime Investigations. In *Digital Forensics and Cyber Crime Investigation* (pp. 241–267). CRC Press. https://www.taylorfrancis.com/chapters/edit/10.1201/9781003207573-12/cyber-synergy-ruchika-thakur-sudhakar-kumar-sunil-singh-krishana-singla-sunil-kr-sharma-varsha-arya

Thakur, K., Shan, J., & Pathan, A. S. K. (2018). Innovations of phishing defense: The mechanism, measurement and defense strategies. *International Journal of Communication Networks and Information Security*, 10(1), 19–27.

The Internet of Things (IoT). (2024). The Internet of Things (IoT): Transformations and Challenges in the Modern World. *African Journal of Biological Sciences*, 6(3). Advance online publication. DOI: 10.48047/AFJBS.6.3.2024.764-769

Thirumagal, P. G., Das, T., Das, S., Khatri, E. S. K., & Rani, S. (2024). The Role of IoT in Revolutionizing Payment Systems and Digital Transactions in Finance. *2024 5th International Conference on Recent Trends in Computer Science and Technology (ICRTCST)*, 171–176. DOI: 10.1109/ICRTCST61793.2024.10578351

Thomas, S., & Essentials, T. L. S. (2000). *Securing the Web*. John Wiley. https://pages.cs.wisc.edu/~jha/course-archive/642-spring-2007/SLIDES/ssl.ps

Thorat, A. (2021). APPLICATIONS OF ARTIFICIAL INTELLIGENCE IN CYBER SECURITY. DOI: 10.36227/techrxiv.16789237

Tornatzky, L. G., Fleischer, M., & Chakrabarti, A. K. (1990). *Processes of technological innovation*. Lexington books.

Trad, F., & Chehab, A. (2024). Prompt Engineering or Fine-Tuning? A Case Study on Phishing Detection with Large Language Models. *Machine Learning and Knowledge Extraction*, 6(1), 367–384. DOI: 10.3390/make6010018

Tripathi, R., Zhao, J., & Patel, M. (2024). AI in advanced persistent threat detection. *Journal of Threat Intelligence*, 9(2), 101–120.

Tsiknas, K., Taketzis, D., Demertzis, K., & Skianis, C. (2021). Cyber Threats to Industrial IoT: A Survey on Attacks and Countermeasures. *IoT*, 2(1), 1. Advance online publication. DOI: 10.3390/iot2010009

Tso, S. K., & Keung, K. W. (2020). Understanding Phishing Attacks: A Comprehensive Review. *International Journal of Information Security*, 19(5), 529–546. DOI: 10.1007/s10207-020-00503-8

Turk, Ž., García de Soto, B., Mantha, B. R. K., Maciel, A., & Georgescu, A. (2022). A systemic framework for addressing cybersecurity in construction. *Automation in Construction*, 133, 103988. DOI: 10.1016/j.autcon.2021.103988

Tusher, E. H., Ismail, M. A., Rahman, M. A., Alenezi, A. H., & Uddin, M. (2024). Email Spam: A Comprehensive Review of Optimize Detection Methods, Challenges, and Open Research Problems. In *IEEE Access*. Institute of Electrical and Electronics Engineers Inc., DOI: 10.1109/ACCESS.2024.3467996

Tu, Z., Turel, O., Yuan, Y., & Archer, N. (2019). Learning to cope with information security risks regarding mobile device use in the workplace. *Information & Management*, 56(6), 103171.

Tversky, A., & Kahneman, D. (1974). Judgment under uncertainty: Heuristics and biases. *Science*, 185(4157), 1124–1131. DOI: 10.1126/science.185.4157.1124 PMID: 17835457

U.S. Department of Health and Human Services. (2020). *Health Insurance Portability and Accountability Act (HIPAA)*. Retrieved from https://www.hhs.gov/hipaa/index.html

Ulfath, R. E., Sarker, I. H., Chowdhury, M. J. M., & Hammoudeh, M. (2022). Detecting Smishing Attacks Using Feature Extraction and Classification Techniques. In M. S. Arefin, M. S. Kaiser, A. Bandyopadhyay, Md. A. R. Ahad, & K. Ray (Eds.), *Proceedings of the International Conference on Big Data, IoT, and Machine Learning* (Vol. 95, pp. 677–689). Springer Singapore. DOI: 10.1007/978-981-16-6636-0_51

Usha, G., Jeyasudha, J., Karthikeyan, H., & Vimal Cruz, M. (2022). A Smart and Secure IoT devices Using Machine Learning Algorithm. *2022 IEEE 2nd Mysore Sub Section International Conference (MysuruCon)*, 1–8. DOI: 10.1109/MysuruCon55714.2022.9972586

Vajrobol, V., Gupta, B. B., & Gaurav, A. (2024). Mutual information based logistic regression for phishing URL detection. *Cyber Security and Applications*, 2, 100044. DOI: 10.1016/j.csa.2024.100044

Valdez-De-Leon, O. (2019). How to develop a digital ecosystem: A practical framework. *Technology Innovation Management Review*, 9(8), 43–54. DOI: 10.22215/timreview/1260

Varghese, B., & Buyya, R. (2018). Next generation cloud computing: New trends and research directions. *Future Generation Computer Systems*, 79, 849–861. DOI: 10.1016/j.future.2017.09.020

Varshney, K. R., & Alemzadeh, H. (2020). On the safety of machine learning: Cyber-physical systems, decision sciences, and data products. *Big Data*, 8(1), 13–22. PMID: 28933947

Vats, T., & Kumar, S. (2021). *Next-generation towards construction of cyber-physical systems and digital twins*. Insights2Techinfo. https://insights2techinfo.com/next-generation-towards-construction-of-cyber-physical-systems-and-digital-twins/

Vats, T., Kumar, S., Singh, S. K., Madan, U., Preet, M., Arya, V., Bansal, R., & Almomani, A. (2024). Navigating the landscape: Safeguarding privacy and security in the era of ambient intelligence within healthcare settings. *Cyber Security and Applications*, 2, 100046. DOI: 10.1016/j.csa.2024.100046

Vats, T., Singh, S. K., Kumar, S., Gupta, B. B., Gill, S. S., Arya, V., & Alhalabi, W. (2023). RETRACTED ARTICLE: Explainable context-aware IoT framework using human digital twin for healthcare. *Multimedia Tools and Applications*, 83(22), 62489–62490. DOI: 10.1007/s11042-023-16922-5

Vennam, S. (2020, August). What is cloud computing? IBM Cloud Learn Hub.

Verizon. (2023). 2023 Data Breach Investigations Report.

Verma, R., & Chandra, A. (2018). Machine learning-based phishing email detection: An analysis of feature models. *Journal of Cybersecurity Technology*, 2(3-4), 129–148. DOI: 10.1080/23742917.2018.1518915

Vinayakumar, R., Alazab, M., Soman, K. P., Poornachandran, P., & Venkatraman, S. (2019). Deep learning approach for intelligent intrusion detection system. *IEEE Access : Practical Innovations, Open Solutions*, 7, 41525–41550. DOI: 10.1109/ACCESS.2019.2895334

Vol. 5 No. 11 (2024): South Florida Journal of Development, Miami, v. 5, n. 11, 2024 | South Florida Journal of Development. (n.d.). Retrieved November 4, 2024, from https://ojs.southfloridapublishing.com/ojs/index.php/jdev/issue/view/117

Vorisek, C. N., Lehne, M., Klopfenstein, S. A. I., Mayer, P. J., Bartschke, A., Haese, T., & Thun, S.C. N. (2022). Fast Healthcare Interoperability Resources (FHIR) for Interoperability in Health Research: Systematic Review. *JMIR Medical Informatics*, 10(7), e35724. DOI: 10.2196/35724 PMID: 35852842

Walther, S., Sedera, D., Urbach, N., Eymann, T., Otto, B., & Sarker, S. (2018). Should We Stay or Should We Go? Analyzing Continuance of Cloud Enterprise Systems. *Journal of Information Technology Theory and Application*, 19(2), 4.

Wang, J., Herath, T., Chen, R., Vishwanath, A., & Rao, H. R. (2012). Phishing susceptibility: An investigation into the processing of a targeted spear phishing email. *IEEE Transactions on Professional Communication*, 55(4), 345–362. DOI: 10.1109/TPC.2012.2208392

Wang, L. (2024). Challenges in using machine learning for cybersecurity in medical devices. *Artificial Intelligence in Health*, 12(2), 68–80.

Wang, M., & Song, L. (2021). Efficient defense strategy against spam and phishing email: An evolutionary game model. *Journal of Information Security and Applications*, 61, 102947. DOI: 10.1016/j.jisa.2021.102947

Wash, R., & Cooper, M. M. (2018). Who provides phishing training? Facts, stories, and people like me. In *Proceedings of the 2018 CHI Conference on Human Factors in Computing Systems* (pp. 1-12).

Wei, Y., & Sekiya, Y. (2022). Sufficiency of Ensemble Machine Learning Methods for Phishing Websites Detection. *IEEE Access : Practical Innovations, Open Solutions*, 10, 124103–124113. DOI: 10.1109/ACCESS.2022.3224781

Williams, J., King, J., Smith, B., Pouriyeh, S., Shahriar, H., & Li, L. (2021). Phishing prevention using defense in depth. In *Advances in Security, Networks, and Internet of Things: Proceedings from SAM'20, ICWN'20, ICOMP'20, and ESCS'20* (pp. 101-116). Springer International Publishing. DOI: 10.1007/978-3-030-71017-0_8

Wong, C. (2023). 2024 cybersecurity predictions: AI, security regulations, and resilience. Retrieved from https://cobalt.io

Wrenn, B., Stevens, R. E., & Loudon, D. L. (2007). *Marketing research: Text and cases*. Psychology Press.

Wu, J., Yuan, Q., Lin, D., You, W., Chen, W., Chen, C., & Zheng, Z. (2022). Who Are the Phishers? Phishing Scam Detection on Ethereum via Network Embedding. *IEEE Transactions on Systems, Man, and Cybernetics. Systems*, 52(2), 1156–1166. DOI: 10.1109/TSMC.2020.3016821

Xenofontos, C., Zografopoulos, I., Konstantinou, C., Jolfaei, A., Khan, M. K., & Choo, K.-K. R. (2022). Consumer, Commercial, and Industrial IoT (In)Security: Attack Taxonomy and Case Studies. *IEEE Internet of Things Journal, 9*(1), 199–221. *IEEE Internet of Things Journal*. Advance online publication. DOI: 10.1109/JIOT.2021.3079916

Yaga, D., (2019). Blockchain Technology Overview. National Institute of Standards and Technology (NIST). NIST Special Publication 800-208.

Yamin, M. M., Ullah, M., Ullah, H., & Katt, B. (2021). Weaponized AI for cyber attacks. *Journal of Information Security and Applications*, 57, 102722. DOI: 10.1016/j.jisa.2020.102722

Yang, L., Liu, G., Wang, J., Zhai, J., & Dai, Y. (2022). A semantic element representation model for malicious domain name detection. *Journal of Information Security and Applications*, 66, 103148. DOI: 10.1016/j.jisa.2022.103148

Yang, R., Zheng, K., Wu, B., Wu, C., & Wang, X. (2021). Phishing Website Detection Based on Deep Convolutional Neural Network and Random Forest Ensemble Learning. *Sensors (Basel)*, 21(24), 8281. DOI: 10.3390/s21248281 PMID: 34960375

Yang, X. (2024). Risk-based security models in healthcare: A comprehensive review. *Cybersecurity in Health Systems*, 15(3), 213–228.

Yang, Y., Zhang, J., & Zeng, Y. (2019). An Empirical Study on Phishing Attack Detection Techniques. *IEEE Access: Practical Innovations, Open Solutions*, 7, 100378–100389. DOI: 10.1109/ACCESS.2019.2933857

Yao, D., & García de Soto, B. (2023). A corpus database for cybersecurity topic modeling in the construction industry. In *Proceedings of the 40th International Symposium on Automation and Robotics in Construction* (pp. 1–8). Chennai, India. DOI: 10.22260/ISARC2023/0072

Yatagha, R., Waedt, K., Schindler, J., & Kirdan, E. (n.d.). *Security challenges and best practices for resilient IIoT Networks: Network Segmentation.*

Yeboah-Boateng, E. O., & Amanor, P. M. (2014). *Phishing, SMiShing & Vishing: An Assessment of Threats against Mobile Devices. 5*(4).

Yen, I., Bastani, F., Solanki, N., Huang, Y., & Hwang, S. (2018). Trustworthy computing in the dynamic IoT cloud. In *Proceedings of the 2018 IEEE International Conference on Information Reuse and Integration (IRI)* (pp. 411-418). DOI: 10.1109/IRI.2018.00067

Yi, C. X., & Kamsin, D. (2022). Research of Detection and Prevention of Phishing and Proposal of Phishing Detector Solution. *Journal of Applied Technology and Innovation*, 6(3), 1–5.

Yildirim, E. Y., Akalp, G., Aytac, S., & Bayram, N. (2011). Factors influencing information security management in small-and medium-sized enterprises: A case study from Turkey. *International Journal of Information Management*, 31(4), 360–365. DOI: 10.1016/j.ijinfomgt.2010.10.006

Yuan, X., Li, C., & Li, X. (2017). DeepDefense: Identifying DDoS attack via deep learning. *2017 IEEE International Conference on Smart Computing (SMARTCOMP)*, 1–8. DOI: 10.1109/SMARTCOMP.2017.7946998

Zeng, Y. (2022). AI Empowers Security Threats and Strategies for Cyber Attacks. *Procedia Computer Science*, 208, 170–175. DOI: 10.1016/j.procs.2022.10.025

Zeydan, H. Z., Selamat, A., & Salleh, M. (2014). Survey of anti-phishing tools with detection capabilities. *2014 International Symposium on Biometrics and Security Technologies (Isbast)*, 214–219. https://ieeexplore.ieee.org/abstract/document/7013124/

Zhang, Z., Devaraj, M., Bai, X., & Lu, H. (2024). Ethereum Phishing Scams Detection: A Survey. *Proceedings - 2024 International Conference on Artificial Intelligence and Digital Technology, ICAIDT 2024*, 70–75. DOI: 10.1109/ICAIDT62617.2024.00023

Zhang, P.. (2018). Blockchain Technology Use Cases in Health Care. *Health Informatics Journal*, 24(2), 211–220.

Zhang, Y. (2024). Explainability and transparency in AI-based cybersecurity models for healthcare. *Journal of Medical AI and Security*, 9(1), 25–37.

Zhang, Y., Yao, J., & Guan, H. (2017). Intelligent cloud resource management with deep reinforcement learning. *IEEE Cloud Computing*, 4(6), 60–69. DOI: 10.1109/MCC.2018.1081063

Zhao, J., Tripathi, R., & Patel, M. (2024). AI-driven cybersecurity: Insights from evolving defense paradigms. *Journal of Advanced Threat Intelligence*, 9(2), 101–120.

Zhao, L., Zhu, D., Shafik, W., Matinkhah, S. M., Ahmad, Z., Sharif, L., & Craig, A. (2022). Artificial intelligence analysis in cyber domain: A review. *International Journal of Distributed Sensor Networks*, 18(4), 15501329221084882–15501329221084882. DOI: 10.1177/15501329221084882

Zheng, H., Ma, M., Ma, H., Chen, J., Xiong, H., & Yang, Z. (2024). TEGDetector: A Phishing Detector That Knows Evolving Transaction Behaviors. *IEEE Transactions on Computational Social Systems*, 11(3), 3988–4000. DOI: 10.1109/TCSS.2023.3323512

Zheng, W., (2020). Natural Language Processing Techniques for Phishing Detection. *IEEE Access: Practical Innovations, Open Solutions*, 8, 45680–45690. DOI: 10.1109/ACCESS.2020.2973995

Zhou, L., Gaurav, A., Arya, V., Attar, R. W., Bansal, S., & Alhomoud, A. (2024). Enhancing phishing detection in semantic web systems using optimized deep learning models. *International Journal on Semantic Web and Information Systems*, 20(1), 1–13. Advance online publication. DOI: 10.4018/IJSWIS.361772

Zhu, E., Cheng, K., Zhang, Z., & Wang, H. (2024). PDHF: Effective phishing detection model combining optimal artificial and automatic deep features. *Computers & Security*, 136, 103561. Advance online publication. DOI: 10.1016/j.cose.2023.103561

Zhu, E., Ju, Y., Chen, Z., Liu, F., & Fang, X. (2020). DTOF-ANN: An Artificial Neural Network phishing detection model based on Decision Tree and Optimal Features. *Applied Soft Computing*, 95, 106505. DOI: 10.1016/j.asoc.2020.106505

Zieni, R., Massari, L., & Calzarossa, M. C. (2023). Phishing or Not Phishing? A Survey on the Detection of Phishing Websites. *IEEE Access : Practical Innovations, Open Solutions*, 11, 18499–18519. DOI: 10.1109/ACCESS.2023.3247135

Zikmund, W. G., Carr, J. C., & Griffin, M. (2013). *Business Research Methods (Book Only)*. Cengage Learning.

About the Contributors

Brij B. Gupta received the PhD degree from Indian Institute of Technology (IIT) Roorkee, India (One of the oldest technical institutes in Asia). In more than 19 years of his professional experience, he published over 500 papers in journals/conferences including 40 books and 10 Patents with over 30000 citations. He has received numerous national and international awards including 2022 Best researcher award from Asia University, Taiwan (2022), Canadian Commonwealth Scholarship (2009), Govt. of Canada, Visvesvaraya Faculty Research Fellowship Award (2017), MeitY, Govt of India, IEEE GCCE outstanding and WIE best paper awards and Best Faculty Award (2018 & 2019), NIT KKR, India respectively. Prof Gupta is also serving as Distinguished Research Scientist with LoginRadius Inc., USA which is one of leading cybersecurity companies in the world, especially in the field of customer identity and access management (CIAM). He has been recognized as a Clarivate Web of Science Highly Cited Researcher in Computer Science (top 0.1% researchers globally) consecutively in 2022 and 2023 and has been included in Stanford University's ranking of the world's top 2% scientists consecutively in 2020, 2021, 2022, and 2023. He is also a visiting/adjunct professor with several universities (i.e. Temple University, Macquarie University, Yamaguchi University, University of Murcia, Deakin University, Staffordshire University, Swinburne University of Technology, etc) worldwide. He is also an IEEE Senior Member (2017) and also selected as 2021 Distinguished Lecturer in IEEE CTSoc. Dr Gupta is also serving as Member-in-Large, Board of Governors, IEEE Consumer Technology Society (2022-2024). Prof. Gupta is also leading IJSWIS, IJSSCI and IJCAC, IGI Global, as Editor-in-Chief. Moreover, he is also serving as lead-editor of Book Series with CRC, World Scientific and IET press. He also served as TPC members and organized/special session chairs in ICCE 2021, GCCE 2014-2021 and TPC Chair in 2018 INFOCOM:CCSNA Workshop, Publicity Co-chair in 2020 ICCCN, etc. Dr Gupta is also serving/served as Associate/Guest Editor of IEEE TII, IEEE TITS, IoT, IEEE Big Data, ASOC, FGCS, etc. At present, Prof. Gupta is working as Director, International Center for AI and Cyber Security Research and Innovations, and Distinguished Professor with the Department of Computer Science and Information Engineering (CSIE), Asia University, Taiwan. His research interests include cyber security, cloud computing, artificial intelligence, intrusion detection, blockchain technologies, cyber physical systems, social media and networking.

***

Zeinab Ahmed With a robust foundation in computer engineering and networking, my tenure as an Assistant Professor at the University of Gezira and a Postdoctoral Research Fellow at IIUM has been marked by a commitment to advancing the field of wireless communication networks. At the core of my professional journey lies a passion for research and education, empowering students and peers through knowledge dissemination and innovative project engagement. My competencies in data analysis and software tools, exemplified by proficiency in Microsoft Power BI and Python, have fueled multiple research endeavors. These skills have not only enhanced the academic landscape but also facilitated the publication of numerous research papers. Our team's dedication to excellence in e-learning and programming continues to contribute significantly to the higher education industry, fostering an environment ripe for breakthroughs in networking technology.

Sumit Bawa, a Cyber security leader with 18+ years of experience in empowering organizations to build efficient security engineering programs, proficient in complex regulatory landscapes, including GDPR, HIPAA, PCI DSS, ISO 27001, skilled in risk assessment, incident response, and data privacy governance.

Kwok Tai Chui received the B.Eng. degree in electronic and communication engineering - Business Intelligence Minor and Ph.D. degree from City University of Hong Kong. He had industry experience as Senior Data Scientist in Internet of Things (IoT) company. He joined the Department of Technology, School of Science and Technology, at The Open University of Hong Kong as Research Assistant Professor. He was the recipient of 2nd Prize Award (Postgraduate Category) of 2014 IEEE Region 10 Student Paper Contest. Also, he received Best Paper Award in IEEE The International Conference on Consumer Electronics-China, in both 2014 and 2015. He has more than 45 research publications including edited books, book chapters, journal papers, and conference papers. His research interests include computational intelligence, data science, energy monitoring and management, intelligent transportation, smart metering, healthcare, machine learning algorithms and optimization.

Susanta Das is a seasoned educator with a proven record of teaching and mentoring diverse students, working at multiple institutions, and providing service to the various initiatives of organizations. He received his Ph.D. and M.A. degrees from Western Michigan University (WMU), USA, and M.Sc. degree from Banaras Hindu University (BHU), India all in Physics. He continued his research as a Marie-Curie post-doctoral fellow at Stockholm University, Stockholm, Sweden on beam diagnostics for the DESIREE (Double ElectroStatic Ion Ring ExpEriment) in the project DITANET (Diagnostic Techniques for particle Accelerators – a Marie-Curie initial training NETwork), at the Indian Institute of Science Education and Research-Kolkata, India on high-pressure physics as a Project Scientist-B, and at the University of Electro-Communications, Tokyo, Japan on ion-surface interactions as a Post-doctoral fellow. Throughout his career, Dr. Das worked and collaborated with many researchers, Ph.D., master, and visiting students from different countries. He further visited many countries to discuss research and an international conference participant (UK, Italy, Germany, Greece, Belgium, Bulgaria, Romania, Brazil etc.). He co-authored several research articles in WoS/Scopus indexed international journals, conference proceedings, and scholarly book chapters published by renowned international publishing houses. Beyond his research endeavors, Dr. Das has a storied history of service to academic and administrative committees, exhibiting his commitment to the growth and development of educational institutions. His experience includes tenure at Central University South Bihar, Sri Sri University, and P.K. University before assuming his current role at Ajeenkya DY Patil University. He received the Marie-Curie post-doctoral fellowship in Sweden, Science Academies' Summer Research Fellowship in India, Gwen Frostic Doctoral Fellowship, Department Graduate Research and Creative Scholar Award by WMU, and Leo R. Parpart Doctoral Fellowship by Dept. of Physics, WMU, among many others, throughout his academic journey. At present, Dr. Das continues to delve into cutting-edge fields, with a keen interest in nanotechnology, quantum computing, and data science. His multifaceted contributions, spanning teaching, research, and administrative leadership, showcase a dedicated professional who is instrumental in advancing the vision and mission of the institutions he serves.

Madhumitha Kulandaivel pursuing as Research Scholar in PSG college of Technology, Coimbatore, India. Her area of interest includes Adhoc networks, Sensor networks, and wireless communication. She is currently working as Assistant Professor, Department of Computer Science, SRM University, Chennai.

Kulandaivel Sindhumitha received her master of engineering degree in communication systems from Anna University, Chennai, Tamil Nadu, India, in 2019. She is currently working toward a PhD in the Department of Electronics and Communication Engineering, National Institute of Technology, Tiruchirappalli, India. Her research interests include optical communication and artificial intelligence in optical communication.

Sudhakar Kumar is working on the post of Assistant Professor(CSE) in Chandigarh College of Engineering and Technology, Sector 26, Chandigarh (under Chandigarh UT Administration). He has pursued his Ph.D. degree in High Performance Computing(Algorithm) and Compiler optimization from Panjab University, Chandigarh, India. He has done his Master in Technology(M. Tech.) degree from Indian Institute of Technology(IIT), Guwahati. His area of specializations are High Performance Computing(HPC), Compiler Optimization, Machine Learning(ML), Artificial Intelligence(AI) and Human Computer Interaction(HCI). He has published more than 90 research papers in different Journals, Conferences, Book Chapters and 2 Design Patents.

Sachithra Lokuge is a Lecturer at the University of Southern Queensland, Australia. She is passionate about investigating the impact of technological advances on organizations and individuals. She has been researching on technology led innovation, digital innovation, social media use on individuals, entrepreneurship, and impact of digital technologies on both firm and individual level. Her work has been published in the Information & Management, Communications of the AIS, Information Technology & People, Journal of Information Technology Theory and Application (JITTA), The International Conference on Information Systems, Academy of Management conference, The Americas Conference, European Conference and The Pacific Asia Conference on Information Systems.

Keerthana N V is an Assistant Professor with 8 Years of experience in teaching and 1-year experience in research (IUCAA LIGO Data Centre, Pune). Her area of interest is Network Security, Blockchain Security, and Machine Learning Algorithms. She is pursuing PhD at Anna University in Security in Blockchain. She has a working experience in High-Performance Computing (HTCondor) in LIGO INDIA Project. She has written many research articles in Network Security and assisted Scientists in analyzing Datasets in HTCondor.

Ruwan Nagahawatta is a Senior Lecturer in the Sydney International School of Technology and Commerce based in the Melbourne Campus, Australia. Ruwan hold a PhD in Cyber Security from RMIT University, Australia, where he has primarily focused on the critical security and privacy factors influencing the adoption of cloud computing. He obtained a BSc Hons from University of Kelaniya and has completed a Master of Information Technology at the University of Colombo, Sri Lanka. Ruwan has received professional recognition as a Certified Professional from the Australian Computer Society. Ruwan's research is interdisciplinary, and he has published numerous articles at the world's leading conferences and high-impact journals. His research spans several areas in Cloud Computing Security and Privacy, Human-Centric Security, Gamification and IT Ethics. He has been serving on numerous information systems, cyber security and privacy conferences.

Suresh P is currently working as Senior Associate Professor in the School of Computer Science and Engineering at Vellore Institute of Technology, Vellore, Tamil Nadu, India. He has 18 years of teaching and academic experience. He has completed Ph.D in Anna University, Chennai. He has published around 55 research papers in reputed international journals indexed by Scopus/SCI/WoS and presented around 35 papers in National and International Conferences. He has authored 6 books and 20 book chapters. His areas of interest include Networks, Cloud Computing, Data Analytics, Machine Learning and Deep Learning. He has received grants from various funding agencies like DRDO, ICMR, and CSIR towards the conduct of seminars and workshops. He has received Best Faculty Award and Best Performer in Academics, Research and consultancy from Kongu Engineering College, Erode, Tamil Nadu. He has received Faculty Research Award for the year 2022 from Vellore Institute of Technology, Vellore. He is serving as Reviewer and Editorial Board member in reputed journals.

Jagruti Patni, currently pursuing Master's degree in Forensic Accounting and Financial Investigations at Rashtriya Raksha University, Gandhinagar.

Mosiur Rahman, a Research Assistant at the International Center for AI and Cyber Security Research and Innovations (CCRI) at Asia University, Taiwan, holds a PhD in Computer Science and Information Engineering and master's degrees in Business Management and Computer Science and Engineering. With prior roles as a Research Assistant in AI and an Assistant Professor in Computer Science, he has extensive experience in academia. Dr. Rahman has been actively involved in international conferences, serving in significant roles, and is a part-time lecturer in Humanities and Social Science. His research interests include AI, Neural Networks, and Security, and he is a dedicated peer reviewer for over 50 journals, showcasing his commitment to research and academic excellence.

Sunil Singh, his areas of expertise are high-performance computing, Linux/Unix, Data Mining, Internet of Things, Machine Learning, Computer Architecture & Organization, Embedded System and Computer Network

Rohini Tarade is working as an Assistant Professor in the School of Engineering, Ajinkya D Y Patil University. She qualified NET and SET and is pursuing a Ph.D. in Computer Science. She has 18 years of experience in academics. Her areas of interest are machine learning and data mining. She has published research papers. She actively participates in outreach activities, workshops, conferences, short-term training courses, and faculty development programs. She is deeply committed to education and has taught a variety of courses at both the undergraduate and graduate levels. She is known for her engaging teaching style, which combines rigorous theoretical foundations with practical, hands-on experience. Mrs. Rohini actively mentors students, guiding them in their academic and research pursuits. She has also worked on various Examination committees such as Paper-Setter, Moderator, and Senior Supervisor. Outside of academia, she enjoys singing and exploring new technologies.

Matthew Warren is a Professor of Information Systems at Deakin University, Australia. Professor Warren is a researcher in the areas of Information Security, Computer Ethics and Cyber Security. He has authored and co-authored over 300 books, book chapters, journal papers and conference papers. He has received numerous grants and awards from national and international funding bodies, such as: Australian Research Council (ARC); Engineering Physical Sciences Research Council (EPSRC) in the United Kingdom; National Research Foundation (NRF) in South Africa and the European Union. Professor Warren gained his PhD in Information Security Risk Analysis from the University of Plymouth, United Kingdom and he has taught in Australia, Finland, Hong Kong and the United Kingdom.

Index

A

B

C

D

E

F

H

I

M

N

P

R

S

T

U

V

Z

www.ingramcontent.com/pod-product-compliance
Lightning Source LLC
LaVergne TN
LVHW060401300926
849162LV00006B/1320